Dark Age of Camelot™

The Atlas

An
Incan Monkey God Studios
Production

Prima Games
A Division of Random House, Inc.
3000 Lava Ridge Court
Roseville, CA 95661
(800) 733-3000

For valuable updates to this book, check out our website!
www.primagames.com

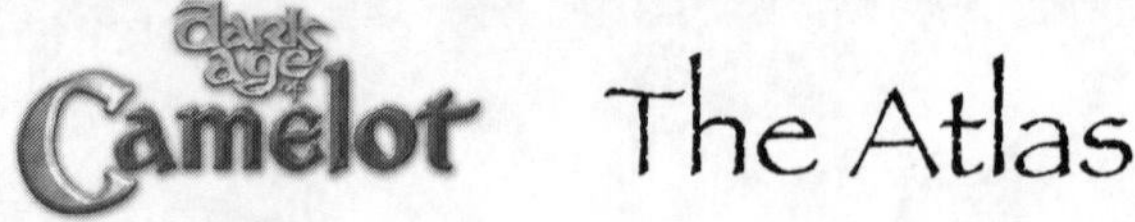

Credits

IMGS Project Lead — Melissa Tyler
Statistics and Editing — David Ladyman
Interior Graphic Design — Sharon Freilich
Interior Layout — Jeffrey M. Phillips, Jan Milstead, Margaret Irene Holden, True M. Hardt, Raini Madden
Border Knotwork Art — Cari Buziak

Gallant and Wise Team Members

Matt Firor, Spike Alexander, Lori Silva, Erik Krebs, Mark Davis, Walter Yarbrough, Eugene Evans

Worldly and Wise Woman

Robin "Maia" Harris (She who said, "you should make a book of maps" and then was invaluable in making it happen.)

Friends Indeed: James Heath, Gordon Vincent

Splendid and Dauntless Panelists

Beau "MacGyani" Stribling
Chris "Kirstena" Yone
Ethan "Esis" Kidhardt
Steve "Larian LeQuella" Lundquist
Heather "Orlena" Rothwell
aka "Treasure Namer Extraordinaire"
Jim "Oakleif" Rothwell
Todd "Jubal" Wharton
Marc "Biggs" Quesnel
Matt "Kyle Draconeco" Shirley
Monica "Seraphym" Hayes
Dave "i3ullseye" Maynor
Georgia "Olivia" Wall
Kevin "Morgan" McLaughlin
DJ "Aphexplotz"Larkin
Jim "Skam" Skamarakas
Joe "Varnarok" Bayley
Mike "Muse" Swiernik
Brian "MrMoose" Beck
Adam "Prior Tuck" Fritz
Jennifer "Ellyndria" Beaulieu
Harold "Mindeater" Pontious
Doug "Kaiser" Fernandez
Cory "Bonham" Magel
Eric "Bubski" Bramblett
Ian "Iain ap Conlan" Wright
James "Aralyanna" Himes

Important:
Prima Games has made every effort to determine that the information contained in this book is accurate. However, the publisher makes no warranty, either expressed or implied, as to the accuracy, effectiveness, or completeness of the material in this book; nor does the publisher assume liability for damages, either incidental or consequential, that may result from using the information in this book. The publisher cannot provide information regarding game play, hints and strategies, or problems with hardware or software. Questions should be directed to the support numbers provided by the game and device manufacturers in their documentation. Some game tricks require precise timing and may require repeated attempts before the desired result is achieved.

ISBN: 0-7615-4041-5

Library of Congress Catalog Card Number: 2002108306

Printed in the United States of America

01 02 03 04 DD 10 9 8 7 6 5 4 3 2 1

Table of Contents

How To Get Places

Albion

Hibernia

The Atlas

Realm of Midgard

Realm vs. Realm

Appendices

How to Get Places

NAVIGATE USING /LOC

When you type **/loc**, you get a message that says something like **In Malmohus: loc=21444,53878,2824 dir=214.**

The first part's easy. It tells you the name of the zone you're in. Nothing could be simpler.

The second part — the three loc numbers — is exactly where you are in the zone. **The first number is how far east you are.** The very westernmost point in the zone is 0. As you go farther east, the first number gets larger. The very easternmost part of the zone is around 63,000. **The second number is how far south you are.** The top of the map is 0, and the second number gets larger the farther south you go. The very southernmost part of the zone is also around 63,000. **The third number is how high you are.** In general you can ignore that number.

So if you are in the northwest corner of the zone, you'll be close to loc=0,0,214. If you are in the middle of the zone, you'll be near loc=30000,30000,214. If you're in the southeast corner, you'll be around loc=63000,63000,214

The third part — **dir** stands for direction, by the way — lets you know what direction you are facing. (It doesn't matter if you're looking up or down, it tells the direction you'd be walking if you were to move ahead.) This is the part that can get confusing, so we've added a compass with the appropriate numbers to every map. It works like a 360-degree circle, with north being the top of the circle. **0=North, 90=East, 180=South, 270=West.** Since by the time you turn a full circle you're pretty much facing the same direction you started, the closer you are to 360, the closer you are to north. At 360 the numbers start over with 0.

HORSE ROUTES

ALBION

Stable — St.Master	*Tickets to*
Adribard's Retreat — Grank	*West Downs* *Castle Sauvage*
Caer Ulfwych — Idian	*Cornwall Station*
Caer Witrin — Jhular	*Western Cornwall*
Camelot Hills — Haruld	*North Camelot Gates*
East Camelot Gates — Vuloch	*Snowdonia Station* *Campacorentin Station*
North Camelot Gates — Bombard	*Camelot Hills*
Camelot Hills — Fluvon	*Campacorentin Forest*
Campacorentin Station — Ridder	*Camelot Hills* *East Camelot Gates*
Castle Sauvage — Uliam	*Ludlow* *Adribard's Retreat* *Snowdonia Fortress*
Castle Snowdonia — Flambon	*Castle Sauvage*
Cornwall Station — Pethos	*Caer Ulfwych*
Humberton Village — *Gracchus*	*Snowdonia Fortress*
Ludlow Village — Yaren	*Castle Sauvage*
Snowdonia Station — Trachon	*East Camelot Gates*
Western Cornwall — Addard Yardly	*Caer Witrin*
West Downs — Edarg	*Adribard's Retreat*

HIBERNIA

Stable — Stable Master	*Tickets to*
Ardagh — Edricar	*Tir Urphost* *Connla*
Ardee — Freagus	*East Lough Derg*
Connla — Aelerogh	*Druim Ligen* *Innis Carthaig* *Culraid*
Culraid — Mulgraighy	*Innis Carthaig* *Connla*
Druim Cain — Chuchear	*Tir na mBeo* *Druim Ligen*
Druim Ligen — Ullios	*Connla*
East Lough Derg — Rheagul	*Druim Cain* *Ardagh*
Howth — Pheuloc	*Innis Carthaig* *Mag Mell*
Innis Carthaig — Breachus	*Tir na mBeo* *Culraid* *Druim Cain*
Mag Mell — Rumdor	*Howth*
Tir Urphost — Luergor	*Ardagh*
Tirn Na mBeo — Truichon	*Druim Ligen*

MIDGARD

Stable — Stable Master	*Tickets to*
Audliten — Fraglock	*Mularn*
Fort Atla — Rundorik	*Galplen* *Mularn*
Fort Veldon — Arskar	*Gna Faste*
Galplen — Treflun	*Fort Atla* *Vasudheim* *Gna Faste*
Gna Faste — Wolgrun	*Raumarik* *Fort Veldon* *Galplen* *Huginfel*
Haggerfel — Yolafson	*Vasudheim*
Huginfel — Prulgar	*Svasud Faste* *Gna Faste*
Mularn — Gularg	*Audliten* *Ft. Atla*
Nalliten — Eryklan	*Vindsaul Faste*
Raumarik — Larsson	*Gna Faste*
Svasud Faste — Vorgar	*Huginfel* *Vindsaul Faste*
Vasudheim — Harlfug	*Haggerfel* *Galplen*
Vindsaul Faste — Ulufgar	*Nalliten* *Svasud Faste*

The Atlas

Albion Merchants

LOCATION KEYS

(Ad. Ret.)	Adribard's Retreat	**(C. Wit.)**	Caer Witrin	**(Co. Stn.)**	Cornwall Station	**(Nob's Farm)**	Nob's Farm
(Av. M. W.)	Avalon Marsh Wharf	**(Cam.)**	Camelot City	**(Cot. V.)**	Cotswold Village	**(Pry. Kp.)**	Prydwen Keep
(C. Bn.)	Caer Benowyc	**(C.H. Tow.)**	Camelot Hills Tower	**(E. C. G.)**	East Camelot Gates	**(Sn. F.)**	Snowdonia Fortress
(C. Bk.)	Caer Berkstead	**(Ca.Stn.)**	Campacorentin Station	**(Gr. Farm)**	Gronyr's Farm	**(S.Stn.)**	Snowdonia Station
(C. Bol.)	Caer Boldiam	**(C. C. En.)**	Castle Camelot Entr.	**(H. Out.)**	Hibernia Outpost	**(SW Tower)**	SW Tower
(C. Era.)	Caer Erasleigh	**(Cam. Entr.)**	Castle Camelot Entrance	**(Hum. V.)**	Humberton Village	**(Sw. K.)**	Swanton Keep
(C. Ren.)	Caer Renaris	**(C. Ex.)**	Castle Excalibur	**(L. Asn.)**	Lethantis Association	**(W. Dn.)**	West Downs
(C. Sur.)	Caer Sursbrook	**(C. My.)**	Castle Myrddin	**(Lud. V.)**	Ludlow Village	**(W. Crn.)**	Western Cornwall
(C. Ulf.)	Caer Ulfwych	**(C. Sau.)**	Castle Sauvage	**(M. Out.)**	Midgard Outpost		

Armor

Boned studded
(Cam.) Jana Hickey
(Cam. Entr.) Lan
(Hum. V.) Dun Mra
(Hum. V.) Zenob Mra
(S.Stn.) Aldys Meccus

Chain
(C. Ulf.) Stephan Fall
(C. Wit.) Azrael Mucto
(Cam.) Serena Muftar
(Ca.Stn.) Junger Gannon
(Co. Stn.) Sar Aldar
(Cot. V.) Col Aldar
(S.Stn.) Aelda

Cymric leather
(Cam.) Geor Nadren
(Ca.Stn.) Fluitha Sufron

Lamellar studded
(C. Wit.) Geofram Hael
(Cam.) Jeffrey Kenric
(Ca.Stn.) Rundeg Faerweth

Mithril chain, mail, lamellar
(Cam.) Lora Theomund

Mithril plate armor
(Cam.) Torr Upton

Plate
(Ad. Ret.) Tathan
(Cam.) Hafgan Corley
(Cot. V.) Gill Hoxley
(Pry. Kp.) Karn Graem
(S.Stn.) Cranly

Quilted
(Ad. Ret.) Anga Weaver
(Cam.) Colby Dalston
(Cam.) Mori Godric
(Cam.) Raggart Bruce
(Cot. V.) Farma Hornly
(Hum. V.) Bline Tengit
(L. Asn.) Sebil Lenut
(Lud. V.) Seamstress Marie
(W. Dn.) Erwin Holdyn

Robe
(Ad. Ret.) Tersa Weaver
(Cam.) Radek Silven
(Cot. V.) Jon Smythe
(Hum. V.) Siom Felanis
(L. Asn.) Epin Lenut
(Lud. V.) Seamstress Lynnet
(S.Stn.) Guyon
(W. Dn.) Aric Barlow

Roman
(Ad. Ret.) Morin Davem
(Cam.) Yoren Shazra
(Cot. V.) Lundeg Tranyth
(Pry. Kp.) Hugh Gallen

Scaled plate
(Cam.) Fuston Talgurt
(Co. Stn.) Jack Landrey
(Hum. V.) Gert Elm

Siluric leather
(Cam.) Elzbet Sable
(Cam.) Warren Gibson
(Hum. V.) Tria Ellowis
(Lud. V.) Fost Mra
(S.Stn.) Boc

Studded
(Av. M. W.) Leshorm Hael
(Cam.) Lara Weathers
(Cot. V.) Ellyn Weyland
(W. Dn.) Garvyn Kensington

Sylvan cloth
(Cam.) Meccus Yrre

Weapons

2-handed
(Ad. Ret.) Tathal
(Cam.) Dougal Heathis
(Ca.Stn.) Malin Cullan
(Cot. V.) Bedamor Routh
(Sw. K.) Jerad

Arrows
(Av. M. W.) Allyn Fletcher
(C. Bol.) Muenian
(C. Era.) Adwu
(C. Sur.) Abila
(C. Sur.) Fiderccorre
(C. Ulf.) Fellya Fletcher
(Cam.) Jana Fletcher
(C.H. Tow.) Meran Fletcher
(Ca.Stn.) Falin Fletcher
(C. Sau.) Lenia Fletcher
(Co. Stn.) Iohannes Aldar
(Cot. V.) Braenwyn Fletcher
(Hum. V.) Nelda Fletcher
(Lud. V.) Gilley Fletcher
(Sn. F.) Pejar
(S.Stn.) Edrea Fletcher
(Sw. K.) Agrakor Fletcher
(W. Dn.) Ainsley Fletcher

Bolts
(Av. M. W.) Boudron Fletcher
(C. Bk.) Gwerra
(C. Ulf.) Eiddin Walelden
(Cam.) Sasha Fletcher
(C.H. Tow.) Mateus Fletcher
(Ca.Stn.) Goodwin Fletcher
(C. Sau.) Allia Fletcher
(Co. Stn.) Heylyn Aldar
(Cot. V.) Yetta Fletcher
(Hum. V.) Alden Fletcher
(Lud. V.) Nulb Pew
(S.Stn.) Gleda Fletcher
(Sw. K.) Dwira Fletcher
(W. Dn.) Radella Fletcher

Bows
(Av. M. W.) Epheria Brighteye
(C. Ulf.) Elger Leafblade
(Cam.) Sara Graston
(C.H. Tow.) Lauryn Swiftrun
(Ca.Stn.) Flaudin Bowman
(Cot. V.) Grum Bowman
(Hum. V.) Feren Erimen
(Lud. V.) Argus Bowman
(S.Stn.) Staeven Bowman
(Sw. K.) Lynd Moidg
(W. Dn.) Aldrin Collyer

Crushing
(Ad. Ret.) Theois Gwynt
(C. Ulf.) Ellard Gram
(C. Wit.) Gregor Lannis
(Cam. Entr.) Fash
(Hum. V.) Stephon Bash
(Pry. Kp.) Barric Camber
(S.Stn.) Elwyn

Iron/Steel
(Cam.) Landry Woden

Miscellaneous
(Cam.) Ordra Yaney
(S.Stn.) Osric

Mithril
(Cam.) Wyne Scead

Polearm
(Av. M. W.) William Oswy
(Cam.) Moira Camber
(Ca.Stn.) Balthaz. Encambrion
(Cot. V.) Rayn Olwyc
(Sw. K.) Ley Manton

Slashing
(Ad. Ret.) Tyngyr Blade
(C. Ulf.) Langston Fall
(Cam.) Ethan Farley
(Cam. Entr.) Joffrey
(Cot. V.) Grannis Ynos
(Hum. V.) Ban Ronem
(Pry. Kp.) Alburn Hale
(S.Stn.) Ember

Staff
(Cam.) Brother Salvar
(Cam.) Colby Dalston
(Cam.) Marius Caest
(Cam.) Mori Godric
(Ad. Ret.) Nai Whit
(Ca.Stn.) Archibald Oakheart
(Cot. V.) Samwell Hornly
(Hum. V.) Mif Feit
(Lud. V.) Sals Pew
(Sw. K.) Nia Leof

Throwing
(C. Bol.) Galaenyth
(C. Ren.) Kederi

Thrusting
(Av. M. W.) Sywno
(Cam.) Fenris Blakely
(Ca.Stn.) Geston Lurger
(Cot. V.) John Weyland
(Hum. V.) Alhrick Duglas
(Lud. V.) Crep Pew
(Pry. Kp.) Elvar Tambor
(S.Stn.) Jonalyn

Shields

(Ad. Ret.) Devyn Godric
(C. Ulf.) Grindan Halig
(Cam.) Ver Nuren
(Cam. Entr.) Chad Denisc
(Cot. V.) Lar Rodor
(Hum. V.) Heorot Kenway
(Pry. Kp.) Ryce Scrydan
(S.Stn.) Cedd Aethelbert

Focus Items

Cabalist staff
(C. Wit.) Wina Wyman
(Cam.) Olaevia Wyman
(Cot. V.) Odelia Wyman
(L. Asn.) Elga Wyman
(Lud. V.) Andrya Wyman

Sorcerer staff
(Ad. Ret.) Wylie Edyn
(Cam.) Pedrith Edyn
(Cot. V.) Cauldir Edyn
(L. Asn.) Norvel Edyn
(Lud. V.) Calldir Edyn

Theurgist staff
(Ad. Ret.) Graeme Dalston
(C. Ulf.) Gery Dalston
(Cam.) Cigolin Dalston
(Cot. V.) Cudbert Dalston
(Lud. V.) Farl Dalston

Wizard staff
(Ad. Ret.) Daisi Egesa
(Cam.) Edmee Heolstor
(Cam.) Gardowen Egesa
(Cot. V.) Doreen Egesa
(L. Asn.) Loretta Egesa
(Lud. V.) Eabae Egesa

Other Goods

Boards and Planing tools
(Cam.) Brach Leof
(Cam.) Freyne Aeoelred

Cloth dye
(Ad. Ret.) Blueheart
(Ad. Ret.) Dyemstr Camdene
(Cam.) Dyemaster Edare
(Cam.) Dyemaster Vandras
(Ca.Stn.) Gwen Arlington
(Cot. V.) Dyemaster Alwin
(Cot. V.) Eowyln Astos
(Hum. V.) Dyemaker Bal
(Hum. V.) Dyemaster Brun
(Lud. V.) Aileen Wyatt
(Lud. V.) Dyemaster Cor
(Pry. Kp.) Arleigh Penn
(Pry. Kp.) Dyemaster Arthw

Drums
(C. Bol.) Ricci
(C. Ren.) Vor

Enamel dye
(Av. M. W.) Dyemstr. Carye
(Av. M. W.) Dyemstr. Godric
(C. Ulf.) Dyemaster Eldred
(C. Ulf.) Dyemaster Nedda
(Cam.) Dyemaster Kael
(Cam.) Dyemaster Marna
(Cot. V.) Dyemaster Edra
(Cot. V.) Dyemaster Octe

Feathers
(Cam.) Gremain Watford
(Cam.) Kippar Row
(Cam.) Willa Dalston

Fletching/tailoring supplies
(C. Bn.) Vrudon

Instruments
(Ad. Ret.) Trill
(Av. M. W.) Bruna
(Cam.) Silura Starish
(Cot. V.) Eileen Morton
(L. Asn.) Sleria
(Lud. V.) Greta Songbird

Iron/Steel Weapons & Armor
(Cam.) Larcwide Wirt
(Cam.) Odella Cerdic
(Cam.) Tait Nerian

Leather dye
(Av. M. W.) Dyemaster Earh
(Av. M. W.) Dyemaster Kaly
(C. Ulf.) Dyemaster Druce
(C. Ulf.) Dyemaster Esme
(Cam.) Dyemaster Emma
(Cam.) Dyemaster Lendand
(Ca.Stn.) Dyemaster Esme
(C. C. En.) Dyemaster Bren
(C. C. En.) Dyemaster Irwin
(Cot. V.) Dyemaster Leax
(Cot. V.) Dyem. Wanetta

Leather/Cloth tradeskill items
(Cam.) Corley Nodens
(Cam.) Coventina Bordin
(Cam.) Cyllena Watford
(Cam.) Shayly Parke

Metal
(Cam.) Anyon Becket

Metalworking equipment
(C. Bn.) Heargh

Misc. expensive items
(SW Tower) Guard Dafydd
(W. Dn.) Farley Daegal

Misc. items
(Cam.) Heolstor Wyman
(Cam.) Holt Finan
(Cam.) Iden Wissan
(Cam.) Lynna Lang

Poison (1)
(Av. M. W.) Wiceit
(C. Bk.) Aleac
(C. Bol.) Lotheria
(C. Era.) Levnadhbh
(C. Ren.) Boedithirse
(C. Ren.) Cynidd
(Cam.) Kedoenad
(Ca.Stn.) Linidd
(C. Sau.) Onyg
(Cot. V.) Unendaldan
(Hum. V.) Nydomath

Poison (2)
(C. Bk.) Eilgriarhe
(C. Era.) Pienn
(C. Sur.) Adale
(C. Wit.) Etie
(Cam.) Velmis
(C. Sau.) Melannon
(Sn. F.) Downifrita
(Sn. F.) Galea
(Sw. K.) Glaeric

Siegecraft items
(C. Bn.) Blaugh
(C. Bn.) Grummond
(C. Bn.) Luthor
(C. Sau.) Cameron
(H. Out.) Malrin
(M. Out.) Bergvall
(Sn. F.) Alaric

Smith/tailoring supplies
(C. Bn.) Olafsson
(Cam.) Chelseigh Stilman
(Cam.) Hector Darian
(Lud. V.) Ochan Aethelhere

Strips
(Cam.) Trina Andreason

Tailoring equipment
(C. Bn.) Brenford
(Co. Stn.) Adaliae Ruthic
(Sw. K.) Yorel Anbidian

Tailoring supplies
(C. Bn.) Crachon

Tradeskill Items
(C. Bn.) Hollach
(C. Bn.) Kedohan
(C. Ex.) Kathlynne Snowe
(C. My.) Eythan Greene
(Co. Stn.) Thule Ruthic

Services

Bounty
(Cam.) Aklee Edelmar
(Cam.) Calldir Edelmar
(Cam.) Dare Edelmar
(Cam.) Freya Edelmar
(Cam.) Maye Edelmar

Enchanter
(Ad. Ret.) EnchanterBraesia
(Cam.) Enchanter Evala
(Cot. V.) Enchanter Grumwold
(Hum. V.) Enchanter Haephus

Guild Registrar
(Cam.) Lord Christopher

Healer
(Cam.) Brother Michel
(Hum. V.) Brother Demay
(Hum. V.) Brother Sabutai
(Pry. Kp.) Brother Maynard
(S.Stn.) Odaro Hengist
(W. Dn.) Master Gerol

Name Registrar
(Cam.) Lady Charlitte

Smith
(Cam.) Judan Hammerfel
(Ca.Stn.) Dafyd Graham
(Cot. V.) Elvar Ironhand
(Hum. V.) Parisch Ealyn
(Lud. V.) Master Sceley
(Pry. Kp.) Gram Ironhand
(S.Stn.) Thol Dunnin
(W. Dn.) Lillian Brydger

Stable
(Ad. Ret.) Grank
(C. Ulf.) Idian
(C. Wit.) Jhular
(Ca.Stn.) Ridder
(Cam. Entr.) Bombard
(C. Sau.) Uliam
(Co. Stn.) Pethos
(E. C. G.) Vuloch
(Gr. Farm) Fluvon
(Hum. V.) Gracchus
(Lud. V.) Yaren
(Nob's Farm) Haruld
(Sn. F.) Flambon
(S.Stn.) Trachon
(W. Dn.) Edarg
(W. Crn.) Addard Yarley

Vault
(Ad. Ret.) Trulion Vrundon
(Cam.) Lord Urqhart
(C. Sau.) Earl Grael
(Co. Stn.) Kalea Eldwig

Trainer

Acolyte
(Ad. Ret.) Sister Chael
(Hum. V.) Brother Dupre
(Pry. Kp.) Sister Gwendolyn

Armorsmith Master
(Cam.) Loraine Elgen

Armsman
(C. Ulf.) Captain Falron
(Cam.) Captain Alphin
(Cam.) Captain Rion
(Sw. K.) Captain Presan

Cabalist
(C. Wit.) Magus Dimos
(Cam.) Magus Agyfen
(Cam.) Magus Isen
(L. Asn.) Magus Sacyn
(Sw. K.) Magus Jeril

Cleric
(Ad. Ret.) Lady Lynn
(C. Ulf.) Collen Blist
(Cam.) Lady Fridwulf
(Cam.) Lady Winchell

Elementalist
(Cot. V.) Master Stearn
(L. Asn.) Mistress Trethia

Emblemeer
(Cam.) Lord Oachley

Engineer Master
(Cam.) Grummond Attor

Fighter
(Ad. Ret.) Master Dyrin
(Ca.Stn.) Master Lorik
(Hum. V.) Master Torr
(Pry. Kp.) Master Graent

Fletcher Master
(Cam.) Acey Dalston
(Cam.) Runthal Devyn

Friar
(Ad. Ret.) Brother Caun
(C. Ulf.) Brother Spilr
(Cam.) Brother Ethelbald
(Cam.) Brother Sterlyn
(Sw. K.) Brother Daniel

Infiltrator
(C. Wit.) Master Noijan
(Cam.) Master Eadig
(Cam.) Master Edric
(L. Asn.) Master Qilith
(Sw. K.) Master Brignun

Mage
(Ad. Ret.) Magus Saloc
(Cot. V.) Magus Aelle
(L. Asn.) Magus Oreal
(Lud. V.) Magus Aldred

Mercenary
(C. Wit.) Master Dohajan
(Cam.) Master Almund
(Cam.) Master Arenis
(Ca.Stn.) Master Astyp
(Sw. K.) Master Kel

Minstrel
(Ad. Ret.) Master Liennon
(Cam.) Master Berwick
(Cam.) Master Dubri
(L. Asn.) Master Glorous
(Sw. K.) Master Hanis

Paladin
(Ad. Ret.) Lord Adribard
(C. Ulf.) Lord Ulfwych
(Cam.) Lady Triss
(Cam.) Lord Prydwen

Rogue
(Ca.Stn.) Master Hadis
(Cot. V.) Master Sorac
(Lud. V.) Master Odon

Scout
(Ad. Ret.) Lieut. Crosean
(C. Ulf.) Lieutenant Mhoudi
(Cam.) Lieutenant Kaherdin
(Cam.) Lieutenant Rydderac
(Sw. K.) Lieutenant Fisra

Sorcerer
(Ad. Ret.) Magus Edaev
(Cam.) Magess Tena
(Cam.) Magus Cormac
(L. Asn.) Magus Crystolos
(Sw. K.) Magus Sarun

Tailoring Master
(Cam.) Arliss Eadig

Theurgist
(Ad. Ret.) Mistress Jeryssa
(C. Ulf.) Mistress Frina
(Cam.) Master Cear
(Cam.) Mistress Welss
(Sw. K.) Mistress Cessa

Weaponsmithing Master
(Cam.) Hephas Elgen

Wizard
(Ad. Ret.) Master Traoyr
(Cam.) Master Grundelth
(Cam.) Mistress Ladriel
(L. Asn.) Master Arbaedes
(Sw. K.) Mistress Alarisa

Avalon Marsh

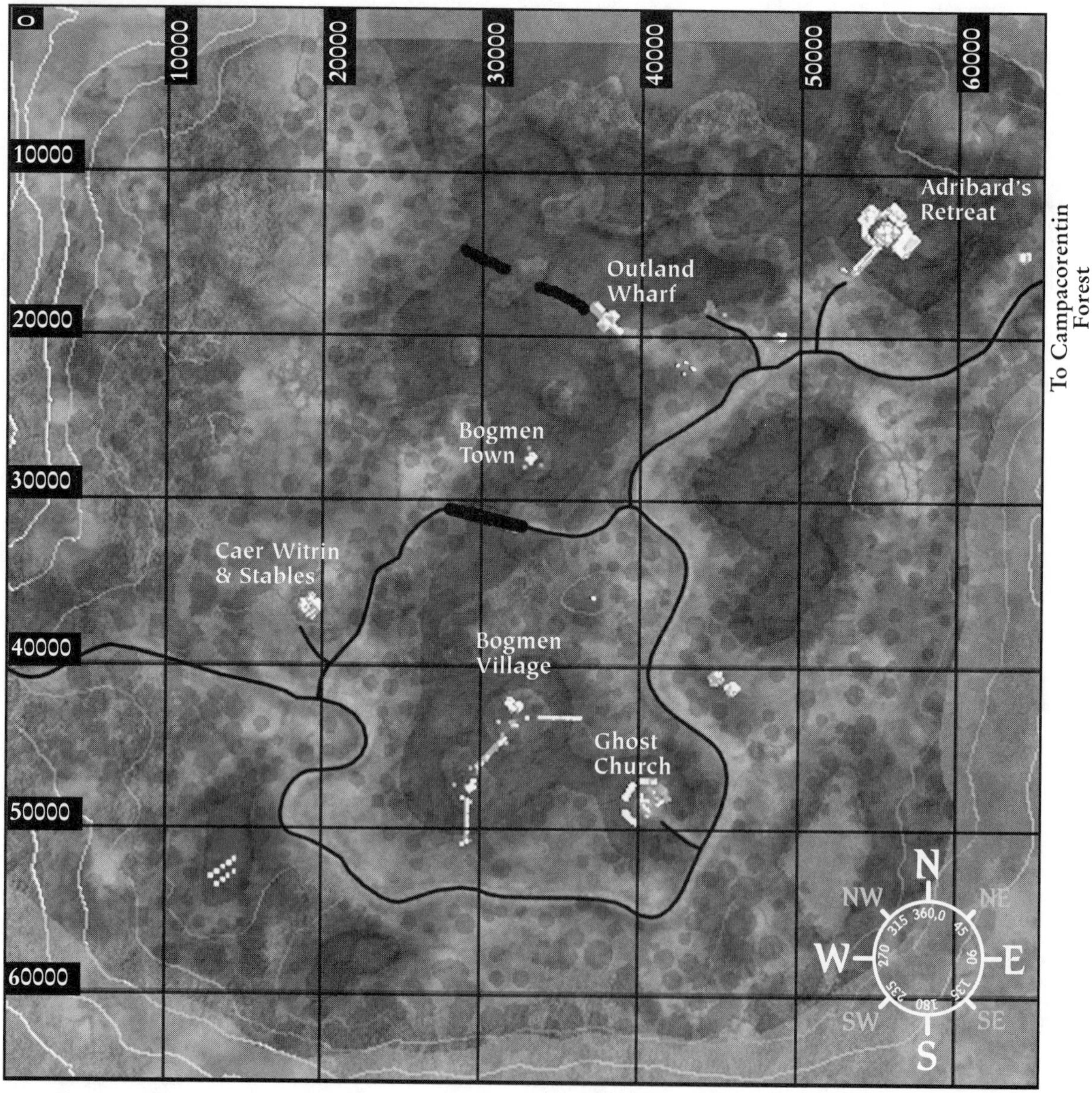
0
10000
20000
30000
40000
50000
60000
10000
20000
30000
40000
50000
60000
Adribard's Retreat
Outland Wharf
To Campacorentin Forest
Bogmen Town
Caer Witrin & Stables
To Snowdonia
Bogmen Village
Ghost Church
N
NW
NE
W
E
SW
SE
S
360,0
45
90
135
180
225
270
315

GHOULS =

wisp ghoul
ghoul footman
ghoul knight
ghoul lord

OGRES =

wood ogre scourge
wood ogre berserker
wood ogre seer

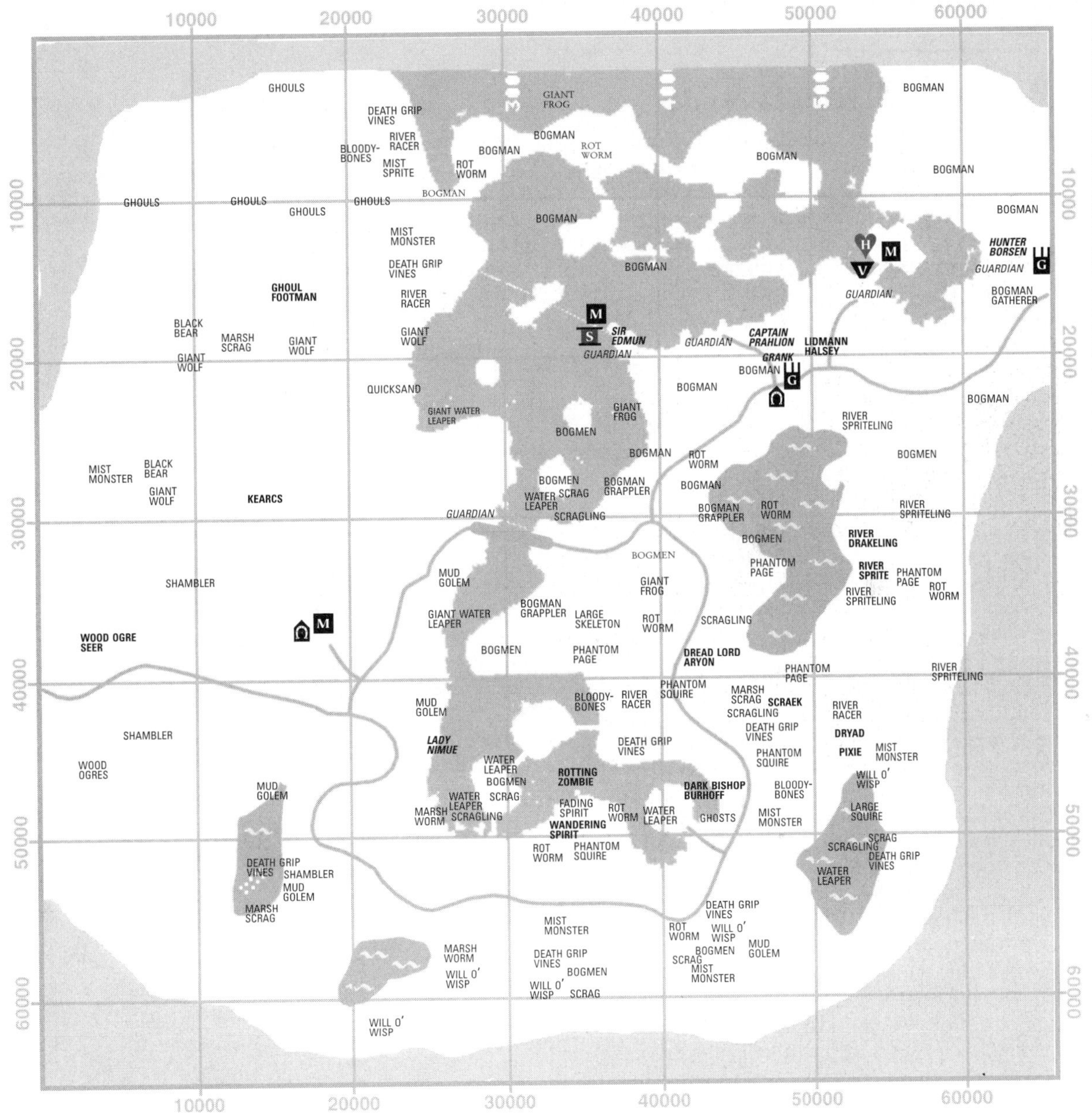

Lower-level monsters not shown on map:

Creature	Lvl	Location
bogman	3	NC,NE,C,EC
carrion crab	2	NC,NE,C
creeping crud	2	NC,NE,C,EC
decayed zombie	3	NC,C,EC
impling	0	NE
muck snake	1	NC,NE
mud worm	0	NC,NE
outcast rogue	1	NE
puny skeleton	1	NE
river drake hatchling	3	NE,EC
river spriteling	3	NE,EC
rotting skeleton	1	NC
scrawny bogman	2	NC,NE,C,EC
scum toad	0	NC,NE
skeleton	2	NC,NE,C
slime lizard	1	NC,NE
slough serpent	0	NC,NE
spiny eel	3	NE
swamp slime	3	NC,NE,C,E
wisp ghoul	0	NC,NE

Avalon Marsh Tips

Avalon Marsh has fewer bindstones than other newbie areas, and aggressive "teenage" monsters make this zone less favorable for newbies than Camelot Hills or Black Mountains. This is a great place to go once you reach level 10 or so, though, because class trainers are available. Trainers do not, however, give "epic" quests, and the quests which start in this area are fewer than around Camelot — Avalon Marsh is probably not the best place to quest. "Named" guards for kill tasks are also rare.

Also, players looking for treasure and quests are not going to be as happy here as they would be in other zones of the same level. Anyone without a ranged attack for pulling won't do as well here because most monsters tend to "group up."

Solo Friendly? This zone is moderately solo-friendly for the teens character and has many static camps of monsters with easy-to-figure-out pathing. Camp bonuses tend to be high, but disappear quickly, meaning the solo-er must move a lot to keep high bonuses.

Group Friendly? Groups can also do well here. Though there aren't as many areas for the right level group to hunt, most monsters in the zone don't BAF, meaning you don't have to worry about crowd control. Keep the members of your group close, though, because having a monster attack your back at just the wrong moment is a recipe for a quick death. Loot doesn't drop as often as it does in other zones, but when it does, it sells for as much as the many little pieces off other monsters. The problem is, though, that if the group is only together for a short time, each individual's "take" might be less.

Don't tackle which areas alone? Be careful wandering over the bridge to Caer Witrin alone. There's a nasty band of wolves off to the right (as you are coming from Adribard's) that will gang up on you if you're not careful. The other area to watch out for in this zone is the Haunted Ruins. The guards here have learned to fight together, and they do it well.

Who loves this area? Clerics, in particular, love Avalon Marsh. The mudmen that spawn around the waters are both Smite- and Crush-susceptible. Undead are also a Cleric's dream. Anyone who uses Crush should be quite happy, in fact. Scouts and casters also like the mudmen because they are naturally slower, allowing more damage on "incoming" than with some other monsters.

- Heather "Orlena" & Jim "Oakleif" Rothwell

One of the greatest benefits to this zone is having guild trainers readily available for most classes. Since they are not in a separate zone, this removes the need for buff or pet recasting, or in the case of Sorcerers, the need to acquire an entirely new pet at each training stop.

One of the nice features is a high concentration of linked monsters. Sometimes at lower levels, it's hard to hunt relying on the BAF code. If you're solo, you pull one, when you can usually handle two or more. But if you hunt in a small group, the BAF code causes the monsters to bring extra, but the composition of the group that comes is not very favorable. With a high concentration of 2 and 3 monster links one can effectively solo the linked monsters benefiting greatly from the bonus experience generated.

Overall this zone offers a lot for just about any class. The number of humanoids makes hunting here with a Sorcerer relatively painless. Some unique drops appear in this zone, including gems and staves from the Mud Golems. There are a few quests that center in this zone, but the wide level range of targets is what makes this zone most appealing.

- Dave "i3ullseye" Maynor

Solo and Group Levelling Tips

Solo

1-5	usual newbie monsters
5-10	bogmen, deathgrip vines, skeletons
10-15	bogmen, shamblers, mud golems
15-20	wolves, quicksands, giant water-leapers

Group

1-5	same as solo
5-10	bogmen, deathgrip vines, skeletons, mud golems, shamblers
15-20	wolves, quicksands, giant water leapers

- Matt "Kyle Draconeco" Shirley

Loot

black bear [16] (23%) Black Bear Pelt • (2.5%) Pristine Black Bear Pelt • (50%) Bloody Bear Fang • (25%) Black Bear Tongue • (1.5%) Long Animal Fang

bloody-bones [7] (80%) Bloody Thigh Bone • (60%) Bloody Little Finger • (70%) Bloody Arm Bone • (0.5%) <Pilfered Prizes>

bogman [3-4] (35%) Lizard-Foot Amulet (x2) • (20%) Aventurine • (1%) Jade • (1%) <Only Just Begun>

bogman fisher [9] (80%) Can of Bait • (70%) Silver Fish Hook • (57%) Elm Fishing Pole • (0.5%) <Of a Sylvan Glade>

bogman gatherer [8] (80%) Gathering Bag • (70%) Digging Stick • (67%) Pale Bumpy Roots • (0.5%) <Pilfered Prizes>

bogman grappler [5] (30%) Crab-Shell Cap • (2%) Mud-Man Totem • (1%) <Only Just Begun>

bogman hunter [11] (80%) Tanned Animal Skin • (75%) Animal Gland • (60%) Chunk of Preserved Meat • (0.5%) <Of a Sylvan Glade>

bogman trapper [10] (70%) Small Animal Trap • (80%) Trap Bait • (63%) Animal Gland • (0.5%) <Of a Sylvan Glade>

carrion crab [2] (40%) Chitin Shard • (27%) Huge Crab Claw

creeping crud [2] (5%) Pitted Shimmering Great Sword • (15% each piece) Tattered Shimmering Leather • (45%) Onyx • (10%) Moonstone • (1%) <Only Just Begun>

Dark Bishop Burhoff [17] (80%) Dark Skull • (30%) Azurite • (10%) Topaz • (1%) Pearl • (0.3%) <Out of the Woods>

death grip vines [7] (10%) Writhing Roots • (70%) Short Piece of Vine • (30%) Long Piece of Vine

decayed zombie [3] (65% each) Aventurine, Leathery Skin • (5%) Aventurine • (8% each piece) Tattered Leather and Quilted • (0.5%) <Only Just Begun>

Dread Lord Aryon [15] (15%) Skull-Embossed Gauntlets • (30%) Lapis Lazuli • (10%) Azurite • (1%) Topaz • (0.3%) <Out of the Woods> • (3%) Night's Fall Halberd ***or*** Hammer

dryad [7] (70% each) Oaken Medallion, Heartwood Amulet • (20%) Vine-Carved Totem • (0.5%) <Of a Sylvan Glade> • (1.5%) Grass Choker

fading spirit [8] (45%) Faded Green Slime • (35%) Tattered Woolen Robes • (25%) Tattered Brown Boots • (50%) Spinel • (1%) Bloodstone • (0.5%) <Pilfered Prizes>

ghostly knight [8-10] (30%) Tarnished Spurs • (35%) Chryoprase • (1%) Amethyst • (0.5%) <Of a Sylvan Glade> • (1.5%) Skull-Embossed Gauntlets

ghoul footman [17] (50%) Footman's Pack • (70%) Footman's Ration • (40%) Bronze Medal • (3%) APOA: Footman's Chain ***or*** Kite Shield • (0.6% each) Ghoul Knight Leggings ***or*** Helm • (0.3%) Night's Edge Bill • (0.3%) <Out of the Woods>

ghoul knight [18] (55%) Heavy Silver Chain • (60%) Knight's Ration • (40%) Silver Medal • (1.5%) APOA: Lion Embossed • (0.6% each) Ghoul Knight Leggings ***or*** Helm • (0.3%) Night's Edge Bill • (0.3%) <Out of the Woods>

ghoul lord [19] (40%) Human-Hide Belt • (60%) Golden Chain • (60%) Illegible Map • (1.5%) APOA: Lion Embossed • (0.6% each) Ghoul Knight Leggings ***or*** Helm • (0.3%) Night's Edge Bill • (0.3%) <Salisbury Stock 1>

giant frog [4] (50%) Frog Legs

giant water leaper [15] (80%) Giant Leaper Leg • (60%) Leaper Eye Earrings • (60%) Leaper Tongue Belt • (2%) Leaper Gut Rapier

giant wolf [15-16] (75%) Giant Wolf Skin • (20%) Giant Wolf Fang

horse [10] (75%) Horse Hair • (10%) Auburn Mane • (80%) Ruined Horse Skin • (35%) Horse Skin • (60%) Horse Hair

impling [0] (50%) Impling Eye • (70%) Impling Claw • (80%) Impling Wing • (1%) <Only Just Begun>

Kearcs [15] (2%) Kearcs' Mattock • (30%) Tattered Cloth Tunic • (20%) Tattered Quilted Pants • (20%) Pitted Main Gauche • (40%) Obsidian • (12%) Chryoprase • (0.5%) <Grave Goods>

large skeleton [5] (50%) Bloody Skull • (70%) Jewels 45 • (1.5%) Old Iron Dagger • (0.3% each piece) Roman Leather • (1%) <Only Just Begun>

marsh scrag [11] (30%) Tattered Cloth Tunic • (20%) Tattered Quilted Pants • (20%) Pitted Main Gauche • (40%) Obsidian • (12%) Chryoprase • (0.5%) <Grave Goods>

marsh worm [9/11] (80%) Worm Skin [9] • (55%) Worm Skin Bracelet [11] • (50/80%) Brown Stone • (40/75%) Marsh Worm Gland

mist monster [16] (30%) Necklace of Swirling Mist • (80%) Misty Gray Stone • (80%) Globe of Swirling Mist • (0.3%) <Out of the Woods>

mist sprite [6] (15%) Misty Gray Stone • (35%) Moonstone • (20%) Jade • (10%) Obsidian • (1%) <Pilfered Prizes>

muck snake [1] (75%) Snake's Head • (10%) Snakeskin • (5%) Snake Meat

mud golem [14] (1.5%) Glowing Ball of Mud • (35%) Obsidian Spear Tip • (0.3%) <Out of the Woods>

mud worm [0] (85%) Worm-Acid Gland

outcast rogue [1] (12%) String of Polished Beads • (8%) Flask of Whiskey • (4% each) Copper Brooch, Silver Armband • (0.2%) <Pilfered Prizes> • (40%) APOA: Tattered Leather • (0.3% each) Bonecharm Amulet, Faithbound Ring • (0.2%) Aged Leather Baldric • (0.1% each) Mildewed Sleeves, Tunic • (20% each piece) Tattered Leather and Quilted

phantom page [4-5] (20%) Bloodied Banner

phantom squire [6-7] (20%) Bloodied Banner • (24%) Spinel • (6%) Chryoprase

pixie [7] (85%) Amber Nugget • (20%) Vine-Carved Totem • (35%) Jade • (2.5%) Grass Choker • (1%) <Pilfered Prizes>

puny skeleton [1] (50%) Bloody Skull • (30%) Jewels 45 • (8% each piece) Tattered Leather and Quilted • (1%) <Only Just Begun>

putrid zombie [4] (50%) Bloody Skull • (70%) Jewels 45 • (1.5%) Old Iron Dagger • (0.3% each piece) Roman Leather • (1%) <Only Just Begun>

quicksand [16] (70%) Fossilized Sand • (50%) Crystalized Sand • (77%) Pile of Sand • (0.5%) <Out of the Woods>

river drake hatchling [3] (70%) Drake Meat • (48%) Drakeling Scales • (10%) Drakeling Eye

river drakeling [5] (70% each) Drake Meat, Drakeling Scales • (10%) Drakeling Eye • (50%) Spiney Drakeling Tail

river racer [7] (95%) Snakeskin • (30%) Snake Scales • (90%) Snake Meat (x2) • (60%) Dead Mouse

river sprite [6] (70% each) Polished River Rock, Moonstone • (5%) Obsidian • (20%) Driftwood Totem • (5%) Jade • (1.5%) Tarnished Silver Torc • (0.5%) <Pilfered Prizes>

river spriteling [3-4] (57%) Half-Eaten Fish • (10% each) Round, Flat ***or*** Thin Flint Chert, Small Pearl • (1.5%) Tarnished Silver Torc • (1%) <Only Just Begun>

rot worm [5] (50% each) Worm-Acid Gland, Worm Skin

rotting skeleton [1] (50%) Bloody Skull • (30%) Jewels 45 • (8% each piece) Tattered Leather and Quilted • (1%) <Only Just Begun>

rotting zombie [5-6] (65% each) Aventurine, Leathery Skin • (5%) Aventurine • (8% each piece) Tattered Leather and Quilted • (0.5%) <Only Just Begun>

Scraek [13] (2%) Scraek's Crusher • (30%) Tattered Cloth Tunic • (20%) Tattered Quilted Pants • (20%) Pitted Main Gauche • (40%) Obsidian • (12%) Chryoprase • (0.5%) <Grave Goods>

scrag [8] (50%) Obsidian • (40%) Spinel • (20%) Pitted Main Gauche • (0.5%) <Of a Sylvan Glade>

scragling [6] (90%) Onyx • (70%) Shiny Trinket • (1%) <Pilfered Prizes>

scrawny bogman [2] (35%) Lizard-Foot Amulet (x2) • (20%) Aventurine • (1%) Jade • (1%) <Only Just Begun>

scum toad [0] (45%) Wart-Covered Toad Skin • (45%) Toad Slime

shambler [12-13] (27%) Shambler Branch (x2) • (1%) Pitted Shambler Staff • (25%) Wooden Shambler Heart • (0.3%) <Grave Goods>

skeleton [2] (55%) Bloody Skull • (40%) Jewels 45 • (8% each piece) Tattered Leather and Quilted • (1%) <Only Just Begun>

slime lizard [1] (65%) Lizard's Head

slough serpent [0] (80%) Serpent Scale • (75%) Serpent Fillet • (60%) Serpent Eggs

spiny eel [3] (30%) Derg Fillet (x2)

swamp rat [4] (50%) Rat Tail • (10%) Rat Fur

swamp slime [3] (10%) Pitted Great Sword • (20% each piece) Tattered Leather • (45%) Onyx • (35%) Moonstone • (1%) <Only Just Begun>

wandering spirit [9] (45%) Glowing Blue Slime • (35%) Pitted Wooden Shield • (25%) Tattered Leather Hood • (15%) Tattered Brown Boots • (50%) Obsidian • (8%) Chryoprase • (1%) Amethyst • (0.5%) <Of a Sylvan Glade>

water leaper [10] (75%) Leaper Tongue • (70%) Leaper Eye • (60%) Clear Green Stone • (80%) Leaper Leg

water leaper [8] (50%) Leaper Tongue • (70%) Leaper Leg • (40%) Clear Green Stone

will o' wisp [9/10/11] (43/60/50%) Globe of Blue Mist • (20/30/50%) Pile of Glowing Dust • (2/3/3%) Glowing Globe of Blue Mist

wisp ghoul [0] (80%) Rotting Flesh • (70%) Ghoul Brains • (50%) Rotting Finger

wood ogre berserker [14-15] (85%) Bloodstone • (45%) Carnelian • (65%) Dried Pork, Muffin, Canteen of Water, ***or*** Bottle of Elderberry Wine • (1.5%) <Ogre Skins> • (3%) APOA: Faded • (0.3%) <Out of the Woods> • (0.8%) Wormskin Helm • (0.4% each) Wormskin Leggings, Wormskin Boots, Sword of the Unruly

wood ogre scourge [12-13] (85%) Chryoprase • (45%) Amethyst • (65%) Dried Pork, Muffin, Canteen of Water, ***or*** Bottle of Elderberry Wine • (1.5%) <Ogre Skins> • (3%) APOA: Faded • (0.3%) <Grave Goods>

wood ogre seer [14] (75%) Chryoprase • (50%) Amethyst • (10%) Lapis Lazuli • (50%) Dried Pork, Muffin, Canteen of Water, ***or*** Bottle of Elderberry Wine • (1.5%) <Ogre Skins> • (3%) APOA: Faded • (0.3%) <Out of the Woods>

Quest NPCs

Avalon Marsh	
Lady Nimue	Barbaric Tales (lvl Guild Track - 15)
Lady Nimue	Legend of the Lake (lvl Guild Track - 15)
Caer Witrin	
Dugan Advien	Dugan's Magic Totem (lvl 19)
Adribard's Retreat	
Aiellana	The Heretical Hermit (lvl 21)
Anga Weaver	Slythcur Cloak (lvl 13)
Blade	Tyngyr's Daughter (lvl 9)
Brother Onoloth	Ivy Weave Gloves (lvl 16)
Camdene	Camdene's Components (lvl 6)

Key. [X] = level(s) • (X%) = chance to get item (if a list, just one) • (X% each) = chance for ***each*** item • hi-lo = most to least likely • APOA = a piece of armor • (x2) = item can drop twice

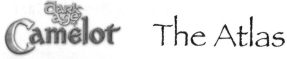

Black Mountains North

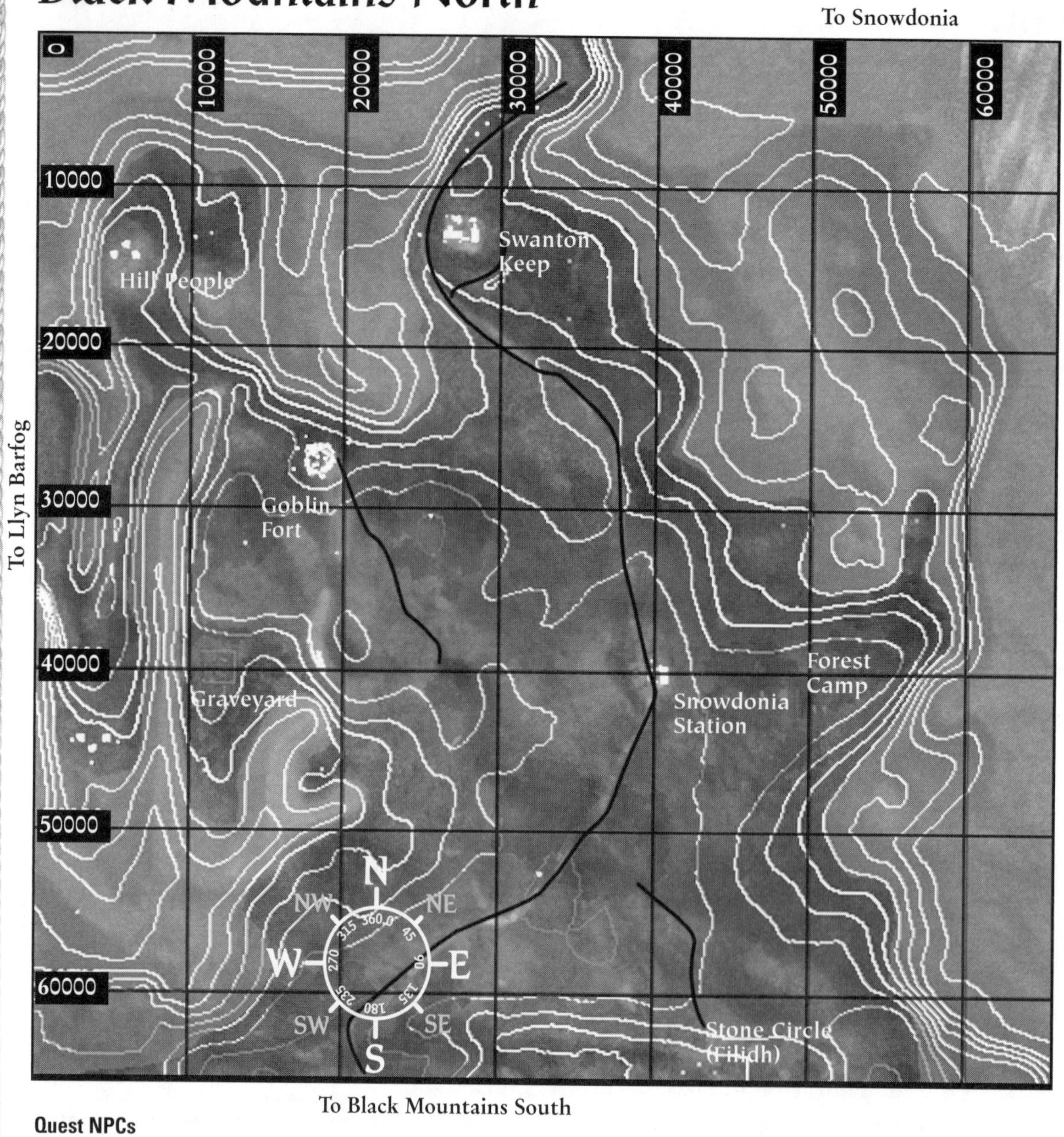
To Snowdonia
To Llyn Barfog
To Black Mountains South
0
10000
20000
30000
40000
50000
60000
Hill People
Swanton Keep
Goblin Fort
Graveyard
Snowdonia Station
Forest Camp
Stone Circle (Filidh)
N
NE
E
SE
S
SW
W
NW
360,0
45
90
135
180
225
270
315

Quest NPCs

Black Mountains North	
Amano	Deserter Amano (lvl Guild Track - 20
Forest Sauvage	
Rob Ria)	The Forest Plot (lvl 40)
Fort Snowdonia	
Sir Defi	Intervention (lvl 10)

Snowdonia Station	
Cranly	Thinking Cap (lvl 9)
Ember	Dragon ant Charm (lvl 10)
Mathien	Mathien's Metal (lvl 13)
Swanton Keep	
Heather Barclay	Secret Orders (lvl 41)
Yorel Anbidian	Wizard's demand (lvl 32)

Snowdonia	
Captain Rhodri	Regal Nobility (lvl Guild Track - 25)
Captain Rhodri	Path of the Renegade (lvl Guild Track - 20)
Lt. Brude	Simple Request (lvl 5)
Lt. Brude	Departed Hero (lvl 10)

Albion: Black Mountains North

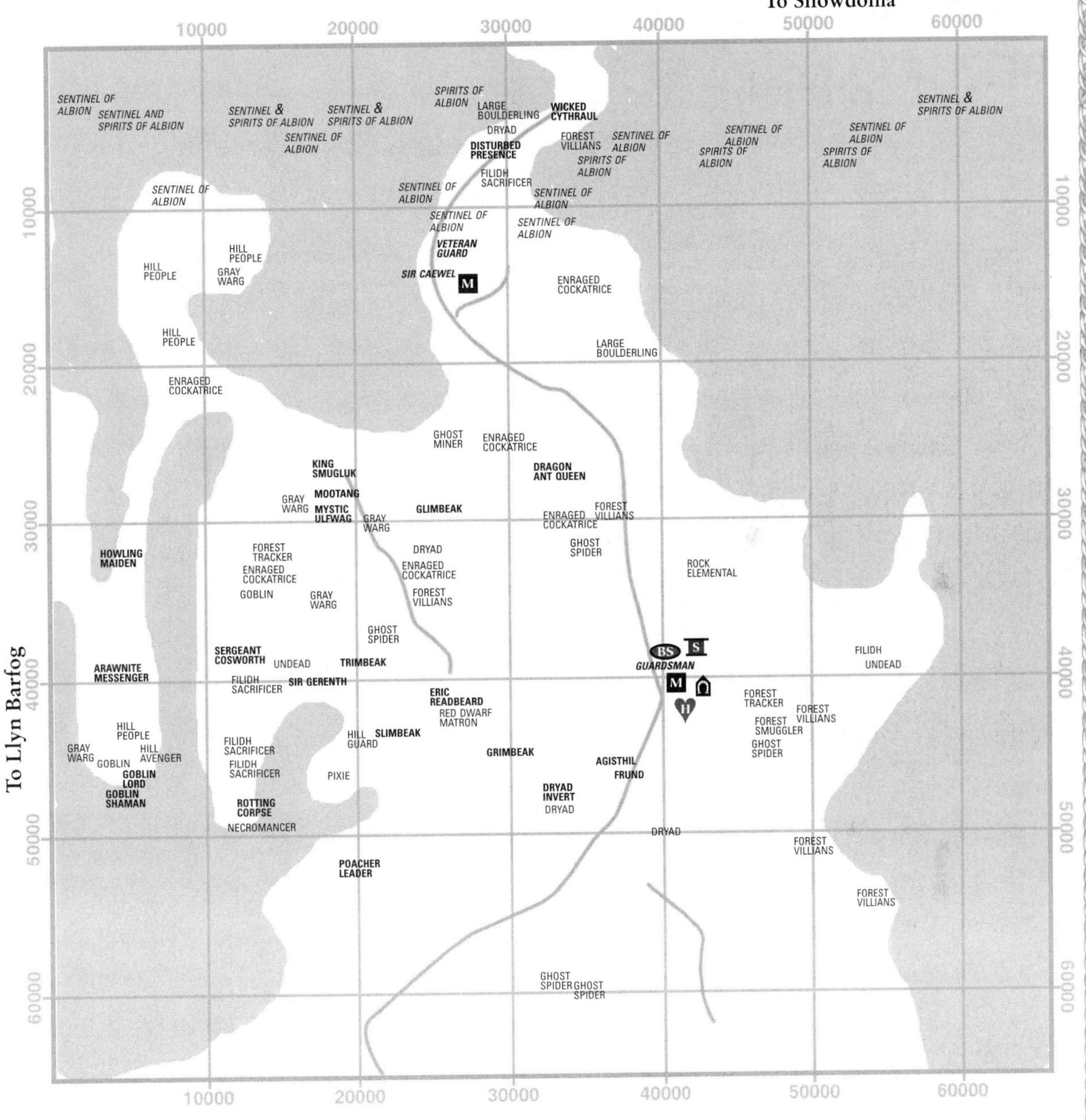

Lower-level monsters (below 9) not shown on map:

Creature	Lvl	Location
poacher	4	SW
small bear	4	WC,C,EC,SW,SC,SE
dragon ant worker	5	C
emerald snake	5	NC
poacher leader	5	SW
undead filidh	5	WC
forest lion	6	WC,C,EC,SW,SC,SE
giant spider	6	WC,C,EC
pixie	6	SW
undead filidh	6	WC
Agisthil	7	SC
dragon ant soldier	7	C
dryad	7	SC
filidh	7	WC
Frund	7	SC
giant spider	7	EC,SC
goblin scout	7	WC,C,SW
pixie	7	SW
red dwarf matron	7	C
undead filidh	7	WC
bear	8	NC,WC,C,EC,SW,SC,SE
devout filidh	8	WC,EC
dragon ant drone	8	C
dryad	8	C,SC
filidh	8	WC,EC
giant spider	8	EC,SC
goblin	8	WC,SW
goblin warrior	8	WC
pixie scout	8	C,SW
red dwarf matron	8	C
undead druid	8	WC

Black Mountains North Tips

This zone is more a connecting point than anything else. There are some good charmable monsters (for Sorcerers), and a few decent camps to hunt, but its real points of interest are its two towns. The first is Snowdonia Station, with the northernmost bindstone in the realm, and the second is Swanton Keep. The keep houses merchants, healers and a few trainers (but only high level poisons).

Heading farther to the north brings you to Snowdonia, the northernmost point of the Albion realm.

- Dave "i3ullseye" Maynor

Black Mountains North Solo and Group Levelling Tips

5-10	forest cats/lions, bears, goblins, druids, wargs
10-15	goblins, wargs, undead miners, dryads
15-20	foresters

Notes: There are plenty of charmables for Sorcerers and easy access to bindstones. It also has healers plus merchants and trainers of all kinds (although only high level poisons).

- Matt "Kyle Draconeco" Shirley

Frontier Tips

All four of the frontier zones are about the same when it comes to risk — you can be killed at any moment if you're not careful. The difference in them is that both Forest Sauvage and Snowdonia offer some excellent hunting for mid-level groups or mid-to-high solo Albion warriors. Snowdonia offers many good charmable monsters for a Sorcerer, and nice, tightly knit clusters of enemies to hunt. Forest Sauvagehas some great hunting spots for mid-20s groups. Forest giants are exceptionally good hunting, and have decent armor drops for some of the more melee oriented classes.

But overall, there is no real safe or sound strategy for hunting in *any* of these four zones. One rogue can turn your best hunt into your worst nightmare. Be on guard at *all* times.

- Dave "i3ullseye" Maynor

Solo and Group Levelling Tips

Forest Sauvage

Solo

15-20	forest snakes, deathstalkers
20-25	forest giants, fellwoods
25-50	fellwoods

Group

15-20	forest giants
20-50	fellwoods

- Matt "Kyle Draconeco" Shirley

Hadrian's Wall

Solo

30-50	midgard/hibernia invaders (mobs, not players), cave faireys, pictish druids/warriors

Group

30-45	same as solo
45-50	templars

Pennine Mountains

Solo

35-40	freybugs, worms
40-45	fellwoods
45-50	angry bwca

Group

35-45	western basilisks, padfoots, isolationists, giant boars, ellyll
45-50	above, plus cythreaths

Snowdonia

Solo

20-25	small rock bounders, faint grims
25-30	knife maidens, fairey frogs
30-40	arawnites
40-45	hollowmen
45-50	tegs, angrie bwca

Group

20-25	knife maidens
25-30	fairey frogs, knife maidens
30-35	arawnites
40-50	tegs, angry bwca

Loot

Agisthil [7] (24%) Pitted Dagger • (20%) Pitted Short Sword • (12%) Pitted Hand Axe • (8% each) Pitted Broadsword, Scimitar • (4% each) Pitted Great Sword, Bastard Sword • (24%) String of Polished Beads • (16%) Flask of Whiskey • (8% each) Copper Brooch, Silver Armband • (1%) <Pilfered Prizes>

Arawnite Messenger [19] (no loot)

bear [8] (33%) Bear Skin • (25%) Bear Fang • (5%) Pitted Sharp Claw

devout filidh [8-9] (40%) Brown Adder Stone • (60%) Obsidian • (25%) Chryoprase • (2%) Bloodstone • (15%) Pitted Wooden Shield, Tattered Cloth Tunic, Tattered Leather Hood, ***or*** Tattered Brown Boots • (20%) Dried Pork, Muffin, Canteen of Water, ***or*** Bottle of Elderberry Wine • (0.5%) <Of a Sylvan Glade>

disturbed presence [13] (60%) Glowing Green Slime • (50%) Bloodstone • (20%) Lapis Lazuli • (1%) Azurite • (1.5%) <Mounds of Salisbury> • (0.5%) <Grave Goods>

dragon ant drone [8] (80%) Dragon Ant Carapace • (35%) Dragon Ant Larva • (45%) Dragon Ant Mandible

dragon ant queen [10] (95%) Dragon Ant Mandible • (90% each) Dragon Ant Carapace, Larva

dragon ant soldier [7] (80%) Dragon Ant Carapace • (55%) Dragon Ant Larva • (15%) Dragon Ant Mandible

dragon ant worker [5] (50%) Dragon Ant Carapace • (40%) Dragon Ant Larva • (1%) Dragon Ant Mandible

dryad [7-9] (70% each) Oaken Medallion, Heartwood Amulet • (20%) Vine-Carved Totem • (0.5%) <Of a Sylvan Glade> • (1.5%) Grass Choker

dryad invert [9] (70% each) Oaken Medallion, Heartwood Amulet • (20%) Vine-Carved Totem • (0.5%) <Of a Sylvan Glade> • (1.5%) Grass Choker

emerald snake [5] (50% each) Emerald Snake Fang, Soft Snakeskin • (35% each) Snake's Head, Snake Meat • (1.5%) Sharp Snake Fang

enraged cockatrice [12] (no loot)

Erick Redbeard [12] (no loot)

filidh [7-8] (40%) Brown Adder Stone • (60%) Obsidian • (25%) Chryoprase • (2%) Bloodstone • (15%) Pitted Wooden Shield, Tattered Cloth Tunic, Tattered Leather Hood, ***or*** Tattered Brown Boots • (20%) Dried Pork, Muffin, Canteen of Water, ***or*** Bottle of Elderberry Wine • (0.5%) <Of a Sylvan Glade>

filidh sacrificer [9-10] (40%) Brown Adder Stone • (60%) Obsidian • (25%) Chryoprase • (2%) Bloodstone • (15%) Pitted Wooden Shield, Tattered Cloth Tunic, Tattered Leather Hood, ***or*** Tattered Brown Boots • (20%) Dried Pork, Muffin, Canteen of Water, ***or*** Bottle of Elderberry Wine • (0.5%) <Of a Sylvan Glade>

forest chief [19] (5%) Pitted Main Gauche • (65%) Bloodstone • (55%) Carnelian • (30%) Pearl • (45%) Dried Pork, Muffin, Canteen of Water, ***or*** Bottle of Elderberry Wine • (0.3%) <Rogue's Clothes>

forest lion [6] (99%) Lion Skin (x2)

forest smuggler [17] (5%) Pitted Rapier • (50%) Chryoprase • (45% each) Amethyst, Lapis Lazuli • (45%) Dried Pork, Muffin, Canteen of Water, ***or*** Bottle of Elderberry Wine • (0.3%) <King's Ransom>

forest tracker [15] (5% each) Pitted Short Sword, Tattered Studded Gauntlets • (35%) Carnelian • (50%) Bloodstone • (65%) Spinel • (0.3%) <King's Ransom> • (45%) Dried Pork, Muffin, Canteen of Water, ***or*** Bottle of Elderberry Wine

Frund [7] (24%) Pitted Dagger • (20%) Pitted Short Sword • (12%) Pitted Hand Axe • (8% each) Pitted Broadsword, Scimitar • (4% each) Pitted Great Sword, Bastard Sword • (24%) String of Polished Beads • (16%) Flask of Whiskey • (8% each) Copper Brooch, Silver Armband • (1%) <Pilfered Prizes>

ghost miner [11-12] (no loot)

giant spider [6-8] (99%) Spider Silk

Glimbeak [15] (no loot)

goblin [8-10] (24%) String of Polished Beads • (16%) Flask of Whiskey • (8% each) Copper Brooch, Silver Armband • (0.5%) <Pilfered Prizes> • (24%) Pitted Dagger • (20%) Pitted Short Sword • (12%) Pitted Hand Axe • (8% each) Pitted Broadsword, Scimitar • (4% each) Pitted Great Sword, Bastard Sword • (80%) APOA: Tattered Leather • (0.5%) <Of a Sylvan Glade>

goblin lord [11] (24%) String of Polished Beads • (16%) Flask of Whiskey • (8% each) Copper Brooch, Silver Armband • (0.5%) <Pilfered Prizes> • (24%) Pitted Dagger • (20%) Pitted Short Sword • (12%) Pitted Hand Axe • (8% each) Pitted Broadsword, Scimitar • (4% each) Pitted Great Sword, Bastard Sword • (80%) APOA: Tattered Leather • (0.5%) <Of a Sylvan Glade>

goblin scout [7] (24%) String of Polished Beads • (16%) Flask of Whiskey • (8% each) Copper Brooch, Silver Armband • (0.5%) <Pilfered Prizes> • (24%) Pitted Dagger • (20%) Pitted Short Sword • (12%) Pitted Hand Axe • (8% each) Pitted Broadsword, Scimitar • (4% each) Pitted Great Sword, Bastard Sword • (80%) APOA: Tattered Leather • (0.5%) <Of a Sylvan Glade>

goblin shaman [9] (24%) String of Polished Beads • (16%) Flask of Whiskey • (8% each) Copper Brooch, Silver Armband • (0.5%) <Pilfered Prizes> • (24%) Pitted Dagger • (20%) Pitted Short Sword • (12%) Pitted Hand Axe • (8% each) Pitted Broadsword, Scimitar • (4% each) Pitted Great Sword, Bastard Sword • (80%) APOA: Tattered Leather • (0.5%) <Of a Sylvan Glade>

goblin warrior [8] (1.4% each) Arm-Bone Scepter, Troll Hide Sleeves • (10%) Bloodstone • (60%) Spinel • (0.5%) <Pilfered Prizes>

gray warg [9-11] (80%) Grey Warg Skin • (40%) Bloody Warg Fang • (60% each) Large Warg Paw, Hunk of Warg Meat

Grimbeak [15] (no loot)

hill avenger [12] (25%) Bag of Herbs • (65%) 50 Feet of Rope • (1.5%) Herb Gatherer's Gloves • (45%) Tanned Bear Hide • (0.3%) <Of a Sylvan Glade>

hill chief [14] (53%) Bag of Herbs • (72%) 50 Feet of Rope • (1.5%) Herb Gatherer's Gloves • (25%) Tanned Bear Hide • (0.3%) <Grave Goods>

hill guard [11] (25%) Bag of Herbs • (65%) 50 Feet of Rope • (1.5%) Herb Gatherer's Gloves • (45%) Tanned Bear Hide • (0.3%) <Of a Sylvan Glade>

hill shaman [12] (60%) 50 Feet of Rope • (30%) Bag of Herbs • (40%) Tanned Bear Hide • (1.5%) Herb Gatherer's Gloves • (0.3%) <Grave Goods>

hill warrior [10] (25%) Bag of Herbs • (65%) 50 Feet of Rope • (1.5%) Herb Gatherer's Gloves • (45%) Tanned Bear Hide • (0.3%) <Of a Sylvan Glade>

horse [10] (75%) Horse Hair • (10%) Auburn Mane • (80%) Ruined Horse Skin • (35%) Horse Skin • (60%) Horse Hair

howling maiden [24] (50% each) Warm Patched Hide Blanket, Flask of Fire Wine, Small Silver Statue • (10% each) Agate, Garnet • (5% each) Citrine, APOA: Mithril Chain • (1.5%) Knifeman's Gold, Crystal ***or*** Silver Dagger, Snowdonian Bandit Bow, Frosted Scimitar, Furlined Cloak, Snowdonian Bandit Warmer • (0.3%) <Arthurian Artifacts 4>

King Smugluk [13] (1.4% each) Arm-Bone Scepter, Troll Hide Sleeves • (80%) Chryoprase • (40%) Carnelian • (0.3%) <Of a Sylvan Glade>

large boulderling [11] (60%) Amethyst • (30%) Carnelian • (1%) Lapis Lazuli

large boulderling [12] (60%) Carnelian • (30%) Lapis Lazuli • (1%) Agate

Mootang [11] (1.4% each) Troll Hide Sleeves, Arm-Bone Scepter • (80%) Chryoprase • (10%) Carnelian • (0.3%) <Of a Sylvan Glade>

Mystic Ulfwag [12] (1.4% each) Arm-Bone Scepter, Troll Hide Sleeves • (80%) Chryoprase • (40%) Carnelian • (0.3%) <Of a Sylvan Glade>

necromancer [31-33] (no loot)

pixie [6-7] (85%) Amber Nugget • (20%) Vine-Carved Totem • (35%) Jade • (2.5%) Grass Choker • (1%) <Pilfered Prizes>

pixie scout [8] (60%) Heartwood Amulet • (80%) Ash Talisman • (10%) Vine-Carved Totem • (2%) Grass Choker • (0.5%) <Of a Sylvan Glade> • (5%) Chryoprase

poacher [4] (5%) Moonstone • (70% each) Snakeskin, Wolf Skin • (5%) Tattered Lionskin • (1.2%) Pitted Dagger • (1%) Pitted Short Sword • (0.6%) Pitted Hand Axe • (0.4% each) Pitted Broadsword, Scimitar • (0.2% each) Pitted Great Sword, Bastard Sword • (20%) APOA: Tattered Leather • (1%) <Only Just Begun>

poacher leader [5] (5%) Moonstone • (70% each) Snakeskin, Wolf Skin • (5%) Tattered Lionskin • (1.2%) Pitted Dagger • (1%) Pitted Short Sword • (0.6%) Pitted Hand Axe • (0.4% each) Pitted Broadsword, Scimitar • (0.2% each) Pitted Great Sword, Bastard Sword • (20%) APOA: Tattered Leather • (1%) <Only Just Begun>

red dwarf matron [7-8] (24%) Pitted Dagger • (20%) Pitted Short Sword • (12%) Pitted Hand Axe • (8% each) Pitted Broadsword, Scimitar • (4% each) Pitted Great Sword, Bastard Sword • (24%) String of Polished Beads • (16%) Flask of Whiskey • (8% each) Copper Brooch, Silver Armband • (1%) <Pilfered Prizes>

rock elemental [11] (60%) Amethyst • (30%) Carnelian • (1%) Lapis Lazuli

rock elemental [12] (60%) Carnelian • (30%) Lapis Lazuli • (1%) Agate

Sergeant Cosworth [10] (no loot)

Sir Gerenth [10] (5%) Sacrificial Dagger • (40%) Citrine • (20%) Malachite • (1%) Green Tourmaline • (25%) Pitted Wooden Shield, Tattered Cloth Tunic, Tattered Leather Hood, ***or*** Tattered Brown Boots • (25%) Dried Pork, Muffin, Canteen of Water, ***or*** Bottle of Elderberry Wine • (1.5%) APOA: of the Resolute • (0.3%) <Out of the Woods> • (1.5%) Vest, Gloves ***or*** Sleeves of the Lost

Slimbeak [15] (no loot)

small bear [4] (33%) Bear Skin • (25%) Bear Fang • (5%) Pitted Sharp Claw

Trimbeak [15] (no loot)

undead druid [8-10] (80%) Brown Adder Stone • (40%) Chryoprase • (20%) Bloodstone • (1%) Amethyst • (25%) Dried Pork, Muffin, Canteen of Water, ***or*** Bottle of Elderberry Wine • (1.5%) <Crystal Visions> • (0.5%) <Of a Sylvan Glade>

undead filidh [5-7] (50%) Brown Adder Stone • (40%) Jade • (20%) Obsidian • (1%) Spinel • (25%) Dried Pork, Muffin, Canteen of Water, ***or*** Bottle of Elderberry Wine • (1.5%) <Crystal Visions> • (0.5%) <Pilfered Prizes>

wicked cythraul [26] (40%) Sunstone • (10%) Black Star Diopside • (1%) Cat's Eye Tourmaline • (1.5%) APOA: Ancient • (0.3%) <Arthurian Artifacts 1>

Key. [X] = level(s) • (X%) = chance to get item (if a list, just one) • (X% each) = chance for ***each*** item • hi-lo = most to least likely • APOA = a piece of armor • (x2) = item can drop twice

Black Mountains South

To Black Mountains North

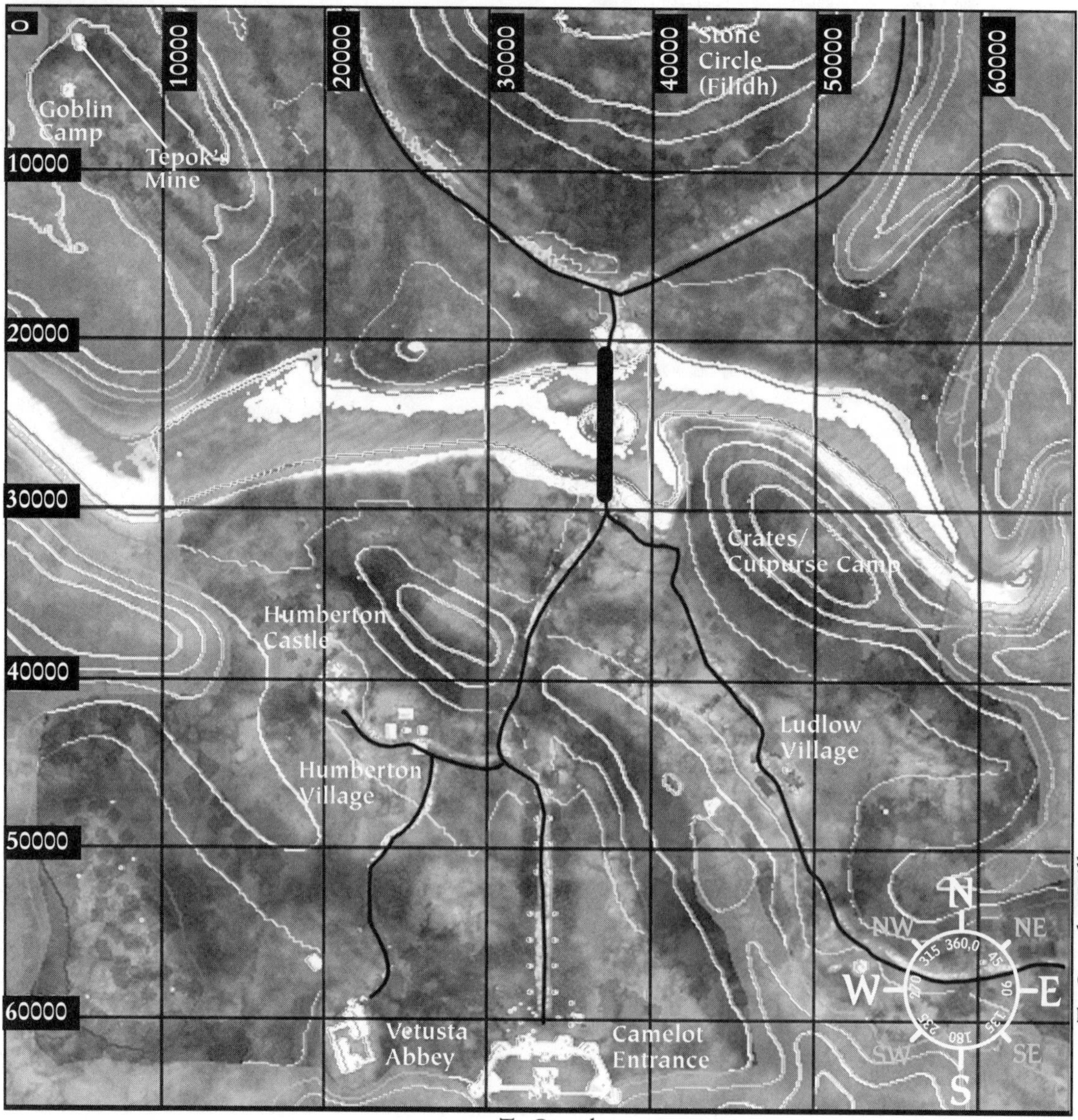

0
10000
20000
30000
40000
50000
60000

Goblin Camp
Tepok's Mine
Stone Circle (Filidh)
Crates/ Cutpurse Camp
Humberton Castle
Ludlow Village
Humberton Village
Vetusta Abbey
Camelot Entrance

N
NW
NE
W
E
SW
SE
S
360,0
45
90
135
180
225
270
315

To Camelot Hills

To Camelot

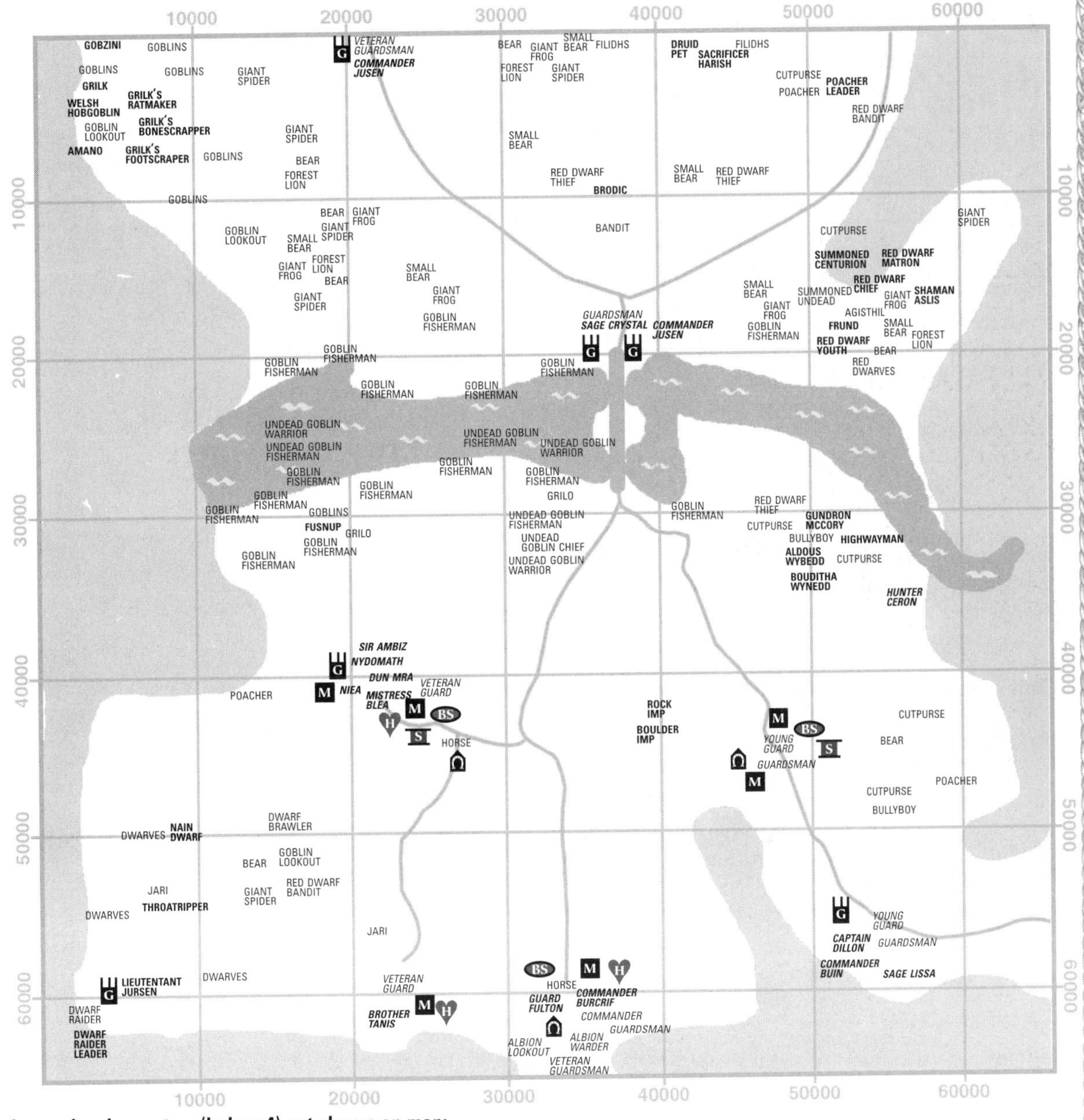

Lower-level monsters (below 4) not shown on map:

Creature	Lvl	Location
green snake	0	WC,C,EC,SW,SC,SE
robber	0	NC
slith broodling	0	SC
spirit hound	0	WC,C,EC,SW,SC,SE
water snake	0	WC,C,EC
worker ant	0	WC,C,EC,SW,SC,SE
black wolf pup	1	WC,C,EC,SW,SC,SE
boar piglet	1	WC,C,EC,SW,SC,SE
large ant	1	C,SW,SC,SE
puny skeleton	1	C,EC
weak skeleton	1	WC,C,EC,SW,SE
ant drone	2	C,SW,SC,SE
bear cub	2	WC,EC,SE
eel	2	WC,C,EC
moldy skeleton	2	C,SW,SE
skeleton	2	C,EC
spriggarn	2	WC,SE
wild sow	2	WC,C,EC,SW,SE
black wolf	3	NW,NC,NE,C,EC,SW,SE
decayed zombie	3	C
dwarf brawler	3	SW
forest snake	3	NC,NE,C,SW,SE
giant frog	3	NW,NC,NE
red lion	3	C,SW
rock imp	3	C
Slith	3	SC
snake	3	NC,NE,C,EC,SW
young cutpurse	3	EC,SE
young poacher	3	SW,SE

Black Mountains South Tips

This area has a lot of smaller towns to hunt from, and many quests involved. The level range is very good for starting characters. Some of the higher points are Goblin Fishermen and a group of Skeletons near the river's edge. Both have fairly good loot for their level, and humanoids (including undead) are the best option for lower-level characters to acquire armor without paying for it. The zone itself feels very sparse, with high-density pockets of enemies.

For a Sorcerer, the number of humanoids is very favorable for hunting. Having fast access to a lot of merchants, and access to the city of Camelot itself, is a great benefit at lower levels when you gain levels faster. Some buffs will have to be recast on zoning, and Sorcerers will have to acquire new pets at each training juncture, but at the lower levels the ready supply of pets lessens this burden.

One other point of interest is the entrance to Tepoks Mine in the northwest. This is a great dungeon for Sorcerers, since it's stocked with humanoids, and you should be able to charm the bears and scorpions by the time you are high enough level to hunt there.

- Dave "i3ullseye" Maynor

Other Notes. This zone has easy access to bindstones. It also has healers and merchants of all kinds.

- Matt "Kyle Draconeco" Shirley

Solo and Group Levelling Tips

Solo

1-5	wolf pups, puny skeletons, cutpurses, boars
5-10	goblin fishermen, bears, giant spiders, dwarfs

Group

1-5	same as solo
5-10	same as solo + druids

- Matt "Kyle Draconeco" Shirley

Quest NPCs

Camelot	
Albion Runner	Impossible Mission (lvl 33)
Bedelia	Bedelia's Grief (lvl 15)
Brother Lensar	Bishop Burhoff's Curse (lvl 19)
Gaevin Sebryn or Aonghas Prirerd	Lady Judith's Circlet (lvl 13)
Lady Triss	Departed Fellowship (lvl Guild Track - 40)
Laurenna	Long Lion Fang (lvl 30)
Magus Agyfen	Hidden Insurrection (lvl Guild Track - 40)
Master Vismer	Arc of Ages (lvl Guild Track - 40)
Master Vismer	Legione perso (lvl Guild Track - 30)
Sir Kenley	Bandit Camp (lvl 12)
Sister Elaydith	Lord Aryon's Box (lvl 17)
Sister Rhigwyn	The Captured Courier (lvl 13)
Vadri Pade	The Stolen Spells (lvl 17)
Vismer	La morti parla (lvl Guild Track - 20)
Vismer	Animare il morti (lvl Guild Track - 25)
Your Trainer	Fortune of Few (lvl 11)
Your Trainer	List of denial (lvl 11)
Your Trainer	Wisdom (lvl 11)
Your Trainer	Craft of Retribution, The (lvl Guild Track - 40)
Your Trainer	Abolishment of Sacrifice (lvl Guild Track - 15)
Your Trainer	Rebellion Accepted (lvl Guild Track - 15)
Your Trainer	Scura tragedia (lvl Guild Track - 15)
your trainer	Wizard Lost (lvl Guild Track - 15)
Your Trainer	Point of Reason (lvl Guild Track - 25)
Your Trainer	Chains of Death (lvl Guild Track - 30)
Your Trainer	Hands of Fate (lvl Guild Track - 30)
Your Trainer	Entry into Tomorrow (lvl 11)
Camelot West Tower Outpost	
Lt. Jursen	Ripper (lvl 5)
Cotswald	
Leridia	Cloak of Shades Part 1 (lvl 11)
Eowyln Astos	Heart of Sephucoth (lvl 7)
Frip	Father Hugrath (lvl 8)
Nob the Stableboy	Search for Sil (lvl 7)
Humberton Keep	
Contyn	Contyth's Hammer (lvl 17)
Niea	Niea's Missing Brother (lvl 11)
Siom Felanis	Siom's Staff (lvl 14)
Sir Gleran	Barnett's Shield (lvl 13)
Steward Willie	Wolf Pelt Cloak (lvl 1)
Ludlow	
Dunan	Dunan's bear tooth (lvl 9)
Sals Pew	Sals' Jar (lvl 11)
North Camelot Gates	
Commander Burcrif	Hunt for Slith (lvl 4)
Prydwen Keep	
Hugh Gallen	Cleric Mulgrut (lvl 5)
Master Graent	Association (lvl 3)
Sir Jerem	Guarding the Stone (lvl 12)
Sir Quait	Lady Leana (lvl 8)
Llewellyn Camber	Staff of Life (lvl 11)
Sgt. Alain	The Growling Ghost (lvl 13)

Loot

Agisthil [7] *see red dwarf bandit [6-8]*

Aldous Wynedd [10] (30%) String of Polished Beads • (20%) Flask of Whiskey • (10% each) Copper Brooch, Silver Armband • (0.5%) <Pilfered Prizes>

Amano [10] *see goblin [8-10]*

ant drone [2] (80%) Ant Parts • (60%) Ant Parts

bandit [5-6] (70% each) Aventurine, Bent Lockpick • (5%) Moonstone • (8%) Bandit's Ear • (0.3% each piece) Roman Leather • (0.5%) <Only Just Begun>

bear [8] (33%) Bear Skin • (25%) Bear Fang • (5%) Pitted Sharp Claw

bear cub [2] (15%) Bear Skin • (22%) Bear Fang • (7%) Pitted Sharp Claw

black wolf [3] (50%) Wolf Fang • (70%) Wolf Skin • (1.5%) Wolf Fang (x2) • (1%) Wolf Hide Leggings

black wolf pup [1] (30%) Wolf Fang • (60%) Wolf Skin • (0.5%) Wolf Fang (x2) • (0.4%) Wolf Hide Leggings

boar piglet [1] (50%) Boar Tusk • (25%) Raw Pork • (0.8%) Boar Tusk (x2) • (0.5%) Sharp Tusk (x3)

Bouditha Wynedd [9] (30%) String of Polished Beads • (20%) Flask of Whiskey • (10% each) Copper Brooch, Silver Armband • (0.5%) <Pilfered Prizes> • (40%) Gnarled Staff

boulder imp [7] (30% each) Rock Imp Head, Hand • (30%) Obsidian • (20%) Spinel • (1%) Chryoprase • (10% each) Round, Thin, Flat Flint Chert • (0.5%) <Pilfered Prizes>

Brodic [11] (50%) Ghostly Roman Lantern • (5%) Bronze Buckled Roman Belt • (20%) Jewels 26 • (2.4%) Roman Short Sword ***or*** Gladius • (0.6%) Roman Shield • (1.5%) Tacticians Ornamental Honor • (0.5%) <Grave Goods>

bullyboy [5-6] (30%) String of Polished Beads • (20%) Flask of Whiskey • (10% each) Copper Brooch, Silver Armband • (0.5%) <Pilfered Prizes>

cutpurse [4] (12%) String of Polished Beads • (8%) Flask of Whiskey • (4% each) Copper Brooch, Silver Armband • (0.2%) <Pilfered Prizes> • (40%) APOA: Tattered Leather • (0.3% each) Bonecharm Amulet, Faithbound Ring • (0.2%) Aged Leather Baldric • (0.1% each) Mildewed Sleeves, Tunic • (20% each piece) Tattered Leather and Quilted

decayed zombie [3] (65% each) Aventurine, Leathery Skin • (5%) Aventurine • (8% each piece) Tattered Leather and Quilted • (0.5%) <Only Just Begun>

devout filidh [8-9] (40%) Brown Adder Stone • (60%) Obsidian • (25%) Chryoprase • (2%) Bloodstone • (15%) Pitted Wooden Shield, Tattered Cloth Tunic, Tattered Leather Hood, ***or*** Tattered Brown Boots • (20%) Dried Pork, Muffin, Canteen of Water, ***or*** Bottle of Elderberry Wine • (0.5%) <Of a Sylvan Glade>

druid pet [4] (60%) Heartwood Amulet • (80%) Ash Talisman • (10%) Vine-Carved Totem • (2%) Grass Choker • (0.5%) <Of a Sylvan Glade> • (5%) Chryoprase

dwarf brawler [3-4] (7.2% each) Pitted Dagger, String of Polished Beads • (6%) Pitted Short Sword • (3.6%) Pitted Hand Axe • (2.4% each) Pitted Broadsword, Pitted Scimitar, Copper Brooch, Silver Armband • (1.2% each) Pitted Great Sword, Bastard Sword • (0.3%) <Pilfered Prizes> (x2) • (40%) Chicken • (20%) Sack of Grain • (15%) Dwarf Skullcap • (10%) APOA: Tattered Leather • (1%) <Only Just Begun>

dwarf pillager [4-5] *see dwarf brawler [3-4]*

dwarf raider [5-6] *see dwarf brawler [3-4]*

Dwarf Raider Leader [8] *see dwarf brawler [3-4]*

eel [2] (30%) Derg Fillet (x2)

filidh [7-8] (40%) Brown Adder Stone • (60%) Obsidian • (25%) Chryoprase • (2%) Bloodstone • (15%) Pitted Wooden Shield, Tattered Cloth Tunic, Tattered Leather Hood, ***or*** Tattered Brown Boots • (20%) Dried Pork, Muffin, Canteen of Water, ***or*** Bottle of Elderberry Wine • (0.5%) <Of a Sylvan Glade>

filidh sacrificer [9-10] (40%) Brown Adder Stone • (60%) Obsidian • (25%) Chryoprase • (2%) Bloodstone • (15%) Pitted Wooden Shield, Tattered Cloth Tunic, Tattered Leather Hood, ***or*** Tattered Brown Boots • (20%) Dried Pork, Muffin, Canteen of Water, ***or*** Bottle of Elderberry Wine • (0.5%) <Of a Sylvan Glade>

forest lion [6] (99%) Lion Skin (x2)

forest snake [3] (70% each) Large Snake Skin, Head • (1.3%) Snake Scales • (1%) Snake Meat • (0.02%) Sharp Snake Fang

Frund [7] *see red dwarf bandit [6-8]*

giant frog [3-4] (50%) Frog Legs

giant spider [6-8] (99%) Spider Silk

goblin [8-10] (24%) String of Polished Beads • (16%) Flask of Whiskey • (8% each) Copper Brooch, Silver Armband • (0.5%) <Pilfered Prizes> • (24%) Pitted Dagger • (20%) Pitted Short Sword • (12%) Pitted Hand Axe • (8% each) Pitted Broadsword, Scimitar • (4% each) Pitted Great Sword, Bastard Sword • (80%) APOA: Tattered Leather • (0.5%) <Of a Sylvan Glade>

goblin fisherman [4-6] (1%) <Only Just Begun> • (40%) APOA: Tattered Leather • (3%) Pitted Dagger • (2.5%) Pitted Short Sword • (1.5%) Pitted Hand Axe • (1% each) Pitted Broadsword, Scimitar • (0.5% each) Pitted Great Sword, Bastard Sword • (12%) String of Polished Beads • (8%) Flask of Whiskey • (4% each) Copper Brooch, Silver Armband • (0.5%) <Pilfered Prizes> • (40%) Derg Fillet

goblin lookout [8] *see goblin [8-10]*

goblin scout [7] *see goblin [8-10]*

goblin shaman [9-10] *see goblin [8-10]*

green snake [0] (45%) Snake's Head • (15%) Snakeskin • (7.5%) Snake Scales • (10%) Snake Meat • (0.4%) Snake Scales • (0.5%) Snake Meat • (0.01%) Sharp Snake Fang

Grilk [13] *see goblin [8-10]*

Grilo [7] *see goblin fisherman [4-6]*

Gundron McCory [9] (30%) String of Polished Beads • (20%) Flask of Whiskey • (10% each) Copper Brooch, Silver Armband • (0.5%) <Pilfered Prizes> • (70%) Iron-Strapped Shield • (30%) String of Polished Beads • (20%) Flask of Whiskey • (10% each) Copper Brooch, Silver Armband • (0.5%) <Pilfered Prizes>

highwayman [7] (30%) String of Polished Beads • (20%) Flask of Whiskey • (10% each) Copper Brooch, Silver Armband • (0.5%) <Pilfered Prizes>

horse [10] (75%) Horse Hair • (10%) Auburn Mane • (80%) Ruined Horse Skin • (35%) Horse Skin • (60%) Horse Hair

Jari [8] (80%) Boar Tusk (x2) • (50%) Sharp Tusk (x3)

large ant [1] (80%) Ant Parts • (60%) Ant Parts

moldy skeleton [2] (55%) Bloody Skull • (40%) Jewels 45 • (8% each piece) Tattered Leather and Quilted • (1%) <Only Just Begun>

Nain Dwarf [9] *see dwarf brawler [3-4]*

Pebble [4] *see rock imp [3-5]*

poacher [4] (5%) Moonstone • (70% each) Snakeskin, Wolf Skin • (5%) Tattered Lionskin • (1.2%) Pitted Dagger • (1%) Pitted Short Sword • (0.6%) Pitted Hand Axe • (0.4% each) Pitted Broadsword, Scimitar • (0.2% each) Pitted Great Sword, Bastard Sword • (20%) APOA: Tattered Leather • (1%) <Only Just Begun>

poacher leader [5] *see poacher [4]*

puny skeleton [1] (50%) Bloody Skull • (30%) Jewels 45 • (8% each piece) Tattered Leather and Quilted • (1%) <Only Just Begun>

red dwarf bandit [6-8] (24%) Pitted Dagger • (20%) Pitted Short Sword • (12%) Pitted Hand Axe • (8% each) Pitted Broadsword, Scimitar • (4% each) Pitted Great Sword, Bastard Sword • (24%) String of Polished Beads • (16%) Flask of Whiskey • (8% each) Copper Brooch, Silver Armband • (1%) <Pilfered Prizes>

red dwarf chief [10] *see red dwarf bandit [6-8]*

red dwarf matron [7-8] *see red dwarf bandit [6-8]*

red dwarf thief [5-7] *see red dwarf bandit [6-8]*

red dwarf youth [5] *see red dwarf bandit [6-8]*

red lion [3] (30%) Tattered Lionskin

robber [0] (70% each) Aventurine, Bent Lockpick • (5%) Moonstone • (8%) Bandit's Ear • (0.3% each piece) Roman Leather • (0.5%) <Only Just Begun>

rock imp [3-5] (5%) Rock Imp Head • (30%) Aventurine • (15%) Moonstone • (15%) Jade • (1%) Obsidian • (1%) <Only Just Begun>

Sacrificer Harish [9] (5%) Sacrificial Dagger • (40%) Citrine • (20%) Malachite • (1%) Green Tourmaline • (25%) Pitted Wooden Shield, Tattered Cloth Tunic, Tattered Leather Hood, ***or*** Tattered Brown Boots • (25%) Dried Pork, Muffin, Canteen of Water, ***or*** Bottle of Elderberry Wine • (1.5%) APOA: of the Resolute • (0.3%) <Out of the Woods> • (1.5%) Vest, Gloves ***or*** Sleeves of the Lost

Shade of Harish [13] *see Sacrificer Harish [9]*

Shaman Aslis [18] *see red dwarf bandit [6-8]*

skeleton [2] (55%) Bloody Skull • (40%) Jewels 45 • (8% each piece) Tattered Leather and Quilted • (1%) <Only Just Begun>

Slith [3] (35%) Snake Scales • (50%) Snake Meat • (1.5%) Sharp Snake Fang

slith broodling [0] *see green snake [0]*

small bear [4] (33%) Bear Skin • (25%) Bear Fang • (5%) Pitted Sharp Claw

snake [3] (70% each) Large Snake Skin, Head • (1.3%) Snake Scales • (1%) Snake Meat • (0.02%) Sharp Snake Fang

spirit hound [0] (99%) Tattered Moldy Collar • (80%) Spirit Fang

spriggarn [2] (55%) Spotted Mushroom • (10%) Polished Wooden Bowl • (17%) Jewels 45 • (25%) Round, Flat ***or*** Thin Flint Chert • (8% each piece) Tattered Leather and Quilted • (1%) <Only Just Begun>

summoned centurion [17] (no loot)

summoned skeleton [20-21] (no loot)

summoned spirit [10-11] (45%) Glowing Blue Slime • (35%) Pitted Wooden Shield • (25%) Tattered Leather Hood • (15%) Tattered Brown Boots • (50%) Obsidian • (8%) Chryoprase • (1%) Amethyst • (0.5%) <Of a Sylvan Glade>

Throatripper [5] (50%) Wolf Fang (x2) • (35%) Wolf Hide Leggings

undead goblin chief [6] (50%) Bloody Skull • (70%) Jewels 45 • (1.5%) Old Iron Dagger • (0.3% each piece) Roman Leather • (1%) <Only Just Begun>

undead goblin fisherman [4] (50%) Bloody Skull • (70%) Jewels 45 • (1.5%) Old Iron Dagger • (0.3% each piece) Roman Leather • (1%) <Only Just Begun>

undead goblin warrior [5] (50%) Bloody Skull • (70%) Jewels 45 • (1.5%) Old Iron Dagger • (0.3% each piece) Roman Leather • (1%) <Only Just Begun>

water snake [0] (30%) Derg Fillet (x2)

weak skeleton [1] (60%) Bloody Skull • (1.2%) Pitted Dagger • (1%) Pitted Short Sword • (0.6%) Pitted Hand Axe, Bonecharm Amulet • (0.4% each) Pitted Broadsword, Pitted Scimitar, Faithbound Ring • (0.2% each) Pitted Great Sword, Bastard Sword • (0.02%) Faerie Charm Necklace • (18% each) Tattered Leather and Quilted • (25%) Onyx

Welsh hobgoblin [17] (25% each) Bloody Hobgoblin Eyeball (x2), Severed Hobgoblin Toe (x2) • (1%) Mutilated Hobgoblin Hand • (0.3%) <Out of the Woods> • (1.5%) APOA: Bloodied Leather

wild sow [2] (50%) Boar Tusk • (40%) Raw Pork • (1.6%) Boar Tusk (x2) • (1%) Sharp Tusk (x3)

worker ant [0] (99%) Ant Parts

young cutpurse [3] *see cutpurse [4]*

young poacher [3] *see poacher [4]*

Key. [X] = level(s) • (X%) = chance to get item (if a list, just one) • (X% each) = chance for ***each*** item • hi-lo = most to least likely • APOA = a piece of armor • (x2) = item can drop twice

Camelot Hills

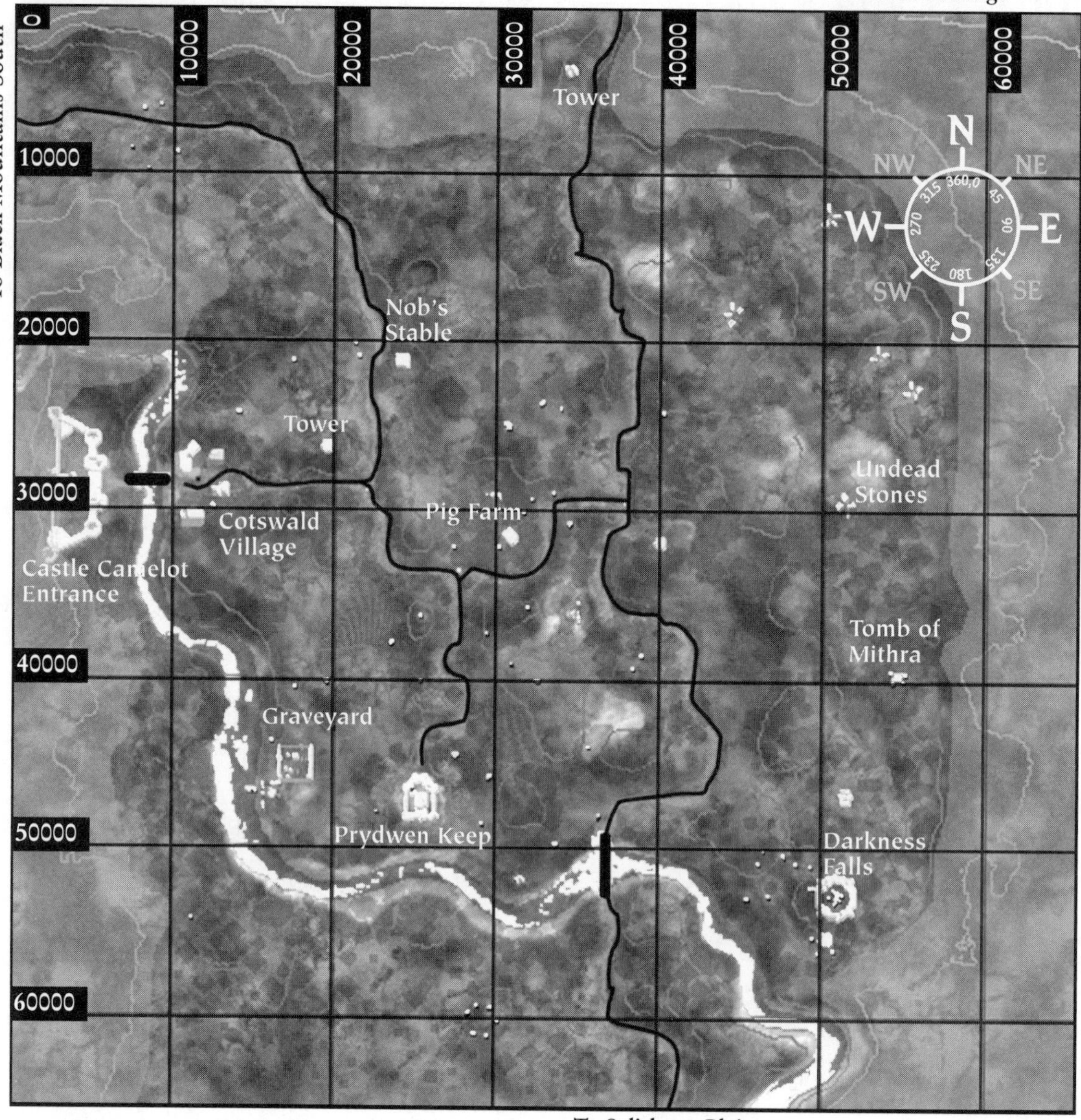

BANDITS =
- bandit
- bandit henchman
- bandit leader
- bandit lieutenant
- bandit messenger
- bandit thaumaturge

BROWNIE =
- brownie
- brownie nomad

SNAKE =
- emerald snake
- grass snake
- adder
- forest snake
- small snake
- snake

HOUND =
- gray wolf
- gray wolf pup
- spirit hound
- small gray wolf

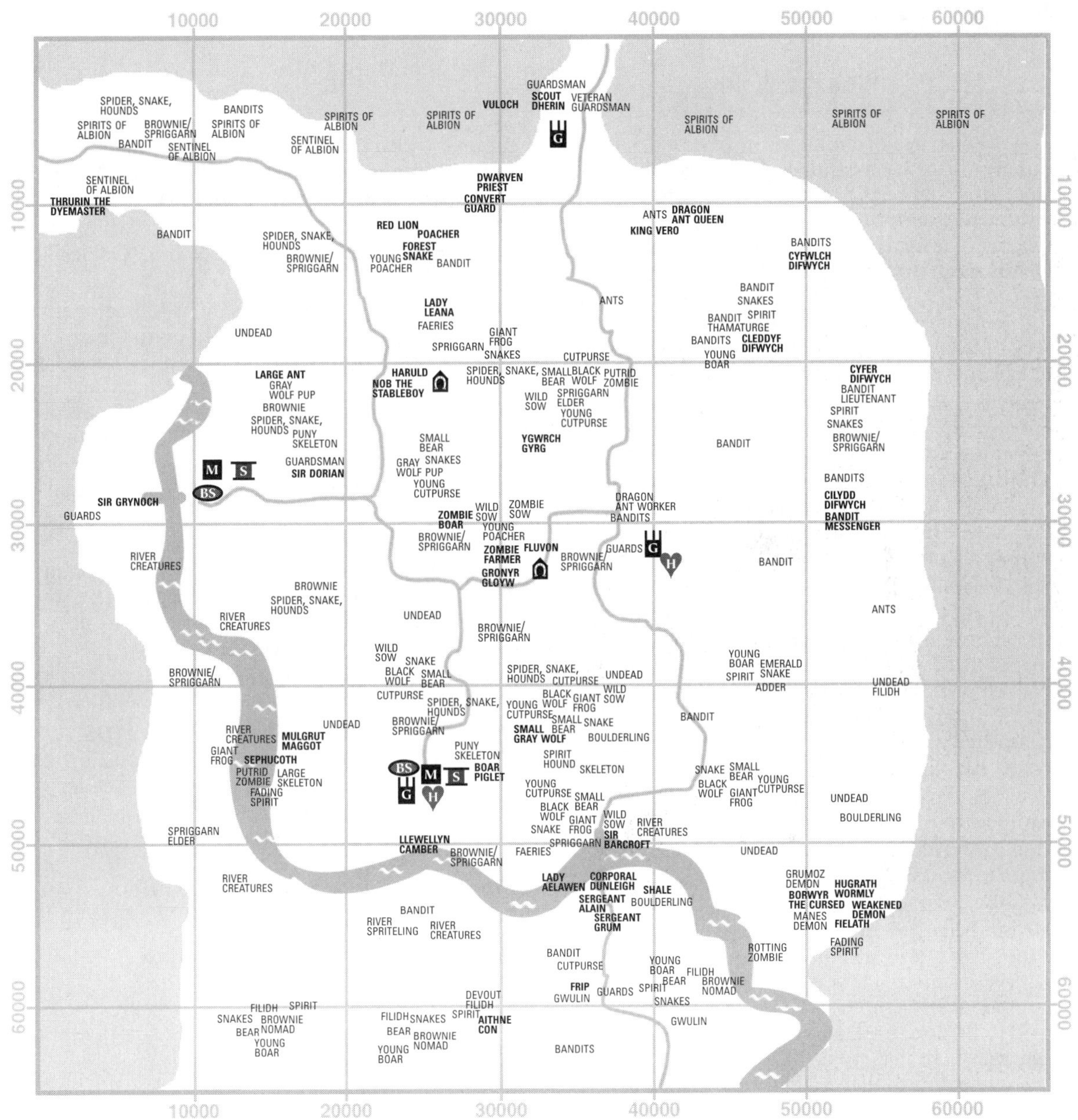

RIVER CREATURES =
- river drake hatchling
- river drakeling
- river sprite
- river spriteling

ANTS =
- dragon ant drone
- dragon ant soldier
- dragon ant worker

spriggarn =
- spriggarn
- spriggarn elder

UNDEAD =
- decayed zombie
- large skeleton
- puny skeleton
- putrid zombie
- undead filidh
- rotting zombie
- skeleton
- undead druid

FAERIES =
- faerie bell-wether
- faerie mischief-maker
- faerie wolf-crier

Camelot Hills Tips

The starting area of choice for most new players, this area is always bustling with activity. Numerous landmarks and bindstones make it easy to learn your way around and get from point A to point B quickly. The many camps of monsters and named guards mean that small groups as well as solo players can get fast experience. Many of the best quests for young characters start in this zone, and the history of Camelot can be learned from the various inhabitants of the towns and villages in the area.

However, anyone who is expecting to start low and move gradually outward toward ever-greater challenges is going to be disappointed by Camelot Hills. The layout of the zone is more "clumps" of mixed-level monsters. There really is no one class type that does worse than any other at this level, though, so if you watch your back, you should do fine.

Solo Friendly? This is definitely the place to be for the young solo character. Low level monsters drop starter armor. The spriggarns drop cherts of various shapes that can be turned in for a starter weapon. Named guards are easy to find and close to bindstones, meaning that kill tasks can be found and completed quickly.

While safe on horseback on the roads, the solo traveler should use caution when traveling the known pathways through the hills. Bandits and highwaymen have been known to attack the weary road traveler, and though the guards try to keep roads safe, they don't always succeed.

Group Friendly? Less group friendly than other zones, this is primarily because grouping at the lowest levels is not the best way to gain experience. The number of static camps is low, and respawn times tend to be slow, meaning that larger groups quickly run out of anything to do. There are, of course, a few exceptions to this. Bandits (and giant ants) plague the hills, and can keep a group busy for quite some time. Most groups that form in Camelot Hills, however, soon find themselves gravitating toward the Tomb of Mithra, where magical loot is more plentiful and the undead seem to never cease.

Who loves this area? The area has something for everyone. There are undead for Clerics and others who use crush weapons. Bandits are susceptible to anyone with a slashing weapon. And animals abound for the thrusting weapon wielder. Anyone who is young and in need of loot to get started is going to like Camelot Hills the best.

- Heather "Orlena" Rothwell & Jim "Oakleif" Rothwell

Both your first and last dungeon in Albion opens into this area. The Tomb of Mithra is to the east, and just south of it is the entrance to Darkness Falls. In the Tomb you will likely start forging your first real grouping skills, but if you are of the Sorcerous profession you will find it impossible to charm a slave in this ruin. Darkness Falls, however, presents targets and Sorcerer pets, from levels 15 or so, all the way through level 50.

There are *many* quests in and around Camelot Hills, and there are many task NPCs to be found. This zone also connects to Forest Sauvage, by way of Castle Sauvage, the jumping-off point to all Battlezone and RvR expeditions.

- Dave "i3ullseye" Maynor

Solo and Group Levelling Tips

1-5	wolf pups, puny skeletons, brownies, cutpurses, zombies, beetles
5-10	bandits, dragon ants, boulderlings

- Matt "Kyle Draconeco" Shirley

Note: See p. 34 for Tomb of Mithra tips.

Quest NPCs

Camelot	
See p. 49 for Camelot quest NPCs.	
Camelot West Tower Outpost	
Lt. Jursen	Ripper (lvl 5)
Cotswald	
Leridia	Cloak of Shades Part 1 (lvl 11)
Eowyln Astos	Heart of Sephucoth (lvl 7)
Frip	Father Hugrath (lvl 8)
Nob the Stableboy	Search for Sil (lvl 7)
Prydwen Keep	
Hugh Gallen	Cleric Mulgrut (lvl 5)
Master Graent	Association (lvl 3)
Sir Jerem	Guarding the Stone (lvl 12)
Sir Quait	Lady Leana (lvl 8)
Llewellyn Camber	Staff of Life (lvl 11)
Sgt. Alain	The Growling Ghost (lvl 13)

Key. [X] = level(s) • (X%) = chance to get item (if a list, just one) • (X% each) = chance for ***each*** item • hi-lo = most to least likely • APOA = a piece of armor • (x2) = item can drop twice

Loot

adder [7] (50% each) Adder Skin, Fang • (8%) Adder Poison Sac • (1.5%) Sharp Snake Fang

Aithne Con [10] (no loot)

bandit [5-6,8] (70% each) Aventurine, Bent Lockpick • (5%) Moonstone • (8%) Bandit's Ear • (0.3% each piece) Roman Leather • (0.5%) <Only Just Begun>

bandit henchman [9] (70% each) Bent Lockpick, Jade • (20%) Obsidian • (48%) Bandit's Ear • (0.3% each piece) Roman Leather • (3%) <Of a Sylvan Glade>

bandit leader [11] (70% each) Bent Lockpick, Jade • (20%) Obsidian • (48%) Bandit's Ear • (0.3% each piece) Roman Leather • (3%) <Of a Sylvan Glade>

bandit lieutenant [9] (70% each) Bent Lockpick, Jade • (20%) Obsidian • (48%) Bandit's Ear • (0.3% each piece) Roman Leather • (3%) <Of a Sylvan Glade>

bandit messenger [9] (no loot)

bandit thaumaturge [8] (10%) Pitted Staff • (70%) Jade • (50%) Chryoprase • (48%) Bandit's Ear • (0.5% each piece) Quilted • (0.5%) <Pilfered Prizes>

bear [8] (33%) Bear Skin • (25%) Bear Fang • (5%) Pitted Sharp Claw

black wolf [3] (50%) Wolf Fang • (70%) Wolf Skin • (1.5%) Wolf Fang (x2) • (1%) Wolf Hide Leggings

boar piglet [1] (50%) Boar Tusk • (25%) Raw Pork • (0.8%) Boar Tusk (x2) • (0.5%) Sharp Tusk (x3)

Borwyr the Cursed [13] (15%) Pitted Staff • (0.3%) <Grave Goods>

boulderling [9] (50%) Jewels 45 • (50%) Spinel • (25%) Bloodstone • (1.5%) Stone Heart of the Earth Spirit • (0.5%) <Pilfered Prizes>

brownie [0] (40%) Spotted Mushroom • (15%) Jewels 45 • (1%) <Only Just Begun>

brownie nomad [8] (40%) Large Spotted Mushroom • (50%) Obsidian • (1%) Spinel • (1.5%) Grass Choker • (0.5%) <Of a Sylvan Glade>

Cilydd Difwych [11] (no loot)

Cleddyf Difwych [11] (70% each) Bent Lockpick, Jade • (20%) Obsidian • (48%) Bandit's Ear • (0.3% each piece) Roman Leather • (3%) <Of a Sylvan Glade>

convert guard [9] (no loot)

cutpurse [4] (12%) String of Polished Beads • (8%) Flask of Whiskey • (4% each) Copper Brooch, Silver Armband • (0.2%) <Pilfered Prizes> • (40%) APOA: Tattered Leather • (0.3% each) Bonecharm Amulet, Faithbound Ring • (0.2%) Aged Leather Baldric • (0.1% each) Mildewed Sleeves, Tunic • (20% each piece) Tattered Leather and Quilted

Cyfer Difwych [11] (10%) Pitted Staff • (70%) Jade • (50%) Chryoprase • (48%) Bandit's Ear • (0.5% each piece) Quilted • (0.5%) <Pilfered Prizes>

Cyfwlch Difwych [11] (70% each) Bent Lockpick, Jade • (20%) Obsidian • (48%) Bandit's Ear • (0.3% each piece) Roman Leather • (3%) <Of a Sylvan Glade>

decayed zombie [3] (65% each) Aventurine, Leathery Skin • (5%) Aventurine • (8% each piece) Tattered Leather and Quilted • (0.5%) <Only Just Begun>

devout filidh [8-9] (40%) Brown Adder Stone • (60%) Obsidian • (25%) Chryoprase • (2%) Bloodstone • (15%) Pitted Wooden Shield, Tattered Cloth Tunic, Tattered Leather Hood, ***or*** Tattered Brown Boots • (20%) Dried Pork, Muffin, Canteen of Water, ***or*** Bottle of Elderberry Wine • (0.5%) <Of a Sylvan Glade>

dragon ant drone [8] (80%) Dragon Ant Carapace • (35%) Dragon Ant Larva • (45%) Dragon Ant Mandible

dragon ant queen [10] (95%) Dragon Ant Mandible • (90% each) Dragon Ant Carapace, Larva

dragon ant soldier [7] (80%) Dragon Ant Carapace • (55%) Dragon Ant Larva • (15%) Dragon Ant Mandible

dragon ant worker [5] (50%) Dragon Ant Carapace • (40%) Dragon Ant Larva • (1%) Dragon Ant Mandible

Dwarven Priest [9] (no loot)

emerald snake [5] (50% each) Emerald Snake Fang, Soft Snakeskin • (35% each) Snake's Head, Snake Meat • (1.5%) Sharp Snake Fang

fading spirit [7] (45%) Faded Green Slime • (35%) Tattered Woolen Robes • (25%) Tattered Brown Boots • (50%) Spinel • (1%) Bloodstone • (0.5%) <Pilfered Prizes>

faerie bell-wether [5] (70%) Toadstool Stalk • (5%) Bronze Rose Pin • (60%) Polished Wooden Bowl • (0.5%) <Only Just Begun> • (19% each piece) Tattered Quilted

faerie mischief-maker [3] (70%) Toadstool Stalk • (5%) Bronze Rose Pin • (60%) Polished Wooden Bowl • (0.5%) <Only Just Begun> • (19% each piece) Tattered Quilted

faerie wolf-crier [4] (70%) Toadstool Stalk • (5%) Bronze Rose Pin • (60%) Polished Wooden Bowl • (0.5%) <Only Just Begun> • (19% each piece) Tattered Quilted

Fielath [12] (no loot)

filidh [7-8] (40%) Brown Adder Stone • (60%) Obsidian • (25%) Chryoprase • (2%) Bloodstone • (15%) Pitted Wooden Shield, Tattered Cloth Tunic, Tattered Leather Hood, ***or*** Tattered Brown Boots • (20%) Dried Pork, Muffin, Canteen of Water, ***or*** Bottle of Elderberry Wine • (0.5%) <Of a Sylvan Glade>

forest snake [3] (70% each) Large Snake Skin, Head • (1.3%) Snake Scales • (1%) Snake Meat • (0.02%) Sharp Snake Fang

Ghost of Hugrath Wormly [8] (no loot)

giant frog [3-4] (50%) Frog Legs

grass snake [5] (95%) Snakeskin • (30%) Snake Scales • (90%) Snake Meat (x2) • (60%) Dead Mouse

gray wolf [4] (20%) Wolf's Ear • (50%) Torn Wolf Pelt • (5%) Pristine Wolf Pelt

gray wolf pup [1] (70% each) Ragged Wolf Pup Pelt, Wolf Pup's Ear

grumoz demon [10-11] (80% each) Smoking Pumice, Chunk of Sulfur • (53%) Charred Grumoz Hoof • (5%) Bloodstone • (1.5%) Brimstone Ring • (0.3%) <Of a Sylvan Glade>

Gwulin [9] (no loot)

horse [10] (75%) Horse Hair • (10%) Auburn Mane • (80%) Ruined Horse Skin • (35%) Horse Skin • (60%) Horse Hair

Hugrath Wormly [8] (40%) Wand of Pestilence • (5% each) Tattered Chain Legs, Sleeves, Mittens • (10%) Small Silver Nugget • (70%) Jade • (0.3%) <Pilfered Prizes>

Lady Leana [6] (10%) Willow Wand • (3%) Tarnished Silver Torc • (70% each) Polished River Rock, Moonstone • (20%) Driftwood Totem • (5% each) Obsidian, Jade • (0.5%) <Pilfered Prizes>

large ant [1] (80%) Ant Parts • (60%) Ant Parts

large skeleton [5] (50%) Bloody Skull • (70%) Jewels 45 • (1.5%) Old Iron Dagger • (0.3% each piece) Roman Leather • (1%) <Only Just Begun>

manes demon [7-8] (80%) Charred Hoof • (40% each) Chunk of Sulfur, Obsidian • (1.5%) Brimstone Ring • (5%) Chryoprase • (0.5%) <Pilfered Prizes>

Mulgrut Maggot [5] (5% each) Tattered Chain Sleeves, Jade • (10%) Obsidian • (5% each) Tattered Chain Mittens, Spinel, Pitted Short Sword • (1%) <Only Just Begun>

plague spider [0] (80%) Spider Legs • (70%) Spider Legs • (50%) Spider Claw

poacher [4] (5%) Moonstone • (70% each) Snakeskin, Wolf Skin • (5%) Tattered Lionskin • (1.2%) Pitted Dagger • (1%) Pitted Short Sword • (0.6%) Pitted Hand Axe • (0.4% each) Pitted Broadsword, Scimitar • (0.2% each) Pitted Great Sword, Bastard Sword • (20%) APOA: Tattered Leather • (1%) <Only Just Begun>

puny skeleton [1] (50%) Bloody Skull • (30%) Jewels 45 • (8% each piece) Tattered Leather and Quilted • (1%) <Only Just Begun>

putrid zombie [4] (50%) Bloody Skull • (70%) Jewels 45 • (1.5%) Old Iron Dagger • (0.3% each piece) Roman Leather • (1%) <Only Just Begun>

red lion [3] (30%) Tattered Lionskin

river drake hatchling [3] (70%) Drake Meat • (48%) Drakeling Scales • (10%) Drakeling Eye

river drakeling [5] (70% each) Drake Meat, Drakeling Scales • (10%) Drakeling Eye • (50%) Spiney Drakeling Tail

river sprite [6] (70% each) Polished River Rock, Moonstone • (5%) Obsidian • (20%) Driftwood Totem • (5%) Jade • (1.5%) Tarnished Silver Torc • (0.5%) <Pilfered Prizes>

river spriteling [3-4] (57%) Half-Eaten Fish • (10% each) Round, Flat ***or*** Thin Flint Chert, Small Pearl • (1.5%) Tarnished Silver Torc • (1%) <Only Just Begun>

rotting zombie [5-6] (65% each) Aventurine, Leathery Skin • (5%) Aventurine • (8% each piece) Tattered Leather and Quilted • (0.5%) <Only Just Begun>

Sephucoth [7] Cask of Apple Brandy • (80%) Carved Fishbone Necklace • (1%) <Pilfered Prizes>

Shale [11] (no loot)

skeleton [2] (55%) Bloody Skull • (40%) Jewels 45 • (8% each piece) Tattered Leather and Quilted • (1%) <Only Just Begun>

small bear [4] (33%) Bear Skin • (25%) Bear Fang • (5%) Pitted Sharp Claw

small gray wolf [3] (20%) Wolf's Ear • (50%) Torn Wolf Pelt • (5%) Pristine Wolf Pelt

small snake [0] (75%) Snake's Head • (10%) Snakeskin • (5%) Snake Meat

snake [3] (70% each) Large Snake Skin, Head • (1.3%) Snake Scales • (1%) Snake Meat • (0.02%) Sharp Snake Fang

spirit [6] (43%) Faded Blue Slime • (30%) Tarnished Dagger • (20%) Tattered Brown Gloves • (1%) Spinel • (50%) Jade • (1%) <Pilfered Prizes>

spirit hound [0] (99%) Tattered Moldy Collar • (80%) Spirit Fang

spriggarn [2] (55%) Spotted Mushroom • (10%) Polished Wooden Bowl • (17%) Jewels 45 • (25%) Round, Flat ***or*** Thin Flint Chert • (8% each piece) Tattered Leather and Quilted • (1%) <Only Just Begun>

spriggarn elder [3] (55%) Spotted Mushroom • (10%) Polished Wooden Bowl • (17%) Jewels 45 • (25%) Round, Flat ***or*** Thin Flint Chert • (8% each piece) Tattered Leather and Quilted • (1%) <Only Just Begun>

undead druid [9-10] (80%) Brown Adder Stone • (40%) Chryoprase • (20%) Bloodstone • (1%) Amethyst • (25%) Dried Pork, Muffin, Canteen of Water, ***or*** Bottle of Elderberry Wine • (1.5%) <Crystal Visions> • (0.5%) <Of a Sylvan Glade>

undead filidh [5-6] (50%) Brown Adder Stone • (40%) Jade • (20%) Obsidian • (1%) Spinel • (25%) Dried Pork, Muffin, Canteen of Water, ***or*** Bottle of Elderberry Wine • (1.5%) <Crystal Visions> • (0.5%) <Pilfered Prizes>

Weakened demon [6] (80%) Charred Hoof • (40% each) Chunk of Sulfur, Obsidian • (1.5%) Brimstone Ring • (5%) Chryoprase • (0.5%) <Pilfered Prizes>

wild sow [2] (50%) Boar Tusk • (40%) Raw Pork • (1.6%) Boar Tusk (x2) • (1%) Sharp Tusk (x3)

Ygwrch Gyrg [7] (no loot)

young boar [6] (90% each) Boar Tusk, Boar Skin • (60%) Raw Pork

young cutpurse [3] (12%) String of Polished Beads • (8%) Flask of Whiskey • (4% each) Copper Brooch, Silver Armband • (0.2%) <Pilfered Prizes> • (40%) APOA: Tattered Leather • (0.3% each) Bonecharm Amulet, Faithbound Ring • (0.2%) Aged Leather Baldric • (0.1% each) Mildewed Sleeves, Tunic • (20% each piece) Tattered Leather and Quilted

young poacher [3] (5%) Moonstone • (70% each) Snakeskin, Wolf Skin • (5%) Tattered Lionskin • (1.2%) Pitted Dagger • (1%) Pitted Short Sword • (0.6%) Pitted Hand Axe • (0.4% each) Pitted Broadsword, Scimitar • (0.2% each) Pitted Great Sword, Bastard Sword • (20%) APOA: Tattered Leather • (1%) <Only Just Begun>

zombie boar [5] (60% each) Rotting Hog Tail, Rotting Pig Skin, Decayed Pig Hoof

zombie farmer [7] (1.5%) Porcine Amulet • (0.5% each) Mildewed Tunic, Mildewed Sleeves, Farmers Gloves • (65% each) Obsidian, Moonstone • (5%) Chryoprase

zombie sow [4] (60% each) Rotting Hog Tail, Rotting Pig Skin, Decayed Pig Hoof

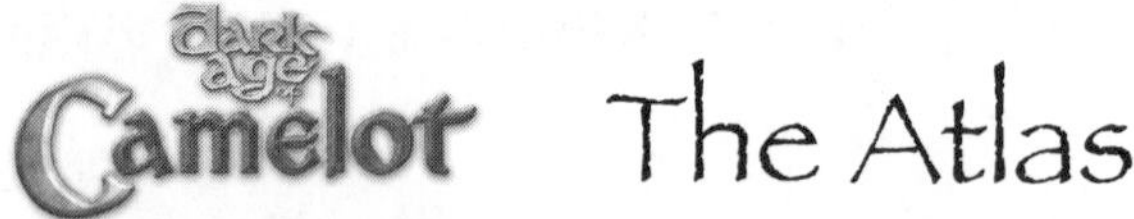

Campacorentin Forest

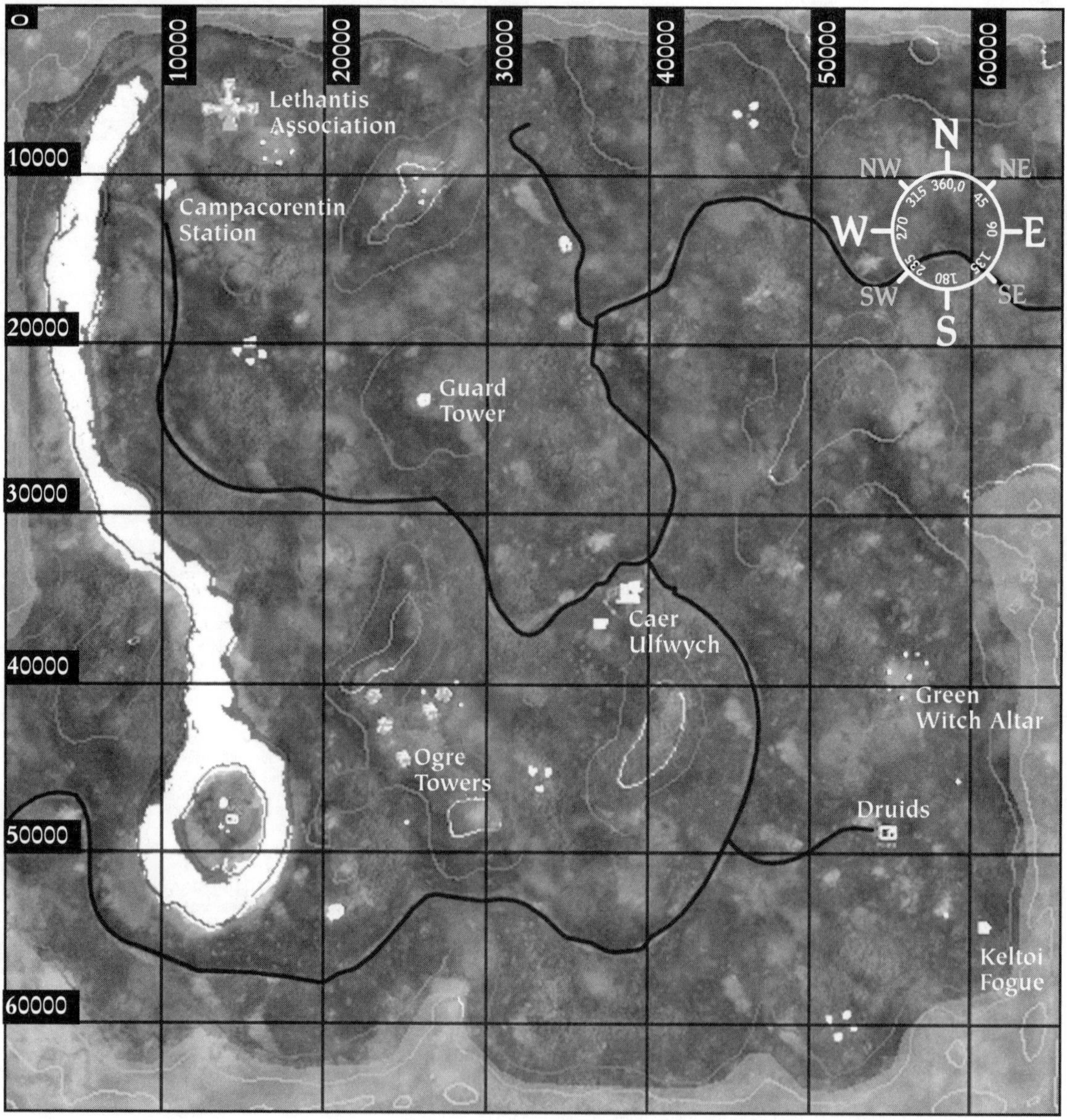

Monsters with levels lower than 4 are not marked on map.

Huntsmen almost always travel with Woodsman companions

LYNX = dappled lynx

WOLF = gray wolf

GOBLIN = Sylvan Goblin

TREES = ashen fellwood, ebony fellwood, oaken fellwood, oak man

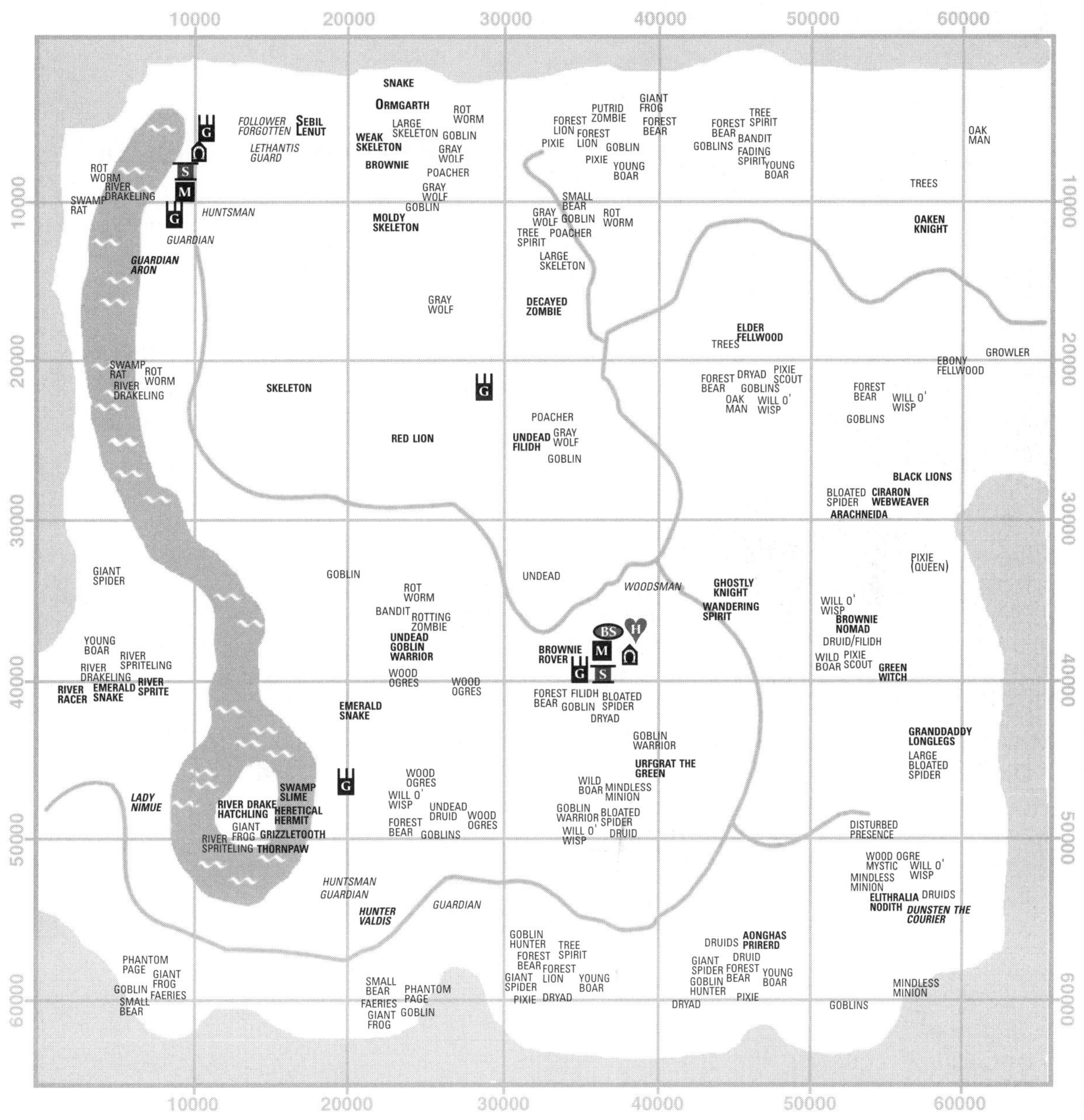

Lower-level monsters not shown on map:

Creature	Lvl	Location
brownie	0	NW
dappled lynx cub	0	NW
Interactions - Lethantis	0	NW
pixie imp	0	NW,WC
robber	0	NW
small snake	0	NC
tree snake	0	NW
dryad twig	1	NW,NC,WC
gray wolf pup	1	NW
rotting skeleton	1	NC,WC
weak skeleton	1	NW
ant drone	2	NW,WC
dappled lynx	2	NW,WC,SW
moldy skeleton	2	NC
skeleton	2	WC
spriggarn	2	NW,NC,WC
tree spider	2	NW,SW
dappled lynx	3	NC,C
decayed zombie	3	WC
forest bear cub	3	NW,NC,WC,C,SW
giant frog	3	SW
red lion	3	C
river drake hatchling	3	SW
river spriteling	3	SW
scrawny red lion	3	NW,WC,SW
small gray wolf	3	NW,NC,WC,SW
snake	3	NC
spriggarn elder	3	NW,WC
swamp slime	3	SW
sylvan goblin whelp	3	NW,NC,WC,C,SE

Campacorentin Forest Tips

If you start in Camp Forest, you will likely be near the Lethantis Association. All the basic trainers are nearby, and a few advanced trainers as well. The forest is overrun with good hunting targets, and many areas even have linked spawns. Humanoids are not as readily available here unless you find camps of them, but once you do, they provide ample pets to the aspiring Sorcerer. The animals are numerous here, as are the undead.

One nice target is the high concentration of Skeletal undead near Lethantis, and the various Spiders and Beetles throughout the forest. Many of these have a weakness to blunt weapons, and when you are low level your staff hits just as hard in your hands as it would in the hands of any warrior.

This zone also houses the entrance to Keltoi Fogou, which is a great dungeon for Sorcerers, since the vast majority of its inhabitants are readily available for charming. Many class quests also involve hunting higher level targets deep in this dungeon, so it is usually one of the busier dungeons and a good spot for finding groups.

- Dave "i3ullseye" Maynor

Solo and Group Levelling Tips

Solo

1-5	usual newbie monsters (brownies, wold pups, etc.)
5-10	goblins, bears
10-15	bloated spiders, druids
15-20	large bloated spiders

Group

1-5	same as solo
5-10	goblins, bears
10-15	bloated spiders, large bloated spiders, druids
15-20	large bloated spiders

- Matt "Kyle Draconeco" Shirley

Quest NPCs

Campacorentin Forest	
Growler	Growler Mace (lvl 13)
Growler	Growler's Necklace (lvl 13)
Campacorentin Station	
Olorustos	Outcast Ormgarth (lvl 6)
Kealan	The Hunt for Arachneida (lvl 14)

Caer Ulfwhych	
Cayla	Oaken Boots (lvl 14)
Fianya Waleldan	The Walelden's Pendant (lvl 16)
Cear Ulfwych	
Huntress Lenna	Goblin Hunting (lvl 7)

Lethantis Association	
Mairi Ralilden	Amulet of the Planes (lvl 16)
Nenet	Nenet's Research (lvl 10)

Loot

ant drone [2] (80%) Ant Parts • (60%) Ant Parts

Aonghas Prirerd [11] (no loot)

Arachneida [12] (60%) Bloated Spider Carapace • (90%) Bloated Spider Legs • (80%) Bloated Spider Claw • (2%) Lost Soul's Gauche

ashen fellwood [16-17] (90%) Ashen Fellwood Branch • (50%) Pitted Ashen Fellwood Staff • (7%) Fellwood Heartwood • (10%) Endearment Dagger ***or*** Ashen Spirit Staff

bandit [5-6] (70% each) Aventurine, Bent Lockpick • (5%) Moonstone • (8%) Bandit's Ear • (0.3% each piece) Roman Leather • (0.5%) <Only Just Begun>

black lion [30] (1.5% each) Black Lion-Hide Jerkin, Black Lion-Skin Cloak • (67%) Black Lion Skin • (2%) Pristine Black Lion Skin

black lioness [30] (1.5%) Black Lion-Skin Cloak • (70%) Black Lion Skin • (2%) Pristine Black Lion Skin

bloated spider [10-11] (60%) Bloated Spider Carapace • (30% each) Bloated Spider Legs, Claw

brownie [0] (40%) Spotted Mushroom • (15%) Jewels 45 • (1%) <Only Just Begun>

brownie nomad [8] (40%) Large Spotted Mushroom • (50%) Obsidian • (1%) Spinel • (1.5%) Grass Choker • (0.5%) <Of a Sylvan Glade>

brownie rover [12] (40%) Giant Spotted Mushroom • (35%) Jewels 39 • (0.3%) <Grave Goods> • (1.4% each) Pulsing Ruby, Grass Choker

Ciraron Webweaver [12] (no loot)

dappled lynx [2-3] (50%) Dappled Lynx Skin • (10%) Pitted Shimmering Sharp Claw

dappled lynx cub [0] (50%) Tattered Dappled Lynx Skin • (10%) Dappled Lynx Skin • (15%) Pitted Sharp Claw

Key. [X] = level(s) • (X%) = chance to get item (if a list, just one) • (X% each) = chance for ***each*** item • hi-lo = most to least likely • APOA = a piece of armor • (x2) = item can drop twice

decayed zombie [3] (65% each) Aventurine, Leathery Skin • (5%) Aventurine • (8% each piece) Tattered Leather and Quilted • (0.5%) <Only Just Begun>

devout filidh [8-9] *see druid [7-8]*

disturbed presence [13-14] (60%) Glowing Green Slime • (50%) Bloodstone • (20%) Lapis Lazuli • (1%) Azurite • (1.5%) <Mounds of Salisbury> • (0.5%) <Grave Goods>

druid [7-8] (40%) Brown Adder Stone • (60%) Obsidian • (25%) Chryoprase • (2%) Bloodstone • (15%) Pitted Wooden Shield, Tattered Cloth Tunic, Tattered Leather Hood, ***or*** Tattered Brown Boots • (20%) Dried Pork, Muffin, Canteen of Water, ***or*** Bottle of Elderberry Wine • (0.5%) <Of a Sylvan Glade>

druid sacrificer [9] *see druid [7-8]*

druid seer [8] *see druid [7-8]*

dryad [7-9] (70% each) Oaken Medallion, Heartwood Amulet • (20%) Vine-Carved Totem • (0.5%) <Of a Sylvan Glade> • (1.5%) Grass Choker

dryad twig [1] (10% each piece) Tattered Leather • (50%) Elm Talisman • (25%) Aventurine • (8% each piece) Tattered and Quilted

ebony fellwood [13-14] (80%) Ebony Fellwood Branch (x2)

Elder Fellwood [21] (60%) Elder Fellwood Branch • (7.1%) Elder Fellwood Staff • (7%) Fellwood Heartwood • (2%) Elder Staff of Wintry Winds ***or*** Earthen Fire

Elithralia Nodith [11] (no loot)

emerald snake [5] (50% each) Emerald Snake Fang, Soft Snakeskin • (35% each) Snake's Head, Snake Meat • (1.5%) Sharp Snake Fang

fading spirit [7-8] (45%) Faded Green Slime • (35%) Tattered Woolen Robes • (25%) Tattered Brown Boots • (50%) Spinel • (1%) Bloodstone • (0.5%) <Pilfered Prizes>

faerie bell-wether [5] (70%) Toadstool Stalk • (5%) Bronze Rose Pin • (60%) Polished Wooden Bowl • (0.5%) <Only Just Begun> • (19% each piece) Tattered Quilted

faerie wolf-crier [4] *see faerie bell-wether [5]*

filidh [8] *see druid [7-8]*

filidh sacrificer [9-10] *see druid [7-8]*

forest bear [7-9] (30%) Bear Skin • (60%) Bear Fang (x2) • (80% each) Bear Tongue, Pitted Sharp Claw

forest bear cub [3] (18%) Bear Skin • (30% each) Pitted Sharp Claw, Bear Tongue

forest lion [6] (99%) Lion Skin (x2)

ghostly knight [8] (30%) Tarnished Spurs • (35%) Chryoprase • (1%) Amethyst • (0.5%) <Of a Sylvan Glade> • (1.5%) Skull-Embossed Gauntlets

giant frog [3-4] (50%) Frog Legs

giant spider [6-7] (99%) Spider Silk

Granddaddy Longlegs [15] *see Arachneida [12]*

gray wolf [4] (20%) Wolf's Ear • (50%) Torn Wolf Pelt • (5%) Pristine Wolf Pelt

gray wolf pup [1] (70% each) Ragged Wolf Pup Pelt, Wolf Pup's Ear

Green Witch [14] (10%) Stick-Figure Totem • (2.5%) Tattered Lamellar Arms • (5%) Tattered Boned Arms

Grizzletooth [23] (80%) Pristine Wolf Pelt • Torn Wolf Pelt

Growler [11] (no loot)

Growler's remains [11] (no loot)

heretical hermit [20] (30%) Topaz • (15%) Pearl • (1%) Green Tourmaline • (0.3%) <Salisbury Stock 1> • (2%) Mace of the Meek

horse [10] (75%) Horse Hair • (10%) Auburn Mane • (80%) Ruined Horse Skin • (35%) Horse Skin • (60%) Horse Hair

large bloated spider [13-14] (50%) Large Bloated Spider Carapace • (70%) Large Bloated Spider Legs • (65%) Large Bloated Spider Claw

large skeleton [5] (50%) Bloody Skull • (70%) Jewels 45 • (1.5%) Old Iron Dagger • (0.3% each piece) Roman Leather • (1%) <Only Just Begun>

mindless minion [8-10] (3.5%) Pulsing Ruby • (3%) Rotting Robes • (0.3%) <Pilfered Prizes>

moldy skeleton [2] *see skeleton [2]*

oak man [7-9] (60%) Oak Branch (x2)

oaken fellwood [18] (5%) Pitted Fellwood Cudgel • (50%) Oaken Fellwood Branch • (6%) Fellwood Heartwood

Oaken Knight [12] (50%) Oaken Fellwood Branch

Ormgarth [5] (50%) Snake's Head Charm • (2%) Snakehead Axe

phantom page [5] (20%) Bloodied Banner

pixie [6-7] (85%) Amber Nugget • (20%) Vine-Carved Totem • (35%) Jade • (2.5%) Grass Choker • (1%) <Pilfered Prizes>

pixie imp [0] *see dryad twig [1]*

Pixie Queen [14] (no loot)

pixie scout [8] (60%) Heartwood Amulet • (80%) Ash Talisman • (10%) Vine-Carved Totem • (2%) Grass Choker • (0.5%) <Of a Sylvan Glade> • (5%) Chryoprase

poacher [4] (5%) Moonstone • (70% each) Snakeskin, Wolf Skin • (5%) Tattered Lionskin • (1.2%) Pitted Dagger • (1%) Pitted Short Sword • (0.6%) Pitted Hand Axe • (0.4% each) Pitted Broadsword, Scimitar • (0.2% each) Pitted Great Sword, Bastard Sword • (20%) APOA: Tattered Leather • (1%) <Only Just Begun>

putrid zombie [4] *see large skeleton [5]*

red lion [3] (30%) Tattered Lionskin

river drake hatchling [3] (70%) Drake Meat • (48%) Drakeling Scales • (10%) Drakeling Eye

river drakeling [5] (70% each) Drake Meat, Drakeling Scales • (10%) Drakeling Eye • (50%) Spiney Drakeling Tail

river racer [7] (95%) Snakeskin • (30%) Snake Scales • (90%) Snake Meat (x2) • (60%) Dead Mouse

river sprite [6] (70% each) Polished River Rock, Moonstone • (5%) Obsidian • (20%) Driftwood Totem • (5%) Jade • (1.5%) Tarnished Silver Torc • (0.5%) <Pilfered Prizes>

river spriteling [3-4] (57%) Half-Eaten Fish • (10% each) Round, Flat ***or*** Thin Flint Chert, Small Pearl • (1.5%) Tarnished Silver Torc • (1%) <Only Just Begun>

robber [0] *see bandit [5-6]*

rot worm [5] (50% each) Worm-Acid Gland, Worm Skin

rotting skeleton [1] (50%) Bloody Skull • (30%) Jewels 45 • (8% each piece) Tattered Leather and Quilted • (1%) <Only Just Begun>

rotting zombie [5] *see decayed zombie [3]*

scrawny red lion [3] (30%) Tattered Lionskin

skeleton [2] (55%) Bloody Skull • (40%) Jewels 45 • (8% each piece) Tattered Leather and Quilted • (1%) <Only Just Begun>

small bear [4] (33%) Bear Skin • (25%) Bear Fang • (5%) Pitted Sharp Claw

small gray wolf [3] (20%) Wolf's Ear • (50%) Torn Wolf Pelt • (5%) Pristine Wolf Pelt

small snake [0] (75%) Snake's Head • (10%) Snakeskin • (5%) Snake Meat

snake [3] (70% each) Large Snake Skin, Head • (1.3%) Snake Scales • (1%) Snake Meat • (0.02%) Sharp Snake Fang

spriggarn [2] (55%) Spotted Mushroom • (10%) Polished Wooden Bowl • (17%) Jewels 45 • (25%) Round, Flat ***or*** Thin Flint Chert • (8% each piece) Tattered Leather and Quilted • (1%) <Only Just Begun>

spriggarn elder [3] *see spriggarn [2]*

swamp rat [4] (50%) Rat Tail • (10%) Rat Fur

swamp slime [3] (10%) Pitted Great Sword • (20% each piece) Tattered Leather • (45%) Onyx • (35%) Moonstone • (1%) <Only Just Begun>

sylvan goblin [5] (50% each) Yellowed Bone Nosering, Rusty Iron Ring • (5% each) Fingerbone Necklace, Crude Stone Idol • (0.5%) <Pilfered Prizes>

sylvan goblin chief [16] (20%) Bloody Scepter • (40%) Topaz • (1%) Pearl • (20%) Large Gold Tooth • (0.3%) <Out of the Woods> • (2%) Snivel, Shrug ***or*** Sure Shot Crossbow

sylvan goblin hunter [6-8] (50% each) Rusty Iron Ring, Yellowed Bone Nosering • (5% each) Crude Stone Idol, Rancid Fur Cape • (25%) Tarnished Silver Earring • (0.5%) <Pilfered Prizes>

sylvan goblin magician [10] (20%) Amethyst • (30%) Carnelian • (80%) Tarnished Silver Earring • (0.5%) <Of a Sylvan Glade> • (1%) Carnelian

sylvan goblin warrior [12] (30% each) Large Gold Tooth, Crude Stone Idol, Yellowed Bone Nosering, Bloodstone, Carnelian • (1%) Agate

sylvan goblin warrior [9-10] (30% each) Carnelian, Crude Stone Idol • (5%) Filthy Hide Pants • (35%) Yellowed Bone Nosering • (10%) Tarnished Silver Earring • (0.3%) <Of a Sylvan Glade>

sylvan goblin whelp [3] (no loot)

Thornpaw [14] Torn Wolf Pelt (x2) • (50%) Pristine Wolf Pelt (x3)

tree snake [0] *see small snake [0]*

tree spider [2] (80%) Spider Legs • (70%) Spider Legs • (50%) Spider Claw

tree spirit [6] (43%) Faded Blue Slime • (30%) Tarnished Dagger • (20%) Tattered Brown Gloves • (1%) Spinel • (50%) Jade • (1%) <Pilfered Prizes>

undead druid [8-10] (80%) Brown Adder Stone • (40%) Chryoprase • (20%) Bloodstone • (1%) Amethyst • (25%) Dried Pork, Muffin, Canteen of Water, ***or*** Bottle of Elderberry Wine • (1.5%) <Crystal Visions> • (0.5%) <Of a Sylvan Glade>

undead filidh [5] (50%) Brown Adder Stone • (40%) Jade • (20%) Obsidian • (1%) Spinel • (25%) Dried Pork, Muffin, Canteen of Water, ***or*** Bottle of Elderberry Wine • (1.5%) <Crystal Visions> • (0.5%) <Pilfered Prizes>

undead goblin warrior [5] *see large skeleton [5]*

Urfgrat the Green [17] *see sylvan goblin chieftain [16]*

wandering spirit [9] (45%) Glowing Blue Slime • (35%) Pitted Wooden Shield • (25%) Tattered Leather Hood • (15%) Tattered Brown Boots • (50%) Obsidian • (8%) Chryoprase • (1%) Amethyst • (0.5%) <Of a Sylvan Glade>

weak skeleton [1] (60%) Bloody Skull • (1.2%) Pitted Dagger • (1%) Pitted Short Sword • (0.6%) Pitted Hand Axe, Bonecharm Amulet • (0.4% each) Pitted Broadsword, Pitted Scimitar, Faithbound Ring • (0.2% each) Pitted Great Sword, Bastard Sword • (0.02%) Faerie Charm Necklace • (18% each) Tattered Leather and Quilted • (25%) Onyx

wild boar [10] (20%) Small Tusk • (50%) Cloven Hoof • Raw Pork • Pig Tail

will o' wisp [9/10/11] (43/60/50%) Globe of Blue Mist • (20/30/50%) Pile of Glowing Dust • (2/3/3%) Glowing Globe of Blue Mist

wood ogre berserker [14-15] (85%) Bloodstone • (45%) Carnelian • (65%) Dried Pork, Muffin, Canteen of Water, ***or*** Bottle of Elderberry Wine • (1.5%) <Ogre Skins> • (3%) APOA: Faded • (0.3%) <Out of the Woods> • (0.8%) Wormskin Helm • (0.4% each) Wormskin Leggings, Wormskin Boots, Sword of the Unruly

wood ogre lord [16] (85%) Amethyst • (45%) Lapis Lazuli • (65%) Dried Pork, Muffin, Canteen of Water, ***or*** Bottle of Elderberry Wine • (1.5%) <Ogre Skins> • (3%) APOA: Faded • (0.3%) <Out of the Woods> • (0.6%) Wormskin Sleeves • (0.4% each) Wormskin Gloves, Jerkin • (0.3% each) Ogre King's Decider, Demolisher

wood ogre mystic [11] (80%) Obsidian • (60%) Spinel • (10%) Bloodstone • (1.5%) Ogre Forged Quarterstaff • (50%) Dried Pork, Muffin, Canteen of Water, ***or*** Bottle of Elderberry Wine • (3%) APOA: Faded • (0.3%) <Grave Goods>

wood ogre scourge [12-13] (85%) Chryoprase • (45%) Amethyst • (65%) Dried Pork, Muffin, Canteen of Water, ***or*** Bottle of Elderberry Wine • (1.5%) <Ogre Skins> • (3%) APOA: Faded • (0.3%) <Grave Goods>

wood ogre seer [14] (75%) Chryoprase • (50%) Amethyst • (10%) Lapis Lazuli • (50%) Dried Pork, Muffin, Canteen of Water, ***or*** Bottle of Elderberry Wine • (1.5%) <Ogre Skins> • (3%) APOA: Faded • (0.3%) <Out of the Woods>

young boar [6] (90% each) Boar Tusk, Boar Skin • (60%) Raw Pork

Cornwall

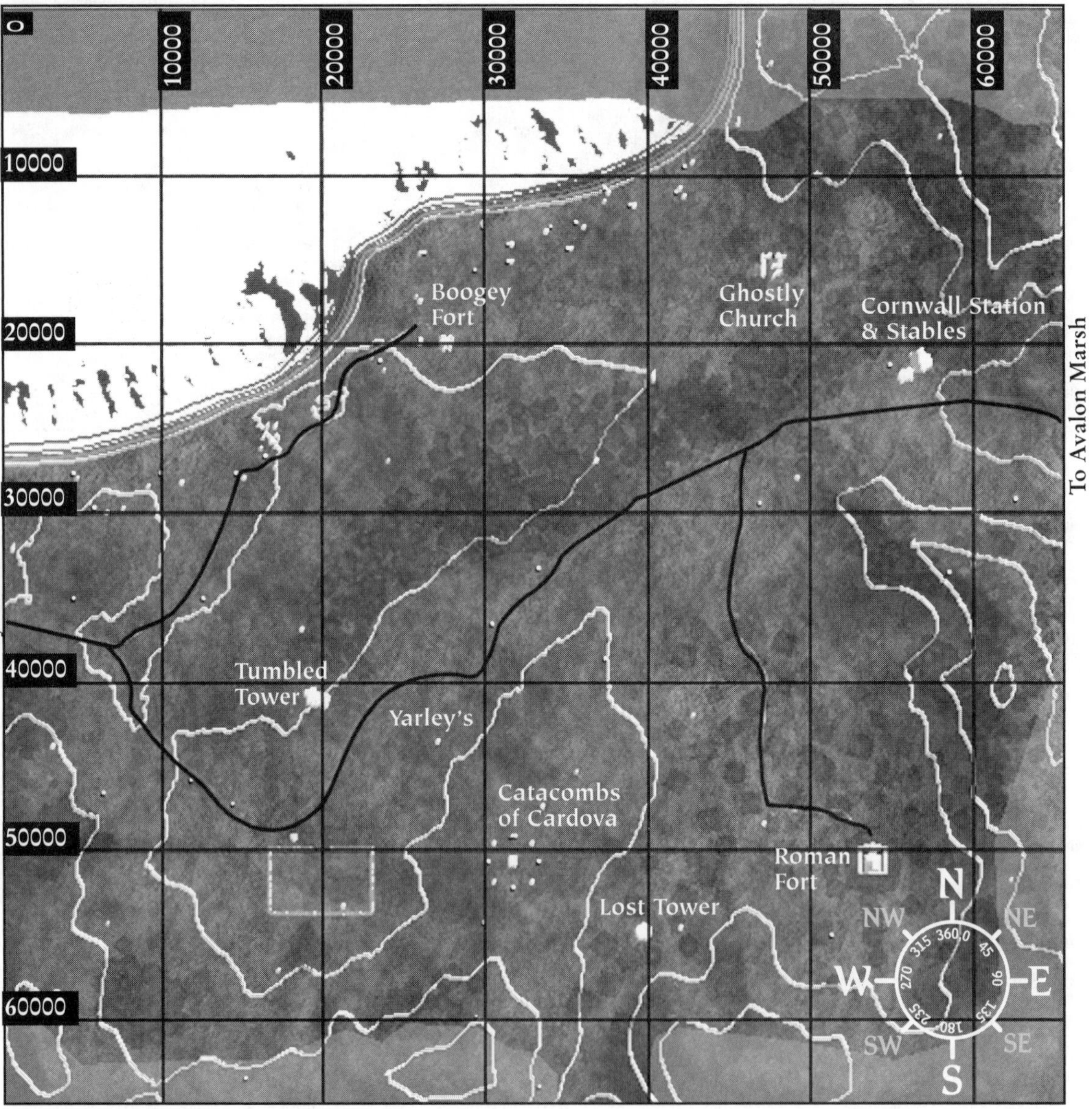

0
10000
20000
30000
40000
50000
60000

Boogey Fort
Ghostly Church
Cornwall Station & Stables
To Avalon Marsh
To Lyonesse
Tumbled Tower
Yarley's
Catacombs of Cardova
Roman Fort
Lost Tower
N
NW
NE
W
E
SW
SE
S
360/0
45
90
135
180
225
270
315
To Dartmoor

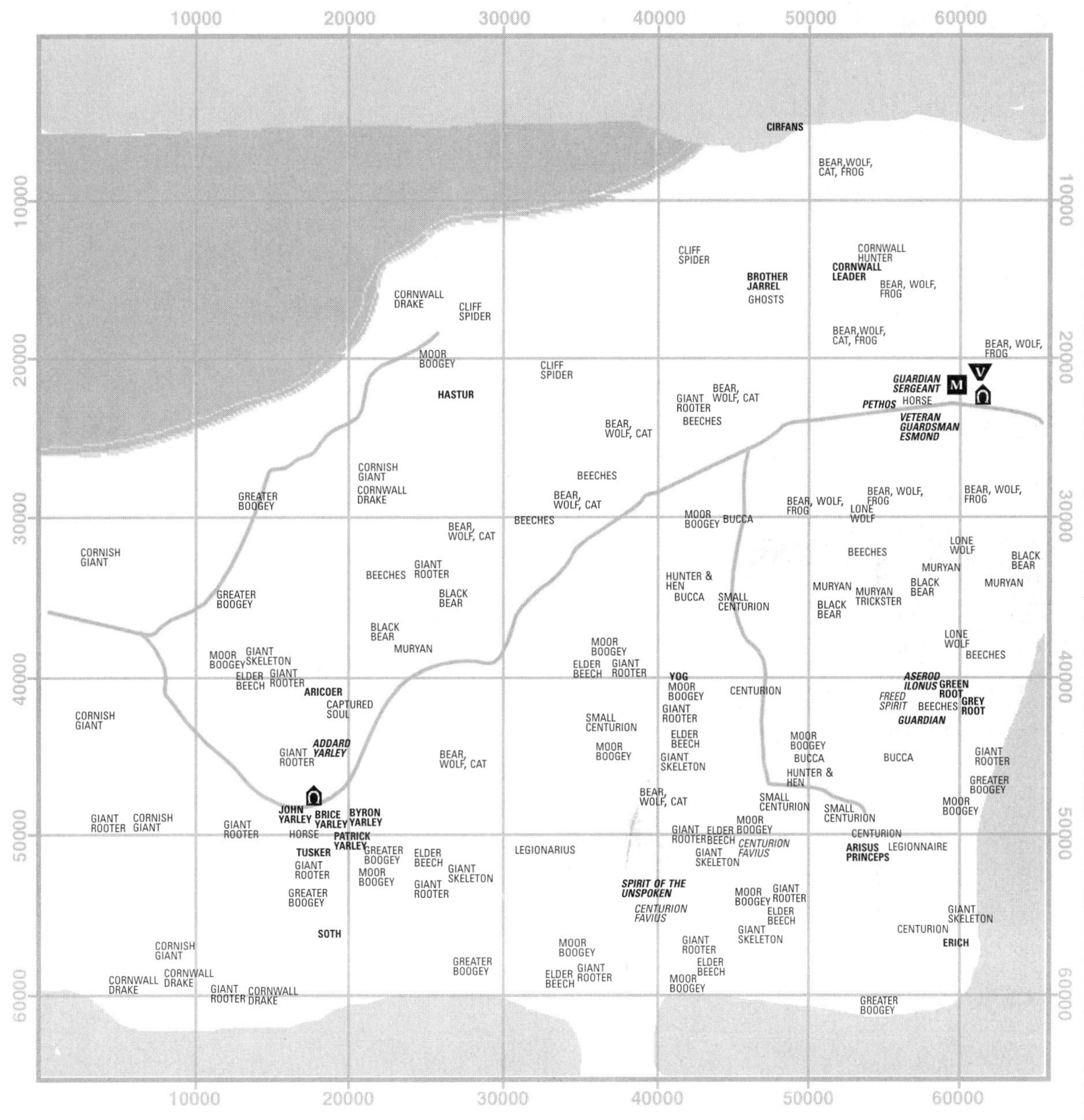

CENTURION = Skeletal centurion
LEGIONNAIRE = Skeletal legionnaire
HUNTER & HEN = Cornish hunter, Cornish Hen

Lower-level monsters not shown on map:

Creature	Lvl	Location	Creature	Lvl	Location	Creature	Lvl	Location	Creature	Lvl	Location
brown bear	15	NE,C,EC,SC	death stalker	17	NE,C,SC	muryan trickster	20	EC	small skeletal centurion	17	EC,SE
cliff spiderling	14	NC,NE	moor den mother	17	NE,C,SC	muryan trickster	21	EC	young brown bear	13	NE,EC
Cornish giant	40	WC,SW	moor pack leader	15	NE,C,SC	skeletal centurion	21	EC,SE			
Cornish hen	24	C,SE	moor wolf	14	NE,C,EC,SC	skeletal legionnaire	18	SE			

Cornwall Tips

This zone is another heavily traveled zone. It connects to both Lyonesse and Dartmoor, and contains the dungeon known as the Catacombs. Pets are plentiful for Sorcerers of most levels, as are many items that you need to grab for use in the next zones. Many epic quests will bring you to this zone to battle the undead that infest a vast portion of this land.

Often overlooked are the cliff spiders, which generate good XP for a solo hunter, and (due to their chitinous nature) are relatively weak to most common attack types. Their poison is not nearly as deadly as it seems on first bite, so the risk is lower than initially perceived.

In Cornwall Station you can find tradeskill merchants, and even a forge. There is also a vault keeper in residence, the southernmost in all of Albion.

- Dave "i3ullseye" Maynor

The Yarleys are not friendly to pig hunters. If you find they do not like you or your money anymore, try killing more boogeys and fewer of their pigs to help with your faction.

The wooded hillside along the road past Cornwall Station is a nice place to hunt. Trees of gradually increasing levels wander the hillside. This area can support careful solo'ers up to full groups. Trees really don't like fire much so it makes them good prey for wizards' fire spells.

Be wary approaching the entrance to Catacombs, it is ringed by undead guards.

- Chris "Kirstena" Yone

Solo and Group Levelling Tips

Solo

15-20	wolves, bears
20-25	roman centurions
25-30	roman legionnaires, hamadryads, moor boogeys
30-35	giant rooters, great boogeys
35-45	great boogeys, cornish giants

Group

15-20	roman centurions
20-25	roman centurions, legionnaires
25-30	roman legionnaires, hamadryads, moor boogeys
30-35	giant rooters, great boogeys, cornish giants
35-40	great boogeys, cornish giants

- Matt "Kyle Draconeco" Shirley

Loot

Aged beech [30] (55%) Petrified Beech Branch • (30%) Beech Root Herb • (25%) Beech Tree Seeds • (1.5%) Sheet of Aged Beech Bark • (0.3%) <In a Spider's Web>

Aricoer [20] (no loot)

Arisus princeps [24] (60%) Roman Commanders Seal • (30%) Small Silver Statue • (50%) Jewels 26 • (1.4%) APOA: Bloodied Leather • (1.4%) Decorated Roman Dagger ***or*** Stiletto, ***or*** Roman Tactician Bracer • (0.3%) <Salisbury Stock 1>

Aserod Ilonus [38] (10% each) Water Opal, Rhodolite,Peridot, Yellow Tourmaline, Kornerupine, Pink Sapphire, Alexandrite, Chrysoberyl, Black Sapphire ***or*** Precious Heliodor

black bear [16-17] (23%) Black Bear Pelt • (2.5%) Pristine Black Bear Pelt • (50%) Bloody Bear Fang • (25%) Black Bear Tongue • (1.5%) Long Animal Fang

black bear [20-21] (80%) Black Bear Claw • (50% each) Black Bear Claw, Paw • (45%) Black Bear Pelt • (5%) Pristine Black Bear Pelt

Brice Yarley [40] (no loot)

Brother Jarrel [14] (no loot)

brown bear [15] (23%) Brown Bear Pelt • (2.5%) Pristine Brown Bear Pelt • (37%) Bloody Bear Fang (x2)

bucca [23-24] (80% each) Topaz, Citrine • (0.3%) Manaweave Ring • (0.6% each) Smoldering, Netherworldly Robes • (0.3%) <Arthurian Artifacts 4> • (9%) Silver Mirror

Byron Yarley [40] (no loot)

captured soul [14-15] (no loot)

Centurion Favius [20] (60%) Roman Commanders Seal • (30%) Small Silver Statue • (50%) Jewels 26 • (1.4%) APOA: Bloodied Leather • (1.4%) Decorated Roman Dagger ***or*** Stiletto, ***or*** Roman Tactician Bracer • (0.3%) <Salisbury Stock 1>

Cirfans [50] (50% each) Cornwall Drake Tooth, Claw • (40%) Cornwall Drake Meat • (45%) Pristine Cornwall Drake Skin • (2.5% each) Long Drake Talon, Fang

cliff spider [18] (38%) Spider Carapace • (70%) Cliff Spider Legs • (80%) Cliff Spider Claw • (60%) Cliff Spider Silk

cliff spiderling [14] (25%) Spiderling Carapace • (60%) Cliff Spiderling Legs • (70%) Cliff Spiderling Claw • (80%) Spiderling Silk

Cornish frog [13] (30%) Giant Frog Tongue • (50%) Giant Frog Skin • (70%) Giant Frog Legs (x2)

Cornish giant [40] (20%) Dented Pewter Urn • (12%) Jewels 21 • (1.5%) Giant Ring of Tenacity, Wits ***or*** Dedication

Cornish hen [24] (35%) Cornish Hen Feathers • (0.3%) <Salisbury Stock 1> • (10%) Cornish Hen Tail

Cornwall Drake [40/42/44] (24/27/26%) Cornwall Drake Tooth • (26%) Cornwall Drake Claw [44] • (50/50/40%) Cornwall Drake Meat • (24/29/25%) Pristine Cornwall Drake Skin • (1.5% each) Long Drake Fang [40,44], Long Drak Talon [42,44]

Cornwall hunter [23] (50%) Agate Studded Waterskin • (15%) Footed Bodkin Arrows • (40%) Jewels 26 • (1.4%) Cornwall Hunter's Rapier ***or*** Light Hunter's Cloak • (1.4%) Hunter's Gauntlets, Boots ***or*** Helm • (25%) Leather Sack • (0.3%) <Salisbury Stock 1>

Cornwall hunter [25] (50%) Leather Sack • (40%) Agate Studded Waterskin • (20%) Footed Bodkin Arrows • (50%) Jewels 26 • (1.4%) Hunter's Vest, Leggings ***or*** Sleeves • (1.4%) Light Hunter's Bow ***or*** Guardian's Necklace • (0.3%) <Arthurian Artifacts 1>

Cornwall Leader [25] (50%) Leather Sack • (40%) Agate Studded Waterskin • (20%) Footed Bodkin Arrows • (50%) Jewels 26 • (1.4%) Hunter's Vest, Leggings ***or*** Sleeves • (1.4%) Light Hunter's Bow ***or*** Guardian's Necklace • (0.3%) <Arthurian Artifacts 1>

death stalker [16-27] (80%) Death Stalker Hide • (24%) Death Stalker Fang

elder beech [23-24/26-28] (45/50%) Petrified Beech Branch • (15/20%) Beech Root Herb • (10/16%) Beech Tree Seeds • (0.3%) <Salisbury Stock 1> [23-24] • (1.5%) Petrified Elder Beech Fruit [26-28] • (0.3%) <Arthurian Artifacts 1> [26-28]

Erich [30] (10%) Stick-Figure Totem • (2.5%) Tattered Lamellar Arms • (5%) Tattered Boned Arms

forest cat [16] (25% each) Forest Cat Tooth, Claw • (60%) Forest Cat Claw • (19%) Forest Cat Skin • (2.1%) Pristine Forest Cat Skin • (1.5%) Long Animal Fang

Freed Spirit [20,25] (50%) Leather Sack • (40%) Agate Studded Waterskin • (20%) Footed Bodkin Arrows • (50%) Jewels 26 • (1.4%) Hunter's Vest, Leggings ***or*** Sleeves • (1.4%) Light Hunter's Bow ***or*** Guardian's Necklace • (0.3%) <Arthurian Artifacts 1>

ghostly cleric [12] (no loot)

ghostly paladin [12-13] (no loot)

giant rooter [30/32/34] (30/45/50%) Rooter Feet • (50%) Rooter Meat • (20/25/37%) Pristine Rooter Skin

giant skeleton [27-28] (50% each) Skeleton Skull, Large Bleached Bone • (0.3%) Manaweave Ring • (0.6% each) Smoldering ***or*** Netherworldly Robes • (1.4%) Jeweled Left ***or*** Right Eye • (0.3%) <Cuisinart>

greater boogey [35-41] (8%) Glowing Soul Gem

Hastur [60] (8%) Glowing Soul Gem

horse [10] (75%) Horse Hair • (10%) Auburn Mane • (80%) Ruined Horse Skin • (35%) Horse Skin • (60%) Horse Hair

John Yarley [40] (no loot)

legionarius [29] (8%) Tarnished Ornate Goblet • (6%) Small Gold-Stitched Pouch • (4%) Orb of the Restless Eye • (2%) Jewel Studded Circlet • (15%) Jewels 54 • (5%) Jewels 47 • (1.6%) Molded Leather Gloves, Boots ***or*** Helm • (1.6%) Despoiled Gladius ***or*** Gauche, Decaying Legion Battle Bracer, ***or*** Tactician's Belt

lone wolf [20] (50%) Lone Wolf Fang (x2) • (23%) Lone Wolf Pelt • (2.5%) Pristine Lone Wolf Pelt • (1.5%) Long Animal Fang

moor boogey [25-27/28-30] (8%) Glowing Soul Gem • (0.3%) <Arthurian Artifacts 1>/<In a Spider's Web>

moor den mother [17] (27%) Moor Wolf Skin • (3%) Pristine Moor Wolf Skin • (53%) Wolf Fang (x2) • (1.5%) Long Animal Fang

moor pack leader [15] (18%) Moor Wolf Skin • (2%) Pristine Moor Wolf Skin • (48%) Wolf Fang (x2) • (1.5%) Long Animal Fang

moor wolf [14] (18%) Moor Wolf Skin • (2%) Pristine Moor Wolf Skin • (50%) Wolf Fang • (1.5%) Long Animal Fang

muryan [18-19/20] (25%) Muryan Leg • (20/23%) Cracked Muryan Carapace • (10/15%) Pristine Muryan Carapace • (0.3%) <Out of the Woods>

muryan trickster [20-21] (25%) Muryan Leg • (23%) Cracked Muryan Carapace • (15%) Pristine Muryan Carapace • (0.3%) <Out of the Woods>

Patrick Yarley [40] (no loot)

skeletal centurion [21] (60%) Roman Commanders Seal • (30%) Small Silver Statue • (50%) Jewels 26 • (1.4%) APOA: Bloodied Leather • (1.4%) Decorated Roman Dagger ***or*** Stiletto, ***or*** Roman Tactician Bracer • (0.3%) <Salisbury Stock 1>

skeletal legionnaire [18] (50%) Ghostly Roman Lantern • (40%) Roman Commanders Seal • (30%) Jewels 26 • (1.4%) Ruined Roman Hauberk, Leggings ***or*** Sleeves • (1.4%) Decorated Roman Dagger ***or*** Stiletto, ***or*** Roman Tactician Bracer • (0.3%) <Salisbury Stock 1>

small skeletal centurion [17] (1%) Tattered Leather Jerkin • (15% each) Pitted Tower Shield, Short Sword, Topaz • (30%) Azurite • (2.7%) Ancient Body Shield, Ancient Battle Bracer, Battleworn Gladius, ***or*** Shimmering Etheric Helm • (0.3%) Blade of Etheric Mist • (1%) Pearl

Soth [44] (8%) Glowing Soul Gem

Spirit of the unspoken [11] (45%) Glowing Blue Slime • (35%) Pitted Wooden Shield • (25%) Tattered Leather Hood • (15%) Tattered Brown Boots • (50%) Obsidian • (8%) Chryoprase • (1%) Amethyst • (0.5%) <Of a Sylvan Glade>

Tusker [38] (60% each) Rooter Feet, Meat • (55%) Pristine Rooter Skin

Yog [33] (8%) Glowing Soul Gem • (0.3%) <In a Spider's Web>

young brown bear [13] (18%) Brown Bear Pelt • (2%) Pristine Brown Bear Pelt • (35%) Bloody Bear Fang • (50%) Brown Bear Paw

Key. [X] = level(s) • (X%) = chance to get item (if a list, just one) • (X% each) = chance for ***each*** item • hi-lo = most to least likely • APOA = a piece of armor • (x2) = item can drop twice

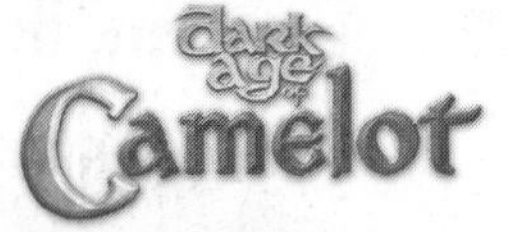

Dartmoor

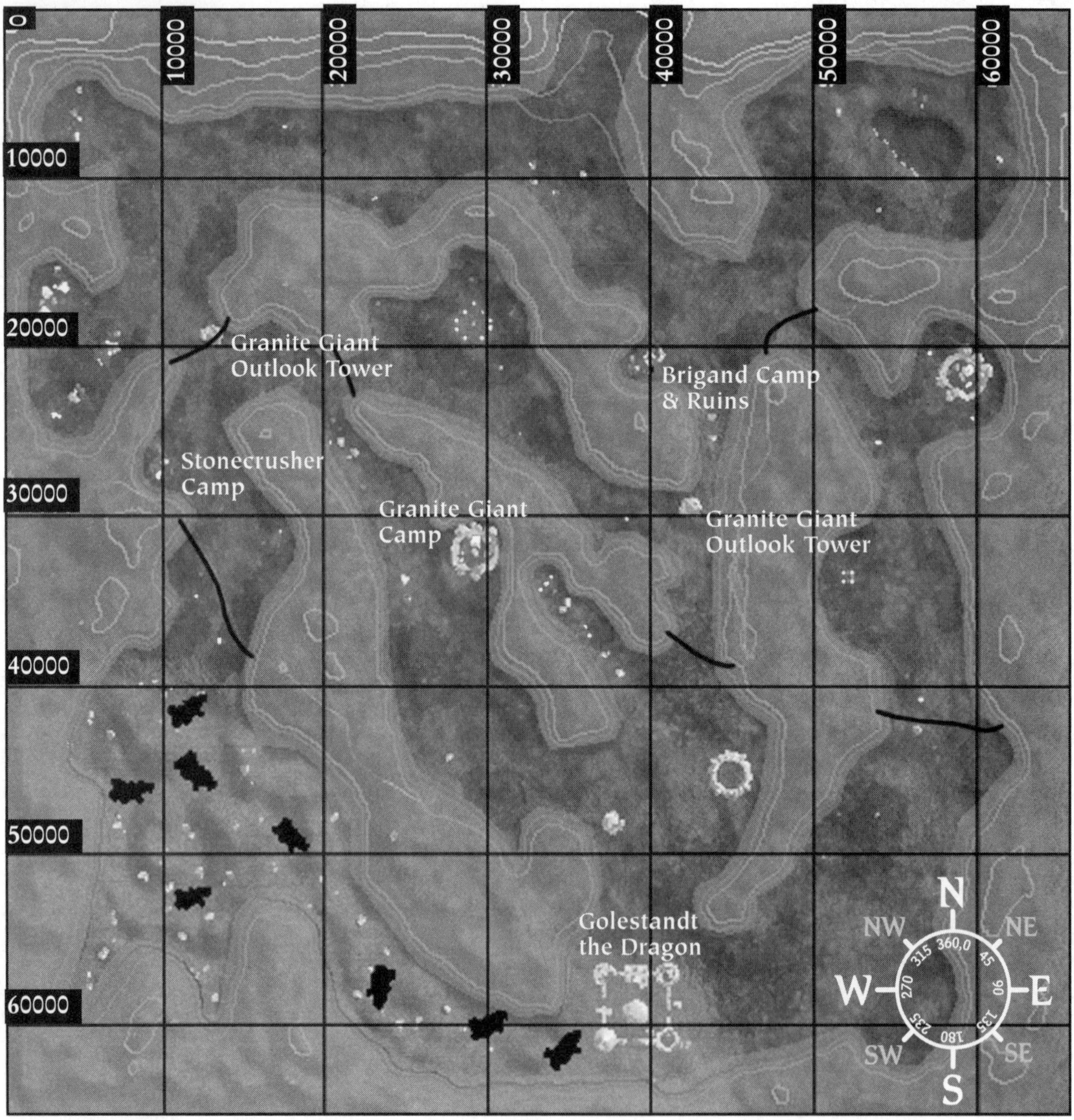

To Cornwall
0
10000
20000
30000
40000
50000
60000
10000
20000
30000
40000
50000
60000
Granite Giant Outlook Tower
Brigand Camp & Ruins
Stonecrusher Camp
Granite Giant Camp
Granite Giant Outlook Tower
Golestandt the Dragon
N
NW
NE
W
E
SW
SE
S
360,0
45
90
135
180
225
270
315

SC = Stonecrush
GG = Granite Giant
H = Granite Giant Herdsman
H&P = Granite Giant Herdsman & Dartmoor Ponies
SHAPER = Granite Giant Stoneshaper
CALLER = Granite Giant Stonecaller
MENDER = Granite Giant stonemender
ORACLE = Granite Giant oracle
OUTLOOKER = Granite Giant Outlooker
GATHERER = Granite Giant gatherer
POUNDER = GG pounder

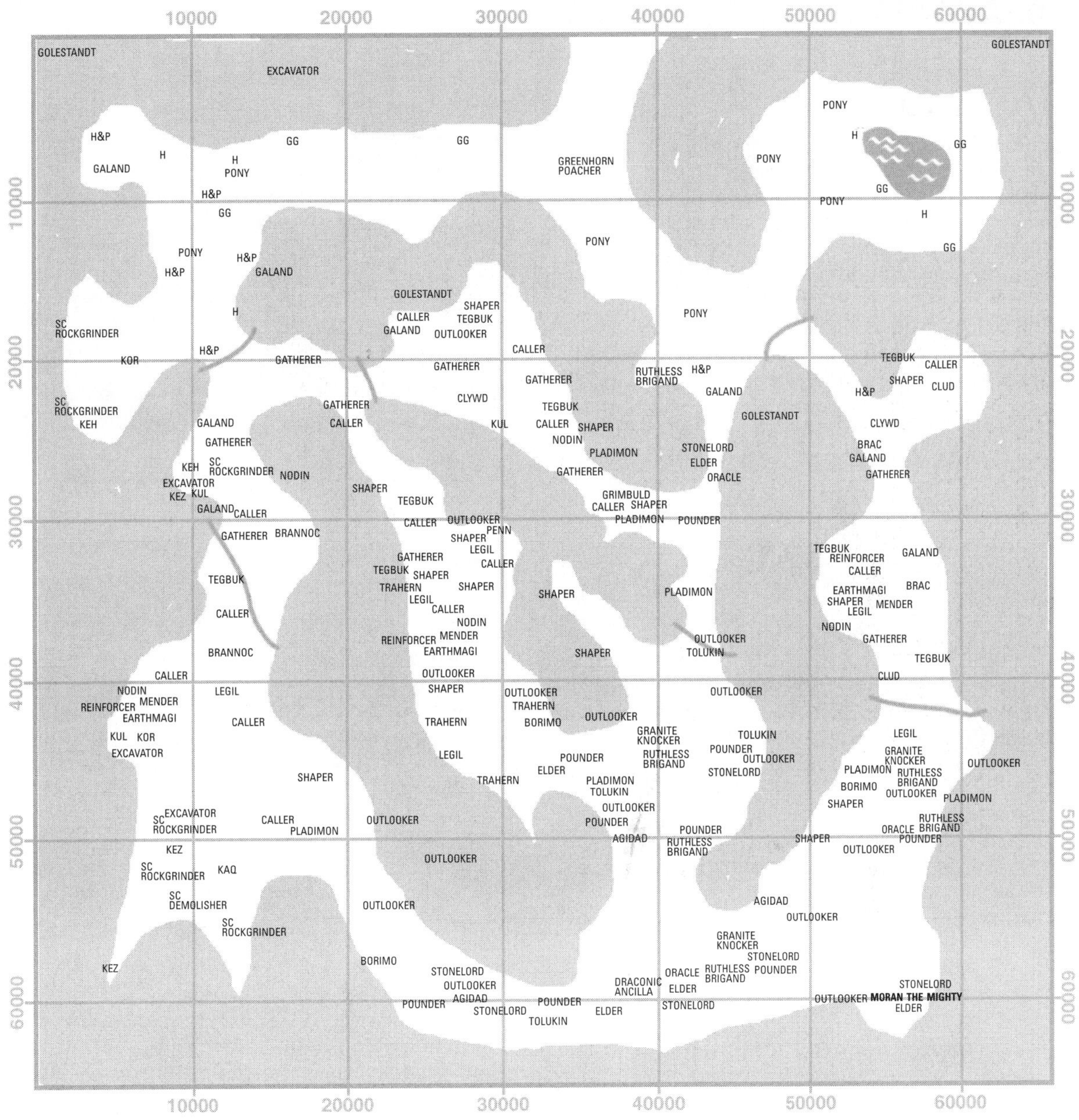

STONELORD = Granite Giant stonelord
EARTHMAGI = Granite Giant earthmagi
REINFORCER = Granite Giant reinforcer
STONEMENDER = Granite Giant stonemender
ELDER = Granite Giant elder

EXCAVATOR = Stonecrush excavator
PONY = Dartmoor pony
Named monsters have unusually large ranges. Note the common areas you'll find them in the monster notes.

Dartmoor Tips

Ponies, ponies, and more ponies. There are many things of interest to hunt here, and a vast amount of giants, but your first experience here will likely be ponies. There are some pets available, but they are usually substandard to what you are hunting here. If you're in your late 20s or early 30s, grab a pet on the way in from Cornwall.

What does make this zone nice, along with Lyonesse, is how isolated it can be from the rest of the realm. Basically when you hit these areas you are there to hunt, nothing more and nothing less. No possibility for enemies to raid your camp, and no lower levels running through looking for a hand-out.

- Dave "i3ullseye" Maynor

Tomb of Mithra

(For map of Tomb of Mithra Dungeon, see p. 71.)

Home to low-level undead, the Tomb is a treasure trove for the low-level character. This is where most players learn grouping techniques and "get their feet wet" with some of the monster AI in the game. The undead in Mithra tend to be social in some way, whether by bringing friends when attacked, or by links to other undead. This is also the first time that having to clear your way to a camping spot is a requirement rather than just a possibility. The deeper you go into this tomb, the harder things get — the young character can spend hours exploring the Tomb of Mithra and still never see the bottom.

Solo Friendly? Not solo friendly until the monsters near the entrance are blue con, the Tomb is still somewhere that the solo player can do well. It's a cleric's dreamland because everything in the zone is Smite-vulnerable. Archers can use their short-range arrows in here rather than having to spend coin they might not have yet on long-range arrows. All classes will find that the magic loot that drops in this area is useful until you can afford crafted gear at higher levels.

Group Friendly? Definitely the place to go if you want to group. Experience comes fast and furious here, especially if you have a good group that knows what it's doing. Camp bonuses and grouped monster bonuses add up very quickly, making the time it takes to gain a level go by so fast, sometimes you wonder if you're cheating somehow. Bindstones are very close so that even if the whole group does die and there is no Cleric high enough to rez, the time it takes to recover from a mistake is minimal.

Don't tackle which areas alone? Don't try to go to any of the rooms alone. Stick to hallways and watch where monsters spawn if you're going to solo in Mithra. Many of the monsters wander in and out of rooms, and one extra monster at just the wrong moment will prove deadly for a single player. And as with any dungeon, make sure you know your way back out so that if you need to leave in a hurry, you don't bring the whole dungeon down on your head. Everything in the zone is aggressive, and while most things have a small aggro radius, if you don't know where you're going, you have little hope of getting out alive.

Who hates this area? All players who lose their sense of direction easily, who become frustrated by other players interfering with their game, or who get mad at the occasional death are not going to like Tomb of Mithra. This place can be dangerous, no question about it.

- Heather "Orlena" Rothwell & Jim "Oakleif" Rothwell

Loot

Agidad [55] (10%) Crushed Helm *or* Boots • (10%) Protector of the Stone Lords • (10%) Crushed Sleeves *or* Leggings • (10%) Protector of the Stone Oracles • (10%) Holy *or* Sturdy Crushed Breastplate *or* Gauntlets • (10%) Lava Forged Sword

Borimo [53] *see Agidad [55]*

Brac [45] (18%; hi-lo) Stonepin Woven Cap, Protector of the Harvest *or* Band of Eldspar • (18%; hi-lo) Stonepin Woven Vest, Protector of the Stone Elders *or* Band of Eldspar • (18%; hi-lo) Stonepin Woven Sleeves, Stone Cutter *or* Band of Eldspar

Braen [45] *see Brac [45]*

Brannoc [47] (18%; hi-lo) Stonepin Woven Gloves, Caller Shard *or* Belt of Granite Enhancement • (18%; hi-lo) Stonepin Woven Pants, Shard of the Stonewatch *or* Belt of Granite Enhancement • (18%; hi-lo) Stonepin Woven Boots, Molten Magma Sword *or* Belt of Granite Enhancement

Clud [47] *see Brannoc [47]*

Clywd [49] (12%) Magmas Imbued Helm *or* Gloves, *or* Helm *or* Gloves of Opposition • (12%) Magmas Imbued Leggings *or* Boots, *or* Leggings *or* Boots of Opposition • (12%) Feather Light Granite Axe *or* Opposition Pin • (12%) Magmas Imbued Robe *or* Sleeves, *or* Jerkin *or* Sleeves of Opposition • (12%) Feather Light Granite Gauche *or* Dark Crystal Mattock

Dartmoor pony [34/36] (95/90%) Dartmoor Pony Hide • (5/10%) Pristine Dartmoor Pony Hide

draconic ancilla [50] (no loot)

Galand [45] *see Brac [45]*

Golestandt [80] *see Moran the Mighty [73], plus* • (99%) <Timeless Treasures> • (99%) <Hearts of the North>

granite giant [36/38/40] (12/16/15%) Granite Finger • (6/8.1/7.5%) Broken Flint • (2/2.7/2.5%) Powdered Granite • (20%) Jewels 21 • (2%; hi-lo) Stonewatch Helm/Breastplate/Arms, Point of the Infidel [36,38]/Unforgiving Mace [40], *or* Magma Imbued Cloak • (5%) Ancient Granite Stone

granite giant earthmagi [65] (no loot)

granite giant elder [62] (15%) Fused Quartz Stone • (20%) Jewels 63 • (1.7%) Granite Seer's Cap of the Spirit *or* the Mind, Granite Seer's Boots, Fire *or* Wind Imbued Cap, *or* Matter Imbued Boots • (1.7%) Polished Granite Staff of Body *or* Matter, *or* Band of Ircon

granite giant elder [64] (15%) Fused Quartz Stone • (20%) Jewels 63 • (1.7%) Granite Seer's Vest of the Body *or* Sleeves of Matter, Lava Imbued Vest, *or* Cold Imbued Sleeves • (1.7%) Polished Granite Staff of Spirit *or* Mind

granite giant gatherer [42/44/46] (4.5/4.5/6% each) Grass Stained Stone, Powdered Ircon • (20%) Jewels 30 • (2%; hi-lo) Stonepin Woven Cap/Vest/Sleeves, Protector of the Harvest/Protector of the Stone Elders/Stone Cutter, *or* Band of Eldspar • (9%) Ancient Granite Stone

granite giant herdsman [39] (12%) Flint • (6%) Cracked Granite Horseshoe • (2%) Granite Horseshoe • (20%) Jewels 21 • (2%; hi-lo) Stonewatch Gauntlets, Granite Drum, *or* Ring of the Stonewatch • (5%) Ancient Granite Stone

granite giant herdsman [41] (10%) Flint • (5.1%) Cracked Granite Horseshoe • (1.7%) Granite Horseshoe • (17%) Jewels 30 • (2%; hi-lo) Stonewatch Leggings, Polished Granite Lute, *or* Jagged Granite Staff • (9%) Ancient Granite Stone

granite giant herdsman [43] (12%) Flint • (6%) Cracked Granite Horseshoe • (2%) Granite Horseshoe • (20%) Jewels 30 • (2%; hi-lo) Stonewatch Boots, Polished Granite Flute, Polished Ilmenite Staff, *or* Stonewatch Pin • (9%) Ancient Granite Stone

granite giant oracle [62/64] (15/17%) Polished Eldspar Stone • (20%) Jewels 63 • (1.7%) Granite Seer's Gloves of the Spirit *or* Mind, Granite Seer's Pants, Fire *or* Wind Imbued Gloves, *or* Matter Imbued Pants [62]/Robe of the Spirit Stone, Eternal Wind *or* Stone Speaking, *or* Lava Imbued Robes [64] • (1.7%) Polished Granite Staff of Earth *or* Cold, *or* Band of Ilmenite

granite giant outlooker [51/53/55] (20/20/25%) Polished Granite Stone • (20%) Jewels 63 • (1.7%) Dark Crystalline Helm *or* Boots/Arms *or* Legs/Vest *or* Gauntlets • (1.7%) Ilmenite *or* Eldspar Crafted Crossbow, *or* Stonewatch Bill/Bow *or* Hammer of the Stonewatch/Enlicimun, *or* Halberd of the Stonewatch • (5%) Ancient Granite Stone

granite giant pounder [52/54/56] (20%) Ircon Stone • (20%) Jewels 63 • (1.7%) Crushed Helm *or* Boots/Crushed Sleeves *or* Leggings/Holy *or* Sturdy Crushed Breastplate *or* Gauntlets • (1.7%) Protector of the Stone Lords/Protector of the Stone Oracles/Lava Forged Sword • (2.5%) Ancient Granite Stone [52]

granite giant reinforcer [65] (no loot)

granite giant stonecaller [45/47/49] (6/6/7.5%) Reflective Stone • (2/2/2.5%) Powdered Ilmenite • (20%) Jewels 30 • (2%; hi-lo) Stonepin Woven Gloves/Pants/Boots, Caller Shard/Shard of the Stonewatch/Molten Magma Sword, *or* Belt of Granite Enhancement • (9%) Ancient Granite Stone

granite giant stonelord [57] (20%) Ilmenite Shard • (20%) Jewels 63 • (1.7%) Coif *or* Leggings (Polished of Eldspar, Ilmenite Laced Chain *or* Ircon Bound Chain) • (1.7%) Belt of the Protector

granite giant stonelord [59] (20%) Ilmenite Shard • (20%) Jewels 63 • (1.7%) Polished Sleeves *or* Boots of Eldspar, Ilmenite Laced Chain Sleeves *or* Boots, *or* Ircon Bound Chain Sleeves • (1.7%) Darksword of Granite *or* Crush Born Sword

granite giant stonelord [61] (20%) Ilmenite Shard • (20%) Jewels 63 • (1.7%) Mittens *or* Hauberk (Polished of Eldspar, Ilmenite Laced Chain *or* Ircon Bound Chain) • (1.7%) Facimil

granite giant stonemender [65] (no loot)

granite giant stoneshaper [48/50/52] (5.4%) Powdered Quartz • (1.8%) Granite Shard • (20%) Jewels 30/Jewels 30/Jewels 63 • (2%) Magmas Imbued Helm *or* Gloves/Leggings *or* Boots/Robe *or* Sleeves, *or* Helm *or* Gloves/Leggings *or* Boots/Jerkin *or* Sleeves of Opposition • (9%) Ancient Granite Stone • (1.7%) Feather Light Granite Axe *or* Opposition Pin [50] • (1.7%) Feather Light Granite Gauche *or* Dark Crystal Mattock • (5%) Ancient Granite Stone [52]

granite knocker [47] (80%) Granite Chisel

greenhorn poacher [25/27/29/31] (70/20/10/10%) Silver Cup • (0/40/50/60%) Bent Silver Spoon

Grimbuld [51] (10%) Dark Crystalline Helm *or* Boots • (10%) Ilmenite *or* Eldspar Crafted Crossbow, *or* Stonewatch Bill • (10%) Dark Crystalline Arms *or* Legs • (10%) Bow *or* Hammer of the Stonewatch • (10%) Dark Crystalline Vest *or* Gauntlets • (10%) Enlicimun *or* Halberd of the Stonewatch

Kaq [55] (20%; hi-lo) Gloves of the Stoneharvest, Fiery Pious Bludgeoner *or* Polished Granite Pin • (20%; hi-lo) Leggings of the Stoneharvest, Rift Sealer *or* Feather Light Granite Hammer • (20%; hi-lo) Boots of the Stoneharvest, Polished Hammer of Eldspar *or* Polished Granite Pin

Keh [49] (20%; hi-lo) Coif of the Stoneharvest, Stone Breaker *or* Stonewatch Bracer • (10%) Hauberk of the Stoneharvest • (5% each) Sulfurous Basher, Granite Pulverizer • (20%; hi-lo) Sleeves of the Stoneharvest, Hammer of Crushing Might *or* Stonewatch Bracer

Kez [53] *see Kaq [55]*

Kor [47] (10%) Stonecrush Leggings *or* Helm • (10%) Rift Finder *or* Stonesoul Staff • (10%) Stonecrush Vest *or* Boots • (10%) Stone Splitter *or* Sheer Granite-Slicer • (10%) Stonecrush Arms *or* Gauntlets • (10%) Stone Gutter, Powder Maker, *or* Ring of Granite Enhancement

Kul [45] *see Kor [47]*

Legil [53] *see Agidad [55]*

Moran the Mighty [73] (15%) Magmas Imbued Helm *or* Gloves, *or* Helm *or* Gloves of Opposition • (15%) Magmas Imbued Leggings *or* Boots, *or* Leggings *or* Boots of Opposition • (15%) Feather Light Granite Axe *or* Opposition Pin • (15%) Magmas Imbued Robe *or* Sleeves, *or* Jerkin *or* Sleeves of Opposition • (15%) Feather Light Granite Gauche *or* Dark Crystal Mattock • (15%) Dark Crystalline Helm *or* Boots • (15%) Ilmenite *or* Eldspar Crafted Crossbow, *or* Stonewatch Bill • (15%) Dark Crystalline Arms *or* Legs • (15%) Bow *or* Hammer of the Stonewatch • (15%) Dark Crystalline Vest *or* Gauntlets • (15%) Enlicimun *or* Halberd of the Stonewatch • (15%) Crushed Helm *or* Boots • (15%) Protector of the Stone Lords • (15%) Crushed Sleeves *or* Leggings • (15%) Protector of the Stone Oracles • (15%) Holy *or* Sturdy Crushed Breastplate *or* Gauntlets • (15%) Lava Forged Sword • (15%) Coif *or* Leggings: Polished of Eldspar, Ilmenite Laced Chain *or* Ircon Bound Chain • (15%) Belt of the Protector • (15%) Polished Sleeves *or* Boots of Eldspar, Ilmenite Laced Chain Sleeves *or* Boots, *or* Ircon Bound Chain Sleeves • (15%) Darksword of Granite *or* Crush Born Sword • (15%) Polished Hauberk *or* Mittens of Eldspar, Ilmenite Laced Chain Hauberk *or* Mittens, *or* Ircon Bound Chain Hauberk • (15%) Facimil • (22%) Granite Seer's Gloves of the Spirit *or* the Mind, Granite Seer's *or* Matter Imbued Pants, *or* Fire *or* Wind Imbued Gloves • (22%) Polished Granite Staff of Earth *or* Cold, *or* Band of Ilmenite • (22%) Robe of the Spirit Stone, the Eternal Wind *or* Stone Speaking, *or* Lava Imbued Robes • (22%) Polished Granite Staff of Wind *or* Fire • (22%) Granite Seer's Cap of the Spirit *or* the Mind, Granite Seer's *or* Matter Imbued Boots, *or* Fire *or* Wind Imbued Cap • (22%) Polished Granite Staff of Body *or* Matter, *or* Band of Ircon • (22%) Granite Seer's Vest of the Body *or* Sleeves of Matter, Lava Imbued Vest, *or* Cold Imbued Sleeves • (22%) Polished Granite Staff of Spirit *or* Mind

Nodin [49] *see Clywd [49]*

Penn [49] *see Clywd [49]*

Pladimon [51] *see Grimbuld [51]*

ruthless brigand [39/41/43] (15/20/20%) Dented Defenders Helm • (20%) Jewels 21/Jewels 21/Jewels 30 • (2%; hi-lo) Magma Hardened Leather Helm *or* Leggings/Jerkin *or* Boots/Sleeves *or* Gloves, *or* Sword of Avengement *or* Longsword of Rancor [39]/Shield of Scorn [41,43]

Stonecrush demolisher [51/53/55] (9/12/12%) Stonehand Shovel • (4.5/6/6%) Stonefinger Necklace • (20/15/20%) Jewels 63 • (2%; hi-lo) Gloves/Leggings/Boots of the Stoneharvest, Fiery Pious Bludgeoner *or* Polished Granite Pin [51]/Rift Sealer *or* Feather Light Granite Hammer [53]/Polished Hammerof Eldspar *or* Polished Granite Pin [55]

Stonecrush excavator [45/47/49] (12%) Bag of Ilmenite Powder • (6%) Bag of Quartz Powder • (20%) Jewels 30 • (1.7%) Stonecrush Leggings *or* Helm/Vest *or* Boots/Arms *or* Gauntlets • (1.7%) Rift Finder *or* Stonesoul Staff [45]/Stone Splitter *or* Sheer Granite-Slicer [47]/Stone Gutter, Powder Maker *or* Ring of Granite Enhancement [49]

Stonecrush rockgrinder [48/50/52] (12%) Stonefoot Press • (4%) Cracked Ircon Ring • (20%) Jewels 30 [48,50] • (15%) Jewels 63 [52] • (2%; hi-lo) Coif/Hauberk/Sleeves of the Stoneharvest, *or* Stone Breaker *or* Stonewatch Bracer [48]/Sulfurous Basher *or* Granite Pulverizer [50]/Hammer of Crushing Might *or* Stonewatch Bracer [52]

Tegbuk [47] *see Brannoc [47]*

Tolukin [55] *see Agidad [55]*

Trahern [51] *see Grimbuld [51]*

Key. [X] = level(s) • (X%) = chance to get item (if a list, just one) • (X% each) = chance for ***each*** item • hi-lo = most to least likely • APOA = a piece of armor • (x2) = item can drop twice

Llyn Barfog

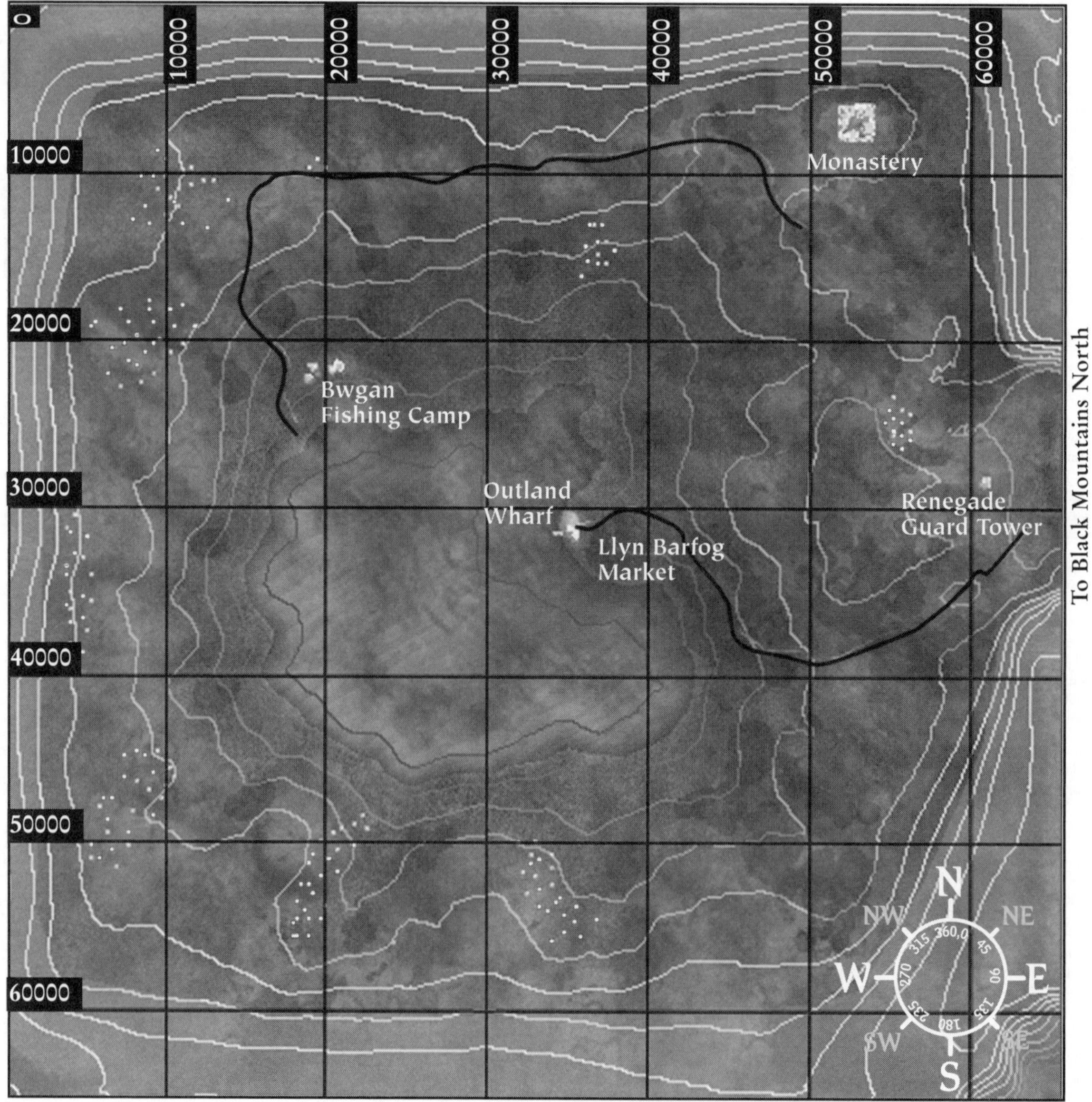

Monsters with levels lower than 22 are not marked.

FF = Frenzied Feeder
ND = Needletooth Devourer
BG = Bearded Gorger
TOAD = Diamondback Toad

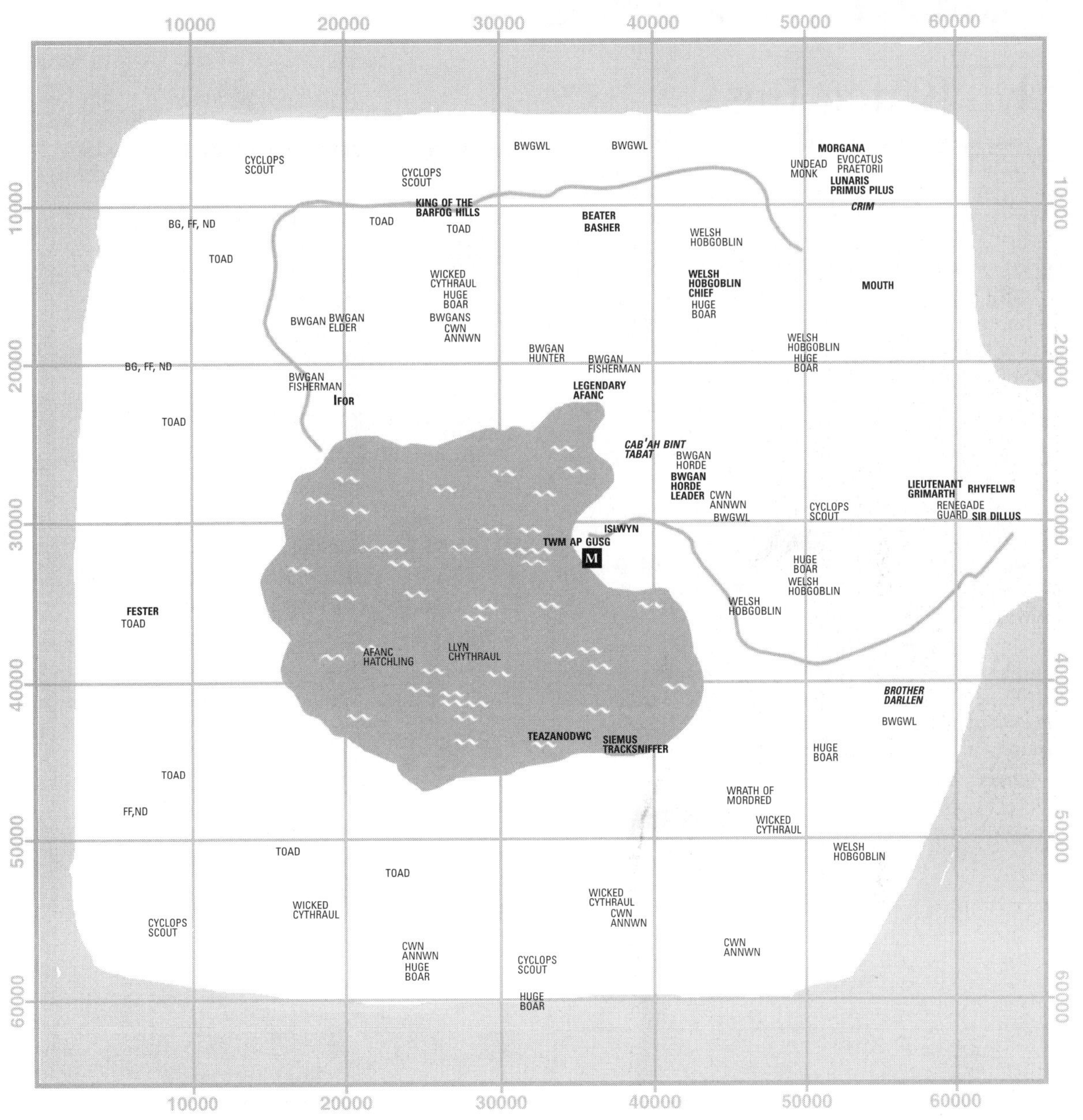

Lower-level monsters not shown on map:

Creature	Lvl	Location
lake adder	10	WC,C
gwr-drwgiaid	15	NW,NC
Rhyfelwr	15	EC
black bear	16	NE,C,EC,SC,SE
gwr-drwgiaid	16	NC,WC,SC
black bear	17	NE,C,EC,SC,SE
gwr-drwgiaid	17	NC,WC
Welsh hobgoblin	17	NC,NE,WC,EC,SE
huge boar	18	NC,EC,SW
Twr ap Alsig	18	C
huge boar	19	NW,NC,NE,WC,SC
renegade guard	19	EC
Welsh hobgoblin	19	NC,NE,WC,EC
cwn annwn	20	NC,C,SW,SC
cythraul	20	NW,NC,NE,WC,EC,SW,SC
Fallen	20	NW
renegade guard	20	EC
Welsh hobgoblin chief	20	NE
cwn annwn	21	SW,SC
cythraul	21	WC,EC,SW,SC
Lieutenant Grimarth	21	EC
bwgan	22	SW

Llyn Barfog Tips

This is an isolated zone off of Black Mountains North. Lots of higher level quest monsters reside here, including little pocket groups of monsters. Most are not linked, but the BAF triggers very easily in many of the camps. There are plenty of good pets for a Sorcerer here, and quite a few off the wall quests.

One unique feature here is the fishing village. By default they will not trade with you (and in some rare cases may even attack you). But once you have hunted the native scourge of the region, the welsh hobgoblins, they eventually warm to you and allow you to use their merchants for trade.

- Dave "i3ullseye" Maynor

Be careful — the local merchants can be aggressive depending on monsters fought. If you fight hobgoblins they like you more, but if you take on the guards they are definitely unfriendly.

- Matt "Kyle Draconeco" Shirley

A single group (1-2 healers, a theurgist, 4 tanks, and a rogue — all lvls 47-50) can often handle the circuit of Epic monsters in this zone ... except for the Shade of Mordred. It never hurts to have more for them though, or a res-er on standby.

- Chris "Kirstena" Yone

Solo and Group Levelling Tips

Solo

15-20	black bears, welsh hobgoblins
20-25	black bears, welsh hobgoblins, cythreals, bwgan fishermen, renegade guards
25-30	welsh hobgoblins, cythreals, bwgan fishermen
30-35	skeletal monks

Group

15-20	welsh hobgoblins, cythreals, renegade guards
20-25	bwgan fishermen, renegade guards
25-30	skeletal monks
40-50	diamondback toads, frenzied feeders, bearded gorgers

- Matt "Kyle Draconeco" Shirley

Loot

afanc hatchling [25] (4%) Pristine Alfanc Hide • (35%) Alfanc Fang • (10%) Alfanc Fang • (50%) Alfanc Eye (x2) • (5%) Serrated Alfanc Tooth • (9%) Alfanc Tongue

Anfri ap Even [29] (70%) Citrine • (65%) Pearl • (50%) Malachite • (80%) Topaz

Basher [42] (60% each) Cyclops Eye, Ear • (80%) Cyclops Toes • (1.4%) Flattened Eye Shield, Basher's Sash, Cyclop's Pupil ***or*** Pulsing Gem • (1.4%) Conquerer's Cloak, Beater's Bludgeon, Basher's Finger ***or*** Beater's Poked Eye

Beater [42] (60% each) Cyclops Eye, Ear • (80%) Cyclops Toes • (1.4%) Flattened Eye Shield, Basher's Sash, Cyclop's Pupil ***or*** Pulsing Gem • (1.4%) Conquerer's Cloak, Beater's Bludgeon, Basher's Finger ***or*** Beater's Poked Eye

black bear [16-17] (23%) Black Bear Pelt • (2.5%) Pristine Black Bear Pelt • (50%) Bloody Bear Fang • (25%) Black Bear Tongue • (1.5%) Long Animal Fang

bwgan [22/23] (40%) Pearl • (10%) Fire Opal/Green Tourmaline • (1%) Chrome Diopside/Jasper • (0.3%) <Salisbury Stock 1> • (1.5%) Animal Skin Shield ***or*** Bwgan Skinning Dirk • (5% each) Severed Bwgan Hand, Leg [23]

bwgan elder [24] (5% each) Severed Bwgan Leg, Hand, Elder Head • (30%) Malachite • (10%) Sunstone • (1%) Black Star Diopside • (0.3%) <Salisbury Stock 1> • (1.5%) Animal Skin Shield ***or*** Bwgan Skinning Dirk

bwgan fisherman [23] (40%) Pearl • (10%) Green Tourmaline • (1%) Jasper • (5% each) Severed Bwgan Hand, Leg • (0.3%) <Salisbury Stock 1> • (1.5%) Bwgan Fishing Pole ***or*** Fish Scale Vest

bwgan fisherman [26-27] (5% each) Severed Bwgan Hand, Leg, Elder Head • (30%) Malachite • (10%) Sunstone • (1%) Sphene • (0.3%) <Arthurian Artifacts 1> • (1.5%) Bwgan Fishing Pole ***or*** Fish Scale Vest

bwgan horde [23] (40%) Pearl • (10%) Green Tourmaline • (1%) Jasper • (5% each) Severed Bwgan Hand, Leg • (0.3%) <Salisbury Stock 1> • (1.5%) Ring of the Leader ***or*** Hoarde Hammer

bwgan horde leader [24] (40%) Pearl • (10%) Green Tourmaline • (1%) Jasper • (5% each) Severed Bwgan Hand, Leg • (0.3%) <Salisbury Stock 1> • (1.5%) Ring of the Leader ***or*** Hoarde Hammer

bwgan hunter [22-23] (40%) Pearl • (10%) Green Tourmaline • (1%) Jasper • (5% each) Severed Bwgan Hand, Leg • (0.3%) <Salisbury Stock 1> • (1.5%) Bwgan's Hunting Bow ***or*** Arrow of the Bwagan • (9%) Bwgan Hunter Eye

bwgwl [28-29] (25% each) Severed Bwgwl Leg (x2), Severed Bwgwl Hand (x2) • (1%) Bloody Bwgwl Finger • (1.5%) APOA: Ancient • (0.3%) <Arthurian Artifacts 1>

cwn annwn [20-22] (62%) Cwn Annwn Pelt • (27%) Sharp Cwn Annwn Fang • (25%) Cwn Annwn Paw • (32%) Cracked Cwn Annwn Claw • (1%) Red Tipped Cwn Annwn Ear

cyclops scout [32] (30%) Rotten Tooth • (60%) Animal Pelt • (80%) Jeweled Eye • (1.5%) Eye-Studded Tunic ***or*** Mace

cythraul [20-21] (40%) Pearl • (10%) Fire Opal • (1%) Sunstone • (0.3%) <Out of the Woods> • (1.5%) Razor Bone Edge ***or*** Cythraul's Dirk

Duncan Curan [28] (70%) Citrine • (65%) Pearl • (50%) Malachite • (80%) Topaz

Evocatus praetorii [26] (60%) Roman Commanders Seal • (30%) Small Silver Statue • (50%) Jewels 26 • (1.4%) APOA: Bloodied Leather • (1.4%) Decorated Roman Dagger ***or*** Stiletto, ***or*** Roman Tactician Bracer • (0.3%) <Salisbury Stock 1>

Fallen [20] (40%) Pearl • (10%) Fire Opal • (1%) Sunstone • (0.3%) <Out of the Woods>

Forsaken [40] (no loot)

Gwallter ap Trevls [29] (70%) Citrine • (65%) Pearl • (50%) Malachite • (80%) Topaz

gwartheg y llyn [25] (no loot)

gwr-drwgiaid [15-17] (25% each) Severed Gwr-Drwgiaid Hand (x2), Severed Gwr-Drwgiaid Leg (x2) • (1%) Bloody Gwr-Drwgiaid Finger • (0.7%) Ponderer • (0.3% each) Resilient Sleeves, Gloves • (0.3%) <Grave Goods> • (1.3%) APOA: Impish Leather ***or*** Frock • (1.3%) Impish Cloak, Ring, Necklace, Bracer ***or*** Gem

huge boar [18-19] (50% each) Huge Boar Hide, Huge Cloven Hoof • (20% each) Bloody Boar Tusk, Large Pig Tail • (15%) Huge Boar Tusk

Ifor [29] (5% each) Severed Bwgan Hand, Leg, Elder Head • (30%) Malachite • (10%) Sunstone • (1%) Sphene • (0.3%) <Arthurian Artifacts 1> • (30%) Islwyn's Bead Necklace ***or*** Ifor's Headband

Islwyn [29] (5% each) Severed Bwgan Hand, Leg, Elder Head • (30%) Malachite • (10%) Sunstone • (1%) Sphene • (0.3%) <Arthurian Artifacts 1> • (30%) Islwyn's Bead Necklace ***or*** Ifor's Headband

lake adder [10] (10%) Pristine Eel Skin • (45%) Eel Meat (x2) • (20%) Eel Poison Gland

Lieutenant Grimarth [21] (10%) Stolen Supplies • (35%) Stolen Rations • (0.15%) Lion Faced Shield • (0.85%) Lion Etched Sword • (1%) APOA: Lion Embossed • (5%) Jewels 57

Llyn Chythraul [41] (45%) Alfanc Eye (x2) • (35% each) Large Alfanc Fang, Serrated Alfanc Tooth • (10% each) Large Alfanc Fang, Serrated Alfanc Tooth, Alfanc Hide • (50%) Alfanc Tongue

Lunaris primus pilus [30] (60%) Roman Commanders Seal • (30%) Small Silver Statue • (50%) Jewels 26 • (1.4%) APOA: Bloodied Leather • (1.4%) Decorated Roman Dagger ***or*** Stiletto, ***or*** Roman Tactician Bracer • (0.3%) <Salisbury Stock 1>

Morgana [90] (10%) Stick-Figure Totem • (2.5%) Tattered Lamellar Arms • (5%) Tattered Boned Arms

Olvryn Wynford [30] (10%) Stolen Supplies • (35%) Stolen Rations • (0.15%) Lion Faced Shield • (0.85%) Lion Etched Sword • (1%) APOA: Lion Embossed • (5%) Jewels 57

renegade guard [19-20] (10%) Stolen Supplies • (35%) Stolen Rations • (0.15%) Lion Faced Shield • (0.85%) Lion Etched Sword • (1%) APOA: Lion Embossed • (5%) Jewels 57

Rhyfelwr [15] (10%) Stolen Supplies • (35%) Stolen Rations • (0.15%) Lion Faced Shield • (0.85%) Lion Etched Sword • (1%) APOA: Lion Embossed • (5%) Jewels 57

Siemus Tracksniffer [29] (5% each) Severed Bwgan Hand, Leg, Elder Head • (30%) Malachite • (10%) Sunstone • (1%) Sphene • (0.3%) <Arthurian Artifacts 1> • (1.5%) Bwgan Fishing Pole ***or*** Fish Scale Vest

Sir Dillus [22] (70%) Stolen Rations • (20%) Stolen Supplies • (1%) APOA: Lion Embossed • (0.15%) Lion Faced Shield • (0.9%) Lion Etched Sword • (10%) Jewels 57

Tewdwr ap Greid [29] (70%) Citrine • (65%) Pearl • (50%) Malachite • (80%) Topaz

Thomas ap Seyton [30] (70%) Citrine • (65%) Pearl • (50%) Malachite • (80%) Topaz

Twm ap Gusg [29] (70%) Citrine • (65%) Pearl • (50%) Malachite • (80%) Topaz

Twr ap Alsig [18] (no loot)

undead monk [29-30] (40%) Black Star Diopside • (10% each) Dried Monk Skull, Cat's Eye Tourmaline • (1%) Cat's Eye Apatite • (0.3%) Werewolf Tooth Necklace, Shadowhands Gloves ***or*** Cloak, ***or*** Majestical Ring • (1.3%) Leg Bone Quarterstaff ***or*** Ghost Robes • (1.3%) APOA: Ghastly Mendicant ***or*** Frock • (1.3%) Ghastly Mendicant Cloak, Ring, Necklace, Bracer ***or*** Gem

Welsh hobgoblin [17,19] (25% each) Bloody Hobgoblin Eyeball (x2), Severed Hobgoblin Toe (x2) • (1%) Mutilated Hobgoblin Hand • (0.3%) <Out of the Woods> • (1.5%) APOA: Bloodied Leather

Welsh hobgoblin chief [20] (30%) Bloody Hobgoblin Eyeball (x2) • (25%) Severed Hobgoblin Toe (x2) • (10%) Mutilated Hobgoblin Hand • (0.3%) <Out of the Woods> • (1.5%) APOA: Bloodied Leather

wicked cythraul [26-27] (40%) Sunstone • (10%) Black Star Diopside • (1%) Cat's Eye Tourmaline • (1.5%) APOA: Ancient • (0.3%) <Arthurian Artifacts 1>

Key. [X] = level(s) • (X%) = chance to get item (if a list, just one) • (X% each) = chance for ***each*** item • hi-lo = most to least likely • APOA = a piece of armor • (x2) = item can drop twice

Lyonesse

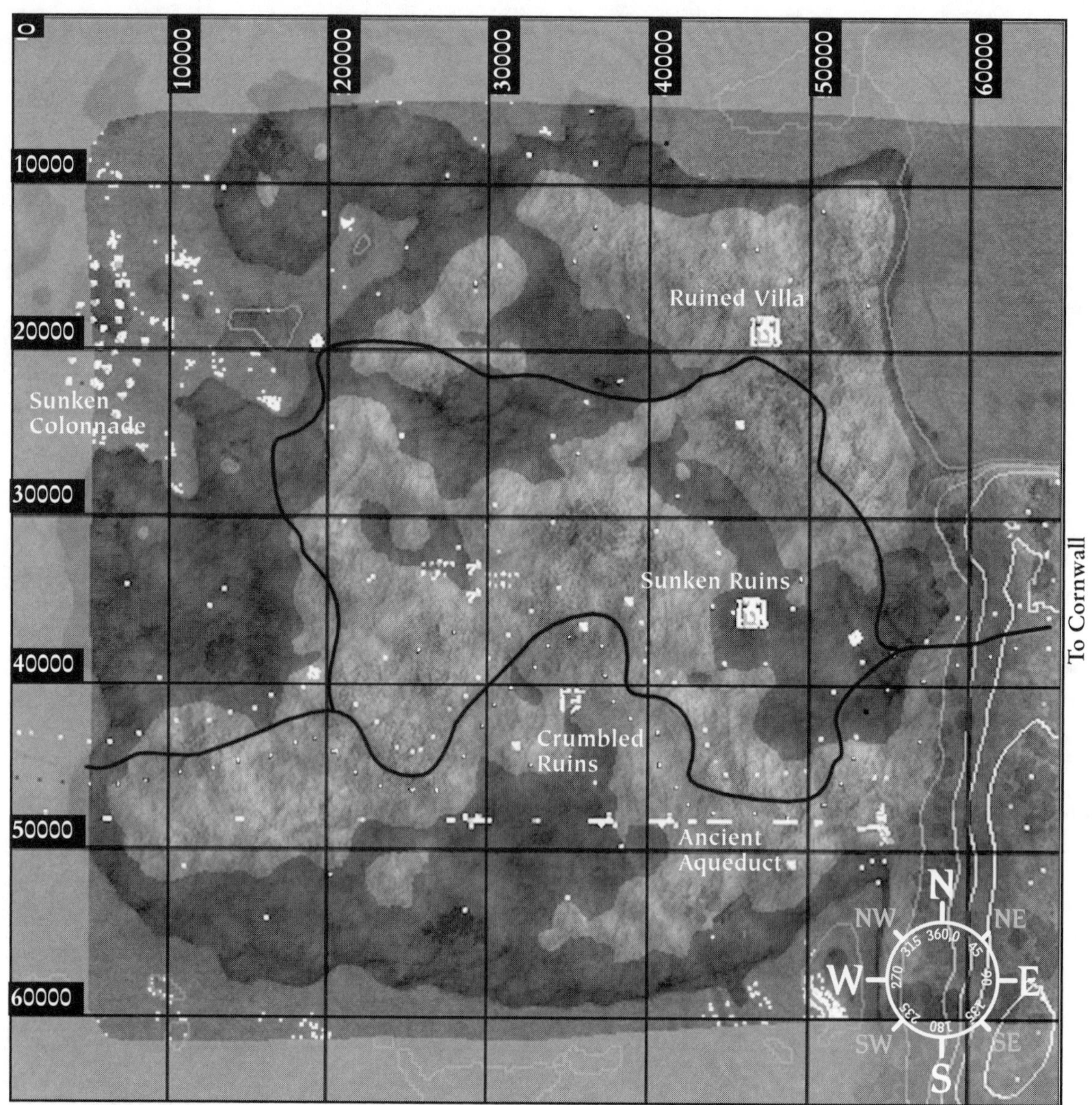
0
10000
20000
30000
40000
50000
60000
10000
20000
30000
40000
50000
60000
Ruined Villa
Sunken Colonnade
Sunken Ruins
Crumbled Ruins
Ancient Aqueduct
To Cornwall
N
NW
NE
W
E
SW
SE
S
360/0
45
90
135
180
225
270
315

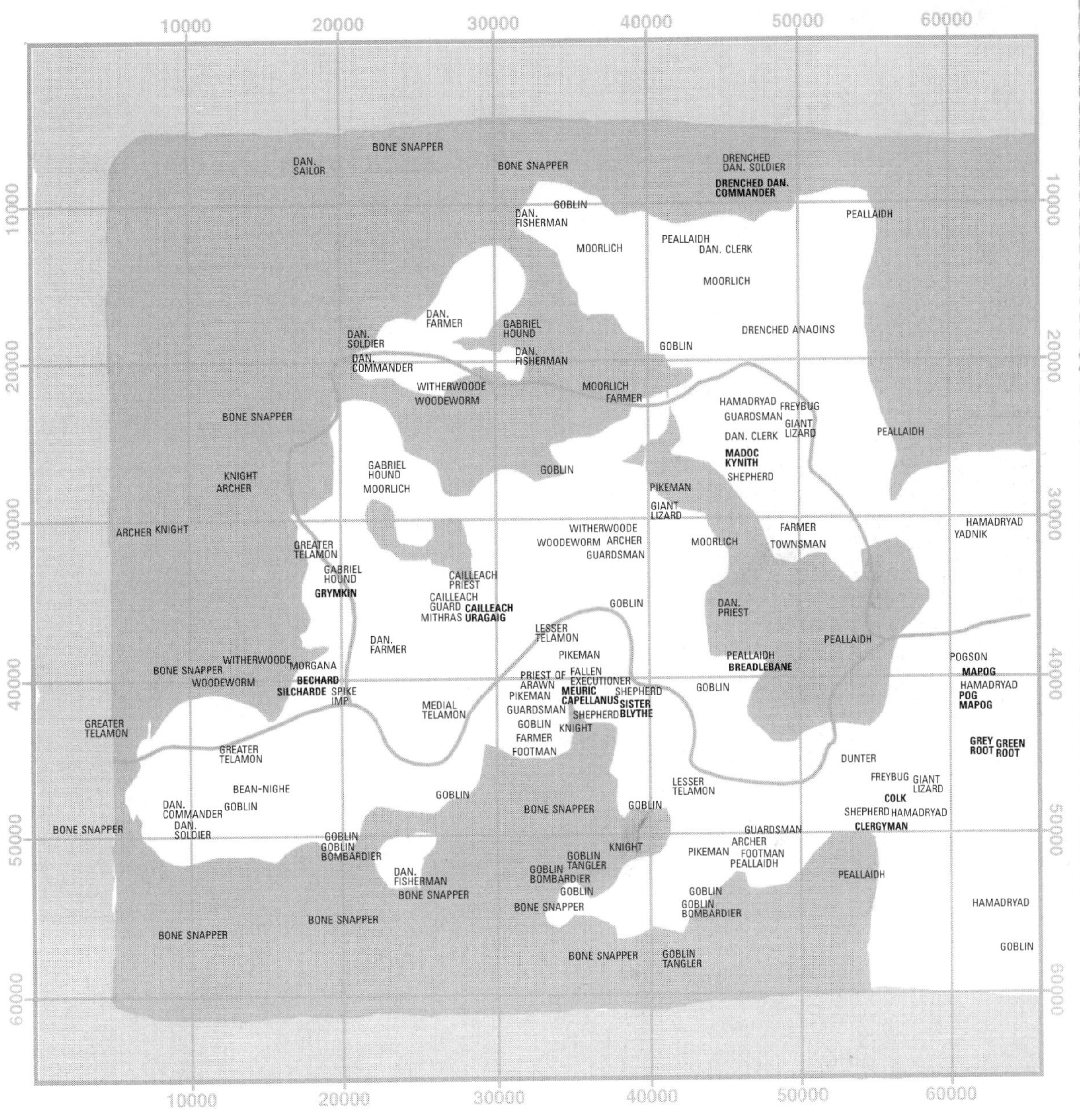

GOBLIN = Pygmy goblin
DAN. = Danaoin

Lyonesse Tips

Lyonesse has become something of a sweet spot for most Albion groups. Some of the fastest non-dungeon XP to be had is found in this area, and you can solo here as low as level 30 (depending on your class). If you're a Sorcerer, grab a good rooter or bogey from Cornwall on your way down, and you can comfortably manage many of the lower level creatures in this zone.

Its real strength lies in its camp for large groups at higher levels: Pygmy goblins, dunters, telamons, and so forth. As far as soloing goes, this zone is only good very early (dunters) or very late when you can harvest large amounts of green and blue targets. Be warned, the BAF in this zone can be very unforgiving at certain camps.

- Dave "i3ullseye" Maynor

One of the most popular high level camps is the witherwoode/worms — it gives fast, steady experience, although it can be rather tedious.

- Matt "Kyle Draconeco" Shirley

Solo and Group Levelling Tips

Solo

30-35	dunters
35-45	lesser telemons, pygmies
45-50	lesser telemons, pygmies, pikemen

Group

30-40	lesser telemons, pygmies
40-50	medial/greater telemons, danaoin soldiers, witherwoode, woodeworm

- Matt "Kyle Draconeco" Shirley

Loot

archer [45] (40%) Jewels 14 • (1.5%) APOA: Aqueous Coral Studded • (1.5%) Fallen Archer's Stiletto ***or*** Dagger • (1.5%) Fallen Archer's Great Bow • (1.5%) Arrows of the Fallen

bean-nighe [50/52-53/54] (20/25/27%) Souless Gem Dust • (1.6%) APOA: Cursed Malcontent's • (1.6%) Bracer of Eternal Screams ***or*** Restless Souls

bone snapper [63] (20%) Chewed Asterium Metal • (1.2% each) APOA: Cursed Malcontent's, Danaoin Nightwatcher, Ageless Telamon, Danaoin Lightwatcher, Cailiondar • (50%) Jewels 14 • (25%) <Mists of Lyonesse> • (1.6%) APOA: Adamant Coral • (1.6%) Avenging Knight's Hammer ***or*** Cloak

Breadlebane [45] (45%) Jewels 27 • (0.6% each) Mind, Spirit, Bloody, Dissolution, Fiery, Windy, Earthen ***or*** Frozen Staff

cailleach guard [60/62/64/66] (10/11/12/13%) Jeweled Coffer • (10/12/14/16%) Jewels 02 • (1.6%) Cailiondar Rapier, Bastard Sword, Mace ***or*** Longbow • (1.6%) APOA: Cailiondar • (1%) Cailiondar Bracer of Battle

cailleach priest [64/66/67] (10/10/15%) Jeweled Coffer • (30/40/45%) Jewels 02 • (1.6%) APOA: Cailiondar • (1.6%) Cailiondar Mace • (1%) Cailiondar Bracer of Piety

Cailleach Uragaig [70] (10%) Jeweled Coffer • (15%) Jewels 02 (x2) • (6.5% each) Celestial Cailiondar Robe, Jerkin, Vest • (6.5%) Cailiondar Battle Robe • (7% each) Celestial Cailiondar Hauberk, Breastplate

clergyman [36] (30%) Jewels 31 • (15%) <Mists of Lyonesse> • (1.5%) APOA: Aqueous • (0.8% each) Clergyman's Mace ***or*** Shield • (0.4%) Clergyman's Pious Mantle

Colk [40] (25%) Water Seers Stone • (1.6%) APOA: Deluged Kelp • (1.6%) Deluged Drum • (25%) Jewels 14

Danaoin clerk [35/37/39] (15/16/17%) <Mists of Lyonesse> • (15/16/17%) Jewels 14 • (1.6%) APOA: Deluged Kelp • (1.6%) Ring of Etiquette • (5/7/14%) Danaoin Poison

Danaoin commander [60] (40%) Jewels 27 • (20%) <Gone Fishin'> • (1.6%) APOA: Danaoin Lightwatcher • (1.6%) Danaoin War Pick, Two-Handed Sword ***or*** Great Hammer

Danaoin farmer [44,46] (25%) Jewels 14 • (10%) <Gone Fishin'> • (1.6%) APOA: Aqueous Coral Studded • (1.6%) <Danaoin Delights>

Danaoin fisherman [40/42] (20%) Jewels 14 • (8/10%) <Gone Fishin'> • (1.7%) Danaoin Harpoon ***or*** Virulent Fishing Hook • (12%) Danaoin Fishing Fly

Danaoin priest [42,44] (15%) Jewels 27 • (10%) <Gone Fishin'> • (1.6%) APOA: Banded Coral • (0.6% each) Clergyman's Mace ***or*** Shield • (0.3%) Clergyman's Pious Mantle

Danaoin sailor [44,46] (25%) Jewels 14 • (10%) <Gone Fishin'> • (1.6%) APOA: Banded Coral • (1.6%) <Danaoin Delights>

Danaoin soldier [50/52/54] (25/30/35%) Jewels 27 • (11/12/13%) <Gone Fishin'> • (1.6%) APOA: Danaoin Nightwatcher [50,52]/Lightwatcher [54] • (1.6%) Danaoin War Pick/Two-Handed Sword/Great Hammer

dunter [30-31/32-33/34] (20/24/25%) Water Seers Stone • (1.6%) APOA: Aqueous [30-33]/Deluged Kelp [34] • (1.6%) Deluged Lute/Flute/Drum • (7/7/13%) Dunter Head

farmer [32] (20%) Jewels 31 • (10%) <Mists of Lyonesse> • (1.6%) APOA: Aqueous • (1.6%) Studded Farmer's Belt ***or*** Farmer's Stump Cutter • (12%) Sack of Grain

footman [45] (45%) Jewels 14 • (1.5%) APOA: Adamant Coral • (1.5%) Fallen Soldier's Pike, Axe ***or*** Hammer • (1.5%) Symbol of Loyalty

gabriel hound [40/42/44/46] (10/12/14/16%) Fiery Hound Skin • (1.1/1.3/1.6/1.8%) Pristine Fiery Hound Skin • (19/19/20/23%) Fiery Hound Tooth • (1/1/1.1/1.3%) Fiery Hound Tooth

gabriel hound [48] (18%) Fiery Hound Skin • (2%) Pristine Fiery Hound Skin • (24%) Fiery Hound Tooth • (1.3%) Fiery Hound Tooth • (1.6%) Immolated Hound Skin Cloak

giant lizard [36,38] (70%) Giant Lizard Hide • (7.5%) Fell Creature's Tooth • (11%) Giant Lizard Sinew

greater telamon [54] (29%) Smooth Golem Stone • (1.5%) APOA: Ageless Telamon • (1.5%) Greater Telamon Scimitar • (1.5%) Hollow Telamon Head

Grymkin [52] (25%) Fiery Hound Skin • (2.8%) Pristine Fiery Hound Skin • (26%) Fiery Hound Tooth • (1.5%) Fiery Hound Tooth • (1.6%) Immolated Hound Skin Cloak

Guardsman [45] (40%) Jewels 14 • (20%) <Mists of Lyonesse> • (1.5%) APOA: Adamant Coral • (0.6% each) Fallen Guardsman's Sword ***or*** Shield • (0.3%) Symbol of Loyalty

hamadryad [30/32/34] (10/13/18%) Vial of Green Tree Blood • (2%) Sheet of Shimmering Bark • (1.5%) Knotted Dryroot Band • (1.5%) APOA: Softened Bark ***or*** Frock • (1.5%) <Death's Door>

hamadryad [36/38] (19/20%) Vial of Green Tree Blood • (3/4.5%) Sheet of Shimmering Bark • (1.5%) Knotted Hamadryad Staff • (1.5%) APOA: Softened Bark ***or*** Frock • (1.5%) <Death's Door>

knight [49] (50%) Jewels 14 • (25%) <Mists of Lyonesse> • (1.6%) APOA: Adamant Coral • (1.6%; hi-lo) Avenging Knight's Hammer ***or*** Cloak

lesser telamon [44] (17%) Smooth Golem Stone • (1.6%) APOA: Aqueous Coral • (1.6%) Lesser Telamon Scimitar

Madoc Kynith [46] (40%) Jewels 14 • (20%) <Mists of Lyonesse> • (1.5%) APOA: Adamant Coral • (0.6% each) Fallen Guardsman's Sword ***or*** Shield • (0.3%) Symbol of Loyalty

Mapog [62] (75%) Jewels 27 • (1.7%) APOA: Cailiondar

medial telamon [49] (24%) Smooth Golem Stone • (1.6%) APOA: Aqueous Coral Studded • (1.6%) Lesser Telamon Scimitar

Meuric Capellanus [60] (40%) Jewels 27 • (1.6%) APOA: Cailiondar

moorlich [48] (20%) Souless Gem Dust • (1.2%) Mystic Robes of Bedazzlement ***or*** Restless Robes • (1.6%) APOA: Adamant Coral

peallaidh [35/37/39/41] (20/25/30/35%) Jewels 27 • (1.6%) a Staff: Earthen ***or*** Frozen/Fiery ***or*** Windy/Bloody ***or*** Dissolution/Mind ***or*** Spirit • (12%) Giant Lizard Sinew

pikeman [45] (45%) Jewels 14 • (1.5%) APOA: Adamant Coral • (1.5%) Fallen Soldier's Pike, Axe ***or*** Hammer • (1.5%) Symbol of Loyalty

Pog Mapog [52] (60%) Jewels 27 • (1.7%) APOA: Adamant Coral

pogson [42] (50%) Jewels 27 • (1.7%) APOA: Aqueous Coral Studded

Priest of Arawn [50] (no loot)

pygmy goblin [43] (5%) Pygmy Sized Ruby Idol • (10%) Jewels 27 • (25%) Pygmy Death Beads • (1.5%) APOA: Banded Coral • (1.5%) Pygmy Needle Mace ***or*** Oversized Pygmy Crossbow

pygmy goblin tangler [45] (5%) Pygmy Sized Ruby Idol • (10%) Jewels 27 • (25%) Pygmy Death Beads • (1.5%) APOA: Banded Coral • (1.5%) Pygmy Needle Mace ***or*** Oversized Pygmy Crossbow

shepherd [34] (30%) Jewels 31 • (15%) <Mists of Lyonesse> • (1.6%) APOA: Aqueous • (1.6%) Bracer of Martial Skill, Shepherd's Shod Staff, ***or*** Shepherd's Robes

Sister Blythe [69] (5%) Ring of Arawn • (1.5%) Cyclops Headsman's Axe, Cyclops Eye, ***or*** Ghost Wolf Hide Cloak • (5%) Yellow Tourmaline • (4%) Aquamarine Beryl • (3%) Kornerupine

townsman [30] (20%) Jewels 31 • (10%) <Mists of Lyonesse> • (1.6%) Muck Crusted Ruby Locket ***or*** Mithril Building Hammer • (9%) Key of the Lost

witherwoode [57] (28%) Ancient Witherwoode Bark • (1.4%) Gnarled Witherwood Staff

woodeworm [55] (23%) Ancient Witherwoode Bark • (1.2%) Ancient Witherwoode Bark • (1.6%) Gnarled Witherwood Staff

Yadnik [44] (24%) Vial of Green Tree Blood • (9%) Sheet of Shimmering Bark • (1.5%) Knotted Hamadryad Staff • (1.5%) <Death's Door> • (1.5%) APOA: Softened Bark ***or*** Frock

Key. [X] = level(s) • (X%) = chance to get item (if a list, just one) • (X% each) = chance for ***each*** item • hi-lo = most to least likely • APOA = a piece of armor • (x2) = item can drop twice

Salisbury Plains

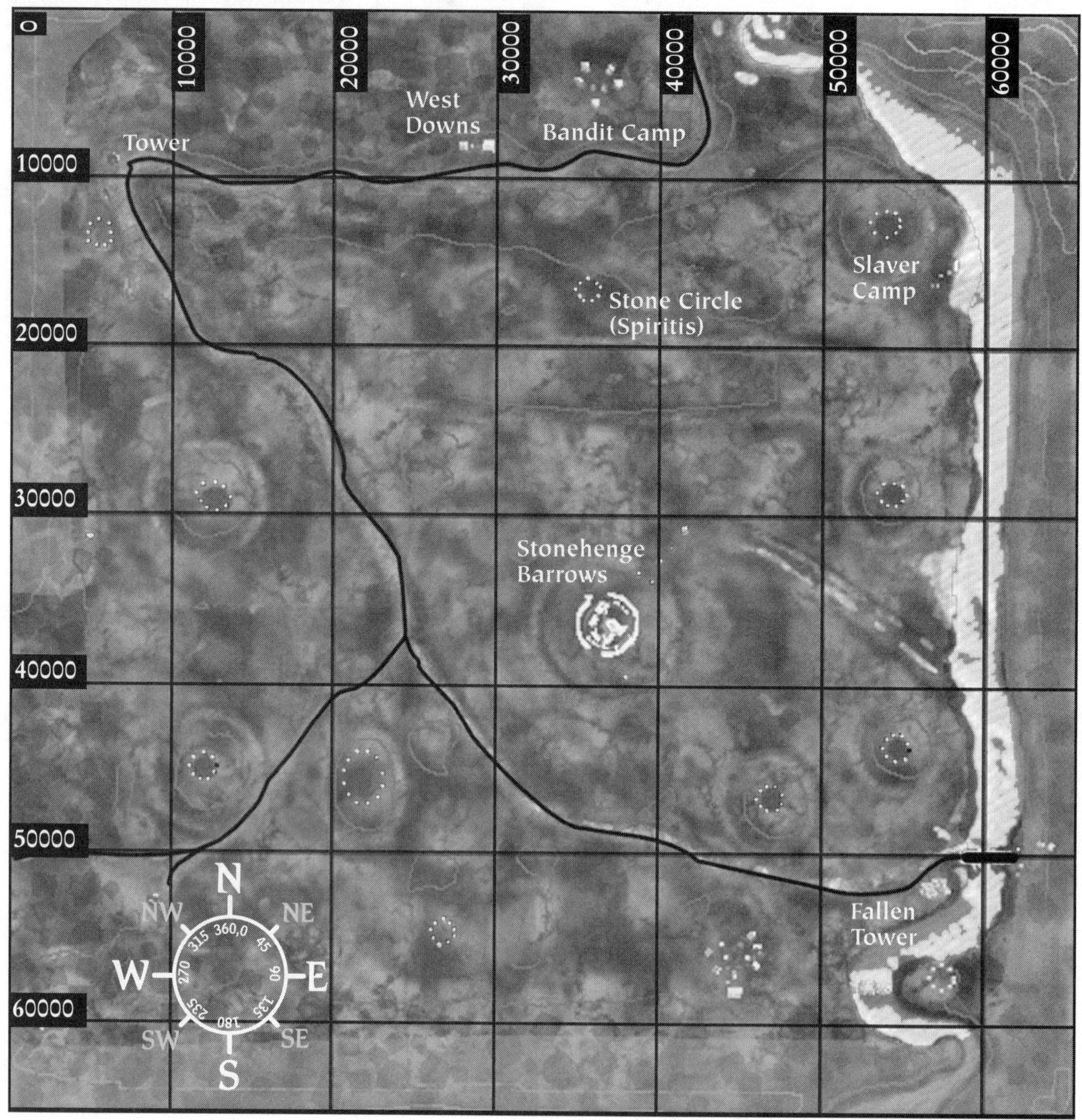

Lower-level monsters not shown on map:

Creature	Lvl	Location
bandit	5	NC
bandit	6	NC,NE
brownie grassrunner	7	NW,NC,NE,WC,C
fading spirit	7	NW,NC,NE,WC
filidh	7	NW,NC,SC
grass snake	5	NW,NC,C
river racer	7	NC,NE
spirit	6	NW,NC,WC
undead filidh	5	NW
undead filidh	6	NW,WC
undead filidh	7	NW,WC

Albion: Salisbury Plains

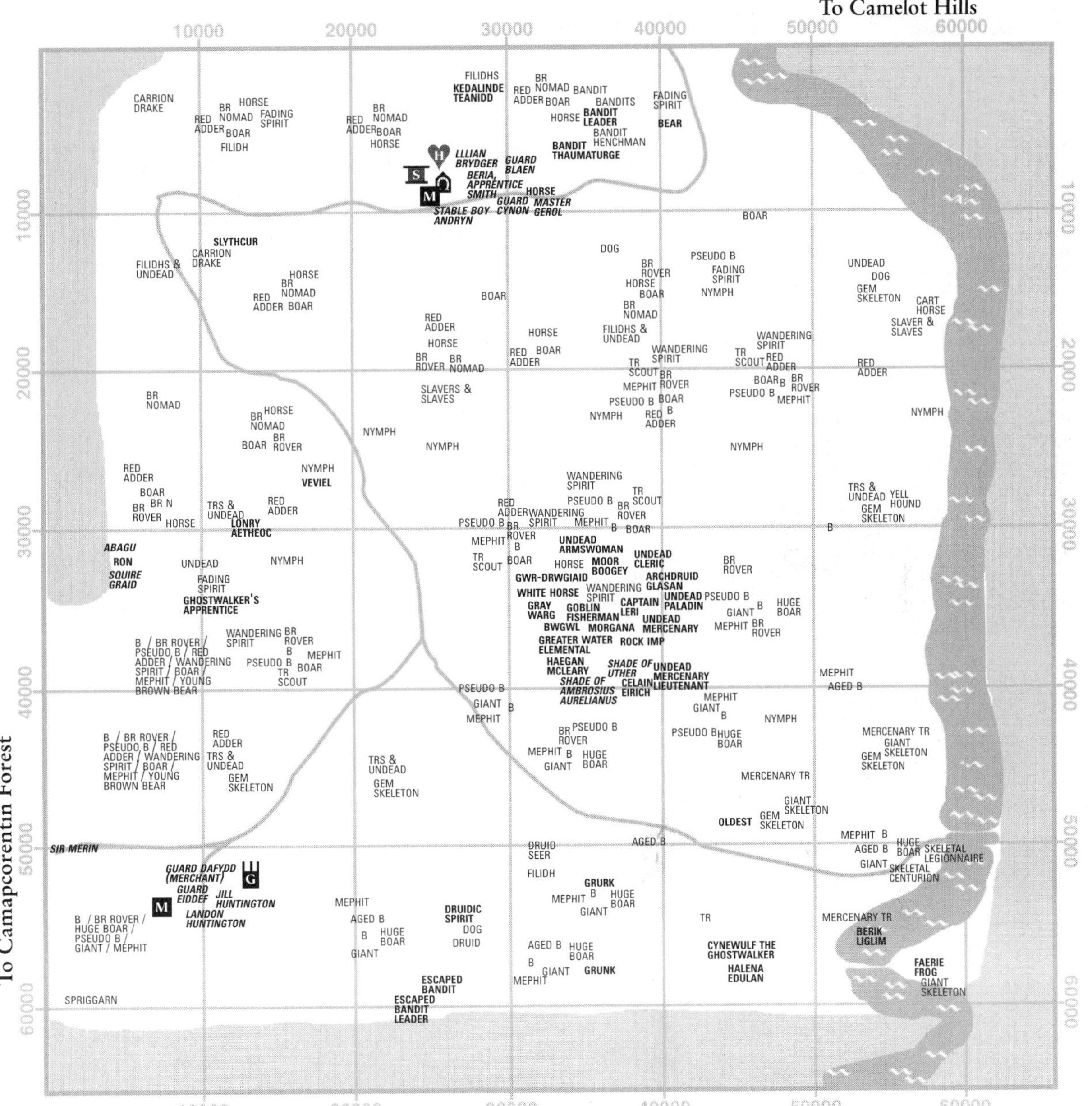

Monsters with levels lower than 8 are not marked on map, but general areas where they can be found are noted in the monster list.

B = Baslisk

BR = Brownie

TR = Tomb Raider

GIANT = Salisbury Giant

MEPHIT = wind mephit

HORSE = wild mare and/or wild stallion

DOG = black dog

BOAR = wild boar

UNDEAD =
- undead druid
- undead filidh
- undead mercenary
- undead mercenary lieutenant
- undead paladin
- undead paladin lieutenant

Salisbury Plains Tips

The Plains are a large open area great for hunting solo or in a group. The tasks given at the southernmost guard tower are easy to accomplish, because of the relatively easy path to get to most creatures in the area. Giants are a good source of coin, and are frequently hunted by groups.

If you're a Sorcerer, there are plenty of pets to charm in this area, including the druids who sometimes have the added benefit of spellcasting to aid you. The tomb raiders and slavers are also very durable pets, and now have the ability to use weapon styles in your favor. There are a few quests in the area, and a few monsters have some unique drops available. This area holds the entrance to the Stonehenge Barrows, a rather high level dungeon crawling with undead.

There are some humanoids or animals within, but they are normally of too low a level to be of use while hunting the massive amount of undead within.

- Dave "i3ullseye" Maynor

Solo and Group Levelling Tips

Solo

5-10	Druids/filidh, boars, bears, bandits
10-15	pseudo basilisk, basilisk, tomb raiders, adders, boars, stallions, nymphs
15-20	basilisk, mephits, tomb raiders, nymphs, slave master/bodyguard
20-25	huge boars, giants
25-35	fairy frogs, giant skeletons

Group

5-10	same as solo
10-15	same as solo
15-20	huge boars, giants
20-25	fairy frogs, giant skeletons

- Matt "Kyle Draconeco" Shirley

Quest NPCs

Salisbury Guard Tower	
Guard	Escaped Bandits (lvl 20)
Landon Huntington	Druid Medicine (lvl 18)
West Downs	
Andryn	Sir Gleran's Lost Necklace (lvl 11)
Beria	Supplies for Lillian (lvl 15)
Guard	Escaped Bandits (lvl 20)

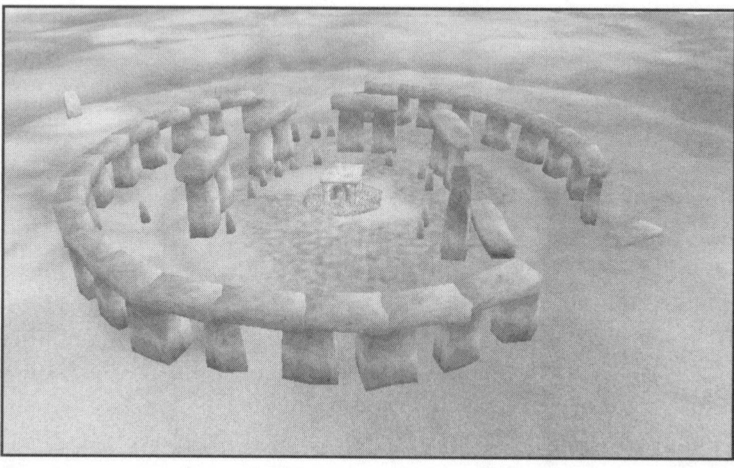

Key. [X] = level(s) • (X%) = chance to get item (if a list, just one) • (X% each) = chance for *each* item • hi-lo = most to least likely • APOA = a piece of armor • (x2) = item can drop twice

Loot

aged basilisk [19] (55%) Basilisk Meat (x4) • (30%) Basilisk Skull ***or*** Fine Basilisk Hide

bandit [5-6] (70% each) Aventurine, Bent Lockpick • (5%) Moonstone • (8%) Bandit's Ear • (0.3% each piece) Roman Leather • (0.5%) <Only Just Begun>

bandit henchman [9] (70% each) Bent Lockpick, Jade • (20%) Obsidian • (48%) Bandit's Ear • (0.3% each piece) Roman Leather • (3%) <Of a Sylvan Glade>

bandit leader [11] *see bandit henchman [9]*

bandit lieutenant [9] *see bandit henchman [9]*

bandit thaumaturge [8] (10%) Pitted Staff • (70%) Jade • (50%) Chryoprase • (48%) Bandit's Ear • (0.5% each piece) Quilted • (0.5%) <Pilfered Prizes>

basilisk [15] (80%) Basilisk Meat • (40% each) Basilisk Meat, Average Basilisk Hide • (20%) Basilisk Meat

bear [8] (33%) Bear Skin • (25%) Bear Fang • (5%) Pitted Sharp Claw

black dog [9-10] (60%) Tattered Black Canine Pelt • (15%) Gnawed Femur • (1%) Sleek Black Skin • (40%) Black Dog Paw (x3) • (15%) Bloody Canine Fang (x2)

brownie grassrunner [7] (40%) Large Spotted Mushroom • (50%) Obsidian • (1%) Spinel • (1.5%) Grass Choker • (0.5%) <Of a Sylvan Glade>

brownie nomad [8-9] *see brownie grassrunner [7]*

brownie rover [12] (40%) Giant Spotted Mushroom • (35%) Jewels 39 • (0.3%) <Grave Goods> • (1.4% each) Pulsing Ruby, Grass Choker

carrion drake [8-9] (65%) Gnawed Bone • (70%) Lump of Carrion • (45%) Carrion Drake Tongue • (35%) Pitted Carrion Drake Talon • (33%) Carrion Drake Tooth • (49%) Small Carrion Drake Scale • (20%) Medium Carrion Drake Scale

cart horse [10] *see horse [10]*

Celain Eirich [36] (no loot)

Cynewulf the Ghostwalker [19] (no loot)

devout filidh [8-9] *see filidh [7-8]*

disturbed presence [12-14] (60%) Glowing Green Slime • (50%) Bloodstone • (20%) Lapis Lazuli • (1%) Azurite • (1.5%) <Mounds of Salisbury> • (0.5%) <Grave Goods>

druid [18-19] (5%) Sacrificial Dagger • (40%) Citrine • (20%) Malachite • (1%) Green Tourmaline • (25%) Pitted Wooden Shield, Tattered Cloth Tunic, Tattered Leather Hood, ***or*** Tattered Brown Boots • (25%) Dried Pork, Muffin, Canteen of Water, ***or*** Bottle of Elderberry Wine • (1.5%) APOA: of the Resolute • (0.3%) <Out of the Woods> • (1.5%) Vest, Gloves ***or*** Sleeves of the Lost

druid sacrificer [20-21] *see druid [18-19]*

druid seer [15] (60%) Large Rock Crystal • (40%) Topaz • (10%) Citrine • (2%) Pearl • (25%) Tarnished Dagger, Torch, Tattered Brown Gloves, Tattered Woolen Robes, ***or*** Chipped Mirror • (25%) Dried Pork, Muffin, Canteen of Water, ***or*** Bottle of Elderberry Wine • (1.5%) Cap, Pants ***or*** Boots of the Lost • (0.3%) <Out of the Woods>

druid seer [19-20] *see druid [18-19]*

druidic spirit [21] *see druid [18-19]*

escaped bandit [18] (75% each) Broken Iron Shackles, Bloodstone • (60%) Carnelian • (20%) Silver Agate Chalice • (1.4%) <Salisbury Stock 4> • (3%) APOA: Faded • (19%) Bandit's Ear • (0.3%) <Salisbury Stock 1> • (1.4%) Warden's Sword

escaped bandit leader [19] *see escaped bandit [18]*

fading spirit [7-8] (45%) Faded Green Slime • (35%) Tattered Woolen Robes • (25%) Tattered Brown Boots • (50%) Spinel • (1%) Bloodstone • (0.5%) <Pilfered Prizes>

faerie frog [28] (55%) Faerie Frog Legs (x2) • (70%) Harness • (10% each) Faerie Frog Skin, Eye

filidh [7-8] (40%) Brown Adder Stone • (60%) Obsidian • (25%) Chryoprase • (2%) Bloodstone • (15%) Pitted Wooden Shield, Tattered Cloth Tunic, Tattered Leather Hood, ***or*** Tattered Brown Boots • (20%) Dried Pork, Muffin, Canteen of Water, ***or*** Bottle of Elderberry Wine • (0.5%) <Of a Sylvan Glade>

filidh sacrificer [9-10] *see filidh [7-8]*

Ghostwalker's Apprentice [10] (no loot)

giant skeleton [27-28] (50% each) Skeleton Skull, Large Bleached Bone • (0.3%) Manaweave Ring • (0.6% each) Smoldering ***or*** Netherworldly Robes • (1.4%) Jeweled Left ***or*** Right Eye • (0.3%) <Cuisinart>

grass snake [5] (95%) Snakeskin • (30%) Snake Scales • (90%) Snake Meat (x2) • (60%) Dead Mouse

green ghast [12-14] (50%) Amethyst • (25%) Lapis Lazuli • (1%) Azurite • (3%) APOA: Footman's Chain ***or*** Kite Shield • (0.5%) <Grave Goods>

grove nymph [10] (75%) Jewels 46 • (70%) Green Mushroom • (30%) Crushed Leaf • (20%) Pile of Amber Dust • (15%) Crushed Mistletoe • (1.4% each) Grass Choker, Ponderer • (0.3%) <Of a Sylvan Glade>

grove nymph [13] (40%) Jewels 39 • (30%) Blue Mushroom • (10%) Curled Leaf • (7.5%) Pile of Glittery Dust • (5%) Mistletoe Leaf • (1.4% each) Grass Choker, Ponderer • (0.3%) <Grave Goods>

grove nymph [15] (60%) Jewels 39 • (40%) Red Mushroom • (21%) Folded Leaf • (11%) Pile of Silvery Dust • (7.5%) Sprig of Mistletoe • (1.3% each) Grass Choker, Ponderer • (0.3%) <Out of the Woods> • (1.3%) Robe of the Lost

grove nymph [18] (20%) Jewels 57 • (5%) Speckled Mushroom • (15%) Perfect Leaf • (10% each) Pile of Golden Dust, Branch of Mistletoe • (0.3%) <Out of the Woods> • (1.5%) Cap of the Keen Mind, Ring of Elemental Fury ***or*** Ring of Alteration

Grunk [22] (40%) Pearl • (10%) Fire Opal • (1%) Sunstone • (1.5%) <Salisbury Stock 4> • (0.3%) <Salisbury Stock 1>

Grurk [21] (40%) Pearl • (10%) Fire Opal • (1%) Sunstone • (1.4%) <Salisbury Stock 4> • (1.4%) Cap, Pants ***or*** Boots of the Lost • (0.3%) <Salisbury Stock 1>

Halena Edulan [15] *see tomb raider scout [13-15]*

horse [10] (75%) Horse Hair • (10%) Auburn Mane • (80%) Ruined Horse Skin • (35%) Horse Skin • (60%) Horse Hair

huge boar [18] (50% each) Huge Boar Hide, Huge Cloven Hoof • (20% each) Bloody Boar Tusk, Large Pig Tail • (15%) Huge Boar Tusk

Kedalinde Teanidd [10] (no loot)

Lonry Aetheoc [13] *see tomb raider digger [10-13]*

mercenary tomb raider [26/28] (9/11%) Stolen Signet Ring

Morgana [90] (10%) Stick-Figure Totem • (2.5%) Tattered Lamellar Arms • (5%) Tattered Boned Arms

Oldest [22] (30%) Fine Basilisk Hide • (35%) Basilisk Meat (x2) • (35%) Clouded Basilisk Eye (x2) • (1.5%) Lost Sword of the Eternals • (0.3%) <Salisbury Stock 1>

pseudo basilisk [12] (40% each) Basilisk Meat, Average Basilisk Hide • (10%) Basilisk Skull ***or*** Fine Basilisk Hide

red adder [10] (95%) Snakeskin • (90%) Snake Meat • (80%) Snake Scales (x2) • (90%) Soft Snakeskin • (95%) Dead Mouse • (90%) Dead Rabbit

river racer [7] *see grass snake [5]*

Salisbury giant [18-21] (40%) Citrine • (10%) Malachite • (1%) Green Tourmaline • (1.4%) <Salisbury Stock 4> • (0.3%) <Salisbury Stock 1> • (1.4%) Head Slicer

skeletal centurion [21] (60%) Roman Commanders Seal • (30%) Small Silver Statue • (50%) Jewels 26 • (1.4%) APOA: Bloodied Leather • (1.4%) Decorated Roman Dagger ***or*** Stiletto, ***or*** Roman Tactician Bracer • (0.3%) <Salisbury Stock 1>

skeletal legionnaire [18] (50%) Ghostly Roman Lantern • (40%) Roman Commanders Seal • (30%) Jewels 26 • (1.4%) Ruined Roman Hauberk, Leggings ***or*** Sleeves • (1.4%) Decorated Roman Dagger ***or*** Stiletto, ***or*** Roman Tactician Bracer • (0.3%) <Salisbury Stock 1>

slave [11] (3.5%) Pulsing Ruby • (3%) Rotting Robes • (0.3%) <Pilfered Prizes>

slave master [13,15] *see slaver [12-15]*

slave master bodyguard [15] (40%) Carnelian • (10%) Agate • (3%) APOA: Footman's Chain ***or*** Kite Shield • (0.3%) <Out of the Woods> • (1.5%) Slaver Axe ***or*** Longbow

slaver [12-15] (40%) Carnelian • (10%) Agate • (3%) APOA: Faded • (0.3%) <Grave Goods> • (1.5%) Slaver Hammer

Slythcur [12] (90%) Gnawed Bone • (80% each) Lump of Carrion, Small Carrion Drake Scale • (60%) Carrion Drake Tongue • (50% each) Pitted Carrion Drake Talon, Carrion Drake Tooth • (40%) Medium Carrion Drake Scale • (30%) Large Carrion Drake Scale • (20%) Carrion Drake Hide

spirit [6] (43%) Faded Blue Slime • (30%) Tarnished Dagger • (20%) Tattered Brown Gloves • (1%) Spinel • (50%) Jade • (1%) <Pilfered Prizes>

spriggarn ambusher [15] (50%) Agate • (20%) Garnet • (2%) APOA: Tattered Hard Leather • (2%) APOA: Footman's Chain ***or*** Kite Shield • (0.3%) <Grave Goods> • (1.5%) Bushwack Mace ***or*** Heart Piercer

spriggarn howler [16] (40%) Agate • (10%) Garnet • (2%) APOA: Tattered Hard Leather ***or*** Shield • (2%) APOA: Footman's Chain ***or*** Shield • (0.3%) <Out of the Woods>

spriggarn waylayer [14] *see spriggarn ambusher [15]*

stable horse [10] *see horse [10]*

tomb raider [16-17] (25% each) Dried Pork, Canteen of Water • (40%) Citrine • (10%) Pearl • (2%) Malachite • (3%) APOA: Footman's Chain, ***or*** Kite Shield • (1.3%) <Salisbury Stock 4> • (1.3%) Rotting Robes, Resilient Sleeves, ***or*** Resilient Gloves • (0.3%) <Out of the Woods> • (1.3%) Spirit Spun Helm, Leggings, ***or*** Boots

tomb raider commander [18-20] (25% each) Dried Pork, Canteen of Water • (40%) Topaz • (10%) Pearl • (1%) Fire Opal • (3%) APOA: Footman's Chain, ***or*** Kite Shield • (1.3%) <Salisbury Stock 4> • (1.3%) Cap of the Keen Mind, Ring of Elemental Fury, ***or*** Ring of Alteration • (0.3%) <Salisbury Stock 1> • (1.5%; hi-lo) Chain Coif, Leggings ***or*** Boots of Disparity, Spirit Crafted Shortbow, ***or*** Shield of Spirit Might

tomb raider digger [10-13] (25% each) Dried Pork, Canteen of Water • (40%) Bloodstone • (20%) Carnelian • (3%) Agate • (1.4%) APOA: Tattered Hard Leather ***or*** a Pitted Hard Leather Shield • (1.4%) <Crystal Visions> • (0.3%) <Grave Goods>

tomb raider scout [13-15] (25% each) Dried Pork, Canteen of Water • (40%) Carnelian • (10%) Agate • (1%) Garnet • (1.4%) <Mounds of Salisbury> • (3%) APOA: Faded • (0.3%) <Grave Goods> • (0.3%) Chain Sleeves of Disparity • (0.2%) Chain Gloves of Disparity • (0.2%) Chain Hauberk of Disparity • (0.1%) Deathscent Mace • (0.1%) Spirit Crafted Shield

undead armswoman [31] (no loot)

undead cleric [31] (no loot)

undead druid [8-10] (80%) Brown Adder Stone • (40%) Chryoprase • (20%) Bloodstone • (1%) Amethyst • (25%) Dried Pork, Muffin, Canteen of Water, ***or*** Bottle of Elderberry Wine • (1.5%) <Crystal Visions> • (0.5%) <Of a Sylvan Glade>

undead filidh [5-7] (50%) Brown Adder Stone • (40%) Jade • (20%) Obsidian • (1%) Spinel • (25%) Dried Pork, Muffin, Canteen of Water, ***or*** Bottle of Elderberry Wine • (1.5%) <Crystal Visions> • (0.5%) <Pilfered Prizes>

undead mercenary [31] (no loot)

undead mercenary lieutenant [31] (no loot)

undead paladin [31] (no loot)

undead paladin lieutenant [31] (no loot)

Veviel [13] *see grove nymph [13]*

wandering spirit [9-11] (45%) Glowing Blue Slime • (35%) Pitted Wooden Shield • (25%) Tattered Leather Hood • (15%) Tattered Brown Boots • (50%) Obsidian • (8%) Chryoprase • (1%) Amethyst • (0.5%) <Of a Sylvan Glade>

White Horse [18] (90% each) Horse Hair (x2), Ruined Horse Skin • (60%) Horse Skin

wild boar [10] (20%) Small Tusk • (50%) Cloven Hoof • Raw Pork • Pig Tail

wild mare [9] *see horse [10]*

wild stallion [10] *see horse [10]*

wind mephit [14] (75%) Wind Mephit Essence • (25%) Mephit Skull • (0.3%) <Grave Goods>

yell hound [15-16] (40%) Yell Hound Skin • (80%) Bloody Canine Fang (x2) • (1.5%) Hound Tooth

young brown bear [13] (18%) Brown Bear Pelt • (2%) Pristine Brown Bear Pelt • (35%) Bloody Bear Fang • (50%) Brown Bear Paw

Camelot

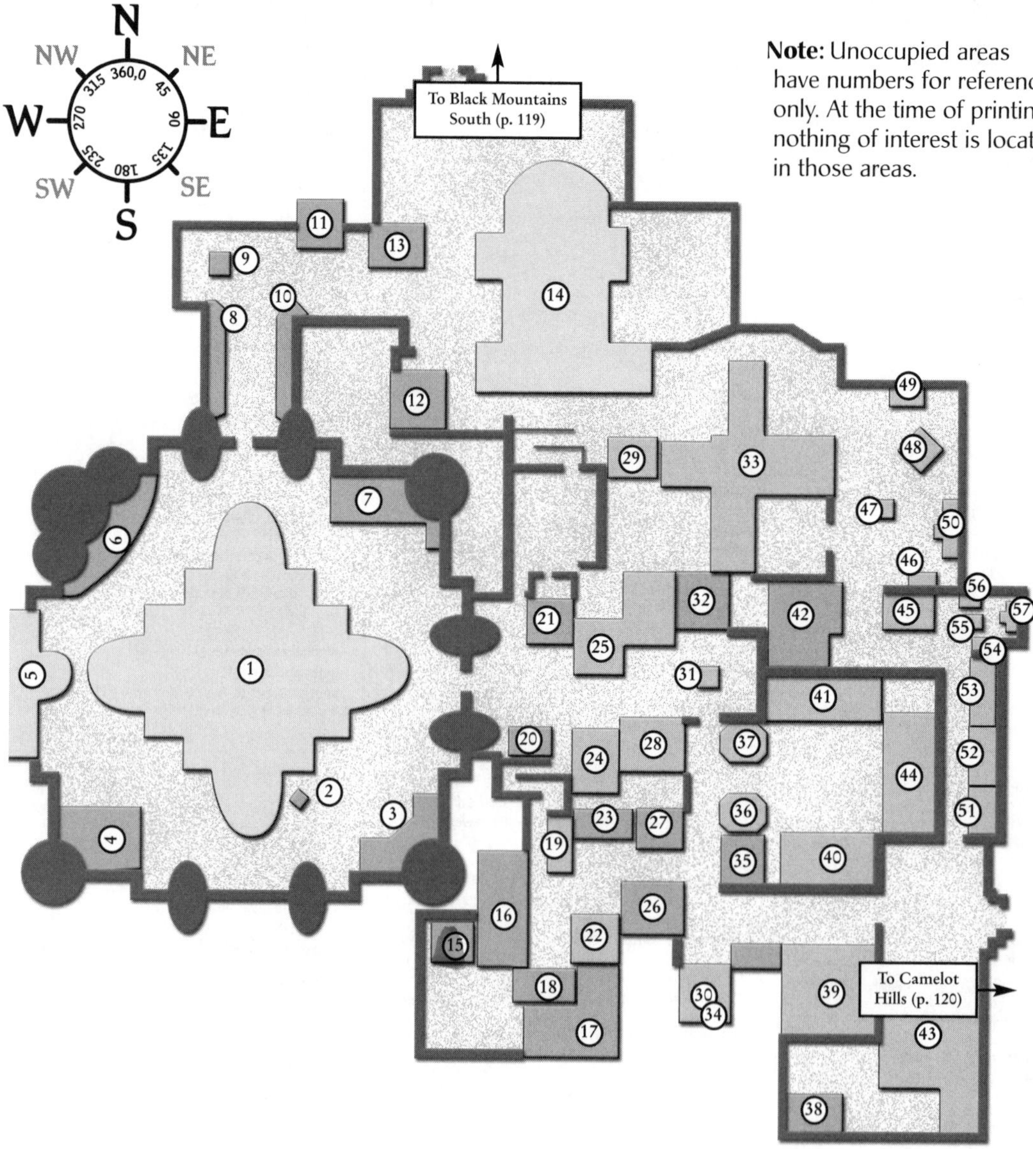

N
NW NE
W E
SW SE
S
360,0 45 90 135 180 225 270 315

To Black Mountains South (p. 119)

Note: Unoccupied areas have numbers for reference only. At the time of printing, nothing of interest is located in those areas.

1 2 3 4 5 6 7 8 9 10 11 12 13 14 15 16 17 18 19 20 21 22 23 24 25 26 27 28 29 30 31 32 33 34 35 36 37 38 39 40 41 42 43 44 45 46 47 48 49 50 51 52 53 54 55 56 57

To Camelot Hills (p. 120)

1 **Lord Urqhart** Vault Keeper
3 **Edmee Heolstor** Embossed Leather Armor
3 **Grummond Attor** Engineers Master
3 **Hector Darian** Smithing Equipment
3 **Hephas Elgen** Weaponsmiths Master
3 **Jeffrey Kenric** Mithril Armor
3 **Lora Theomund** Mithril Armor
3 **Loraine Elgen** Armorsmith Master
3 **Meccus Yrre** Sylvan Cloth Armor
3 **Runthal Devyn** Fletcher Master
3 **Shallah**
3 **Torr Upton** Mithril Plate Armor
3 **Wyne Scead** Mithril weapons
4 **Lady Charlitte** Name Registrar
4 **Lord Christopher** Guild Registrar
4 **Lord Oachley** Guild Emblemeer
5 **Scribe Veral**
6 **Calldir Edelmar** Bounty
6 **Magess Islia**
13 **Corley Nodens** Tailoring Equipment
13 **Laurenna**
14 **Aklee Edelmar** Bounty
14 **Brother Lensar**
14 **Brother Michel** Healer Trainer
14 **Lady Fridwulf** Cleric Trainer
14 **Lady Triss** Paladin Trainer
14 **Lady Winchell** Cleric Trainer
14 **Lord Prydwen** Paladin Trainer
14 **Lynna Lang** Tanned Cymric Armor, Steel Studded Armor, Bashing Weapons
14 **Sister Elaydith**
14 **Sister Rhigwyn**
14 **Tait Nerian** Iron Studded and Steel Chain Armor, Shields, Swords
15 **Magus Isen** Cabalist Trainer
15 **Master Edric** Infiltrator Trainer
16 **Magus Agyfen** Cabalist Trainer
16 **Master Arenis** Mercenary Trainer
16 **Olaevia Wyman** Cabalist Staves
17 **Freya Edelmar** Bounty
17 **Landry Woden** Armor, Weapons
17 **Larcwide Wirt** Armor, Weapons
17 **Master Almund** Mercenary Trainer
17 **Master Eadig** Infiltrator Trainer
19 **Acey Dalston** Fletcher Master
19 **Jana Fletcher** Arrow
19 **Kedoenad** Poison
19 **Sara Graston** Bows
19 **Sasha Fletcher** Crossbow Bolts
19 **Velmis** Poison
19 **Willa Dalston** Feathers
21 **Berenger Brennar**
21 **Gaevin Sebryn**
25 **Bedelia**
25 **Hamon Sallitt**
26 **Sir Kenley**
28 **Barkeep Broec**
28 **Brother Ethelbald** Friar Trainer
28 **Gamel Platfoot**
30 **Andri**
30 **Barkeep Dwerrav**
30 **Sandre Stanhill**
30 **Sephere Lade**
31 **Master Dubri** Minstrel Trainer
31 **Silura Starish** Bard Instruments
39 **Brother Sterlyn** Friar Trainer
39 **Cigolin Dalston** Theurgist Staves
39 **Colby Dalston** Quilted Armor, Staves
39 **Dare Edelmar** Bounty
39 **Iden Wissan** tanned Cymric, Steel Studded, Maces
39 **Lieutenant Rydderac** Scout Trainer
39 **Master Cear** Theurgist Trainer
39 **Mistress Welss** Theurgist Trainer
39 **Odella Cerdic** Tanned Cymric and Steel Studded Armor, Arrows, Bows, Rapiers
40 **Librarian Ophus**
40 **Maye Edelmar** Bounty
41 **Holt Finan** Bard Instruments, Tanned Siluric Armor, Steel Studded Armor, Pierce Weapons
41 **Mori Godric** Quilted Armor, Staves
41 **Ulyius Feu-Ame**
42 **Enchanter Evala** Enchanter
42 **Marius Caest** Staves
42 **Vadri Pade**
43 **Captain Alphin** Armsman Trainer
43 **Captain Rion** Armsman Trainer
43 **Catelyn Boltar**
43 **Elzbet Sable** Siluric Leather
43 **Heolstor Wyman** Leather
43 **Lieutenant Kaherdin** Scout Trainer
43 **Ordra Yaney** Alloy Weapons (all)
43 **Stephon the Crier**
44 **Gardowen Egesa** Wizard Staves
44 **Loremaster Alain**
44 **Magess Tena** Sorcerer Trainer
44 **Magus Cormac** Sorcerer Trainer
44 **Master Berwick** Minstrel Trainer
44 **Master Grundelth** Wizard Trainer
44 **Master Vismer**
44 **Mistress Ladriel** Wizard Trainer
44 **Pedrith Edyn** Sorcerer Staves
45 **Arliss Eadig** Tailor Master
45 **Coventina Bordin** Tailoring Equipment
45 **Dyemaster Edare** Green/brown/grey/orange/yellow cloth dye
45 **Dyemaster Emma** Blue/turquoise/teal/red/purple leather dye
45 **Dyemaster Kael** Blue/turquoise/teal/red/purple enamel dye
45 **Dyemaster Lendand** Green/brown/grey/orange/yellow leather dye
45 **Dyemaster Mara** Green/brown/grey/orange/yellow enamel dye
45 **Dyemaster Vandras** Blue/turquoise/teal/red/purple cloth dye
45 **Radek Silven** Robes
45 **Raggart Bruce** Quilted Armor
46 **Guardsman Exeter**
46 **Lara Weathers** Studded Armor
46 **Serena Muftar** Chain Armor
46 **Ver Nuren** Shields
48 **Ethan Farley** Alloy/steel Armor
48 **Fenris Blakely** Pierce Weapons
49 **Jana Hickey** Boned Leather Armor
54 **Geor Nadren** Cymric Leather Armor
55 **Dougal Heathis** 2-Handed
55 **Judan Hammerfel** Smith
55 **Yoren Shazra** Roman Leather Armor
56 **Moira Camber** Polearms
57 **Fuston Talgurt** Scaled Plate Armor
57 **Hafgan Corley** Plate/full Armor
57 **Warren Gibson** Siluric Leather Armor

Adribard's Retreat (Avalon Marsh)

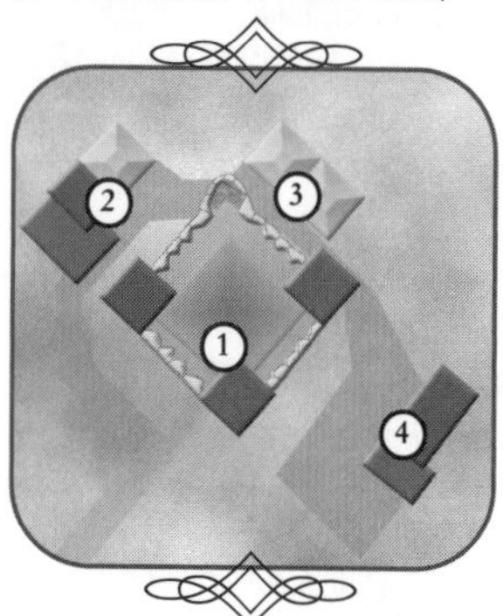

1 Aiellana
1 Brother Caun *Friar Tr.*
1 Brother Onoloth
1 Daisi Egesa *Wizard staff W.*
1 Graeme Dalston *Theurgist staff W.*
1 Lady Lynn *Cleric Tr.*
1 Lieutenant Crosean *Scout Tr.*
1 Lord Adribard *Paladin Tr.*
1 Magus Edaev *Sorcerer Tr.*
1 Magus Saloc *Mage Tr.*
1 Master Dyrin *Fighter Tr.*
1 Master Liennon *Minstrel Tr.*
1 Master Traoyr *Wizard Tr.*
1 Mistress Jeryssa *Theurgist Tr.*
1 Salwis the crier
1 Scribe Eril
1 Sister Chael *Acolyte Tr.*
1 Sister Endri *Healer*
1 Wylie Edyn *Sorcerer staff W.*
2 Blueheart *Dyes*
2 Dyemaster Camdene *Dyes*
2 Enchanter Braesia *Enchanter*
2 Tersa Weaver *Robe A.*
2 Trulion Vrundon *Vault Keeper*
3 Anga Weaver *Quilted A.*
3 Morin Davem *Roman leather A.*
3 Nai Whit *Staff W.*
3 Tathal *2-handed W.*
3 Tathan *Plate A.*
4 Devyn Godric *Shields*
4 Theois Gwynt *Crushing W.*
4 Trill *Bard instruments*
4 Tyngyr Blade *Slashing W.*

Caer Ulfwych (Campacorentin Forest)

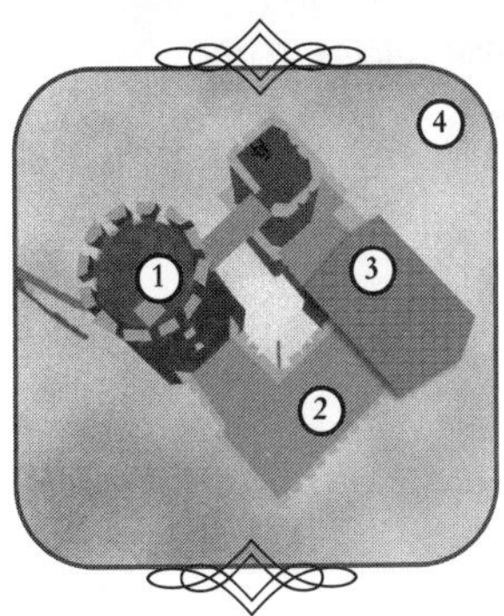

1 Aclee Marlow
1 Calya
1 Collen Blist *Cleric Tr.*
1 Dyemaster Eldred *Dyes*
1 Dyemaster Nedda *Dyes*
1 Huntress Lenna
1 Lord Ulfwych *Paladin Tr.*
2 Brother Eurius *Healer*
2 Brother Spilr *Friar Tr.*
2 Captain Falron *Armsman Tr.*
2 Elger Leafblade *Bows*
2 Fellya Fletcher *Arrows*
2 Gery Dalston *Theurgist staff W.*
2 Mistress Frina *Theurgist Tr.*
3 Dyemaster Druce *Dyes*
3 Dyemaster Esme *Dyes*
3 Gral Bermorn
4 Eiddin Walelden *Bolts*
4 Ellard Fall *Smith*
4 Ellard Gram *Crushing W*
4 Fianya Walelden
4 Grindan Halig *Shields*
4 Idian *Stable*
4 Langston Fall *Slashing W.*
4 Lieutenant Mhoudi *Scout Tr.*
4 Stephan Fall *Chain A.*
Guardian
Guardian Sergeant
Huntsman

Caer Witrin (Avalon Marsh)

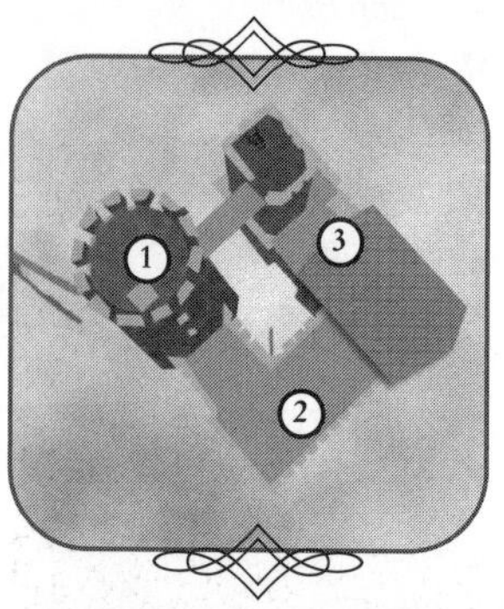

1 Dugan Advien
1 Jhular *Stable*
1 Master Dohajan
1 Master Eadberth *Mercenary Tr.*
1 Sister Lilly *Healer*
1 Tyna Blade
2 Azrael Mucto *Chain A.*
2 Elvinia Dareal
2 Fread Gramley *Smith*
2 Geofram Hael
2 Gregor Lannis *Crushing W.*
2 Magus Dimos *Cabalist Tr.*
2 Wina Wyman *Cabalist Staff*
3 Etie *Poisons*
3 Master Noijan *Infiltrator Tr.*
Guardian
Guardian Sergeant

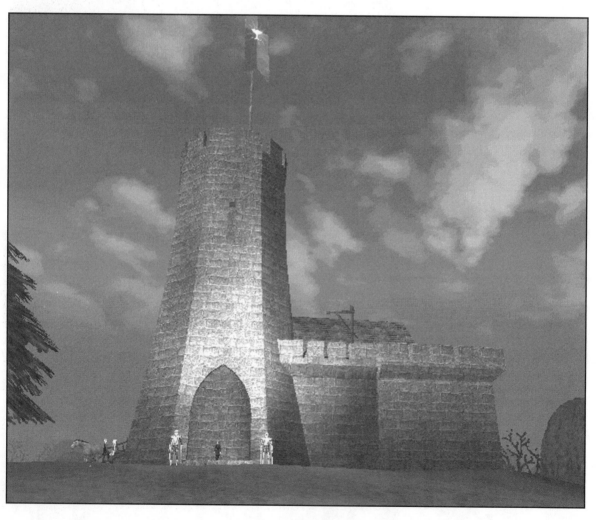

Camelot Entrance (Black Mtn. South)

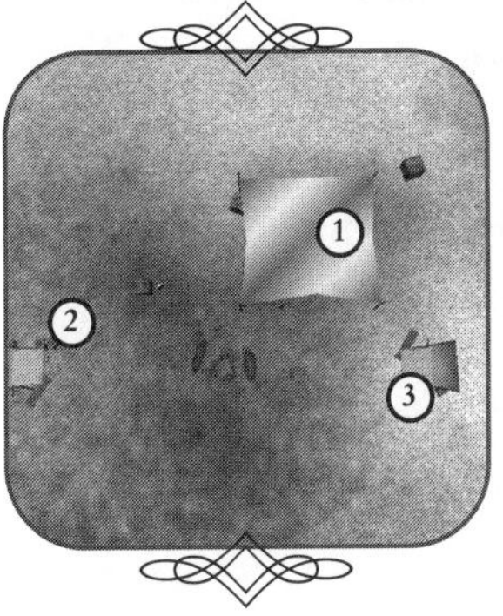

1 Brother Penric *Healer*
1 Dyemaster Bren *Dyes*
1 Dyemaster Irwin *Dyes*
1 Fash *Crushing W.*
1 Joffrey *Slashing W.*
2 Chad Denisc *Shield*
3 Lan *Boned A.*

Camelot Hills Tower (Camelot Hills)

Brother Willem *Healer*
Elsbeth *Crossbows*
Hunter Derwyn
Lauryn Swiftrun *Bows*
Mateus Fletcher *Bolts*
Meran Fletcher *Arrows*
Sage Nelson

Campacorentin Station (Campacorentin Forest)

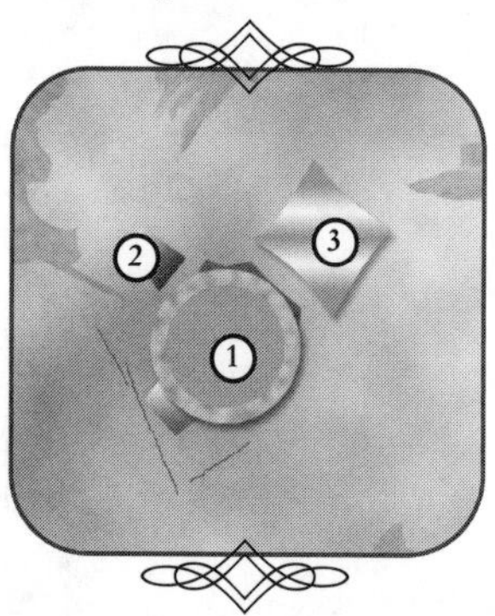

1 Hunter Kenwin

1 Kealan

***1 Master Hadis** Rogue Tr.*

***1 Master Lorik** Fighter Tr.*

***2 Balthazar Encambrion** Polearm W.*

***2 Dyemaster Esme** Dyes*

2 Grin the crier

***2 Gwendolyn Arlington** Dyes*

***2 Junger Gannon** Chain A.*

***2 Linidd** Poisons*

***2 Ridder** Stable*

***3 Archibald Oakheart** Staff*

***3 Dafyd Graham** Smith*

***3 Emyr** Crossbows*

***3 Falin Fletcher** Arrows*

***3 Flaudin Bowman** Bows*

***3 Fluitha Sufron** Cymric leather A.*

***3 Geston Lurger** Thrusting W.*

***3 Goodwin Fletcher** Bolts*

***3 Malin Cullan** 2-handed W.*

***3 Master Astyp** Mercenary Tr.*

***3 Rundeg Faerweth** Lamellar studded A.*

Cornwall Station (Cornwall)

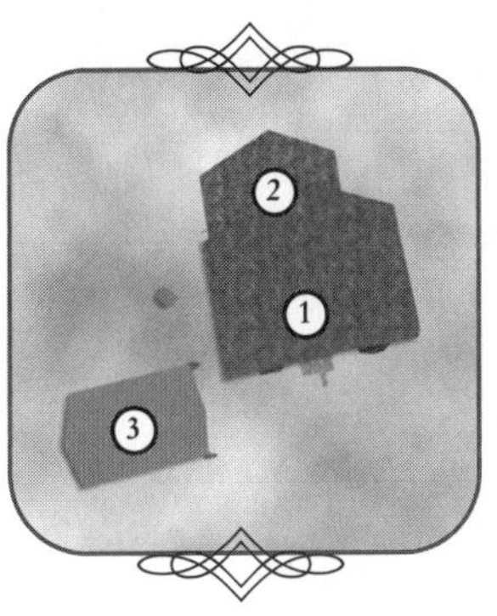

1 Adaliae Ruthic *Tailoring Equipment*

1 Edern *Crossbow*

1 Heylyn Aldar *Bolts*

1 Iohannes Aldar *Arrows*

1 Jack Landrey *Plate A.*

1 Kalea Eldwig

1 Larel Esric *Recharger*

1 Sar Aldar *Chain A.*

1 Veteran Guardsman Edmond

2 Eugene Aldar

2 Eva Aldar *Healer*

2 Roben Fraomar

2 Seysild Aldar *Smith*

2 Thule Ruthic *Smithing/Tailoring Supplies*

3 Pethos *Stable*

Cotswold Village (Camelot Hills)

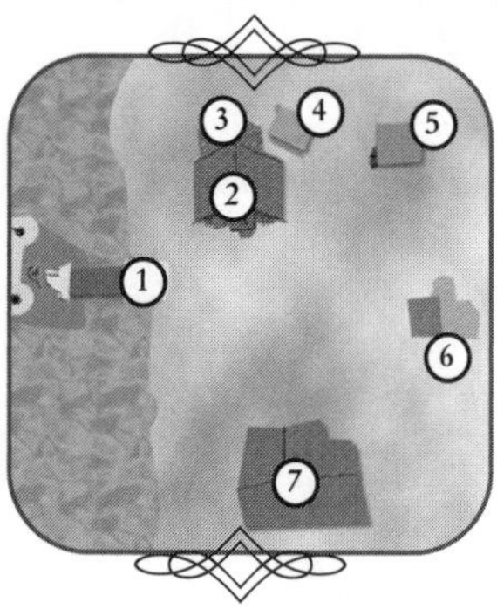

1 Enchanter Grumwold *Enchanter*
1 Master Sorac *Rogue Tr.*
2 Andrew Wyatt
2 Daniel Edwards
2 Eileen Morton *Bard instruments*
2 Godaleva Dowden
2 Jonathan Lee
2 Ydenia Philpott
3 Odelia Wyman
3 Unendaldan
4 Braenwyn Fletcher *Arrows*
4 Cullen Smyth
4 Grum Bowman *Bows*
4 Pellam *Crossbows*
4 Yetta Fletcher *Bolts*
5 Bedamor Routh *2-handed W.*
5 Col Aldar *Chain A.*
5 Cudbert Dalston *Theurgist staff*
5 Ellyn Weyland *Studded A.*
5 Elvar Ironhand *Smith*
5 Gill Hoxley *Steel/alloy plate A.*
5 Grannis Ynos *Slashing*
5 John Weyland *Thrusting*
5 Lar Rodor *Shields*
5 Rayn Olwyc *Polearm W.*
6 Doreen Egesa *Wizard staff*
6 Dyemaster Edra *Enamel dye*
6 Dyemaster Leax *Leather dye*
6 Dyemaster Octe *Enamel dye*
6 Dyemaster Wanetta *Leather dye*
6 Laridia the Minstrel
6 Master Kless
6 Master Stearn *Elementalist Tr.*
6 Pompin the Crier
7 Cauldir Edyn *Sorcerer staff*
7 Dyemaster Alwin *Cloth dye*
7 Eowyln Astos *Cloth dye*
7 Farma Hornly *Quilted A.*
7 Jon Smythe *Robes*
7 Lundeg Tranyth *Roman A.*
7 Magus Aelle *Mage Tr.*
7 Samwell Hornly *Staff*
7 Stonemason Glover
7 Brother Lawrence

Humberton Castle (Black Mtn. South)

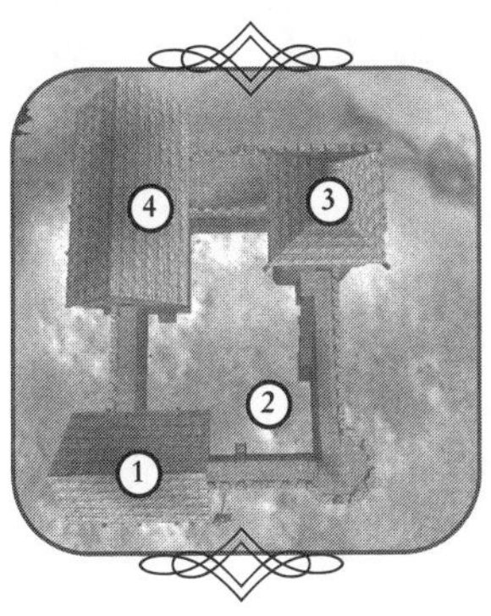

1 Mistress Blea

2 Dun Mra *Boned A.*

2 Niea

2 Steward Willie

2 Ta'ifah Alhambra

3 Nydomath *Poison*

3 Sir Ambiz

4 Belef

4 Brother Dupre *Acolyte Tr.*

4 Brother Sabutai *Healer*

4 Colina Darksky

4 Fearchar Mac a'Bhaird

4 Gaemis Aer'Taimor

4 Iomharr Buchanan

4 Malcolm Shaw

4 Sachin

4 Sir Gleran

4 Tavish Camshron

4 Tredim

Humberton Village (Black Mtn. South)

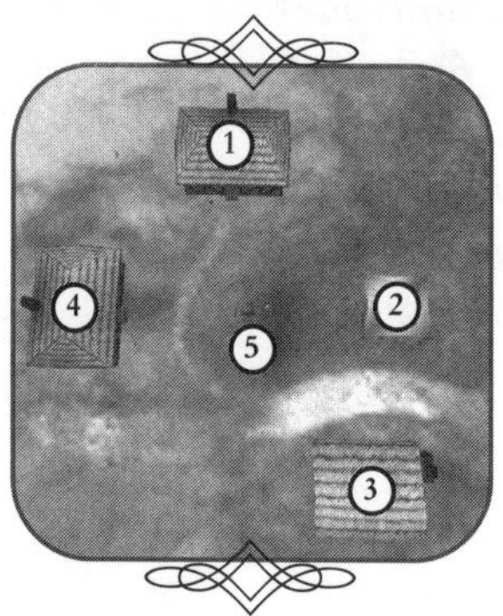

1 Master Torr *Fighter Tr.*
1 Mif Feit *Staff*
1 Siom Felanis *Robe A.*
1 Tria Ellowis
2 Dyemaker Bal *Dyes*
2 Dyemaster Brun *Dyes*
2 Gert Elm *Scaled plate A.*
2 Stephon Bash *Crushing W.*
3 Alhrick Duglas *Thrusting W.*
3 Ban Ronem *Slashing W.*
3 Contyth *apprentice smith*
3 Enchanter Haephus *Enchanter*
3 Gracchus *Stable*
3 Heorot Kenway *Shields*
3 Parisch Ealyn
4 Alden Fletcher *Bolts*
4 Bline Tengit *Quilted A.*
4 Brother Demay *Healer*
4 Feren Erimen *Bows*
4 Nelda Fletcher *Arrows*
4 Olwyn *Crossbows*
5 Barnarn the crier
5 Captain Ryder
5 Guard Reed

Lethantis Association (Campacorentin Forest)

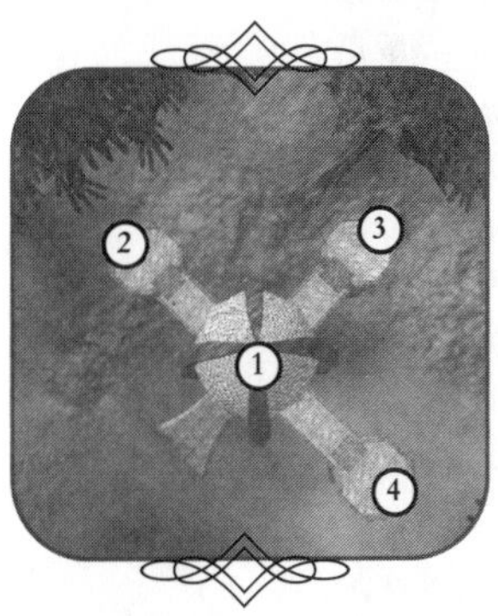

1 Loretta Egesa *Wizard staff W.*
1 Magus Crystolos *Sorcerer Tr.*
1 Magus Oreal *Mage Tr.*
1 Master Arbaedes *Wizard Tr.*
1 Mistress Trethia *Elementalist Tr.*
1 Norvel Edyn *Sorcerer staff W.*
1 Olorustos
1 Scholar Nenet
2 Elga Wyman *Cabalist Staff*
2 Magess Axton
2 Magus Sacyn *Cabalist Tr.*
3 Master Qilith *Infiltrator Tr.*
4 Epin Lenut *Robe A.*
4 Mairi Ralilden
4 Master Glorous *Minstrel Tr.*
4 Sebil Lenut *Quilted A.*
4 Sleria *Bard instruments*

Ludlow Village (Black Mtn. South)

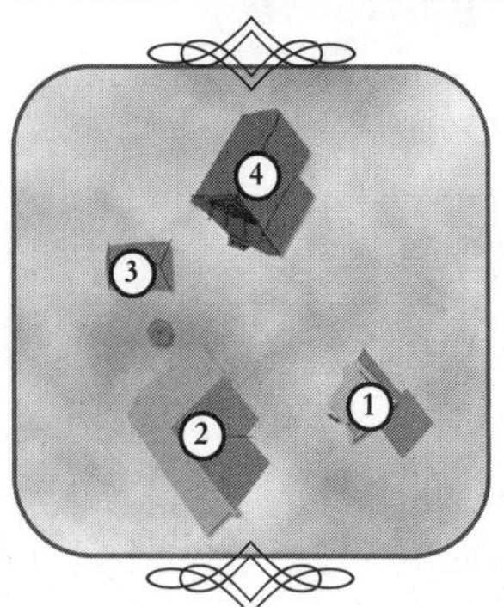

1 Calldir Edyn *Sorcerer staff*
1 Eabae Egesa *Wizard staff*
1 Farl Dalston *Theurgist staff*
1 Sals Pew *staff*
2 Argus Bowman *Bows*
2 Crep Pew *Thrusting W.*
2 Fost Mra *Siluric leather A.*
2 Gilley Fletcher *Arrows*
2 Laudine *Crossbow*
2 Magus Aldred *Mage Tr.*
2 Master Odon *Rogue Tr.*
2 Nulb Pew *Bolts*
2 Ochan Aethelhere *Trade skill items*
2 Varrin the crier
3 Aileen Wyatt *Dyes*
3 Dyemaster Cor *Dyes*
3 Seamstress Lynnet *Robes A.*
3 Seamstress Marie *Quilted A.*
3 Stonemason Harwin
3 Yaren *Stable*
4 Andrya Wyman *Cabalist staff*
4 Bouncer Corwin
4 Charlotte Salter
4 Graham Mal'toinia
4 Greta Songbird
4 Guy Reed
4 Haskis Mordoo
4 Jezzy Piper
4 Keenar Woedin
4 Maggie McClellan
4 Pebble
4 Phyllis Darksky
4 Trini Piper
4 Yasminea Darden
Apprentice Dunan
Guard Wynn
Master Sceley *Smith*

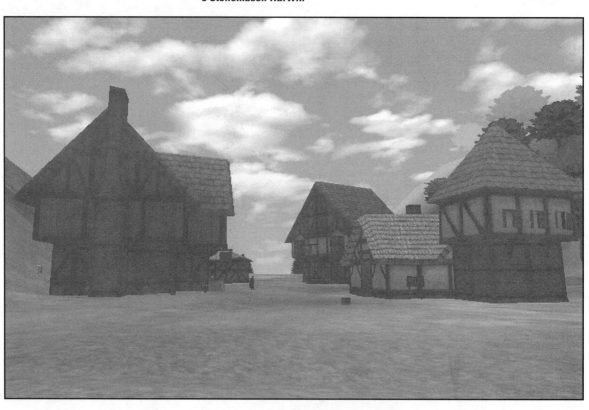

Llyn Barfog Market (Llyn Barfog)

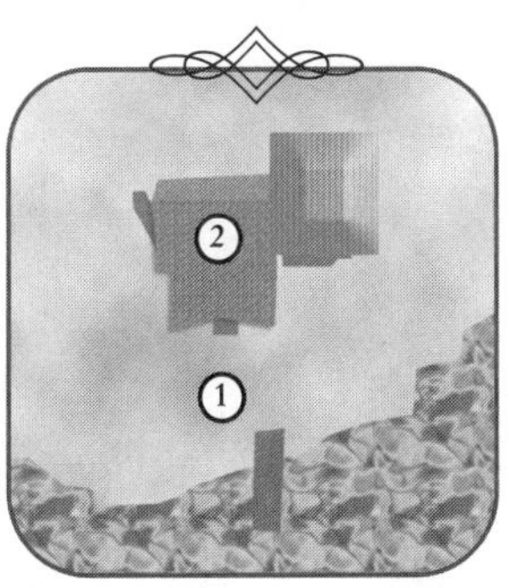

1 Edern *Crossbow*
1 Gwallter ap Trevls *Slashing W.*
1 Thomas ap Seyton *Plate A.*
1 Twm ap Gusg *Siluric leather A.*
2 Anfri ap Even *Weapons*
2 Duncan Curan *Arrows*
2 Olvryn Wynford *Smith*
2 Tewdwr ap Greid *Quilted A.*
2 Twr ap Alsig

Outland Wharf (Avalon Marsh)

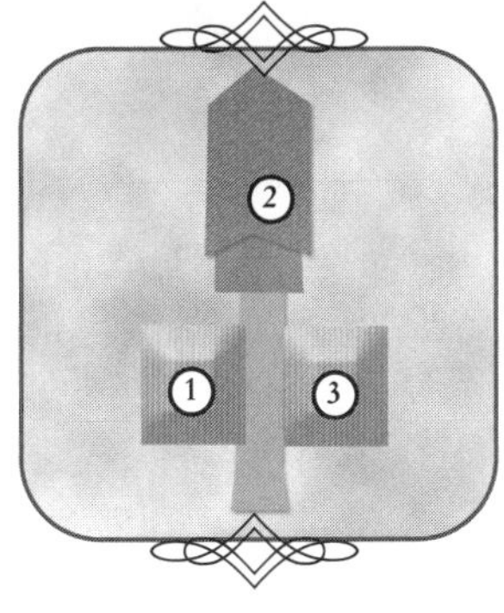

1 Allyn Fletcher *Arrows*
1 Boudron Fletcher *Bolts*
1 Bruna *Instrument Tr.*
2 Dyemaster Carye *Dyes*
2 Dyemaster Earh *Dyes*
2 Dyemaster Godric *Dyes*
2 Dyemaster Kaly *Dyes*
2 Erstal Furlan *Blacksmith*
2 Leshorm Hael *Studded A.*
2 Wiceit *Poisons*
3 Epheria Brighteye *Bows W.*
3 Sywno *Pierce W.*
3 William Oswy *Polearm W.*

Prydwen Keep (Camelot Hills)

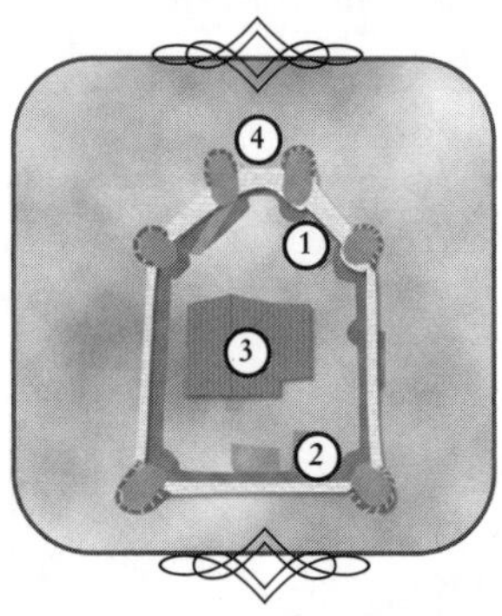

1 Alburn Hale *Slashing W.*
1 Barric Camber *Crushing W.*
1 Elvar Tambor *Thrusting W.*
1 Ryce Scrydan *Shields*
1 Sister Gwendolyn *Acolyte Tr.*
2 Arleigh Penn *Dyes*
2 Captain Bonswell
2 Dyemaster Arthw *Dyes*
2 Gram Ironhand *Smith*
2 Hugh Gallen *Roman leather A.*
2 Karn Graem *Plate A.*
2 Meran the Weaver
3 Atheleys Sy'Lian
3 Brother Maynard *Healer*
3 Licrin the crier
3 Master Graent *Fighter Tr.*
4 Sir Quait

Snowdonia Station (Black Mtn. North)

1 Aldys Meccus *Boned Studded A.*
1 Cranly *Plate A.*
1 Edrea Fletcher *Arrows*
1 Gerb *Crossbow W.*
1 Gleda Fletcher *Bolts*
1 Mathien
1 Staeven *Bowman Bows*
1 Thol Dunnin *Smith*
2 Aelda *Chain A.*
2 Boc *Siluric leather A.*
2 Cedd Aethelbert *Shields*
2 Elrigh
2 Elwyn *Crushing W.*
2 Ember *Slashing W.*
2 Jonalyn *Thrusting W.*
2 Odaro Hengist *Healer*
3 Guyon *Robe A.*
3 Osric *Slash, Crush, Pierce W.*
3 Trachon *Stable*

Swanton Keep (Black Mtn. North)

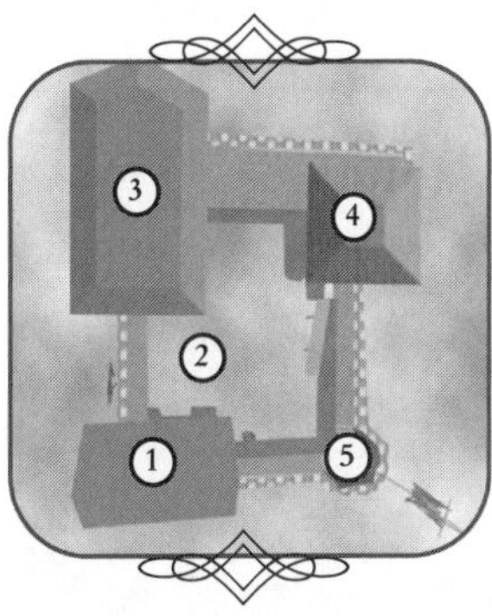

1 Magus Jeril *Cabalist Tr.*
1 Master Kel *Mercenary Tr.*
1 Sir Verin
2 Agrakor Fletcher *Arrows*
2 Dwira Fletcher *Bolts*
2 Guards' Armorer
2 Ither *Crossbows*
2 Ley Manton
2 Lynd Moidg *Bows*
2 Nia Leof *Staff W.*
3 Father Turnis *Cleric Tr.*
3 Magus Sarun *Sorcerer Tr.*
3 Master Hanis *Minstrel Tr.*
3 Mistress Alarisa *Wizard Tr.*
3 Mistress Cessa *Theurgist Tr.*
3 Omis
3 Sir Caewel *Paladin Tr.*
4 Bertie Dracon
4 Brother Daniel *Friar Tr.*
4 Captain Presan *Armsman Tr.*
4 Glaeric *Poisons*
4 Heather Barclay
4 Jerad *2-handed W.*
4 Master Brignun *Infiltrator Tr.*
4 Yorel Anbidian *Tailoring equipment*
5 Lieutenant Fisra *Scout Tr.*

Vetusta Abbey (Black Mtn. South)

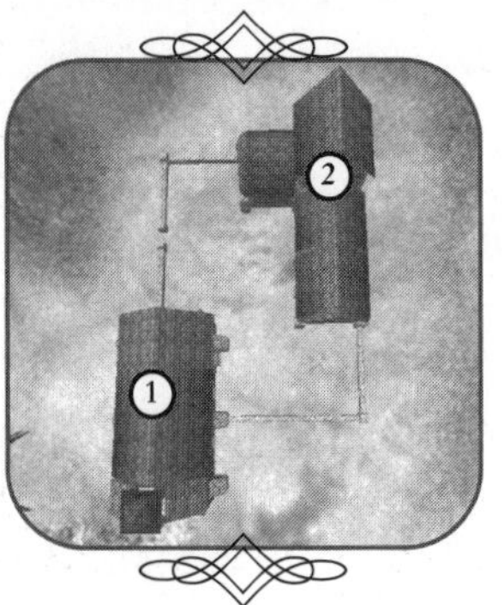

1 Brother Don
2 Brother Darren
2 Brother Tanis *Healer*
2 Sister Deane
2 Zenob Mra *Boned A.*

West Downs (Salisbury)

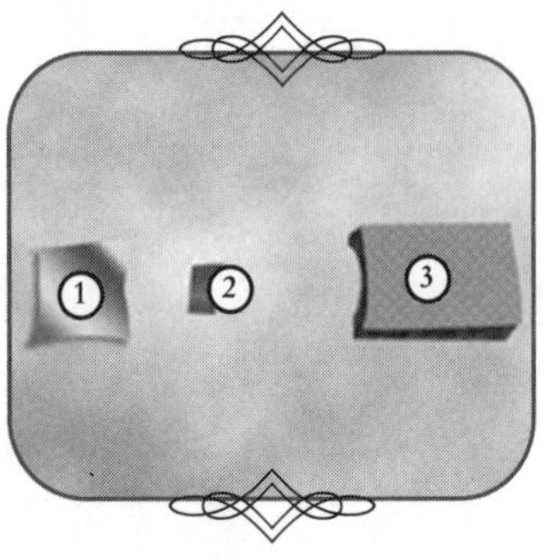

1 Aric Barlow *Robes A.*
1 Beria *apprentice Smith*
1 Garvyn Kensington *Studded A.*
1 Lillian Brydger *Smith*
1 Radella Fletcher *Bolts*
2 Ainsley Fletcher *Arrows*
2 Aldrin Collyer *Bows*
2 Bodwyn *Crossbow*
2 Erwin Holdyn *Quilted A.*
2 Farley Daegal *Expensive Trade Skill Items*
3 Edarg *Stable*
3 Master Gerol *Healer*
3 Stable Boy Andryn

Catacombs of Cardova

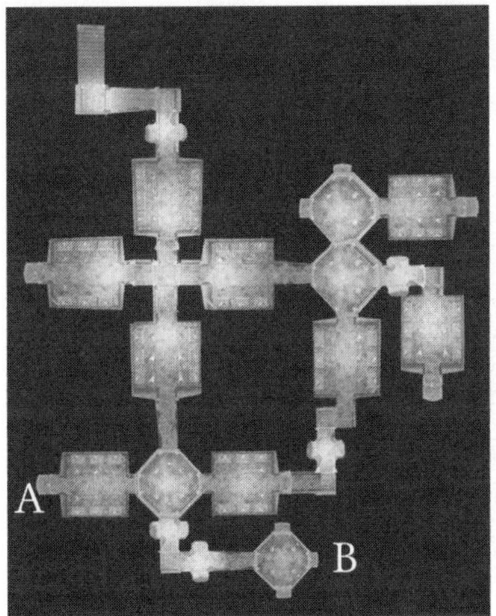

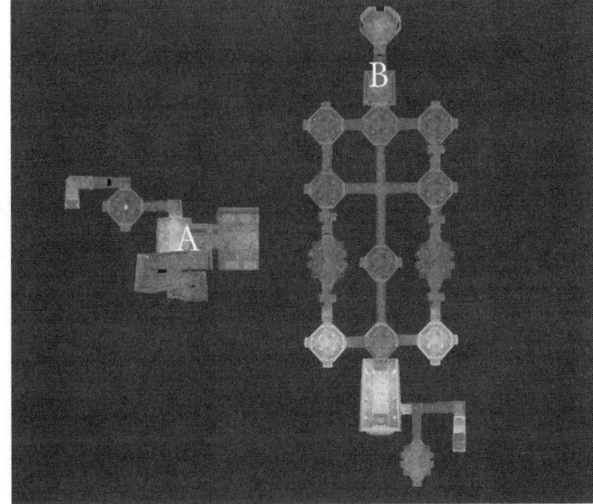

Loot

Note (1) These all have: (8%) Tarnished Ornate Goblet • (6%) Small Gold-Stitched Pouch • (4%) Orb of the Restless Eye • (2%) Jewel Studded Circlet • (15%) Jewels 54 • (5%) Jewels 47

Note (2) These all have: (8%) Tarnished Ornate Bracer • (6%) Tattered Gold-Stitched Standard • (4%) Small Studded Golden Chest • (2%) Golden Seal of Rome • (15%) Jewels 54 • (5%) Jewels 47

Note (3) These all have: (20%) Jewels 54 • (5%) Jewels 47 • (1.6%) Tarnished Ornate Bracer • (1.2%) Tattered Gold-Stitched Standard • (0.8%) Small Studded Golden Chest • (0.4%) Golden Seal of Rome • (1.6%) Vae Inimicus Sagittae

actarius [31] *see Note 1, plus* • (1.6%) Despoiled Gloves, Coif ***or*** Boots • (1.6%) Despoiled Two-Handed Sword ***or*** Lochaber Axe, Ancient Roman Signet, ***or*** Antiquated Cloak

Amminus pilus [36] *see Note (3), plus* • (1.6%) Vae Inimicus Caduceus, Scutum, ***or*** Aegis **centurio princeps praetorii [32]** *see Note (3), plus* • (1.6%) Vae Inimicus Emerald ***or*** Ruby Ring, ***or*** Compes

aquilifer [31] *see Note 1, plus* • (1.6%) Legions Scaled Gauntlets, Boots ***or*** Helm • (1.6%) Despoiled Great Hammer ***or*** Lucerne Hammer, Ancient Roman Signet, ***or*** Antiquated Cloak

centurio manipularis [31] *see Note 1, plus* • (1.6%) Rigid Roman Vest, Legs ***or*** Arms • (1.6%; hi-lo) Despoiled Lute, Flute ***or*** Drum, Ancient Roman Signet, ***or*** Antiquated Cloak

centurio pilus posterior [31] *see Note 1, plus* • (1.6%) Despoiled Mail, Legs ***or*** Sleeves • (1.6%) Despoiled Two-Handed Sword ***or*** Lochaber Axe, Ancient Roman Signet, ***or*** Antiquated Cloak • (11%) Gem of the Despoiled

centurio primus ordines [31] *see Note 1, plus* • (1.6%) Despoiled Mail, Legs ***or*** Sleeves • (1.6%) Despoiled Great Hammer ***or*** Lucerne Hammer, Ancient Roman Signet, ***or*** Antiquated Cloak

centurio primus pilus [32] *see Note 2, plus* • (1.6%) Despoiled Mail, Legs ***or*** Sleeves • (1.6%) Decaying Legions Shield, Despoiled War Shield, Restless Centurion Belt, ***or*** Bracer of the Pious Defender

Centurio Crotus praetorii [31] *see praetor [31]*

centurio manipularis [31] *see Note (1), plus* • (2%) Jewel Studded Circlet • (1.6%) Rigid Roman Vest, Legs ***or*** Arms • (1.6%; hi-lo) Despoiled Lute, Flute ***or*** Drum, Ancient Roman Signet, ***or*** Antiquated Cloak

Centurio Olivarius praetorii [31] *see praetor [31]*

Centurio Taras praetorii [31] *see praetor [31]*

cohorstalis [30] *see Note 1, plus* • (1.6%) Molded Leather Breastplate, Greaves ***or*** Armplates • (1.6%) Despoiled Mace ***or*** Flanged Mace, ***or*** Decaying Roman Ring ***or*** Necklace

Crotus princeps praetorii [33] *see Note (3), plus* • (1.6%) Vae Inimicus War Mattock, Lucerne Pike, ***or*** Dirk

crypt snake [29] (no loot)

decurion [31] *see Note 1, plus* • (1.6%) Molded Leather Breastplate, Greaves ***or*** Armplates • (1.6%) Despoiled Mattock ***or*** Bill, Ancient Roman Signet ***or*** Antiquated Cloak

draconarius [31] *see Note 1, plus* • (1.6%) Legions Scaled Gauntlets, Boots ***or*** Helm • (1.6%) Decaying Legions Shield, Despoiled War Shield, Restless Centurion Belt, ***or*** Bracer of the Pious Defender

dux [32] *see Note 2, plus* • (1.5%) Antiquated Noble's Gloves, Cap ***or*** Boots • (1.5%) Tribunus Staff of the Damned (x4) • (1.5%) Restless Centurion Belt, Bracer of the Pious Defender, ***or*** Resplendant ***or*** Resplendant Ring

Emperor Seleucus [40] *see forgotten emperor [35]*

eques [34] *see Note (3), plus* • (1.6%) Vae Inimicus Jewel, Golden Chain, ***or*** Velvet Cloak

evocatus Augusti [33] *see Note (3), plus* • (1.6%) Vae Inimicus Diamond ***or*** Sapphire Ring, ***or*** Armilla

forgotten emperor [35] (8%) Tarnished Ornate Bracer • (6%) Tattered Gold-Stitched Standard • (4%) Small Studded Golden Chest • (2%) Golden Seal of Rome • (15%) Jewels 54 • (10%) Jewels 47 • (1.4%) Legions Scaled Gauntlets, Boots ***or*** Helm • (1.6%) Legions Scaled Breastplate, Greaves ***or*** Armplates • (1.4%) Mantle of Resplendance ***or*** Forgotten Jewel • (1.4%) Spiked War Scepter

imaginifer [31] *see Note 1, plus* • (1.6%) Legions Scaled Gauntlets, Boots ***or*** Helm • (1.6%) Despoiled Mattock ***or*** Bill, Ancient Roman Signet, ***or*** Antiquated Cloak

immunis [29] *see Note 1, plus* • (1.6%) Molded Leather Gloves, Boots ***or*** Helm • (1.6%) Despoiled War Sword ***or*** Short Sword, Decaying Legion Battle Bracer, ***or*** Tactician's Belt

juggernaut [32] (20%) Jewels 18 • (1.5%) APOA: Woebegone Miner • (1.5%) <Mined from the Deep> • (1.5%) <Goblin' It Up>

legatio [33] *see Note 2, plus* • (1.3%) War Torn ***or*** Antiquated Robe • (0.3%) Robe of the Abyss • (1.6%) Wisened Staff of the Enforcer, Large Despoiled War Shield, ***or*** Resplendant Necklace ***or*** Ring

legionarius [29] *see Note 1, plus* • (1.6%) Molded Leather Gloves, Boots ***or*** Helm • (1.6%) Despoiled Gladius ***or*** Gauche, Decaying Legion Battle Bracer, ***or*** Tactician's Belt

magister [32] *see Note 2, plus* • (1.5%) Antiquated Noble's Vest, Pants ***or*** Sleeves • (1.5%) Tribunus Staff of the Damned (x4) • (1.5%) Restless Centurion Belt, Bracer of the Pious Defender, ***or*** Resplendant ***or*** Resplendant Ring

manipularis [30] *see Note 1, plus* • (1.6%) Rigid Roman Gauntlets, Boots ***or*** Helm • (1.6%) Despoiled Mace ***or*** Flanged Mace, ***or*** Decaying Roman Ring ***or*** Necklace

Olivarius princeps praetorii [32] *see Note (3), plus* • (1.6%) Vae Inimicus Hammer, Lucerne Hammer, ***or*** Mace

optio [31] *see Note 1, plus* • (1.6%) Despoiled Gloves, Coif ***or*** Boots • (1.6%) Despoiled Great Hammer ***or*** Lucerne Hammer, Ancient Roman Signet, ***or*** Antiquated Cloak

praefectus [32] *see Note 2, plus* • (1.4%) Legions Scaled Gauntlets, Boots ***or*** Helm • (1.5%) Tribunus Staff of the Damned (x4) • (1.5%) Restless Centurion Belt, Bracer of the Pious Defender, ***or*** Resplendant ***or*** Resplendant Ring

praetor [31] *see Note 1, plus* • (1.6%) Despoiled Gloves, Coif ***or*** Boots • (1.6%) Despoiled Mattock ***or*** Bill, Ancient Roman Signet, ***or*** Antiquated Cloak

praetorian guard [33] *see Note 2, plus* • (1.6%) Legions Scaled Breastplate, Greaves ***or*** Armplates • (1.6%) Bow of the Decaying Legions, Antiquated Crossbow ***or*** Bow, ***or*** Praetorian Gladius

princep [32] *see Note 2, plus* • (1.6%) Despoiled Mail, Legs ***or*** Sleeves • (1.6%) Decaying Legions Shield, Despoiled War Shield, Restless Centurion Belt, ***or*** Bracer of the Pious Defender

signifier [31] *see Note 1, plus* • (1.6%) Legions Scaled Gauntlets, Boots ***or*** Helm • (1.6%) Despoiled Two-Handed Sword ***or*** Lochaber Axe, Ancient Roman Signet, ***or*** Antiquated Cloak

singular [33] *see Note 2, plus* • (1.6%) Legions Scaled Breastplate, Greaves ***or*** Armplates • (1.6%; hi-lo) Wisened Staff of the Enforcer ***or*** Singular War Sword

Skull Eater [34] (no loot)

Spirit of the Emperor [36] *see Note (2), plus* • (1.6%) Despoiled Mail, Legs ***or*** Sleeves • (1.6%) Decaying Legions Shield, Despoiled War Shield, Restless Centurion Belt, ***or*** Bracer of the Pious Defender

Taras princeps praetorii [33] *see Note (3), plus* • (1.6%) Vae Inimicus Great Sword, Lochaber Axe, ***or*** Gladius

tribune [32] *see Note 2, plus* • (1.5%) Legions Scaled Gauntlets, Boots ***or*** Helm • (1.5%) Tribunus Staff of the Damned (x4) • (1.5%) Restless Centurion Belt, Bracer of the Pious Defender, ***or*** Resplendant Necklace ***or*** Ring

tribunus laticlavicus [33] *see Note 2, plus* • (1.4%) Legions Scaled Gauntlets, Boots ***or*** Helm • (1.4%) Legions Scaled Breastplate, Greaves ***or*** Armplates • (1.4%) Tribunus Staff of the Damned (x8) ***or*** Wisened Staff of the Enforcer • (1.4%) Resplendant Necklace ***or*** Ring

vigilis [29] *see Note 1, plus* • (1.5%) Molded Leather Gloves, Boots ***or*** Helm • (1.5%) Molded Leather Breastplate, Greaves ***or*** Armplates • (1.5%) Despoiled War Sword ***or*** Short Sword, Decaying Legion Battle Bracer, ***or*** Tactician's Belt

Key. [X] = level(s) • (X%) = chance to get item (if a list, just one) • (X% each) = chance for *each* item • hi-lo = most to least likely • APOA = a piece of armor • (x2) = item can drop twice

Keltoi Fogou

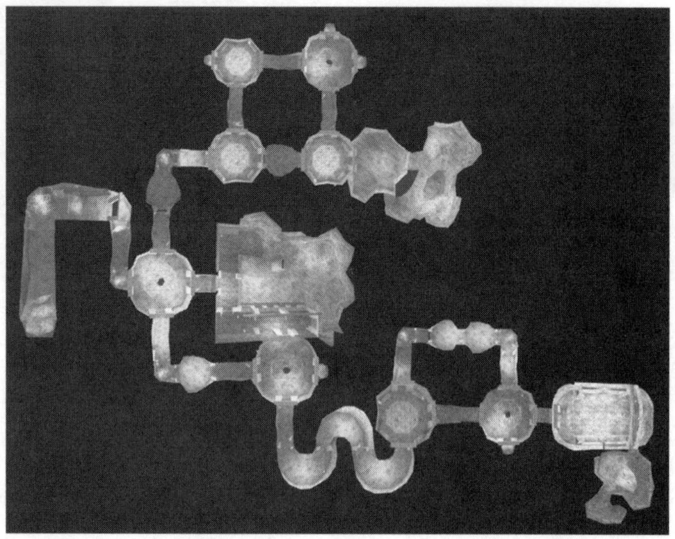

Loot

Note (1) These all have: (29%) Celtic Bracelet • (24%) Ornamental Necklace • (19%) Keltoi Crafted Belt • (14%) Traveling Backpack • (9.5%) Thick Rope • (95%) Jewels 09 • (5%) Blue, Red *or* Light Teal Colors

Archdruid Cadwallen [35] *see Dai [26]*

Beven [21] (27%) Celtic Bracelet • (23%) Ornamental Necklace • (18%) Keltoi Crafted Belt • (14%) Traveling Backpack • (9%) Thick Rope • (2%) <The Spy's Satchel> • (90%) Jewels 09 • (2%) Jewels 60 • (1.5%) APOA: Dusk-Walkers *or* Vindicator's • (1.5%) <Sacred Jewelry> • (1.5%) <Drako's Droppings> • (0.5%) <Salisbury Stock 2>

Dai [26] *see Note (1), plus* • (25%) <The Spy's Satchel> • (25%) Jewels 60 • (1.5%) APOA: Insurgent's, Observer's, *or* Prey-Stalker's, *or* Keltoi Infiltrators Disguise • (1.5%) <To Hang My Sporran> • (1.5%) <Celtic Wonders> • (0.5%) <Arthurian Artifacts 2>

Fane [25] *see Dai [26]*

gremlin [20-21] (27%) Celtic Bracelet • (23%) Ornamental Necklace • (18%) Keltoi Crafted Belt • (14%) Traveling Backpack • (9%) Thick Rope • (2%) <The Spy's Satchel> • (90%) Jewels 09 • (2%) Jewels 60 • (5%) Blue, Red *or* Light Teal Colors • (1.5%) APOA: Dusk-Walkers *or* Vindicator's • (1.5%) <Sacred Jewelry> • (1.5%) <Drako's Droppings> • (0.5%) <Salisbury Stock 2>

Gwern [24] *see Note (1), plus* • (15%) <The Spy's Satchel> • (15%) Jewels 60 • (1.5%) APOA: Insurgent's, Observer's, *or* Prey-Stalker's, *or* Keltoi Infiltrators Disguise • (1.5%) <Celtic Wonders> • (0.5%) <Salisbury Stock 2>

keltoi banisher [22-23] (27%) Celtic Bracelet • (23%) Ornamental Necklace • (18%) Keltoi Crafted Belt • (14%) Traveling Backpack • (9%) Thick Rope • (5%) <The Spy's Satchel> • (90%) Jewels 09 • (5%) Jewels 60 • (5%) Blue, Red *or* Light Teal Colors • (1.5%) APOA: Dusk-Walkers *or* Vindicator's • (1.5%) <To Hang My Sporran> • (1.5%) <Celtic Wonders> • (0.5%) <Salisbury Stock 2>

keltoi eremite [21] (27%) Celtic Bracelet • (23%) Ornamental Necklace • (18%) Keltoi Crafted Belt • (14%) Traveling Backpack • (9%) Thick Rope • (2%) <The Spy's Satchel> • (90%) Jewels 09 • (2%) Jewels 60 • (5%) Blue, Red *or* Light Teal Colors • (1.5%) APOA: Dusk-Walkers *or* Vindicator's • (1.5%) <Sacred Jewelry> • (1.5%) <Drako's Droppings> • (0.5%) <Salisbury Stock 2> • (29%) Celtic Bracelet • (24%) Ornamental Necklace • (19%) Keltoi Crafted Belt • (14%) Traveling Backpack • (9.5%) Thick Rope

keltoi familiar [23/25] (20/30%) Sleek Black Pelt • (80% each) Razor Sharp Claw, Sharp Tooth • (20/40% each) Razor Sharp Claw, Sharp Tooth

keltoi initiate [20] (24%) Celtic Bracelet • (20%) Ornamental Necklace • (16%) Keltoi Crafted Belt • (12%) Traveling Backpack • (8%) Thick Rope • (2%) <The Spy's Satchel> • (80%) Jewels 09 • (2%) Jewels 60 • (5%) Blue, Red *or* Light Teal Colors • (1.5%) APOA: Dusk-Walkers *or* Vindicator's • (1.5%) <Sacred Jewelry> • (1.5%) <Drako's Droppings> • (0.5%) <Salisbury Stock 2>

keltoi recluse [22] *see Note (1), plus* • (2%) <The Spy's Satchel> • (2%) Jewels 60 • (1.5%) APOA: Dusk-Walkers *or* Vindicator's • (1.5%) <Sacred Jewelry> • (1.5%) <Drako's Droppings> • (0.5%) <Salisbury Stock 2>

keltoi ritualist [23] *see Note (1), plus* • (10%) <The Spy's Satchel> • (10%) Jewels 60 • (1.5%) APOA: Insurgent's, Observer's, *or* Prey-Stalker's, *or* Keltoi Infiltrators Disguise • (1.5%) <To Hang My Sporran> • (1.5%) <Celtic Wonders> • (0.5%) <Salisbury Stock 2> • (10%) Ring of Insane Might

keltoi spiritualist [25] *see Note (1), plus* • (20%) <The Spy's Satchel> • (20%) Jewels 60 • (1.5%) APOA: Insurgent's, Observer's, *or* Prey-Stalker's, *or* Keltoi Infiltrators Disguise • (1.5%) <To Hang My Sporran> • (1.5%) <Celtic Wonders> • (0.5%) <Arthurian Artifacts 2>

keltoi visionary [21-22] *see Note (1), plus* • (2%) <The Spy's Satchel> • (2%) Jewels 60 • (1.5%) APOA: Dusk-Walkers *or* Vindicator's • (1.5%) <Sacred Jewelry> • (1.5%) <Drako's Droppings> • (0.5%) <Salisbury Stock 2>

Meurig [25] *see Note (1), plus* • (20%) <The Spy's Satchel> • (20%) Jewels 60 • (1.5%) APOA: Insurgent's, Observer's, *or* Prey-Stalker's, *or* Keltoi Infiltrators Disguise • (1.5%) <To Hang My Sporran> • (1.5%) <Celtic Wonders> • (0.5%) <Arthurian Artifacts 2>

muryan emmisary [25] *see Note (1), plus* • (20%) <The Spy's Satchel> • (20%) Jewels 60 • (1.5%) APOA: Insurgent's, Observer's, *or* Prey-Stalker's, *or* Keltoi Infiltrators Disguise • (1.5%) <To Hang My Sporran> • (1.5%) <Celtic Wonders> • (0.5%) <Arthurian Artifacts 2>

Key. [X] = level(s) • (X%) = chance to get item (if a list, just one) • (X% each) = chance for *each* item • hi-lo = most to least likely • APOA = a piece of armor • (x2) = item can drop twice

Stonehenge Barrows

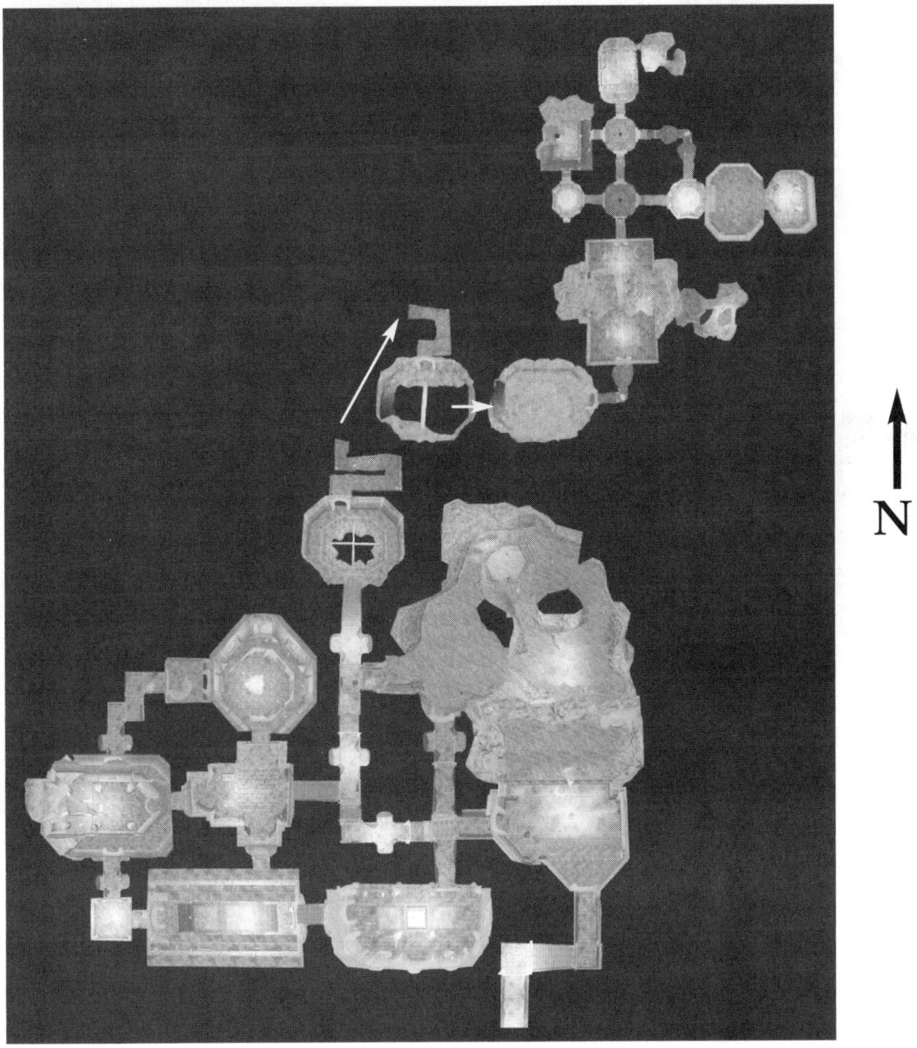

Stonehenge Barrows Loot

barrow wight [43] (30%) Magical Soul Anchor • (10%) Malefic Spirit Orb • (50%) Jewels 32 • (2%) Jewels 15 • (3.6%) Blue, Red ***or*** Light Teal Colors • (0.4%) Light Turquoise, Teal ***or*** Dark Gray Colors • (1.5%) <Death's Door> • (1%) <Frigg's Gift> • (0.2%) <Glimmer Gear> • (0.2%) <Asterite Attic> • (1.5%; hi-lo) APOA: Scarlet of the Covetous, Ebony of the Corrupt, Runic Ravenbone, Sable of Dementia, ***or*** Delusional Power

barrow wight [44] (30%) Magical Soul Anchor • (10%) Malefic Spirit Orb • (35%) Jewels 19 • (0.8%) Jewels 52 • (4.5%) Turquoise, Purple ***or*** Charcoal Colors • (0.5%) Black, Royal Blue ***or*** Crimson Colors • (1.5%) <Mantles of Magic> • (0.5%) <Ebony and Ivory> • (0.5%) <Heart of Darkness> • (0.5%) <Hand of Darkness> • (1.5%) APOA: Ancient Ebony, Corrupt Greatheart, Ghostly Light, Baleful Dead, ***or*** Eternal Midnight

cave hound [38] (24%) Cave Hound Tooth • (42%) Cave Hound Claw (x2) • (23%) Cave Hound Skin • (2.5%) Pristine Cave Hound Skin • (1.7%) Great Hound Tooth

Celtic lich [50] (33%) Ancient Sacrificial Goblet • (1.8%) Ancient Sacrificial Goblet • (10%) Ancient Burial Wrap • (40%) Jewels 19 • (0.8%) Jewels 52 • (4.5%) Turquoise, Purple ***or*** Charcoal Colors • (0.5%) Black, Royal Blue ***or*** Crimson Colors • (1.5%) <Mantles of Magic> • (1%) <Ebony and Ivory> • (0.2%) <Heart of Darkness> • (0.2%) <Hand of Darkness> • (1.5%; hi-lo) APOA: Ancient Ebony, Baleful Dead, Ghostly Light, Corrupt Greatheart, ***or*** Eternal Midnight • (2%) Jewels 14

Celtic sepulchre chieftain [52] (33%) Ancient Sacrificial Goblet • (1.8%) Ancient Sacrificial Goblet • (20%) Ancient Burial Wrap • (40%) Jewels 19 • (0.8%) Jewels 52 • (4.5%) Turquoise, Purple ***or*** Charcoal Colors • (0.5%) Black, Royal Blue ***or*** Crimson Colors • (1.5%) <Mantles of Magic> • (1%) <Heart of Darkness> • (0.2%) <Hand of Darkness> • (0.2%) <Ebony and Ivory> • (1.5%; hi-lo) APOA: Corrupt Greatheart, Eternal Midnight, the Baleful Dead, the Ghostly Light, ***or*** Ancient Ebony

Celtic sepulchre warrior [47] (10%) Ancient Golden Baldric • (25%) Ancient Beaded Bag • (40%) Jewels 19 • (0.8%) Jewels 52 • (4.5%) Turquoise, Purple ***or*** Charcoal Colors • (0.5%) Black, Royal Blue ***or*** Crimson Colors • (1.5%) <Mantles of Magic> • (1%) <Heart of Darkness> • (0.2%) <Hand of Darkness> • (0.2%) <Ebony and Ivory> • (1.5%; hi-lo) APOA: Corrupt Greatheart, Eternal Midnight, the Baleful Dead, the Ghostly Light, ***or*** Ancient Ebony

creeping ooze [42] (15%) Crude Barbed Shackle • (15%) Jeweled Redbone Skull • (15%) Old Scaled Baldric • (15%) Deathly Reanimated Bones • (30%) Jewels 32 • (2%) Jewels 15 • (3.6%) Blue, Red ***or*** Light Teal Colors • (0.4%) Light Turquoise, Teal ***or*** Dark Gray Colors • (1.5%) <Death's Door> • (0.5%) <Asterite Attic> • (0.5%) <Frigg's Gift> • (0.5%) <Glimmer Gear> • (1.5%) APOA: Delusional Power, Sable of Dementia, Runic Ravenbone, Scarlet of the Covetous, Ebony of the Corrupt

dark fire [42] (30%) Ember of Darkfire • (50%) Jewels 32 • (2%) Jewels 15 • (3.6%) Blue, Red ***or*** Light Teal Colors • (0.4%) Light Turquoise, Teal ***or*** Dark Gray Colors • (1.6%) <Dark Knight Wear> • (2.8%) <Merlin's Closet> • (0.6%) <Freedon's Gift> • (0.6%) <Tanks for the Loot> • (1.6%; hi-lo) APOA: Delusional Power, Runic Ravenbone, Sable of Dementia, Scarlet of the Covetous, Ebony of the Corrupt

decayed barbarian [40] (15%) Deathly Reanimated Bones • (30%) Old Scaled Baldric • (45%) Jewels 32 • (2%) Jewels 15 • (3.6%) Blue, Red ***or*** Light Teal Colors • (0.4%) Light Turquoise, Teal ***or*** Dark Gray Colors • (1.6%) <Dark Knight Wear> • (2.8%) <Freedon's Gift> • (0.6%) <Tanks for the Loot> • (0.6%) <Merlin's Closet> • (1.2%) APOA: Risen, Dejected, Blackheart, Dissolution, ***or*** Mortification

decayed barbarian chieftain [42] (15%) Ancient Beaded Bag • (30%) Burial Wrap • (45%) Jewels 32 • (2%) Jewels 15 • (3.6%) Blue, Red ***or*** Light Teal Colors • (0.4%) Light Turquoise, Teal ***or*** Dark Gray Colors • (1.5%) <Death's Door> • (0.5%) <Asterite Attic> • (0.5%) <Frigg's Gift> • (0.5%) <Glimmer Gear> • (1.5%; hi-lo) APOA: Delusional Power, Runic Ravenbone, Sable of Dementia, Scarlet of the Covetous, Ebony of the Corrupt

decaying tomb raider [36] (30%) Torn Luminescent Skin • (5%) Cursed Golden Statue • (45%) Jewels 32 • (2%) Jewels 15 • (3.6%) Blue, Red ***or*** Light Teal Cloth Dye • (0.4%) Light Turquoise, Teal ***or*** Dark Gray Colors • (1.7%) Cloak of the Blackheart, Ghastly Ring of Bone, Necklace of the Dark Soul, ***or*** Bracer of Shaved Bone • (2.8%) <Freedon's Gift> • (0.6%) <Tanks for the Loot> • (0.6%) <Merlin's Closet> • (4%) APOA: Risen (Faded), Dejected (Faded), Blackheart (Worn), Dissolution (Worn), ***or*** Mortification (Worn)

deep goblin [42] (30%) Jeweled Skull Totem • (10%) Cursed Golden Statue • (50%) Jewels 32 • (2%) Jewels 15 • (3.6%) Blue, Red ***or*** Light Teal Colors • (0.4%) Light Turquoise, Teal ***or*** Dark Gray Colors • (1.5%) <Death's Door> • (1%) <Frigg's Gift> • (0.2%) <Glimmer Gear> • (0.2%) <Asterite Attic> • (1.5%; hi-lo) APOA: Scarlet of the Covetous, Ebony of the Corrupt, Runic Ravenbone, Sable of Dementia, ***or*** Delusional Power • (1.5%; hi-lo) APOA: Scarlet of the Covetous, Ebony of the Corrupt, Runic Ravenbone, Sable of Dementia, ***or*** Delusional Power

deep goblin blighter [43] (30%) Jeweled Skull Totem • (10%) Cursed Golden Statue • (50%) Jewels 32 • (2%) Jewels 15 • (3.6%) Blue, Red ***or*** Light Teal Colors • (0.4%) Light Turquoise, Teal ***or*** Dark Gray Colors • (1.5%) <Death's Door> • (1%) <Glimmer Gear> • (0.2%) <Asterite Attic> • (0.2%) <Frigg's Gift> • (1.5%; hi-lo) APOA: Scarlet of the Covetous, Ebony of the Corrupt, Runic Ravenbone, Sable of Dementia, ***or*** Delusional Power

diseased rat [38] (41%) Glowing Rat Claw (x2) • (23%) Diseased Rat Skin • (2.5%) Pristine Diseased Rat Skin • (1.7%) Diseased Rat Tail

echo of life [41] (10%) Malefic Spirit Orb • (25%) Essence of the Haunted • (50%) Jewels 32 • (1%) Jewels 15 • (3.6%) Blue, Red ***or*** Light Teal Colors • (0.4%) Light Turquoise, Teal ***or*** Dark Gray Colors • (1.5%) <Dark Knight Wear> • (0.5%) <Merlin's Closet> • (0.5%) <Freedon's Gift> • (0.5%) <Tanks for the Loot> • (1.5%) APOA: of the Risen, the Dejected, the Blackheart, Dissolution, ***or*** Mortification

ectoplasm [41] (30%) Ectoplasmic Goo • (15%) Residue of the Cremated • (45%) Jewels 32 • (2%) Jewels 15 • (3.6%) Blue, Red ***or*** Light Teal Colors • (0.4%) Light Turquoise, Teal ***or*** Dark Gray Colors • (1.5%) <Dark Knight Wear> • (0.5%) <Merlin's Closet> • (0.5%) <Freedon's Gift> • (0.5%) <Tanks for the Loot> • (1.5%) APOA: Risen, Dejected, Blackheart, Dissolution, ***or*** Mortification

fallen warrior [41] (20%) Spined Death Claw Bracelet • (30%) Burial Wrap • (45%) Jewels 32 • (2%) Jewels 15 • (3.6%) Blue, Red ***or*** Light Teal Colors • (0.4%) Light Turquoise, Teal ***or*** Dark Gray Colors • (1.5%) <Dark Knight Wear> • (1%) <Tanks for the Loot> • (2.3%) <Merlin's Closet> • (2.3%) <Freedon's Gift> • (1.6%) APOA: Risen, Dejected, Blackheart, Dissolution, ***or*** Mortification

ghoulic viper [42] (56%) Ghoulic Viper Fang • (24%) Ghoulic Viper Skin • (2.6%) Pristine Ghoulic Viper Skin • (1.7%) Ghoulish Viper Fang

glowing goo [36] (30%) Glowing Viscous Goo • (45%) Jewels 32 • (2%) Jewels 15 • (3.6%) Blue, Red ***or*** Light Teal Cloth Dye • (0.4%) Light Turquoise, Teal ***or*** Dark Gray Colors • (1.6%) <Dark Knight Wear> • (2.8%) <Merlin's Closet> • (0.6%) <Freedon's Gift> • (0.6%) <Tanks for the Loot> • (1.6%) APOA: Risen (Faded), Dejected (Faded), Blackheart (Worn), Dissolution (Worn), ***or*** Mortification (Worn)

grave goblin [40] (10%) Jeweled Skull Totem • (30%) Spined Death Claw Bracelet • (45%) Jewels 32 • (2%) Jewels 15 • (3.6%) Blue, Red ***or*** Light Teal Cloth Dye • (0.4%) Light Turquoise, Teal ***or*** Dark Gray Colors • (1.6%) <Dark Knight Wear> • (2.8%) <Freedon's Gift> • (0.6%) <Tanks for the Loot> • (0.6%) <Merlin's Closet> • (1.6%) APOA: Risen, Dejected, Blackheart, Dissolution, ***or*** Mortification

grave goblin shaman [38] (30%) Torn Luminescent Skin • (10%) Shamanic Death Beads • (40%) <Pilfered Prizes> • (12%) Enchanted Metal Stud • (2%) Jewels 15 • (4.5%) Turquoise, Purple ***or*** Charcoal Colors • (0.5%) Black, Royal Blue ***or*** Crimson Colors • (1.6%) <Dark Knight Wear> • (2.8%) <Merlin's Closet> • (0.6%) <Freedon's Gift> • (0.6%) <Tanks for the Loot> • (1.2%) APOA: Risen (Faded), Dejected (Faded), Blackheart (Worn), Dissolution (Worn), ***or*** Mortification (Worn) • (0.4%) APOA: Risen, Dejected, Blackheart, Dissolution, ***or*** Mortification

grave goblin whelp [28,30,32] (no loot)

High Priestess Ywera [47] *see skeletal high priestess [46]*

king's wight [50] (10%) Soul Anchor Lock • (30%) Essence of the Fervent Defender • (40%) Jewels 19 • (0.8%) Jewels 52 • (4.5%) Turquoise, Purple ***or*** Charcoal Colors • (0.5%) Black, Royal Blue ***or*** Crimson Colors • (1.5%) <Mantles of Magic> • (0.5%) <Ebony and Ivory> • (0.5%) <Heart of Darkness> • (0.5%) <Hand of Darkness> • (1.5%) APOA: Ancient Ebony, Corrupt Greatheart, Ghostly Light, Baleful Dead, ***or*** Eternal Midnight

Lifeblighter [43] (30%) Jeweled Skull Totem • (10%) Cursed Golden Statue • (50%) Jewels 32 • (2%) Jewels 15 • (3.6%) Blue, Red ***or*** Light Teal Colors • (0.4%) Light Turquoise, Teal ***or*** Dark Gray Colors • (1.5%) <Death's Door> • (1%) <Glimmer Gear> • (0.2%) <Asterite Attic> • (0.2%) <Frigg's Gift> • (1.5%) APOA: Delusional Power, Sable of Dementia, Runic Ravenbone, Scarlet of the Covetous, ***or*** Ebony of the Corrupt

malefic phantom [47] (25%) Malefic Spirit Orb • (50%) Jewels 19 • (0.8%) Jewels 52 • (4.5%) Turquoise, Purple ***or*** Charcoal Colors • (0.5%) Black, Royal Blue ***or*** Crimson Colors • (1.5%) <Mantles of Magic> • (0.5%) <Ebony and Ivory> • (0.5%) <Heart of Darkness> • (0.5%) <Hand of Darkness> • (1.5%) APOA: Ancient Ebony, Corrupt Greatheart, Ghostly Light, Baleful Dead, ***or*** Eternal Midnight

marrow leech [38] (43%) Residue of the Cremated • (23%) Marrow Leech Carapace • (2.5%) Pristine Leech Carapace • (1.7%) Symbiotic Leech Bracer

megalith wight [46] *see barrow wight [44]*

megalithic terror [49] (10%) Soul Anchor Lock • (25%) Malefic Spirit Orb • (40%) Jewels 19 • (0.8%) Jewels 52 • (4.5%) Turquoise, Purple ***or*** Charcoal Colors • (0.5%) Black, Royal Blue ***or*** Crimson Colors • (1.5%) <Mantles of Magic> • (0.5%) <Ebony and Ivory> • (0.5%) <Heart of Darkness> • (0.5%) <Hand of Darkness> • (1.5%) APOA: Ancient Ebony, Corrupt Greatheart, Ghostly Light, Baleful Dead, ***or*** Eternal Midnight

Mikolas [43] (25%) Spined Death Claw Bracelet • (30%) Burial Wrap • (45%) Jewels 32 • (2%) Jewels 15 • (3.6%) Blue, Red ***or*** Light Teal Colors • (0.4%) Light Turquoise, Teal ***or*** Dark Gray Colors • (1.5%) <Death's Door> • (0.5%) <Asterite Attic> • (0.5%) <Frigg's Gift> • (0.5%) <Glimmer Gear> • (1.5%) APOA: Delusional Power, Sable of Dementia, Runic Ravenbone, Scarlet of the Covetous, Ebony of the Corrupt

ossuary guardian [48] (10%) Essence of the Fervent Defender • (30%) Magical Soul Anchor • (1.5%) <Mantles of Magic> • (40%) Jewels 19 • (0.8%) Jewels 52 • (4.5%) Turquoise, Purple ***or*** Charcoal Colors • (0.5%) Black, Royal Blue ***or*** Crimson Colors • (1%) <Heart of Darkness> • (0.2%) <Hand of Darkness> • (0.2%) <Ebony and Ivory> • (1.5%; hi-lo) APOA: Corrupt Greatheart, Eternal Midnight, the Baleful Dead, the Ghostly Light, ***or*** Ancient Ebony

pendragon ardent [48] (20%) Essence of the Fervent Defender • (10%) Ancient Golden Baldric • (45%) Jewels 19 • (0.8%) Jewels 52 • (4.5%) Turquoise, Purple ***or*** Charcoal Colors • (0.5%) Black, Royal Blue ***or*** Crimson Colors • (1.5%) <Mantles of Magic> • (1%) <Heart of Darkness> • (0.2%) <Hand of Darkness> • (0.2%) <Ebony and Ivory> • (1.5%; hi-lo) APOA: Corrupt Greatheart, Eternal Midnight, the Baleful Dead, the Ghostly Light, ***or*** Ancient Ebony

pendrake [48] (47%) Pendrake Claw • (48%) Pendrake Fang • (23%) Pendrake Skin • (2.5%) Pristine Pendrake Skin • (1.7%) Sheer Ruby Scale-Splitter

petrified grovewood [43] (39%) Horrific Petrified Branch • (33%) Bloody Root • (0.6%) Gnarled Branch of Grovewood • (0.6%) Shield of Grovewood Bark • (0.6%) Shard of Grovewood

Priestess of Purity [44] (no loot)

reanimated foe [37-38] (30%) Torn Luminescent Skin • (10%) Deathly Reanimated Bones • (45%) Jewels 32 • (2%) Jewels 15 • (3.6%) Blue, Red ***or*** Light Teal Cloth Dye • (0.4%) Light Turquoise, Teal ***or*** Dark Gray Colors • (1.6%) <Dark Knight Wear> • (2.8%) <Tanks for the Loot> • (0.6%) <Merlin's Closet> • (0.6%) <Freedon's Gift> • (1.2%) APOA: Risen (Faded), Dejected (Faded), Blackheart (Worn), Dissolution (Worn), ***or*** Mortification (Worn) • (0.4%) APOA: Risen, Dejected, Blackheart, Dissolution, ***or*** Mortification

redbone skeleton [37] (5%) Jeweled Redbone Skull • (30%) Spined Death Claw Bracelet • (45%) Jewels 32 • (2%) Jewels 14 • (3.6%) Blue, Red ***or*** Light Teal Cloth Dye • (0.4%) Light Turquoise, Teal ***or*** Dark Gray Colors • (1.6%) <Dark Knight Wear> • (2.8%) <Tanks for the Loot> • (0.6%) <Merlin's Closet> • (0.6%) <Freedon's Gift> • (1.2%) APOA: Risen (Faded), Dejected (Faded), Blackheart (Worn), Dissolution (Worn), ***or*** Mortification (Worn) • (0.4%) APOA: Risen, Dejected, Blackheart, Dissolution, ***or*** Mortification

repentant follower [37] (30%) Torn Luminescent Skin • (30%) Old Scaled Baldric • (45%) Jewels 32 • (2%) Jewels 15 • (3.6%) Blue, Red ***or*** Light Teal Cloth Dye • (0.4%) Light Turquoise, Teal ***or*** Dark Gray Colors • (1.6%) <Dark Knight Wear> • (2.8%) <Merlin's Closet> • (0.6%) <Freedon's Gift> • (0.6%) <Tanks for the Loot> • (1.2%) APOA: Risen (Faded), Dejected (Faded), Blackheart (Worn), Dissolution (Worn), ***or*** Mortification (Worn) • (0.4%) APOA: Risen, Dejected, Blackheart, Dissolution, ***or*** Mortification

sacrificial soul [43] (30%) Torn Luminescent Skin • (20%) Crude Barbed Shackle • (50%) Jewels 19 • (0.8%) Jewels 52 • (4.5%) Turquoise, Purple ***or*** Charcoal Colors • (0.5%) Black, Royal Blue ***or*** Crimson Colors • (1.5%) <Death's Door> • (1%) <Glimmer Gear> • (0.2%) <Asterite Attic> • (0.2%) <Frigg's Gift> • (1.5%) APOA: Delusional Power, Sable of Dementia, Runic Ravenbone, Scarlet of the Covetous, Ebony of the Corrupt

saxonbone skeleton [40] *see decayed barbarian [40]*

scaled fiend [42] (48%) Scaled Fiend Tooth • (50%) Scaled Fiend Tail • (23%) Scaled Fiend Skin • (2.5%) Pristine Scaled Fiend Skin • (1.7%) Claw of the Rending

Shade of Ambrosius Aurelianus [54] (25%) Essence of the Fervent Defender • (15%) Ancient Golden Baldric • (50%) Jewels 19 • (0.8%) Jewels 52 • (4.5%) Turquoise, Purple ***or*** Charcoal Colors • (0.5%) Black, Royal Blue ***or*** Crimson Colors • (1.5%) <Mantles of Magic> • (1%) <Heart of Darkness> • (0.2%) <Hand of Darkness> • (0.2%) <Ebony and Ivory> • (1.5%; hi-lo) APOA: Corrupt Greatheart, Eternal Midnight, the Baleful Dead, the Ghostly Light, ***or*** Ancient Ebony

Shade of Uther Pendragon [55] (30%) Essence of the Fervent Defender • (15%) Ancient Golden Baldric • (55%) Jewels 19 • (0.8%) Jewels 52 • (4.5%) Turquoise, Purple ***or*** Charcoal Colors • (0.5%) Black, Royal Blue ***or*** Crimson Colors • (1.5%) <Mantles of Magic> • (1%) <Heart of Darkness> • (0.2%) <Hand of Darkness> • (0.2%) <Ebony and Ivory> • (1.5%; hi-lo) APOA: Corrupt Greatheart, Eternal Midnight, the Baleful Dead, the Ghostly Light, ***or*** Ancient Ebony

skeletal druid [44] (33%) Ancient Sacrificial Goblet • (1.8%) Ancient Sacrificial Goblet • (50%) Jewels 32 • (2%) Jewels 15 • (3.6%) Blue, Red ***or*** Light Teal Colors • (0.4%) Light Turquoise, Teal ***or*** Dark Gray Colors • (1.5%) <Death's Door> • (1 %) <Asterite Attic> • (0.2%) <Frigg's Gift> • (0.2%) <Glimmer Gear> • (1.5%; hi-lo) APOA: Delusional Power, Runic Ravenbone, Sable of Dementia, Scarlet of the Covetous, Ebony of the Corrupt • (10%) Malefic Spirit Orb

skeletal druidess [44] *see skeletal druid [44]*

skeletal high priestess [46] (10%) Malefic Spirit Orb • (33%) Ancient Sacrificial Goblet • (1.8%) Ancient Sacrificial Goblet • (35%) Jewels 19 • (0.8%) Jewels 52 • (4.5%) Turquoise, Purple ***or*** Charcoal Colors • (0.5%) Black, Royal Blue ***or*** Crimson Colors • (1.5%) <Mantles of Magic> • (1%) <Ebony and Ivory> • (0.2%) <Heart of Darkness> • (0.2%) <Hand of Darkness> • (1.5%; hi-lo) APOA: Ancient Ebony, Baleful Dead, Ghostly Light, Corrupt Greatheart, ***or*** Eternal Midnight

soul harvester [41] (10%) Residue of the Cremated • (30%) Jeweled Skull Totem • (45%) Jewels 32 • (2%) Jewels 15 • (3.6%) Blue, Red ***or*** Light Teal Colors • (0.4%) Light Turquoise, Teal ***or*** Dark Gray Colors • (1.5%) <Dark Knight Wear> • (1%) <Tanks for the Loot> • (.2%) <Merlin's Closet> • (.2%) <Freedon's Gift> • (1.5%) APOA: Risen, Dejected, Blackheart, Dissolution, ***or*** Mortification

spectral essence [46-47] (25%) Spectral Essence • (10%) Malefic Spirit Orb • (45%) Jewels 19 • (0.8%) Jewels 52 • (4.5%) Turquoise, Purple ***or*** Charcoal Colors • (0.5%) Black, Royal Blue ***or*** Crimson Colors • (0.5%) <Ebony and Ivory> • (0.5%) <Heart of Darkness> • (0.5%) <Hand of Darkness> • (1.5%) APOA: Ancient Ebony, Corrupt Greatheart, Ghostly Light, Baleful Dead, ***or*** Eternal Midnight • (1.5%) <Mantles of Magic>

spectral wizard [47] (25%) Malefic Spirit Orb • (10%) Ancient Book • (45%) Jewels 19 • (0.8%) Jewels 52 • (4.5%) Turquoise, Purple ***or*** Charcoal Colors • (0.5%) Black, Royal Blue ***or*** Crimson Colors • (1.5%) <Mantles of Magic> • (1%) <Ebony and Ivory> • (0.2%) <Heart of Darkness> • (0.2%) <Hand of Darkness> • (1.5%; hi-lo) APOA: Ancient Ebony, Baleful Dead, Ghostly Light, Corrupt Greatheart, ***or*** Eternal Midnight

spiritual advisor [48] (30%) Residue of the Cremated • (15%) Ancient Book • (50%) Jewels 19 • (0.8%) Jewels 52 • (4.5%) Turquoise, Purple ***or*** Charcoal Colors • (0.5%) Black, Royal Blue ***or*** Crimson Colors • (1.5%) <Mantles of Magic> • (1%) <Ebony and Ivory> • (0.2%) <Heart of Darkness> • (0.2%) <Hand of Darkness> • (1.5%; hi-lo) APOA: Ancient Ebony, Baleful Dead, Ghostly Light, Corrupt Greatheart, ***or*** Eternal Midnight

stone sentinel [48/50] (25/31%) Ancient Molded Stone • (78/81%) Jewels 19 • (0.8%) Jewels 52 • (1.5%) <Mantles of Magic> • (1%) <Hand of Darkness> • (0.2%) <Ebony and Ivory> • (0.2%) <Heart of Darkness> • (1.5%; hi-lo) APOA: Corrupt Greatheart, Eternal Midnight, the Baleful Dead, the Ghostly Light, ***or*** Ancient Ebony

tomb keeper [41] (10%) Malefic Spirit Orb • (25%) Essence of the Haunted • (60%) Jewels 32 • (2%) Jewels 15 • (3.6%) Blue, Red ***or*** Light Teal Colors • (0.4%) Light Turquoise, Teal ***or*** Dark Gray Colors • (1.5%) <Dark Knight Wear> • (0.5%) <Merlin's Closet> • (0.5%) <Freedon's Gift> • (0.5%) <Tanks for the Loot> • (1.5%) APOA: of the Risen, the Dejected, the Blackheart, Dissolution, ***or*** Mortification

Templar Avenger [54] (no loot)

tomb wight [42] (25%) Malefic Spirit Orb • (50%) Jewels 32 • (2%) Jewels 15 • (3.6%) Blue, Red ***or*** Light Teal Colors • (0.4%) Light Turquoise, Teal ***or*** Dark Gray Colors • (1.5%) <Death's Door> • (1%) <Frigg's Gift> • (0.2%) <Glimmer Gear> • (0.2%) <Asterite Attic> • (1.5%; hi-lo) APOA: Scarlet of the Covetous, Ebony of the Corrupt, Runic Ravenbone, Sable of Dementia, ***or*** Delusional Power

tunneler [37] (42%) Tunneler Fang (x2) • (23%) Tunneler Skin • (2.5%) Pristine Tunneler Skin • (1.7%) Tunneler Eye

undead retainer [36-37] (10%) Torn Luminescent Skin • (30%) Old Scaled Baldric • (45%) Jewels 32 • (2%) Jewels 14 • (3.6%) Blue, Red ***or*** Light Teal Colors • (0.4%) Light Turquoise, Teal ***or*** Dark Gray Colors • (1.7%) Cloak of the Blackheart, Ghastly Ring of Bone, Necklace of the Dark Soul, ***or*** Bracer of Shaved Bone • (2.8%) <Merlin's Closet> • (0.6%) <Freedon's Gift> • (0.6%) <Tanks for the Loot> • (4%) APOA: Risen (Faded), Dejected (Faded), Blackheart (Worn), Dissolution (Worn), ***or*** Mortification (Worn)

vigilant soul [46] (10%) Malefic Spirit Orb • (30%) Ancient Runic Scroll • (40%) Jewels 19 • (0.8%) Jewels 52 • (4.5%) Turquoise, Purple ***or*** Charcoal Colors • (0.5%) Black, Royal Blue ***or*** Crimson Colors • (1.5%) <Mantles of Magic> • (1.5%) <Heart of Darkness> • (1.5%) APOA: Ancient Ebony, Corrupt Greatheart, Ghostly Light, Baleful Dead, ***or*** Eternal Midnight

Wizard Lichas [48] *see spectral wizard [47]*

Key. [X] = level(s) • (X%) = chance to get item (if a list, just one) • (X% each) = chance for *each* item • hi-lo = most to least likely • APOA = a piece of armor • (x2) = item can drop twice

Tepok's Mine

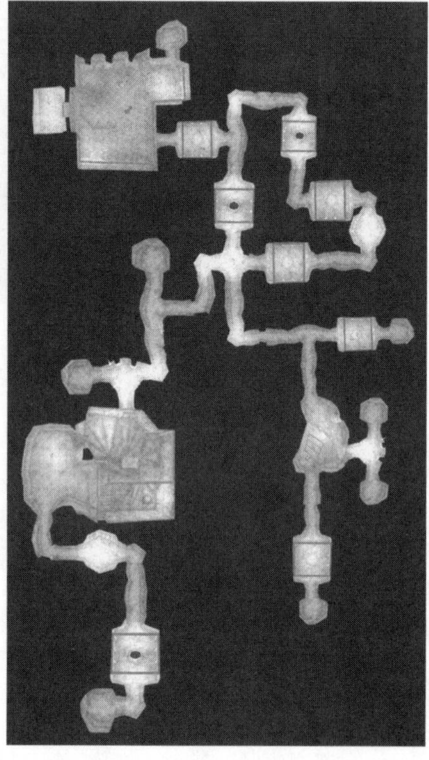

Loot

angler [28] (18%) Angler Leg Tip • (4.6%) Angler Poison Sac

apprentice beastmaster [31] *see goblin beastmaster [31]*

cave bear [24/26/35] (18/20/23%) Cave Bear Pelt • (2/2.2/2.5%) Pristine Cave Bear Pelt

cave bear cub [16-17] (18%) Cave Bear Cub Pelt • (2%) Pristine Cave Bear Cub Pelt

cave fisher [22/24] (16/18%) Cave Fisher Leg Tip • (4/4.4%) Cave Fisher Poison Sac

cave lion [24/25/26] (20/22/24%) Cave Lion Pelt • (2.2/2.4/2.7%) Pristine Cave Lion Pelt

Director Botok [35] (10%) < Goblin's Cellar> • (10%) Jewels 18 • (1.5%) APOA: Woebegone Miner • (1.5%) <Mined from the Deep> • (1.5%) <Goblin' It Up> • (35%) Director's Devastator

Emissary Sebian [33] *see Sarel Sebian [32]*

fisher hatchling [15/16/17] (18/20/22%) Fisher Hatcher Leg Tip • (4.4/5/5.6%) Fisher Hatcher Carapace

goblin [25-26] (10%) <Miner Midden> • (10%) Jewels 33 • (1.5%) APOA: Goblin-Forged • (1.5%) <Thrym's Dream> • (1.5%) <Goblin's Forge>

goblin [28-29] (8%) < Goblin's Cellar> • (8%) Jewels 18 • (1.5%) APOA: Goblin Goldminer • (1.5%) <Thrym's Dream> • (1.5%) <Goblin's Forge>

goblin apprentice [24] (8%) <Miner Midden> • (8%) Jewels 33 • (1.5%) APOA: Hob Hunter ***or*** Silken Robe • (1.5%) <Tepok Treasures 1> • (1.5%) <Tepok Treasures 2>

goblin beastmaster [31] (9%) < Goblin's Cellar> • (9%) Jewels 18 • (1.5%) APOA: Goblinskin • (1.5%) <Thrym's Dream> • (1.5%) <Goblin's Forge>

goblin cleaner [30] (8%) < Goblin's Cellar> • (8%) Jewels 18 • (1.5%) APOA: Goblinskin • (1.5%) <Thrym's Dream> • (1.5%) <Goblin's Forge>

goblin crawler [23-24] (9%) <Miner Midden> • (9%) Jewels 33 • (1.5%) APOA: Hob Hunter ***or*** Silken Robe • (1.5%) <Tepok Treasures 1> • (1.5%) <Tepok Treasures 2>

goblin imperator [31] (9%) < Goblin's Cellar> • (9%) Jewels 18 • (1.5%) APOA: Woebegone Miner • (1.5%) <Thrym's Dream> • (1.5%) <Goblin's Forge>

goblin monitor [33] *see goblin imperator [31]*

goblin patrol leader [27] (12%) <Miner Midden> • (12%) Jewels 33 • (1.5%) APOA: Goblin-Forged • (1.5%) <Thrym's Dream> • (1.5%) <Goblin's Forge>

goblin snatcher [31] (8%) < Goblin's Cellar> • (8%) Jewels 18 • (1.5%) APOA: Woebegone Miner • (1.5%) <Thrym's Dream> • (1.5%) <Goblin's Forge>

goblin watcher [20-22] (8%) <Miner Midden> • (8%) Jewels 33 • (1.5%) APOA: Fire-Forged • (1.5%) <Tepok Treasures 1> • (1.5%) <Tepok Treasures 2>

goblin whip [30-32] (9%) < Goblin's Cellar> • (9%) Jewels 18 • (1.5%) APOA: Woebegone Miner • (1.5%) <Mined from the Deep> • (1.5%) <Goblin' It Up>

juggernaut [32] (20%) Jewels 18 • (1.5%) APOA: Woebegone Miner • (1.5%) <Mined from the Deep> • (1.5%) <Goblin' It Up>

Morvel Glyne [34] (10%) < Goblin's Cellar> • (10%) Jewels 18 • (1.5%) APOA: Goblinskin • (1.5%) <Mined from the Deep> • (1.5%) <Goblin' It Up> • (65%) Morvel Mauler

Overseer Tepok [39] (10%) < Goblin's Cellar> • (10%) Jewels 18 • (1.5%) APOA: Woebegone Miner • (1.5%) <Mined from the Deep> • (1.5%) <Goblin' It Up> • (35%) Robe of the Overseer

phantom [2] (no loot)

red dwarf youth [25-26] *see goblin crawler [23-24]*

Sarel Sebian [32] (10%) < Goblin's Cellar> • (10%) Jewels 18 • (1.5%) APOA: Goblin-Forged • (1.5%) <Thrym's Dream> • (1.5%) <Goblin's Forge> • (65%) Sarel Sebian Smasher

Savant [34] (10%) < Goblin's Cellar> • (10%) Jewels 18 • (1.5%) APOA: Woebegone Miner • (1.5%) <Thrym's Dream> • (1.5%) <Goblin's Forge>

stalker [18/19/20/21] (18/20/22/24%) Stalker Pelt • (2/2.2/2.5/2.7%) Pristine Stalker Pelt

Tuder Glyne [34] (10%) < Goblin's Cellar> • (10%) Jewels 18 • (1.5%) APOA: Goblinskin • (1.5%) <Mined from the Deep> • (1.5%) <Goblin' It Up> • (65%) Sarel Sebian Smasher

undead miner [20-22] (7%) <Miner Midden> • (7%) Jewels 33

Whisperer [35] (10%) < Goblin's Cellar> • (10%) Jewels 18 • (1.5%) APOA: Goblinskin • (1.5%) <Mined from the Deep> • (1.5%) <Goblin' It Up> • (35%) Whisperer of Death

wight [26] (9%) <Miner Midden> • (9%) Jewels 33 • (1.5%) APOA: Goblin-Forged • (1.5%) <Thrym's Dream> • (1.5%) <Goblin's Forge>

Tomb of Mithra

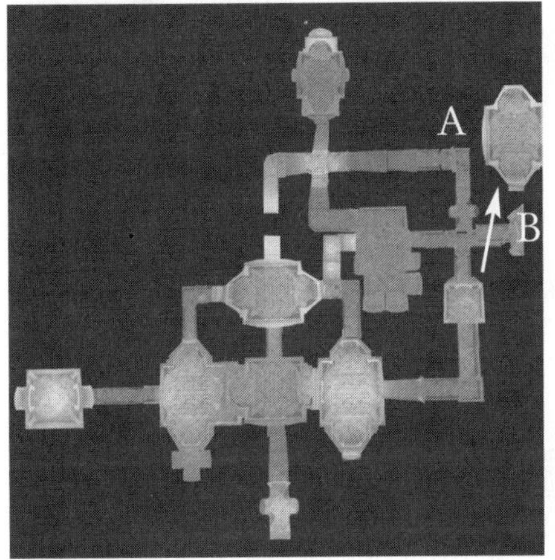

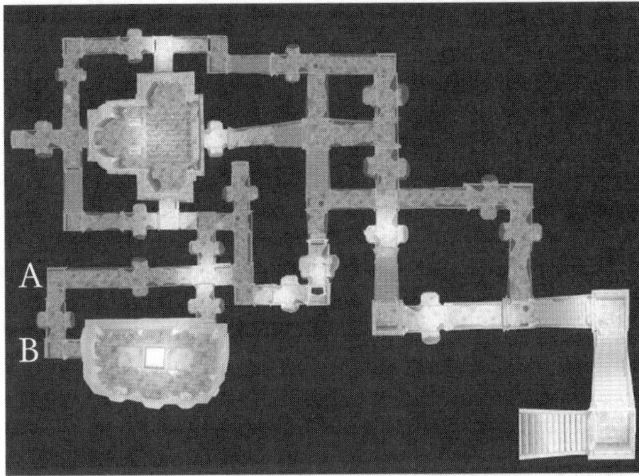

Loot

Acolyte Nascita [13] (40%) Lute, Flute ***or*** Drum of Sacred Hymns, ***or*** Underling Priest Protector

aged bleeder [13] (45%) Bleeder Tail • (35%) Shredded Bleeder Skin • (25%) Pristine Bleeder Skin

Anilius [14] (33%) Vial of Embalming Fluid • (23%) Ground Bone and Onyx Dust • (15%) Mortar and Pestle • (3.7%) Detailed Carved Bone Brooch • (75%) Jewels 55 • (1.5%) APOA: Ancient Mithrian Cloth, Musty Leather, Preserved Studded ***or*** of the Forlorn • (1.5%) <Vaulted Weaponry> • (5%) Light Blue, Light Green ***or*** Light Red Colors • (2%) Jewels 01 • (1.5%) <It's Golden> • (0.5%) <Grave Goods>

bleeder [10] (48%) Forgotten Silver Key • (29%) Blackened Silver Locket • (19%) Old Silver Lined Map Case • (95%) Jewels 43 • (5%) Light Blue, Light Green ***or*** Light Red Colors • (4%) APOA: Cracked Leather, Worn Studded, Aged Mithrian Cloth ***or*** of the Forlorn • (4%) <Sepulchral Secrets> • (1.7%) <Bone Up On Your Loot> • (0.5%) <Of a Sylvan Glade> • (2%) Jewels 08

bleeder broodmother [11] (32%) Bleeder Tail • (20%) Shredded Bleeder Skin • (15%) Pristine Bleeder Skin • (10%) Bleeder Broodmother Egg

bleeder hatchling [9] (40%) Bleeder Hatchling Tail • (30%) Shredded Hatchling Skin • (25%) Pristine Hatchling Skin

botched sacrifice [11] *see fallen paladin [11]*

chilled presence [10] *see bleeder [10]*

controlled bleeder [10] (30%) Bleeder Tail • (24%) Shredded Bleeder Skin • (15%) Pristine Bleeder Skin

cursed believer [13] (64%) Etheric Sash of Honor • (16%) Spirit Orb of the Forlorn • (80%) Jewels 55 • (2%) Jewels 01 • (1.5%) APOA: Ancient Mithrian Cloth, Musty Leather, Preserved Studded ***or*** of the Forlorn • (1.5%) <Vaulted Weaponry> • (1.5%) <It's Golden> • (0.5%) <Grave Goods>

decaying spirit [8] (56%) Essence of the Anguished Soul • (14%) Spirit Orb of the Wretched • (70%) Jewels 43 • (4%) APOA: Cracked Leather, Worn Studded, Aged Mithrian Cloth ***or*** of the Forlorn • (4%) <Sepulchral Secrets> • (1.7%) <Bone Up On Your Loot> • (0.5%) <Of a Sylvan Glade>

devout follower [9] (45%) Forgotten Silver Key • (27%) Blackened Silver Locket • (18%) Old Silver Lined Map Case • (90%) Jewels 43 • (5%) Light Blue, Light Green ***or*** Light Red Colors • (4%) APOA: Cracked Leather, Worn Studded, Aged Mithrian Cloth ***or*** the Forlorn • (4%) <Sepulchral Secrets> • (1.7%) <Bone Up On Your Loot> • (0.5%) <Of a Sylvan Glade> • (2%) Jewels 08

disturbed initiate [13] *see cursed believer [13]*

doomed minion [12] (72%) Etheric Sash of Honor • (18%) Spirit Orb of the Forlorn • (90%) Jewels 43 • (2%) Jewels 08 • (4%) APOA: Cracked Leather, Worn Studded, Aged Mithrian Cloth ***or*** of the Forlorn • (4%) <Sepulchral Secrets> • (1.7%) <Bone Up On Your Loot> • (0.5%) <Of a Sylvan Glade>

dreadful cadaver [8] (38%) Forgotten Silver Key • (23%) Blackened Silver Locket • (15%) Old Silver Lined Map Case • (75%) Jewels 43 • (5%) Light Blue, Light Green ***or*** Light Red Colors • (4%) APOA: Cracked Leather, Worn Studded, Aged Mithrian Cloth ***or*** the Forlorn • (4%) <Sepulchral Secrets> • (1.7%) <Bone Up On Your Loot> • (0.5%) <Of a Sylvan Glade>

Erisus [13] (45%) Silverlined Leather Baldric • (35%) Locket of the Forlorn • (20%) Ancient Vellum Book • Jewels 43 • (1.5%) APOA: Ancient Mithrian Cloth, Musty Leather, Preserved Studded ***or*** the Forlorn • (1.5%) <Vaulted Weaponry> • (5%) Light Blue, Light Green ***or*** Light Red Colors • (2%) Jewels 01 • (1.5%) <It's Golden> • (0.5%) <Grave Goods>

eternal scream [14] (56%) Essence of the Vengeful Spirit • (19%) Shimmering Painted Skull • (80%) Jewels 55 • (2%) Jewels 01 • (1.5%) APOA: Ancient Mithrian Cloth, Musty Leather, Preserved Studded ***or*** of the Forlorn • (1.5%) <Vaulted Weaponry> • (1.5%) <It's Golden> • (0.5%) <Grave Goods>

fallen cleric [10] *see bleeder [10]*

fallen paladin [11] (36%) Silverlined Leather Baldric • (28%) Locket of the Forlorn • (16%) Ancient Vellum Book • (90%) Jewels 43 • (4%) APOA: Cracked Leather, Worn Studded, Aged Mithrian Cloth ***or*** the Forlorn • (4%) <Sepulchral Secrets> • (5%) Light Blue, Light Green ***or*** Light Red Colors • (2%) Jewels 08 • (1.7%) <Bone Up On Your Loot> • (0.5%) <Of a Sylvan Glade>

Favonius Facilis [16] (43%) Vial of Embalming Fluid • (29%) Ground Bone and Onyx Dust • (19%) Mortar and Pestle • (4.7%) Detailed Carved Bone Brooch • (95%) Jewels 55 • (1.5%) APOA: Ancient Mithrian Cloth, Musty Leather, Preserved Studded ***or*** of the Forlorn • (1.5%) <Vaulted Weaponry> • (5%) Light Blue, Light Green ***or*** Light Red Colors • (2%) Jewels 01 • (1.5%) <It's Golden> • (0.5%) <Grave Goods>

forgotten promise [9] *see tortured soul [9]*

haunting gloom [8] *see decaying spirit [8]*

High Priest Andania [15] (no loot)

insidious whisper [14] *see eternal scream [14]*

last breath [15] (60%) Essence of the Vengeful Spirit • (20%) Shimmering Painted Skull • (90%) Jewels 55 • (2%) Jewels 01 • (1.5%) APOA: Ancient Mithrian Cloth, Musty Leather, Preserved Studded ***or*** the Forlorn • (1.5%) <Vaulted Weaponry> • (1.5%) <It's Golden> • (0.5%) <Grave Goods>

lingering shade [11] *see cursed believer [13]*

living entombed [11] *see fallen paladin [11]*

malevolent disciple [13] *see cursed believer [13]*

menacing presence [8] see dreadful cadaver [8]

Mithra acolyte [10] (25%) Silken Prayer Cloth • (20%) Dusty Golden Idol • (15%) Golden Prayer Beads • (10%) Priestly Pin of Servitude • (5%) Bottle of Blessed Oils • (5%) Light Blue, Light Red, ***or*** Light Green Colors • (10%; hi-lo) Jewels 08 • (25%) Jewels 43

Mithra acolyte [10] (40%) High Priest's: Gem of Rejuvenation ***or*** Retribution, Bracer of Defense, Signet Ring, Velvet Cape, Golden Prayer Chain, ***or*** Silken Vestment

Mithra acolyte [10] (40%; hi-lo) Dented Pewter Chalice, Tattered Rope Belt, Brass Insignia Ring, ***or*** Old Mildewed Diary • (5%) Light Blue, Light Red, ***or*** Light Green Colors • (10%; hi-lo) Jewels 08 • (25%) Jewels 43

Mithra fanatic [13] (1.7%) Fanatical Great Sword, War Mattock, Mithran Crusher, ***or*** Mithran Slasher • (40%; hi-lo) Vial of Embalming Fluid, Ground Bone And Onyx Dust, Mortar And Pestle, ***or*** Detailed Carved Bone Brooch • (20%) Jewels 55 • (18%) Jewels 01 • (5%) Light Blue, Light Red, ***or*** Light Green Colors

priest of Mithra [12] (1.7%) Crossbow ***or*** Mace of the Penitent, ***or*** Ceremonial Dirk ***or*** Dagger • (30%; hi-lo) Silverlined Leather Baldric, Locket of the Forlorn, ***or*** Ancient Vellum Book • (18%) Jewels 01 • (5%) Light Blue, Light Red, ***or*** Light Green Colors • (30%) Jewels 55

putrid sacrificer [9] *see devout follower [9]*

rogue bleeder [13] *see aged bleeder [13]*

rotting tombraider [9] *see devout follower [9]*

sacrificed slave [10] (72%) Essence of the Anguished Soul • (18%) Spirit Orb of the Wretched • (90%) Jewels 43 • (2%) Jewels 08 • (4%) APOA: Cracked Leather, Worn Studded, Aged Mithrian Cloth ***or*** of the Forlorn • (4%) <Sepulchral Secrets> • (1.7%) <Bone Up On Your Loot> • (0.5%) <Of a Sylvan Glade>

spiteful wraith [10] *see sacrificed slave [10]*

suffering apparition [12] *see doomed minion [12]*

tortured soul [9] (64%) Essence of the Anguished Soul • (16%) Spirit Orb of the Wretched • (80%) Jewels 43 • (2%) Jewels 08 • (4%) APOA: Cracked Leather, Worn Studded, Aged Mithrian Cloth ***or*** of the Forlorn • (4%) <Sepulchral Secrets> • (1.7%) <Bone Up On Your Loot> • (0.5%) <Of a Sylvan Glade>

undead builder [9] *see tortured soul [9]*

undead guardsman [9] *see tortured soul [9]*

undead poacher [9] *see tortured soul [9]*

unfortunate pragmatic [9] *see devout follower [9]*

Virilis [15] (35%) Vial of Embalming Fluid • (26%) Ground Bone and Onyx Dust • (17%) Mortar and Pestle • (4.3%) Detailed Carved Bone Brooch • (85%) Jewels 55 • (1.5%) APOA: Ancient Mithrian Cloth, Musty Leather, Preserved Studded ***or*** of the Forlorn • (1.5%) <Vaulted Weaponry> • (5%) Light Blue, Light Green ***or*** Light Red Colors • (2%) Jewels 01 • (1.5%) <It's Golden> • (0.5%) <Grave Goods>

Key. [X] = level(s) • (X%) = chance to get item (if a list, just one) • (X% each) = chance for *each* item • hi-lo = most to least likely • APOA = a piece of armor • (x2) = item can drop twice

Hibernia Merchants

LOCATION KEYS

(A.Out.)	Albion Outpost	**(D.Ail.)**	Dun Ailinne	**(Dr.C.)**	Druim Cain	**(mBeo.)**	Tir na mBeo
(Al.B.)	Alainn Bin	**(D.Bol.)**	Dun Bolg	**(Dr.L.)**	Druim Ligen	**(SEBr.)**	Shannon Estuary Bridge
(Arda.)	Ardagh	**(D.Cri.)**	Dun Crimthainn	**(FuC.)**	Fuath Camp	**(Sio.)**	Siopa
(Arde.)	Ardee	**(D.Cru.)**	Dun Cruachan	**(How.)**	Howth	**(SMc.)**	Camp
(Bas.)	Basar	**(D.nG.)**	Dun na nGed	**(I.Car.)**	Innis Carthaig	**(SMc.)**	Silvermine Mtn. Camp
(Cail.)	Caille	**(D.Sca.)**	Don Scathaig	**(M.M.)**	Mag Mell	**(T.Urp.)**	Tir Urphost
(Cean.)	Ceannai	**(Dain.)**	Daingean	**(M.Out.)**	Midgard Outpost	**(Tir.N.)**	Tir na Nog
(Cnl.)	Connla	**(DdB.)**	Dun da Behnn	**(Mard.)**	Mardagh	**Palace**	Palace

Armor

Amber Reimbursed
(Arde.) Caoimhin
(Tir.N.) Banyell
(Tir.N.) Taleai

Brea leather
(Arde.) Fianait
(Cnl.) Erskine
(M.M.) Kylirean
(Tir.N.) Ermid

Cailiocht reinforced
(Al.B.) Cragen
(Arda.) Roise
(How.) Twm
(I.Car.) Mariota
(Mard.) Akira
(Tir.N.) Nolan

Carbide scale
(Tir.N.) Keya

Cloak
(Arda.) Moesen
(I.Car.) Feoras
(M.M.) Oistin
(Sio.) Murchadh
(Tir.N.) Conary

Constaic leather
(Bas.) Neb
(SMc.) Elder Finian
(How.) Kenna
(Mard.) Brody
(Sio.) Caron
(Tir.N.) Vaughn

Cruaigh leather
(Al.B.) Dympna
(Bas.) Arzhela
(SMc.) Aeveen
(I.Car.) Gorawen
(Mard.) Ebril
(Tir.N.) Gemma
(Tir.N.) Tomas

Cruanach scale
(Al.B.) Finghin
(How.) Iain
(I.Car.) Kian
(mBeo.) Una
(Tir.N.) Laurence
(T.Urp.) Mosby

Daingean scale
(Bas.) Cristin
(Cean.) Unarla
(I.Car.) Talriese
(mBeo.) Teleri
(Tir.N.) Maxen

Embossed leather
(Tir.N.) Sharon

Nadurtha reinforced
(Arde.) Evan
(Bas.) Anna
(How.) Bevin
(mBeo.) Boyd
(Tir.N.) Renny
(T.Urp.) Tavie

Osnadurtha scale
(Arda.) Noreen
(Cean.) Vivienne
(Cnl.) Colm
(Sio.) Devin
(mBeo.) Aidaila
(Tir.N.) Hywela
(Tir.N.) Tristan

Robes
(Sio.) Raghnall
(Arda.) Brisen
(Arde.) Ailfrid
(SMc.) Elder Brona
(Cnl.) Sorcha
(I.Car.) Slaine
(M.M.) Eluned
(mBeo.) Kaenia
(Tir.N.) Sissy

Sylvan woven
(FuC.) Ciara the Dark
(Tir.N.) Lerena

Tacuil reinforced
(Bas.) Cubert
(How.) Kevain
(Mard.) Ardal
(Tir.N.) Kralla

Woven
(Arde.) Qunilan
(Cail.) Lysagh
(Cnl.) Ronan
(M.M.) Anice
(mBeo.) Duer
(mBeo.) Elith
(Tir.N.) Aulif
(Tir.N.) Eachann
(Tir.N.) Kado
(Tir.N.) Kinnat

Weapon

Arrows
(Al.B.) Liam
(Arda.) Celder
(Bas.) Tara
Camp Lorcan
(Cnl.) Edana
(D.Sca.) Aibfathane
(Dr.L.) Llalla
(DdB.) Iionadhbh
(How.) Blayne
(I.Car.) Deirdre
(M.M.) Aillig
(Mard.) Calder
Palace Lila
(Tir.N.) Connor
(Tir.N.) Kelsi
(Tir.N.) Seren

Blade
(Arda.) Ysbail
(Arde.) Garnock
Camp Onora
(Cnl.) Eira
(How.) Ainbe
(I.Car.) Asthore
(M.M.) Wony
(Mard.) Dirmyg
(Sio.) Broc
(Tir.N.) Lulach
(Tir.N.) Seva

Blunt
(Arda.) Nyle
(Arde.) Aideen
(Bas.) Deryn
(Cnl.) Alun
(Mard.) Eimhin
(Sio.) Alar
(Tir.N.) Franseza

Bows
(Al.B.) Maureen
(Arda.) Rhodry
(Arde.) Rhona
(Bas.) Zinna
(Cnl.) Kiara
(M.M.) Mannix
(Tir.N.) Briana
(Tir.N.) Isibael
(Tir.N.) Kenzia
(T.Urp.) Daracha

Carbide
(FuC.) Cinaed the Pure
(Tir.N.) Deverry

Celtic spear
(Arda.) Iaine
(Arde.) Eleri
(Cean.) Izold
(Cnl.) Marus
(How.) Cait
(Mard.) Mearchian
(Tir.N.) Jiskarr de'Mordan
(Tir.N.) Romney

Large
(Al.B.) Alaiina
(Cnl.) Erwana
(How.) Ffion
(I.Car.) Drummond
(Mard.) Thady
(mBeo.) Achaius
(Tir.N.) Drumnail
(Tir.N.) Ffiara
(T.Urp.) Callough

Piercing
(Al.B.) Helori
(Arde.) Mahon
(Bas.) Briac
(M.M.) Lachlan
(Cean.) Yann
(How.) Gaenor
(Tir.N.) Muirne

Staff
(Arde.) Ierna
(Arda.) Seana
(Cean.) Fallon
(Cnl.) Peadar
(How.) Anra
(I.Car.) Barra
(M.M.) Sian
(Mard.) Muadhnait
(mBeo.) Anrai
(Tir.N.) Adrai
(Tir.N.) Ewen

Shields

(Cean.) Wynda
(Cnl.) Gavina
(Dain.) Slevin
(How.) Blaez
(M.M.) Cafell
(Sio.) Morag
(Tir.N.) Cleit
(T.Urp.) Yvon

Focus Items

Eldritch staff
(Al.B.) Iama
(Arda.) Brenna
(Arde.) Creirwy
(Cail.) Keir
(Cnl.) Glyn
(I.Car.) Glennard
(mBeo.) Lavena
(Tir.N.) Kedric

Enchanter staff
(Al.B.) Aisling
(Arda.) Illaliel
(Arda.) Torlan
(Arde.) Daron
(Cail.) Brynn
(Cnl.) Bryanna
(I.Car.) Crayg
(Sio.) Emhyr
(mBeo.) Liadan
(Tir.N.) Brianna

Mentalist staff
(Arde.) Naomhan
(Cail.) Ariana
(Cnl.) Edmyg
(I.Car.) Amynda
(M.M.) Sedric
(Tir.N.) Aghna

Other Goods

Bard instruments
(Arda.) Della
(Cnl.) Edernola
(How.) Irksa
(Mard.) Edsoner
(mBeo.) Cian
(Tir.N.) Fingal
(Tir.N.) Rhosyn

Cloth dye
(Arda.) Mabli
(Arda.) Reeni
(Tir.N.) Blanche
(Tir.N.) Cinnie
(Tir.N.) Dierdra
(Tir.N.) Madarl
(Tir.N.) Nealcail

Enamel dye
(Mard.) Dilith
(mBeo.) Rhian
(Tir.N.) Cristolia
(Tir.N.) Kirsta

Expensive trade skill items
(Bas.) Erech
(M.M.) Jahan

Feathers
(I.Car.) Trahern
(Tir.N.) Brigacos
(Tir.N.) Izall

Fletching/tailoring supplies
(D.Cru.) Svenrir

Leather dye
(How.) Dyvyr
(How.) Tyree
(Tir.N.) Jeanna
(Tir.N.) Krianna

Metal
(I.Car.) Syvwlch
(Tir.N.) Aurnia
(Tir.N.) Baran

Metalworking equipment
(D.Cru.) Haelrach
(I.Car.) Yealcha

Poison (1)
(Arde.) Lexie
(Cnl.) Kinney
(D.Sca.) Lotheam
(D.Ail.) Downerit
(D.Cri.) Onalelin
(D.nG.) Kedalil
(D.nG.) Snarf
(How.) Kalla
(Tir.N.) Deante
(Tir.N.) Roibyn

Poison (2)
(Al.B.) Lirla
(Cean.) Dorran
(Dr.L.) Riber
(D.Ail.) Cadalennon
(D.Bol.) Halenyth
(D.Bol.) Iiono
(D.Cri.) Bearidhella
(DdB.) Peap
(I.Car.) Sarena
(mBeo.) Borlai
(Tir.N.) Malior
(Tir.N.) Nona

Sewing (1)
(Arde.) Arshan
(Tir.N.) Cathal
(Tir.N.) Darcy
(Tir.N.) Saffa

Sewing skill supplies
(I.Car.) Whiltierna

Siegecraft items
(A.Out.) Katarin
(Dr.L.) Renwisk
(Dr.C.) Sulvan
(D.Cru.) Bradford
(D.Cru.) Ellyoron
(D.Cru.) Gundor
(M.Out.) Ursula

Smith/tailoring supplies
(D.Cru.) Igor

Smithing tradeskill items
(Tir.N.) Morolt

Tailoring supplies
(D.Cru.) Aenris
(I.Car.) Amhlaoibh
(I.Car.) Macharan
(Tir.N.) Darova
(Tir.N.) Geryn

Tradeskill Items
(D.Cru.) Chanirasha

Vault
(Dain.) Ghearic Chauclon
(Dr.L.) Yralun Trallae
(I.Car.) Blanchefleur
(Tir.N.) Bhreagar Hylvian

Wood skill supplies
(I.Car.) Accalon
(Tir.N.) Caley
(Tir.N.) Cedric

Wood, Metal, Leather
(D.Cru.) Allun
(D.Cru.) Willem

Services

Bounty
(Tir.N.) Aghaistin
(Tir.N.) Ailson
(Tir.N.) Antaine
(Tir.N.) Grainne
(Tir.N.) Kiley

Enchanter
(Arda.) Iola
(Arde.) Eiral
(Cail.) Ainrebh
(Cnl.) Eli
(I.Car.) Kern
(M.M.) Dera
(mBeo.) Dicra
(mBeo.) Tangi
(Tir.N.) Caolan
(Tir.N.) Sadhbh
(T.Urp.) Cleary

Guild Emblemeer
(Tir.N.) Ffhionbarr

Guild Registrar
(Tir.N.) Filidh Fadywn

Healer
(Al.B.) Ceri
(Arda.) Fyrsil
(Arde.) Llyn
(Cean.) Kyle
(Cnl.) Keagan
(How.) Gralon
(I.Car.) Blyanche
(M.M.) Epona
(Mard.) Beli
(Sio.) Kerwin
(mBeo.) Ionhar
(Tir.N.) Vaddon
(Tir.N.) Waljan

Name Registrar
(Tir.N.) Filidh Filiara

Smith
(Al.B.) Dalladva
(Arde.) Criostoir
(Cnl.) Sarff
(How.) Alwyn
(I.Car.) Siobhan
(M.M.) Ilisa
(Mard.) Grizel
(mBeo.) Lainie
(Tir.N.) Banon
(Tir.N.) Kiam

Stable
(Arda.) Edricar Stable
(Arde.) Freagus
(Cnl.) Aelerogh
(Dr.L.) Ullios
(Dr.C.) Chuchear
(How.) Pheuloc
(I.Car.) Breachus
(M.M.) Rumdor
(mBeo.) Truichon
(T.Urp.) Luergor

Trainer

Armorsmith Master
(Tir.N.) Dunstan
(Tir.N.) Tegvan

Bard
(Cnl.) Dempsey
(Dr.C.) Kiernan
(How.) Maille
(Tir.N.) Selia

Blademaster
(Arda.) Ea
(Cnl.) Allistar
(Dr.C.) Meriel
(Tir.N.) Luighseach

Champion
(Arda.) Siodhachan
(Cnl.) Cordelia
(Dr.C.) Echlin
(Tir.N.) Lasairiona

Druid
(Dain.) Torrance
(Dr.C.) Erli
(How.) Bidelia
(Tir.N.) Daray

Eldritch
(Arda.) Coman
(Cnl.) Nainsi
(Dr.C.) Ina
(Tir.N.) Aodh

Enchanter
(Arda.) Talaith
(Cnl.) Eyslk
(Dr.C.) Mhari
(Tir.N.) Anwar

Fletcher Master
(Tir.N.) Arziqua

Guardian
(Arde.) Flannery
(Cnl.) Ailill
(How.) Kaley
(M.M.) Meadghbh

Hero
(Cnl.) Searlas
(Dr.C.) Sheelah
(How.) Nevin
(Tir.N.) Riofach

Magician
(Arde.) Auliffe
(Cnl.) Ennis
(How.) Adair
(M.M.) Etain

Mentalist
(Arda.) Aindreas
(Cnl.) Treise
(Tir.N.) Ena
(Tir.N.) Lovernios

Naturalist
(Arde.) Caoimhe
(Cnl.) Benen
(How.) Daibheid
(M.M.) Breeda

Nightshade
(Arda.) Leachlainn
(Dain.) Rooney
(Dr.C.) Yseult
(Tir.N.) Blathnaid

Ranger
(Arda.) Teague
(Cnl.) Sile
(Dr.C.) Crimthan
(Tir.N.) Mavelle

Stalker
(Arde.) Daithi
(Cnl.) Bran
(How.) Damhnait
(M.M.) Ula

Tailor Master
(Tir.N.) Armin

Warden
(Arda.) Uilliam
(SEBr.) Bebhinn
(Dr.C.) Vevina
(Tir.N.) Labhras

Weaponsmith Master
(Tir.N.) Hendrika

Bog of Cullen

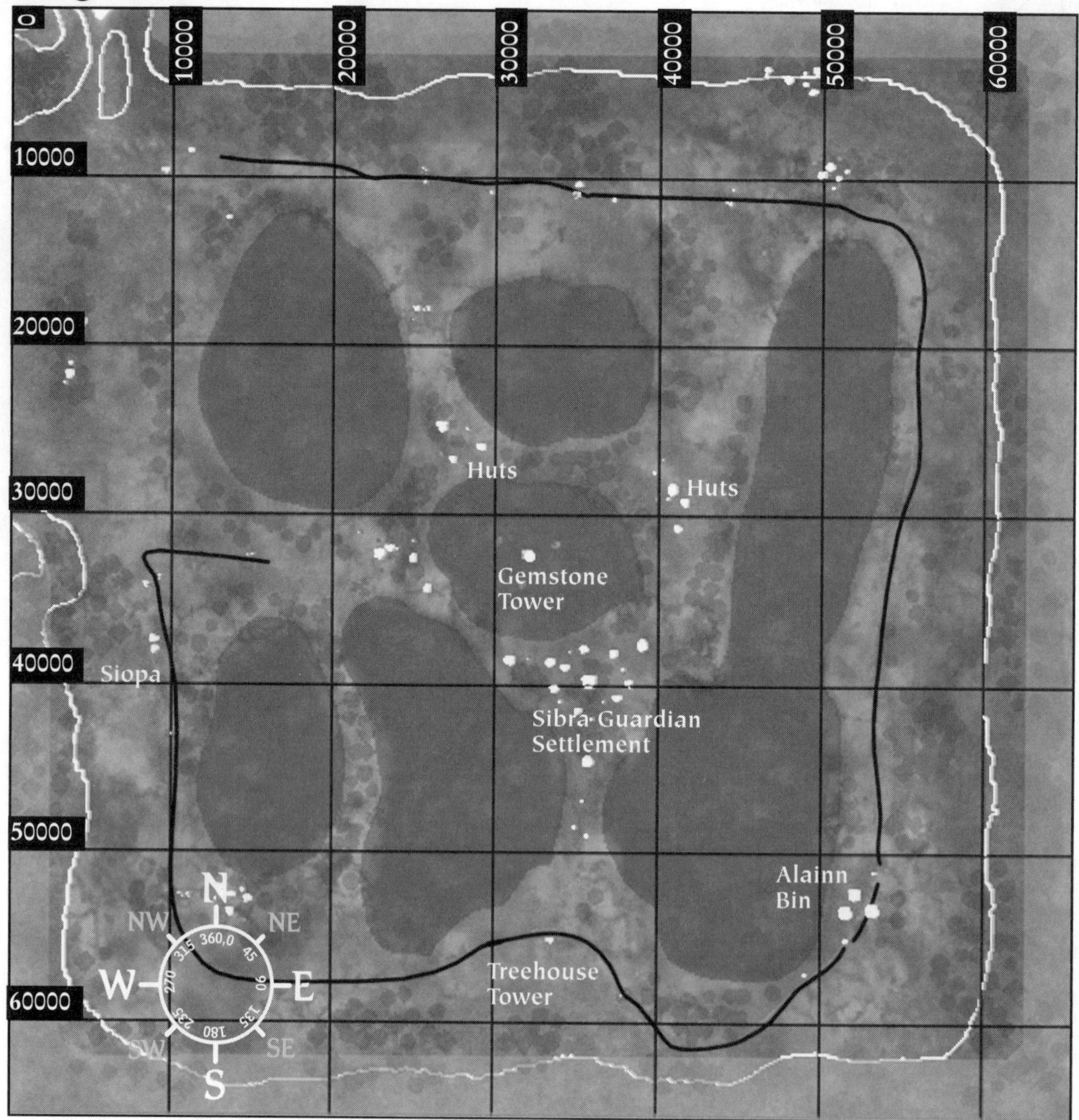

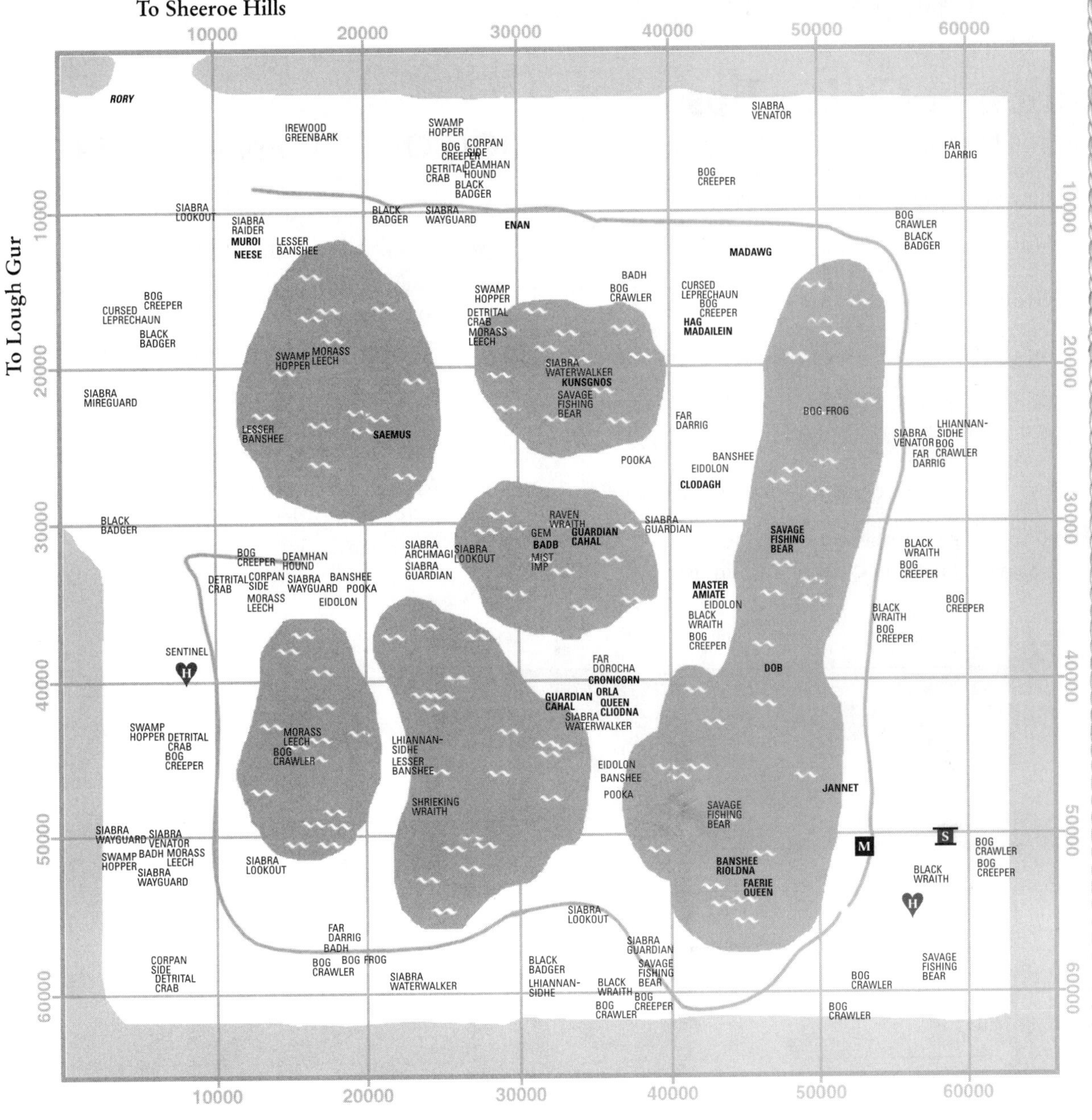

Lower-level monsters not shown on map:

Creature	Lvl	Location
alp luachra	30	NW,WC
alp luachra	31	NW,WC
amadan touched	30	NW,WC
amadan touched	31	NW,WC
amadan touched	34	NC,WC

Creature	Lvl	Location
aughisky	32	NW
aughisky	33	NW
black badger	36	NW,WC
bog worm	30	NW,NC,WC,EC,SW,SC,SE

Creature	Lvl	Location
fog wraith	30	NW,WC
irewood sapling	21	NW,NC
irewood sapling	22	NW,NC
merman	36	NW,WC
siabra seeker	30	NW

Creature	Lvl	Location
siabra seeker	31	NW
wiggle worm	0	NC,NE,WC,EC,SW,SC,SE

Bog of Cullen Tips

Solo Friendly?

This is *the* zone Rangers end up going to once they hit 40! The Irewood Greenbarks stay through day and night here (just past the Sheeroe Hills entrance). Not only that, you have lesser banshees and Siabra to pick off as well.

Group Friendly?

There are bears galore here for groups. Also getting into the Siabra cities and the wayguard areas can make for excellent grouping. Quite often the Siabra BAF (Bring a Friend), so the group bonus is nice as well.

Loot make-up?

I seem to be collecting a *lot* of caster-specific armor, as well as a lot of staffs. The Siabra also drop some nice Stalker type items.

- Steve "Larian LeQuella" Lundquist

BOG OF CULLEN HUNTING

21-24 Look for Irewood Saplings outside of Ceannai and use fire-based attacks.

23-25 Hunt Mermans during these levels. They're vulnerable to cold-based attacks, so concentrate on those.

41-45 Scour the area for Greenbarks — there are plenty of them here.

49-50 This is a good, though remote, site to find Far Darrigs.

46-50 Around Alainn Binn, you can find plenty of Black Wraiths, Banshees and Guardians to keep you occupied.

Loot

alp luachra [30/31] (25/30%) Alp Luachra Hand (x2) • (25/20%) Alp Luachra Eye • (8/10%) Alp Luachra Head

amadan touched [29-30/31-32/33-34] (1.5%) Ring of the Amadan ***or*** Ring of Undead Might • (40/40/20%) Worn Carnielian Studded Belt • (8/12/20%) Forgotten Silver Jasper Locket • (80% each) Well Crafted Lantern, Flint • (60%) Copper Amethyst Bracelet • (10/20/40%) Small Silver Laden Box • (0.3%) <The Four Elements>

aughisky [32-33] (85%) Patch of Aughisky Hide • (70%) Pristine Aughisky Hide • (45%) Aughisky Mane

Badb [62] (65%) Ghostly Banshee Hair • (45%) Wailing Essence Gem • (35%) Banshee Essence • (1.5%) Obsidian Kite, Tower ***or*** Round Shield • (1.5%) Glistening Broadsword ***or*** Great Sword • (20%) Jewels 64 • (1.5%) <Rogue Pendants (Mid)>

badh [46-47] (60%) Ghostly Banshee Hair • (40%) Wailing Essence Gem • (10%) Banshee Essence • (15%) Jewels 64 • (1.5%) <Rogue Pendants (Mid)>

banshee [55-56/58-59] (60/65%) Ghostly Banshee Hair • (40/45%) Wailing Essence Gem • (20/25%) Banshee Essence • (20%) Jewels 64 • (1.3%) Obsidian Kite, Tower ***or*** Round Shield • (1.5%) <Rogue Pendants (Mid)> • (1.3%) Glistening Broadsword ***or*** Great Sword • (1.3%) APOA: Manifested Terror

Banshee Rioldna [56] (20%) Howling Stone of the Banshee • (80% each) Manifested Terror Cloth, Banshee Essence • (20% each) Kornerupine, Precious Jasper • (1.5%) APOA: Manifested Terror

black badger [36-37/39-40] (75%) Black Badger Tooth (x2) • (65/70%) Black Badger Claw (x2) • (35/75%) Black Badger Meat (x2) • (15/20%) Pristine Black Badger Pelt • (1.5%) Badger Pelt Shield/Helm ***or*** Cloak

black wraith [52-55] (30% each) Wraith Essence, Shadowy Gem • (45%) Etheric Spirit Shackles • (25%) Jewels 64 • (1.6%) <Arcane Artifacts> • (1.6%) Phantom Gem

bog crawler [46-47] (44%) Bog Crawler Leg Tip (x2) • (35%) Bog Crawler Chiten Shell • (44%) Bog Crawler Leg (x2) • (40%) Bog Crawler Mandible

bog creeper [42-43/44] (40/45%) Bog Creeper Leg (x2) • (30/37% each) Bog Creeper Carapace, Poison Sac • (60%) Bog Creeper Eye (x2) • (40/45%) Bog Creeper Leg Tip (x2)

bog frog [47-48/49-50] (20/25%) Bog Frog Skin • (82/90%) Bog Frog Leg (x2)

bog worm [30] (80%) Bog Worm Husk • (45%) Bog Worm Husk • (45%) Bog Worm Setae (x2)

Clodagh [38] (no loot)

corpan side [40/41] (80% each) Changeling Hair, Changeling Skin • (20/30% each) Jasper Beetle Chitin Necklace, Changeling Blood • (1.5%) Giant Gutter ***or*** Spine Splitter

cronicorn [68] (no loot)

cursed leprechaun [63] (no loot)

deamhan hound [40-41/42] (68/72%) Deamhan Hound Tooth (x2) • (72/65%) Deamhan Hound Claw • (40/55%) Deamhan Hound Claw • (20%) Deamhan Hound Pelt • (1.2%) Infernal Edge, Flute ***or*** Cloak/Infernal Bane ***or*** Bracer

detrital crab [42] (25% each) Chunk of Clay (x2), Glob of Mud (x2) • (40%) Detrital Crab Claw (x2) • (49%) Detrital Crab Meat (x2)

Dob [55] (35%) Savage Fishing Bear Skin (x2) • (20%) Pristine Bear Skin • (45%) Savage Fishing Bear Tooth (x2) • (65%) Savage Fishing Bear Meat (x2) • (1.7%) Bear Claw Talisman

eidolon [58/60/62/64] (40/40/40/50%) Etheric Spirit Shackles • (20/25/25/25%) Pendant of Calling • (30/30/32/35%) Shadowy Gem • (1.6%) APOA: Dusk Dweller • (25%) Jewels 64 • (1.6%) Glistening War Spear ***or*** Stiletto

Enan [43] (no loot)

Faerie Queen [60] (no loot)

far darrig [46-47/48] (80%) Briar Horror Mask • (40/60%) Thorny Green Sapphire Bracelet • (1.4%) APOA: Mischievious Greenbriar • (1.4%) Wicked Thorn

far dorocha [62] (no loot)

fishing bear [21] (40%) Fishing Bear Skin • (65%) Bear Tooth (x2) • (65%) Bear Meat (x2)

fog wraith [30] (80%) Dark Heart of the Vindictive Spirit • (20%) Fog Wraith Essence • (1.5%) Spirit Searer • (5%) Cat's Eye Tourmaline • (0.3%) <De'velyn's Delights>

Guardian Cahal [66] (44%) Vial of Elvish Essence • (35% each) Ruby Dust, Diamond Dust • (1.5%) APOA: Ensorcelled Explorer • (1.5%) Noble Lord, Royal Guardian ***or*** Noble Overlord Pendant • (1.5%) Soul Reaver ***or*** Empyreal Golden Reaver • (28%) Jewels 64

irewood greenbark [40] (80%) Irewood Greenbark Branch (x2) • (30%) Glowing Irewood Greenbark Sap • (20%) Bundle of Greenbark Branches • (1.4%) APOA: Hardened Cloth • (1.4%) Bardic Wonder, ***or*** Staff of Thought, Destruction ***or*** Enchantments (All Petrified)

irewood sapling [21-22] (75%) Ire Wood Sapling Branch (x2) • (55%) Bundle of Sapling Branches (x2) • (5%) Pitted Glowing Ng Kit Ire Wood Sapling Staff

Kunsgnos [52] (25%) Vial of Elvish Essence • (21%) Ruby Dust • (12%) Diamond Dust • (27%) Jewels 17 • (17%) Jewels 64 • (1.7%) Supernal ***or*** Paradisiacal Cloak

lesser banshee [36-37] (40%) Lesser Banshee Essence • (35%) Ghostly Banshee Hair • (5%) Wailing Essence Gem • (15%) Jewels 62 • (1.5%) APOA: Darkened Spirit • (1.5%) Staff of Ominous Void, Staff of Ominous Enchantment, ***or*** Staff of the Ominous Mind • (1.5%) Alluvion Sword ***or*** Great Sword, Sinister Alluvion Falcata, ***or*** Rubigo Kite Shield

lhiannan-sidhe [49] (80%) Briar Horror Mask • (60%) Thorny Green Sapphire Bracelet • (1.4%) APOA: Mischievious Greenbriar • (1.4%) Wicked Thorn

lunger [1] (no loot)

Master Amiate [66] (50%) Etheric Spirit Shackles • (25%) Pendant of Calling • (35%) Shadowy Gem • (1.6%) APOA: Dusk Dweller • (25%) Jewels 64 • (1.6%) Glistening War Spear ***or*** Stiletto

merman [36] (75% each) Merman Scales, Green Tourmaline • (50%) Orb of Swirling Sea Water • (5%) Red Spinel • (1.4%) APOA: Algae Covered Coral ***or*** Sidhe Spine Barbed Spear • (1.4%) Braided Kelp Belt, Bracelet ***or*** Necklace, ***or*** Coral Ring

morass leech [41-43] (58%) Worn Leech Skin (x2) • (15%) Pristine Leech Skin (x2) [43] • (25%) Pristine Leech Skin [41-42] • (1.7%) Leech Husk Bracer

Muroi [40] (32%) Vial of Elven Essence • (22%) Emerald Dust • (32%) Sapphire Dust • (22%) Jewels 17 • (1.5%) General ***or*** Noble Lord Pendant • (1.5%) APOA: Turbid Waters • (1.5%) <Bogman's Bundle>

Neese [40] (32%) Vial of Elven Essence • (22%) Emerald Dust • (32%) Sapphire Dust • (22%) Jewels 17 • (1.5%) General ***or*** Noble Lord Pendant • (1.5%) APOA: Turbid Waters • (1.5%) <Bogman's Bundle>

pooka [57] (60%) Shape Changer's Hide • (80% each) Shape Changer's Skull, Tooth • (1.5%) <No Such Thing as the Bogeyman>

Queen Cliodna [70] (8% each) Moonstruck Mire Robe, Jerkin, Vest, Hauberk

raven wraith [58/60/62/64] (25%) Wraith Essence • (40/40/41/42%) Etheric Spirit Shackles • (25%) Shadowy Gem • (20%) Shiftless Soul Anchor • (20/22/23/24%) Jewels 64 • (1.5%) APOA: Lucent Spirit • (1.5%) Glistening Shillelagh ***or*** Spiked Club • (1.5%) Noble Lord, Royal Guardian ***or*** Noble Overlord Pendant

savage fishing bear [52-53] (40%) Savage Fishing Bear Skin • (25%) Pristine Bear Skin • (45%) Savage Fishing Bear Tooth • (1.7%) Bear Claw Talisman • (40%) Savage Fishing Bear Tooth • (60%) Savage Fishing Bear Meat (x2)

siabra archmagi [59/61/63/65] (41/42/43%) Vial of Elvish Essence • (31/32/33% each) Ruby Dust, Diamond Dust • (1.5%) <Magi Pendants (Higher)> • (1.5%) APOA: Manifested Terror • (1.5%) <Arch-Mage Artifacts> • (26%) Jewels 64

siabra guardian [56/58/60,62/64] (40/41/42/43%) Vial of Elvish Essence • (30/31/32/33% each) Ruby Dust, Diamond Dust • (1.5%) APOA: Ensorcelled Explorer • (1.5%) Noble Lord, Royal Guardian ***or*** Noble Overlord Pendant • (1.5%) Soul Reaver ***or*** Empyreal Golden Reaver • (25%) Jewels 64

siabra lookout [47] (30% each) Vial of Elven Essence, Emerald Dust, Sapphire Dust • (20%) Jewels 64 • (1.5%) Siabrian Arcane Methods, Ring of Delightful Deception, Necklace of Combat, ***or*** Bracer of Zo'arkat • (1.5%) Ruby Death Bringer • (1.5%) Crimson Heart-Stoppers

siabra mireguard [38] (30%) Vial of Elven Essence • (20%) Emerald Dust • (30%) Sapphire Dust • (20%) Jewels 17 • (1.2%) General ***or*** Noble Lord Pendant • (1.2%) APOA: Turbid Waters • (1.2%) <Bogman's Bundle> • (1.2%) APOA: Cath, ***or*** Cath Drum

siabra raider [37/39] (30/40% each) Vial of Elven Essence, Sapphire Dust • (20%) Emerald Dust • (20%) Jewels 17 • (1.5%) <Rogue Pendants (Mid)> • (1.6%) Alluvion Rapier ***or*** Spear, Sinister Alluvion Stiletto, ***or*** Rubigo Heater Shield

siabra seeker [30] (30%) Tattered Scroll • (30%) Luminescent Orb • (30%) Orb of Viewing • (10%) Primrose Eye • (1.5%) Spectral Legs, Gloves, Arms ***or*** Boots, Thumper, ***or*** Slicer • (50%) Bolt of Soft Gossamer

siabra seeker [31] (35%) Primrose Eye • (35%) Siog Brandy • (35%) Topaz • (1.3%) Spectral Tunic, Helm ***or*** Shadow, ***or*** Bracer of Might • (1.3%) Smiter's Belt, Smiter, ***or*** Siog's Might • (50%) Bolt of Soft Gossamer • (1.3%) Cath Lute, Shield, Spear, Cloak ***or*** Charms

siabra venator [46-47/48] (25%) Vial of Elven Essence • (25/30% each) Emerald Dust, Sapphire Dust • (20/25%) Jewels 64 • (1.5%) General ***or*** Noble Lord Pendant • (1.5%) Ruby Death Bringer • (1.5%) APOA: Bog Strider • (1.5%) Crimson Heart-Stoppers

siabra waterwalker [49-50/52] (25%) Vial of Elvish Essence • (20/21%) Ruby Dust • (10/12%) Diamond Dust • (25/27%) Jewels 17 • (15/17%) Jewels 64 • (1.6%) Supernal ***or*** Paradisiacal Cloak • (1.6%) <Treasures of the Magi>

siabra wayguard [43-44] (25% each) Vial of Elven Essence, Sapphire Dust • (20%) Emerald Dust • (25%) Jewels 17 • (1.5%) <Rogue Pendants (Mid)> • (1.5%) APOA: Mire Walker's • (1.5%) Ruby Death Bringer • (1.5%) Crimson Heart-Stoppers

swamp hopper [43-44] (20%) Swamp Hopper Skin • (79%) Hopper Leg (x2)

wiggle worm [0] (80%) Worm Fishing Bait • (10%) Worm Fishing Bait

Cliffs of Moher

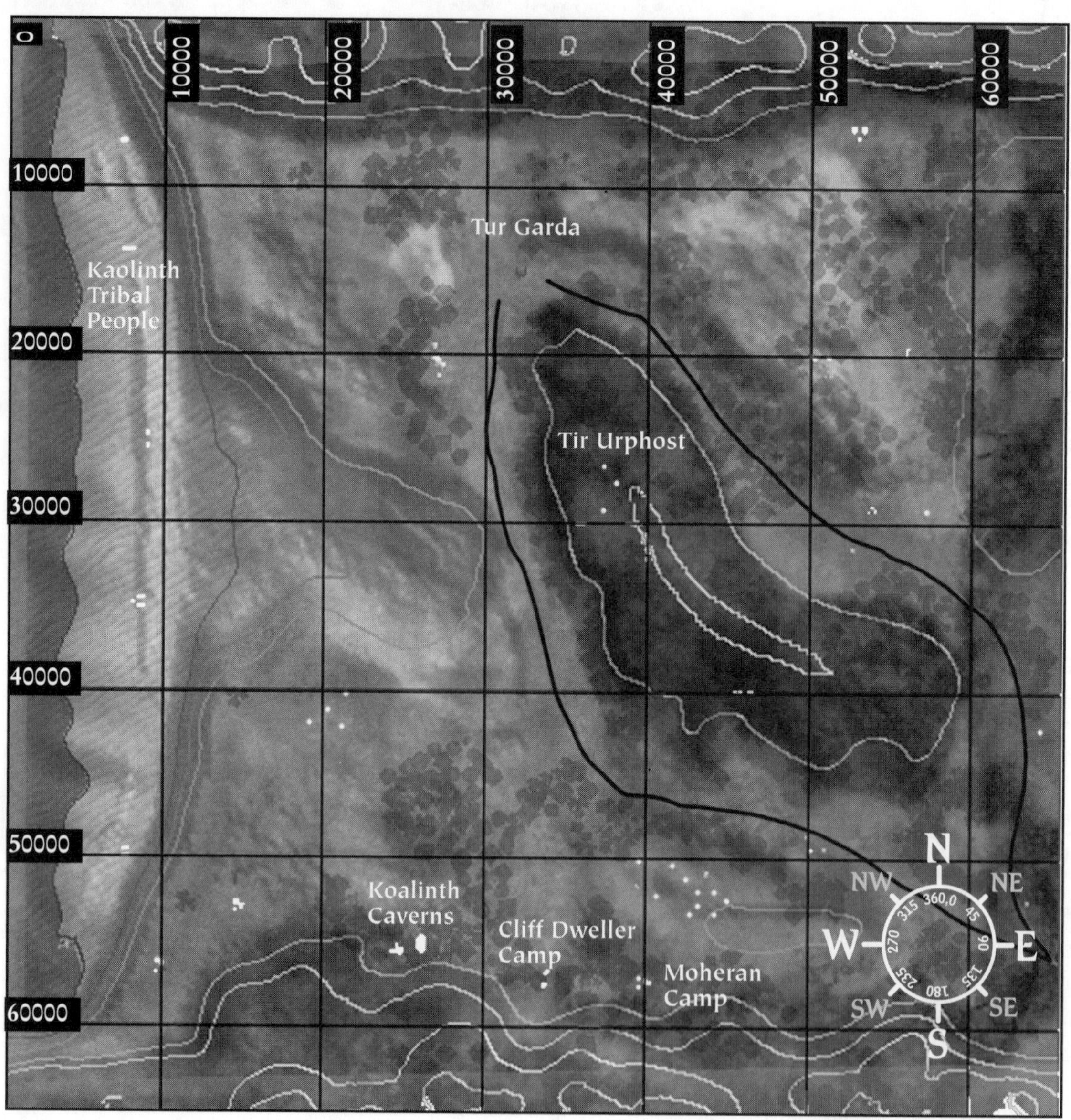

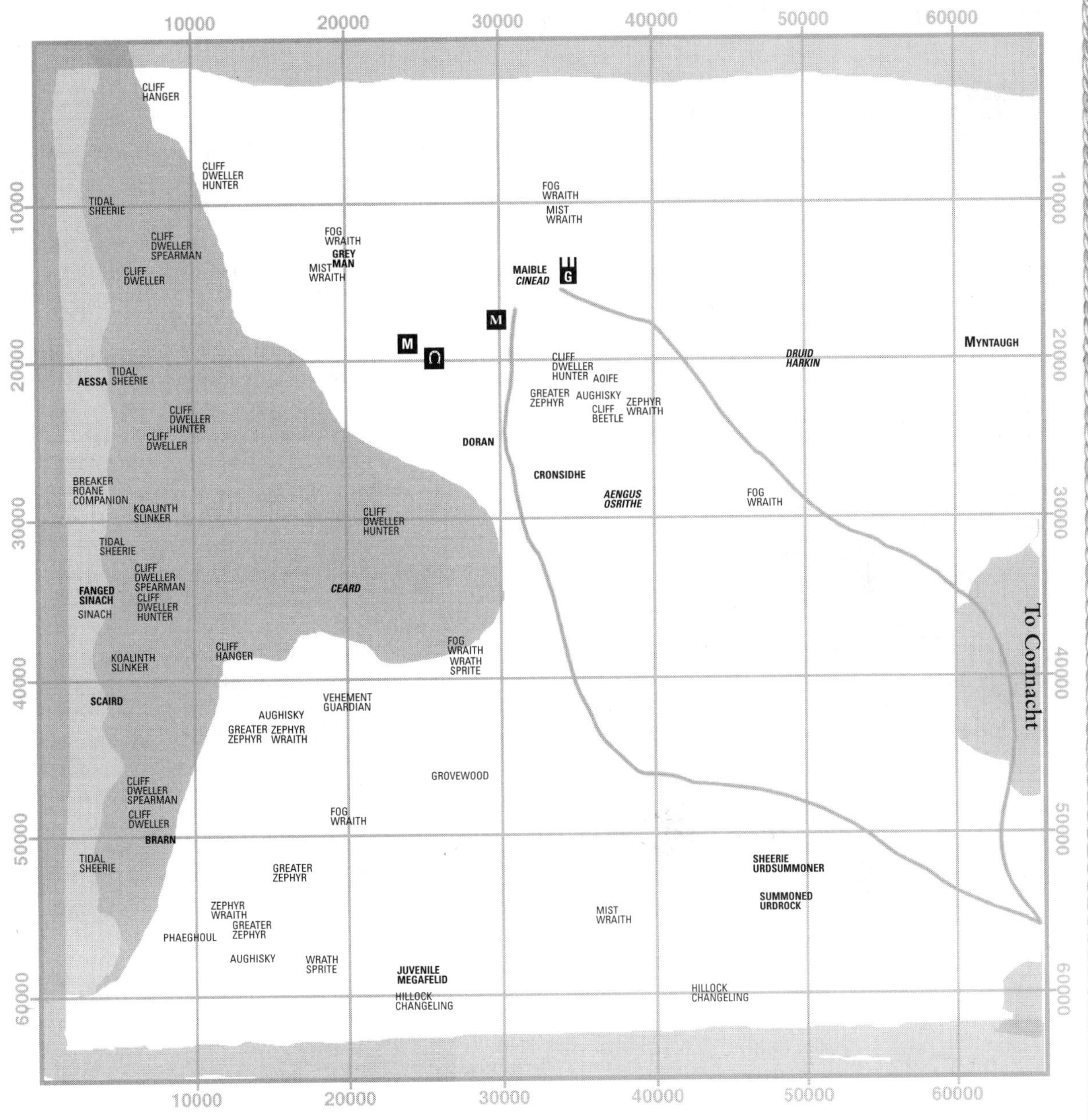

Lower-level monsters not shown on map:

Creature	Lvl	Location
bantam spectre	15	C,EC,SC,SE
bocan	15	NC,NE,C,EC,SC,SE
fetch	15	C,EC,SC,SE
fog phantom	21	NC,NE,EC
fog phantom	22	NC,NE,EC
fog phantom	23	NC,NE,EC
fury sprite	15	SE
fury sprite	16	SE
Gala	19	C,EC,SC,SE
gale	16	C,EC,SC,SE
gale	17	C,EC,SC,SE
gale	18	C,EC,SC,SE
ghoulie	20	NC,NE,EC
ghoulie	21	NC,NE,EC
ghoulie	22	NC,NE,EC
giant beetle	20	C,EC,SC,SE
giant beetle	21	C,EC,SC,SE
grass sheerie	15	SE
koalinth sentinel	18	SC
moheran beast	19	SC
moheran distorter	17	NE
moheran distorter	18	NE,C,EC,SC,SE
moheran distorter	19	NE,SC
rock sheerie	18	SC,SE
rock sheerie	19	SC,SE
vindictive bocan	20	NE
vindictive bocan	21	NE
vindictive bocan	22	NE

Cliffs of Moher Tips

Solo Friendly?

Mostly for folks with range! (This applies to all outdoor zones really, but especially this one since it's nice and wide open.) You can probably start to think of soloing here around level 28. Stay away from the Grovewoods. You can easily get the whole forest after you!

Group Friendly?

There are quite a few areas with camps for groups to take on. The lower-level monsters here for group hunting can start at level 25 or so, and there's plenty to keep a group hunting here until the early 40s.

Loot make-up?

Most of the items here are just sell-for-cash items. There is a nice level 25 or so sword (Spirit Searer) that drops here.

- Steve "Larian LeQuella" Lundquist

CLIFFS OF MOHER HUNTING

11-15 Between these two levels, you should be able to handle the Spectres, Grass Sheeries and Bocan that live in this area.

18-20 The cliff area is populated by Gales and other miscellaneous creatures. If you can use Stealth, that increases your chances for a good hunt.

19 - 21 Head north from Tir na Nog, then pick up the road traveling west. Seek out Spectres, Gales and Fetch for a ton of gold and experience.

21 - 23 The cliff area also hides Giant Beetles and some Siabra Distorters.

28 - 31 Mist wraiths wandering around in this area are a tough kill, but can be worth the effort.

31 Fog Wraiths also roam the zone, but are more difficult to find. For a rewarding hunt off the beaten path, load up on arrows, find a horse and ride from Ardagh to Tir Urphost. Head west from Tir Urphost to find them.

36 - 40 Concentrate on Grovewoods for a while, or go after them whenever you can't find anything else to hunt.

38-39 Finally, as you approach level 40, you're strong enough to take on the Cliff Dwellers. Several of their camps are scattered throughout this zone.

The Cliffs of Moher is a good traveling zone. If you start on the main path and follow it from the first tower north north-west to Tir Uphost you'll find steady variety of mobs. Instead of "camping" one area, you can move slowly along the path. This style of hunting will best suit a group hunting mobs in the level range of high teens to low twenties. While you can do the same solo, it is risky due to wandering aggressive/hostile mobs. If you attempt it solo, keep a watch out for all directions and have an escape plan. Gales are casters but with a bow (short or recurve) you can interrupt their casting enough to cause them to charge in for melee combat. Moheran Distorters are casters as well, but a bit more deadly because of insta-cast capabilities. Groups are recommended because like all Siabra, Moheran Distorters like to bring a friend along when out numbered. There are a few camps where the Moheran Distorters like to keep Morheran Beasts as pets. So again, be careful. As you advance in level you can move up to larger game. If your target hunting mob rangers in the high twenties to thirty, north-west of Tir Uphost you can find Mist Wraiths (27-28) and Fog Wraiths (28-30). You can group to hunt these but if you choose to solo hunt, watch your back for wanderers. You can keep coming back to the Cliffs as you level higher and higher. If your target hunting range includes mid-thirties to forty then you can find Cliff Dwellers and Grovewoods. Overall this is a well designed zone. Because there is only one entry — through Connacht — fewer players visit this zone. Thus you'll normally find less competition and higher camp bonuses.

– Beau "MacGyani" Stribling

Quest NPCs

Tir Urphorst Tower	
Cinead	The Anxious Healer (lvl 31)

Loot

Aengus Osrithe [29] (80%) Dark Heart of the Vindictive Spirit • (20%) Zeypher Wraith Essence • (1.5%) Zephyr Belt, Eluvium Belt, Crystalline Band of Wind, ***or*** Windy Crusher • (5%) Black Star Diopside • (0.3%) <The Four Elements>

Aoife [35] (70% each) Zephyr's Windy Essence, Expended Commanding Stone • (1.4%) Zephyr's Commanding Stone • (20%) Sphene • (5%) Cat's Eye Apatite • (0.3%) <The Four Elements> • (1.4%) APOA: Eluvium

aughisky [31-33] (85%) Patch of Aughisky Hide • (70%) Pristine Aughisky Hide • (45%) Aughisky Mane

bantam spectre [15] (1.5%) Spectral Shroud • (40%) Spectral Essence • (0.3%) <Muire's Riches 2>

bocan [15] (1% each piece) Tattered Shimmering Sapphire Tacuil • (80%) Chryoprase • (70%) Carnelian • (5%) Topaz • (0.3%) <Muire's Riches 2>

Brarn [40] (1.5%) APOA: Furtive Cavedweller • (10%) Golden Sunstone Necklace • (25%) Gold Lined Drinking Horn • (50%) Primitive Fire Opal Eyed Totem • (48%) Carved Granite Bracer (x2)

breaker roane companion [46-47] (1.4%) Selkie Skin • (1.4%) Topaz Studded Shell Flute • (5%) Water Opal Shell Bracelet • (45%) Threaded Silver Net • (85%) Jeweled Roane Choker

cliff beetle [31-33/34-35/36-37] (65%) Cliff Beetle Leg (x2) • (48/60/55%) Cliff Beetle Leg Tip (x2) • (15/25/40%) Cliff Beetle Mandible • (5/10/15%) Cliff Beetle Carapace

cliff dweller [36-38] (1.5%) APOA: Furtive Cavedweller • (5%) Golden Sunstone Necklace • (10%) Gold Lined Drinking Horn • (40%) Primitive Fire Opal Eyed Totem • (50%) Carved Granite Bracer (x2)

cliff dweller hunter [37-38] (1.5%) APOA: Furtive Cavedweller • (5%) Golden Sunstone Necklace • (20%) Gold Lined Drinking Horn • (40%) Primitive Fire Opal Eyed Totem • (50%) Carved Granite Bracer (x2)

cliff dweller spearman [38-39/40] (1.5%) Cliff Dweller Hammer, Sword, Skewer, Recurved Bow, Drum ***or*** Lute • (5/10%) Golden Sunstone Necklace • (25%) Gold Lined Drinking Horn • (50/55%) Primitive Fire Opal Eyed Totem • (56/58%) Carved Granite Bracer (x2)

cliff hanger [36-37/38-39] (60%) Cliff Hanger Leg (x2) • (50%) Cliff Hanger Leg Tip (x2) • (35/37%) Cliff Hanger Mandible • (8/15%) Cliff Hanger Carapace

cronsidhe [41] (60%) Giant Water Skin • (90%) Giant Hide Loin Cloth • (50%) Rotten Fanged Tooth • (1.4%) Cronsidhe Biter ***or*** Cronsidhe's Red Eye • (1.4%) Jewels 20

fetch [15] (15%) Fetch's Magical Skin • (80%) Bloodstone • (50%) Carnelian • (0.3%) <Muire's Riches 2>

fog phantom [21-22/23] (80%) Phantom Essence • (20/30%) Dark Heart of the Vindictive Spirit • (1.4% each) Phantom Arrows, Phantom Short Bow • (0.3%) <Muire's Riches 3> • (8/10%) Cracked Dark Heart

fog wraith [28-29/30] (80%) Dark Heart of the Vindictive Spirit • (10/20%) Fog Wraith Essence • (1.5%) Spirit Searer • (5%) Red Spinel/Cat's Eye Tourmaline • (0.3%) <De'velyn's Delights>

fury sprite [15/16] (40%) Pouch of Magic Dust • (35/40%) Jewels 38 • (0.3%) <Treasures of the Fey>/<Muire's Riches 2> • (1.5%) APOA: Riven Silk

Gala [19] (10%) Gale's Essence • (70% each) Bloodstone, Agate • (10%) Citrine • (0.3%) <Muire's Riches 2> • (1.5%) Mariner Ring

gale [16-17/18] (5/10%) Gale's Essence • (60/70%) Bloodstone • (60%) Carnelian [16-17] • (10%) Citrine [18] • (25/70%) Agate • (0.3%) <Muire's Riches 2> • (1.5%) Mariner Ring

ghoulie [20-21/22] (1.5%) Ghoulish Shackle • (80%) Ghoul Skin • (80%) Carnelian/Agate • (40%) Ghoul Skin • (20/30%) Azurite • (5% each) Forgotten Silk Coth, Citrine • (0.3%) <Muire's Riches 3>

giant beetle [20-21] (60%) Giant Beetle Leg (x2) • (40%) Giant Beetle Leg Tip (x2) • (18%) Giant Beetle Mandible (x2) • (5%) Giant Beetle Carapace

grass sheerie [15] (50%) Glimmering Clump of Grass • (25%) Pouch of Faerie Dust • (20%) Jewels 03 • (0.3%) <Treasures of the Fey> • (1.5%) Hardened Grass Bracer

greater zephyr [31-32/33] (70% each) Zephyr's Windy Essence, Expended Commanding Stone • (1.4%) Zephyr's Commanding Stone • (10%) Chrome Diopside [31-32] • (20%) Sphene [33] • (5%) Black Star Diopside/Cat's Eye Apatite • (0.3%) <The Four Elements> • (1.4%) APOA: Eluvium

Grey Man [31] (80%) Dark Heart of the Vindictive Spirit • (20%) Fog Wraith Essence • (1.5%) Spirit Searer • (5%) Cat's Eye Tourmaline • (0.3%) <De'velyn's Delights>

grovewood [38-40] (12%) Grovewood Bark

hillock changeling [35] (no loot)

horse [10] (75%) Horse Hair • (10%) Auburn Mane • (80%) Ruined Horse Skin • (35%) Horse Skin • (60%) Horse Hair

juvenile megafelid [35] (8%) Dangerous Tooth

koalinth sentinel [18] (8%) <Flecks O' Gold> • (8%) Jewels 56 • (1.5%) APOA: Abandoned Crustacean • (1.5%) <Wealth of an Empire> • (1.5%) <Fathoms Below>

koalinth slinker [34-35/36-37/38] (1.4%) APOA: Algae Covered Coral, ***or*** Sidhe Spine Barbed Spear • (1.4%) Sharkskin Cloak • (5/10/10%) Jeweled Merman Skull • (80% each) Sharkskin Bag, Sharktooth Necklace • (35/35/40%) Cat's Eye Apatite • (5%) Blue Spinel [36-37]/Green Sapphire [38]

mist wraith [27-28] (80%) Dark Heart of the Vindictive Spirit • (10%) Mist Wraith Essence • (1.5%) Wraith Necklace, Mist Necklace ***or*** Etheric Bludgeoner • (0.3%) <De'velyn's Delights>

moheran beast [19] (no loot)

moheran distorter [17-19] (80% each) Sulfur, Pixie Dust • (40%) Empty Crystal Vial • (20%) Luminescent Liquid • (10%) Alchemy Mixing Bowl [19] • (3%) Robes of the Arcane Order • (1.5%) <Magi Pendants> • (0.3%) <Muire's Riches 2>

Myntaugh [19] (80% each) Sulfur, Pixie Dust • (40%) Empty Crystal Vial • (20%) Luminescent Liquid • (10%) Alchemy Mixing Bowl • (3%) Robes of the Arcane Order • (1.5%) <Magi Pendants> • (0.3%) <Muire's Riches 2>

Orik [15] (50%) Glimmering Clump of Grass • (25%) Pouch of Faerie Dust • (20%) Jewels 03 • (0.3%) <Treasures of the Fey> • (1.5%) Hardened Grass Bracer

phaeghoul [37] (12%) Phaeghoul Red Hand

rock sheerie [18-19] (5% each) Smooth Sling Stones, Fine Unworked Stone • (90%) Unworked Stone • (1.5%) Rock Sherrie Bracer • (0.3%) <Muire's Riches 2>

Scaird [39] (70% each) Tidal Sheerie's Shimmering Hair, Gilded Star Fish Necklace • (5%) Fire Opal Shell Belt Buckle • (50%) Polished Sea Shell Box • (1.4%) Kelp Bracelet • (1.4%) APOA: Mariner • (12%) Sack of Grain

sheerie urdsummoner [26] (5% each) Smooth Sling Stones, Fine Unworked Stone • (90%) Unworked Stone • (1.5%) Rock Sherrie Bracer • (0.3%) <Muire's Riches 2>

sinach [49-50/51] (75/80%) Sinach Meat (x2) • (75/70%) Sinach Claw (x2) • (65/70%) Sinach Fang • (25/50%) Sinach Femur • (1.5%) Sinach's Great Tooth • (10%) Pristine Sinach Hide

summoned urdrock [25] (no loot)

tidal sheerie [35-36/37-38/39] (70% each) Tidal Sheerie's Shimmering Hair, Gilded Star Fish Necklace • (5%) Fire Opal Shell Belt Buckle • (20/30/50%) Polished Sea Shell Box • (1.4%) Kelp Bracelet • (1.4%) APOA: Mariner • (12%) Sack of Grain

vehement guardian [40-41] (12%) Vehement Gizzard

vindictive bocan [20-21/22] (1% each piece) Tattered Stone Cailiocht/Tattered Cailiocht • (80%) Agate/Topaz • (40%) Topaz/Pearl • (5%) Green Tourmaline/Fire Opal • (0.3%) <Muire's Riches 3>

wrath sprite [27-28] (80%) Bleached Leg Bone • (60%) Softly Glowing Orb • (50%) Red Spinel • (1.5%) Spritely Stiletto ***or*** Shield

zephyr wraith [29-30/31-32] (80%) Dark Heart of the Vindictive Spirit • (20/25%) Zeypher Wraith Essence • (1.5%) Zephyr Belt, Eluvium Belt, Crystalline Band of Wind, ***or*** Windy Crusher • (5%) Black Star Diopside/Red Spinel • (0.3%) <The Four Elements>

Connacht

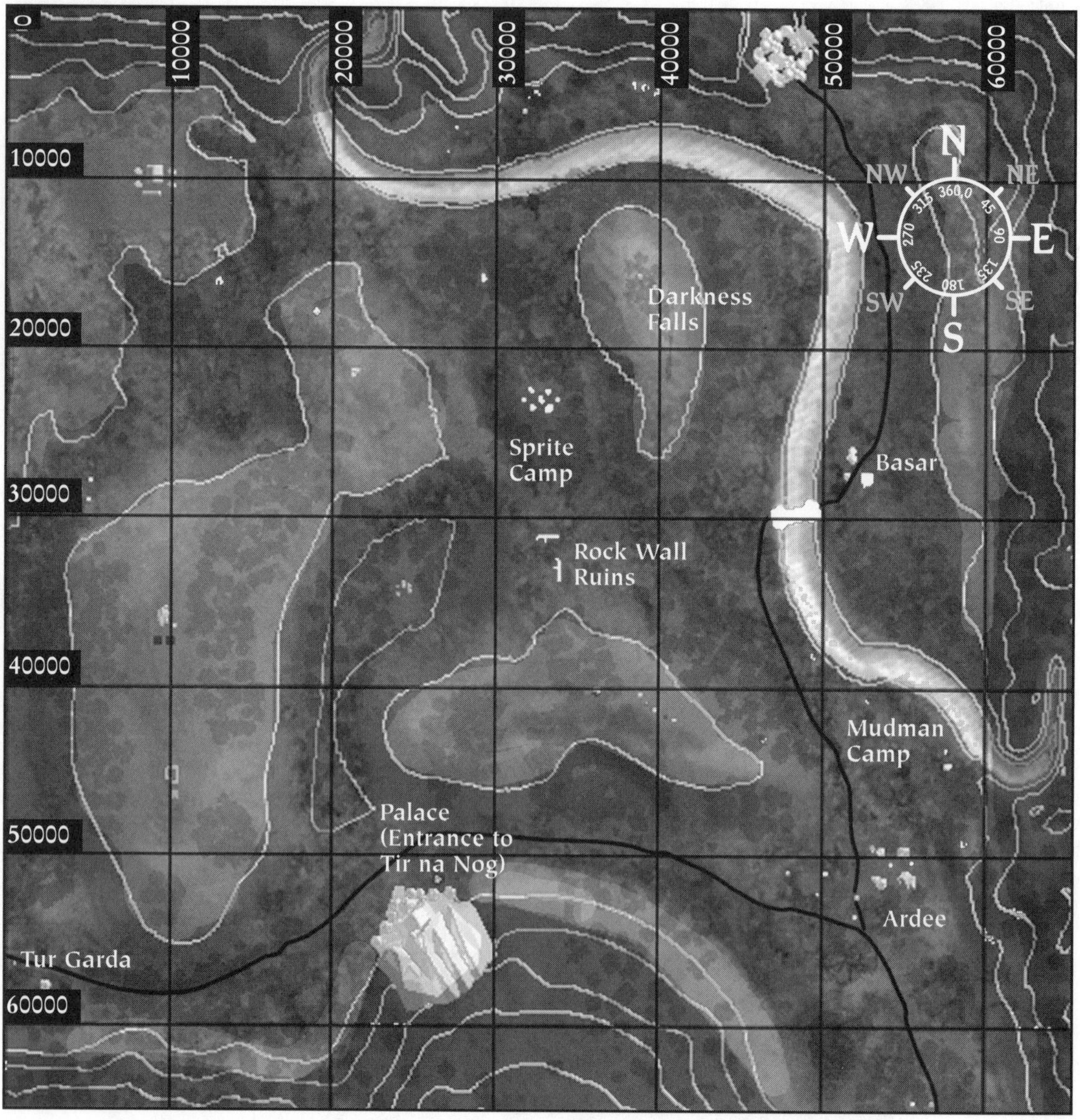

Lower-level monsters not shown on map:

Creature	Lvl	Location
anger sprite	11	NW,NC,WC,C
annoying lucradan	0	SE
badger cub	0	SE
bodachan sabhaill	4	SC
changeling	11	NW,NC,WC,C
eirebug	4	SC
eirebug	5	SW,SC,SE
feccan	1	SE
feccan	2	SE
feckless lucragan	4	SC
ghostly siabra	11	C,SW
hill toad	5	C,SE
hill toad	6	C
hill toad	7	C
large eirebug	10	WC,C
large frog	0	SE
large frog	1	EC,SE
lugradan whelp	5	C,EC,SW,SC
lugradan whelp	6	C,EC,SW,SC
lunantishee	8	WC,SW

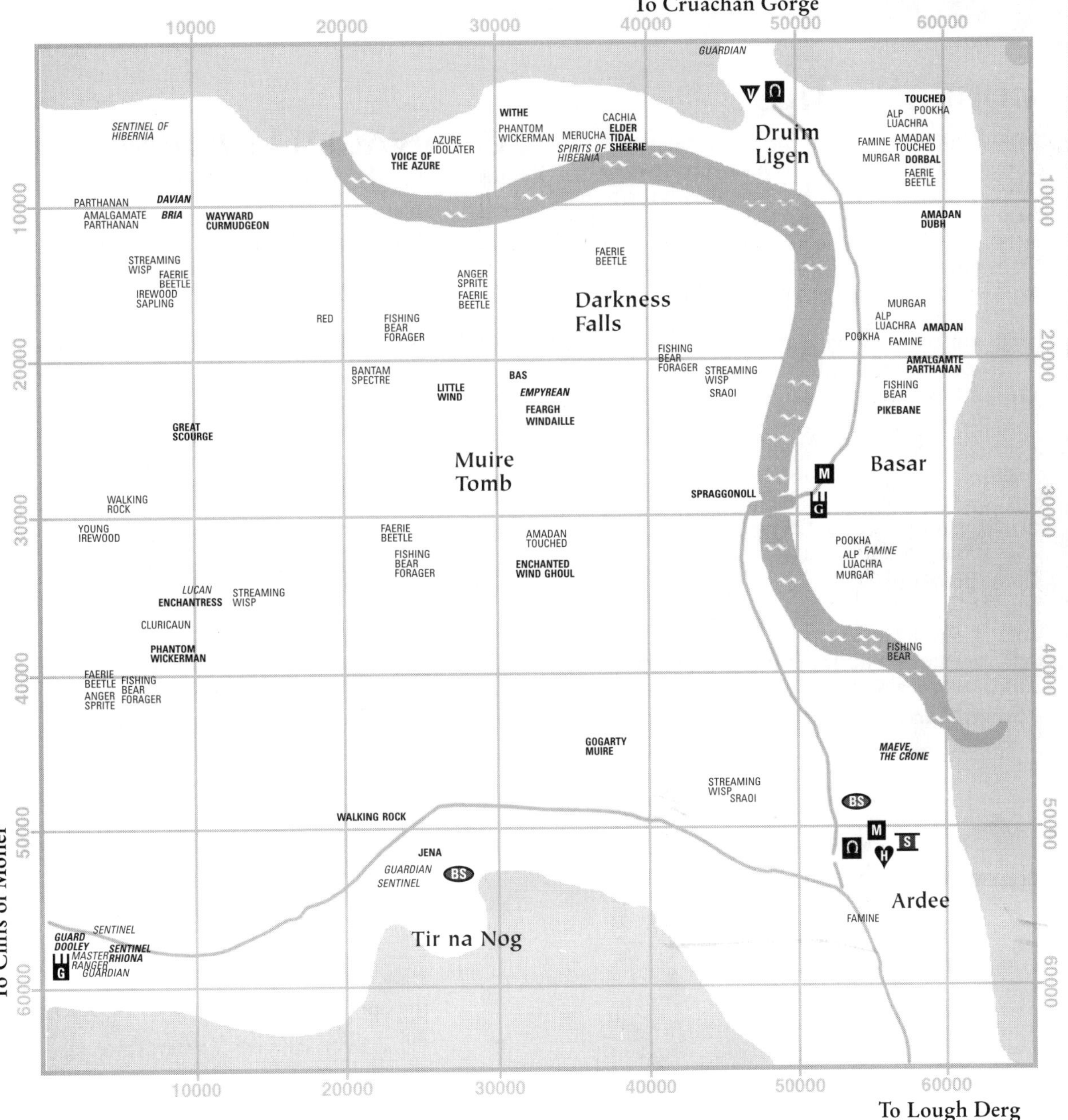

Lower-level monsters not shown on map:

Creature	Lvl	Location
moss sheerie	10	WC,C
mudman	2	EC,SE
mudman	3	EC,SE
mudman	4	NC,WC,C,EC,SW,SE
orchard nipper	6	C,EC
rowdy	5	C,SC
rowdy	6	C,EC,SC
skeletal minion	4	C,SC
skeletal pawn	1	SE
skeletal pawn	2	SE
spraggon	3	SE
spraggon	4	SE
spraggon	5	EC,SW,SC
spraggonite	5	C
spraggonite	6	C,EC,SW,SC
villainous youth	3	SE
villainous youth	4	C
water beetle	6	EC
water beetle	7	EC
water beetle	8	EC
water beetle collector	5	EC
water beetle larva	0	SE
water beetle larva	1	SE
wild crouch	5	SW
wild crouch	6	SW
wild lucradan	9	WC,SW
wind ghoul	7	NC,WC,C

Connacht Tips

Solo Friendly?

Starting as low as level 7 you can go after the Wind ghoul. Everyone is familiar with the water beetle area north of Ardee as well — a nice beginners area. North of the TNN entrance, you can start working the lower 20s on the Irewood saplings and faire beetles near the farm (and parths are there as well). As you go up in level, then you go up to the Young irewoods. This can keep you busy through level 29.

Group Friendly?

Low-level groups can go after the camps of Clurican, ghouls and siabra in this zone. (This will only keep you busy as a group for your first few levels.) Once you're higher, it's good to group against the pookhas and amadan touched near Basar and Drum Ligen.

Loot make-up?

The *Mythical* Archer's bracer is supposed to come from the pookhas or amadan touched in the area, but some folks think they are just fables. The pookhas also drop several nice cloaks.

- Steve "Larian LeQuella" Lundquist

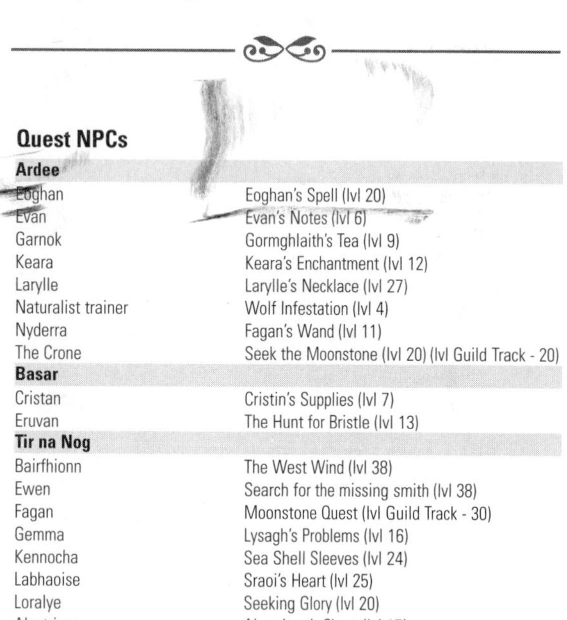

Quest NPCs

Ardee	
Eoghan	Eoghan's Spell (lvl 20)
Evan	Evan's Notes (lvl 6)
Garnok	Gormghlaith's Tea (lvl 9)
Keara	Keara's Enchantment (lvl 12)
Larylle	Larylle's Necklace (lvl 27)
Naturalist trainer	Wolf Infestation (lvl 4)
Nyderra	Fagan's Wand (lvl 11)
The Crone	Seek the Moonstone (lvl 20) (lvl Guild Track - 20)
Basar	
Cristan	Cristin's Supplies (lvl 7)
Eruvan	The Hunt for Bristle (lvl 13)
Tir na Nog	
Bairfhionn	The West Wind (lvl 38)
Ewen	Search for the missing smith (lvl 38)
Fagan	Moonstone Quest (lvl Guild Track - 30)
Gemma	Lysagh's Problems (lvl 16)
Kennocha	Sea Shell Sleeves (lvl 24)
Labhaoise	Sraoi's Heart (lvl 25)
Loralye	Seeking Glory (lvl 20)
Alastriona	Alastriona's Chest (lvl 17)

CONNACHT HUNTING

5-8	In your youth, try your hand at killing Water Beetles. They're particularly vulnerable to cold attacks and can be found near Mag Mell and Mardagh, as well as Ardee and the lake behind Tir na mBeo.
7-9	Just north and west of Ardee, you can find Wind Ghouls. Try making this hunt during daylight, as nighttime brings out the Amadan-Touched spawns. Also, cold attacks work well against them.
15-17	By this point, you should be prepared to take on Fishing Bear Foragers.
21-24	Right outside Ceannai, you can find Irewood Saplings that are vulnerable to fire attacks.
23-24	Head for the north gate at Tir na Nog, then head northwest to find Cluricans. They're hard to target and kill because they're constantly moving, but you can score a great armor drop if you manage to bring one down. There are plenty of other intermediate-level creatures to hunt here as well.
23-25	Look for more fire-vulnerable Young Irewoods near the Cluricans.
24-27	Also northwest of Tir na Nog, you have the opportunity to hunt Walking Rocks.
35 -36	Close to Basar, you can start tracking Phookas — cross the bridge and head past Ardee to find them.

Loot

alp luachra [29-30/31] (25/30%) Alp Luachra Hand (x2) • (25/20%) Alp Luachra Eye • (8/10%) Alp Luachra Head

Amadan [39] (1.5%) Ring of the Amadan ***or*** Ring of Undead Might • (80% each) Worn Carnielian Studded Belt, Well Crafted Lantern, Copper Amethyst Bracelet • (50%) Forgotten Silver Jasper Locket • (40%) Small Silver Laden Box

amadan touched [29-30/31-32/33-34] (1.5%) Ring of the Amadan ***or*** Ring of Undead Might • (40/40/20%) Worn Carnielian Studded Belt • (8/12/20%) Forgotten Silver Jasper Locket • (80% each) Well Crafted Lantern, Flint • (60%) Copper Amethyst Bracelet • (10/20/40%) Small Silver Laden Box • (0.3%) <The Four Elements>

amalgamate parthanan [26] (75% each) Malicious Black Heart, Black Clawed Hand • (3% each) Parthanan Head, Pearl • (10%) Lapis Lazuli • (0.3%) <Muire's Riches 2> • (1.5%) Parthanon Fist ***or*** Ether Ring

anger sprite [11-12/13] (5/20%) Faerie Anger Dust • (80/60%) Expended Thin Copper Wand • (80/70%) Anger Sprite Wing • (20/70%) Anger Sprite Wing • (1.4% each) Sprite Vine Helm, Anger Sprite Dirk • (0.3%) <Engraved Enchantments>/<Treasures of the Fey>

annoying lucradan [0] (5%) Poteen Wine Flask • (70%) Onyx • (1%) <Braided Beauties> • (8% each piece) Tattered Brea and Tattered Woven

azure idolater [24-26] (no loot)

badger cub [0] (60%) Badger Cub Fur • (40%) Badger Cub Tooth • (50%) Badger Cub Claw

bantam spectre [15] (1.5%) Spectral Shroud • (40%) Spectral Essence • (0.3%) <Muire's Riches 2>

Bas [6] (no loot)

bodachan sabhaill [4] (75%) Onyx • (2%) Copper Charm • (25%) Oil Flask • (10% each piece) Tattered Brea and Tattered Woven • (1%) <Braided Beauties>

Cachia [30] (80%) Seal Skin Bag • (60%) Silver Pearl Ring • (40%) Silver Pearl Necklace • (1.5%) Coral Vest • (5%) Green Tourmaline • (50%) Topaz • (0.3%) <The Four Elements>

changeling [11] (10%) Changeling Skin • (1.5%) Hood of the Forsaken • (80%) Obsidian • (60%) Bloodstone • (0.3%) <Engraved Enchantments>

cluricaun [22] (5%) Silver Goblet • (75% each) Pouch of Ill Gotten Gain, Forgetful Dust • (1.3%) <Hedge Clippers> • (1.3%) APOA: Woven Hedge Weed • (0.3%) <Muire's Riches 3> • (0.8%) Lucky Lauean, Lucky Muinneelyn ***or*** Lucky Failm • (0.5%) Mollachd Coin

Dorbal [34] (1.5%) Ring of the Amadan ***or*** Ring of Undead Might • (20%) Worn Carnielian Studded Belt • (20%) Forgotten Silver Jasper Locket • (80% each) Well Crafted Lantern, Flint • (60%) Copper Amethyst Bracelet • (40%) Small Silver Laden Box • (0.3%) <The Four Elements>

eirebug [4-5] (75%) Eirebug Leg (x2) • (10%) Eirebug Mandible • (5%) Eirebug Carapace

enchanted wind ghoul [7] (20% each) Gem of Swirling Wind, Wind Ghoul Essence • (80%) Aventurine • (60%) Jade • (0.5%) <Celtic Knots>

Enchantress [50] (no loot)

faerie beetle [17] (80%) Faerie Beetle Leg (x2) • (10%) Faerie Beetle Mandible • (5% each) Faerie Beetle Carapace, Faerie Dust

Famine [32] (30%) Alp Luachra Hand (x2) • (20%) Alp Luachra Eye • (10%) Alp Luachra Head

Fearg [6] (no loot)

feccan [1-2] (5%) Feccan Skin • (75%) Onyx • (10%) Aventurine • (1%) <Braided Beauties> • (10% each piece) Tattered Brea and Tattered Woven

feckless lucragan [4] (70% each) Poteen Wine Flask, Onyx • (2%) Leather Pouch • (1%) <Braided Beauties>

fishing bear [18-19/20-21] (20/40%) Fishing Bear Skin • (70/65%) Bear Tooth (x2) • (70/65%) Bear Meat (x2)

fishing bear forager [13-14] (20%) Fishing Bear Forager Skin • (80%) Fishing Bear Forager Tooth • (40%) Fishing Bear Forager Tooth • (80%) Fishing Bear Forager Meat • (40%) Fishing Bear Forager Meat

ghostly siabra [11] (80% each) Etched Wooden Bowl, Obsidian • (20% each) Etched Wooden Cup, Chryoprase • (1.4%) Siabrian Gloves • (1.5%) <Craftsman Pendants> • (0.5%) <Engraved Enchantments>

great scourge [30] (60% each) Diseased Tail, Crystalized Eye • (80%) Tough Hide • (1.5%) Jewels 34 • (80%) Milky Membrane • (40%) Pointed Fang

hill toad [5-7] (75%) Frog Legs • (60%) Frog Legs • (10%) Hill Toad Skin

horse [10] (75%) Horse Hair • (10%) Auburn Mane • (80%) Ruined Horse Skin • (35%) Horse Skin • (60%) Horse Hair

irewood sapling [21-22] (75%) Ire Wood Sapling Branch (x2) • (55%) Bundle of Sapling Branches (x2) • (5%) Pitted Glowing Ng Kit Ire Wood Sapling Staff

large eirebug [10] (80%) Large Eirebug Leg (x2) • (40%) Large Eirebug Mandible • (10%) Large Eirebug Carapace

large frog [0-1] (65%) Frog Legs • (5%) Frog Legs

Little Wind [8] (20% each) Gem of Swirling Wind, Wind Ghoul Essence • (80%) Aventurine • (60%) Jade • (0.5%) <Celtic Knots>

lugradan whelp [4-5/6] (5%) Silver Coin • (5%) Moonstone/Jade • (80%) Onyx/Aventurine • (5%) Jade [6] • (60/20%) Poteen Wine Flask • (1%) <Braided Beauties>/(0.5%) <Celtic Knots> • (1% each piece) Tattered Brea and Tattered Woven

lunantishee [8] (15%) Onyx Figurine • (60%) Luna Dust • (1.5%) Blackthorn Club • (3%) APOA: Blackthorn • (0.2%) APOA: Spiked Blackthorn, ***or*** a Blackthorn Wreath • (0.5%) <Celtic Knots>

merucha [30] (80%) Seal Skin Bag • (60%) Silver Pearl Ring • (40%) Silver Pearl Necklace • (1.5%) Coral Vest • (5%) Green Tourmaline • (50%) Topaz • (0.3%) <The Four Elements>

moss sheerie [10] (50%) Clump of Moss • (20%) Pouch of Faerie Dust • (10%) Jewels 24 • (0.3%) <Engraved Enchantments> • (1.5%) Hardened Moss Bracer

mudman [2-3/4] (80%) Ball of Clay • (30/40%) Small Amount of Clay • (5/10%) Block of Clay • (1%) <Braided Beauties>

Murgar [36] (30%) Pooka Skin • (80%) Pooka Hair (x2) • (1.5%) Horse, Goblin, Boogieman, Eagle ***or*** Goatman Mantle

orchard nipper [6] (75% each) Small Copper Ring, Red Apples • (5% each) Small Copper Bracelet, Bag of Fruit • (1%) <Braided Beauties>

parthanan [17-18] (75% each) Malicious Black Heart, Black Clawed Hand • (3% each) Parthanan Head, Pearl • (10%) Lapis Lazuli • (0.3%) <Muire's Riches 2>

phantom wickerman [28] (80%) Phantom Essence • (30%) Manifested Phantom Terror Claw (x2) • (1.5%) Phantom Bastard Sword • (8%) Darkened Terror Claw

Pikebane [22] (50%) Fishing Bear Skin • (70%) Bear Tooth (x2) • (63%) Bear Meat (x3)

pookha [33-34/35] (20/30%) Pooka Skin • (70/80%) Pooka Hair (x2) • (1.5%) Horse, Goblin, Boogieman, Eagle ***or*** Goatman Mantle • (0.3%) <The Four Elements> [33-34]

Red [15] (20%) Faerie Anger Dust • (60%) Expended Thin Copper Wand • (1.4% each) Sprite Vine Helm, Anger Sprite Dirk • (70%) Anger Sprite Wing (x2) • (0.3%) <Treasures of the Fey>

rowdy [5-6] (no loot)

skeletal minion [4] (5%) Pitted Broadsword • (75%) Onyx • (60%) Onyx • (8% each piece) Tattered Brea and Tattered Woven • (1%) <Braided Beauties>

skeletal pawn [1-2] (70%) Onyx • (10%) Aventurine • (8% each piece) Tattered Brea and Tattered Woven • (1%) <Braided Beauties>

spraggon [3-5] (15%) Chipped Mirror • (75%) Oil Flask • (5%) Pint of Grog • (1%) <Braided Beauties> • (10% each piece) Tattered Brea and Tattered Woven

spraggonite [5-6] (5%) Pitted Stiletto • (5%) Pint of Grog • (75%) Moonstone • (25%) Chipped Mirror • (1%) <Braided Beauties> • (10% each piece) Tattered Brea and Tattered Woven

spraggonoll [7] (5%) Pitted Spiked Mace • (25%) Pint of Grog • (75%) Moonstone • (15%) Jade • (1%) <Braided Beauties>

Sraoi [25] (85%) Streaming Wisp Essence • (70%) Streaming Wisp Gem • (30%) Streaming Wisp Husk

streaming wisp [21-22/23-24] (80/85%) Streaming Wisp Essence • (65%) Streaming Wisp Gem • (10/20%) Streaming Wisp Husk

villainous youth [3-4] (no loot)

Voice of the Azure [27] (no loot)

walking rock [24] (5% each) Smooth Sling Stones, Chunk of Silver • (25%) Fine Unworked Stone • (45%) Unworked Stone • (50%) Malachite • (60% each) Silver Nugget, Chunk of Copper • (0.3%) <De'velyn's Delights> • (1.5%) Mineralized Ring

water beetle [6-8] (75%) Water Beetle Leg (x2) • (50%) Water Beetle Mandible • (25%) Water Beetle Carapace

water beetle collector [5] (80%) Water Beetle Leg • (45%) Water Beetle Leg

water beetle larva [0-1] (75%) Worm Fishing Bait • (15%) Worm Fishing Bait

wayward curmudgeon [24] (40%) Smooth Bone Necklace • (20%) Smooth Bone Totem • (1.5%) Pelt Punch, Hunting Spear, ***or*** Sewn Cloak of Might • (3%) APOA: Patched Hide • (0.15%) APOA: Sewn Hide • (0.5%) <Engraved Enchantments>

wild crouch [5-6] (75%) Moonstone • (10%) Jade • (3%) Pitted Stiletto • (25%) Small Copper Bracelet • (1%) <Braided Beauties>

wild lucradan [9] (3%) Bottle of Poteen Wine • (80% each) Leather Pouch, Spinel • (20%) Silver Coin • (0.5%) <Engraved Enchantments>

wind ghoul [7] (20% each) Gem of Swirling Wind, Wind Ghoul Essence • (80%) Aventurine • (60%) Jade • (0.5%) <Celtic Knots>

Windaille [6] (no loot)

Withe [29] (80%) Phantom Essence • (30%) Manifested Phantom Terror Claw (x2) • (1.5%) Phantom Bastard Sword • (8%) Darkened Terror Claw

young irewood [24-25] (75%) Ire Wood Sapling Branch (x2) • (55%) Bundle of Sapling Branches (x2) • (5%) Pitted Glowing Ng Kit Ire Wood Sapling Staff

Cursed Forest

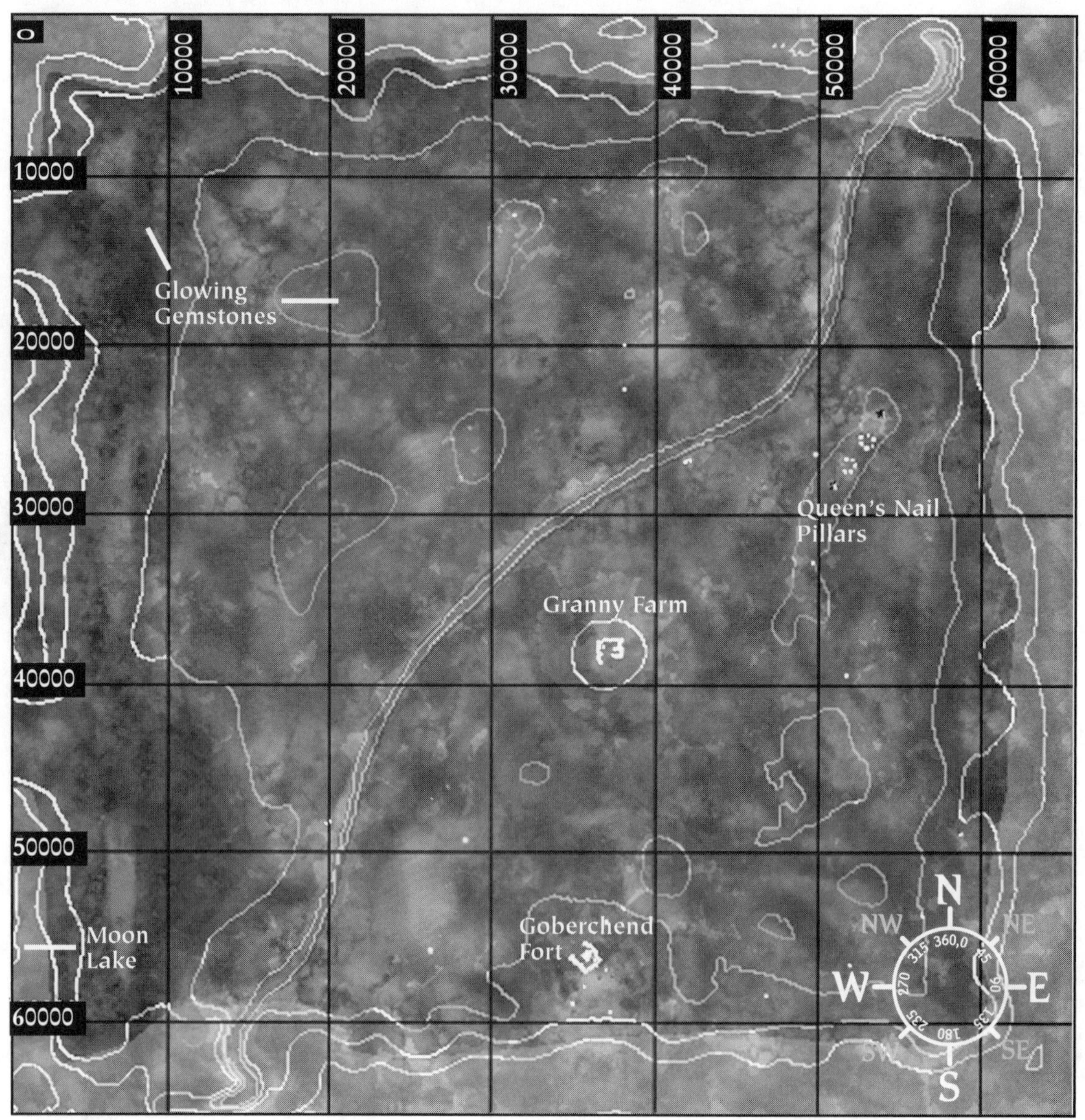

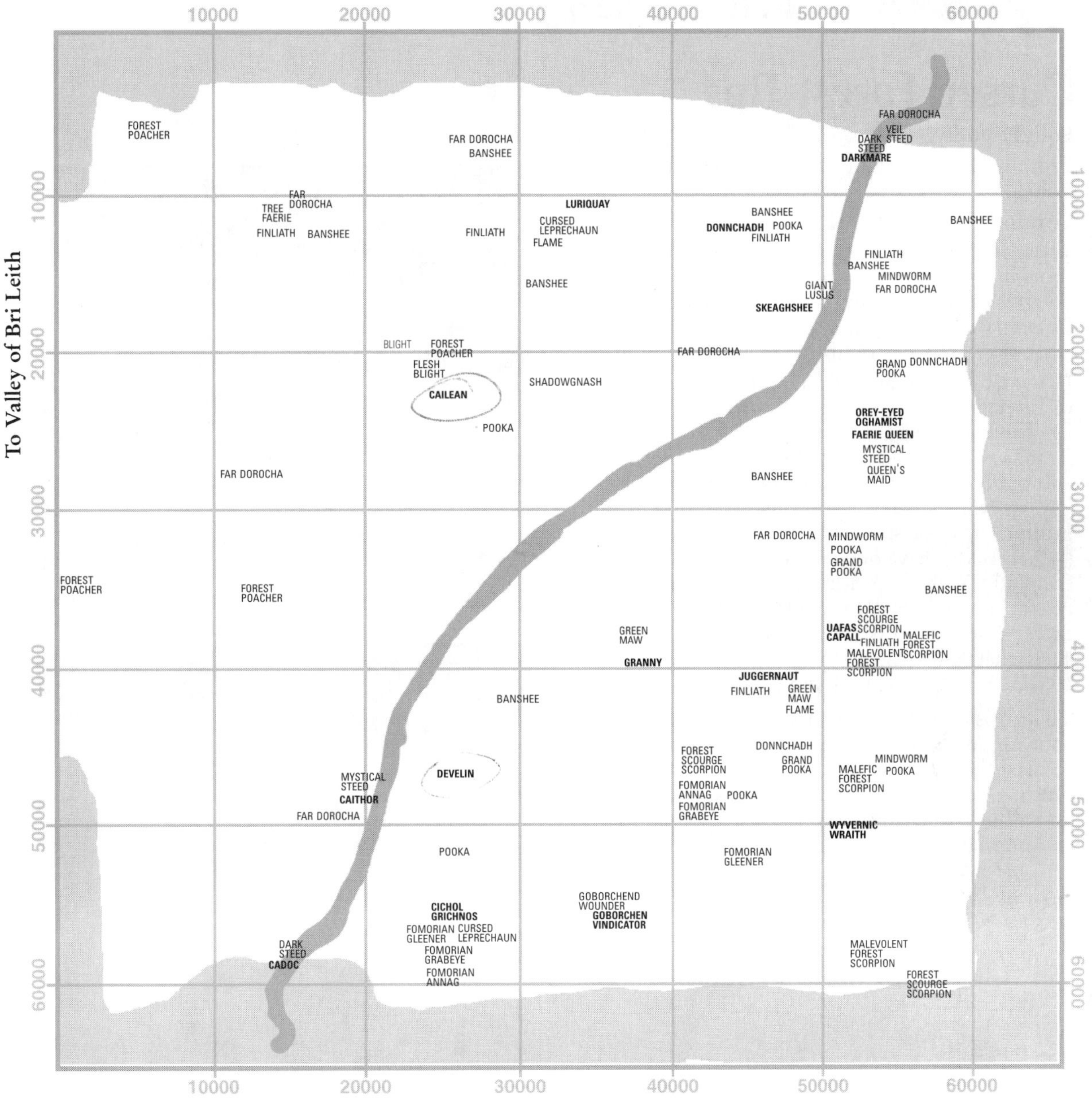

Lower-level monsters not shown on map:

Creature	Lvl	Location
black wraith	52	SW
black wraith	53	NE
black wraith	54	NE
far dorocha	55	EC
far dorocha	56	SW
Fomorian grencher	52	SW
gan ceanach	50	NW
gan ceanach	51	NW
goborchend gasher	52	SC
goborchend gasher	55	SC
goborchend piercer	50	SC
goborchend piercer	51	SC
goborchend piercer	52	SC
goborchend piercer	53	SC
goborchend wounder	54	SC
goborchend wounder	55	SC
goborchend wounder	56	SC
leprechaun	50	NW
levian-al	50	NW
levian-al	51	NW
Luriquay	50	NC
mindworm	57	SE
pooka	52	SW
pooka	53	NE,SW
pooka	54	NE
Queen's Maid	56	EC
spectral manslayer	50	C
spectral manslayer	53	NE
unearthed cave bear	50	NW
unearthed cave bear	51	NW

Cursed Forest Tips

Solo Friendly?

From what I can tell, it's a deathtrap to solo folks!

Group Friendly?

The classic PBAoE group (see note) absolutely *rocks* in this zone! Starting at around 40, you can go after the leprechauns, after that it's the Fins. Be prepared to wait on a list for the Fins though, since they are so incredibly popular.

Note: PBAoE Group. This is a Point Blank Area of Effect group. Ideally it consists of an Enchanter or Eldritch with a good PBAoE spell, 3 tanks with a good taunt, a Warden for healing and bubble, a Bard for endurance song and healing, and then whatever you can use to fill out the group. The basic strategy is to pull the Fins (which BAF), have one tank on each Fin, get them all bunched up close together, and the caster gets in the middle and rapid fires off the PBAoE. Sweet when it works, dangerous if folks aren't sure what to do.

- Steve "Larian LeQuella" Lundquist

This zone is a favorite for levels 45-50. A favorite spot for AOE groups, many players gather here to blast their final levels away. There is easier hunting near the zoneline (bears and leprechauns) and more challenging areas deeper in (finlaiths and banshees are common spots).

- Todd "Jubal" Wharton

Loot

banshee [55-56,58-59] (60%) Ghostly Banshee Hair • (40%) Wailing Essence Gem • (20%) Banshee Essence • (20%) Jewels 64 • (1.3%) Obsidian Kite, Tower ***or*** Round Shield • (1.5%) <Rogue Pendants (Mid)> • (1.3%) Glistening Broadsword ***or*** Great Sword • (1.3%) APOA: Manifested Terror

black wraith [52-55] (30% each) Wraith Essence, Shadowy Gem • (45%) Etheric Spirit Shackles • (25%) Jewels 64 • (1.6%) <Arcane Artifacts> • (1.6%) Phantom Gem

Blight [70] (90%) Shard of Light ***or*** Deleterious Pall

Caithor [66] (no loot)

cursed leprechaun [63] (no loot)

Faerie Queen [57] (no loot)

far dorocha [53,55,56,59] [some have no loot] (15%) Jewels 05 • (5%) <Mementoes> • (1.5%) Far Dorocha Devastator • (0.5%) <Valor's Heart>

finliath [58-60] (10%) Jewels 61 • (3.5%) Translucent Finliath Tooth • (1.5%) Pouch of Fettered Screams • (2%) Box of Childrens Toys • (3%) Bloodstained Golden Splinter • (1.5%) Finliath Firebrand • (0.5%) <Valor's Heart>

Flame [64,79] (no loot)

Fomorian annag [55-56] (10%) Jewels 61 • (1.5%) Small Annag Head • (1%) Large Annag Head • (3.5%) Rune Etched Seashell • (4%) Glowing Ultramarine Stone • (1.6%) Diabolical Fomorian Vest ***or*** Robe • (0.4%) <Valor's Heart>

Fomorian grencher [50-52] (10%) Jewels 05 • (2.5%) Cask of Fomorian Swill • (1%) Orb of the Sea • (2.5%) Glowing Ultramarine Stone • (2%) Polished and Painted Seashell • (2%) Rune Etched Seashell • (1.5%) Diabolical Eldritch Boots • (0.5%) <Granny's Basket>

gan ceanach [50-51,53] (10%) Jewels 04 • (3.5%) Lock of Silver Hair • (3.3%) Pungent Ruddy Spirits • (2.7%) Wound Fine Silver Thread • (0.5%) Fulgent Dusklight Gem • (1.6%) Cursed Lute • (0.4%) <Granny's Basket>

giant lusus [58-61] (9%) Jewels 61 • (9%) <Lusus Lootus> • (1.6%) Twisted Melody Boots ***or*** Twisted Lusus Boots • (0.4%) <Valor's Heart>

Goborchen Vindicator [60] (4%) Vindicator's Staff of the Void, of Enchantments, of Mentalism, of Light ***or*** of Mana

goborchend gasher [52/55] (10/15%) Jewels 05 • (3/4.5%) Preserved Human Heart • (2.5/3.8%) Viscous Fragrant Fluid • (1/1.5%) Restless Ethereal Eye • (3.5/5.3%) Goborchend Hoof • (1.6%) Shagreen Fighter's Coif ***or*** Shagreen Coif/Shagreen Leggings • (0.4%) <Granny's Basket>/<Valor's Heart>

goborchend piercer [50/51/52/53] (10/12/14/14%) Jewels 04 • (3/3.6/4.2/4.2%) Preserved Human Heart • (2.5/3/3.5/3.5%) Viscous Fragrant Fluid • (1/1.2/1.4/1.4%) Restless Ethereal Eye • (3.5/4.2/5.5/5.5%) Goborchend Hoof • (1.6%) Shagreen Champion/Hero/Druid/Warden Boots • (0.4%) <Granny's Basket>

goborchend wounder [54/55/56] (10/12/15%) Jewels 05 • (2/2/2.4%) Preserved Human Heart • (2.4/2.4/2.9%) Viscous Fragrant Fluid • (3/3/3.6%) Restless Ethereal Eye • (2.6/2.6/3.1%) Goborchend Hoof • (1.6%) Shagreen Gloves/Sleeves/Hauberk • (0.4%) <Valor's Heart>

grand pooka [61-62] (7.5%) Jewels 61 • (0.8%) Fuliginous Mane Hairs • (2%) Pooka's Luminous Horseshoe • (4%) Broken Carved Music Box • (3%) Grand Pooka Hoof • (1.5%) Pooka's Broken Horn • (0.5%) <Valor's Heart>

granny [50] (2.3%) Bag of Glowing Seeds • (5.3%) Leafy Silver Stemmed Vine • (6%) Luminous Golden Flower • (1.5%) Exotic Herbs • (2%) Granny's Shawl, Kettle ***or*** Needle

Green Maw [54-56,58,65,68] (no loot)

Juggernaut [75] (90%) Juggernaut Great Falcata ***or*** Stoney Links of Magic

leprechaun [48-50] (1.7%) Forest Green ***or*** Royal Green Enamel • (0.3%) Black, Royal Purple ***or*** Dark Purple Enamel • (2%) <Lucky Charms> • (15%) Jewels 49 • (1.5%) Leprechaun's Staff of the Void • (0.5%) <Granny's Basket>

levian-al [50-54] (9%) Cracked Levian-Al Fang • (6%) Levian-Al Fang • (9%) Broken Levian-Al Claw • (6%) Levian-Al Claw • (16%) Slashed Levian-Al Pelt • (12%) Flayed Levian-Al Pelt • (3.1%) August Levian-Al Pelt

Luriquay [50,65] (no loot)

mindworm [57-59] (7.5%) Translucent Mindworm Fang • (6%) Mindworm Poison Gland • (1.5%) Renitent Mindworm Skin

Mystical Steed [70] (80%) Faerie Steed Mane • (30%) Faerie Steed Pelt • (90%) Faerie Steed Tail

Orey-eyed Oghamist [73] (90%) Oghamist Pick Hammer ***or*** Eye of Fire

pooka [52-55,57] (50%) Shape Changer's Hide • (75% each) Shape Changer's Skull, Tooth • (1.5%) <No Such Thing as the Bogeyman>

Queen's Maid [56] (no loot)

Skeaghshee [71] (90%) Crescent of Light ***or*** Mischievous Bracer

spectral manslayer [50-53] (2.4%) Runed Pitcher of Ashes • (5%) Gold Embossed Parchment • (3.9%) Ash and Gold Dust Mix • (10%) Jewels 04 • (1.6%) Spectral Impaler [50]/Spectral Crusher [52]/Finliath Firebrand [53] • (0.4%) <Granny's Basket> [level 51 currently has no loot]

Uafas Capall [72] (90%) Luminescent Sickle of the Unicorn ***or*** Braided Unicorn Mane

unearthed cave bear [49-51] (6.6%) Bloodstained Bear Claw • (4.3%) Gnarled Bear Tooth • (1.2%) Bloody Broken Bear Trap • (5%) Slashed Bear Pelt • (3.6%) Fine Bear Pelt • (1.2%) Supple Bear Pelt

Wyvernic Wraith [74] (90%) Wyvern Spear of Light ***or*** Ring of Elements

Lough Derg

To Connacht

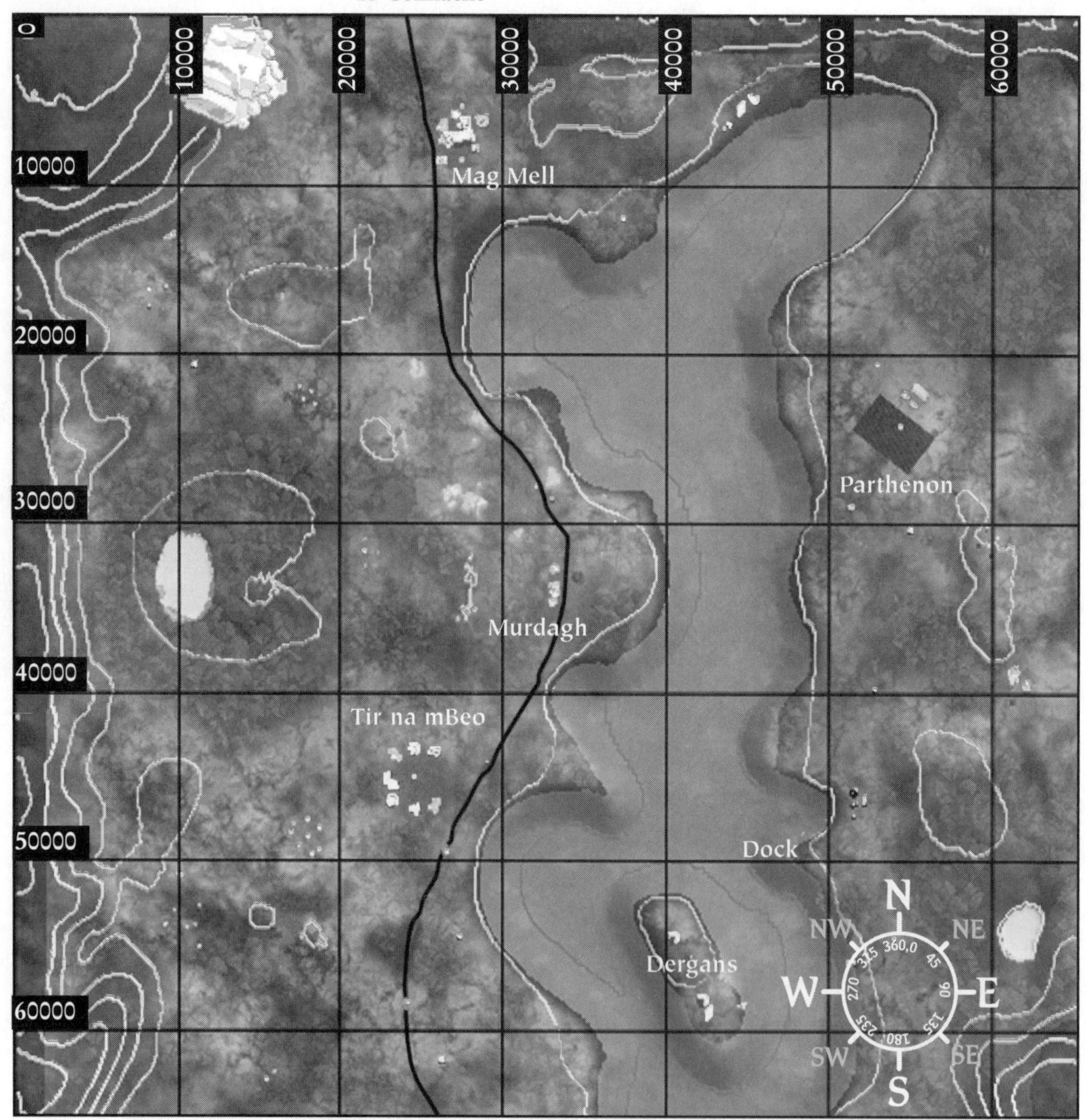

To Silvermine Mountains

Lower-level monsters not shown on map:

Creature	Lvl	Location
annoying lucradan	0	NC
badger cub	0	NC
Caoranach	6	NC
Caoranach	7	NC
cluricaun trip	7	NW,NC,WC
derg monster	5	NC,SC

Creature	Lvl	Location
eirebug	4	NW,NC,WC,SW,SC,SE
eirebug	5	NC,WC,C,SW,SC
feckless lucragan	4	NW,NC,WC,C,SW,SC
grass spirit	1	NC
hill toad	5	NC

Creature	Lvl	Location
hill toad	6	NW,NC
hill toad	7	NW,NC,WC
large frog	0	NC,SE
large frog	1	NC
lough wolf	7	NW,NC,WC,SW
lough wolf cadger	2	NC

Creature	Lvl	Location
lough wolf cadger	3	NW,NC,SW,SC
lugradan whelp	5	NW,NC
minor changeling	1	NC
minor changeling	2	NW,NC
mudman	2	NC
mudman	3	NC
mudman	4	NC,SC

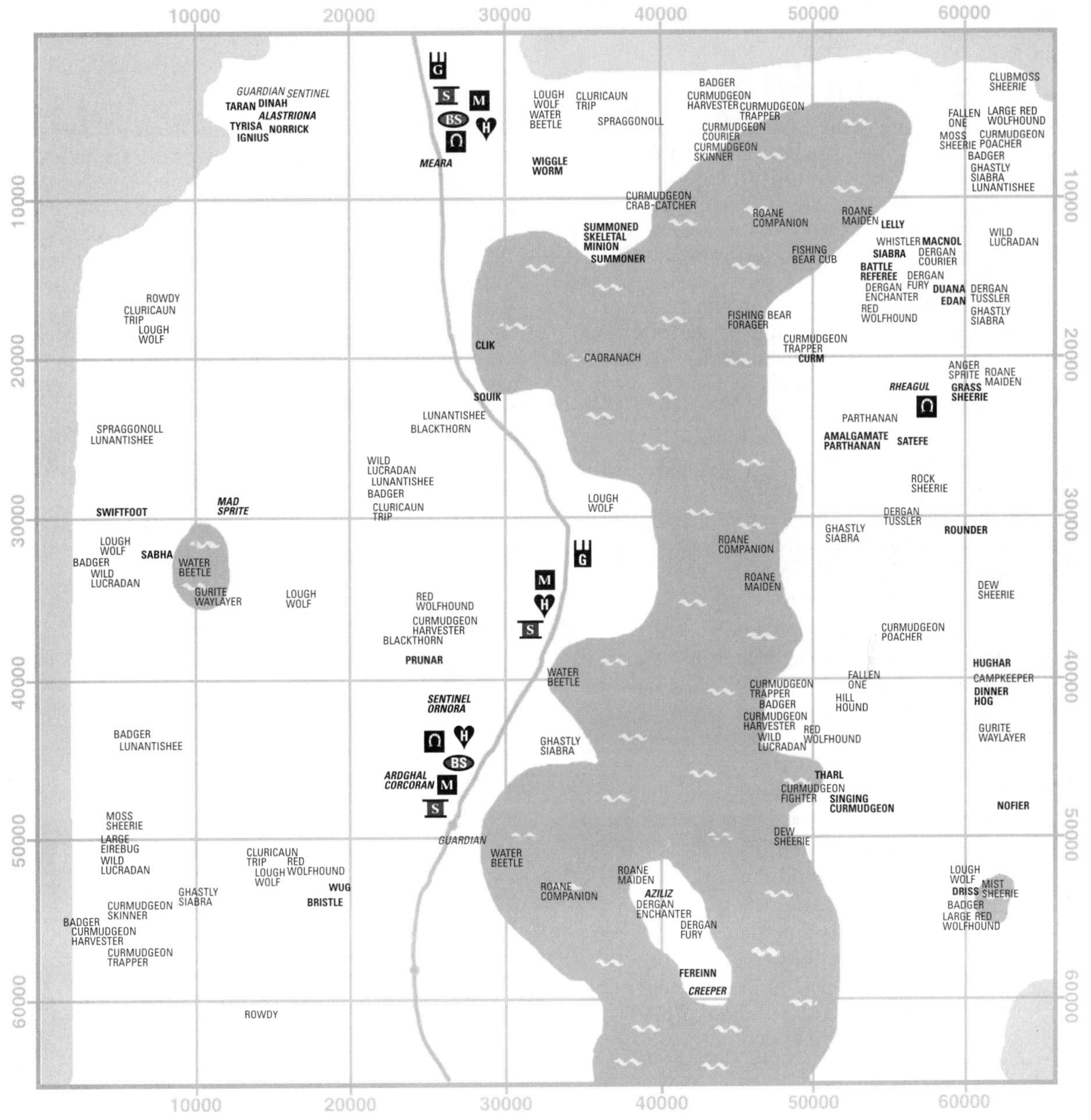

Creature	Lvl	Location
orchard nipper	5	NW,NC,SC
orchard nipper	6	NW,NC,WC,SC
rat boy	3	NW,NC,SW,SC
rowdy	5	NW,SW
rowdy	6	NW
rowdy	7	NW,WC
skeletal minion	3	NW,NC,SW
skeletal minion	4	NC
skeletal pawn	1	NC
skeletal pawn	2	NW,NC
slough serpent	0	NC,SC
small freshwater crab	4	NC
spraggon	5	NW,NC
spraggonite	6	NW,NC
spraggonoll	7	NW,NC,WC
villainous youth	3	NW,SW,SC
villainous youth	4	SW
water beetle	6	NC,WC,SC
water beetle	7	NC,WC,SC
water beetle collector	4	NC,WC,SC
water beetle collector	5	NC,WC,SC
water beetle larva	0	NC,WC,C,SC
water beetle larva	1	NC,WC,SC
wild crouch	5	NC,SW,SC
wild crouch	6	NW,NC,WC
young badger	7	NC,NE,WC,C,EC,SW

Lough Derg Tips

A popular starting zone, Lough Derg holds Mag Mell, Tir na Nog, and the Parthanan Farm. Just outside Mag Mell is great for soloing your first few levels. The large castle is Tir na Nog, where you can find anything from trainers to merchants. The Parthanan Farm is good for levels 15-18 and is considered East Lough Derg; the easiest way to get there is a horse from the stable in Ardee, if you have the silver to shell out. Tir na mBeo is a popular place to bind for the defenders of the realm, as there is a horse route directly to Druim Ligen.

- Steve "Larian LeQuella" Lundquist

Lough Derg really is the perfect Hibernia newbie zone. If you start around Mag Mell you can slowly progress farther away as you level. Below are some of the monsters you can hunt, by level. The farther from Mag Mell you go, the higher the level of the monsters — a perfect progression.

1	badger cubs, large frogs, water beetle larva, annoying lucradan
2	minor changelings, grass spirits, large frogs, water beetle larva, skeletal pawns
3	minor changelings, mud men, lough wolf cadgers, skeletal pawns
4	villainous youths, skeletal minions, rat boys, mud men, lough wolf cadgers
5	eirebugs, mud men, water beetle collectors, skeletal minions
6	wild crouch, hill toads, water beetle collectors, orchard nippers, lough derg pike

And so on ...

Between Mag Mell and Tir na nOg, you'll find everything you need in the way of quests, tasks, kill tasks and equipment. If tasks or kill tasks come up short in Mag Mell, it's only a short run north to Ardee in Connacht or south to Mardagh in Lough Derg. The only downside to this zone is the very thing that makes it so great. Because it is a newbie zone and so well laid out, overcrowding might become a problem. This zone continues to accommodate various player levels through the mid-to-high teens and low twenties with the ever popular Parthanan Farm across the lake from Mag Mell and still farther on. It isn't uncommon for players to spend a large portion of their characters' lives in or around Lough Derg.

- Beau "Garvyn MacGyani" Stribling

Quest NPCs

Broken Tower of mBeo	
Talking Wolves	Seek the Moonstone (lvl 25) (lvl Guild Track - 25)
Mag Mell	
Anise	Sheerie Mischief (lvl 22)
Mardagh (lvl guard tower)	
Riona	Riona's Revenge (lvl 17)
Siabra distorter camp	
Druid Harkin	Cad Goddeau (lvl 20) (lvl Guild Track - 20)
Siabra island	
Azilize	Search for Nasco's Spear (lvl 27)
Tir Na mBeo	
Guardian Andraste	Essence of Hostility (lvl 24)
Kaenia	Bria's Savior (lvl 24)
Reidie	Little Wind (lvl 9)
Tavie	Beautiful Music (lvl 14)
Tavie	Magic's scar (lvl 36)

Loot

rat boy [3] (10%) Small Copper Ring • (80%) Small Mirror • (1%) <Braided Beauties> • (8% each piece) Tattered Brea and Tattered Woven

fishing bear forager [13-14] (20%) Fishing Bear Forager Skin • (80% each) Fishing Bear Forager Tooth, Meat • (40% each) Fishing Bear Forager Tooth, Meat

grass spirit [1] (23%) Small Copper Ring • (75%) Grass Ring • (1%) <Braided Beauties> • (8% each piece) Tattered Brea and Tattered Woven

dergan enchanter [12] (30%) Pixie Dust • (30%) Sulfur • (30%) Jewels 24 • (1.5%) Jewels 38 • (1.5%) <Magi Pendants> • (1.4%) Studied Eldritch ***or*** Mentalist Staff, ***or*** Dergan Enchanter's Staff • (3%) APOA: Dergan Enchanter's • (0.2%) APOA: Enchanter's Fine • (0.5%) <Engraved Enchantments>

lugradan whelp [5] (5% each) Silver Coin, Moonstone • (80%) Onyx • (60%) Poteen Wine Flask • (1%) <Braided Beauties> • (1% each piece) Tattered Brea and Tattered Woven

rounder [21] (5% each) Smooth Sling Stones, Fine Unworked Stone • (90%) Unworked Stone • (1.5%) Rock Sherrie Bracer • (0.3%) <Muire's Riches 2>

campkeeper [15] (5% each) Tattered Sapphire Brea Sleeves, Helm • (25% each) Ivory Handled Skinning Knife, Smooth Bone Totem, Pristine Wolf Pelt, Pristine Badger Hide • (80% each) Smooth Bone Necklace, Torn Wolf Pelt • (0.3%) <Treasures of the Fey>

curmudgeon fighter [16-18] *see campkeeper [15]*

curmudgeon poacher [15] *see campkeeper [15]*

Hughar [16] *see campkeeper [15]*

singing curmudgeon [17] *see campkeeper [15]*

Tharl [19] *see campkeeper [15]*

spraggonoll [7] (5%) Pitted Spiked Mace • (25%) Pint of Grog • (75%) Moonstone • (15%) Jade • (1%) <Braided Beauties>

spraggonite [6] (5%) Pitted Stiletto • (5%) Pint of Grog • (75%) Moonstone • (25%) Chipped Mirror • (1%) <Braided Beauties> • (10% each piece) Tattered Brea and Tattered Woven

annoying lucradan [0] (5%) Poteen Wine Flask • (70%) Onyx • (1%) <Braided Beauties> • (8% each piece) Tattered Brea and Tattered Woven

anger sprite [12/13] (5/20%) Faerie Anger Dust • (80/60%) Expended Thin Copper Wand • (80/70%) Anger Sprite Wing • (20/70%) Anger Sprite Wing • (1.4% each) Sprite Vine Helm, Anger Sprite Dirk • (0.3%) <Engraved Enchantments>/<Treasures of the Fey>

clubmoss sheerie [11] *see moss sheerie [10]*

moss sheerie [10] (50%) Clump of Moss • (20%) Pouch of Faerie Dust • (10%) Jewels 24 • (0.3%) <Engraved Enchantments> • (1.5%) Hardened Moss Bracer

grass sheerie [13] (50%) Glimmering Clump of Grass • (25%) Pouch of Faerie Dust • (20%) Jewels 03 • (0.3%) <Treasures of the Fey> • (1.5%) Hardened Grass Bracer

badger cub [0] (60%) Badger Cub Fur • (40%) Badger Cub Tooth • (50%) Badger Cub Claw

feckless lucragan [4] (70% each) Poteen Wine Flask, Onyx • (2%) Leather Pouch • (1%) <Braided Beauties>

derg monster [5] (70%) Derg Fillet • (40%) Derg's Toothed Jaw

amalgamate parthanan [26] (75% each) Malicious Black Heart, Black Clawed Hand • (3% each) Parthanan Head, Pearl • (10%) Lapis Lazuli • (0.3%) <Muire's Riches 2> • (1.5%) Parthanon Fist ***or*** Ether Ring

parthanan [17-18] (75% each) Malicious Black Heart, Black Clawed Hand • (3% each) Parthanan Head, Pearl • (10%) Lapis Lazuli • (0.3%) <Muire's Riches 2>

Satefe [19] *see parthanan [17-18]*

dew sheerie [16-17/18-19] (75%) Chryoprase [16-17] • (50%) Lapis Lazuli [18-19] • (75/80%) Amethyst • (15/30%) Waterproof Satchel • (1.5%) Glowing Sherrie Beads • (5%) Intricate Sea Shell Bracelet • (0.3%) <Muire's Riches 2>

horse [10] (75%) Horse Hair • (10%) Auburn Mane • (80%) Ruined Horse Skin • (35%) Horse Skin • (60%) Horse Hair

Driss [21] *see mist sheerie [20-21]*

mist sheerie [20-21] (75%) Lapis Lazuli • (75%) Waterproof Satchel • (10%) Topaz • (3%) Sheeries Fearsome Shroud • (1%) Rattling Sherrie Beads • (0.3%) <Muire's Riches 3>

Duana [14] (75%) Sharp Hound Claw (x2) • (30%) Pristine Redhound Pelt

Edan [13] (75%) Sharp Hound Claw (x2) • (30%) Pristine Redhound Pelt

fallen one [17] (80% each) Etched Wooden Bowl, Amethyst • (20% each) Etched Wooden Cup, Chryoprase • (1.4%) Siabrian Gloves • (5%) Azurite • (1.5%) <Craftsman Pendants> • (0.3%) <Treasures of the Fey>

ghastly siabra [13-14/15] (80% each) Etched Wooden Bowl, Spinel/Amethyst • (20% each) Etched Wooden Cup, Chryoprase • (1.4%) Siabrian Gloves • (3%) Lapis Lazuli [13-14] • (5%) Azurite [15] • (1.5%) <Craftsman Pendants> • (0.3%) <Treasures of the Fey>

mudman [2-3/4] (80%) Ball of Clay • (30/40%) Small Amount of Clay • (5/10%) Block of Clay • (1%) <Braided Beauties>

fishing bear cub [12] (80%) Bear Meat • (40%) Bear Meat • (80%) Bear Tooth • (40%) Bear Tooth • (30%) Fishing Bear Skin

dergan tussler [14] (80%) Leather Pouch • (2%) Siabra Skirmisher's Head • (60%) Spinel • (0.3%) <Treasures of the Fey> • (5%) Pitted Short Bow • (10%) Flight Bodkin Arrows (x2) • (1.4%) Siabrian Sword Baldric • (3%) APOA: Worn Dark Guardian, Sword ***or*** Shield • (1.5%) <Military Pendants>

dergan fury [13-15] (80%) Leather Pouch • (20%) Writ of Station • (2%) Siabrian Fury's Head • (80%) Spinel • (20%) Chryoprase • (20%) Bloodstone • (1.4%) Siabrian Sword Baldric • (3%) APOA: Worn Dark Guardian, Sword ***or*** Shield • (1.5%) <Military Pendants> • (0.3%) <Treasures of the Fey>

Macnol [16] *see dergan fury [13-15]*

slough serpent [0] (80%) Serpent Scale • (75%) Serpent Fillet • (60%) Serpent Eggs

nofier [23] (80%) Small Skeletal Head • (30%) Polished Bones • (60%) Ground Bone Chips • (1.5%) Blunted Femur ***or*** Bloodied Bone

wiggle worm [0] (80%) Worm Fishing Bait • (10%) Worm Fishing Bait

curmudgeon crab-catcher [11] (no loot)

dinner hog [14] (no loot)

hill hound [22] (no loot)

Mad Sprite [6] (no loot)

Sabha [3] (no loot)

small freshwater crab [4] (no loot)

summoned skeletal minion [4] (no loot)

Summoner [3] (no loot)

whistler [13] (no loot)

Caoranach [6-7/8-9] (10/50%) Caoranach Hide • (80%) Caoranach Toothed Jaw

large frog [0-1] (65%) Frog Legs • (5%) Frog Legs

water beetle larva [0-1] (75%) Worm Fishing Bait • (15%) Worm Fishing Bait

minor changeling [1-2] *see rat boy [3]*

skeletal pawn [1-2] (70%) Onyx • (10%) Aventurine • (8% each piece) Tattered Brea and Tattered Woven • (1%) <Braided Beauties>

lough wolf cadger [2-3] (60%) Chunk of Wolf Meat • (75%) Wolf Fang • (5%) Torn Wolf Pelt

skeletal minion [3-4] (5%) Pitted Broadsword • (75%) Onyx • (60%) Onyx • (8% each piece) Tattered Brea and Tattered Woven • (1%) <Braided Beauties>

villainous youth [3-4] (no loot)

spraggon [4-5] (15%) Chipped Mirror • (75%) Oil Flask • (5%) Pint of Grog • (1%) <Braided Beauties> • (10% each piece) Tattered Brea and Tattered Woven

eirebug [4-5] (75%) Eirebug Leg (x2) • (10%) Eirebug Mandible • (5%) Eirebug Carapace

water beetle collector [4-5] (80%) Water Beetle Leg • (45%) Water Beetle Leg

red wolfhound [10-11/112-13] (75%) Sharp Hound Claw (x2) • (5/30%) Pristine Redhound Pelt

rock sheerie [18-19/20] (90/80%) Unworked Stone • (5/30%) Fine Unworked Stone • (5%) Smooth Sling Stones/Garnet • (1.5%) Rock Sherrie Bracer • (0.3%) <Muire's Riches 2>/<Muire's Riches 3>

orchard nipper [5-6] (75% each) Small Copper Ring, Red Apples • (5% each) Small Copper Bracelet, Bag of Fruit • (1%) <Braided Beauties>

wild crouch [5-6] (75%) Moonstone • (10%) Jade • (3%) Pitted Stiletto • (25%) Small Copper Bracelet • (1%) <Braided Beauties>

hill toad [5-7] (75%) Frog Legs • (60%) Frog Legs • (10%) Hill Toad Skin

rowdy [5-8] (no loot)

Clik [9] *see water beetle [6-8]*

water beetle [6-8] (75%) Water Beetle Leg (x2) • (50%) Water Beetle Mandible • (25%) Water Beetle Carapace

lunantishee [8-9] (15%) Onyx Figurine • (60%) Luna Dust • (1.5%) Blackthorn Club • (3%) APOA: Blackthorn • (0.2%) APOA: Spiked Blackthorn, ***or*** a Blackthorn Wreath • (0.5%) <Celtic Knots>

large red wolfhound [17,19] (50%) Pristine Redhound Pelt • (75%) Large Red Hound Claw (x2)

lough wolf [7-9] (20%) Sharp Wolf Claw • (80%) Chunk of Wolf Meat • (70%) Pristine Wolf Pelt

Swiftfoot [9] *see lough wolf [7-9]*

cluricaun trip [7-9] (5% each) Silver Coin, Leather Pouch • (80% each) Poteen Wine Flask, Moonstone • (5%) Pitted Dirk • (0.5%) <Celtic Knots>

Prunar [10] *see lunantishee [8-9]*

blackthorn [8-9] (no loot)

wild lucradan [9-10] (3%) Bottle of Poteen Wine • (80% each) Leather Pouch, Spinel • (20%) Silver Coin • (0.5%) <Engraved Enchantments>

Wug [10] *see wild lucradan [9-10]*

large eirebug [9-10] (80%) Large Eirebug Leg (x2) • (40%) Large Eirebug Mandible • (10%) Large Eirebug Carapace

curmudgeon harvester [9-11] (40%) Smooth Bone Necklace • (20%) Smooth Bone Totem • (1.5%) Pelt Punch, Hunting Spear, ***or*** Sewn Cloak of Might • (3%) APOA: Patched Hide • (0.15%) APOA: Sewn Hide • (0.5%) <Engraved Enchantments>

badger [9-11] (70%) Badger Tooth • (60%) Badger Claw • (50%) Pristine Badger Hide

Bristle [12] *see badger [9-11]*

young badger [7] *see badger [9-11]*

curmudgeon skinner [10-11] (10%) Smooth Bone Necklace • (10%) Smooth Bone Totem • (20%) Ivory Handled Skinning Knife • (25%) Pristine Wolf Pelt • (25%) Pristine Badger Hide • (1.5%) Pelt Punch, Hunting Spear, ***or*** Sewn Cloak of Might • (3%) APOA: Patched Hide • (0.15%) APOA: Sewn Hide • (0.5%) <Engraved Enchantments>

curmudgeon trapper [11-12] *see curmudgeon skinner [10-11]*

ghostly siabra [11-12] (80% each) Etched Wooden Bowl, Obsidian • (20% each) Etched Wooden Cup, Chryoprase • (1.4%) Siabrian Gloves • (1.5%) <Craftsman Pendants> • (0.5%) <Engraved Enchantments>

Lelly [13] *see roane maiden [12-13]*

roane companion [12-13] *see roane maiden [12-13]*

roane maiden [12-13] (1.5%) Selkie Skin • (10%) Fish (x2) • (80% each) Fish, Fishing Pole, Obsidian • (10%) Chryoprase • (0.5%) <Engraved Enchantments>

Lough Gur

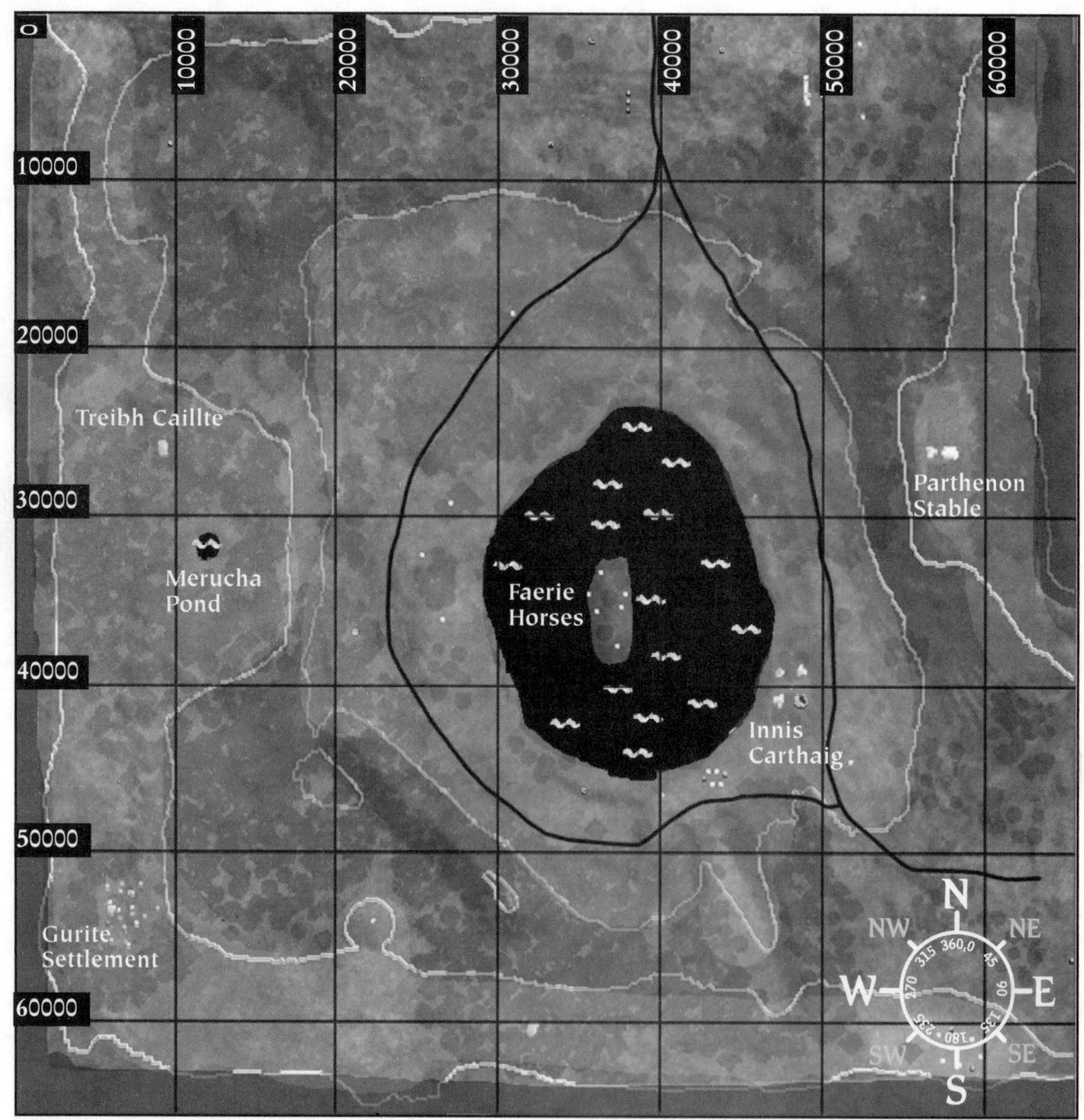

Lower-level monsters not shown on map:

Creature	Lvl	Location
chipstone sheerie	21	SC,SE
cluricaun	22	NE,EC,SE
cluricaun	23	NE,WC,EC,SW,SE
cluricaun	24	NC,NE,SE
curmudgeon fighter	16	NE
curmudgeon fighter	18	EC
curmudgeon poacher	15	NE
curmudgeon scout	15	NE
curmudgeon scout	16	NE,EC
curmudgeon scout	17	EC
dampwood mite	22	NC,SC,SE
dew sheerie	16	EC
dew sheerie	17	NE,EC
dew sheerie	18	EC
Druid	22	WC
faerie beetle	17	NE,EC,SW
faerie horse	23	C
fishing bear	18	C,EC
fishing bear	19	C,EC
fishing bear	20	C,EC
fishing bear	21	C,EC
fishing bear forager	13	C,EC
fishing bear forager	14	C,EC

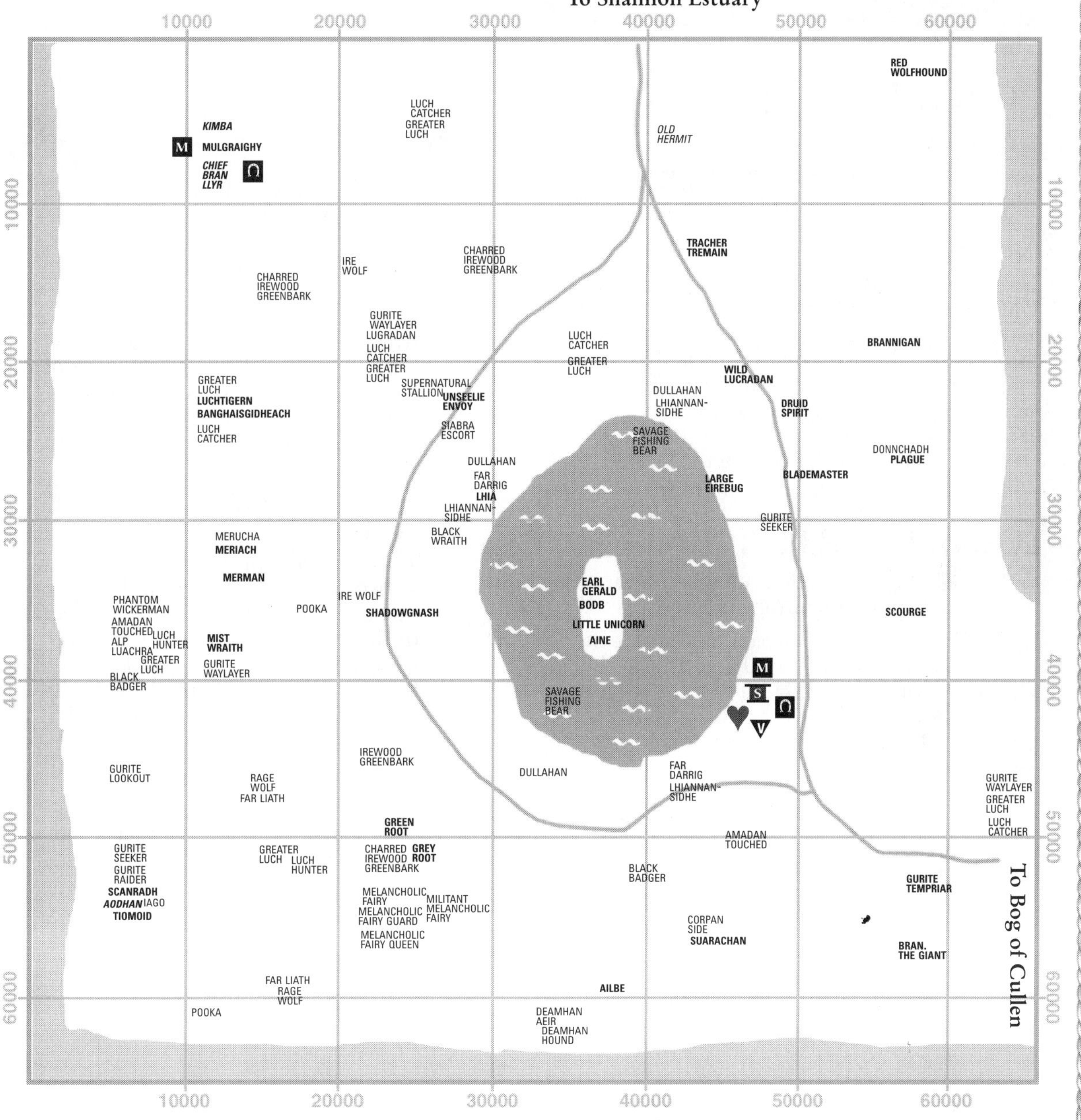

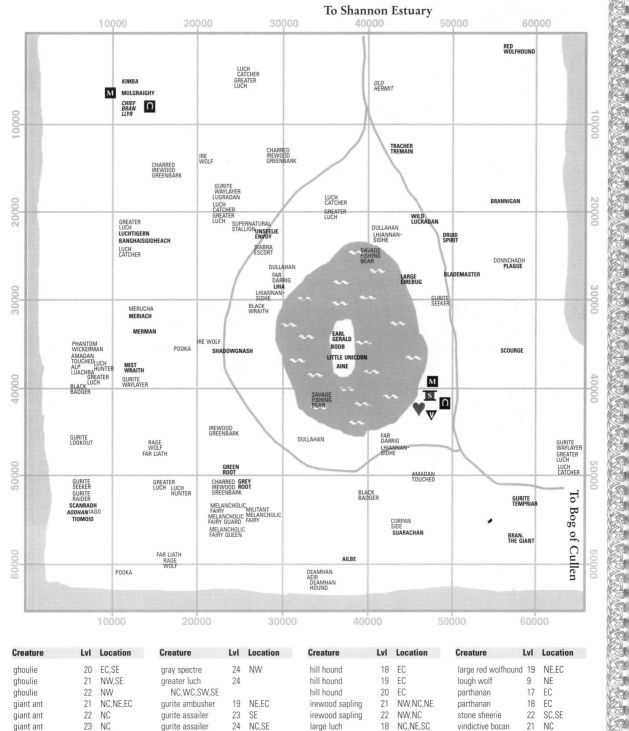

Creature	Lvl	Location
ghoulie	20	EC,SE
ghoulie	21	NW,SE
ghoulie	22	NW
giant ant	21	NC,NE,EC
giant ant	22	NC
giant ant	23	NC
giant ant	24	SE
giant beetle	20	EC
giant beetle	21	NC
gray spectre	23	NW
gray spectre	24	NW
greater luch	24	NC,WC,SW,SE
gurite ambusher	19	NE,EC
gurite assailer	23	SE
gurite assailer	24	NC,SE
gurite footpad	15	NC,NE
gurite footpad	16	NE,EC
gurite piller	19	NC,NE
gurite piller	21	NE
hill hound	18	EC
hill hound	19	EC
hill hound	20	EC
irewood sapling	21	NW,NC,NE
irewood sapling	22	NW,NC
large luch	18	NC,NE,SC
large luch	19	NE,EC
large luch	21	NE,EC
large red wolfhound	17	NE,EC
large red wolfhound	18	NE
large red wolfhound	19	NE,EC
lough wolf	9	NE
parthanan	17	EC
parthanan	18	EC
stone sheerie	22	SC,SE
vindictive bocan	21	NC
vindictive bocan	22	NC

Lough Gur Tips

Solo Friendly?

For rangers, there are the Irewood greenbarks starting at 40 that are just a godsend! Of course, these tend to disappear at night.

Group Friendly?

The whole zone is an excellent grouping area. There is a small parth farm and the dampwood mites for lower levels, and there are a host of creatures for high-level folks to hunt. The pooks are probably the most popular. Nighttime hunting is also popular, and it's close to Innis, so you have a place to run to (for safety or just to sell). Daytime hunting usually goes to the bears.

- Steve "Larian LeQuella" Lundquist

LOUGH GUR HUNTING

15-17 By this point, you should be prepared to take on Fishing Bear Foragers.

21-24 Look for Irewood Saplings outside of Ceannai and use fire-based attacks, but be careful. 23-25 Hunt Mermans during these levels. They're vulnerable to cold-based attacks, so concentrate on those.

22-28 Once you have some basic pet combat abilities, head toward Innis Carthaig and fight a few Dampwood Mites. They'll occasionally bring a friend (which is why a pet is good). Most of these critters will con blue/yellow at the earlier levels in this range, but will go blue, then green as you reach the top of this level bracket. They normally yield a sizeable amount of gold and are vulnerable to cold.

22 - 24 Time for more Irewood Saplings. Go by horseback to Innis, then cross the bridge near Connla. When you ride by a merchant tent, head southwest and take pains to avoid the Guirrite Footman. The first stand of trees contains slow-moving sapling mobs who don't cast. Further southwest, you can find a smaller group. Attack from max range and drop any branches you pick up. The bundles of Ire wood will bring 10s, so haul them back to town. (Take plenty of arrows; the tent merchants don't sell them.

28 - 31 Mist wraiths wandering around in this area are a tough kill, but can be worth the effort.

30 The lower part of this zone is home to Siabria Wayslayers. As with the saplings, ride by horse to Innis and turn toward the bog when the path splits near the merchant tents. As you emerge from the forest, theWayslayers are there. Using a quest bow is an effective way to kill them.

36-38 Spend some time in this level range hunting Deamhan Aeirs.

41-45 Five words — Pooka, Dullahans and Savage Fishing Bears.

49-50 As you approach level 50, Far Darrigs are your best bet for hunting in Lough Gur.

Quest NPCs

Innis Carthaig	
Chieftain	Cad Goddeau (lvl 30) (lvl Guild Track - 30)
Bran the Giant	Secret of Nuada's Silver (lvl 25) (lvl Guild Track - 25)

Loot

Ailbe [43] (72%) Deamhan Hound Tooth (x2) • (60%) Deamhan Hound Claw (x2) • (20%) Deamhan Hound Pelt • (1.5%) Infernal Bane ***or*** Bracer

Aine [61] (1.5%) Deo Hauberk, Reinforced Deo Vest ***or*** Leather Deo Jerkin • (80%) Jewel-Encrusted Eye • (60%) Violet Diamond

alp luachra [29-30/31] (25/30%) Alp Luachra Hand (x2) • (25/20%) Alp Luachra Eye • (8/10%) Alp Luachra Head

amadan touched [29-30/31-32/33-34] (1.5%) Ring of the Amadan ***or*** Ring of Undead Might • (40/40/20%) Worn Carnielian Studded Belt • (8/12/20%) Forgotten Silver Jasper Locket • (80% each) Well Crafted Lantern, Flint • (60%) Copper Amethyst Bracelet • (10/20/40%) Small Silver Laden Box • (0.3%) <The Four Elements>

amalgamate parthanan [26] (75% each) Malicious Black Heart, Black Clawed Hand • (3% each) Parthanan Head, Pearl • (10%) Lapis Lazuli • (0.3%) <Muire's Riches 2> • (1.5%) Parthanon Fist ***or*** Ether Ring

Aodhan [40] (2%) Siabrian Raider's Head • (80%) Eagle Head Brooch • (70%) Jeweled Scabard • (10%) Cat's Eye Apatite • (1.2%) APOA: Raider's Chitin • (1.2%) Left ***or*** Right Bracer of Skill, Siabrian Belt, Mystic Shield ***or*** Crusher, ***or*** Crescent Razor • (1.2%) <Rogue Pendants (Highest)> • (1.2%) Cath Drum ***or*** APOA: Cath

Banghaisgidheach [34] (68%) Luch Tooth (x2) • (75%) Luch Meat (x2) • (80%) Luch Claw • (40%) Luch Claw • (30%) Pristine Luch Hide • (0.5%) Ranger's Last Flight • (0.8%) Silvered Arrow • (0.3%) Aotrom Pearls

black badger [36-37/39-40] (75%) Black Badger Tooth (x2) • (65/70%) Black Badger Claw (x2) • (35/75%) Black Badger Meat (x2) • (15/20%) Pristine Black Badger Pelt • (1.5%) Badger Pelt Shield/Helm ***or*** Cloak

black wraith [52] (30% each) Wraith Essence, Shadowy Gem • (45%) Etheric Spirit Shackles • (25%) Jewels 64 • (1.6%) <Arcane Artifacts> • (1.6%) Phantom Gem

Blademaster [14] (no loot)

Bodb [63] (1.5%) Wraith Necklace, Mist Necklace, ***or*** Etheric Bludgeoner • (80%) Chrysoberyl • (30%) Precious Jasper**Bran the Giant [24]** (no loot)

Brannigan [25] *see cluricaun [24]*

chipstone sheerie [21] (5% each) Smooth Sling Stones, Fine Unworked Stone • (90%) Unworked Stone • (1.5%) Rock Sherrie Bracer • (0.3%) <Muire's Riches 2>

cluricaun [22-23] (5%) Silver Goblet • (75% each) Pouch of Ill Gotten Gain, Forgetful Dust • (1.3%) <Hedge Clippers> • (1.3%) APOA: Woven Hedge Weed • (0.3%) <Muire's Riches 3> • (0.8%) Lucky Lauean, Lucky Muinneelyn ***or*** Lucky Failm • (0.5%) Mollachd Coin

cluricaun [24] (10%) Silver Goblet • (80% each) Pouch of Ill Gotten Gain, Forgetful Dust • (1.3%) <Hedge Clippers> • (1.3%) APOA: Woven Hedge Weed • (0.3%) <De'velyn's Delights> • (1.3%) Lucky Rhusag, Lucky Bootsyn, Lucky Perree ***or*** Lucky Breechyn

corpan side [39-40/41] (80% each) Changeling Hair, Changeling Skin • (20/30% each) Jasper Beetle Chitin Necklace, Changeling Blood • (1.5%) Giant Gutter ***or*** Spine Splitter

curmudgeon fighter [16,18,21] *see curmudgeon poacher [15]*

curmudgeon poacher [15] (5% each) Tattered Sapphire Brea Sleeves, Helm • (25% each) Ivory Handled Skinning Knife, Smooth Bone Totem, Pristine Wolf Pelt, Pristine Badger Hide • (80% each) Smooth Bone Necklace, Torn Wolf Pelt • (0.3%) <Treasures of the Fey>

curmudgeon scout [15-16/17] (5% each) Pitted Recurve Bow, Rough Flight Blunt Arrows • (80% each) 50 Feet of Rope, Leather Pouch • (40%) Waterskin • (20%) Garnet/Citrine • (0.3%) <Muire's Riches 2>

dampwood mite [22] (21% each) Mite Poison Gland, Dampwood Mite Leg, Gnawed Insect Wing

deamhan aeir [35-36/37] (70%) Deamhan Wing (x2) • (70%) Deamhan Claw (x2) • (20/30%) Cat's Eye Opal • (5%) Cat's Eye Apatite/Green Sapphire • (1.4%) Deamhan Circlet of Speed • (1.4%) [Deamhan Aeir Claw ***or*** Screaming Ring]/[Ether Staff, Ether Staff of Thought, Ether Staff of Light, ***or*** Abrasive Necklace] • (12%) Essence of Deamhan Aeir

deamhan hound [40-41/42] (68/72%) Deamhan Hound Tooth (x2) • (72/65%) Deamhan Hound Claw • (40/55%) Deamhan Hound Claw • (20%) Deamhan Hound Pelt • (1.2%) Infernal Edge, Flute ***or*** Cloak/Infernal Bane ***or*** Bracer

dew sheerie [16-17/18] (75% each) Chryoprase, Amethyst [16-17] • (80%) Amethyst [18] • (50%) Lapis Lazuli [18] • (15/30%) Waterproof Satchel • (1.5%) Glowing Sherrie Beads • (5%) Intricate Sea Shell Bracelet • (0.3%) <Muire's Riches 2>

Druid [22] (80% each) Softly Glowing Orb, Draoish Sacrificial Heart • (1.5%) APOA: Draoi, Draoi Shield ***or*** Draoish Sickle • (40%) Faerie Gem

Druid Spirit [30] (no loot)

dullahan [48-49,51] (80%) Dullahan's Skin • (70%) Dullahan's Blackened Heart • (60%) Blood Stained Bag • (1.4%) Harvester of Malign Doom ***or*** Dullahan's Luminescent Head • (1.4%) Dread Blackscale

Earl Gerald [60] *see Aine [61]*

faerie beetle [17] (80%) Faerie Beetle Leg (x2) • (10%) Faerie Beetle Mandible • (5% each) Faerie Beetle Carapace, Faerie Dust

faerie horse [23] (80%) Faerie Horse Mane • (50%) Faerie Horse Pelt • (90%) Faerie Horse Tail

far darrig [46-47/48] (80%) Briar Horror Mask • (40/60%) Thorny Green Sapphire Bracelet • (1.4%) APOA: Mischievious Greenbriar • (1.4%) Wicked Thorn

far liath [31-32] (1.5%) Fog Bound Cape • (80% each) Far Liath Essense, Green Tourmaline • (10%) Black Star Diopside • (0.3%) <The Four Elements>

fishing bear [18-19/20-21] (20/40%) Fishing Bear Skin • (70/65%) Bear Tooth (x2) • (70/65%) Bear Meat (x2)

fishing bear forager [13-14] (20%) Fishing Bear Forager Skin • (80% each) Fishing Bear Forager Tooth, Meat • (40% each) Fishing Bear Forager Tooth, Meat

ghoulie [20-21/22] (1.5%) Ghoulish Shackle • (80%) Ghoul Skin • (80%) Carnelian/Agate • (40%) Ghoul Skin • (20/30%) Azurite • (5% each) Forgotten Silk Coth, Citrine • (0.3%) <Muire's Riches 3>

giant ant [21-22/23-24] (70/80%) Giant Ant Legs (x2) • (40/55%) Giant Ant Mandible • (5/10%) Giant Ant Carapace

giant beetle [20-21] (60%) Giant Beetle Leg (x2) • (40%) Giant Beetle Leg Tip (x2) • (18%) Giant Beetle Mandible (x2) • (5%) Giant Beetle Carapace

gray spectre [23/24] (1.5%) Spectral Shroud • (40/60%) Spectral Essence • (80%) Spirit Shackles • (5%) Green Tourmaline/Chrome Diopside • (0.3%) <Muire's Riches 3> • (1.5%) Orb of Resistance [23] • [remaining are 24 only] (1.1%) Malicious Black Heart • (1.1%) Black Clawed Hand • (0.05%) Parthanan Head • (0.05%) Pearl • (0.2%) Lapis Lazuli • (0.01%) <Muire's Riches 2> • (0.02%) Parthanon Fist ***or*** Ether Ring

greater luch [24-25,27] (55%) Luch Tooth • (75%) Luch Meat • (60%) Luch Meat • (45%) Luch Claw • (10%) Pristine Luch Hide • (1.5%) Puinesean Fang ***or*** Eucail Eye

gurite ambusher [19] (20%) Leather Pouch • (80%) Bandit Sash • (3%) APOA: Worn Dark Shadow • (40%) Carnelian • (0.3%) <Muire's Riches 2> • (15%) Silver Gaming Dice • (2%) Siabrian Ambusher's Head • (1.4%) APOA: Ambusher • (1.5%) <Rogue Pendants (Low)>

gurite assailer [23-24] (80%) Soft Padded Backpack • (70%) Overlord's Orders • (20%) Garnet • (10%) Topaz • (5%) Bracelet of Twisted Silver • (1.3%) Assailer's Curved Blade • (3%) APOA: Worn Dark Shadow • (1.5%) <Rogue Pendants (Higher)> • (0.3%) <Muire's Riches 3> • (1.3%) Soiagh Blade ***or*** Cur Shaghey

gurite footpad [15-16] (25%) Silver Amethyst Ring • (20%) Bloodstone • (15%) Amethyst • (10%) Carnelian • (5%) Siabrian Footpad's Head • (2%) Worn Dark Shadow Rapier • (2%) APOA: Worn Dark Shadow • (0.3%) <Muire's Riches 2>

gurite lookout [37] (30%) Vial of Elven Essence • (20%) Emerald Dust • (30%) Sapphire Dust • (20%) Jewels 17 • (1.2%) General ***or*** Noble Lord Pendant • (1.2%) APOA: Turbid Waters • (1.2%) <Bogman's Bundle> • (1.2%) APOA: Cath, ***or*** Cath Drum

gurite piller [19,21] (35%) Bandit Sash • (25%) Bandit Mask • (15%) Silver Topaz Ring • (5%) Siabrian Piller's Head • (1.5%) Griffonhead Cloak Pin • (2%) APOA: Worn Dark Shadow • (0.3%) <Muire's Riches 3>

gurite raider [37,39] (70%) Eagle Head Brooch • (60%) Jeweled Scabard • (2%) Siabrian Raider's Head • (10%) Cat's Eye Opal • (1.2%) APOA: Raider's Chitin • (1.2%) Left ***or*** Right Bracer of Skill, Siabrian Belt, Mystic Shield ***or*** Crusher, ***or*** Crescent Razor • (1.5%) <Rogue Pendants (Highest)> • (1.2%) Cath Drum ***or*** APOA: Cath

gurite seeker [31] (35%) Primrose Eye • (35%) Siog Brandy • (35%) Topaz • (1.3%) Spectral Tunic, Helm ***or*** Shadow, ***or*** Bracer of Might • (1.3%) Smiter's Belt, Smiter, ***or*** Siog's Might • (50%) Bolt of Soft Gossamer • (1.3%) Cath Lute, Shield, Spear, Cloak ***or*** Charms

gurite tempriar [24] *see gurite assailer [23-24]*

gurite waylayer [26-27] (1.5%) <Rogue Pendants (Higher)> • (1.2%) Siabrian Bandit Helm • (70%) Bandit Mask • (10%) Siabra Waylayer Sash • (1.2%) Waylayer Short Sword, Great Sword, Shillelagh, Spiked Mace, Hammer, Rapier ***or*** Dirk • (40%) Silver Gaming Dice • (20%) Green Tourmaline • (0.3%) <De'velyn's Delights> • (2%) Siabrian Waylayer's Head • (1.2%) Cath Lute, Shield, Spear, Cloak ***or*** Charms

hill hound [18-19/20] (80/85%) Hill Hound Canine (x2) • (30/48%) Pristine Hill Hound Pelt

horse [10,55] (75%) Horse Hair • (10%) Auburn Mane • (80%) Ruined Horse Skin • (35%) Horse Skin • (60%) Horse Hair

ire wolf [25-26/27] (75/80%) Ire Wolf Tooth (x3) • (25/33%) Ire Wolf Pelt • (10%) Ire Wolf Claw [25-26]

irewood greenbark [40] (80%) Irewood Greenbark Branch (x2) • (30%) Glowing Irewood Greenbark Sap • (20%) Bundle of Greenbark Branches • (1.4%) APOA: Hardened Cloth • (1.4%) Bardic Wonder, ***or*** Staff of Thought, Destruction ***or*** Enchantments (all Petrified)

irewood sapling [21-22] (75%) Ire Wood Sapling Branch (x2) • (55%) Bundle of Sapling Branches (x2) • (5%) Pitted Glowing Ng Kit Ire Wood Sapling Staff

large eirebug [10] (80%) Large Eirebug Leg (x2) • (40%) Large Eirebug Mandible • (10%) Large Eirebug Carapace

large luch [18-19/21] (55/50%) Large Luch Tooth • (85/80%) Large Luch Meat • (25/60%) Large Luch Meat • (5/25%) Large Luch Claw • (5/10%) Pristine Large Luch Hide

large red wolfhound [17-19] (50%) Pristine Redhound Pelt • (75%) Large Red Hound Claw (x2)

Lhia [51] *see far darrig [48]*

lhiannan-sidhe [49] *see far darrig [48]*

little unicorn [23] (80%) Faerie Horse Mane • (50%) Faerie Horse Pelt • (90%) Faerie Horse Tail • (1.5%) Tiny ***or*** Hollowed Unicorn Horn

lough wolf [9] (20%) Sharp Wolf Claw • (80%) Chunk of Wolf Meat • (70%) Pristine Wolf Pelt

luch catcher [25/27-28] (55%) Luch Tooth • (70/68%) Luch Meat (x2) • (45/35%) Luch Claw • (11/22%) Pristine Luch Hide • (1.5%) Luch Paw [25] • (1.5%) Missing Caster's Cap, Gloves ***or*** Belt, ***or*** Caster's Missing Eye [27-28]

luch hunter [31/33-34] (60/68%) Luch Tooth • (35/68%) Luch Tooth • (75%) Luch Meat (x2) • (60/80%) Luch Claw • (30/40%) Luch Claw • (22/30%) Pristine Luch Hide • (1.5/0.5%) Ranger's Last Flight • (0.8%) Silvered Arrow [33-34] • (0.3%) Aotrom Pearls [33-34]

Luchtigern [30] (65%) Luch Tooth (x2) • (80%) Luch Meat • (55%) Luch Meat • (40%) Luch Claw • (20%) Pristine Luch Hide • (1.5%) Puinesean Fang ***or*** Eucail Eye

lugradan [28] (75% each) Silver Goblet, Pouch of Ill Gotten Gain • (10%) Golden Clover Brooch • (1.4%) Nearahd Sleeves, Gloves, Coif ***or*** Cloak, ***or*** Pluc • (1.3%) APOA: Woven Hedge Weed • (0.3%) <De'velyn's Delights>

lugradan [30] (80% each) Silver Goblet, Pouch of Ill Gotten Gain • (15%) Golden Clover Brooch • (1.4%) <Hedge Clippers> • (1.4%) Nearahd Hauberk, Leggings ***or*** Boots, Lucky Striker, ***or*** Fainne Necklace • (0.3%) <The Four Elements>

Meriach [50] *see merucha [30]*

merman [36] (75% each) Merman Scales, Green Tourmaline • (50%) Orb of Swirling Sea Water • (5%) Red Spinel • (1.4%) APOA: Algae Covered Coral ***or*** Sidhe Spine Barbed Spear • (1.4%) Braided Kelp Belt, Bracelet ***or*** Necklace, ***or*** Coral Ring

merucha [30] (80%) Seal Skin Bag • (60%) Silver Pearl Ring • (40%) Silver Pearl Necklace • (1.5%) Coral Vest • (5%) Green Tourmaline • (50%) Topaz • (0.3%) <The Four Elements>

mist wraith [27] (80%) Dark Heart of the Vindictive Spirit • (10%) Mist Wraith Essence • (1.5%) Wraith Necklace, Mist Necklace ***or*** Etheric Bludgeoner • (0.3%) <De'velyn's Delights>

parthanan [17-18] (75% each) Malicious Black Heart, Black Clawed Hand • (3% each) Parthanan Head, Pearl • (10%) Lapis Lazuli • (0.3%) <Muire's Riches 2>

phantom wickerman [28] (80%) Phantom Essence • (30%) Manifested Phantom Terror Claw (x2) • (1.5%) Phantom Bastard Sword • (8%) Darkened Terror Claw

pooka [52-54/55,57] (50/60%) Shape Changer's Hide • (75/80% each) Shape Changer's Skull, Tooth • (1.5%) <No Such Thing as the Bogeyman>

rage wolf [31-32] (70%) Rage Wolf Fang (x2) • (70%) Rage Wolf Claw (x2) • (20%) Rage Wolf Pelt • (8%) Dangerous Tooth

red wolfhound [13] (75%) Sharp Hound Claw (x2) • (30%) Pristine Redhound Pelt

savage fishing bear [52-53] (40%) Savage Fishing Bear Skin • (25%) Pristine Bear Skin • (45%) Savage Fishing Bear Tooth • (1.7%) Bear Claw Talisman • (40%) Savage Fishing Bear Tooth • (60%) Savage Fishing Bear Meat (x2)

scanradh [39] (no loot)

Shadowgnash [58] (70%) Shape Changer's Hide • (80% each) Shape Changer's Skull, Tooth • (1.5%) <No Such Thing as the Bogeyman>

siabra escort [48] (25% each) Vial of Elven Essence, Emerald Dust, Sapphire Dust • (20%) Jewels 64 • (1.1%) General ***or*** Noble Lord Pendant • (1.1%) Ruby Death Bringer • (1.1%) APOA: Bog Strider • (1.1%) Crimson Heart-Stoppers • (0.6%) Valorous Mane • (0.6%) Valorous Hauberk ***or*** Sword of Valor

stone sheerie [22] (80%) Unworked Stone • (30%) Fine Unworked Stone • (5%) Fire Opal • (1.5%) Rock Sherrie Bracer • (0.3%) <Muire's Riches 3>

Suarachan [42] *see corpan side [41]*

supernatural stallion [48] (no loot)

Tiomoid [39] (no loot)

Tracker Tremain [24] (no loot)

unseelie envoy [55] (no loot)

vindictive bocan [20-21/22] (1% each piece) Tattered Stone Cailiocht/Tattered Cailiocht • (80%) Agate/Topaz • (40%) Topaz/Pearl • (5%) Green Tourmaline/Fire Opal • (0.3%) <Muire's Riches 3>

wild lucradan [10] (3%) Bottle of Poteen Wine • (80% each) Leather Pouch, Spinel • (20%) Silver Coin • (0.5%) <Engraved Enchantments>

Dark Age of Camelot The Atlas

Shannon Estuary

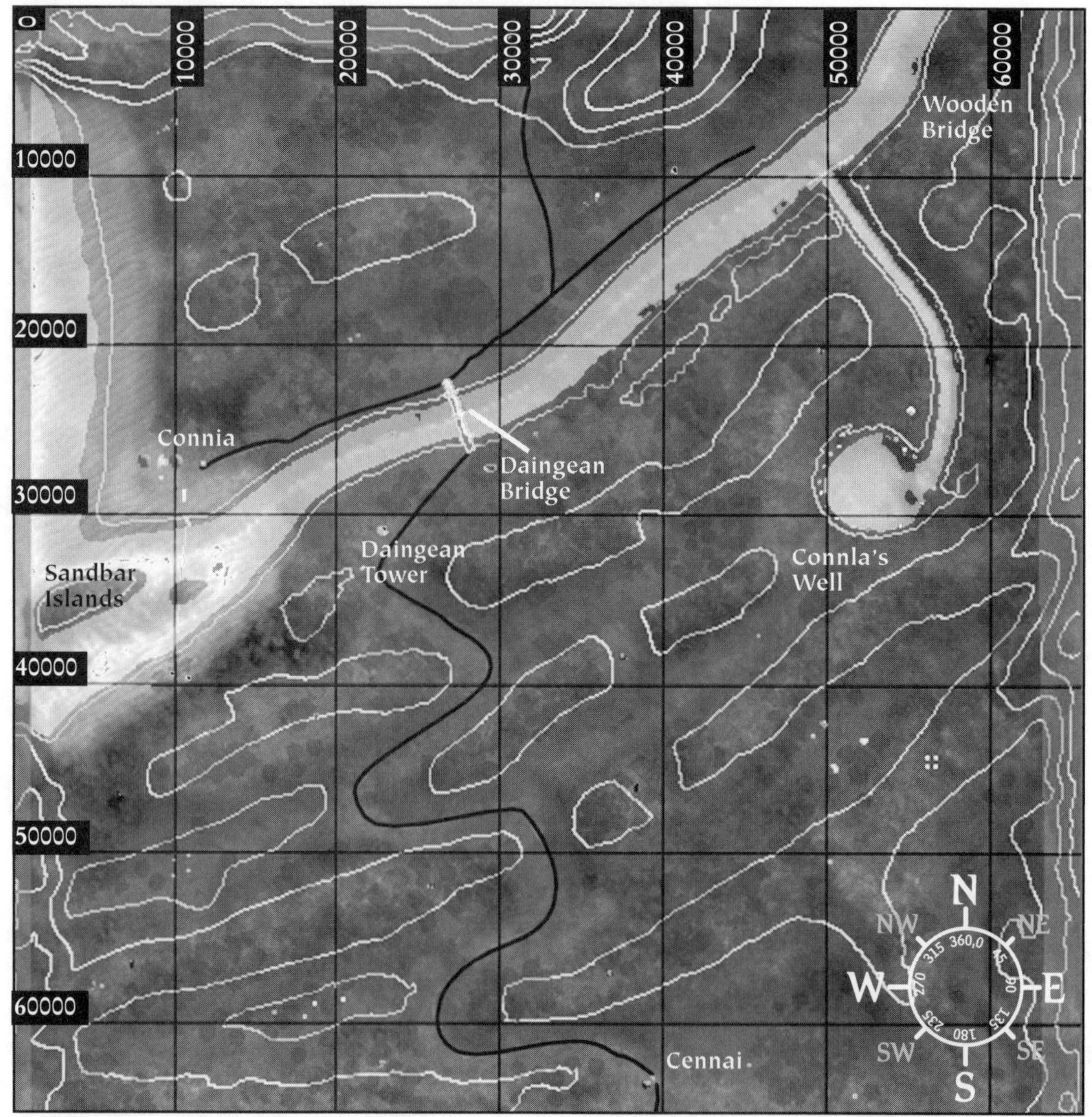

Lower-level monsters not shown on map:

Creature	Lvl	Location
annoying lucradan	0	NW,NC,WC
badger cub	0	NW,NC,WC
beach rat	1	WC
beach rat	2	NW,WC
bodachan sabhaill	3	NC,NE
bodachan sabhaill	4	NC,NE
Caoranach	7	EC
Caoranach	8	EC
Caoranach	9	EC
cluricaun trip	7	SC
cluricaun trip	8	SC
eriu fiscere	13	NW,NE,C
feccan	3	NW,NC,NE
haunted driftwood	1	NW,WC
hill toad	5	NC,NE,WC,C
hill toad	7	SC
large frog	0	NW,NC,WC
large frog	1	NW,NC,WC
Lucan	6	WC
lugradan whelp	4	NW,NC,NE
lugradan whelp	5	NW,NC
lugradan whelp	6	NW,NC
lunantishee	8	SC
moss sheerie	9	WC,SW
moss sheerie	10	WC,SW
moss sheerie	11	WC,SW
moss sheerie	12	WC,SW
mudman	2	NW,NC,WC

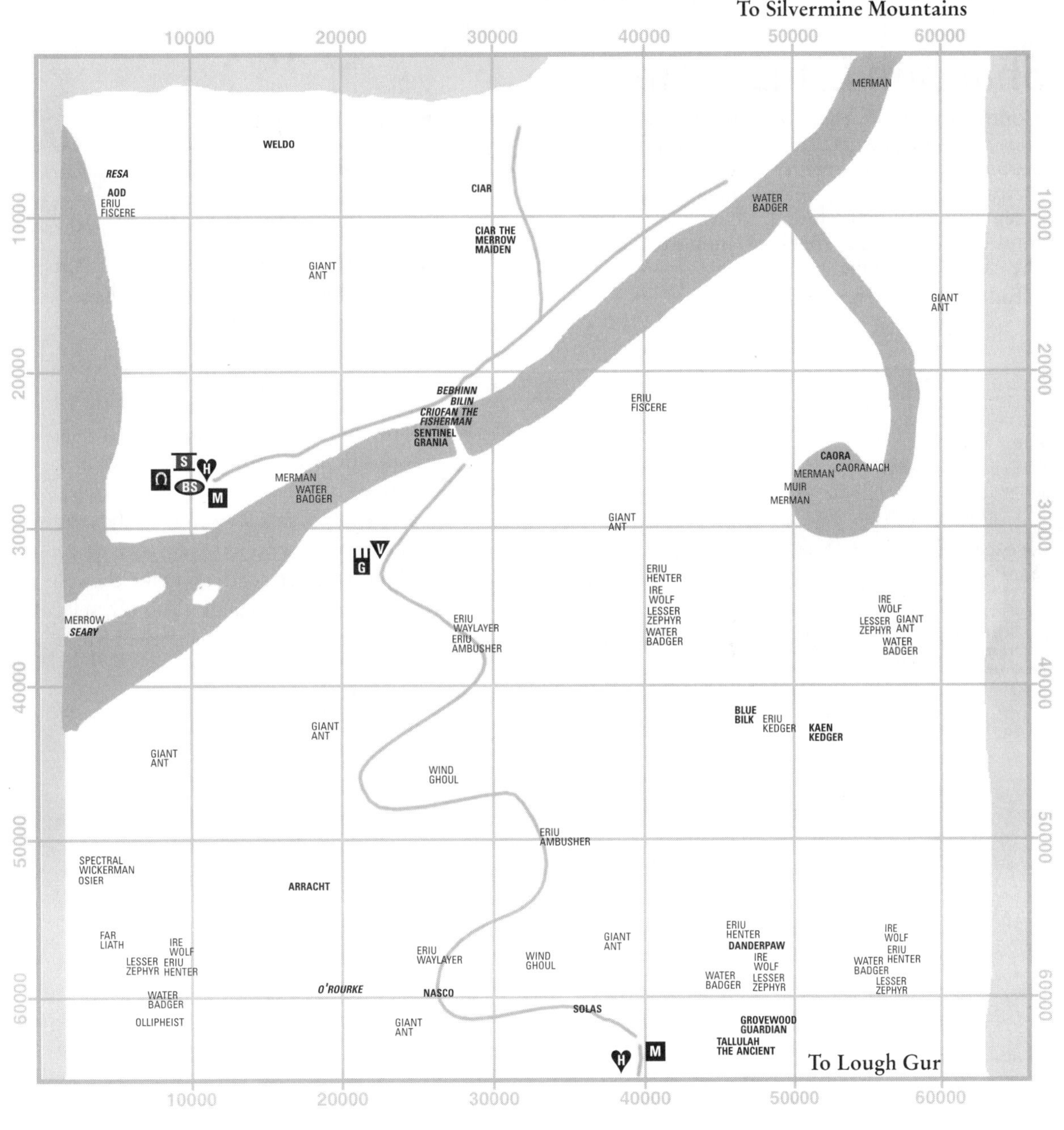

Creature	Lvl	Location
mudman	3	NW,NC,NE,WC,C
mudman	4	NW,NC,NE,WC,C
rat boy	3	NW,NC,NE
roane companion	13	NW,WC
rowdy	5	NW,NC,NE,WC,C
rowdy	6	NC
rowdy	7	NC,WC,SC
rowdy	8	NC,WC,SC
sand crab	0	NW,WC
sand crab	1	NW,WC
sandman	2	NW,WC
sandman	3	NW,WC
sandman	4	NW,WC
skeletal minion	3	NW,NC,NE
skeletal minion	4	NC,NE
skeletal pawn	1	NW,WC
small walking rock	3	NC,NE
spraggon	3	NW
spraggon	4	NC,NE,WC,C
spraggon	5	NC,NE,WC,C
spraggonite	5	NC,NE
villainous youth	3	NW
villainous youth	4	NW,NC,NE,WC,C
water beetle	6	WC
water beetle	7	WC
water beetle collector	4	WC
water beetle collector	5	WC
wiggle worm	0	WC
wind ghoul	7	SC

Shannon Estuary Tips

Connla is found in Shannon Estuary. A starting spot for some players, there are easy hunting grounds for younger players just outside of town. Across the river is a tower in which a Vault Keeper (Bank) can be found. Many players who hunt in Trebh Caille(spelling?) hunt here, as it is the closest bindstone.

- Todd "Jubal" Wharton

Quest NPCs

Bridge in Shannon Estuary	
Criofan	Criofan's Fish (lvl 20)
Connla	
Eira	Storyteller's Tale (lvl 10)
Oran O'Braonain	Sile's Sight (lvl 27)
your trainer	Connla's Fever (lvl 3)
your trainer	Sad tale (lvl 4)
your trainer	Slevin's Powder (lvl 4)
your trainer	Summoner Expulsion (lvl 4)
your trainer	Tale of Cad Goddeau (lvl 4)
Daingean	
Flidh Martin	The Touch of Amadan Dubh (lvl 40)

SHANNON ESTUARY HUNTING

5-8 Once again, your best bet right now is to go after Water Beetles with cold attacks

21-25 The vegetation here attracts Giant Ants, a nice collection to your hunting species.

23-25 Hunt Mermans during these levels. They're vulnerable to cold-based attacks, so concentrate on those.

25-27 Don your swimwear and look for two groups of Water Badgers and Merman north of the bridge near Connla. The badgers are a safe way to steadily earn XP, but when you're bored with that, follow the river north and take the split for even more Mermans. You can sell off your loot at the tower near the bridge, plus a vault's there.

Loot

annoying lucradan [0] (5%) Poteen Wine Flask • (70%) Onyx • (1%) <Braided Beauties> • (8% each piece) Tattered Brea and Tattered Woven

Aod [16] (80% each) Small Fish, Large Fish • (40% each) Fish Catchers Net, Silver Gilded Fishing Pole • (1.4%) APOA: Siabrian • (1.5%) <Craftsman Pendants> • (3%) APOA: Woven Crafter's • (0.3%) <Muire's Riches 2>

Arracht [38] (80%) Ollipheist Meat (x3) • (85% each) Ollipheist Claw, Ollipheist Fang • (50% each) Ollipheist Claw, Ollipheist Fang • (1%) Ollipheist Eye • (23%) Pristine Ollipheist Hide

badger cub [0] (60%) Badger Cub Fur • (40%) Badger Cub Tooth • (50%) Badger Cub Claw

beach rat [1-2] (25%) Beach Rat Fur • (68%) Beach Rat Claw (x2)

blue bilk [26] (80%) Bag of Blue Dyes • (60%) Blue Goblet • (1.5%) APOA: Bilk's Blue ***or*** Bilk's Spear

bodachan sabhaill [3-4] (75%) Onyx • (2%) Copper Charm • (25%) Oil Flask • (10% each piece) Tattered Brea and Tattered Woven • (1%) <Braided Beauties>

Caeoimhin [8] (no loot)

Caora [10] (50%) Caoranach Hide • (80%) Caoranach Toothed Jaw

Caoranach [7/8-9] (10/50%) Caoranach Hide • (80%) Caoranach Toothed Jaw

Chief Gaeth [20] (no loot)

Ciar [6] (no loot)

Ciar the Merrow Maiden [20] (no loot)

cluricaun trip [7-8] (5% each) Silver Coin, Leather Pouch • (80% each) Poteen Wine Flask, Moonstone • (5%) Pitted Dirk • (0.5%) <Celtic Knots>

Danderpaw [28] (80%) Ire Wolf Tooth (x3) • (33%) Ire Wolf Pelt

Driscol [10] (no loot)

Eoin [10] (no loot)

eriu ambusher [19] (20%) Leather Pouch • (80%) Bandit Sash • (3%) APOA: Worn Dark Shadow • (40%) Carnelian • (0.3%) <Muire's Riches 2> • (15%) Silver Gaming Dice • (2%) Siabrian Ambusher's Head • (1.4%) APOA: Ambusher • (1.5%) <Rogue Pendants (Low)>

eriu fiscere [13-14/15] (80% each) Small Fish, Large Fish • (20% each) Fish Catchers Net, Silver Gilded Fishing Pole • (1.4%) APOA: Siabrian • (1.5%) <Craftsman Pendants> • (3%) APOA: Woven Crafter's • (0.3%) <Treasures of the Fey>/<Muire's Riches 2>

eriu henter [19-20/21-22] (80% each) Small Fish, Large Fish • (40%) Large Fish [19-20] • (40%) Silver Gilded Fishing Pole • (20%) Silver Topaz Fishing Hook • (20/40%) Large Fishing Net • (1.4%) APOA: Tidal • (1.5%) <Craftsman Pendants> • (3%) APOA: Woven Crafter's • (0.3%) <Muire's Riches 3>

eriu kedger [16-17/18] (80% each) Small Fish, Large Fish • (40/60%) Large Fish • (10% each) Silver Gilded Fishing Pole, Large Fishing Net • (5/10%) Silver Topaz Fishing Hook • (1.4%) Kedger Short Bow, Recurve Bow, Drum, Flute, Lute, ***or*** Staff of Void Magic, Mentalism ***or*** Enchantment • (1.5%) <Craftsman Pendants> • (3%) APOA: Woven Crafter's • (0.3%) <Muire's Riches 2>

eriu waylayer [26-27] (1.5%) <Rogue Pendants (Higher)> • (1.2%) Siabrian Bandit Helm • (70%) Bandit Mask • (10%) Siabra Waylayer Sash • (1.2%) Waylayer Short Sword, Great Sword, Shillelagh, Spiked Mace, Hammer, Rapier ***or*** Dirk • (40%) Silver Gaming Dice • (20%) Green Tourmaline • (0.3%) <De'velyn's Delights> • (2%) Siabrian Waylayer's Head • (1.2%) Cath Lute, Shield, Spear, Cloak ***or*** Charms

far liath [31-32] (1.5%) Fog Bound Cape • (80% each) Far Liath Essense, Green Tourmaline • (10%) Black Star Diopside • (0.3%) <The Four Elements>

feccan [3] (5%) Feccan Skin • (75%) Onyx • (20%) Aventurine • (10% each piece) Tattered Brea and Tattered Woven • (1%) <Braided Beauties>

Flann [10] (no loot)

giant ant [21-22/23-24] (70/80%) Giant Ant Legs (x2) • (40/55%) Giant Ant Mandible • (5/10%) Giant Ant Carapace

Hagan [10] (no loot)

haunted driftwood [1] (65%) Driftwood (x2)

hill toad [5,7] (75%) Frog Legs • (60%) Frog Legs • (10%) Hill Toad Skin

horse [10] (75%) Horse Hair • (10%) Auburn Mane • (80%) Ruined Horse Skin • (35%) Horse Skin • (60%) Horse Hair

ire wolf [25-26/27] (75/80%) Ire Wolf Tooth (x3) • (25/33%) Ire Wolf Pelt • (10%) Ire Wolf Claw [25-26]

Kaen Kedger [19] (80% each) Small Fish, Large Fish • (60%) Large Fish • (20% each) Silver Gilded Fishing Pole, Large Fishing Net • (10%) Silver Topaz Fishing Hook • (1.4%) Kedger Short Bow, Recurve Bow, Drum, Flute, Lute, ***or*** Staff of Void Magic, Mentalism ***or*** Enchantment • (1.5%) <Craftsman Pendants> • (3%) APOA: Woven Crafter's • (0.3%) <Muire's Riches 2>

Kellan [10] (no loot)

Kiara, Roane Maiden [13] (1.5%) Selkie Skin • (10%) Fish (x2) • (80% each) Fish, Fishing Pole, Obsidian • (10%) Chryoprase • (0.5%) <Engraved Enchantments>

large frog [0-1] (65%) Frog Legs • (5%) Frog Legs

lesser zephyr [23-24] (35%) Swirling Crystal • (1.5%) Zephyr's Band of Power, Glowing Zephyr Gem, ***or*** Ethereal Zephyr Bracelet • (15%) Zephyr's Windy Essence • (0.3%) <Muire's Riches 3> • (10%) Wind Swept Leaves

Lucan [6] (no loot)

lugradan whelp [4-5/6] (5%) Silver Coin • (5%) Moonstone/Jade • (80%) Onyx/Aventurine • (5%) Jade [6] • (60/20%) Poteen Wine Flask • (1%) <Braided Beauties> [4-5] • (0.5%) <Celtic Knots> [6] • (1% each piece) Tattered Brea and Tattered Woven

lunantishee [8-9] (15%) Onyx Figurine • (60%) Luna Dust • (1.5%) Blackthorn Club • (3%) APOA: Blackthorn • (0.2%) APOA: Spiked Blackthorn, ***or*** a Blackthorn Wreath • (0.5%) <Celtic Knots>

Lunn [10] (no loot)

merman [23-24/25] (80% each) Seal Skin Bag, 50ft of Kelp Rope • (20% each) Silver Pearl Ring, Necklace • (1.4%) APOA: Coral • (0.3%) <Muire's Riches 3>/<De'velyn's Delights> • (1.4%) Coral Spear • (20%) Azurite [25]

merrow [20-22] (80% each) Seal Skin Bag, 50ft of Kelp Rope • (20%) Silver Pearl Ring • (10% each) Silver Pearl Necklace, Agate • (1.4%) APOA: Coral • (1.4%) Coral Spear • (0.3%) <Muire's Riches 3>

moss sheerie [9-12] (50%) Clump of Moss • (20%) Pouch of Faerie Dust • (10%) Jewels 24 • (0.3%) <Engraved Enchantments> • (1.5%) Hardened Moss Bracer

mudman [2-3/4] (80%) Ball of Clay • (30/40%) Small Amount of Clay • (5/10%) Block of Clay • (1%) <Braided Beauties>

Muir [25] (80% each) Seal Skin Bag, 50ft of Kelp Rope • (25% each) Silver Pearl Ring, Necklace • (1.4%) APOA: Coral • (20%) Azurite • (1.4%) Coral Spear • (0.3%) <De'velyn's Delights>

Nasco [28] (1.5%) <Rogue Pendants (Higher)> • (1.2%) Siabrian Bandit Helm • (70%) Bandit Mask • (10%) Siabra Waylayer Sash • (1.2%) Waylayer Short Sword, Great Sword, Shillelagh, Spiked Mace, Hammer, Rapier ***or*** Dirk • (40%) Silver Gaming Dice • (20%) Green Tourmaline • (0.3%) <De'velyn's Delights> • (2%) Siabrian Waylayer's Head • (1.2%) Cath Lute, Shield, Spear, Cloak ***or*** Charms

ollipheist [34-35/36-37] (65/75%) Ollipheist Meat (x3) • (80/85% each) Ollipheist Claw, Ollipheist Fang • (40/45% each) Ollipheist Claw, Ollipheist Fang • (1%) Ollipheist Eye • (6/20%) Pristine Ollipheist Hide

Osier [19] (80% each) Spectral Wickerman Essence, Manifested Terror Claw • (40%) Manifested Terror Claw • (1.5%) Spectral Long Sword • (0.3%) <Muire's Riches 3>

rat boy [3] (10%) Small Copper Ring • (80%) Small Mirror • (1%) <Braided Beauties> • (8% each piece) Tattered Brea and Tattered Woven

Resa [13] (1.5%) Selkie Skin • (10%) Fish (x2) • (80% each) Fish, Fishing Pole, Obsidian • (10%) Chryoprase • (0.5%) <Engraved Enchantments>

roane companion [13] (1.5%) Selkie Skin • (10%) Fish (x2) • (80% each) Fish, Fishing Pole, Obsidian • (10%) Chryoprase • (0.5%) <Engraved Enchantments>

rowdy [5-8] (no loot)

sand crab [0/1] (75/70%) Crab Legs • (30/40% each) Crab Legs, Shell

sandman [2-3/4] (80%) Ball of Clay • (30/40%) Small Amount of Clay • (5/10%) Block of Clay • (1%) <Braided Beauties>

Seary [23] (80% each) Seal Skin Bag, 50ft of Kelp Rope • (20% each) Silver Pearl Ring, Necklace • (1.4%) APOA: Coral • (20%) Agate • (1.4%) Coral Spear • (0.3%) <Muire's Riches 3>

skeletal minion [3-4] (5%) Pitted Broadsword • (75%) Onyx • (60%) Onyx • (8% each piece) Tattered Brea and Tattered Woven • (1%) <Braided Beauties>

skeletal pawn [1] (70%) Onyx • (10%) Aventurine • (8% each piece) Tattered Brea and Tattered Woven • (1%) <Braided Beauties>

small walking rock [3] (5%) Sling Stones • (70%) Large Rock Crystal • (1%) <Braided Beauties>

spectral wickerman [14-15/16-17] (20/80%) Spectral Wickerman Essence • (80%) Manifested Terror Claw • (60/20%) Manifested Terror Claw • (1.5%) Spectral Long Sword • (0.3%) <Muire's Riches 2>

spraggon [3-5] (15%) Chipped Mirror • (75%) Oil Flask • (5%) Pint of Grog • (1%) <Braided Beauties> • (10% each piece) Tattered Brea and Tattered Woven

spraggonite [5] (5%) Pitted Stiletto • (5%) Pint of Grog • (75%) Moonstone • (25%) Chipped Mirror • (1%) <Braided Beauties> • (10% each piece) Tattered Brea and Tattered Woven

villainous youth [3-4] (no loot)

water badger [21-22/23] (65%) Water Badger Tooth (x2) • (65%) Water Badger Claw (x2) • (17/31%) Water Badger Pelt • (8%) Ire Wolf Claw [23]

water beetle [6-7] (75%) Water Beetle Leg (x2) • (50%) Water Beetle Mandible • (25%) Water Beetle Carapace

water beetle collector [4-5] (80%) Water Beetle Leg • (45%) Water Beetle Leg

Weldo [6] (5% each) Silver Coin, Jade • (80%) Aventurine • (60%) Moonstone • (20%) Poteen Wine Flask • (0.5%) <Celtic Knots> • (1% each piece) Tattered Brea and Tattered Woven

wiggle worm [0] (80%) Worm Fishing Bait • (10%) Worm Fishing Bait

wind ghoul [7] (20% each) Gem of Swirling Wind, Wind Ghoul Essence • (80%) Aventurine • (60%) Jade • (0.5%) <Celtic Knots>

Sheeroe Hills

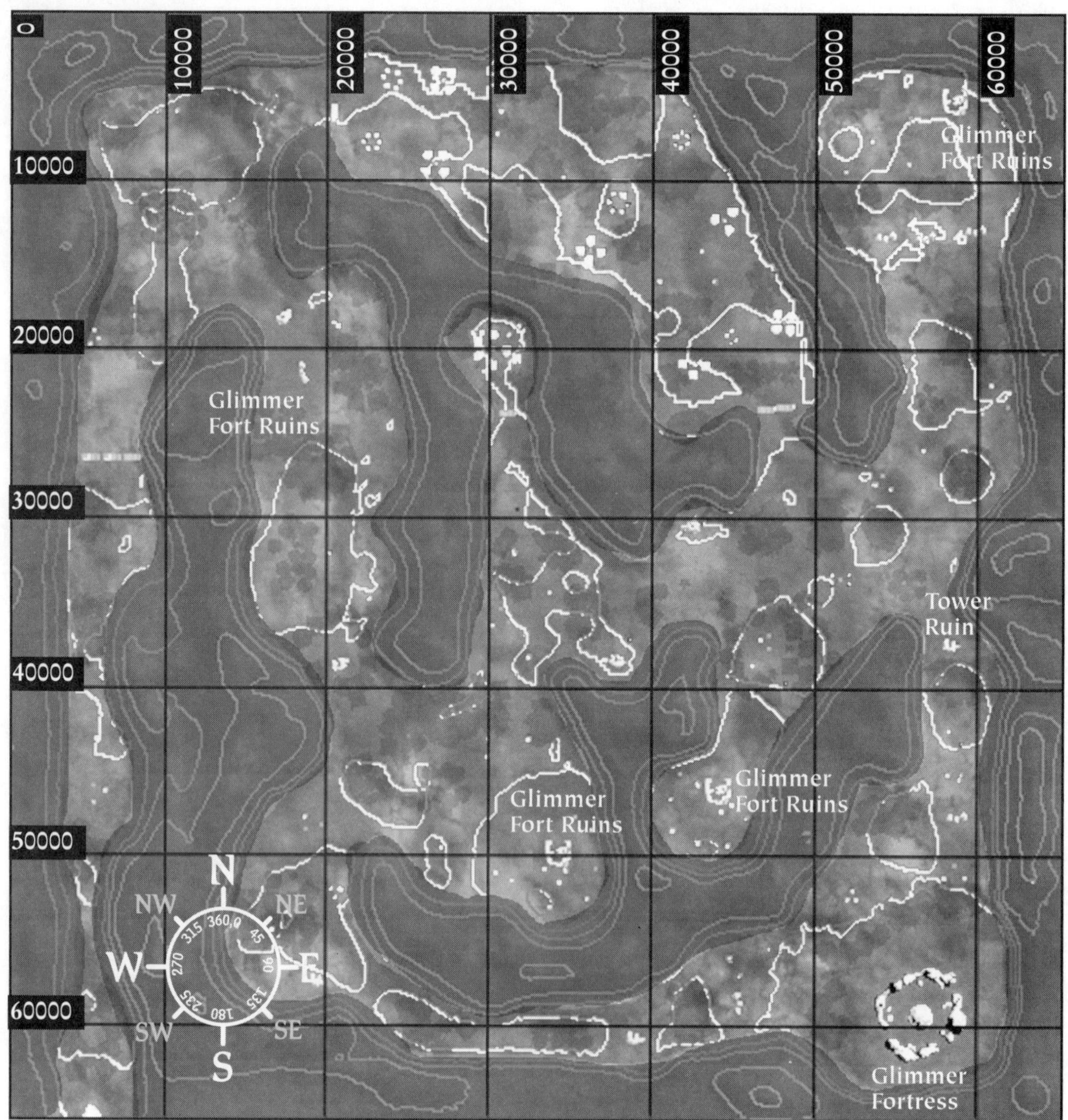

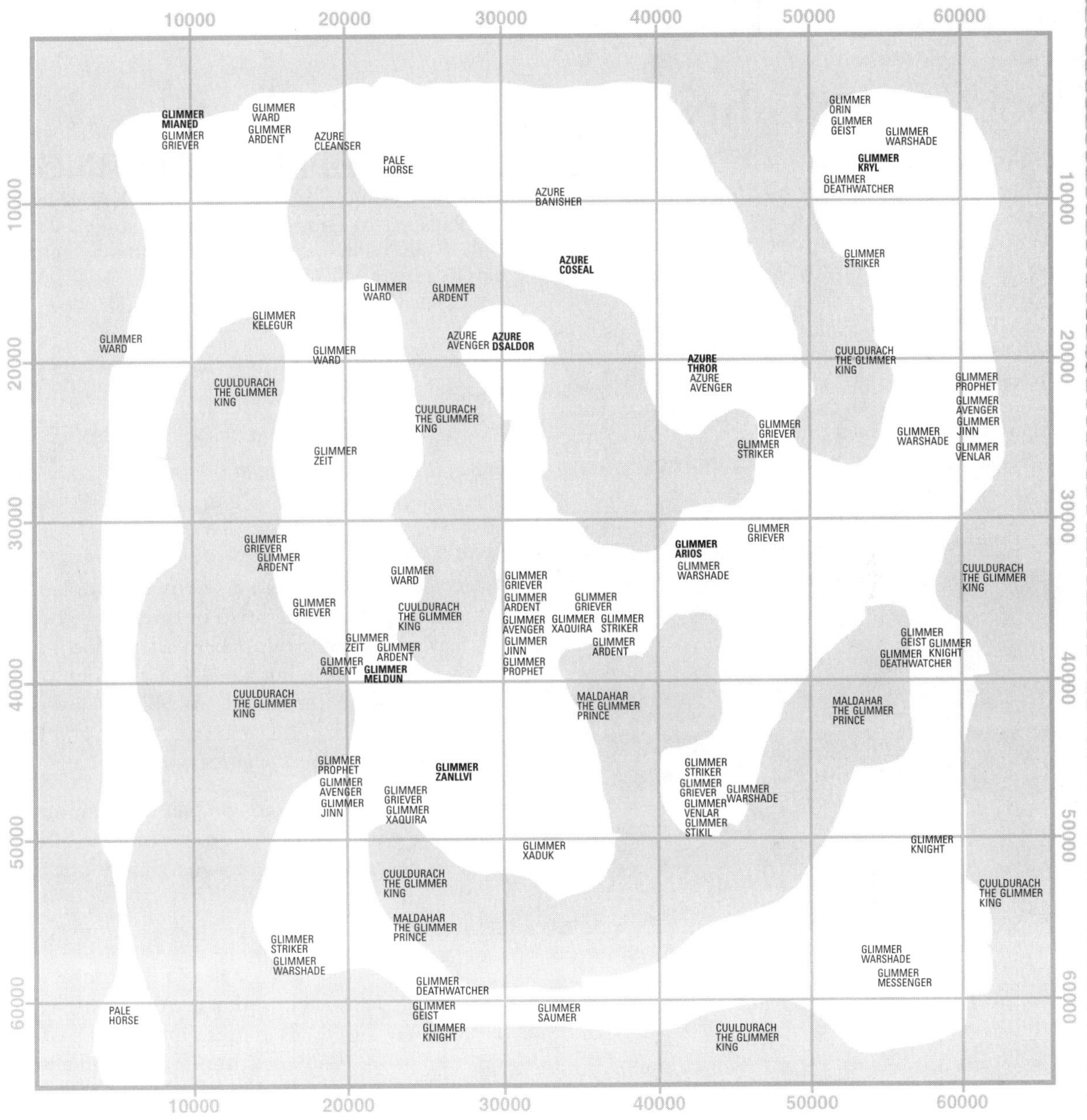

Lower-level monsters not shown on map:

Creature	Lvl	Location
azure cleanser	45	NW,NC,EC
celt spirit	40	SE
elf spirit	40	SE
elfshot madman	34	NC,SW
elfshot madman	36	NC,WC,SW
firbolg spirit	40	SE
glimmer ardent	45	NW,NC,WC,C
glimmer ghoul	39	NW,WC
glimmer ghoul	41	NW,WC
glimmer ghoul	43	NW,NC,WC,C
Glimmer Orist	45	WC
Glimmer Spass	45	NW,C
glimmer spirit	40	SE
glimmer ward	42	NW,NC,WC,C
glimmer ward	44	NW,NC,WC,C
glimmerling	36	WC,SW
glimmerling	38	NW,WC,SW
glimmerling	40	NW,WC,SW
lurikeen spirit	40	SE
raging subverter	39	NC,SW
raging subverter	41	NC,SW
raging subverter	43	NC,SW
Ranger	45	SE

Sheeroe Hills Tips

Solo Friendly?

The entrance area is very nice for a Ranger to solo. Not only that, the kill tasks for 20+ have a drop here (Glimmering Gem or something like that), worth a lot of experience.

Group Friendly?

I think this zone was designed for groups primarily! Once you get deeper into the zone, you will have oodles to hunt. A lower-level group would also have a lot of success near the entrance. Then there's always the dragon!

- Steve "Larian LeQuella" Lundquist

SHEEROE HILLS HUNTING

To hunt solo here, you'd better be at least level 40. All sorts of Glimmers roam this zone, and unless you're an excellent soloer, you may get an early death wish!

40-42	Elf-Shot Madman
40-42	Glimmerling
45-47	Glimmer Ghoul
46-48	Glimmer Ardent
46-48	Glimmer Griever

Group advice

- If you just *have* to go take down the dragon, you're going to need two or three high-level, very organized groups. The eastern side is the easiest approach, but a really large group of level 50 characters could probably try a western angle with good scouting, MCLs, and lots of good area-effect spellcasters.
- You should be able to conquer the Glimmer Prince with a couple of groups of 45 to 50 level characters. It's not a guaranteed loot fest, though.
- The best places to gain XP as a 45 to 49 level group are the multiple-critter type camps past Azures. You'll find a ton of good pullable areas, along with mob loot and dropped loot.

Loot

azure avenger [51/53/55] (15%) Golden Crown • (5%) Scroll of Worshipping Rites • (20%) Jewels 63 • (1.7%)(hi-lo) Gossamer Seolc Sleeves ***or*** Pants, ***or*** Seolc Cap of the Void [51]/(hi-lo) Gossamer Seolc Gloves ***or*** Boots, ***or*** Seolc Cap of Enchantment [53]/(hi-lo) Gossamer Seolc Vest ***or*** Robe, ***or*** Seolc Cap of Mentalism [55] • (1.7%)(hi-lo) Glimmerspirit Sword ***or*** Celestial Gem of the Sky [51]/(hi-lo) Midnight Vengeance Falcata ***or*** Potent Gem of the Sky [53]/(hi-lo) Azure Avenger, Azure Defender ***or*** Ethereal Gem of the Sky [55]

azure banisher [48/50/52] (15%) Mystical Welkin Orb • (5%) Banisher's Signet Ring • (20%) Jewels 30 • (2%; hi-lo) Shining Sheeroe Coif/Boots/Hauberk, Antipodean Short Sword ***or*** Netherworld Flower

azure cleanser [45/47/49] (15%) Sky Worshipper Totem • (5%) Unclouded Jewel Broach • (20%) Jewels 30 • (2%; hi-lo) Welkin Gauntlets ***or*** Sleeves/Helm ***or*** Boots/Leggings ***or*** Vest, Antipodean Club ***or*** Entwined Silken Strand

Azure Coseal [53] (10%) Gossamer Seolc Sleeves ***or*** Pants, ***or*** Seolc Cap of the Void • (10%; hi-lo) Glimmerspirit Sword ***or*** Celestial Gem of the Sky • (10%) Gossamer Seolc Gloves ***or*** Boots, ***or*** Seolc Cap of Enchantment • (10%; hi-lo) Midnight Vengeance Falcata ***or*** Potent Gem of the Sky • (10%) Gossamer Seolc Vest ***or*** Robe, ***or*** Seolc Cap of Mentalism • (10%; hi-lo) Azure Avenger, Azure Defender ***or*** Ethereal Gem of the Sky

Azure Dsaldor [57] *see Azure Coseal [53]*

Azure Thror [52] (10%) Gossamer Seolc Sleeves ***or*** Pants, ***or*** Seolc Cap of the Void • (10%; hi-lo) Glimmerspirit Sword ***or*** Celestial Gem of the Sky • (10%) Gossamer Seolc Gloves ***or*** Boots, ***or*** Seolc Cap of Enchantment • (10%) Gossamer Seolc Vest ***or*** Robe, ***or*** Seolc Cap of Mentalism • (10%; hi-lo) Azure Avenger, Azure Defender ***or*** Ethereal Gem of the Sky

celt spirit [40] (1.4% each piece) Glowing Guile • (4.2% each) Glimmer Spirit Sword, Club, Cloak, Trammel

Cuuldurach the Glimmer King [80] (16% each) Fine Steel Long Sword, Soul Glimmer, Frigid Azure Crusher, Smoldering Crimson Bow, Semi-Ethereal Robe, Gloom Warder's Spear • (14% each) Netherworldy Scale Hauberk, Vest of the Veil Warder, Ghostly Great Falcata, Jerkin of the Ghostly Soul, Gauntlets of the Veil, Ring of Zo'arkat, Cloth Cap • ***plus everything that Maldahar the Glimmer Prince [73] might drop, at about x7 probability (15% instead of 2.3%, and 22% instead of 3.3%)***

elf spirit [40] *see celt spirit [40]*

elfshot madman [34,36] (15%) Shreds of Dingy Cloth • (5%) Bottle of Wine • (20%) Jewels 21

firbolg spirit [40] *see celt spirit [40]*

glimmer ardent [45/47/49] (15%) Glimmering Spirit Orb • (5%) Sheeroe Ardent Earring • (20%) Jewels 30 • (2%; hi-lo) Odyllic Cap/Boots/Vest, Antipodean Club ***or*** Entwined Silken Strand • (9%) Glimmering Gem

Glimmer Arios [53] (10%) Midnight Marauder Helm ***or*** Sleeves • (10%; hi-lo) Moonstrike Mace, Glimmerstrike Drum, ***or*** Shadowstrike Ring • (10%) Midnight Marauder Gloves ***or*** Mystical Moonglade Boots • (10%; hi-lo) Glimmerstrike Crusher ***or*** Glimmer Striker Ring • (10%) Midnight Marauder Jerkin ***or*** Leggings • (10%; hi-lo) Glimmer Wrath Great Hammer, Glimmerstrike Shield ***or*** Shadow Ring

glimmer avenger [65] (no loot)

glimmer deathwatcher [57/59/61] (15%) Sickly Pulsing Orb • (5%) Bottled Stench of Death • (20%) Jewels 63 • (1.7%) Burnished Shanshee Gloves ***or*** Sleeves, ***or*** Heroic Burnished Shanshee Coif [57]/(hi-lo) Burnished Shanshee Boots ***or*** Champion Burnished Shanshee Coif [59]/Burnished Shanshee Hauberk ***or*** Leggings [61] • (1.7%)(hi-lo) Moondeath Mace, Deathwatcher Lute ***or*** Sorcerous Deathwatcher Chain [57]/Warshadow Staff of the Sun ***or*** Moon, ***or*** Potent Deathwatcher Chain [59]/(hi-lo) Deathmoon Rapier, Deathwatcher Ward ***or*** Empathic Deathwatcher Chain [61]

glimmer geist [60/62] (15%) Glimmer Spirit Essence • (5%) Glimmer Spirit Wand • (20%) Jewels 63 • (1.7%)(hi-lo) Melodic Moonglade Sleeves ***or*** Gauntlets [60]/(hi-lo) Masterful Moonglade Gauntlets ***or*** Boots [62] • (1.7%) Glimmering Stiletto ***or*** Calignous Shroud [60]/(hi-lo) Glimmer Geist Spear ***or*** Lurid Mantle [62]

glimmer ghoul [39/41/43] (15%) Scrap of Ghoul Flesh • (5%) Ghoulish Spirit Necklace • (20%) Jewels 21 • (2%; hi-lo) Glowing Guile Helm/Boots/Jerkin, Glimmer Spirit Sword ***or*** Glimmer Spirit Trammel • (6/9/9%) Glimmering Gem

glimmer griever [48/50/52] (15%) Worn Runed Stone • (5%) Griever's Notched Stick • (20%) Jewels 30 • (2%; hi-lo) Shining Sheeroe Gloves/Sleeves/Leggings, Antipodean Short Sword ***or*** Netherworld Flower • (9%) Glimmering Gem

glimmer jinn [65] (no loot)

Glimmer Kelegur [55] *see Glimmer Arios [53]*

glimmer knight [60/62] (15%) Glimmer Spirit Pennant • (5%) Glimmer Knight's Service Scroll • (20%) Jewels 63 • (1.7%; hi-lo) Iridescent Sylph Leggings ***or*** Mossy Moonglade Gauntlets [60]/Mystical Moonglade Helm ***or*** Vest [62] • (1.7%) Calignous Shroud ***or*** Glimmerspirit Recurved Bow [60]/Glimmerspirit Short Bow ***or*** Lurid Mantle [62]

Glimmer Kryl [59] (10%) Burnished Shanshee Gloves ***or*** Sleeves, ***or*** Heroic Burnished Shanshee Coif • (10%; hi-lo) Moondeath Mace, Deathwatcher Lute ***or*** Sorcerous Deathwatcher Chain • (10%; hi-lo) Burnished Shanshee Boots ***or*** Champion Burnished Shanshee Coif • (10%) Warshadow Staff of the Sun ***or*** Moon, ***or*** Potent Deathwatcher Chain • (10%) Burnished Shanshee Hauberk ***or*** Burnished Shanshee Leggings • (10%; hi-lo) Deathmoon Rapier, Deathwatcher Ward ***or*** Empathic Deathwatcher Chain

Glimmer Meldun [47] (20%; hi-lo) Odyllic Cap, Antipodean Club ***or*** Entwined Silken Strand • (20%; hi-lo) Odyllic Boots, Antipodean Club ***or*** Entwined Silken Strand • (20%; hi-lo) Odyllic Vest, Antipodean Club ***or*** Entwined Silken Strand

glimmer messenger [50] (no loot)

Glimmer Mianed [47] *see Glimmer Meldun [47]*

Glimmer Orin [61] *see Glimmer Kryl [59]*

Glimmer Orist [45] *see Glimmer Meldun [47]*

glimmer prophet [65] (no loot)

Glimmer Saumer [64] (10%; hi-lo) Mystical Moonglade Sleeves ***or*** Melodic Moonglade Gauntlets • (10%) Glimmering Stiletto ***or*** Calignous Shroud • (10%; hi-lo) Masterful Moonglade Gauntlets ***or*** Mystical Moonglade Boots • (10%; hi-lo) Glimmer Geist Spear ***or*** Lurid Mantle • (10%; hi-lo) Iridescent Sylph Leggings ***or*** Mossy Moonglade Gauntlets • (10%) Calignous Shroud ***or*** Glimmerspirit Recurved Bow • (10%) Mystical Moonglade Helm ***or*** Vest • (10%) Glimmerspirit Short Bow ***or*** Lurid Mantle

Glimmer Spass [45] *see Glimmer Meldun [47]*

glimmer spirit [40] *see celt spirit [40]*

Glimmer Stikil [55] (10%) Midnight Marauder Helm ***or*** Midnight Marauder Sleeves • (10%; hi-lo) Moonstrike Mace, Glimmerstrike Drum ***or*** Shadowstrike Ring • (10%) Midnight Marauder Gloves ***or*** Mystical Moonglade Boots • (10%; hi-lo) Glimmerstrike Crusher ***or*** Glimmer Striker Ring • (10%) Midnight Marauder Jerkin ***or*** Leggings • (10%; hi-lo) Glimmer Wrath Great Hammer, Glimmerstrike Shield ***or*** Shadow Ring

glimmer striker [51/53/55] (15%) Glimmer Striker Belt • (5%) Tarnished Glimmer Spirit Ring • (20%) Jewels 63 • (1.7%) Midnight Marauder Helm ***or*** Sleeves [51]/Midnight Marauder Gloves ***or*** Mystical Moonglade Boots [53]/Midnight Marauder Jerkin ***or*** Leggings [55] • (1.7%)(hi-lo) Moonstrike Mace, Glimmerstrike Drum ***or*** Shadowstrike Ring [51]/(hi-lo) Glimmerstrike Crusher ***or*** Glimmer Striker Ring [53]/(hi-lo) Glimmer Wrath Great Hammer, Glimmerstrike Shield ***or*** Shadow Ring [55] • (5%) Glimmering Gem

Glimmer Venlar [57] *see Glimmer Kryl [59]*

glimmer ward [42/44/46] (15%) Wayward Traveler Pouch • (5%) Death Ward Token • (20%) Jewels 21 • (2%; hi-lo) Odyllic Gloves/Sleeves/Pants, Glimmer Spirit Rapier ***or*** Glimmer Spirit Band • (9%) Glimmering Gem

glimmer warshade [54/56/58] (15%) Furious Warshade Gem • (5%) Bloody Warshade Axe • (20%) Jewels 63 • (1.7%) Iridescent Sylph Druid Gloves, Sleeves ***or*** Coif/Warden Gloves ***or*** Boots/Hauberk ***or*** Leggings • (1.7%) Warshadow Staff of the Void, Warshadow Flute, ***or*** Deathshadow Bracer [54]/(hi-lo) Warshadow Staff of Mentalism ***or*** Warshadow Bracer [56]/Warshadow Staff of Enchantments, Warshade Protector ***or*** Glimmershade Bracer [58] • (2.5%) Glimmering Gem

Glimmer Xaduk [53] *see Glimmer Stikil [55]*

Glimmer Xaquira [49] *see Glimmer Meldun [47]*

Glimmer Zanllvi [51] (10%; hi-lo) Midnight Marauder Helm ***or*** Sleeves • (10%; hi-lo) Moonstrike Mace, Glimmerstrike Drum ***or*** Shadowstrike Ring • (10%; hi-lo) Midnight Marauder Gloves ***or*** Mystical Moonglade Boots • (10%; hi-lo) Glimmerstrike Crusher ***or*** Glimmer Striker Ring • (10%; hi-lo) Midnight Marauder Jerkin ***or*** Leggings • (10%; hi-lo) Glimmer Wrath Great Hammer, Glimmerstrike Shield ***or*** Shadow Ring

Glimmer Zeit [49] *see Glimmer Meldun [47]*

glimmerling [36/38/40] (15%) Glimmering Gem • (5/5/7%) Glimmering Gem • (5%) Glimmer Spirit Shackle • (20%) Jewels 21 • (2%; hi-lo) Glowing Guile Gloves/Sleeves/Leggings, ***or*** Glimmer Spirit Club ***or*** Cloak

lurikeen spirit [40] *see celt spirit [40]*

Maldahar the Glimmer Prince [73] (2.3%) Midnight Marauder Helm ***or*** Sleeves • (2.3%; hi-lo) Moonstrike Mace, Glimmerstrike Drum ***or*** Shadowstrike Ring • (2.3%) Midnight Marauder Gloves ***or*** Mystical Moonglade Boots • (2.3%; hi-lo) Glimmerstrike Crusher ***or*** Glimmer Striker Ring • (2.3%) Midnight Marauder Jerkin ***or*** Leggings • (2.3%; hi-lo) Glimmer Wrath Great Hammer, Glimmerstrike Shield, ***or*** Shadow Ring • (2.3%) Iridescent Sylph Druid Gloves, Sleeves ***or*** Coif • (2.3%) Warshadow Staff of the Void, Warshade Flute ***or*** Deathshadow Bracer • (2.3%) Iridescent Sylph Boots ***or*** Warden Gloves • (2.3%; hi-lo) Warshadow Staff of Mentalism ***or*** Bracer • (2.3%) Iridescent Sylph Hauberk ***or*** Leggings • (2.3%) Warshadow Staff of Enchantments, Warshade Protector ***or*** Glimmershade Bracer • (2.3%) Burnished Shanshee Gloves ***or*** Sleeves, ***or*** Heroic Burnished Shanshee Coif • (2.3%; hi-lo) Moondeath Mace, Deathwatcher Lute ***or*** Sorcerous Deathwatcher Chain • (2.3%; hi-lo) Burnished Shanshee Boots ***or*** Champion Burnished Shanshee Coif • (2.3%) Warshadow Staff of the Sun ***or*** Moon, ***or*** Potent Deathwatcher Chain • (2.3%) Burnished Shanshee Hauberk ***or*** Leggings • (2.3%; hi-lo) Deathmoon Rapier, Deathwatcher Ward ***or*** Empathic Deathwatcher Chain • (3.3%; hi-lo) Mystical Moonglade Sleeves ***or*** Melodic Moonglade Gauntlets • (3.3%) Glimmering Stiletto ***or*** Calignous Shroud • (3.3%; hi-lo) Masterful Moonglade Gauntlets ***or*** Mystical Moonglade Boots • (3.3%; hi-lo) Glimmer Geist Spear ***or*** Lurid Mantle • (3.3%; hi-lo) Iridescent Sylph Leggings ***or*** Mossy Moonglade Gauntlets • (3.3%) Calignous Shroud ***or*** Glimmerspirit Recurved Bow • (3.3%) Mystical Moonglade Helm ***or*** Vest • (3.3%) Glimmerspirit Short Bow ***or*** Lurid Mantle • (2.3%) Gossamer Seolc Sleeves ***or*** Pants, ***or*** Seolc Cap of the Void • (2.3%; hi-lo) Glimmerspirit Sword ***or*** Celestial Gem of the Sky • (2.3%) Gossamer Seolc Gloves ***or*** Boots, ***or*** Seolc Cap of Enchantment • (2.3%; hi-lo) Midnight Vengeance Falcata ***or*** Potent Gem of the Sky • (2.3%) Gossamer Seolc Vest ***or*** Robe, ***or*** Seolc Cap of Mentalism • (2.3%; hi-lo) Azure Avenger, Azure Defender ***or*** Ethereal Gem of the Sky

pale horse [50] (15%) Worn Pale Horse Pelt • (5%) Pristine Pale Horse Pelt

raging subverter [39,41,43] (15%) Mysterious Glimmering Vial • (5%) Pilfered Draconic Scale • (20%) Jewels 21

Ranger [45] (no loot)

Silvermine Mountains

To Lough Derg

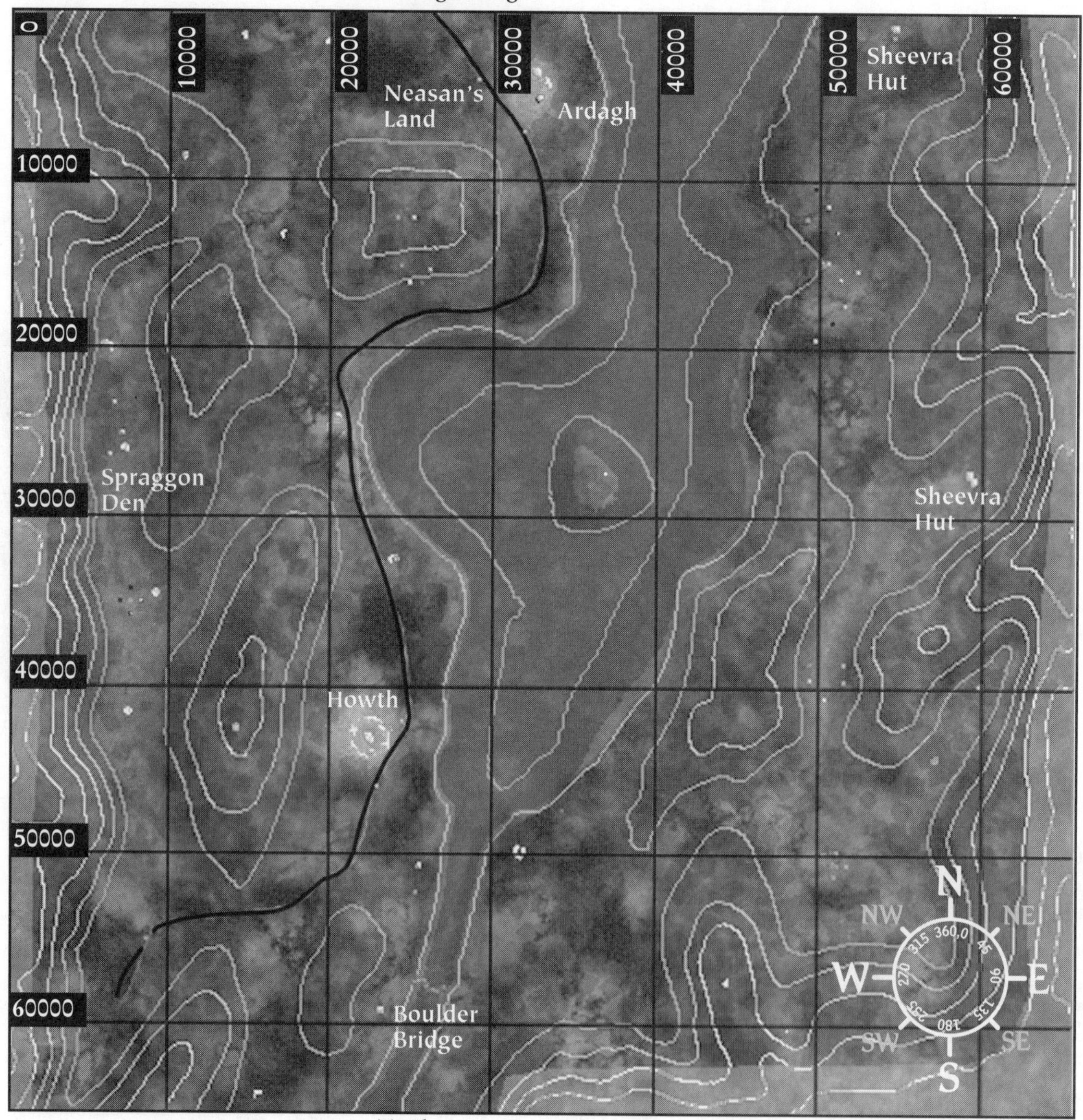

To Shannon Estuary

Lower-level monsters not shown on map:

Creature	Lvl	Location
annoying lucradan	0	WC,C,SW,SC
badger cub	0	WC,C,SW,SC
bodachan sabhaill	2	NC,WC,C,SW
bodachan sabhaill	3	NC,WC
bodachan sabhaill	4	NW,NC,WC,C,SW
cluricaun trip	8	SC,SE
eirebug	4	NW
eirebug	5	NW,SW
feccan	1	WC,C,SW,SC
feccan	2	WC,C,SW
feccan	3	WC
feckless lucragan	4	SW
hill toad	5	NW,NC,WC,SW
hill toad	6	NW,NC,WC,SW
hill toad	7	NW,NC,WC,SW
large frog	0	WC,C,SW,SC
large frog	1	NC,WC,C,SW,SC

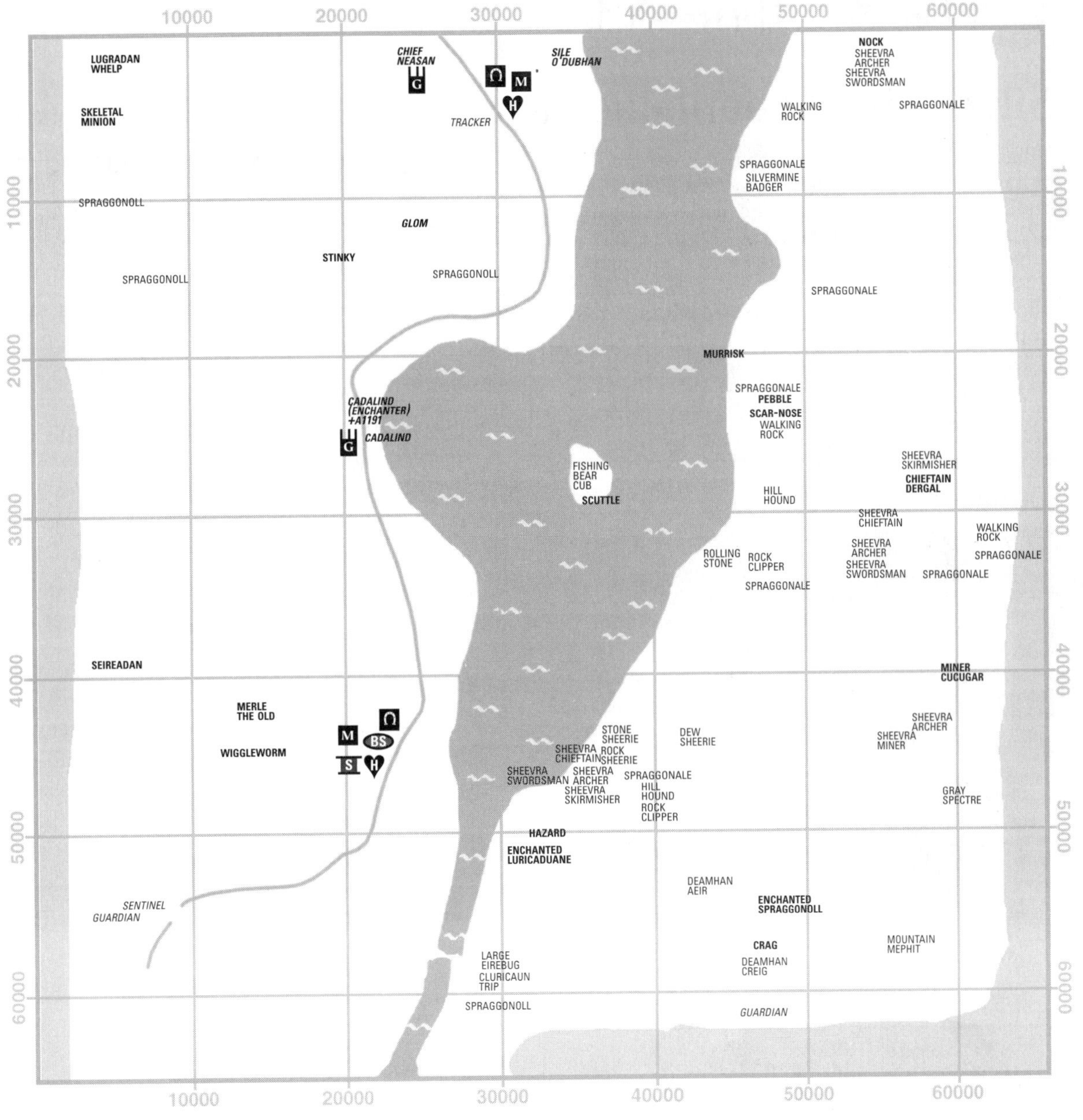

Creature	Lvl	Location
luricaduane	6	NW,WC,SW,SC,SE
luricaduane	7	NW,WC,SW,SC,SE
luricaduane	8	NW,WC,SW,SC,SE
mudman	3	C,SW
mudman	4	C,SW
rat boy	3	SW
rowdy	5	NW,WC,SW
rowdy	6	NW
skeletal pawn	1	WC,C,SW,SC
skeletal pawn	2	NC,WC,C,SW,SC
small walking rock	2	NW,NC,WC,SW
small walking rock	3	NW,NC,WC,C,SW
spraggon	3	NW,NC,WC,C,SW
spraggon	4	NW,NC,WC,C,SW
spraggon	5	NW,NC,SW
spraggonite	5	NW
spraggonite	6	NW
spraggonoll	7	NW,NC
spraggonoll	8	NW,SC,SE
villainous youth	4	NW,WC,SW
water beetle	6	NC,C
water beetle	7	NC
water beetle	8	NC,C
water beetle collector	4	NC,C
water beetle collector	5	NC,C
water beetle larva	0	WC,C
water beetle larva	1	NC,WC,C,SW,SC
wild crouch	6	NW

Silvermine Mountains Tips

Silvermine Mountains is home to Howth and Spraggon Den. Many players in their early 20s bind here for easy access to the den. Spraggon Den, just over the hill from Howth, is a fun adventuring spot for adventurers in their early 20s. Howth is also a popular spot to bind for those in their early 40s, as it provides a horse route to Innis Carthaig.

- Todd "Jubal" Wharton

Quest NPCs

Ardagh	
Caitriona	Clik's Raids (lvl 9)
Fianait	Fearan (lvl 16)
Illaliel	Missing Bard (lvl 43)
Odharnait	Freeing Osier (lvl 19)
Reeni	Sad Fomorie (lvl 10)
Reeni	Returning to the Source (lvl 31)
Seana	Scuttle (lvl 13)
Lochlain	Lochlain's Curse (lvl 12)
Howth	
Banba	Spinner's Cloak (lvl 10)
Banba	Returning for More (lvl 31)
Cathbad	Cad Goddeau (lvl 25) (lvl Guild Track - 25)
Chief of Howth	Stolen Ore (lvl 20) (lvl Guild Track - 20)
Chieftan Pronnias	Secret of Nuada's Silver (lvl 30) (lvl Guild Trace - 30)
Damhnait	Track and Seek (lvl 4)
Kaylee	Balm hunt (lvl 3)
Kaylee	Enchanted Bandit Hunt (lvl 4)
Lasrina	The Feud (lvl 20)
Tyree	Tyree's Dyes (lvl 11)
Piaras	Piaras and Lhia (lvl 50)

SILVERMINE MTS. HUNTING

5-8 Early on, try your hand at killing Water Beetles. They're particularly vulnerable to cold attacks.

15 -17 There's a Miner camp east of Howth and across the water. (Make sure you set your bind point to Howth first.) When you arrive at the campsite, stay up on the hill to accumulate the most XP. Also, you can find a small area of trees just north of the site. There, you can find hard-hitting

Sheevra Miners and Archers, but at least they swing slowly!

18-20 Also across the lake near Howth, you can find Sheeries in the hills.

20-21 Once again, search the eastern Howth hills for your prey — Dreanham Creigs, Hill Wolves, and a Grey Spectre camp.

22-23 The hills are a recurring theme here, if you haven't guessed by now. Crags and Spraggonites lurk in the Silvermine Mountains east of Howth. Their favorite spot is in the hills around the valley containing the Spectre camp.

24-27 Venture east of Howth to find Walking Rocks ...

33-37 .... and Deamhan Aeirs.

Loot

annoying lucradan [0] (5%) Poteen Wine Flask • (70%) Onyx • (1%) <Braided Beauties> • (8% each piece) Tattered Brea and Tattered Woven

badger cub [0] (60%) Badger Cub Fur • (40%) Badger Cub Tooth • (50%) Badger Cub Claw

bodachan sabhaill [2-4] (75%) Onyx • (2%) Copper Charm • (25%) Oil Flask • (10% each piece) Tattered Brea and Tattered Woven • (1%) <Braided Beauties>

Chieftain Dergal [16] (10%) Flask of Elven Spirits • (80% each) Spinel, Chryoprase • (40%) Bloodstone • (10%) Silver Amethyst Ring • (2%) Siabrian Chieftain's Head • (1.4%) Siabrian Sword Baldric • (3%) APOA: Worn Dark Guardian, Sword ***or*** Shield • (1.5%) <Craftsman Pendants> • (0.3%) <Muire's Riches 2>

Ciandra [3] (no loot)

cluricaun trip [8-9] (5% each) Silver Coin, Leather Pouch • (80% each) Poteen Wine Flask, Moonstone • (5%) Pitted Dirk • (0.5%) <Celtic Knots>

Crag [19] (80% each) Chryoprase, Bloodstone • (40%) Lapis Lazuli • (20%) Agate • (5%) Garnet • (1.5%) Swirling Granite • (0.3%) <Muire's Riches 2>

deamhan aeir [34-35/36-37] (70%) Deamhan Wing (x2) • (70%) Deamhan Claw (x2) • (20/30%) Cat's Eye Opal • (5%) Cat's Eye Apatite/Green Sapphire • (1.4%) Deamhan Circlet of Speed • (1.4%) [Deamhan Aeir Claw ***or*** Screaming Ring]/[Ether Staff, Ether Staff of Thought ***or*** Light, ***or*** Abrasive Necklace] • (12%) Essence of Deamhan Aeir

deamhan creig [17-18] (80% each) Chryoprase, Bloodstone • (40%) Lapis Lazuli • (20%) Agate • (5%) Garnet • (1.5%) Swirling Granite • (0.3%) <Muire's Riches 2>

dew sheerie [16-17] (75%) Chryoprase • (75%) Amethyst • (15%) Waterproof Satchel • (1.5%) Glowing Sherrie Beads • (5%) Intricate Sea Shell Bracelet • (0.3%) <Muire's Riches 2>

eirebug [4-5] (75%) Eirebug Leg (x2) • (10%) Eirebug Mandible • (5%) Eirebug Carapace

enchanted luricaduane [7] (5% each) Silver Coin, Leather Pouch • (80% each) Poteen Wine Flask, Moonstone • (5%) Pitted Dirk • (0.5%) <Celtic Knots>

enchanted spraggonoll [7] (5%) Pitted Spiked Mace • (25%) Pint of Grog • (75%) Moonstone • (15%) Jade • (1%) <Braided Beauties>

feccan [1-2/3] (5%) Feccan Skin • (75%) Onyx • (10/20%) Aventurine • (1%) <Braided Beauties> • (10% each piece) Tattered Brea and Tattered Woven

feckless lucragan [4] (70% each) Poteen Wine Flask, Onyx • (2%) Leather Pouch • (1%) <Braided Beauties>

fishing bear cub [11-12] (80%) Bear Meat • (40%) Bear Meat • (80%) Bear Tooth • (40%) Bear Tooth • (30%) Fishing Bear Skin

gray spectre [22-23/24] (1.5%) Spectral Shroud • (40/60%) Spectral Essence • (80%) Spirit Shackles • (5%) Green Tourmaline/Chrome Diopside • (0.3%) <Muire's Riches 3> • (1.5%) Orb of Resistance [22-23] • [Remainder is only 24] (1.1% each) Malicious Black Heart, Black Clawed Hand • (0.05% each) Parthanan Head, Pearl • (0.2%) Lapis Lazuli • (0.01%) <Muire's Riches 2> • (0.02%) Parthanon Fist ***or*** Ether Ring

Guardian [29] (60% each) Carnelian, Agate • (80%) Obsidian • (35%) Jasper • (1.5%) Ether Cloak ***or*** Silvered Eye

Hazard [9] (10%) Silver Coin • (80% each) Leather Pouch, Jade • (5% each) Bottle of Poteen Wine, Pitted Dirk • (0.5%) <Celtic Knots>

hill hound [18-19/20] (80/85%) Hill Hound Canine (x2) • (30/48%) Pristine Hill Hound Pelt

hill toad [5-7] (75%) Frog Legs • (60%) Frog Legs • (10%) Hill Toad Skin

horse [10] (75%) Horse Hair • (10%) Auburn Mane • (80%) Ruined Horse Skin • (35%) Horse Skin • (60%) Horse Hair

large eirebug [9-10/11] (80%) Large Eirebug Leg (x2) • (40/60%) Large Eirebug Mandible • (10/18%) Large Eirebug Carapace

large frog [0-1] (65%) Frog Legs • (5%) Frog Legs

lugradan whelp [5] (5% each) Silver Coin, Moonstone • (80%) Onyx • (60%) Poteen Wine Flask • (1%) <Braided Beauties> • (1% each piece) Tattered Brea and Tattered Woven

luricaduane [6-7/8] (5/10%) Silver Coin • (5/80%) Leather Pouch • (80%) Poteen Wine Flask/Bottle of Poteen Wine • (80%) Moonstone/Jade • (5%) Pitted Dirk • (0.5%) <Celtic Knots>

Merle the Old [30] (no loot)

Miner Cucugar [14] (80% each) Mining Pick, Chunk of Copper • (10% each) Waterskin, Loot Bag, Spinel • (5%) Silver Nugget • (0.3%) <Treasures of the Fey> • (1.4%) Siabrian Gloves • (1.5%) <Craftsman Pendants> • (3%) APOA: Woven Crafter's

mountain mephit [20-22] (80%) Mephit Wing • (40%) Mephit Wing • (80%) Poisonous Mephit Fang • (50%) Poisonous Mephit Fang • (10%) Silvered Bracer • (1.5%) Splintered Mephit Femur • (0.3%) <Muire's Riches 3> • (1.5%) Aeiry Belt ***or*** Forked Mephit Tail

mudman [3/4] (80%) Ball of Clay • (30/40%) Small Amount of Clay • (5/10%) Block of Clay • (1%) <Braided Beauties>

murrisk [28] (80%) Seal Skin Bag • (25% each) Silver Pearl Ring, Necklace • (1.4%) Red Spinel • (80%) 50ft of Kelp Rope • (20%) Cat's Eye Opal • (1.4%) Coral Spear • (0.3%) <De'velyn's Delights> • (1.5%) Jewels 20

Nock [15] (30%) Silver Amethyst Ring • (15%) Rough Flight Bodkin Arrows (x2) • (1.4%) Pitted Recurve Bow • (1.4%) Siabrian Bracer • (1.5%) <Rogue Pendants (Low)> • (0.3%) <Treasures of the Fey>

Pebble [25] (5% each) Smooth Sling Stones, Chunk of Silver • (25%) Fine Unworked Stone • (45%) Unworked Stone • (50%) Malachite • (60% each) Silver Nugget, Chunk of Copper • (0.3%) <De'velyn's Delights> • (1.5%) Mineralized Ring

rat boy [3] (10%) Small Copper Ring • (80%) Small Mirror • (1%) <Braided Beauties> • (8% each piece) Tattered Brea and Tattered Woven

rock sheerie [18-19/20-21] (90/80%) Unworked Stone • (5/30%) Fine Unworked Stone • (5%) Smooth Sling Stones/Garnet • (1.5%) Rock Sherrie Bracer • (0.3%) <Muire's Riches 2>/<Muire's Riches 3>

Rolling Stone [23] (80%) Unworked Stone • (30%) Fine Unworked Stone • (5%) Fire Opal • (1.5%) Rock Sherrie Bracer • (0.3%) <Muire's Riches 3>

rowdy [5-6] (no loot)

Scar-nose [26] (70%) Badger Claw (x2) • (52%) Badger Tooth (x2) • (5%) Pristine Badger Pelt • (1.5%) Badger Pelt Cloak ***or*** Slimed Bracer

Scuttle [13] (80%) Bear Meat • (40%) Bear Meat • (80%) Bear Tooth • (40%) Bear Tooth • (30%) Fishing Bear Skin

Seireadan [3] (no loot)

sheevra archer [14] (30%) Silver Amethyst Ring • (15%) Rough Flight Bodkin Arrows (x2) • (1.4%) Pitted Recurve Bow • (1.4%) Siabrian Bracer • (1.5%) <Rogue Pendants (Low)> • (0.3%) <Treasures of the Fey>

sheevra chieftain [15] (10%) Flask of Elven Spirits • (80% each) Spinel, Chryoprase • (40%) Bloodstone • (10%) Silver Amethyst Ring • (2%) Siabrian Chieftain's Head • (1.4%) Siabrian Sword Baldric • (3%) APOA: Worn Dark Guardian, Sword ***or*** Shield • (1.5%) <Craftsman Pendants> • (0.3%) <Muire's Riches 2>

sheevra miner [13-14] (80% each) Mining Pick, Chunk of Copper • (10% each) Waterskin, Loot Bag, Spinel • (5%) Silver Nugget • (0.3%) <Treasures of the Fey> • (1.4%) Siabrian Gloves • (1.5%) <Craftsman Pendants> • (3%) APOA: Woven Crafter's

sheevra skirmisher [13-14] (80%) Leather Pouch • (2%) Siabra Skirmisher's Head • (60%) Spinel • (0.3%) <Treasures of the Fey> • (5%) Pitted Short Bow • (10%) Flight Bodkin Arrows (x2) • (1.4%) Siabrian Sword Baldric • (3%) APOA: Worn Dark Guardian, Sword ***or*** Shield • (1.5%) <Military Pendants>

sheevra swordsman [12-13] (80%) Etched Wooden Cup • (60%) Etched Wooden Bowl • (10%) Flask of Elven Spirits • (1.4%) Siabrian Gloves • (1.5%) <Craftsman Pendants> • (3%) APOA: Woven Crafter's • (0.5%) <Treasures of the Fey>

silvermine badger [22-23] (70%) Badger Claw (x2) • (52%) Badger Tooth (x2) • (5%) Pristine Badger Pelt • (1.5%) Badger Pelt Cloak ***or*** Slimed Bracer

skeletal minion [4] (5%) Pitted Broadsword • (75%) Onyx • (60%) Onyx • (8% each piece) Tattered Brea and Tattered Woven • (1%) <Braided Beauties>

skeletal pawn [1-2] (70%) Onyx • (10%) Aventurine • (8% each piece) Tattered Brea and Tattered Woven • (1%) <Braided Beauties>

small walking rock [2-3] (5%) Sling Stones • (70%) Large Rock Crystal • (1%) <Braided Beauties>

spraggon [3-5] (15%) Chipped Mirror • (75%) Oil Flask • (5%) Pint of Grog • (1%) <Braided Beauties> • (10% each piece) Tattered Brea and Tattered Woven

spraggonale [21-22/23] (15/20%) Copper Moonstone Flagon • (80/70%) Bottle of Grog • (80/90%) Copper Cryoprase Earring • (40%) Topaz [21-22] • (30%) Pearl [23] • (3%) Pitted Falcata • (5%) Jasper [23] • (0.3%) <Muire's Riches 3> • (1.5%) Dusty Leggings [21-22 only] ***or*** Silvermined Blade

spraggonite [5-6] (5%) Pitted Stiletto • (5%) Pint of Grog • (75%) Moonstone • (25%) Chipped Mirror • (1%) <Braided Beauties> • (10% each piece) Tattered Brea and Tattered Woven

spraggonoll [7-9] (5%) Pitted Spiked Mace • (25%) Pint of Grog • (75%) Moonstone • (15%) Jade • (1%) <Braided Beauties>

Stinky [9] (60%) Badger Cub Fur • (40%) Badger Cub Tooth • (50%) Badger Cub Claw

stone sheerie [19-20/21-22] (80%) Unworked Stone • (20/30%) Fine Unworked Stone • (5%) Topaz/Fire Opal • (1.5%) Rock Sherrie Bracer • (0.3%) <Muire's Riches 3>

villainous youth [4] (no loot)

walking rock [21,24] (5% each) Smooth Sling Stones, Chunk of Silver • (25%) Fine Unworked Stone • (45%) Unworked Stone • (50%) Malachite • (60% each) Silver Nugget, Chunk of Copper • (0.3%) <De'velyn's Delights> • (1.5%) Mineralized Ring

water beetle [6-8] (75%) Water Beetle Leg (x2) • (50%) Water Beetle Mandible • (25%) Water Beetle Carapace

water beetle collector [4-5] (80%) Water Beetle Leg • (45%) Water Beetle Leg

water beetle larva [0-1] (75%) Worm Fishing Bait • (15%) Worm Fishing Bait

wiggle worm [0] (80%) Worm Fishing Bait • (10%) Worm Fishing Bait

wild crouch [6] (75%) Moonstone • (10%) Jade • (3%) Pitted Stiletto • (25%) Small Copper Bracelet • (1%) <Braided Beauties>

Valley of Bri Leith

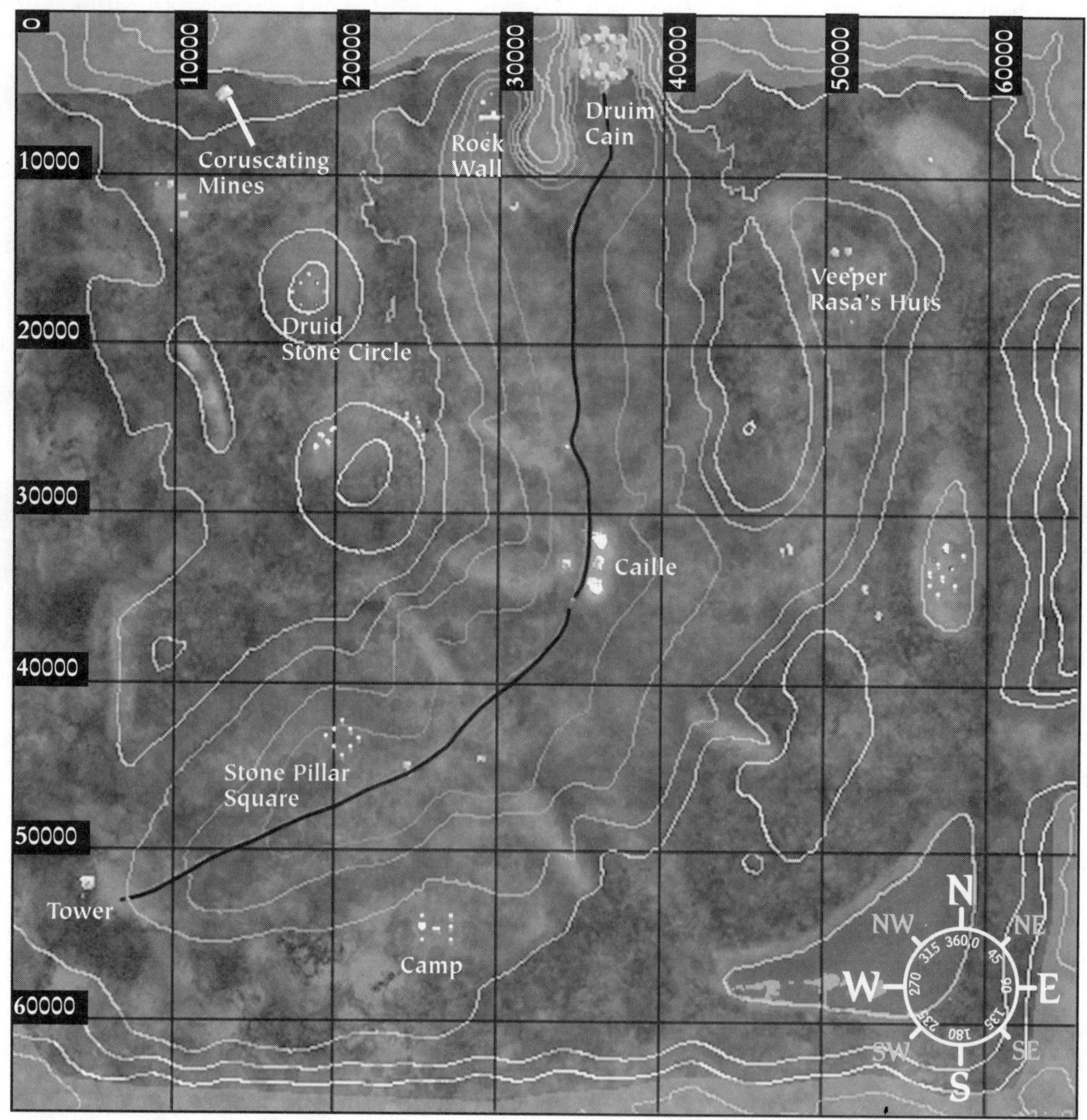

Lower-level monsters not shown on map:

Creature	Lvl	Location
barca	10	NW,NC,WC,C,SW
barca	11	NW,WC,C,SW
barca	12	NW,WC,C,SW
empyrean orb	10	NW,NC,WC,C,SW
empyrean watcher	16	C,EC,SE
empyrean watcher	17	C,EC,SE
empyrean watcher	18	C,EC,SE
empyrean wisp	13	NC,C,SW
empyrean wisp	14	NC,C,SW
empyrean wisp	15	NC,C,SW
faerie drake	20	SW,SC
faerie drake	21	SW,SC
faerie horse	18	SW,SC
faerie horse	19	SW,SC
faerie horse	20	SW,SC
faerie horse	21	SW,SC
faerie steed	19	SW,SC
faerie steed	20	SW,SC
faerie steed	21	SW,SC
fury sprite	14	C

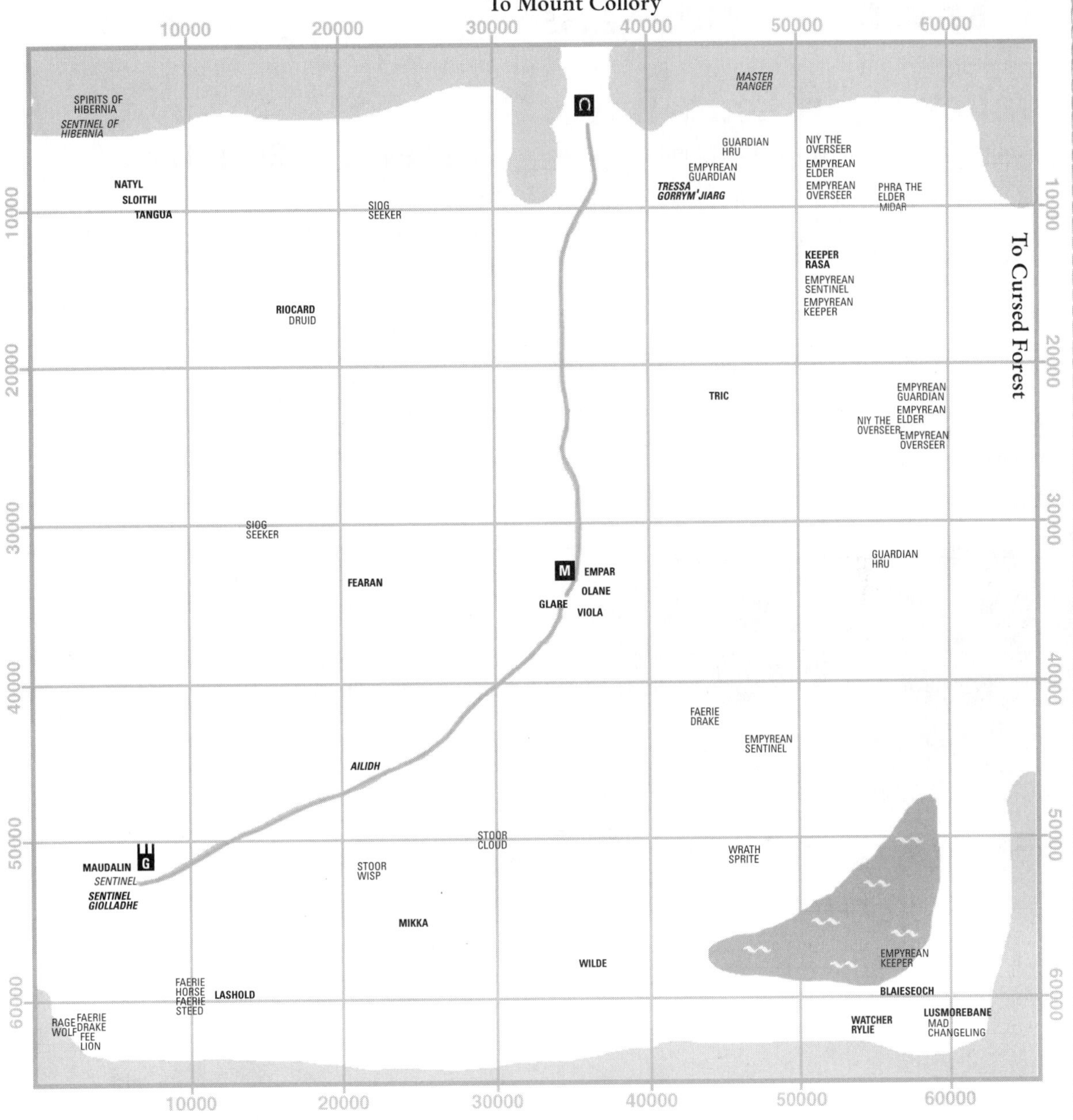

Creature	Lvl	Location
fury sprite	15	C
fury sprite	16	C
grass sheerie	13	NW,WC,C,SW
grass sheerie	14	NW,WC,C,SW
grass sheerie	15	NW,WC,C,SW
moss sheerie	10	NC,C,SW
moss sheerie	11	NC,C,SW
moss sheerie	12	NC,C,SW
primrose	10	NW,NC,WC,C,SW
siog footpad	15	NW
siog footpad	16	NW
siog piller	18	NW
siog piller	19	NW
Tracker	17	SE
Tracker	19	SE
veil wisp	11	NW,WC
veil wisp	12	NW,WC
veil wisp	13	NW,WC

Valley of Bri Leith Tips

Caille, the empyrean city can be found here as well as Druim Caim, the frontier keep. Druim Caim houses merchants and all of the class trainers.

- Todd "Jubal" Wharton

Quest NPCs

Druim Cain	
Oak Man	Aid for Alainn Bin (lvl 50)
Tressa Gorrym'jiarg	Traces of Mad Changlings (lvl 31)

VALLEY OF BRI LEITH HUNTING

6-10	The roads north and south of Caille are popular areas for Barca, Empyrean and Primrose.
11-15	Your next focus should be on Empyrean Wisps.
16 - 20	For the next few levels, hunt for Ghostly Siabras...
21- 25	.... Faerie Horses ...
26 - 30	... and Fee Lions
26-27	Now it's time for a change of pace. Head for the southeast corner of the zone in search of Mad Changelings, just past Moon Lake.
31-32	Last but not least, Siabra seekers inhabit the hills west of Druim Cain.

Loot

barca [10-12] (50%) Ripped Piece of Silk • (25%) Pouch of Faerie Dust • (10%) Jewels 24 • (0.3%) <Engraved Enchantments> • (1.5%) Pilfered Traveler's Mace

Blaieseach [21] (no loot)

Druid [22] (80% each) Softly Glowing Orb, Draoish Sacrificial Heart • (1.5%) APOA: Draoi, Draoi Shield ***or*** Draoish Sickle • (40%) Faerie Gem

Empar [17] (no loot)

empyrean elder [42-44] (20%) Silken Sash • (25%) Empyreal Mist Orb • (5%) Otherworldly Wine • (1.5%) <Ancient Wisdom>

empyrean guardian [34-35/36-37(38)] (15/25%) Drakescale Venom • (10%) Empyrean Wine • (20/15%) Cat's Eye Apatite • (1.5%) Empyreal Leggings ***or*** Sleeves, Empyreal Ranger Gauntlets ***or*** Boots, ***or*** Spectral Flight Arrows [34-35] • (1.8%; hi-lo) Empyreal Vest ***or*** Helm, Spectral Flight Arrows, Spectral Flight, ***or*** Sentinel's Ring [36-37]

empyrean keeper [23-24/25] (20%) Green Tourmaline • (10%) Empyrean Silk • (30/35%) Primrose Eye • (1.5%) Keeper's Shade ***or*** Ring [23-24] • (1.5%) APOA: Keeper's, Keeper's Friend, ***or*** Guardian Shield of the Keeper [25]

empyrean orb [10] (55%) Softly Glowing Orb • (55%) Jewels 24 • (0.5%) <Engraved Enchantments> • (1.5%) Empyrean Ring

empyrean overseer [37-39] (20%) Guardian Veil Ring • (25%) Drakescale Venom • (1.5%) Gossamer Voided, Enchanter ***or*** Mentalist Robe

empyrean sentinel [26-27/28-29] (35%) Orb of Viewing • (5/7%) Empyrean Wine • (15%) Red Spinel • (1.5%) APOA: Twined, ***or*** Twined Piercer/Twined Hauberk ***or*** Sleeves, ***or*** Twined Sentinel

empyrean watcher [16-18] (25% each) Bolt of Soft Gossamer, Primrose Eye

empyrean wisp [13-15] (45%) Softly Glowing Orb • (18%) Jewels 38 • (0.3%) <Treasures of the Fey> • (1.5%) Celestial Pearl Necklace

faerie drake [20-21/22] (60%) Faerie Drakes Rainbow Scale (x3) • (1.5%) Faerie Drakes Eye • (5%) Faerie Drakes Scaled Hide • (50%) Faerie Drakes Tail • (10/15%) Topaz • (5/15%) Pearl • (1.5%) Faerie Charm, ***or*** Luminescent Gloves ***or*** Boots [22] • (8/10%) Faerie Drake Hide

faerie horse [18-19/20-21/22-23] (50/75/80%) Faerie Horse Mane • (20/25/50%) Faerie Horse Pelt • (80/85/90%) Faerie Horse Tail

faerie steed [19-21/22-24] (40/55%) Faerie Steed Mane • (20/25%) Faerie Steed Pelt • (80/90%) Faerie Steed Tail • (1.5%) Faerie Eye/Faerie Saddle Cloak

Fearan [15] (50%) Glimmering Clump of Grass • (25%) Pouch of Faerie Dust • (20%) Jewels 03 • (0.3%) <Treasures of the Fey> • (1.5%) Hardened Grass Bracer

fee lion [25-27] (90%) Fee Lion Meat • (70% each) Fee Lion Tooth, Fee Lion Claw [25-26] • (75%) Fee Lion Tooth (x2) [27] • (50%) Fee Lion Claw (x2) [27] • (20%) Fee Lion Pelt • (1.5%) Blackened Feelion Paw ***or*** Feelion Razor [25-26]

fury sprite [14/15-16] (40%) Pouch of Magic Dust • (35/40%) Jewels 38 • (0.3%) <Treasures of the Fey>/<Muire's Riches 2> • (1.5%) APOA: Riven Silk

Glare [16] (40%) Pouch of Magic Dust • (40%) Jewels 38 • (0.3%) <Muire's Riches 2> • (1.5%) APOA: Riven Silk

grass sheerie [13-15] (50%) Glimmering Clump of Grass • (25%) Pouch of Faerie Dust • (20%) Jewels 03 • (0.3%) <Treasures of the Fey> • (1.5%) Hardened Grass Bracer

Guardian Hru [39] (no loot)

horse [10] (75%) Horse Hair • (10%) Auburn Mane • (80%) Ruined Horse Skin • (35%) Horse Skin • (60%) Horse Hair

Keeper Rasa [26] (10%) Empyrean Silk • (20%) Green Tourmaline • (1.5%) APOA: Keeper's, Keeper's Friend, ***or*** Guardian Shield of the Keeper • (35%) Primrose Eye

Lashold [33] (70%) Rage Wolf Fang (x2) • (70%) Rage Wolf Claw (x2) • (28%) Rage Wolf Pelt

Lusmorebane [30] (35% each) Changeling Ear, Changeling Tongue, Bleached Leg Bone • (1.5%) Wrathfully Righteous Beads • (15%) Topaz

mad changeling [26-27/28] (35% each) Changeling Ear, Changeling Tongue, Bleached Leg Bone • (1.5%) Madder Earring/Wrathfully Righteous Beads • (5/15%) Topaz

Midar [61] (35%) Empyreal Mist Orb • (20%) Silken Sash • (5%) Otherworldly Wine • (1.6%) <Ancient Wisdom>

Mikka [50] (no loot)

moss sheerie [10-12] (50%) Clump of Moss • (20%) Pouch of Faerie Dust • (10%) Jewels 24 • (0.3%) <Engraved Enchantments> • (1.5%) Hardened Moss Bracer

Natyl [17] (70%) Leather Pouch • (60%) Waterskin • (50%) Chryoprase • (40%) Amethyst • (30%) Silver Amethyst Ring • (3%) Siabrian Footpad's Head • (3%) Worn Dark Shadow Rapier • (1.5%) Zephyr's Band of Power, Glowing Zephyr Gem, ***or*** Ethereal Zephyr Bracelet • (3%) APOA: Worn Dark Shadow

Niy the Overseer [40] (20%) Guardian Veil Ring • (25%) Drakescale Venom • (1.5%) Gossamer Voided, Enchanter ***or*** Mentalist Robe

Olane [16] (no loot)

Phra the Elder [47] (30%) Empyreal Mist Orb • (25%) Silken Sash • (5%) Otherworldly Wine • (1.6%) <Ancient Wisdom>

primrose [10] (70%) Shimmering Rose Petal • (20%) Pouch of Faerie Dust • (0.5%) <Engraved Enchantments> • (1.5%) Glowing Rose Petal Chain

rage wolf [31-32] (70%) Rage Wolf Fang (x2) • (70%) Rage Wolf Claw (x2) • (20%) Rage Wolf Pelt • (8%) Dangerous Tooth

Riocard [28] (60% each) Draoish Sacrificial Heart, Faerie Gem • (0.5%) Robe of the Draoi • (1%) Empathetic Jewel

siog footpad [15-16] (25%) Silver Amethyst Ring • (20%) Bloodstone • (15%) Amethyst • (10%) Carnelian • (5%) Siabrian Footpad's Head • (2%) Worn Dark Shadow Rapier • (2%) APOA: Worn Dark Shadow • (0.3%) <Muire's Riches 2>

siog piller [18-19] (35%) Bandit Sash • (25%) Bandit Mask • (15%) Silver Topaz Ring • (5%) Siabrian Piller's Head • (1.5%) Griffonhead Cloak Pin • (2%) APOA: Worn Dark Shadow • (0.3%) <Muire's Riches 3>

siog seeker [28-29] (30%) Tattered Scroll • (30%) Luminescent Orb • (30%) Orb of Viewing • (10%) Primrose Eye • (1.5%) Spectral Legs, Gloves, Arms ***or*** Boots, Thumper, ***or*** Slicer • (50%) Bolt of Soft Gossamer

siog seeker [30-31] (35%) Primrose Eye • (35%) Siog Brandy • (35%) Topaz • (1.3%) Spectral Tunic, Helm ***or*** Shadow, ***or*** Bracer of Might • (1.3%) Smiter's Belt, Smiter, ***or*** Siog's Might • (50%) Bolt of Soft Gossamer • (1.3%) Cath Lute, Shield, Spear, Cloak ***or*** Charms

Sloithi [17] (70%) Leather Pouch • (60%) Waterskin • (50%) Chryoprase • (40%) Amethyst • (30%) Silver Amethyst Ring • (3%) Siabrian Footpad's Head • (3%) Worn Dark Shadow Rapier • (1.5%) Zephyr's Band of Power, Glowing Zephyr Gem, ***or*** Ethereal Zephyr Bracelet • (3%) APOA: Worn Dark Shadow

Tangua [20] (30%) Silver Amethyst Ring • (15%) Rough Flight Bodkin Arrows (x2) • (1.4%) Pitted Recurve Bow • (1.4%) Siabrian Bracer • (1.5%) <Rogue Pendants (Low)> • (0.3%) <Treasures of the Fey>

Tracker [17,19] (no loot)

Tric [23] (60%) Faerie Drakes Rainbow Scale (x3) • (1.5%) Faerie Drakes Eye • (5%) Faerie Drakes Scaled Hide • (50%) Faerie Drakes Tail • (15% each) Topaz, Pearl • (1.5%) Faerie Charm, ***or*** Luminescent Gloves ***or*** Boots • (10%) Faerie Drake Hide

veil wisp [11-13] (50%) Softly Glowing Orb • (25%) Jewels 03 • (0.3%) <Engraved Enchantments>

Viola [16] (no loot)

Watcher Rylie [19] (no loot)

Wilde [24] (80%) Faerie Steed Mane • (30%) Faerie Steed Pelt • (90%) Faerie Steed Tail

wrath sprite [27-28] (80%) Bleached Leg Bone • (60%) Softly Glowing Orb • (50%) Red Spinel • (1.5%) Spritely Stiletto ***or*** Shield

Tir na Nog

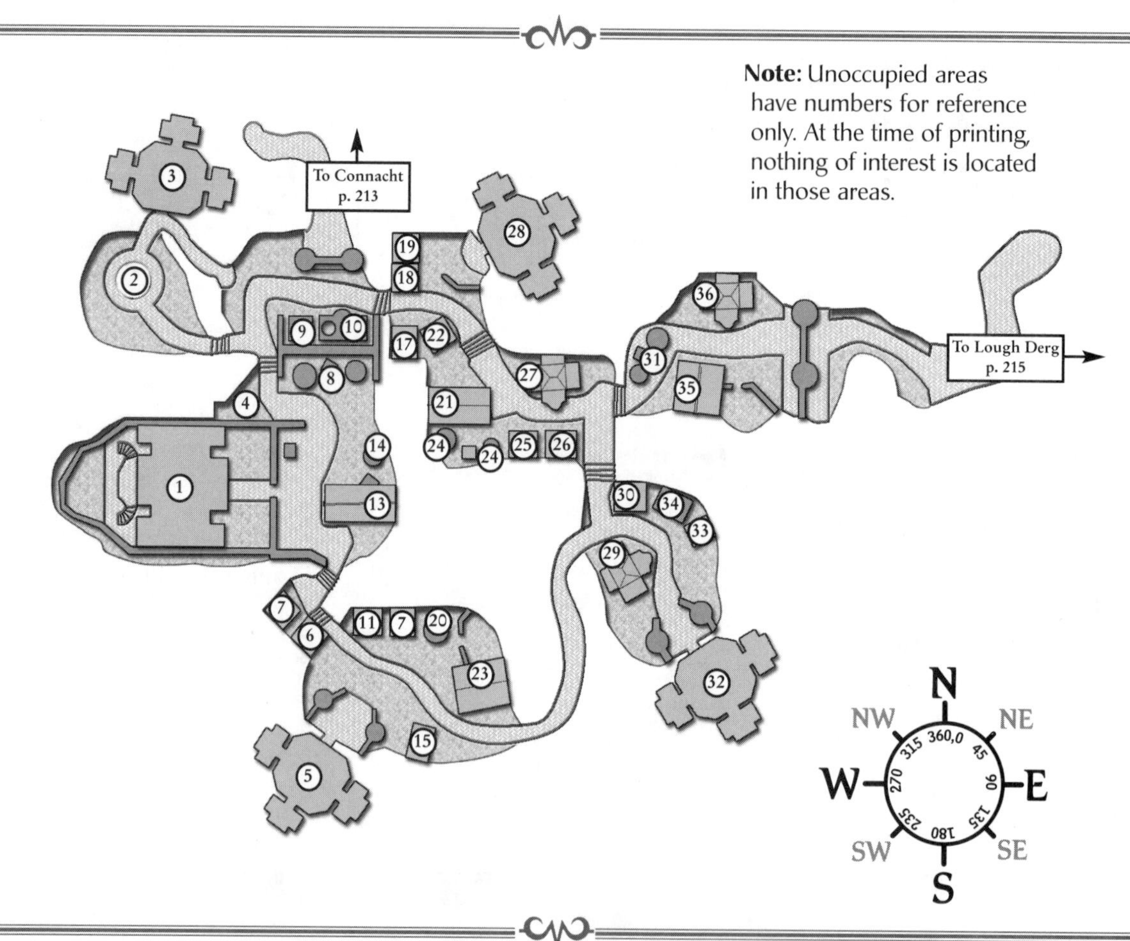
Note: Unoccupied areas have numbers for reference only. At the time of printing, nothing of interest is located in those areas.
To Connacht p. 213
To Lough Derg p. 215
N
NE
E
SE
S
SW
W
NW

1 **Aghaistin** Bounty Store - Crystals
1 **Bhreagar Hylvian** Vault Keeper
1 **Brigit**
1 **Caolan** Enchanter
1 **Ffhionbarr** Guild Emblemeer
1 **Filidh Fadwyn** Guild Registrar
1 **Filidh Filiara** Name Registrar
1 **Harper Eibhilin**
1 **Lauralaye**
1 **Lobais**
1 **Lovernios**
1 **Sentinel Liadin**
1 **Sentinel Llacheu**
1 **Vaddon** Healer
2 **Bard**
2 **Filidh Meilseior**
3 **Daray** Druid Trainer
3 **Grainne** Bounty Store - Crystals
3 **Labhras** Warden Trainer
3 **Selia** Bard Trainer
4 **Ffiara** Large weapons
4 **Geryn** Strips
5 **Antaine** Bounty Store - Crystals
5 **Lasairiona** Champion Trainer
5 **Luighseach** Blademaster Trainer
5 **Riofach** Hero Trainer
8 **Cedric** Boards
8 **Darcy** Tailoring equipment
8 **Ewen** Staff
8 **Hywela** Osnadurtha scale armor
8 **Saffa** Tailoring equipment
8 **Vaughn** Constaic leather armor
10 **Connor** Arrows
10 **Fingal** Bard instruments
10 **Guardian Daire**
10 **Guardian Sima**
10 **Jarlath**
10 **Jezza Blackfingers** Smith
10 **Jiskarr de'Mordan** Celtic spears
10 **Kenzia** Bows
10 **Waljan** Healer
12 **Arziqua** Fletching Master
12 **Izall** Fletching supplies (feathers)
13 **Deante** Poison
13 **Franseza** Blunt
13 **Jeanna** Green/brown/gray/orange/yellow leather dye
13 **Krianna** Blue/teal/red/purple leather dye
13 **Malior** Poison
13 **Tomas** Cruaigh leather armor
14 **Armin** Master Tailor
14 **Baran** Smithing equipment
14 **Dunstan** Armorcraft Master
14 **Hendrika** Weaponcraft Master
14 **Tegvan** Armorcraft Master
19 **Eavan**
19 **Tiarnan**
20 **Cristolia** Green/brown/grey/orange/yellow enamel dye
20 **Drumnail** Large weapons
20 **Kiam** Smith
20 **Kirsta** Blue/turq/teal/red/purple enamel dye
20 **Lulach** Blades
21 **Adrai** Staff
21 **Banyell** Reinforced armor
21 **Deverry** Carbide weapons
21 **Keya** Carbide scale armor
21 **Lerena** Sylvan woven armor
21 **Sharon** Embossed leather armor
21 **Taleai** Amber reinforced armor
24 **Briana** Bows
24 **Dierdra** Green/brown/grey/orange/yellow cloth dye
24 **Gemma** Cruaigh leather armor
24 **Kelsi** Arrows
24 **Laurence** Cruanach scale armor
24 **Sissy** Robes
27 **Banon** Smith
27 **Ermid** Brea leather armor
27 **Guardian Brighid**
27 **Guardian Teadoir**
27 **Romney** Celtic spears
27 **Seva** Blades
28 **Blathnaid** Nightshade Trainer
28 **Kiley** Bounty Store - Crystals
28 **Mavelle** Ranger Trainer
28 **Nona** Poison merchant
28 **Roibin** Poison merchant
29 **Bairfhionn**
29 **Blanche** Blue/teal/turq/red/purple cloth dye
29 **Harper Evelyn**
29 **Isibael** Bows
29 **Muirne** Piercers
29 **Seren** Arrows
29 **Tristan** Osnadurtha scale armor
31 **Cleit** Shields
31 **Cragen** Cailiocht reinforced armor
31 **Eachann** Woven armor
31 **Nolan** Cailiocht reinforced armor
31 **Renny** Nadurtha reinforced armor
31 **Sadhbh** Enchanter
31 **Sentinel Mada**
32 **Aghna** Enchanter staves
32 **Ailson** Bounty Store - Crystals
32 **Anwar** Enchanter Trainer
32 **Aodh** Eldritch Trainer
32 **Aulif** Woven armor
32 **Brianna** Mentalist staves
32 **Cinnie** Cheap cloth dye, robes
32 **Ena** Mentalist Trainer
32 **Kado** Woven armor
32 **Kedric** Eldritch staves
32 **Kinnat** Woven armor
32 **Madarl** Cheap cloth dye, robes
32 **Nealcail** Cheap cloth dye, robes
36 **Ailish**
36 **Bevan Clune**
36 **Conary**
36 **Conleth Cuagain**
36 **Fidelma Breen**
36 **Harper Eveny**
36 **Iarla Clune**
36 **Kieran Breen**
36 **Larla Clune**
36 **Maxen** Daingean scale armor
36 **Rhosyn** Bard instruments
36 **Somhairle Breen**
36 **Treasa Breen**
by 22 **Kennocha**
by 33 **Labhaoise**

Alainn Bin (Bog of Cullen)

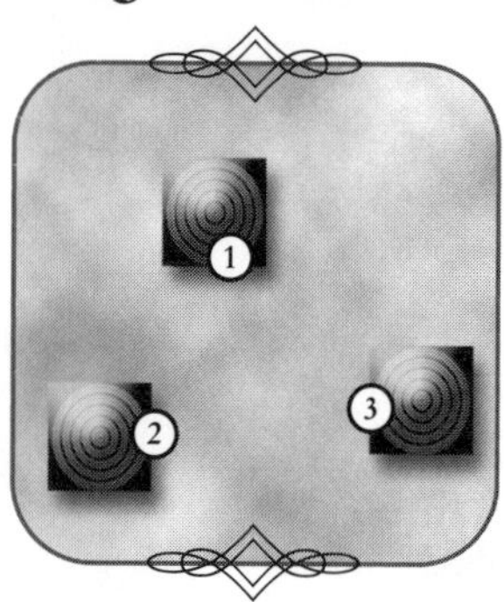

1 **Alaiina** *Large W.*
1 **Chieftess Dana**
1 **Cragen** *Cailiocht reinforced A.*
1 **Dympna** *Cruaigh leather A.*
2 **Iama** *Eldritch staff*
2 **Liam** *Arrows*
2 **Lirla** *Poison (2)*
2 **Maureen** *Bows*
2 **Rois**
3 **Aisling** *Enchanter staff*
3 **Ceri** *Healer*
3 **Dalladva** *Smith*
3 **Finghin** *Cruanach scale A.*
3 **Helori** *Piercing W.*

Ardagh (Silvermine Mts.)

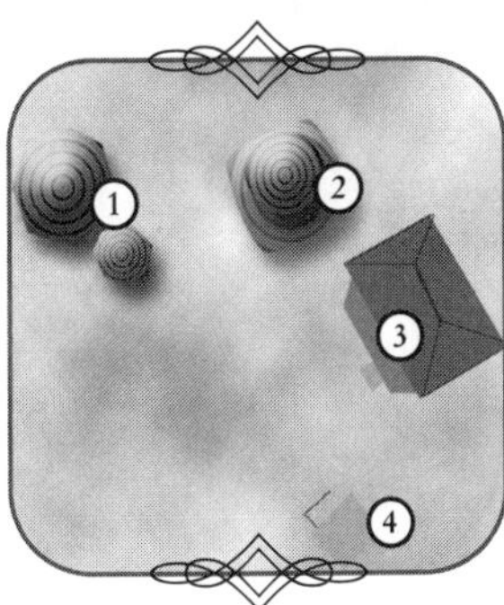

1 **Della** *Bard instruments*
1 **Ea** *Blademaster Tr.*
1 **Edricar Stable** *Stable*
1 **Illaliel** *Enchanter staff*
1 **Noreen** *Osnadurtha scale A.*
1 **Nyle** *Blunt W.*
1 **Reeni** *Cloth dye*
1 **Roise** *Cailiocht reinforced A.*
2 **Caitriona**
2 **Iaine** *Celtic spear*
2 **Leachlainn** *Nightshade Tr.*
2 **Odharnait**
2 **Siodhachan** *Champion Tr.*
2 **Teague** *Ranger Tr.*
2 **Ysbail** *Blade W.*
3 **Aindreas** *Mentalist Tr.*
3 **Brenna** *Eldritch staff*
3 **Brisen** *Robes*
3 **Coman** *Eldritch Tr.*
3 **Iola** *Enchanter*
3 **Lochlain**
3 **Mabli** *Cloth dye*
3 **Moesen** *Cloak A.*
3 **Sentinel Eimile**
3 **Talaith** *Enchanter Tr.*
3 **Torlan** *Enchanter staff*
4 **Celder** *Arrows*
4 **Filidh Medyr**
4 **Fyrsil** *Healer*
4 **Rhodry** *Bows*
4 **Seana** *Staff*
4 **Uilliam** *Warden Tr.*
Guardian
Sentinel

Ardee (Connacht)

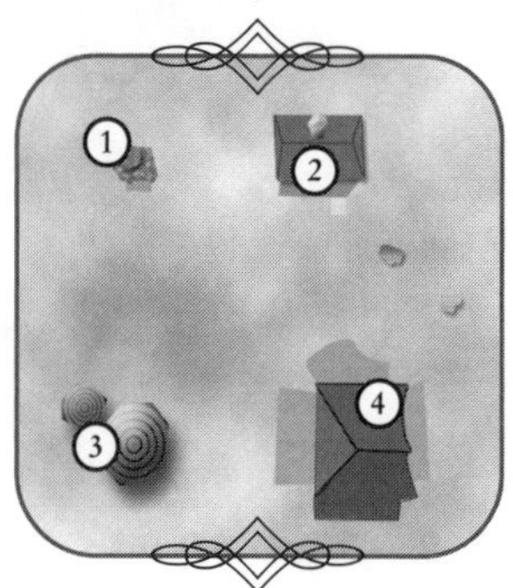

1 **Auliffe** *Magician Tr.*
1 **Caoimhe** *Naturalist Tr.*
1 **Eiral** *Enchanter*
2 **Aideen** *Blunt W.*
2 **Arshan** *Sewing (1)*
2 **Creirwy** *Eldritch staff*
2 **Daron** *Enchanter staff*
2 **Fianait** *Brea leather A.*
2 Flannery Guardian Tr.
2 **Mahon** *Piercing W.*
2 **Naomhan** *Mentalist staff*
2 **Nyderra**
3 **Ailfrid** *Robes*
3 **Eleri** *Celtic spear*
3 **Eoghan**
3 **Freagus** *Stable*
3 **Ierna** *Staff*
3 **Qunilan** *Woven A.*
3 **Rhona** *Bows*
4 **Criostoir** *Smith*
4 **Daithi** *Stalker Tr.*
4 **Evan** *Nadurtha reinforced A.*
4 **Garnock** *Blade W.*
4 **Keara**
4 **Kiana**
4 **Larylle**
4 **Lexie** *Poison (1)*
4 **Llyn** *Healer*
4 Tethra
4 **Tira**
Local Bard
Sentinel Moya

Basar (Connacht)

1 ***Anna*** *Nadurtha reinforced A.*
1 ***Erech*** *Expensive trade skill items*
1 ***Neb*** *Constaic leather A.*
2 ***Arzhela*** *Cruaigh leather A.*
2 ***Deryn*** *Blunt W.*
2 ***Tara*** *Arrows*
2 ***Zinna*** *Bows*
3 ***Briac*** *Piercing W.*
3 ***Cristin*** *Daingean scale A.*
3 ***Cubert*** *Tacuil reinforced A.*
3 ***Eruven***
Guardian
Sentinel
Sentinel Andreasa

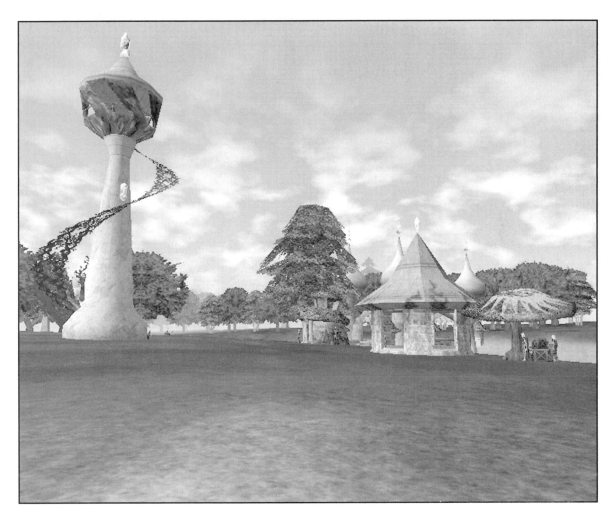

Caille (Valley of Bri Leith)

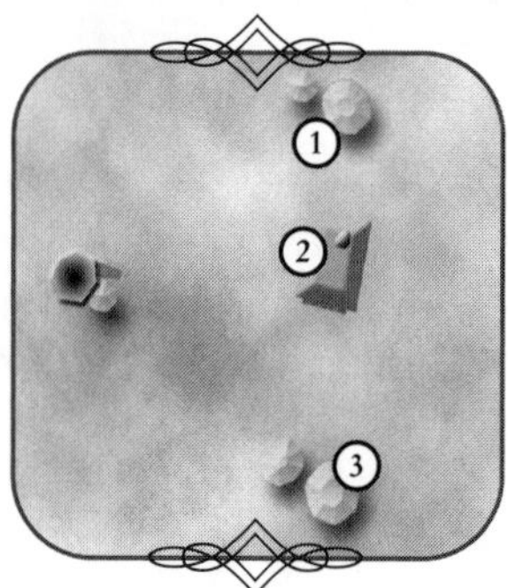

*1 **Empar***
*1 **Olane***
*1 **Saraid***
*2 **Ainrebh** Enchanter*
*2 **Ariana** Mentalist staff*
*2 **Brynn** Enchanter staff*
*2 **Keir** Eldritch staff*
*3 **Lysagh** Woven A.*
*3 **Viola***

Ceannai (Shannon Estuary)

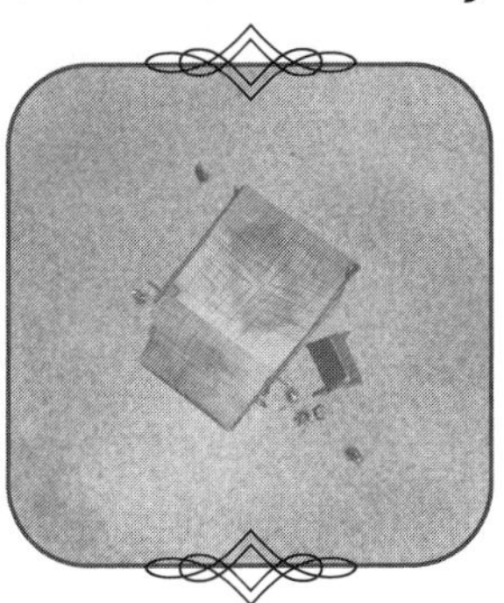

Dorran *Poison (2)*
Fallon *Staff*
Guardian
Izold *Celtic spear*
Kyle *Healer*
Sentinel
Unarla *Daingean scale A.*
Vivienne *Osnadurtha scale A.*
Wynda *Shields*
Yann *Piercing W.*

Connla (Shannon Estuary)

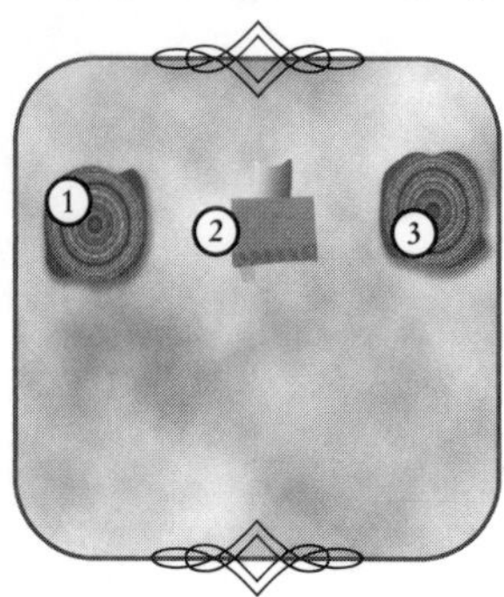

1 **Aelerogh** *Stable*
1 **Allistar** *Blademaster Tr.*
1 **Benen** *Naturalist Tr.*
1 **Bryanna** *Enchanter staff*
1 **Colm** *Osnadurtha scale A.*
1 **Eira** *Blade W.*
1 **Eli** *Enchanter*
1 **Erwana** *Large W.*
1 **Kigua**
1 **Searlas** *Hero Tr.*
1 *Sile Ranger Tr.*
1 **Tadhg**
1 **Uisetan**
2 **Alun** *Blunt W.*
2 **Bran** *Stalker Tr.*
2 **Edana** *Arrows*
2 **Ennis** *Magician Tr.*
2 **Erskine** *Brea leather A.*
2 **Glyn** *Eldritch staff*
2 **Kiara** *Bows*
2 **Kinney** *Poison (1)*
2 **Maire**
2 **Marus** *Celtic spear*
2 **Oran O'Braonain**
2 **Sarff** *Smith*
3 **Ailill** *Guardian Tr.*
3 **Edernola** *Bard instruments*
3 **Edmyg** *Mentalist staff*
3 **Eyslk** *Enchanter Tr.*
3 **Gavina** *Shields*
3 **Keagan** *Healer*
3 **Nainsi** *Eldritch Tr.*
3 **Peadar** *Staff*
3 **Sorcha** *Robes*
3 **Ronan** *Woven A.*
3 **Treise** *Mentalist Tr.*
4 *Ascatinius*
4 *Cordelia Champion Tr.*
4 **Dempsey** *Bard Tr.*
4 **Filidh Mairtin**
4 **Harper Cadwr**
4 **Kyli**
4 *Local Bard*
Guardian
Sentinel
Sentinel Glynis

Daingean (Shannon Estuary)

Ghearic Chauclon *Vault*
Guardian
Iacob
Kaylee
Iunger
Rooney *Nightshade Tr.*
Sentinel
Slevin *Shields*
Torrance Druid Tr.

Druim Ligen (Connacht)

Araisa *Passage Medallion*
Genee
Glasny
horse
Keep Sentinel
Llalla *Arrows*
Master Eldritch
Master Ranger
Medallion Master
Ranger
Renwisk *Siegecraft items*
Riber *Poison (2)*
Seoltoir
Ullios *Stable*
Yralun Trallae *Vault*
PALACE
Guardian
Jena
Lila *Arrows*
Melro
Qunie
Sentinel

Druim Cain (Valley of Bri Leith)

Crimthan Ranger Tr.
Echlin Champion Tr.
Erli Druid Tr.
Ina Eldritch Tr.
Kiernan Bard Tr.
Meriel Blademaster Tr.
Mhari Enchanter Tr.
Sheelah Hero Tr.
Vevina Warden Tr.
Yseult Nightshade Tr.

Howth (Silvermine Mts.)

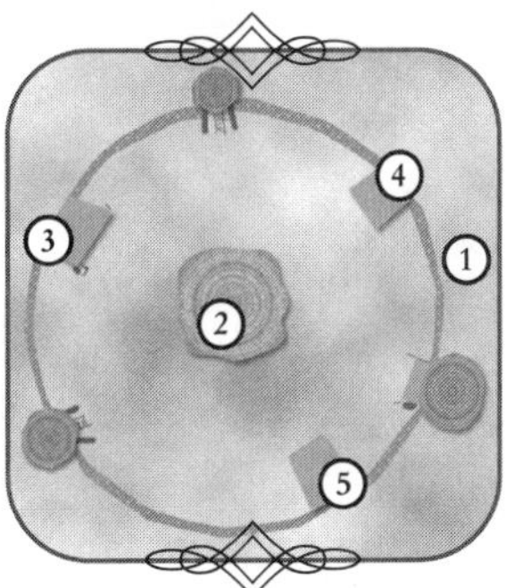

1 **Gormghlaith**
1 **Maille** Bard Tr.
1 **Pheuloc** Stable
1 **Piaras**
1 Sentinel
1 **Sentinel Beacan**
2 **Adair** Magician Tr.
2 **Bidelia** Druid Tr.
2 **Cathbad**
2 **Chief Proinnsias**
2 **Gralon** Healer
2 **Iain** Cruanach scale A.
2 **Kaley** Guardian Tr.
2 **Keriann**
2 **Nevin** Hero Tr.
3 **Ainbe** Blade W.
3 **Alwyn** Smith
3 **Anra** Staff
3 **Blaez** Shields
3 **Blayne** Arrows
3 **Cait** Celtic spear
3 **Ffion** Large W.
3 **Gaenor** Piercing W.
3 **Mairona**
4 **Bevin** Nadurtha reinforced A.
4 **Dyvyr** Leather dye
4 **Kenna** Constaic leather A.
4 **Kevain** Tacuil reinforced A.
4 **Tyree** Leather dye
5 **Daibheid** Naturalist Tr.
5 Damhnait Stalker Tr.
5 **Irksa** Bard instruments
5 **Kalla** Poison (1)
5 **Lasrina**
5 **Troya**
5 **Twm** Cailiocht reinforced A.
Guardian
Local Bard

Innis Carthaig (Lough Gur)

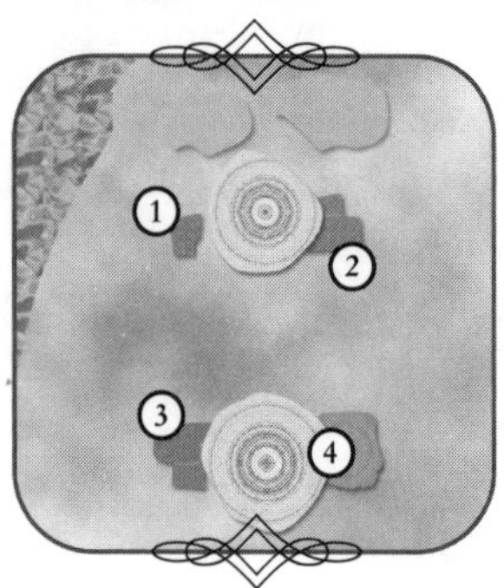

Slaine Robes
1 ***Accalon*** *Wood skill supplies*
1 ***Chieftess Niamh***
1 ***Feoras*** *Cloak A.*
1 ***Gorawen*** *Cruaigh leather A.*
1 ***Harper Brac***
1 ***Kian*** *Cruanach scale A.*
1 ***Macharan*** *Tailoring supplies*
1 ***Sholto***
1 ***Trahern*** *Feathers*
1 ***Yealcha*** *Metalworking equipment*
2 ***Amhlaoibh*** *Tailoring strips*
2 ***Amynda*** *Mentalist staff*
2 ***Crayg*** *Enchanter staff*
2 ***Glennard*** *Eldritch staff*
2 ***Sarena*** *Poison (2)*
2 ***Sentinel Adienna***
2 ***Whiltierna*** *Sewing skill supplies*
3 ***Blanchefleur*** *Vault*
3 ***Blyanche*** *Healer*
3 ***Kern*** *Enchanter*
3 ***Malachy***
3 ***Siobhan*** *Smith*
3 ***Slaine*** *Robes*
4 ***Asthore*** *Blade W.*
4 ***Barra*** *Staff*
4 ***Breachus*** *Stable*
4 ***Deirdre*** *Arrows*
4 ***Drummond*** *Large W.*
4 ***Mariota*** *Cailiocht reinforced A.*
4 ***Talriese*** *Daingean scale A.*
4 ***Syvwlch*** *Metal*
Guardian
Noble Steed
Sentinel Champion

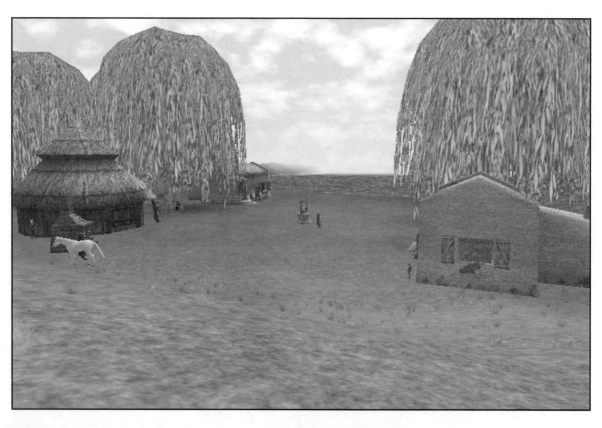

Mag Mell (Lough Derg)

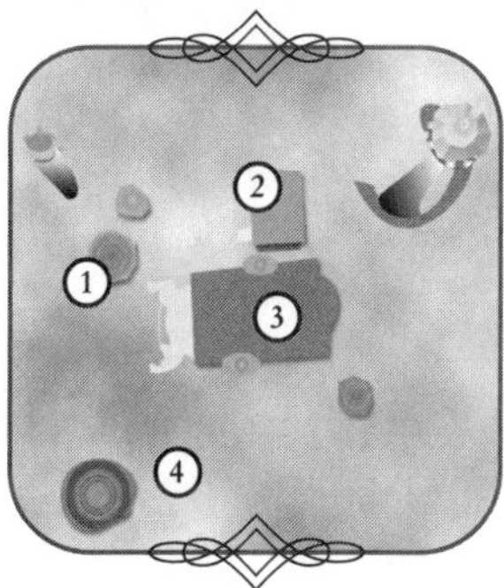

1 Breeda Naturalist Tr.
1 **Cafell** Shields
1 **Ilisa** Smith
1 **Jahan** Expensive trade skill items
1 **Kylirean** Brea leather A.
1 **Sentinel Maitias**
1 **Wony** Blade W.
2 **Anice** Woven A.
2 **Dera** Enchanter
2 **Eluned** Robes
2 **Sedric** Mentalist staff
2 **Sian** Staff
3 **Epona** Healer
3 Etain Magician Tr.
3 **Fagan**
3 **Filidh Morven**
3 **Greagoir**
3 **Harper Cara**
3 **Mandra**
3 **Meadghbh** Guardian Tr.
4 **Aillig** Arrows
4 **Lachlan** Piercing W.
4 **Mannix** Bows
4 **Meara**
4 **Oistin** Cloak A.
4 **Rumdor** Stable
4 **Ula** Stalker Tr.
Guardian
Local Bard
Sentinel

Mardagh (Lough Derg)

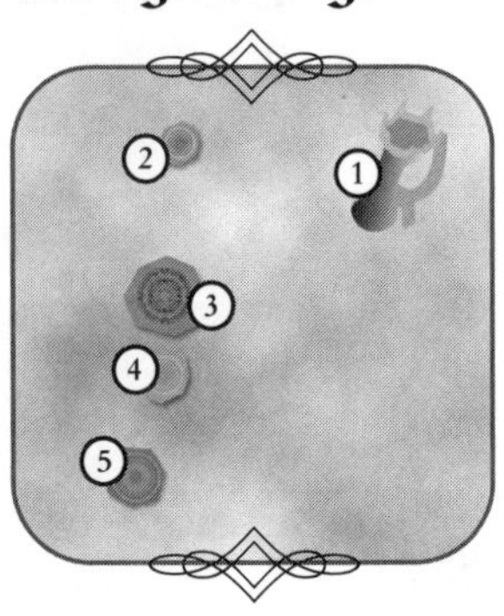

1 ***Riona***
1 ***Rolney***
2 ***Ardal*** *Tacuil reinforced A.*
2 ***Dilith*** *Enamel dye*
2 ***Dirmyg*** *Blade W.*
2 ***Ebril*** *Cruaigh leather A.*
2 ***Thady*** *Large W.*
3 ***Akira*** *Cailiocht reinforced A.*
3 ***Mearchian*** *Celtic spear*
4 ***Beli*** *Healer*
4 ***Edsoner*** *Bard instruments*
4 ***Eimhin*** *Blunt W.*
4 ***Grizel*** *Smith*
4 ***Muadhnait*** *Staff*
5 ***Brody*** *Constaic leather A.*
5 ***Calder*** *Arrows*
Guardian

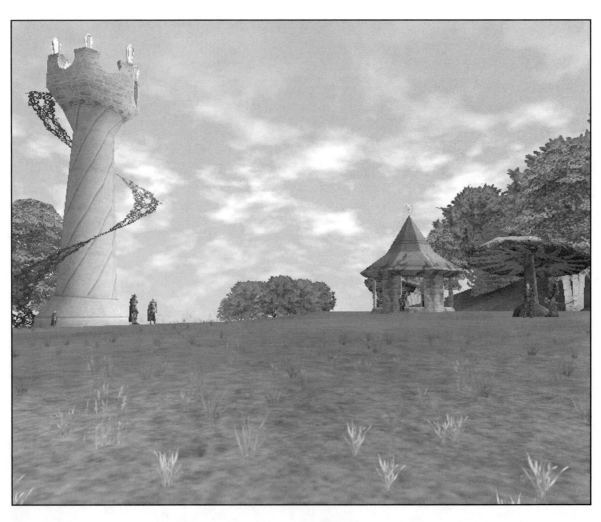

Shannon Estuary Bridge (Shannon Estuary)

Bebhinn *Warden Tr.*

Silvermine Mtns. Camp (Silvermine Mts.)

Aeveen *Cruaigh leather A.*

Elder Brona *Robes*

Elder Finian *Constaic leather A.*

Gobnait

Lorcan *Arrows*

Onora *Blade W.*

Siopa (Bog of Cullen)

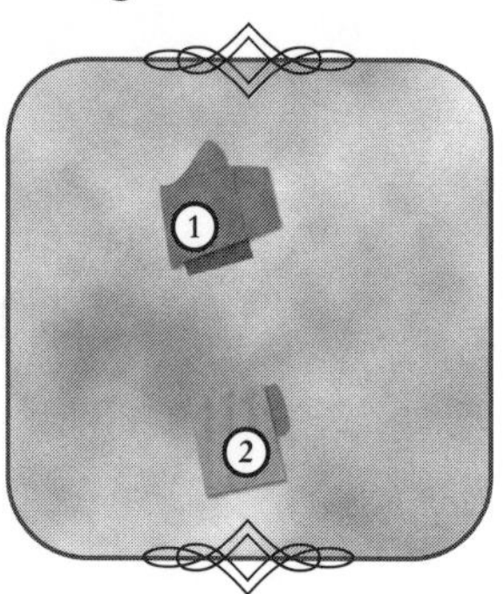

1 ***Caron*** *Constaic leather A.*
1 ***Emhyr*** *Enchanter staff*
1 ***Kerwin*** *Healer*
1 ***Murchadh*** *Cloak A.*
1 ***Raghnall*** *Robes*
3 ***Alar*** *Blunt W.*
3 ***Broc*** *Blade W.*
3 ***Devin*** *Osnadurtha scale A.*
3 ***Morag*** *Shields*
Sentinel

Tir na mBeo (Lough Derg)

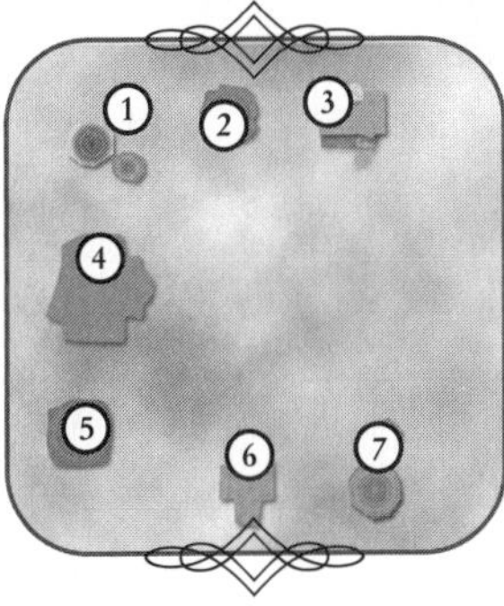

1 **Achaius** Large W.
1 **Liadan** Enchanter staff
1 **Truichon** Stable
2 **Borlai** Poison (2)
2 **Cian** Bard instruments
2 **Harper Jocelin**
2 **Una** Cruanach scale A.
3 **Boyd** Nadurtha reinforced A.
3 Ionhar Healer
3 **Sentinel Ornora**
4 **Ardghal Corcoran**
4 **Dicra** Enchanter
4 **Guardian Andraste**
4 **Kaenia** Robes
4 **Lainie** Smith
4 **Raine**
4 **Reidie**
4 **Tangi** Enchanter
4 Tavie
5 **Rhian** Enamel dye
5 **Teleri** Daingean scale A.
6 **Elith** Woven A.
6 **Kean**
7 **Aidaila** Osnadurtha scale A.
7 **Anrai** Staff
7 **Duer** Woven A.
7 **Lavena** Eldritch staff
Sentinel

Tir Urphost (Cliffs of Mohur)

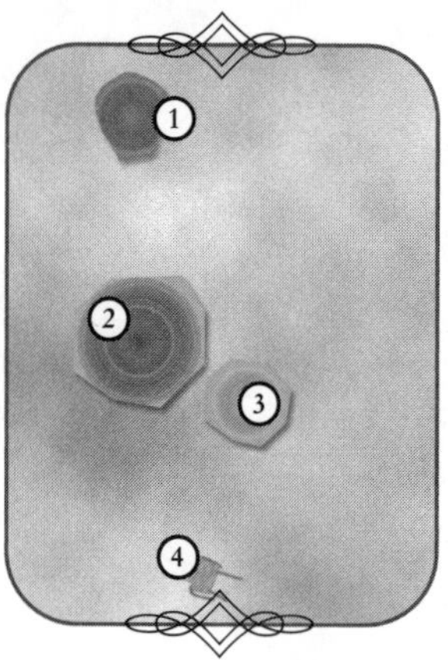

1 ***Cleary*** *Enchanter*
1 ***Luergor*** *Stable*
2 ***Callough*** *Large W.*
2 ***Daracha*** *Bows*
2 ***Yvon*** *Shields*
3 ***Mosby*** *Cruanach scale A.*
3 Tavie Nadurtha reinforced A.
Sentinel
Sentinel Casidhe

Coruscating Mines

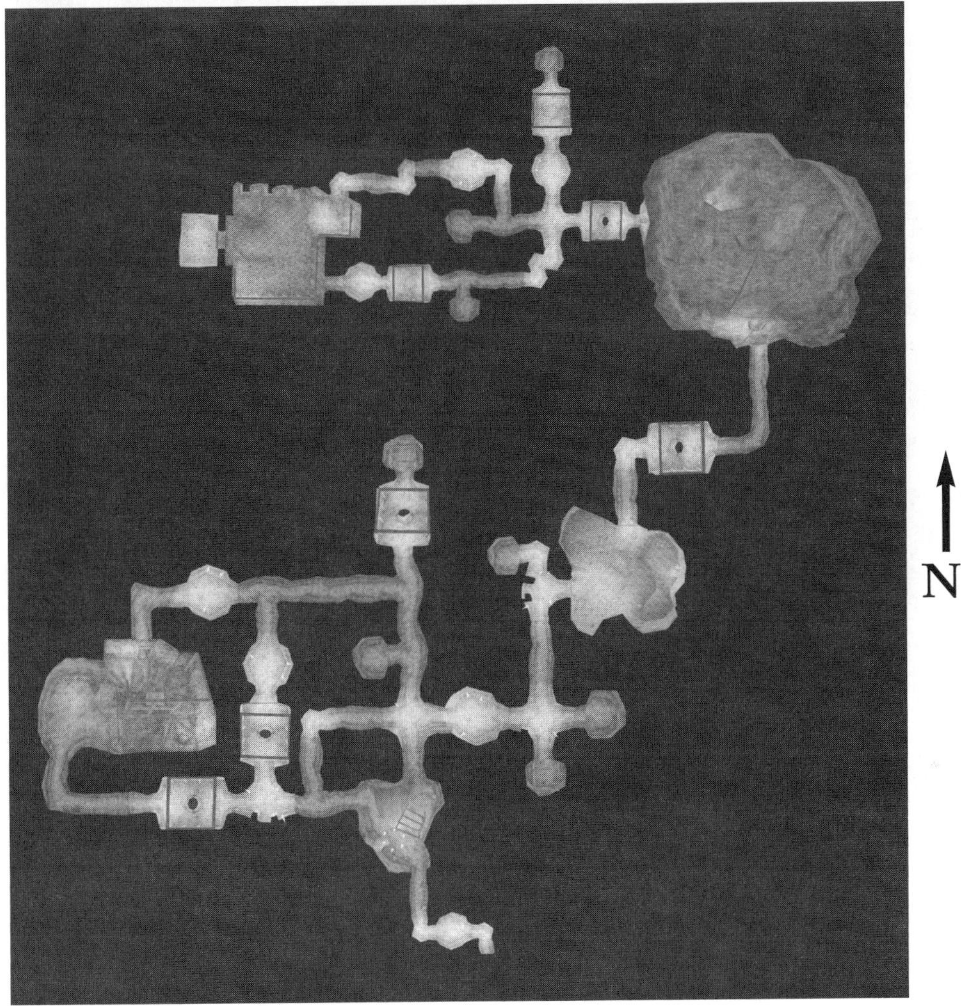

Loot

abysmal [50] (15%) Shadow Crystal • (15%) Abysmal Scraps • (15%) Jewels 07 • (0.5%) Jewels 37 • (1.2%) <Thrym's Gift> • (0.4%) <Fire and Ice> • (1.5%; hi-lo) APOA: Sable Drakescale, Bladed Guardian, Imbued Unseelie, *or* Unseelie Loyalist • (1.5%) <Silverhand's Hoard> • (3.6%) Rust, Charcoal *or* Royal Teal Colors • (0.4%) Crimson, Black *or* Violet Colors

Allyn [36] *see trammer [36]*

Atur [48] (20%) Phantom Miner Essence • (40%) Jewels 07 • (1.2%) Jewels 37 • (3.6%) Rust, Charcoal *or* Royal Teal Colors • (0.4%) Crimson, Black *or* Violet Colors • (0.8%) <Fire and Ice> • (0.8%) <Thrym's Gift> • (1.5%; hi-lo) APOA: Unseelie Loyalist, Imbued Unseelie, Bladed Guardian, *or* Sable Drakescale • (1.5%) <Silverhand's Hoard>

casolith [45] (25%) Shadow Crystal • (30%) Jewels 58 • (0.9%) Jewels 16 • (3.6%) Light Turquoise, Teal *or* Light Purple Colors • (0.4%) Turquoise, Royal Teal *or* Purple Colors • (0.8%) <Glittering Goodies 1> • (0.8%) <Glittering Goodies 2> • (1.5%) APOA: Ghostly Truesilver Cloth *or* Leather, *or* Reinforced *or* Silverhand Truemail • (1.5%) <Flash of Wonders>

coerced groover [45] (20% each) Tarnished Truesilver Collar, Shackle • (15%) Jewels 58 • (0.5%) Jewels 16 • (3.6%) Light Turquoise, Teal *or* Light Purple Colors • (0.4%) Turquoise, Royal Teal *or* Purple Colors • (1.2 %) <Glittering Goodies 1> • (0.4%) <Glittering Goodies 2> • (1.5%; hi-lo) APOA: Ghostly Truesilver Cloth, Ghostly Truesilver Leather, Reinforced Truemail, Silverhand Truemail • (1.5%) <Flash of Wonders>

collared gemgetter [38-39] (30%) Tarnished Truesilver Collar • (5%) Tarnished Truesilver Shackle • (5%) Jewels 42 • (0.6%) Jewels 20 • (3.6%) Light Turquoise, Teal *or* Light Purple Colors • (0.4%) Turquoise, Royal Teal *or* Purple Colors • (0.8%) <Filled with Radiance> • (0.8%) <Luminescence> • (1.5%; hi-lo) APOA: Loyalist Scalemail, *or* Jewel Spiked, Rigid *or* Dusted • (1.5%) <Glint of Brilliance>

Duga [42] (25%) Underviewers Rank Insignia • (10%) Plans For the Mines • (25%) Jewels 42 • (0.6%) Jewels 20 • (3.6%) Light Turquoise, Teal *or* Light Purple Colors • (0.4%) Turquoise, Royal Teal *or* Purple Colors • (0.8%) <Filled with Radiance> • (0.8%) <Luminescence> • (1.5%) APOA: Loyalist Scalemail, *or* Jewel Spiked, Rigid *or* Dusted • (1.5%) <Twinkling Treasures>

enthralled silvier [36/37] (20%) Tarnished Truesilver Collar • (5%) Tarnished Truesilver Shackle • (10/20%) Jewels 42 • (0.6%) Jewels 20 • (3.6%) Light Turquoise, Teal *or* Light Purple Colors • (0.4%) Turquoise, Royal Teal *or* Purple Colors • (3%) <Nobody's Perfect> • (1%) <Seconds of the Best> • (4%) APOA: Worn Jewel Dusted, Pierced *or* Spiked, *or* Worn Loyalist Scale • (1.7%) <Glint of Brilliance>

Frat [38] (25%) Gem Dust Powder • (25%) Jewels 42 • (0.6%) Jewels 20 • (3.6%) Light Turquoise, Teal *or* Light Purple Colors • (0.4%) Turquoise, Royal Teal *or* Purple Colors • (1.3%) <Seconds of the Best> • (1.3%) <Nobody's Perfect> • (0.6%) <Filled with Radiance> • (0.6%) <Luminescence> • (2.8%; hi-lo) APOA: Worn Jewel Dusted, Pierced *or* Spiked, *or* Worn Loyalist Scale • (1.2%; hi-lo) APOA: Jewel Dusted, Rigid *or* Spiked, *or* Loyalist Scalemail • (1.7%) <Glint of Brilliance>

Frit [37] *see silvermine knocker [36-37]*

geas-bound hewer [39] (25%) Affixed Geas Stone • (25%) Jewels 42 • (0.6%) Jewels 20 • (3.6%) Light Turquoise, Teal *or* Light Purple Colors • (0.4%) Turquoise, Royal Teal *or* Purple Colors • (1.2%) <Luminescence> • (0.4%) <Filled with Radiance> • (1.5%; hi-lo) APOA: Jewel Dusted, Rigid *or* Spiked, *or* Loyalist Scale • (1.5%) <Glint of Brilliance>

gemclicker [37/38/39] (23%) Gem Clicker Carapace • (20/23/25%) Gem Clicker Claw • (2.5%) Pristine Gem Clicker Carapace • (1.7%) Gem Encrusted Claw • (10/10/18%) Jewels 42 • (0.6%) Jewels 20

gemclicker horder [40] (23%) Gem Clicker Carapace • (2.5%) Pristine Gem Clicker Carapace • (28%) Gem Clicker Claw • (1.7%) Gem Encrusted Claw • (23%) Jewels 42 • (0.6%) Jewels 20

gem-dusted skeleton [37] (25%) Gem Dusted Bone • (15%) Gem Dusted Skull • (20%) Jewels 42 • (0.6%) Jewels 20 • (3.6%) Light Turquoise, Teal *or* Light Purple Colors • (0.4%) Turquoise, Royal Teal *or* Purple Colors • (3%) <Seconds of the Best> • (1%) <Nobody's Perfect> • (4%) APOA: Worn Jewel Dusted, Pierced *or* Spiked, *or* Worn Loyalist Scale • (1.7%) <Glint of Brilliance>

glow worm [36] (38%) Glow Worm Carapace • (1.6%) Crested Glow Worm Carapace • (20%) Jewels 42 • (0.6%) Jewels 20

Guardian of the Silver Hand [50] (15%) Silverhand Rank Insignia • (15%) Unseelie Signet Ring • (15%) Jewels 07 • (0.5%) Jewels 37 • (3.6%) Rust, Charcoal *or* Royal Teal Colors • (0.4%) Crimson, Black *or* Violet Colors • (1.2%) <Thrym's Gift> • (0.4%) <Fire and Ice> • (1.5%; hi-lo) APOA: Sable Drakescale, Bladed Guardian, Imbued Unseelie, *or* Unseelie Loyalist • (1.5%) <Silverhand's Hoard>

haunting draft [49] (3.6%) Rust, Charcoal *or* Royal Teal Colors • (0.4%) Crimson, Black *or* Violet Colors • (1.2%) <Fire and Ice> • (0.4%) <Thrym's Gift> • (1.5%; hi-lo) APOA: Unseelie Loyalist, Imbued Unseelie, Bladed Guardian, *or* Sable Drakescale • (1.5%) <Silverhand's Hoard>

larval predator [36] (22%) Sparkling Gem Studded Carapace • (2.4%) Dazzling Jeweled Carapace

Lobigan [48] (10%) Shadow Crystal • (20%) Vial of Silver Poisoned Blood • (20%) Jewels 07 • (0.6%) Jewels 37 • (3.6%) Rust, Charcoal *or* Royal Teal Colors • (0.4%) Crimson, Black *or* Violet Colors • (0.8%) <Fire and Ice> • (0.8%) <Thrym's Gift> • (1.5%; hi-lo) APOA: Unseelie Loyalist, Imbued Unseelie, Bladed Guardian, *or* Sable Drakescale • (1.5%) <Silverhand's Hoard>

lode protector [47/48] (20%) Gem of Animation • (60/50%) Jewels 07 • (1.8/1.5%) Jewels 37 • (3.6%) Rust, Charcoal *or* Royal Teal Colors • (0.4%) Crimson, Black *or* Violet Colors • (0.8%) <Glittering Goodies 1>/<Fire and Ice> • (0.8%) <Glittering Goodies 2>/<Thrym's Gift> • (1.5%) APOA: Ghostly Truesilver Cloth *or* Leather, *or* Reinforced *or* Silverhand Truemail [47] • (1.5%; hi-lo) APOA: Unseelie Loyalist, Imbued Unseelie, Bladed Guardian, *or* Sable Drakescale [48] • (1.5%) <Flash of Wonders>/<Silverhand's Hoard>

lode runner [49] (10%) Gem of Animation • (75%) Jewels 07 • (2.2%) Jewels 37 • (3.6%) Rust, Charcoal *or* Royal Teal Colors • (0.4%) Crimson, Black *or* Violet Colors • (0.8%) <Fire and Ice> • (0.8%) <Thrym's Gift> • (1.5%) APOA: Unseelie Loyalist, Imbued Unseelie, Bladed Guardian, *or* Sable Drakescale • (1.5%) <Silverhand's Hoard>

Overman Regnal [50] *see unseelie overman [49]*

Overseer of the Silver Hand [51] (15% each) Silverhand Rank Insignia, Unseelie Signet Ring • (15%) Jewels 07 • (0.5%) Jewels 37 • (3.6%) Rust, Charcoal *or* Royal Teal Colors • (0.4%) Crimson, Black *or* Violet Colors • (1.2%) <Fire and Ice> • (0.4%) <Thrym's Gift> • (1.5%; hi-lo) APOA: Sable Drakescale, Bladed Guardian, Imbued Unseelie, *or* Unseelie Loyalist • (1.5%) <Silverhand's Hoard>

phantom miner [47] (20%) Phantom Miner Essence • (30%) Jewels 07 • (0.9%) Jewels 37 • (3.6%) Rust, Charcoal *or* Royal Teal Colors • (0.4%) Crimson, Black *or* Violet Colors • (1.2%) <Glittering Goodies 2> • (0.4%) <Glittering Goodies 1> • (1.5%; hi-lo) APOA: Ghostly Truesilver Cloth, Ghostly Truesilver Leather, Reinforced Truemail, Silverhand Truemail • (1.5%) <Silverhand's Hoard>

rockbiter [37] (38%) Bitten Truesilver Stone • (22%) Jewels 42 • (0.6%) Jewels 20 • (1.7%) Elemental Heatstone

Scratch [39] *see tunnel imp [38]*

shaft rat [36] (23%) Gem Dusted Rat Pelt • (2.5%) Gem Dusted Pristine Rat Pelt • (25%) Gem Imbedded Rat Fang • (1.7%) Rat Fang Stiletto

silver-flecked skeleton [47] (10% each) Truesilver Covered Skull, Bone • (10%) Jewels 07 • (0.3%) Jewels 37 • (3.6%) Rust, Charcoal *or* Royal Teal Colors • (0.4%) Crimson, Black *or* Violet Colors • (0.8%) <Glittering Goodies 1> • (0.8%) <Glittering Goodies 2> • (1.5%) APOA: Ghostly Truesilver Cloth *or* Leather, *or* Reinforced *or* Silverhand Truemail • (1.5%) <Silverhand's Hoard>

silver-maddened werewolf [47] (10%) Shadow Crystal • (20%) Vial of Silver Poisoned Blood • (20%) Jewels 07 • (0.6%) Jewels 37 • (3.6%) Rust, Charcoal *or* Royal Teal Colors • (0.4%) Crimson, Black *or* Violet Colors • (0.8%) <Glittering Goodies 1> • (0.8%) <Glittering Goodies 2> • (1.5%; hi-lo) APOA: Ghostly Truesilver Cloth, Ghostly Truesilver Leather, Reinforced Truemail, Silverhand Truemail • (1.5%) <Silverhand's Hoard>

silvermine guard [45] (15%) Unseelie Jeweled Baldric • (10%) Silvermine Rank Insignia • (10%) Jewels 58 • (0.3%) Jewels 16 • (3.6%) Light Turquoise, Teal *or* Light Purple Colors • (0.4%) Turquoise, Royal Teal *or* Purple Colors • (1.2%) <Glittering Goodies 2> • (0.4%) <Glittering Goodies 1> • (1.5%; hi-lo) APOA: Silverhand *or* Reinforced Truemail, *or* Ghostly Truesilver Leather *or* Cloth • (1.5%) <Flash of Wonders>

silvermine knocker [36-37] (20%) Gem Dust Powder • (20%) Jewels 42 • (0.6%) Jewels 20 • (3.6%) Light Turquoise, Teal *or* Light Purple Colors • (0.4%) Turquoise, Royal Teal *or* Purple Colors • (3%) <Seconds of the Best> • (1%) <Nobody's Perfect> • (4%) APOA: Worn Jewel Dusted, Pierced *or* Spiked, *or* Worn Loyalist Scale • (1.7%) <Glint of Brilliance>

silvermine sentry [39] (10%) Silvermine Sentry Insignia • (75%) Jewels 42 • (0.6%) Jewels 20 • (3.6%) Light Turquoise, Teal *or* Light Purple Colors • (0.4%) Turquoise, Royal Teal *or* Purple Colors • (1.2%) <Filled with Radiance> • (0.4%) <Luminescence> • (1.5%; hi-lo) APOA: Loyalist Scalemail, *or* Jewel Spiked, Dusted *or* Rigid • (1.5%) <Glint of Brilliance>

trammer [36] (20%) Affixed Geas Stone • (20%) Jewels 42 • (0.6%) Jewels 20 • (3.6%) Light Turquoise, Teal *or* Light Purple Colors • (0.4%) Turquoise, Royal Teal *or* Purple Colors • (3%) <Seconds of the Best> • (1%) <Nobody's Perfect> • (4%) APOA: Worn Jewel Dusted, Pierced *or* Spiked, *or* Worn Loyalist Scale • (1.7%) <Glint of Brilliance>

troglodyte [45] (30%) Troglodyte Eye • (10%) Jewels 58 • (0.3%) Jewels 16 • (3.6%) Light Turquoise, Teal *or* Light Purple Colors • (0.4%) Turquoise, Royal Teal *or* Purple Colors • (0.8%) <Glittering Goodies 1> • (0.8%) <Glittering Goodies 2> • (1.5%) APOA: Ghostly Truesilver Cloth *or* Leather, *or* Reinforced *or* Silverhand Truemail • (1.5%) <Flash of Wonders>

tunnel imp [38] (15% each) Small Shadow Crystal, Imp's Small Jeweled Crown • (30%) Jewels 42 • (0.6%) Jewels 20 • (3.6%) Light Turquoise, Teal *or* Light Purple Colors • (0.4%) Turquoise, Royal Teal *or* Purple Colors • (1.4%) <Seconds of the Best> • (1.4%) <Nobody's Perfect> • (0.6%) <Filled with Radiance> • (0.6%) <Luminescence> • (2.8%) APOA: Worn Jewel Dusted, Pierced *or* Spiked, *or* Worn Loyalist Scale • (1.2%; hi-lo) APOA: Loyalist Scalemail, *or* Jewel Spiked, Dusted *or* Rigid • (1.7%) <Glint of Brilliance>

undead drudger [38/39] (25% each) Truesilver Nugget, Small Shadow Crystal • (25/50%) Jewels 42 • (0.6%) Jewels 20 • (3.6%) Light Turquoise, Teal ***or*** Light Purple Colors • (0.4%) Turquoise, Royal Teal ***or*** Purple Colors • (1.4%) <Seconds of the Best> • (1.4%) <Nobody's Perfect> • (0.6%) <Filled with Radiance> • (0.6%) <Luminescence> • (2.8%) APOA: Worn Loyalist Scale, ***or*** Worn Jewel Spiked, Dusted ***or*** Pierced • (1.2%; hi-lo) APOA: Loyalist Scalemail, ***or*** Jewel Spiked, Dusted ***or*** Rigid • (1.7%) <Glint of Brilliance>

Underviewer Treeal [42] *see unseelie underviewer [42]*

unseelie mango [40] (20%) Underviewers Rank Insignia • (10%) Plans For the Mines • (20%) Jewels 42 • (0.6%) Jewels 20 • (3.6%) Light Turquoise, Teal ***or*** Light Purple Colors • (0.4%) Turquoise, Royal Teal ***or*** Purple Colors • (0.8%) <Filled with Radiance> • (0.8%) <Luminescence> • (1.5%) APOA: Loyalist Scalemail, ***or*** Jewel Spiked, Rigid ***or*** Dusted • (1.5%) <Twinkling Treasures>

unseelie overman [49] (13% each) Unseelie Jeweled Baldric, Truesilver Drinking Horn • (13%) Jewels 07 • (0.4%) Jewels 37 • (3.6%) Rust, Charcoal ***or*** Royal Teal Colors • (0.4%) Crimson, Black ***or*** Violet Colors • (1.2%) <Fire and Ice> • (0.4%) <Thrym's Gift> • (1.5%; hi-lo) APOA: Unseelie Loyalist, Imbued Unseelie, Bladed Guardian, ***or*** Sable Drakescale • (1.5%) <Silverhand's Hoard>

unseelie underviewer [42] (20%) Underviewers Rank Insignia • (10%) Plans For the Mines • (10%) Jewels 58 • (0.3%) Jewels 16 • (3.6%) Light Turquoise, Teal ***or*** Light Purple Colors • (0.4%) Turquoise, Royal Teal ***or*** Purple Colors • (1.2%) <Luminescence> • (0.4%) <Filled with Radiance> • (1.5%; hi-lo) APOA: Loyalist Scalemail, ***or*** Jewel Spiked, Rigid ***or*** Dusted • (1.5%) <Twinkling Treasures>

unseelie viewer [48] (10% each) Unseelie Jeweled Baldric, Truesilver Drinking Horn • (10%) Jewels 07 • (0.3%) Jewels 37 • (3.6%) Rust, Charcoal ***or*** Royal Teal Colors • (0.4%) Crimson, Black ***or*** Violet Colors • (1.2%) <Fire and Ice> • (0.4%) <Thrym's Gift> • (1.5%; hi-lo) APOA: Unseelie Loyalist, Imbued Unseelie, Bladed Guardian, ***or*** Sable Drakescale • (1.5%) <Silverhand's Hoard>

vein golem [49] (20%) Truesilver Lined Stone • (10%) Jewels 07 • (0.3%) Jewels 37 • (3.6%) Rust, Charcoal ***or*** Royal Teal Colors • (0.4%) Crimson, Black ***or*** Violet Colors • (0.8%) <Fire and Ice> • (0.8%) <Thrym's Gift> • (1.5%; hi-lo) APOA: Unseelie Loyalist, Imbued Unseelie, Bladed Guardian, ***or*** Sable Drakescale • (1.5%) <Silverhand's Hoard>

Viewer Etol [49] *see unseelie viewer [48]*

weewere [48-49] (23%) Wee Were Pelt • (2.5%) Pristine Wee Were Pelt • (5%) Jewels 07 • (0.2%) Jewels 37 • (3.6%) Rust, Charcoal ***or*** Royal Teal Colors • (0.4%) Crimson, Black ***or*** Violet Colors • (0.8%) <Fire and Ice> • (0.8%) <Thrym's Gift> • (1.5%; hi-lo) APOA: Unseelie Loyalist, Imbued Unseelie, Bladed Guardian, ***or*** Sable Drakescale • (1.5%) <Silverhand's Hoard>

Koalinth Caverns

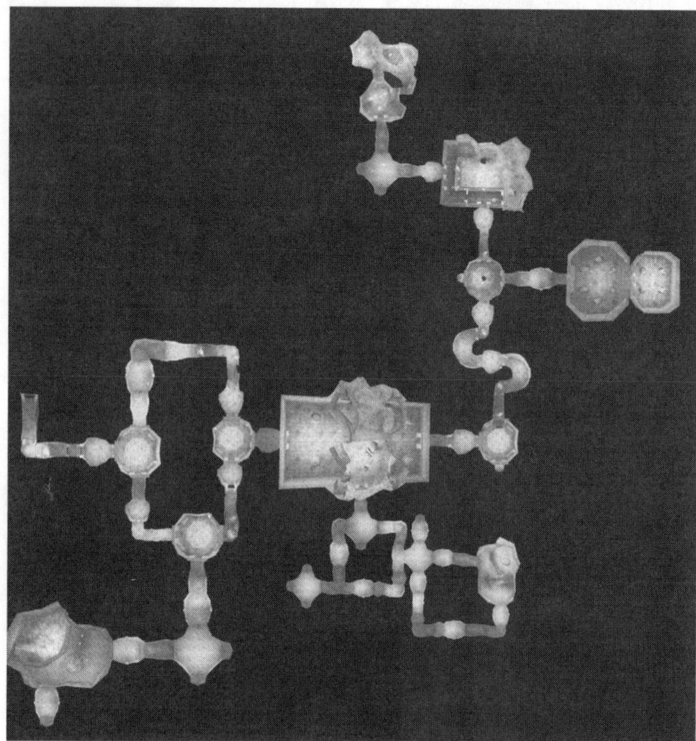

Loot

aqueous slug [23] (23%) Aqueous Slug Carapace • (2.5%) Pristine Slug Carapace • (0.5%) Dark Crystalized Poison Sac

cave toad [22] (23%) Cave Toad Skin • (2.5%) Pristine Cave Toad Skin • (0.5%) Dark Crystalized Poison Sac

horned cave toad [23] (23%) Horned Toad Skin • (2.5%) Pristine Horned Toad Skin • (0.5%) Dark Crystalized Poison Sac

koalinth bouncer [20] (9%) <Flecks O' Gold> • (9%) Jewels 56 • (1.5%) APOA: Abandoned Crustacean • (1.5%) <Wealth of an Empire> • (1.5%) <Fathoms Below>

koalinth castellan [26] (10%) <Crystal Clear> • (10%) Jewels 51 • (1.5%) <Impenetrable Arms> • (1.5%) APOA: Fathomless Deepscale, ***or*** Imperial Sword of the Depths • (1.5%) <Out of the Sea> • (1.5%) Will Shatterer

koalinth diplomat [27] (10%) <Crystal Clear> • (10%) Jewels 51 • (1.5%) <Impenetrable Arms> • (1.5%) APOA: Fathomless Deepscale, ***or*** Imperial Sword of the Depths • (1.5%) <Out of the Sea> • (1.5%) Pearl Rapier

koalinth elder [27] (10%) <Crystal Clear> • (10%) Jewels 51 • (1.5%) <Impenetrable Arms> • (1.5%) APOA: Fathomless Deepscale, ***or*** Imperial Sword of the Depths • (1.5%) <Out of the Sea> • (1.5%) Spear of Elder Pearl

koalinth envoy [23/26] (10%) <Crystal Clear> • (10%) Jewels 56/Jewels 51 • (1.5%) <Carved from Coral> • (1.5%) APOA: Fathomless Deepscale, ***or*** Imperial Sword of the Depths • (1.5%) <Salvaged Goods>/<Out of the Sea> • (1.5%) Sight Blighter [26]

koalinth guardian [24] (10%) <Crystal Clear> • (10%) Jewels 51 • (1.5%) <Impenetrable Arms> • (1.5%) APOA: Fathomless Deepscale, ***or*** Imperial Sword of the Depths • (1.5%) <Out of the Sea>

koalinth sentinel [18] (8%) <Flecks O' Gold> • (8%) Jewels 56 • (1.5%) APOA: Abandoned Crustacean • (1.5%) <Wealth of an Empire> • (1.5%) <Fathoms Below>

koalinth spectator [19] (9%) <Flecks O' Gold> • (9%) Jewels 56 • (1%) APOA: Damp Shell Flecked • (0.5%) APOA: Watery Shell Flecked • (1.5%) <Wealth of an Empire> • (1.5%) <Fathoms Below>

koalinth warden [19] *see koalinth sentinel [18]*

koalinth warder [20] *see koalinth spectator [19]*

koalinth wrestler [20] *see koalinth spectator [19]*

Master of Ceremonies [22] (10%) <Flecks O' Gold> • (10%) Jewels 56 • (1.5%) APOA: Fathomless Deepscale, ***or*** Imperial Sword of the Depths • (1.5%) <Wealth of an Empire> • (1.5%) <Salvaged Goods> • (1.5%) Imperial Golden Hammer

pelagian alliant [28] (10%) Jewels 51 • (1.6%) APOA: Hollowed Crustacean • (1.6%) <Out of the Sea> • (1.6%) Spined Razor Foreclaw

pelagian crab [25-26] (10%) Jewels 51 • (1.6%) APOA: Hollowed Crustacean • (1.6%) <Out of the Sea> • (1.3%) Fathomless Crescent Claw

pelagian guard [28] *see pelagian crab [25-26]*

poisonous cave toad [22] (23%) Poisonous Cave Toad Skin • (2.5%) Pristine Poisonous Toad Skin • (0.5%) Dark Crystalized Poison Sac

shock aqueous slug [24] (23%) Shock Slug Carapace • (2.5%) Pristine Shock Slug Carapace • (0.5%) Dark Crystalized Poison Sac

watery escort [18] *see koalinth bouncer [20]*

Muire Tomb

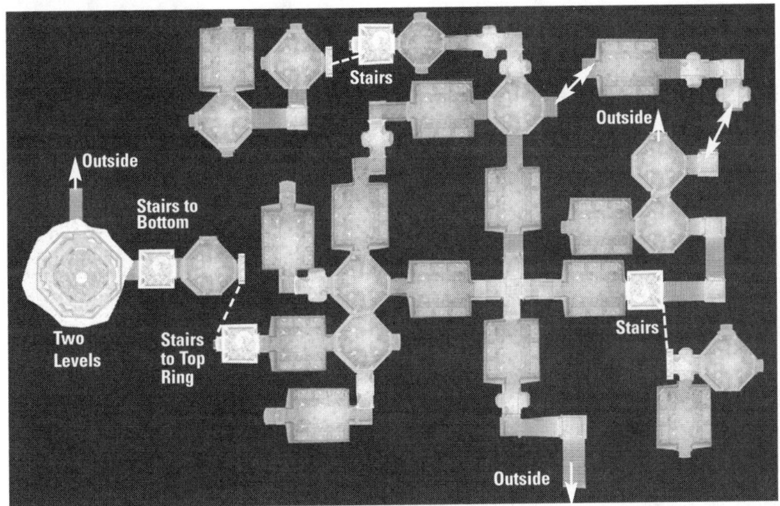

Loot

Note (1) all these monsters have: (5%) Light Blue, Light Red ***or*** Light Green Colors • (1.5%) APOA: Regal Woven, Noble's Leather, Lavish Reinforced, ***or*** Splendid Scale • (1.5%) <Muire's Riches 1>

Alsandair Muire [16] *see Note (1), plus* • (70%) <Quoth the Raven> • (70%) Jewels 03 • (1.5%) <It's a Mad, Mad World> • (0.5%) <Muire's Riches 2>

Beare Muire [18] *see Note (1), plus* • (85%) <Quoth the Raven> • (85%) Jewels 03 • (1.5%) <It's a Mad, Mad World> • (0.5%) <Muire's Riches 2>

carrion scorpionida [15] (20%) Scorpion Carapace • (80%) Scorpion Claw • (48%) Scorpion Tail • (0.3%) <Treasures of the Fey>

Conaire Muire [19] *see Note (1), plus* • (90%) <Quoth the Raven> • (90%) Jewels 03 • (1.5%) <It's a Mad, Mad World> • (0.5%) <Muire's Riches 2>

corpse devourer [16] (15%) Corpse Devourer Silk • (22%) Corpse Devourer Maw • (10%) Corpse Devourer Carapace

crypt spider [10-11/12] (20/45%) Crypt Spider Leg Tip • (10%) Crypt Spider Carapace • (75%) Crypt Spider Leg • (60%) Crypt Spider Silk • (0.3%) <Engraved Enchantments>

death worm [14] (55%) Death Worm Carapace • (65%) Death Worm Maw • (75%) Death Worm Silk • (0.3%) <Treasures of the Fey>

Frang [20] (59%) <Wine Shine> • (15%) Jewels 03 • (1.7%) Morbid Muire Mace ***or*** Outrider's Gem

Guardian Betrayer [19] (55%) <Wine Shine> • (15%) Jewels 03 • (1.7%) Etched Bone Broadsword, Euphonic Gem ***or*** Welkin Gem

Hellhag [14] *see Note (1), plus* • (80%) Hag's Green Hair • (15%) Torn Silk Mummy Wrap • (95%) Jewels 44 • (1.5%) Shield of the Decadent *or* Gold Embossed Shield • (0.5%) <Treasures of the Fey>

Kacey Muire [17] *see Note (1), plus* • (75%) <Quoth the Raven> • (75%) Jewels 03 • (1.5%) <It's a Mad, Mad World> • (0.5%) <Muire's Riches 2>

Muire Champion [19] (55%) <Wine Shine> • (15%) Jewels 03 • (1.7%) Grisly Great Sword ***or*** Gem of A Champion

Muire herbalist [18] (42%) <Wine Shine> • (15%) Jewels 03 • (1.7%) Imbued Shield of Bone ***or*** Shield of Bone

Muire Hero [19] *see Guardian Betrayer [19]*

Muire lady-in-waiting [14, 16] *see Note (1), plus* • (60%) Jeweled Bone Comb • (10%) Stuffed Raven • (60%) Jewels 44 • (1.5%) <It's a Mad, Mad World> • (0.5%) <Treasures of the Fey>

Muire man-at-arms [16] *see Note (1), plus* • (75%) Symbol of Loyalty In Death • (50%) Essence of Madness • (1.5%) <It's a Mad, Mad World> • (0.5%) <Muire's Riches 2>

mummy hag [11-12/13] (80%) Hag's Green Hair • (5/15%) Torn Silk Mummy Wrap • (80/90%) Jewels 44 • (5%) Light Blue, Light Red *or* Light Green Colors • (4%) APOA: Old Silk, Macabre Leather, *or* Old Noble's • (4%) <Gaudy *or* Gorgeous> • (1.7%) <Gaudy Jewelry> • (0.5%) <Engraved Enchantments>

mummy hag wizard [17] (35%) <Wine Shine> • (15%) Jewels 03 • (1.7%) Dancing Bones Lute, Flute ***or*** Drum

murkman [15-16] *see Note (1), plus* • (15%) Golden Muck Covered Pendant • (80%) Muck Crusted Silver Baldric • (90%) Jewels 44 • (1.5%) <It's a Mad, Mad World> • (0.5%) <Muire's Riches 2>

Quillan Muire [23] (85%) <Wine Shine> • (15%) Jewels 03 • (1.7%) Macabre Muire Club ***or*** Morbid Jewel of Skill

Scorpionida Regina [17] (40%) Scorpion Carapace • (80%) Scorpion Claw • (70%) Scorpion Tail • (0.3%) <Muire's Riches 2>

suitor spirit [14-15] *see Note (1), plus* • (80%) Symbol of Loyalty In Death • (5%) Bottle of Poisoned Wine • (80%) Jewels 44 • (1.5%) <It's a Mad, Mad World> • (0.5%) <Treasures of the Fey>

tomb creeper [9] (2%) Creeper Skin • (60%) Creeper Clawed Hand • (15%) Obsidian • (12%) Spinel • (10%) Chryoprase • (7.5%) Bloodstone • (5%) Amethyst • (1.7%) <Gaudy Jewelry> • (5%) Light Blue, Light Green *or* Light Red Colors • (0.5%) <Engraved Enchantments>

tomb creeper [13] (10%) Creeper Skin • (75%) Creeper Clawed Hand • (27%) Obsidian • (23%) Spinel • (18%) Chryoprase • (13%) Bloodstone • (9%) Amethyst • (5%) Light Blue, Light Green *or* Light Red Colors • (4%) APOA: Old Silk, Macabre Leather, *or* Old Noble's • (4%) <Gaudy *or* Gorgeous> • (1.7%) <Gaudy Jewelry> • (0.5%) <Treasures of the Fey>

tomb creeper [16] *see Note (1), plus* • (10%) Creeper Skin • (80%) Creeper Clawed Hand • (80%) Jewels 03 • (1.5%) <It's a Mad, Mad World> • (0.5%) <Muire's Riches 2>

tomb dweller [18] *see tomb creeper [16]*

Spraggon Den

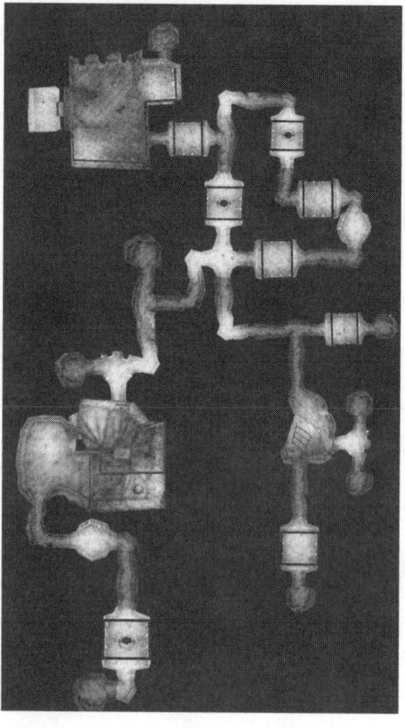

Loot

Dramacus [30] <Arctic Articles> • Jewels 38 • (6%) Green ***or*** Brown Colors • (1.5%) APOA: Earthen Woven Root, Earth Crafted Molded, Earth Crafted, ***or*** Earth Crafted Scale • (1.5%) <Skirnir's Promise> • (1.5%) <Odin's Wish> • (6%) Jewels 25

earth sprite [24-25/26] (75/85%) <Arctic Articles> • (75/85%) Jewels 38 • (5%) Green ***or*** Brown Colors • (1.5%) APOA: Earthen Woven Root, Earth Crafted Molded, Earth Crafted, ***or*** Earth Crafted Scale • (1.5%) <Skirnir's Promise> • (1.5%) <Odin's Wish> • (2%) Jewels 25

Ick [22] (73% each) Large Worm Carapace, Large Worm Jaw • (1.7%) <Bio 101: Dissection>

ick worm [17] (40%) Worm Carapace • (75%) Worm Tooth • (1.7%) <Bio 101: Dissection>

pit boss [23-24] (80%) <Hi Ho, Hi Ho, It's ...> • (80%) Jewels 38 • (5%) Green ***or*** Brown Colors • (1.5%) APOA: Earthen Woven Root, Earth Crafted Molded, Earth Crafted, ***or*** Earth Crafted Scale • (1.5%) <Skirnir's Promise> • (1.5%) <Odin's Wish> • (2%) Jewels 25

pit spraggon [20-21/22] (80/90%) <Hi Ho, Hi Ho, It's ...> • (80/90%) Jewels 22 • (5%) Green ***or*** Brown Colors • (4%) APOA: Dried Woven Root, Molded, Root Reinforced, ***or*** Molded Scale • (4%) <... And Carry a Big Stick> • (1.7%) <Older than Dirt> • (2%) Jewels 40

rock sprite [21-22/23] *see pit spraggon [20-21/22]*

root worm [18-19/20-21] (50/75%) Worm Carapace • (80%) Worm Tooth • (1.7%) <Bio 101: Dissection>

Ruckus [24] *see earth sprite [24-25]*

spraggon cutter [23-24/25] (78%) <Hi Ho, Hi Ho, It's ...>/<Arctic Articles> • (80/75%) Jewels 38 • (5%) Green ***or*** Brown Colors • (1.5%) APOA: Earthen Woven Root, Earth Crafted Molded, Earth Crafted, ***or*** Earth Crafted Scale • (1.5%) <Skirnir's Promise> • (1.5%) <Odin's Wish> • (2%) Jewels 25

spraggon runner [21-22/23] *see pit spraggon [20-21/22]*

spraggon springer [22-23] (90%) <Hi Ho, Hi Ho, It's ...> • (90%) Jewels 22 • (5%) Green ***or*** Brown Colors • (4%) APOA: Dried Woven Root, Molded, Root Reinforced, ***or*** Molded Scale • (4%) <... And Carry a Big Stick> • (1.7%) <Older than Dirt> • (2%) Jewels 40

spraggon springer [24] *see earth sprite [24-25]*

spraggonale [21] (15%) Copper Moonstone Flagon • (80% each) Bottle of Grog, Copper Cryoprase Earring • (40%) Topaz • (3%) Pitted Falcata • (0.3%) <Muire's Riches 3> • (1.5%) Dusty Leggings ***or*** Silvermined Blade

spraggonix [25-26] (85%) <Arctic Articles> • (85%) Jewels 38 • (5%) Green ***or*** Brown Colors • (1.5%) APOA: Earthen Woven Root, Earth Crafted Molded, Earth Crafted, ***or*** Earth Crafted Scale • (1.5%) <Skirnir's Promise> • (1.5%) <Odin's Wish> • (2%) Jewels 25

spraggonote [24-25] (80%) <Arctic Articles> • (80%) Jewels 38 • (5%) Green ***or*** Brown Colors • (1.5%) APOA: Earthen Woven Root, Earth Crafted Molded, Earth Crafted, ***or*** Earth Crafted Scale • (1.5%) <Skirnir's Promise> • (1.5%) <Odin's Wish> • (2%) Jewels 25

Spriggit [26] *see spraggonix [25-26]*

Yadda [27] (90%) <Arctic Articles> • (90%) Jewels 38 • (5%) Green ***or*** Brown Colors • (1.5%) APOA: Earthen Woven Root, Earth Crafted Molded, Earth Crafted, ***or*** Earth Crafted Scale • (1.5%) <Skirnir's Promise> • (1.5%) <Odin's Wish> • (2%) Jewels 25

Treibh Caillte

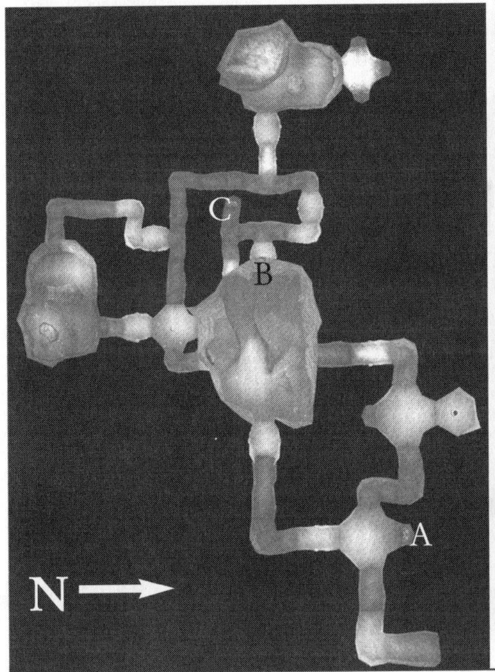

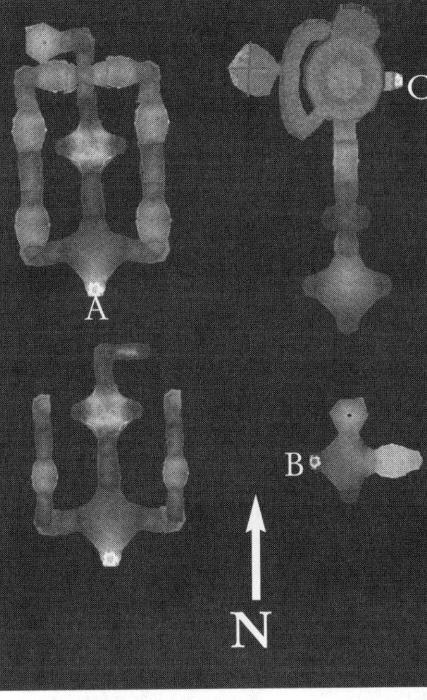

Loot

arachnid [37-38/39] (62%) Arachnid Leg Tip (x2) • (26/32%) Arachnid Carapace • (50% each) Silk Spinnerettes, Arachnid Silk • (26/32%) Arachnid Poison Sac

arachnite [28-29] (70% each) Arachnid Silk, Arachnid Leg Tip • (15%) Arachnid Carapace

arachnite [30] (70% each) Chitin Leg Tip Necklace, Harvested Spider Eggs • (40% each) Spider Catcher, Web Proof Mixture • (1.5%) APOA: Spider Keeper's ***or*** Silk Gatherer's • (1.5%) <Geirrod's Arms> • (1.5%) Shrunken Spider Necklace ***or*** Spider Gem • (2%) Jewels 50

Ceracor [42] *see rock golem [37]*

Dreaded Ursine [46] *see King Vian [40]*

Driff Tinel [40] *see ursine thrall [35-36]*

earth golem [39] *see rock golem [37]*

Cuuldurach the Glimmer King [80] (16% each) Fine Steel Long Sword, Soul Glimmer, Frigid Azure Crusher, Smoldering Crimson Bow, Semi-Ethereal Robe, Gloom Warder's Spear • (14% each) Netherworldy Scale Hauberk, Vest of the Veil Warder, Ghostly Great Falcata, Jerkin of the Ghostly Soul, Gauntlets of the Veil, Ring of Zo'arkat, Cloth Cap • (15%) Midnight Marauder Helm ***or*** Sleeves • (15%; hi-lo) Moonstrike Mace, Glimmerstrike Drum ***or*** Shadowstrike Ring • (15%) Midnight Marauder Gloves ***or*** Mystical Moonglade Boots • (15%; hi-lo) Glimmerstrike Crusher ***or*** Glimmer Striker Ring • (15%) Midnight Marauder Jerkin ***or*** Leggings • (15%; hi-lo) Glimmer Wrath Great Hammer, Glimmerstrike Shield, ***or*** Shadow Ring • (15%) Iridescent Sylph Druid Gloves, Sleeves ***or*** Coif • (15%) Warshadow Staff of the Void, Warshade Flute ***or*** Deathshadow Bracer • (15%) Iridescent Sylph Boots ***or*** Warden Gloves • (15%; hi-lo) Warshadow Staff of Mentalism ***or*** Bracer • (15%) Iridescent Sylph Hauberk ***or*** Leggings • (15%) Warshadow Staff of Enchantments, Warshade Protector ***or*** Glimmershade Bracer • (15%) Burnished Shanshee Gloves ***or*** Sleeves, ***or*** Heroic Burnished Shanshee Coif • (15%; hi-lo) Moondeath Mace, Deathwatcher Lute ***or*** Sorcerous Deathwatcher Chain • (15%; hi-lo) Burnished Shanshee Boots ***or*** Champion Burnished Shanshee Coif • (15%) Warshadow Staff of the Sun ***or*** Moon, ***or*** Potent Deathwatcher Chain • (15%) Burnished Shanshee Hauberk ***or*** Leggings • (15%; hi-lo) Deathmoon Rapier, Deathwatcher Ward ***or*** Empathic Deathwatcher Chain • (22%; hi-lo) Mystical Moonglade Sleeves ***or*** Melodic Moonglade Gauntlets • (22%) Glimmering Stiletto ***or*** Calignous Shroud • (22%; hi-lo) Masterful Moonglade Gauntlets ***or*** Mystical Moonglade Boots • (22%; hi-lo) Glimmer Geist Spear ***or*** Lurid Mantle • (22%; hi-lo) Iridescent Sylph Leggings ***or*** Mossy Moonglade Gauntlets • (22%) Calignous Shroud ***or*** Glimmerspirit Recurved Bow • (22%) Mystical Moonglade Helm ***or*** Vest • (22%) Glimmerspirit Short Bow ***or*** Lurid Mantle • (15%) Gossamer Seolc Sleeves ***or*** Pants, ***or*** Seolc Cap of the Void • (15%; hi-lo) Glimmerspirit Sword ***or*** Celestial Gem of the Sky • (15%) Gossamer Seolc Gloves ***or*** Boots, ***or*** Seolc Cap of Enchantment • (15%; hi-lo) Midnight Vengeance Falcata ***or*** Potent Gem of the Sky • (15%) Gossamer Seolc Vest ***or*** Robe, ***or*** Seolc Cap of Mentalism • (15%; hi-lo) Azure Avenger, Azure Defender ***or*** Ethereal Gem of the Sky

Helminth [37] (60% each) Worm Silk, Silk Spinnerettes • (58% each) Worm Acid Sac, Worm Carapace

Hervelina the hermit [34] *see ursine thrall [33-34]*

Hursk the Alchemist [43] *see ursine thrall [35-36]*

King Vian [40] (60%) Ring of Friendly Gestures • (2%) Ursine Head • (60%) Opal Mosaic Armband • (50%) Ursine War Paint • (1.5%) APOA: Silken Threaded Chitin ***or*** Ursine Forged Scale • (1.5%) <Agnar's Arms> • (1.5%) <Geirrod's Wish> • (2%) Jewels 50

Lair Overseer [37] (65%) Ring of Friendly Gestures • (65%) Chitin Leg Tip Necklace • (65%) Opal Mosaic Armband • (20%) Ursine War Paint • (1.5%) APOA: Silken Threaded Chitin ***or*** Ursine Forged Scale • (1.5%) <Agnar's Arms> • (1.5%) <Geirrod's Wish> • (2%) Jewels 50

lair worm [31/34-35] (60% each) Worm Silk, Silk Spinnerettes • (19/45% each) Worm Carapace, Worm Acid Sac

Pericolias the dreaded [43] *see arachnid [39]*

rock golem [35-36/37] (70/76%) Orb of Animation • (1.7%) Earth Shaker ***or*** Giant Swath-Cutter • (2%) Jewels 50

rocky golem [35] *see rock golem [35-36]*

scragger [30-31] (50%) Scragger's Pouch • Jewels 11 • (4%) APOA: Crude Silk ***or*** Crude Leather • (4%) Crude Club, Crude Spear, ***or*** Large Stone Mace • (1.7%) Scragger's Primitive Necklace • (2%) Jewels 50

Scurry [34] (80%) Scragger's Pouch • Jewels 11 • (4%) APOA: Crude Silk ***or*** Crude Leather • (4%) Crude Club, Crude Spear, ***or*** Large Stone Mace • (1.6%) Scragger's Primitive Necklace • (1.6%) Jewels 50

Thorg [38] *see arachnite [30]*

troglodyte [36-37] (50% each) Chitin Leg Tip Necklace, Harvested Spider Eggs, Spider Catcher, Web Proof Mixture • (1.5%) APOA: Spider Keeper's ***or*** Silk Gatherer's • (1.5%) <Geirrod's Arms> • (1.5%) Shrunken Spider Necklace ***or*** Spider Gem • (2%) Jewels 50

ursine dweller [36] (75%) Ring of Friendly Gestures • (2%) Ursine Head • (50%) Opal Mosaic Armband • (25%) Ursine War Paint • (1.5%) APOA: Silken Threaded Chitin ***or*** Ursine Forged Scale • (1.5%) <Agnar's Arms> • (1.5%) <Geirrod's Wish> • (2%) Jewels 50

ursine patrol [37] *see ursine dweller [36]*

ursine shaman [38] (80%) Ring of Friendly Gestures • (2%) Ursine Head • (55%) Opal Mosaic Armband • (30%) Ursine War Paint • (1.5%) APOA: Silken Threaded Chitin ***or*** Ursine Forged Scale • (1.5%) <Agnar's Arms> • (1.5%) <Geirrod's Wish> • (2%) Jewels 50

ursine sorcerer [39] (60%) Ring of Friendly Gestures • (2%) Ursine Head • (60%) Opal Mosaic Armband • (40%) Ursine War Paint • (1.5%) APOA: Silken Threaded Chitin ***or*** Ursine Forged Scale • (1.5%) <Agnar's Arms> • (1.5%) <Geirrod's Wish> • (2%) Jewels 50

ursine thrall [33-34/35-36] (50/62%) War Torn Baldric • (45/62%) Ring of Compliance • (45/60%) Light Carbide Shackles • (4%) APOA: Faded Spiderweave ***or*** Thrall's Ruined • (4%) <Heavy Handed> • (1.7%) Mantle of Forgotten Prowess

ursine warrior [37] *see ursine dweller [36]*

Webweaver [40] (70%) Arachnid Leg Tip (x2) • (70%) Arachnid Silk • (44% each) Arachnid Carapace, Arachnid Poison Sac

Midgard

Merchants

LOCATION KEYS

(A.Out.)	Albion Outpost
(Arv.)	Arvakr
(Aud.)	Audliten
(Bm.F)	Bledmeer Faste
(Bd.F.)	Blendrake Faste
(Dva.)	Dvalin
(F.F.)	Fensalir Faste
(Ft.A.)	Fort Atla
(Ft.V.)	Fort Veldon
(Gal.)	Galplen
(Gl.F.)	Glenlock Faste
(Gn.F.)	Gna Faste
(Hag.)	Haggerfel
(H.Out.)	Hibernia Outpost
(Hl.F.)	Hledskiaff Faste
(Hug.)	Huginfel
(Jor.)	Jordheim
(M.V.)	Mularn Village
(Nal.)	Nalliten
(Nm.F.)	Nottmoor Faste
(Sv.F.)	Svasud Faste
(Vas.)	Vasudheim
(Vs.F.)	Vindsaul Faste

Armor

Cloth
- (Jor.) Uli Johannsson

Leather Embossed
- (Jor.) Fiora

Mithril
- (Jor.) Hakan
- (Jor.) Tait

Mjuklaedar Leather
- (Aud.) Olav
- (Ft.A.) Og
- (Jor.) Im
- (M.V.) Lene
- (Vas.) Fianna

Padded Cloth
- (Aud.) Tozur
- (Ft.A.) Meeka
- (Gal.) Kaiti
- (Hag.) Culben
- (Hug.) Aylarn
- (Jor.) Torrad Gunderson
- (M.V.) Asta
- (Nal.) Moona
- (Vas.) Gunnar

Pansarkedja Chain
- (Aud.) Geirrid
- (Ft.A.) Ugg
- (Gal.) Thyra
- (Hag.) Den
- (Hug.) Radgar
- (Jor.) Njal
- (M.V.) Bein
- (Nal.) Grungir
- (Vas.) Vidar

Starkakedja Chain
- (Aud.) Deilf
- (Dva.) Alfrig
- (Ft.V.) Kell

Starkalaedar Leather
- (Dva.) Tyrn

Starkaskodd Studded
- (Aud.) Leim
- (Dva.) Laed
- (Ft.V.) Darby Connor
- (Hug.) Enir

Starklaedar Leather
- (Aud.) Pireda
- (Ft.V.) Gerda
- (Ft.V.) Idona Tiu
- (Hug.) Wulfwer
- (Jor.) Morgen

Stelskodd Studded
- (Aud.) Eigil
- (Ft.A.) Lagg
- (Jor.) Keki
- (M.V.) Blyn
- (Vas.) Baldus

Svarkedja Chain
- (Aud.) Gruth
- (M.V.) Vers
- (Vas.) Krip

Svarlaedar Leather
- (Aud.) Jordan
- (Dva.) Rae
- (Hag.) Dritsa
- (Nal.) Tig

Svarskodd Studded
- (Aud.) Ragnar
- (Dva.) Marianne
- (Ft.A.) Trunk
- (Gal.) Nyden
- (Gal.) Nikgor
- (Hag.) Erik
- (Jor.) Hodern
- (Nal.) Dink

Weapon

Arrows
- (Aud.) Inga
- (F.F.) Aeodig
- (Ft.A.) Sillis
- (Gn.F.) Ingrid
- (Hag.) Takker
- (Hug.) Dana
- (Jor.) Asra
- (Jor.) Gerd
- (M.V.) Geir
- (Nal.) Cragg
- (Nm.F.) Legerranad
- (Nm.F.) Ingobneb
- (Sv.F.) Tayte
- (Vas.) Krisst

Axe
- (Aud.) Armond
- (Dva.) Svard
- (Ft.A.) Yop
- (Ft.V.) Hlif
- (Gal.) Gestod
- (Hag.) Burr
- (Hug.) Auda
- (Jor.) Ema
- (Jor.) Gymir
- (M.V.) Hrolf
- (Vas.) Leik

Bows
- (Aud.) Brede
- (Dva.) Brok
- (Ft.A.) Krak
- (Ft.V.) Bitta
- (Gn.F.) Kedin
- (Hag.) Mattie
- (Hug.) Hakon
- (Jor.) Ole
- (Jor.) Thir
- (M.V.) Linna
- (Vas.) Kerr

Hammer
- (Aud.) Frey
- (Dva.) Laran
- (Ft.A.) Stap
- (Ft.V.) Olof
- (Gal.) Helga
- (Hag.) Cort
- (Hug.) Lodin
- (Jor.) Signy
- (M.V.) Gram
- (Vas.) Burl

Large
- (Ft.A.) Isleif
- (Gal.) Galena
- (Hag.) Sinmora
- (Jor.) KalfSaga

Mithril 1-handed
- (Jor.) Dala

Mithri I2-handed
- (Jor.) Tove

Staff
- (Aud.) Eirik
- (Ft.A.) Ruk
- (Gal.) Serilyna
- (Hag.) Eda
- (Hug.) Svala
- (Jor.) Borg
- (M.V.) Brik
- (Vas.) Mildri

Spear
- (Aud.) Josli
- (Ft.A.) Freydis
- (Ft.A.) Looga
- (Gal.) Gudrid
- (Hag.) Fuiren
- (Hug.) Ivara
- (Jor.) Hedin
- (Jor.) Synna
- (M.V.) Grenlyr
- (Vas.) Galagore

Sword
(Aud.) Pater
(Dva.) Vordn
(Ft.A.) Vifil
(Ft.A.) Harald
(Ft.V.) Liv
(Gal.) Stein
(Hag.) Armund
(Hug.) Orm
(Jor.) Flosi
(Jor.) Hrapp
(M.V.) Aren
(Vas.) Gyda

Throwing
(Aud.) Delg
(Ft.A.) Carl
(Gal.) Aki
(Hag.) Bodil
(Hl.F.) Alaonydd
(Hug.) Ryden
(Jor.) Canute
(Jor.) Harry
(M.V.) Hild
(Vas.) Hallfred

Shields

(Aud.) Hulda
(Dva.) Aesirdia
(Ft.A.) Klag
(Ft.V.) Avar
(Gal.) Otkel
(Hag.) Ime
(Hug.) Runolf
(Jor.) Aric
(Jor.) Digby
(M.V.) Marie
(Vas.) Bothe

Focus Items

Runemaster Staff
(Ft.A.) Niniver
(Gal.) Ysunoic
(Hug.) Elengwen
(Jor.) Anya Vinsdottir
(M.V.) Raelyan
(Vas.) Merwdda

Spiritmaster Staff
(Ft.A.) Merarka
(Gal.) Curka
(Hug.) Alyllyra
(Jor.) Magna Vinsdottir
(M.V.) Lyna
(Vas.) Clena

Other Goods

Cloth dye
(Ft.A.) Hrin
(Ft.A.) Ullaria
(Jor.) Alleca Gunderson
(Jor.) Hyndla Gunderson
(Vas.) Thord Gregor

Enamel dye
(Ft.V.) Rulongja
(Ft.V.) Seiml
(Gal.) Ohar
(Gal.) Tallya
(Hag.) Gale
(Hug.) Arnlaug
(Hug.) Ruloia
(Jor.) Greip
(Jor.) Solveig

Leather dye
(Aud.) Serath
(Hag.) Belyria
(Jor.) Ella Johannsson
(Jor.) Ozur Johannsson
(M.V.) Finn
(M.V.) Cale
(Nal.) Rooka
(Nal.) Hallaya

Drums
(Aud.) Ostein
(Ft.A.) Estrilith
(Gal.) Ola
(Hag.) Borghilda
(Hl.F.) Lunt
(Hug.) Rorik
(Jor.) Aaric
(Jor.) Asina
(M.V.) Oken
(Vas.) Wyborn

Poison (1)
(Arv.) Fardokath
(Aud.) Jolgeir
(Ft.A.) Bersi
(Gl.F.) Cuareadh
(Gl.F.) Moekath
(Hl.F.) Aoodip
(Jor.) Oilibhear
(Nm.F.) Kirawyr
(Sv.F.) Svewn

Poison (2)
(Arv.) Eododilny
(Aud.) Osk
(Bd.F.) Daatharbh
(Bd.F.) Gwaeli
(F.F.) Eredrildan
(Ft.A.) Helja
(Hl.F.) Etiand
(Jor.) Ander
(Sv.F.) Sissel

Fletching
(Jor.) Darg
(Jor.) Haylei

Fletching/Tailoring
(Bm.F) Yvigir
(Gn.F.) Jytal

Metal
(Jor.) Amund

Metal Bars
(Jor.) Kkor Borson Om

Metalworking Equipment
(Bm.F) Freagh

Misc. expensive
(Vs.F.) Beni

Siegecraft
(A.Out.) Ronalda
(Bm.F) Hridnon
(Bm.F) Lochun
(Bm.F) Logan
(H.Out.) Melin
(Sv.F.) Filip
(Vs.F.) Jelena

Tailoring equipment
(Vas.) Ingerd

Smith/Tailoring
(Bm.F) Frenrik
(Gn.F.) Ulwatyl

Tailoring
(Bm.F) Crachon
(Jor.) Embla

Tailoring, Leather
(Jor.) Ereck Hemingr
(Jor.) Falla Hemingr
(Jor.) Gro Gunderson
(Jor.) Jorun

Tradeskill
(Bm.F) Vauclua

Wood,Metal,Leather
(Bm.F) Collen
(Bm.F) Daggon

Woodworking
(Hag.) Frikk
(Jor.) Holsvi Hallgrim
(Jor.) Kvasir
(Jor.) Ottar

Services

Enchanter
(Ft.A.) Onund
(Gn.F.) Halldis
(Hag.) Pavar
(Hug.) Raker
(Jor.) Amma
(Jor.) Arve
(M.V.) Elizabeth
(Vas.) Ulf

Healer
(Ft.A.) Kari
(Gal.) Hord
(Hag.) Gustav
(Hug.) Saydyn
(Jor.) Gungir
(Jor.) Nanna Vinsdottir
(M.V.) Kalbin
(Vas.) Aud

Bounty
(Jor.) Jordheim
(Jor.) Jordheim
(Jor.) Jordheim

Guild Emblemeer
(Jor.) Audill
(Jor.) Karis

Guild Registrar
(Jor.) Brit
(Jor.) Oda

Name Registrar
(Jor.) Jarl Uffenlong
(Jor.) Ullag Nottlok

Vault
(Gn.F.) Idonna
(Jor.) Jarl Yuliwyf
(Sv.F.) Hralyvar

Smith
(Aud.) Dahn
(Ft.A.) Eindridi
(Gal.) Gord
(Hag.) Genlu Edrill
(Hag.) Hilde
(Hug.) Kol Smithir
(Jor.) Gris
(Jor.) Kiarr
(Jor.) Morlin Caan
(M.V.) Vahn
(M.V.) Gordin Tuhan
(Vas.) Arnfinn

Stable
(Aud.) Fraglock
(Ft.A.) Rundorik
(Ft.V.) Arskar
(Gal.) Treflun
(Gn.F.) Wolgrun
(Hag.) Yolafson
(Hug.) Prulgar
(M.V.) Gularg
(Nal.) Eryklan
(Sv.F.) Vorgar
(Vas.) Harlfug
(Vs.F.) Ulufgar

Trainer

Berserker
(Ft.A.) Kalli
(Gn.F.) Zalerik
(Vs.F.) Ingemur
(Jor.) Haaken Hodr

Healer
(Ft.A.) Welgen
(Gn.F.) Itesta
(Jor.) Per
(Jor.) Rana
(Vs.F.) Ari

Hunter
(Ft.A.) Budo
(Jor.) Hauk Singrid

Master Armourcraft
(Jor.) Gest

Master Tailoring
(Jor.) Eskil

Master Weaponcraft
(Jor.) Aase

Mystic
(Ft.A.) Lycla
(M.V.) Vigdis
(Vas.) Ragna

Rogue
(Ft.A.) Jucla
(Hag.) Glum
(Vas.) Hrut

Runemaster
(Ft.A.) Thetus
(Jor.) Bera
(Jor.) Signa
(Vs.F.) Var

Seer
(Ft.A.) Hyndia
(Gal.) Canan
(Hag.) Groa
(Vas.) Tosti

Shadowblade
(Ft.A.) Boidoc
(Jor.) Elin
(Jor.) Hreidar
(Vs.F.) Gunnolf

Shaman
(Ft.A.) Korgan
(Gal.) Bec
(Jor.) Dane Grimma
(Vs.F.) Audney

Skald
(Ft.A.) Lalida
(Gal.) Vanah
(Jor.) Leif Sven

Spiritmaster
(Ft.A.) Sarry
(Jor.) Dyre
(Jor.) Galn

Thane
(Ft.A.) Salma
(Gn.F.) Aphriodora
(Jor.) Frode
(Jor.) Katla

Viking
(Gal.) Krek
(M.V.) Skapi
(Vas.) Saeunn

Warrior
(Ft.A.) Halker
(Gn.F.) Khelad
(Jor.) Osten
(Jor.) Thordia

Gotar

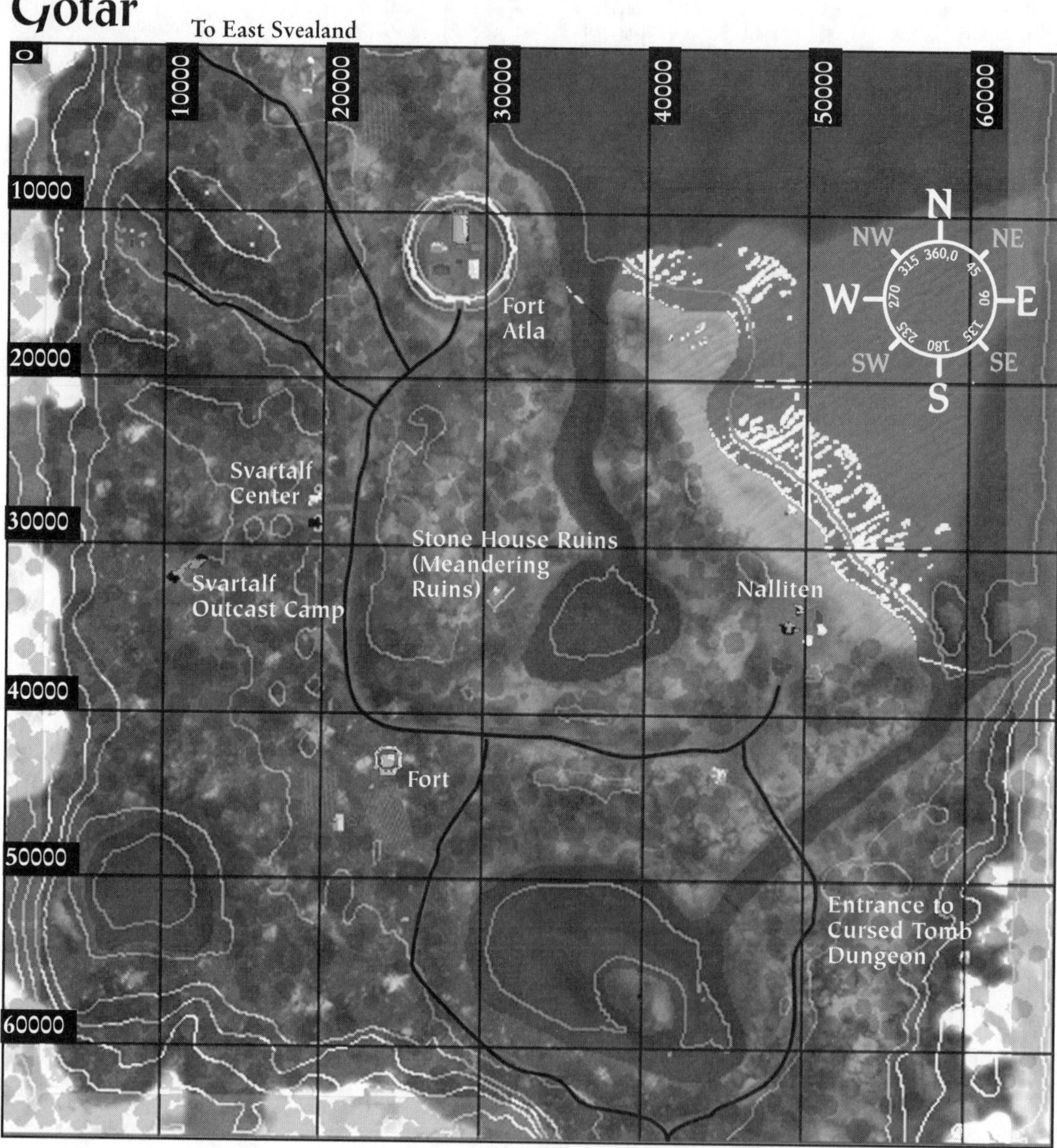

Quest NPCs

Fort Atla	
Amora	Magnild's Cure (lvl 2)
Boidoc	Jewel hunt (lvl 11)
Darrius	Tale of two trolls (lvl 22)
your trainer	Amora's Aid (lvl 1)
Finna	Big Paw (lvl 38)
Finni	Nihm's Secret (lvl 26)

Nallitan	
Gautr	Zrit-zrit's Item (lvl 35)
Geiri	Cargila's Blessing (lvl 40)
Dalla	Furf's reward (lvl 29)
Sveck	Cape of the mother wolf (lvl 14)

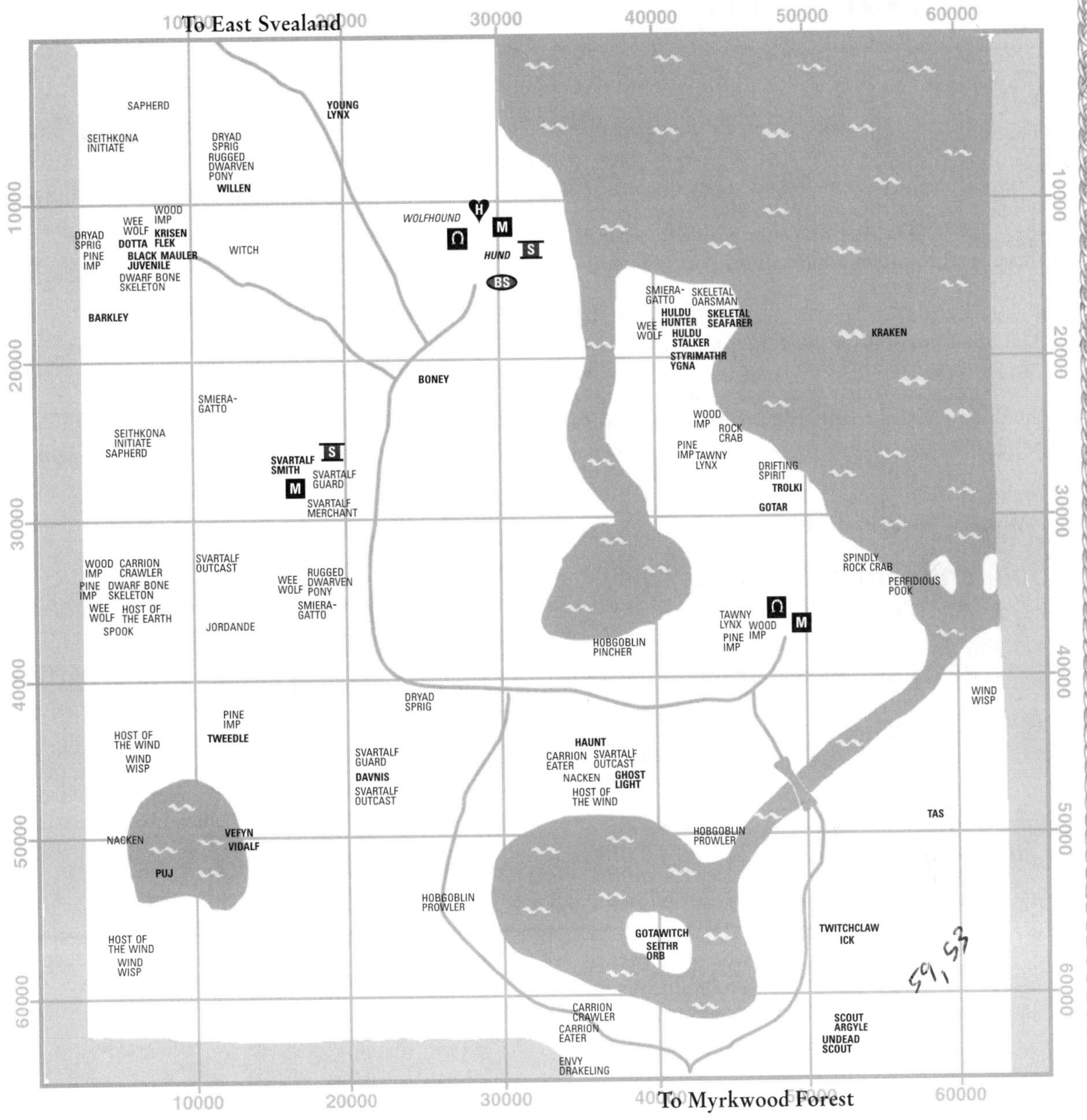

Lower-level monsters not shown on map:

Creature	Lvl	Location
carrion lizard	3	NW,NC
coastal wolf	3	NW,NC,WC
drowned soul	3	NC,NE
dryad sprout	3	NW,WC
escaped thrall	3	NW,WC
fragile skeleton	3	NW,C
green serpent	2	NW,NC,C
hobgoblin fish-catcher	0	NC,WC,C
hobgoblin prankster	3	NW,C,SC
hobgoblin snagger	2	NW,NC,WC,C
hbgbln snake-finder	1	NC,C
huldu lurker	2	NW,C
huldu outcast	1	NW,NC,C
little water goblin	2	NW,NC,WC
meandering spirit	1	C
phantom hound	3	C
rattling skeleton	1	NW,NC,WC,C
scavenger	1	NW,NC,WC,C
sharktooth whelp	1	NW,NC,WC,C
spectral hog	2	NW,C
undead explorer	3	C
vein spiderling	0	NW,NC
water snake	0	NW,NC,WC,C
water strider	1	NC,C
wild hog	2	NW,NC,WC,C
wildling	0	NW,NC,WC
wolf nipper	0	NW,NC,WC,C
young lynx	2	NW

Gotar Tips

There is an island with perfidious pooks that con yellow and orange to level 10. They are also found across on the mainland. They do not BAF when pulling so a solo-er can effectively hunt there. On the border of Gotar and Myrkwood, there is a mountain where a group of tawny lynx's can be found.

These con blue to level 10 and orange/red to level 8. A group or solo-er can function well here. They are aggressive so watch where you stand. There is also a named lynx, Tas, that spawns near the dungeon and roams in the lynx area. This cat has a one time drop of Boots of Cat-like Visage (or something like that).These boots are good for rogue classes.

- Monica "Seraphym" Hayes

Solo and Group Levelling Tips

Solo

1-5 For the adventurous newbie, the ideal place is the pig farm. It's big and rarely camped, so you can often get the camp bonus.

5 Once you're a little more grownup, try the skeletal seafarers on the beach near Fort Atla.

6-8 Level 6 can tackle the skeletal oarsmen. Level 7 is good with the carrion crawlers in the south. Level 8 should look for hobgoblin prowlers and the imps out near Nalliten.

Don't forget the kill tasks! There are some Troll Flayers over near tower, right before Myrkwood Forest. They give kill tasks that are local — hosts of earth and wind, carrion crawlers and pine imps. It can be worth your while to hang out there for a while and just rack up xp.

There's also rock crabs if you're in Fort Atla's neck of the woods, just head out south and a little east.

9-11 At these levels, what you're interested in is hobgoblin prowlers. There are some near the bone bridge near Nalliten, and more over on the western side of the water, just SW of Nalliten.

Near Nalliten are also some spindly rock crabs that are good for level 9.

The carrion crawlers aren't too bad, and they don't BAF.

Crabs/pooks are also pretty good for levels 9 and 10. Pooks drop gems, which makes it convenient to run back and forth from Nalliten, killing crabs as you travel.

Moreover there are tawny lynxes near the Nalliten beach. These are also good at level 9.

12-14 Look around for pooks that are still in your optimum range.

Group

9-11 pooks (with a group of nine)

11-13 pooks (with a group of four)

Who hates this area? No one, there is something there for every class.

Who loves this area? Anyone levels 1–12, great for soloing, and group friendly for low level groups.

Other Notes. Norseman Seer, Kobold Viking, Kobold Rogue, and Kobold Mystic starting place is Fort Alta in Gotar. Zone not overly crowded with other players since most head to Myrkwood Forest as soon as they can to solo, or stay in the Vale of Mularn region, both of which are also starting places for other races/classes.

Also in Gotar: Cursed Tomb (dungeon)

Mix of undead, humanoid and creatures susceptible to crush damage. Just watch out for BAF.

Loot

Barkley [6] (65% each) Necklace of Leaves, Knobby Root • (70%) Twisting Vine

black mauler juvenile [5] (51%) Small Mauler Skin • (25%) Mauler Claw

carrion crawler [6] (45% each) Lump of Carrion, Dead Rabbit, Tawny Lynx Meat, Chunk of Wolf Meat

carrion eater [7] (48% each) Lump of Carrion, Dead Rabbit • (70% each) Tawny Lynx Meat, Chunk of Wolf Meat

carrion lizard [3] (23%) Diseased Claw • (70%) Rotting Carrion

coastal wolf [3] (50% each) Wolf Skin, Dead Fish • (30%) Wolf Tail • (25%) Wolf's Ear

Davnis [9] (70%) Lynx Pelt Bag • (75%) Copper Amber Pin • (85%) Small Packet of Food • (0.5%) <Vafprudnir's Adornment>

Dotta [5] (70% each) Bag of Foul-Smelling Herbs, Initiate's Bracelet • (80%) a Blank Spell Book

drifting spirit [13] (55%) Spirit Shreds • (0.3%) <Brendig's Gear>

drowned soul [3] (80%) Clump of Seaweed • (70%) Dead Fish • (50%) Small Shell • (1%) <Into the Woods> • (10% each piece) Tattered Padded and Mjuklaedar

dryad sprig [4] (75%) Pine Branch • (80%) Pine Seedling • (45%) Pine Talisman • (1%) <Into the Woods>

dryad sprout [3] (70%) Pine Branch • (80%) Pine Seedling • (45%) Pine Talisman • (1%) <Into the Woods> • (8% each piece) Tattered Padded and Mjuklaedar

dwarf bone skeleton [5] (50%) Jewels 45 • (8% each piece) Tattered Padded and Mjuklaedar • (1%) <Into the Woods>

envy drakeling [9] (68% each) Envy Drakeling Hide, Tail

escaped thrall [3] (45%) Broken Iron Shackle • (10%) Jewels 45 • (1%) <Into the Woods>

fragile skeleton [3] (75%) Jewels 45 • (8% each piece) Tattered Padded and Mjuklaedar • (1%) <Into the Woods>

Fressen [15] (no loot)

ghost light [7] (65%) Round Sapphire • (80% each) Square Aquamarine, Small Green Topaz

gotawitch [9] (70%) Bag of Blue Dust • (40% each) Mystical Medallion, Dryad Hide Belt • (60%) Pouch of Hobgoblin Eyes • (0.5%) <Norseman Cache>

green serpent [2] (48%) Green Serpent Skin

haunt [7] (20% each) Rusty Slave's Collar, Obsidian Stone • (40%) Small Silver Nugget • (1%) <Har's Adornments>

hobgoblin fish-catcher [0] (55%) Dead Fish • (80% each) Fishing Pole, Fishing Hook

hobgoblin pincher [4] (80% each) a Hook Shaped Earring, Flat Round Rock • (60%) a Little Hobgoblin Finger • (65%) Garnet Chip • (1%) <Into the Woods>

hobgoblin prankster [3] (50%) Patched Old Sack • (10%) Beaded Hobgoblin Belt • (1.5%) Hobgoblin Hammer • (1%) <Into the Woods> • (20%) Jewels 45

hobgoblin prowler [8] (80%) Beaded Hobgoblin Belt • (40%) Clan Crest • (1.5%) Crusty Old Bracer • (40%) Jewels 45 • (0.5%) <Har's Adornments>

hobgoblin snagger [2] (60%) Shiny Metal Pin • (80%) Little Hobgoblin Toe • (70%) Flat Round Rock • (50%) a Hook Shaped Earring • (1%) <Into the Woods>

hobgoblin snake-finder [1] (50%) Patched Old Sack • (5%) Jewels 45 • (1%) <Into the Woods>

horse [55] (75%) Horse Hair • (10%) Auburn Mane • (80%) Ruined Horse Skin • (35%) Horse Skin • (60%) Horse Hair

host of the earth [6] (45%) Cloudy Green Stone • (65%) Small Green Topaz • (75%) Shiny Brown Rock

host of the wind [7] (54%) Round Sapphire • (80%) Square Aquamarine • (75%) Piece of Lapis Lazuli

huldu hunter [4] (35%) Carved Wood Norseman • (25%) Carved Wood Troll • (15%) Carved Wood Kobold • (5%) Carved Wood Dwarf • (10%) Old Carving Tool • (1%) <Into the Woods> • (1.4%) Huldu Axe • (1.4%) Huldu Mantle of Obscurity

huldu lurker [2] (10%) Carved Wood Norseman • (7.5%) Carved Wood Troll • (5%) Carved Wood Kobold • (2.5%) Carved Wood Dwarf • (10%) Old Carving Tool • (1%) <Into the Woods> • (7.5% each piece) Tattered Padded and Mjuklaedar

huldu outcast [1] (10%) Carved Wood Norseman • (7.5%) Carved Wood Troll • (5%) Carved Wood Kobold • (2.5%) Carved Wood Dwarf • (10%) Old Carving Tool • (1%) <Into the Woods> • (7.5% each piece) Tattered Padded and Mjuklaedar

huldu stalker [5] (35%) Carved Wood Norseman • (25%) Carved Wood Troll • (15%) Carved Wood Kobold • (5%) Carved Wood Dwarf • (10%) Old Carving Tool • (1%) <Into the Woods> • (1.4%) Huldu Axe • (1.4%) Huldu Mantle of Obscurity

Hund [7] (70%) Gnawed Bone • (30%) Wolfhound Pelt • (50%) Large Spiked Collar • (35%) Large Wolfhound Fang

Ick [8] (45%) Dead Rabbit • (80% each) Tawny Lynx Meat, Rotting Carapace • (70%) Chunk of Wolf Meat

Jordande [8] (65%) Necklace of Shiny Brown Rocks • (75%) Small Green Topaz • (80%) Shiny Brown Rock • (50%) Cloudy Green Stone

kraken [20] (80%) Green Decaying Finger • (60%) Flask of Potency • (1.5%) Kraken's Maw ***or*** Lost Tooth

Krisen Flek [26] (no loot)

little water goblin [2] (70%) Clump of Seaweed • (50%) String of Blue Beads • (60%) Dead Fish • (1%) <Into the Woods>

meandering spirit [1] (50%) Jewels 45 • (8% each piece) Tattered Padded and Mjuklaedar • (1%) <Into the Woods>

nacken [8] (50%) Small Pearl • (65%) Pink Pearl • (80%) Pearlized Shell

perfidious pook [10] (80%) Smooth Blue Stone • (50% each) Clouded Beryl, Yellow Quartz • (85%) Round Sapphire • (0.5%) <Grimnir's Adornment>

phantom hound [3] (10%) Phosphorescent Pelt • (70%) Phosphorescent Claw

pine imp [6] (75%) Pine Talisman • (70%) Pine Cone • (50%) Knobby Root • (30%) Crystalized Pine Sap

Puj [9] (65%) Small Pearl • (70%) Pink Pearl • (60%) Pearlized Shell • (45%) Pearl Earring

rattling skeleton [1] (50%) Jewels 45 • (8% each piece) Tattered Padded and Mjuklaedar • (1%) <Into the Woods>

rock crab [7] (50%) Rock Crab Leg (x2) • (30%) Rock Crab Shell • (5%) Rock Crab Leg (x2)

rugged dwarven pony [4] (10%) Pony Hoof • (60%) Pony Hide

sapherd [5] (75%) Pile of Seeds

scavenger [1] (20%) Chunk of Meat • (60% each) Chewed Bone, Dead Bird

Scout Argyle [12] (no loot)

seithkona initiate [5] (70% each) Bag of Foul-Smelling Herbs, Initiate's Bracelet • (80%) a Blank Spell Book

seithr orb [9] (85%) Pile of Orange Dust • (80%) Burned Out Globe • (69%) Glowing Orange Globe

sharktooth whelp [1] (80%) Whelp's Tooth • (70%) Whelp Hide • (50%) String of Blue Beads

skeletal oarsman [5] (85%) Rotting Oar • (75%) Brass Earring • (55%) Carved Whalebone • (65%) Decaying Fishing Net • (1%) <Into the Woods>

skeletal seafarer [4] (40%) Rotting Oar • (70%) Brass Earring • (50%) Carved Whalebone • (70%) Decaying Fishing Net • (1%) <Into the Woods>

smiera-gatto [4] (no loot)

spectral hog [2] (26%) Frigid Hog's Tusk • (23%) Pallid Hog's Hoof

spindly rock crab [9] (50%) Spindly Rock Crab Leg (x2) • (10%) Spindly Rock Crab Leg (x2) • (50%) Rock Crab Shell

spook [6] (20% each) Rusty Slave's Collar, Obsidian Stone • (40%) Small Silver Nugget • (1%) <Har's Adornments>

Styrimathr Ygna [7] (67%) Captain's Spyglass • (80%) Gold Hoop Earring • (75%) Rotting Ship's Log

svartalf guard [10] (70%) Lynx Pelt Bag • (75%) Copper Amber Pin • (85%) Small Packet of Food • (0.5%) <Vafprudnir's Adornment>

svartalf merchant [6] (55%) Lynx Pelt Bag • (70%) Copper Amber Pin • (75%) Small Packet of Food • (0.5%) <Har's Adornments>

svartalf outcast [8] (55%) Lynx Pelt Bag • (70%) Copper Amber Pin • (75%) Small Packet of Food • (0.5%) <Har's Adornments>

svartalf smith [6] (55%) Lynx Pelt Bag • (70%) Copper Amber Pin • (75%) Small Packet of Food • (0.5%) <Har's Adornments>

Tas [9] (57%) Tawny Pelt • (60% each) Lynx Claw, Lynx Skull, Tawny Lynx Meat

tawny lynx [8] (33%) Tawny Pelt • (60% each) Lynx Claw, Tawny Lynx Meat • (40%) Lynx Skull

Trolki [10] (80%) Smooth Blue Stone • (50% each) Clouded Beryl, Yellow Quartz • (85%) Round Sapphire • (0.5%) <Grimnir's Adornment>

Tweedle [7] (85%) Pine Talisman • (80%) Pine Cone • (50% each) Pine Needle Crown, Crystalized Pine Sap

Twitchclaw [8] (70% each) Dead Rabbit, Tawny Lynx Meat, Chunk of Wolf Meat, Lump of Rotting Meat

undead explorer [3] (25%) Obsidian Stone • (15%) Hand-Tooled Belt • (1%; all or none) a Suit of Tattered Shimmering Studded armor, Huntsman's Cloak, Pitted Shimmering Battle Axe

undead scout [10] (no loot)

Vefyn [8] (65%) Round Sapphire • (80%) Square Aquamarine • (75%) Piece of Lapis Lazuli • (40%) Sapphire Necklace

vein spiderling [0] (80%) Spider Legs • (50%) Veined Mandible

Vidalf [10] (85%) Piece of Lapis Lazuli • (80%) Round Sapphire • (85%) Square Aquamarine • (76%) Smooth Blue Stone • (71%) Clear Blue Orb • (0.5%) <Grimnir's Adornment>

water snake [0] (70%) Water Snake Fang • (80%) Water Snakeskin • (50%) Water Snake Meat

water strider [1] (30%) Strider Carapace • (80%) Strider Eye • (70%) Strider Antenna

wee wolf [5] (80%) Wee Wolf Tail • (70%) Wee Wolf Pelt • (45%) Wee Wolf Fang

wild hog [2] (35% each) Curly Hog Tail, Small Hog Hoof • (50% each) Small Hog Tusk, Hide

wildling [0] (50%) Jewels 45 • (8% each piece) Tattered Padded and Mjuklaedar • (1%) <Into the Woods>

Willen [5] (65%) Pile of Seeds

wind wisp [9] (80%) Round Sapphire (x2) • (70%) Clear Blue Orb

Witch [22] (50%) Laering Necklace • (80%) Bag of Blue Dust • (45%) Locked Spell Book • (70%) Crooked Wand • (0.5%) <Norseman Cache>

wolf nipper [0] (35%) Wolf Canine • (70%) Small Wolf Paw • (50%) Patch of Wolf Fur

wolfhound [6] (70%) Gnawed Bone • (30%) Wolfhound Pelt • (55%) Large Spiked Collar

wood imp [5] (70%) Pine Branch • (50%) Pile of Seeds • (45%) Twisting Vine • (40%) Knobby Root • (1%) <Rig's Lament>

young lynx [2] (73%) Small Lynx Skin

Malmohus

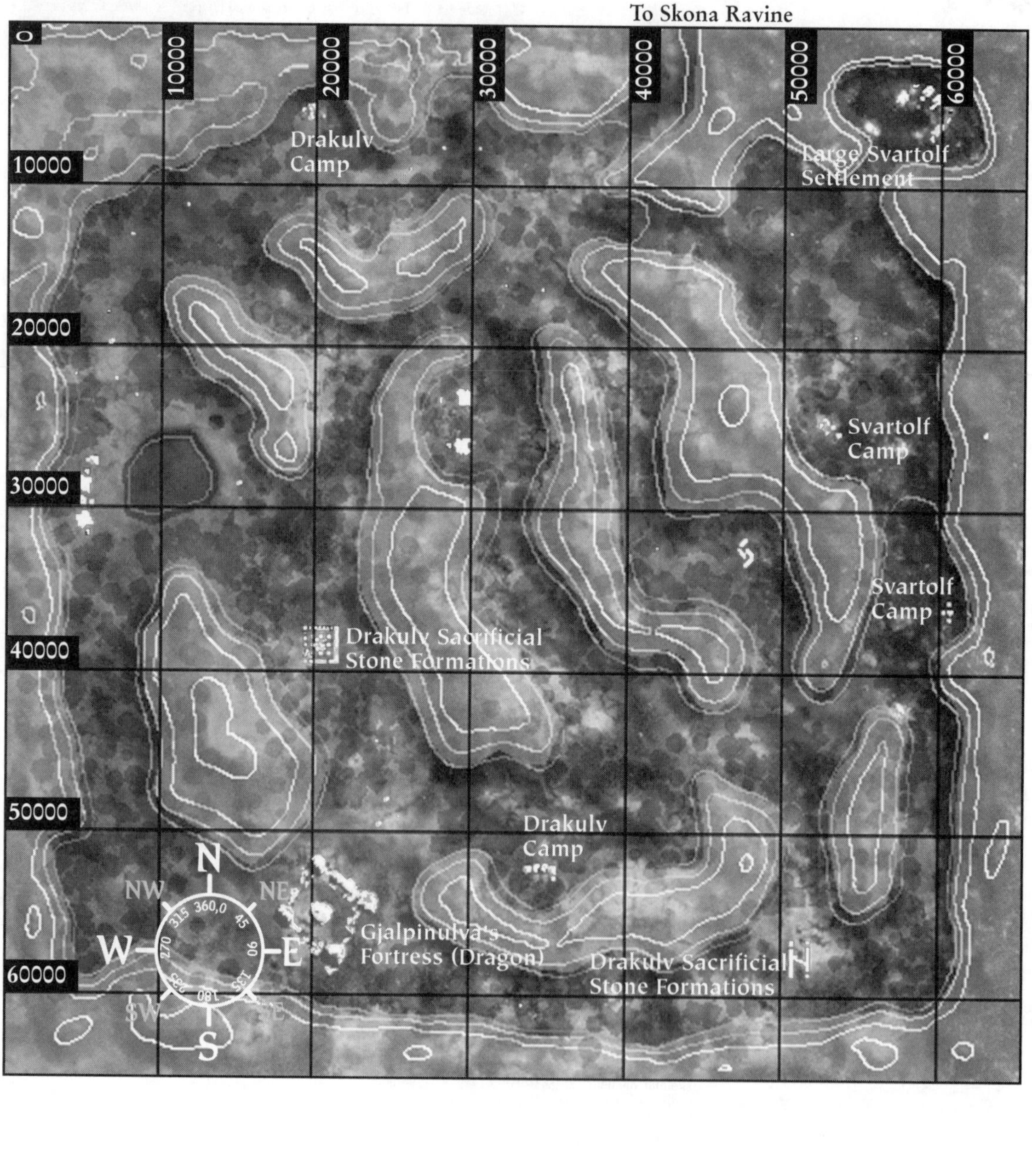

To Skona Ravine

0
10000
20000
30000
40000
50000
60000

Drakulv Camp

Large Svartolf Settlement

Svartolf Camp

Svartolf Camp

Drakulv Sacrificial Stone Formations

Drakulv Camp

Gjalpinulva's Fortress (Dragon)

Drakulv Sacrificial Stone Formations

N
NE
E
SE
S
SW
W
NW
360,0
45
90
135
180
225
270
315

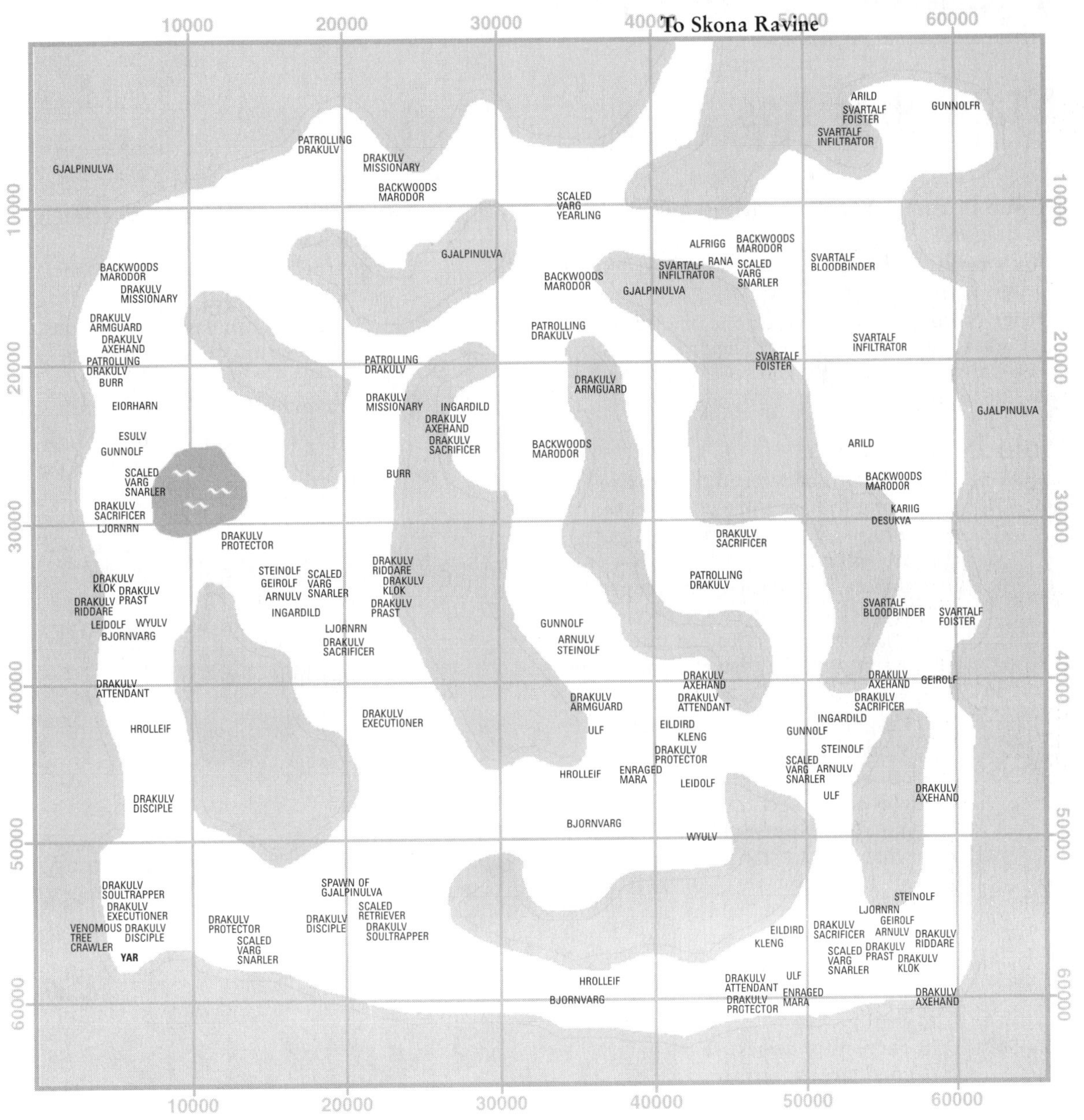
To Skona Ravine
10000
20000
30000
40000
50000
60000
ARILD
SVARTALF FOISTER
GUNNOLFR
SVARTALF INFILTRATOR
PATROLLING DRAKULV
DRAKULV MISSIONARY
GJALPINULVA
BACKWOODS MARODOR
SCALED VARG YEARLING
GJALPINULVA
ALFRIGG
BACKWOODS MARODOR
RANA
SVARTALF INFILTRATOR
SCALED VARG SNARLER
SVARTALF BLOODBINDER
BACKWOODS MARODOR
GJALPINULVA
BACKWOODS MARODOR
DRAKULV MISSIONARY
DRAKULV ARMGUARD
DRAKULV AXEHAND
PATROLLING DRAKULV
BURR
PATROLLING DRAKULV
PATROLLING DRAKULV
SVARTALF FOISTER
SVARTALF INFILTRATOR
DRAKULV ARMGUARD
EIORHARN
DRAKULV MISSIONARY
INGARDILD
DRAKULV AXEHAND
DRAKULV SACRIFICER
GJALPINULVA
ESULV
GUNNOLF
BACKWOODS MARODOR
ARILD
SCALED VARG SNARLER
BURR
BACKWOODS MARODOR
DRAKULV SACRIFICER
LJORNRN
KARIIG
DESUKVA
DRAKULV PROTECTOR
DRAKULV SACRIFICER
DRAKULV RIDDARE
DRAKULV KLOK
DRAKULV PRAST
STEINOLF
GEIROLF
ARNULV
SCALED VARG SNARLER
DRAKULV KLOK
DRAKULV PRAST
DRAKULV RIDDARE
PATROLLING DRAKULV
INGARDILD
SVARTALF BLOODBINDER
SVARTALF FOISTER
LEIDOLF
WYULV
BJORNVARG
LJORNRN
DRAKULV SACRIFICER
GUNNOLF
ARNULV
STEINOLF
DRAKULV ATTENDANT
DRAKULV AXEHAND
DRAKULV AXEHAND
GEIROLF
DRAKULV ARMGUARD
DRAKULV ATTENDANT
DRAKULV SACRIFICER
DRAKULV EXECUTIONER
INGARDILD
HROLLEIF
ULF
EILDIRD
KLENG
GUNNOLF
STEINOLF
DRAKULV PROTECTOR
SCALED VARG SNARLER
ARNULV
HROLLEIF
ENRAGED MARA
LEIDOLF
ULF
DRAKULV DISCIPLE
DRAKULV AXEHAND
BJORNVARG
WYULV
DRAKULV SOULTRAPPER
SPAWN OF GJALPINULVA
STEINOLF
DRAKULV EXECUTIONER
SCALED RETRIEVER
LJORNRN
GEIROLF
VENOMOUS TREE CRAWLER
DRAKULV DISCIPLE
DRAKULV PROTECTOR
DRAKULV DISCIPLE
DRAKULV SOULTRAPPER
EILDIRD
DRAKULV SACRIFICER
ARNULV
DRAKULV RIDDARE
SCALED VARG SNARLER
KLENG
SCALED VARG SNARLER
DRAKULV PRAST
DRAKULV KLOK
YAR
HROLLEIF
DRAKULV ATTENDANT
ULF
ENRAGED MARA
BJORNVARG
DRAKULV PROTECTOR
DRAKULV AXEHAND

Malmohus Tips

Group Friendly? Yes — massive groups, to slay the dragon

Don't tackle which creatures alone? The dragon and his surrounding minions

Other Notes. This is the epic zone of Midgard, and where the dragon resides. The dragon has been known to take flight and scout the zone for players to kill.

Solo Levelling Tips

38-41 First off, be warned that you're going to have to face off a posse of Svakuld Missionaries. These guys are archers, so it's absolutely imperataive that you interrupt them before you get perforated. It's actually okay to just interrup them, you don't have to root them.

39 What you're looking for is Ice Crags, and you can find them by Vindaul Faste, east of the lake. It can be tricky to get there because you need to get up on top of the mountain. It just takes planning, which means starting off a ways and following the mountain wall around the lake. Ice Crags are particularly vulnerable to SC.

40 The wintry dirges are good targets, and so are the ice creatures and blocks of ice. In general you can find them near the bone-eater camps, and oracles. Be careful, because wintry dirges are nearly impossible to see in that environment.

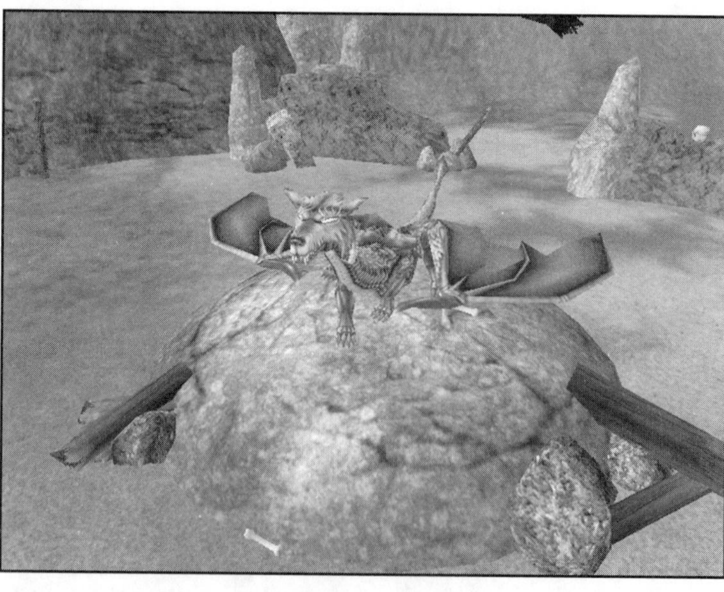

There's a slightly safer bone eater camp west of Grallahorn. It's guarded by blocks of ice, so the invader danger is lower.

(43) Berserkers can have a good time with drak missionaries near the entrance to Malmohus. Not to hard and plenty to pick from.

40-50 Just a note, not really on soloing … sometimes some high-level people will pull like mad right outside the dragon's area, tackle whatever comes out, and then turn around and sell off the loot to whoever shows up. It's kind of like going shopping ... there's not much xp, but you can get a real bargain on something that is pretty nice.

Loot

Alfrigg [45] (20%; hi-lo) Emerald Moonshone Boots, Drakulv Militia Great Hammer, *or* Cloak of the Bloodwolf • (20%; hi-lo) Emerald Moonshone Sleeves, Drakulv Militia Great Sword, *or* Cloak of the Bloodwolf • (20%; hi-lo) Emerald Moonshone Jerkin, Drakulv Militia Great Axe, *or* Cloak of the Bloodwolf

Arild [49] (20%; hi-lo) Gauntlets of the Bloodwolf, Drakulv Militia Hammer, *or* Jade Moonshone Cloak • (20%; hi-lo) Leggings of the Bloodwolf, Drakulv Militia Axe, *or* Jade Moonshone Cloak • (20%; hi-lo) Vest of the Bloodwolf, Drakulv Militia Sword, *or* Jade Moonshone Cloak

Arnulv [49] (20%; hi-lo) Helm of the Bloodwolf, Drakulv Militia Hammer, *or* Drakulv Crescent Talisman • (20%; hi-lo) Boots of the Bloodwolf, Drakulv Militia Axe, *or* Drakulv Crescent Talisman • (20%; hi-lo) Sleeves of the Bloodwolf, Drakulv Militia Sword, *or* Drakulv Crescent Talisman

backwoods marodor [39/41/43] (19%) Bandit's Small Chest • (0.6%) Bandit King's Crown • (25%) Jewels 21 [39] • (30%) Jewels 21 [41] • (20%) Jewels 30 [43] • (2%; hi-lo) Ageless Luminary Pants/Cap/Vest, Runed Bone Staff [39,41]/Spirit Bone Staff [41,43], *or* Marodor Gem

Bjornvarg [55] (10%) Dragon Etched Boots *or* Legs • (10%; hi-lo) Dragon Etched Bracer, *or* Golden Alloy Bastard Sword *or* Kite Shield • (10%) Dragon Etched Sleeves *or* Gloves • (10%; hi-lo) Golden Alloy Great Sword *or* Mystical Golden Scale Belt • (10%; hi-lo) Dragon Etched Hauberk, *or* Ancient *or* Ageless Dragon Etched Coif • (10%; hi-lo) Golden Alloy Great Spear *or* Cloak of the Dragonwolf

Burr [45] (20%; hi-lo) Jet Bloodletter's Sleeves, Drakulv Small Shield *or* Drakulv Mightcaller • (20%; hi-lo) Jet Bloodletter's Leggings, Drakulv Milita Spear *or* Drakulv Mightcaller • (20%; hi-lo) Jet Bloodletter's Helm, Drakulv Militia Composite Bow *or* Drakulv Mightcaller

Desukva [55] (10%) Ancient Bloodbound Boots *or* Pants • (10%; hi-lo) Black Diamond Staff *or* Bloodbound Book • (10%) Ancient Bloodbound Sleeves *or* Gloves • (10%; hi-lo) Blue Diamond Staff *or* Bloodbound Totem • (10%; hi-lo) Ancient Bloodbound Vest, *or* Ageless *or* Runed Bloodbound Cap • (10%) Red *or* Yellow Diamond Staff, *or* Luminescent Diamond Necklace

drakulv armguard [42/44/46] (9/10/11%) Golden Crescent Necklace • (3/3.8/4%) Moonshone Bracelet • (25%) Jewels 21 [42] • (15%) Jewels 30 [44] • (20%) Jewels 30 [46] • (2.5%; hi-lo) Jet Bloodletter's Sleeves/Leggings/Helm, Drakulv Small Shield/Militia Spear/Militia Composite Bow, *or* Drakulv Mightcaller • (9%) Drakulv Scale

drakulv attendant [51/53/55] (15%) Necklace of Servitude • (5%) Forgotten Clan Necklace • (16%) Jewels 63 • (1.7%) Timorous Drakulv Ebon Legs *or* Boots/Sleeves *or* Helm/Gloves *or* Jerkin • (1.7%; hi-lo) Golden Alloy Short Sword/Hammer/Axe *or* Ancient Ebon Bracer/Ebony Flecked Shimmering Cloak/Ancient Ebon Ring • (5%) Drakulv Scale

drakulv axehand [48/50/52] (18%) Etched Silvery Bracer • (5.5/6.3/6.3%) Etched Golden Bracer • (22/25/25%) Jewels 30 • (2.5%; hi-lo) Helm/Boots/Sleeves of the Bloodwolf, Drakulv Militia Hammer/Axe/Sword, *or* Drakulv Crescent Talisman • (9%) Drakulv Scale

drakulv disciple [62/64] (19%) Unprepared Ebony Metal Rod • (6.3%) Prepared Ebony Metal Rod • (25%) Jewels 63 • (1.7%; hi-lo) Soulbinder's Boots, Legs *or* Helm/Jerkin *or* Sleeves, *or* Soulrager's/Soulpiercer's Gauntlets • (1.7%; hi-lo) [Battle Scourge, Soulbound Necklace, *or* Soulbinder's Shield]/[Soul Forge, Golden Alloy Great Bow *or* Bracer of Embodiment]

drakulv executioner [57] (19%) Executioner's Tooth Necklace • (3%) Black Golden-Embossed Hood • (23%) Jewels 63 • (1.7%; hi-lo) Dragon Singed Ebon Legs, Boots *or* Coif, *or* Crackling Ebon Gloves • (1.7%; hi-lo) Immolated Dragonfire Cleaver, Flame Wrought Cloak, *or* Smoldering Ebon Shield

drakulv executioner [59] (19%) Executioner's Tooth Necklace • (0.6%) Black Golden-Embossed Hood • (25%) Jewels 63 • (1.7%; hi-lo) Dragon Singed Ebon Arms, Crackling Ebon Coif *or* Hymn-Weaver's Ebon Gloves • (1.7%; hi-lo) Immolated Great Dragonfire Cleaver *or* Flame Wrought Ring

drakulv executioner [61] (19%) Executioner's Tooth Necklace • (0.6%) Black Golden-Embossed Hood • (25%) Jewels 63 • (1.7%; hi-lo) Dragon Singed Ebon Hauberk, *or* Barbed Ebon Coif *or* Gloves • (1.7%) Immolated Dragonfire Cleaver *or* Great Cleaver, *or* Flame Wrought Belt

drakulv klok [65] (no loot)

drakulv missionary [36/38/40] (12/13/15%) Mystic Dragon Idol • (4/4.3/5%) Small Engraved Scale • (30/35/40%) Jewels 21 • (2.5%; hi-lo) Ageless Luminary Boots/Sleeves/Gloves, Dark Bone Staff/Jaundiced Bone Staff/Runed *or* Spirit Bone Staff, *or* Missionary's Bracer • (2.5/5/7%) Drakulv Scale

drakulv prast [65] (no loot)

drakulv protector [54/56/58] (15%) Golden Ornamental Armguard • (5%) Golden Ornamental Neckguard • (20%) Jewels 63 • (1.7%) Dragon Etched Boots *or* Legs/Sleeves *or* Gloves/Hauberk, *or* Ancient *or* Ageless Dragon Etched Coif [coifs only available to 58] • (1.7%; hi-lo) Golden Alloy Bastard Sword *or* Kite Shield/Great Sword/Great Spear, *or* Dragon Etched Bracer/Mystical Golden Scale Belt/Cloak of the Dragonwolf • (2.5%) Drakulv Scale

drakulv riddare [65] (no loot)

drakulv sacrificer [45/47/49] (15/15/18%) Etched Silver Orb • (5/5/5.8%) Vial of Silvery Blood • (20/25/23%) Jewels 30 • (2.5%; hi-lo) Emerald Moonshone Gloves/Leggings/ Helm, Drakulv Militia Great Hammer/Great Sword/ Great Axe, *or* Cloak of the Unseen Stalker • (9%) Drakulv Scale

drakulv soultrapper [62] (19%) Unprepared Ebony Metal Rod • (6.3%) Prepared Ebony Metal Rod • (25%) Jewels 63 • (1.7%) Soulrager's Gauntlets, Boots, Legs *or* Helm • (1.7%; hi-lo) Battle Scourge, Ring of the Mindwall, *or* Soulbinder's Shield

drakulv soultrapper [64] (19%) Unprepared Ebony Metal Rod • (6.3%) Prepared Ebony Metal Rod • (25%) Jewels 63 • (1.7%; hi-lo) Soulbinder's Jerkin *or* Sleeves, *or* Soulpiercer's Gauntlets • (1.7%; hi-lo) Soul Forge, Golden Alloy Great Bow, *or* Soulbinder's Belt

Eildird [51] (10%) Timorous Drakulv Ebon Legs *or* Boots • (10%; hi-lo) Golden Alloy Short Sword *or* Ancient Ebon Bracer • (10%) Timorous Drakulv Ebon Sleeves *or* Helm • (10%; hi-lo) Golden Alloy Hammer *or* Ebony Flecked Shimmering Cloak • (10%) Timorous Drakulv Ebon Gloves *or* Jerkin • (10%; hi-lo) Golden Alloy Axe *or* Ancient Ebon Ring

Eiorharn [45] *see Burr [45]*

enraged mara [50] (12%) Pristine Mara Pelt • (20%) Enraged Wolf Pelt Cloak

Esulv [45] *see Burr [45]*

Geirolf [47] (20%; hi-lo) Emerald Moonshone Gloves, Drakulv Militia Great Hammer *or* Cloak of the Unseen Stalker • (20%; hi-lo) Emerald Moonshone Leggings, Drakulv Militia Great Sword *or* Cloak of the Unseen Stalker • (20%; hi-lo) Emerald Moonshone Helm, Drakulv Militia Great Axe *or* Cloak of the Unseen Stalker

Gjalpinulva [80] (99%) <Blue Fire Gear> • (99%) Lost Hauberk of Valhalla, Runed Saga Etched Shield, Dragon Bone Bracelet, Bearman Battle Gauntlets *or* Cloth Cap • *plus everything that Yar [73] might drop, at about x7 probability (15% instead of 2.3%, and 22% instead of 3.3%)*

Gunnolf [47] *see Geirolf [47]*

Gunnolfr [48] (19%) Blood-Filled Crystal • (0.6%) Blood-Stained Tiara • (15%) Jewels 63 • (1.7%) Ancient Bloodbound Boots *or* Pants • (1.7%; hi-lo) Black Diamond Staff *or* Bloodbound Book

Hrolleif [55] *see Bjornvarg [55]*

Ingardild [47] *see Geirolf [47]*

Kariig [53] *see Desukva [55]*

Kleng [51] *see Eildird [51]*

Leidolf [53] *see Bjornvarg [55]*

Ljornrn [49] *see Arnulv [49]*

patrolling drakulv [39/41/43] (13/15/19%) Scaled Sword Baldric • (4.3/5/6.3%) Drakulv Patrol Insignia • (3540/50%) Jewels 21 • (2.5%; hi-lo) Jet Bloodletter's Gloves/Boots/Hauberk, Skycaller's Protector/Drakulv Great Shield/Drakulv Shield, *or* Drakulv Defender's Belt • (6/9/9%) Drakulv Scale

Rana [47] *see Alfrigg [45]*

scaled retriever [50] (no loot)

scaled varg snarler [34/36] (22/25%) Scaled Snarler Pelt • (2.4/2.8%) Pristine Scaled Snarler Pelt

scaled varg yearling [25/27/29/31] (14/15/20/24%) Scaled Varg Pelt • (1.5/1.7/2.2/2.7%) Pristine Scaled Varg Pelt

spawn of Gjalpinulva [37] (no loot)

Steinolf [49] *see Arnulv [49]*

svartalf bloodbinder [51/53/55] (19%) Blood-Filled Crystal • (0.6%) Blood-Stained Tiara • (15/17/20%) Jewels 63 • (1.7%) Ancient Bloodbound Boots *or* Pants/Sleeves *or* Gloves/Vest *or* Cap, *or* Runed Bloodbound Cap [level 55 only] • (1.7%; hi-lo) Black/Blue/Red *or* Yellow Diamond Staff, *or* Bloodbound Book/Bloodbound Totem/Luminescent Diamond Necklace

svartalf foister [48/50/52] (19%) Svartalf Asterite Ring • (0.6%) Crown of the Darkheart • (25/30/40%) Jewels 30 • (2%; hi-lo) Gauntlets/Leggings/Vest of the Bloodwolf, Drakulv Militia Hammer/Axe/Sword, *or* Jade Moonshone Cloak

svartalf infiltrator [45/47/49] (19%) Drakulv Nightwalker's Cloak • (0.4% each) Greater Enervating Poison, Greater Enervating Serum [Greater Infectious Serum for 49], Lifebane • (15/15/20%) Jewels 30 • (2%; hi-lo) Emerald Moonshone Boots/Sleeves/Jerkin, Drakulv Militia Great Hammer/Great Sword/Great Axe, *or* Cloak of the Bloodwolf

Ulf [51] *see Eildird [51]*

venomous tree crawler [55] (no loot)

Wyulv [53] *see Bjornvarg [55]*

Yar [73] (2.3%) Timorous Drakulv Ebon Legs *or* Boots • (2.3%; hi-lo) Golden Alloy Short Sword *or* Ancient Ebon Bracer • (2.3%) Timorous Drakulv Ebon Sleeves *or* Helm • (2.3%; hi-lo) Golden Alloy Hammer *or* Ebony Flecked Shimmering Cloak • (2.3%) Timorous Drakulv Ebon Gloves *or* Jerkin • (2.3%; hi-lo) Golden Alloy Axe *or* Ancient Ebon Ring • (2.3%) Dragon Etched Boots *or* Legs • (2.3%; hi-lo) Dragon Etched Bracer, *or* Golden Alloy Bastard Sword *or* Kite Shield • (2.3%) Dragon Etched Sleeves *or* Gloves • (2.3%; hi-lo) Golden Alloy Great Sword *or* Mystical Golden Scale Belt • (2.3%; hi-lo) Dragon Etched Hauberk, *or* Ancient *or* Ageless Dragon Etched Coif • (2.3%; hi-lo) Golden Alloy Great Spear *or* Cloak of the Dragonwolf • (2.3%; hi-lo) Dragon Singed Ebon Legs, Boots *or* Coif, *or* Crackling Ebon Gloves • (2.3%; hi-lo) Immolated Dragonfire Cleaver, Flame Wrought Cloak *or* Smoldering Ebon Shield • (2.3%; hi-lo) Dragon Singed Ebon Arms, Crackling Ebon Coif, *or* Hymn-Weaver's Ebon Gloves • (2.3%; hi-lo) Immolated Great Dragonfire Cleaver *or* Flame Wrought Ring • (2.3%; hi-lo) Dragon Singed Ebon Hauberk, *or* Barbed Ebon Coif *or* Gloves • (2.3%) Immolated Dragonfire Cleaver *or* Great Cleaver, *or* Flame Wrought Belt • (3.3%; hi-lo) Soulbinder's Boots, Legs *or* Helm, *or* Soulrager's Gauntlets • (3.3%; hi-lo) Soulbinder's Jerkin, Sleeves *or* Gauntlets • (3.3%; hi-lo) Battle Scourge, Ring of the Mindwall *or* Soulbinder's Shield • (3.3%; hi-lo) Soul Forge, Golden Alloy Great Bow, *or* Soulbinder's Belt • (3.3%; hi-lo) Soulbinder's Boots, Legs *or* Helm, *or* Soulrager's Gauntlets • (3.3%; hi-lo) Soulbinder's Jerkin *or* Sleeves, *or* Soulpiercer's Gauntlets • (3.3%) Battle Scourge, Soulbound Necklace *or* Soulbinder's Shield • (3.3%; hi-lo) Soul Forge, Golden Alloy Great Bow, *or* Bracer of Embodiment • (2.3%) Ancient Bloodbound Boots *or* Pants • (2.3%; hi-lo) Black Diamond Staff *or* Bloodbound Book • (2.3%) Ancient Bloodbound Sleeves *or* Gloves • (2.3%; hi-lo) Blue Diamond Staff *or* Bloodbound Totem • (2.3%; hi-lo) Ancient Bloodbound Vest, *or* Ageless *or* Runed Bloodbound Cap • (2.3%) Red *or* Yellow Diamond Staff, *or* Luminescent Diamond Necklace

Muspelheim

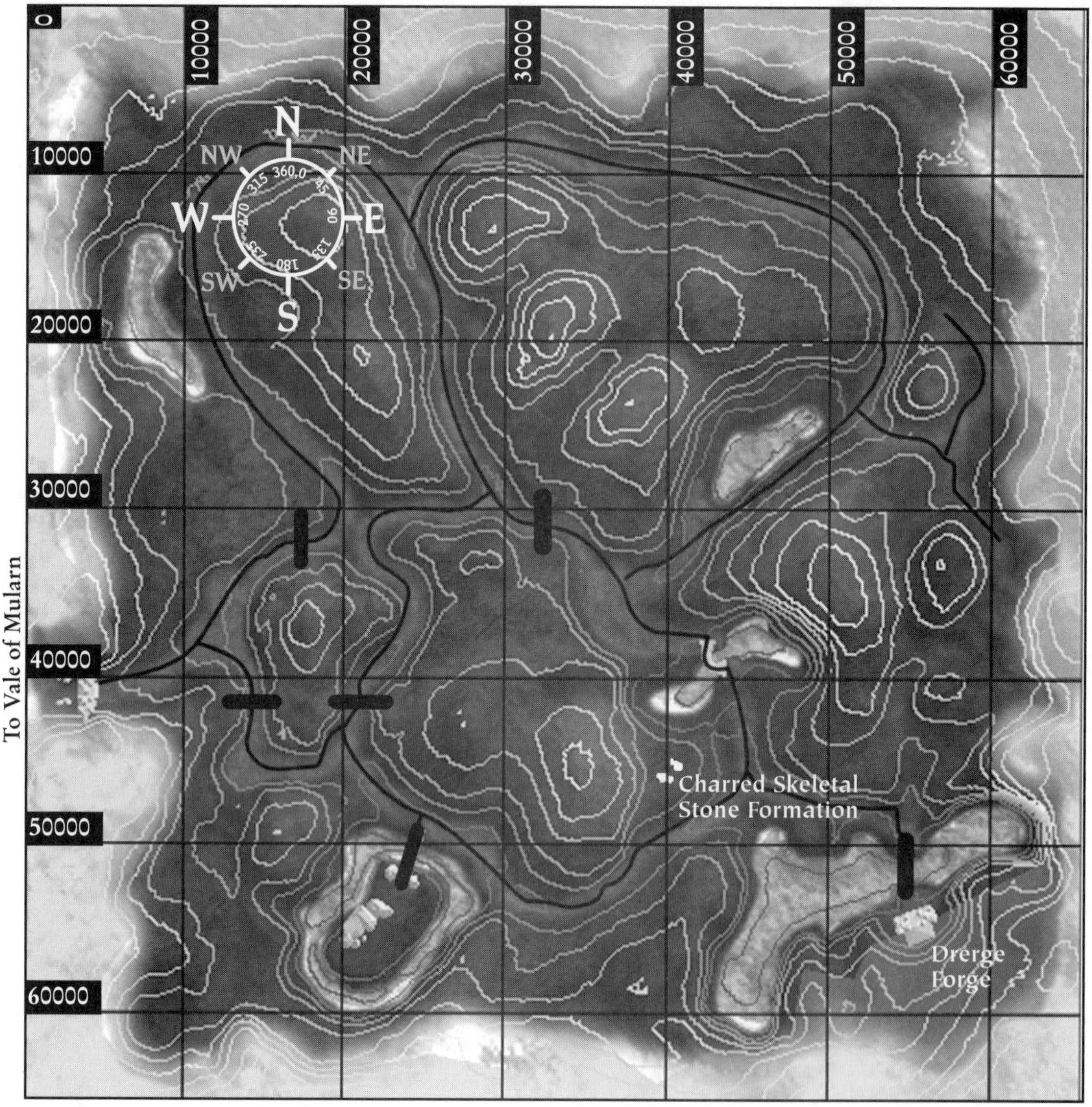

0
10000
20000
30000
40000
50000
60000
N
NE
E
SE
S
SW
W
NW
360,0
45
90
135
180
225
270
315
To Vale of Mularn
Charred Skeletal Stone Formation
Drerge Forge

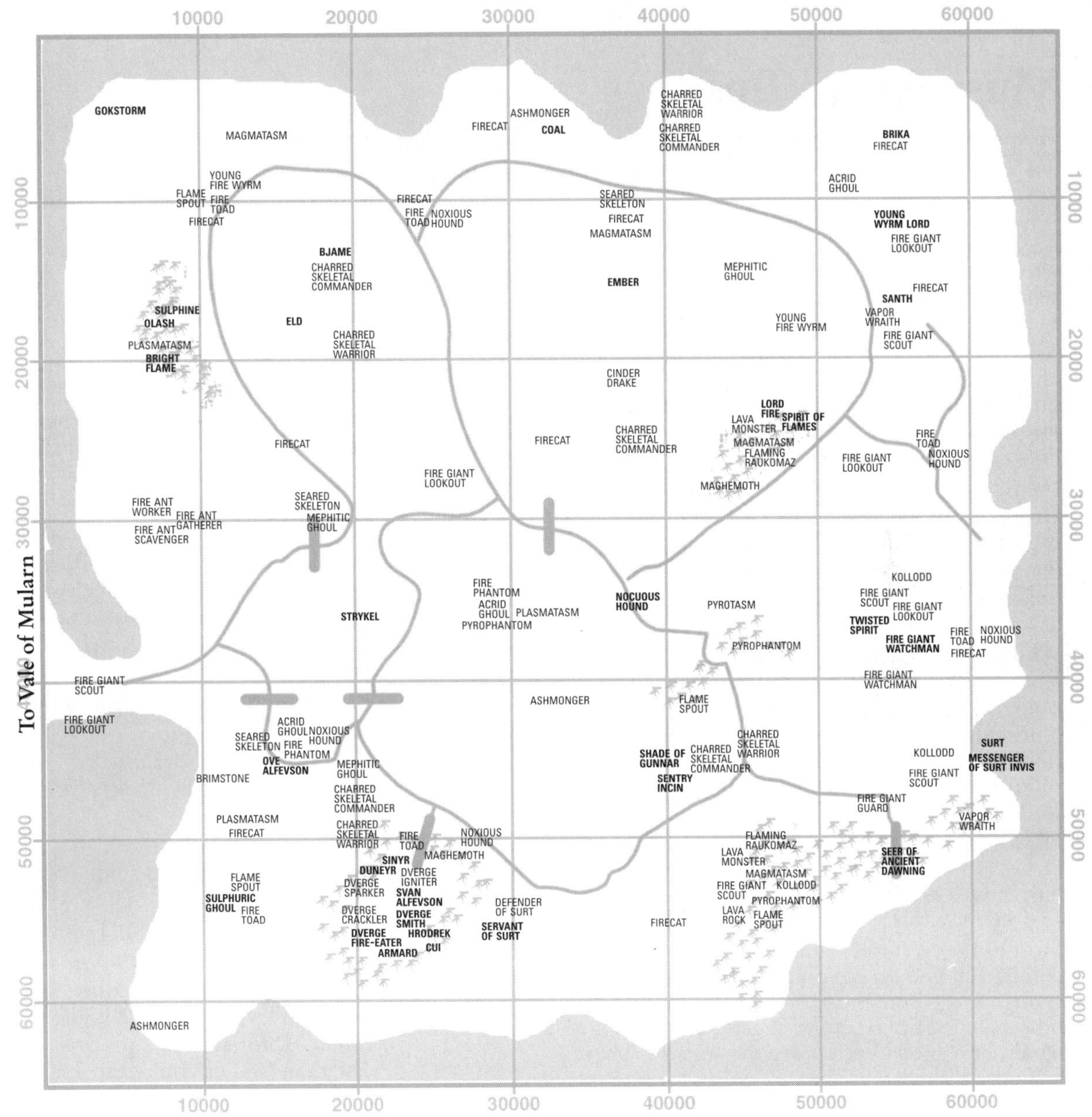
10000
20000
30000
40000
50000
60000
GOKSTORM
MAGMATASM
ASHMONGER
FIRECAT
COAL
CHARRED SKELETAL WARRIOR
CHARRED SKELETAL COMMANDER
BRIKA
FIRECAT
YOUNG FIRE WYRM
FLAME SPOUT
FIRE TOAD
FIRECAT
ACRID GHOUL
FIRECAT
FIRE TOAD
NOXIOUS HOUND
SEARED SKELETON
FIRECAT
MAGMATASM
YOUNG WYRM LORD
FIRE GIANT LOOKOUT
BJAME
CHARRED SKELETAL COMMANDER
EMBER
MEPHITIC GHOUL
FIRECAT
SANTH
SULPHINE
OLASH
ELD
YOUNG FIRE WYRM
VAPOR WRAITH
FIRE GIANT SCOUT
CHARRED SKELETAL WARRIOR
PLASMATASM
BRIGHT FLAME
CINDER DRAKE
LORD FIRE
SPIRIT OF FLAMES
LAVA MONSTER
MAGMATASM
FLAMING RAUKOMAZ
CHARRED SKELETAL COMMANDER
FIRECAT
FIRECAT
FIRE TOAD
NOXIOUS HOUND
FIRE GIANT LOOKOUT
FIRE GIANT LOOKOUT
MAGHEMOTH
SEARED SKELETON
MEPHITIC GHOUL
FIRE ANT WORKER
FIRE ANT GATHERER
FIRE ANT SCAVENGER
To Vale of Mularn
FIRE PHANTOM
ACRID GHOUL
PLASMATASM
PYROPHANTOM
STRYKEL
NOCUOUS HOUND
PYROTASM
KOLLODD
FIRE GIANT SCOUT
FIRE GIANT LOOKOUT
TWISTED SPIRIT
FIRE GIANT WATCHMAN
FIRE TOAD
NOXIOUS HOUND
FIRECAT
PYROPHANTOM
FIRE GIANT SCOUT
FIRE GIANT WATCHMAN
ASHMONGER
FLAME SPOUT
FIRE GIANT LOOKOUT
SEARED SKELETON
ACRID GHOUL
NOXIOUS HOUND
FIRE PHANTOM
OVE ALFEVSON
MEPHITIC GHOUL
BRIMSTONE
CHARRED SKELETAL COMMANDER
SHADE OF GUNNAR
CHARRED SKELETAL COMMANDER
CHARRED SKELETAL WARRIOR
SENTRY INCIN
KOLLODD
SURT
MESSENGER OF SURT INVIS
FIRE GIANT SCOUT
FIRE GIANT GUARD
PLASMATASM
FIRECAT
CHARRED SKELETAL WARRIOR
FIRE TOAD
NOXIOUS HOUND
MAGHEMOTH
FLAMING RAUKOMAZ
LAVA MONSTER
VAPOR WRAITH
SEER OF ANCIENT DAWNING
SINYR
DUNEYR
DVERGE IGNITER
DVERGE SPARKER
FLAME SPOUT
SULPHURIC GHOUL
FIRE TOAD
SVAN ALFEVSON
DVERGE CRACKLER
DVERGE SMITH
DVERGE FIRE-EATER
HRODREK
ARMARD
CUI
DEFENDER OF SURT
SERVANT OF SURT
MAGMATASM
FIRE GIANT SCOUT
KOLLODD
PYROPHANTOM
LAVA ROCK
FLAME SPOUT
FIRECAT
ASHMONGER

Muspelheim Tips

Muspel: start with soot harvesters, then move to fire flowers/crabs/ants/lava lizards/ashen spirits, then ash mongers/low skeletons, then zombies/high skeletons, then fire giants.

Careful with the ants — they're all over, patrol actively, and *will* bring friends from afar (*). At 26 a mob of blue/green ones nicked me and an even con'd Thane to death in no time.

Also the fire lizards past the lava pit that's North of the gates. They don't bring friends, have a small aggro radius and are easy to melee. Some of them nuke but very rarely.

Don't mess with the dogs: they are allied with the Dverge and you'll need their faction at 30.

Group Friendly? Yes

Who hates this area? No one, there is something there for every class. Though folks playing on a small monitor or have gamma set a little off may have a hard time seeing things at night.

Who loves this area? Everyone, generally this zone is regarded as one of the best zones in the game.

Notes about Muspelheim: This a fire and brimstone zone, so well done you can almost smell the sulfur from the steam. Great hunting grouped or solo.

Drawback to this zone is visibility at night, it can be hard to see and when you add rain into the mix and it's even more difficult for gamers with 15-inch monitors.

Most of the creatures in this zone are social and will BAF if you do not pull your target far enough away from their friends. With so many other monsters in the zone to get exp from it would be a good idea to leave the Ants be. They are more trouble than they are worth for hunting, they bring friends in excess, the exp gained is not worth the hassle.

When you enter Musp be on your toes, Fire Giant lookouts and a named fire giant (Golstat (ck spelling)) like to lurk at the entry gates, might not be a bad idea just to take the high road and run up the side of the mountain to enter Musp.

Solo Levelling Tips

20-22	This is a great place to level in the 20s. Next to the more dangerous frontier, this is maybe the best place! At this level, a good soot harvesters (not orange) are the way to go. By 22, soot harvesters are perfect. Just through the gate and to the right is a (usually heavily camped) area, but there's another one to the left up on the mountain. Another reason to go to Musp is that a good 1-time drops from named monsters and a decent cash.
23-24	The best here would be fire flowers. They are casters, so they've got low hp. Be careful, because they BAF. I've usually gotten full camp bonus here.
25-27	Plasmatasms spawn at night in the lava pit.
27-28	Young fire wyrms are usually good. 2 bolts and a dd takes care of a yellow.
28-29	Cinder drakes in the north go down with 2 bolts and a dd.
30-31	Try mephetic zombies. They're slow and usually have full camp bonus. Lots of mana per xp.
30-32	Flaming raukomaz con yellow and orange at level 30, takes 2 bolts and a DD for around 2 mil xp. They can BAF if you're careless. Also fire giants.
35	About lvl 35 is when Muspelheim starts being less useful for leveling purposes.
38-42	Pyrotasm's. At level 42, occasionally you'll see a blue or orange; mostly you'll get yellows. Make sure you're seeing pyrotasms, because it's easy to get the confused with plasmatasms.

Loot

acrid ghoul [29] (58%) Acrid Ghoul Ear • (80% each) Chunk of Ghoul Flesh, Yellow Topaz • (75%) Piece of Polished Onyx • (70%) Red Diamond • (0.3%) <Freya's Dowry>

Armard [27] (75% each) Glowing Ember, Yellow Topaz • (55%) Necklace of Flames • (65%) Fire Opal • (70%) Blood Red Ruby • (0.3%) Hearthwood Branch, Shadowformed Ring **or** Lightbound Ring • (1.5%) <Magma Carta>

ashen spirit [21/23] Pile of Ashes • (40/65%) Obsidian Bracelet • (58/65%) Charred Leg Bone • (48/65%) Piece of Burnt Skin • (0.3%) <Great Balls O' Fire> • (1.5%) Ashen Axe

ashmonger [23] (80% each) Pile of Ashes, Piece of Obsidian • (65%) Hardened Lava Stone • (60%) Fire Opal • (1.5%) <Ashes to Ashes> • (0.3%) <Great Balls O' Fire> • (9%) Polished Piece of Obsidian

ashmonger [25] (80% each) Pile of Ashes, Piece of Obsidian • (70%) Hardened Lava Stone • (68%) Fire Opal • (45%) Blood Red Ruby • (1.5%) <Ashes to Ashes> • (0.3%) <Great Balls O' Fire> • (11%) Polished Piece of Obsidian

Bright Flame [25] (70% each) Glowing Ember, Blood Red Ruby • (77%) Piece of Obsidian • (50% each) Ball of Fire, Necklace of Flames • (1.5%) <Forged in the Cauldron> • (0.3%) <Great Balls O' Fire>

Brika [25] (70%) Firecat Pelt • (60%) Firecat Fang • (52%) Firecat Claw • (40%) Collar of Red Carnelians • (1.5%) Lava Forged Coif **or** Boots, Lava Etched Gloves **or** Sleeves **or** Blunted Fire Cat Tooth

Brimstone [23] (65%) Yellow Topaz • (70% each) Flask of Sulphuric Gas, Yellowed Ghoul Skin • (45%) Large Topaz Ring • (0.3%) <Great Balls O' Fire> • (1.5%; hi-lo) Acid Etched Leggings, Sleeves **or** Gauntlets

burnt skeletal sentry [21] (60%) Burned Skull • (50%) Singed Wristband • (40%) Small Burned Satchel • (1%) Fire Opal • (0.3%) <Great Balls O' Fire>

charred skeletal commander [26] (75%) Charred Finger Bone • (70%) Charred Hide Belt • (65%) Charred Golden Medal • (73%) Fire Opal Ring • (0.3%) <All Fired Up> • (1.5%) <Fire and Rain>

charred skeletal warrior [23] (70%) Small Burned Satchel • (60% each) Fire Opal, Charred Finger Bone • (50%) Charred Hide Belt • (0.3%) <Great Balls O' Fire> • (1.5%) <Fire and Rain>

charred skeletal warrior [25] (70% each) Charred Finger Bone, Hide Belt • (65%) Charred Bronze Medal • (77%) Small Burned Satchel • (1.5%) <Fire and Rain>

cinder drake [28] (65%) Flaming Chunk of Lava • (40%) Large Yellow Topaz • (80%) Pile of Glowing Cinders • (65%) Large Glowing Eye

Coal [25] (40%) Pile of Ashes • (70%) Hardened Lava Stone • (80%) Piece of Obsidian • (72%) Fire Opal • (65%) Blood Red Ruby • (1.5%) <Ashes to Ashes> • (0.3%) <Great Balls O' Fire>

Cui [29] (60%) Heart of Fire • (70%) Necklace of Flames • (85% each) Large Topaz Ring, Red Carnelian • (80%) Blood Red Ruby • (0.3%) <All Fired Up>

Duneyr [31] (70%) Heart of Fire • (75% each) Fire Opal Earring, Crystalized Ball of Flame • (53%) Large Yellow Topaz • (55%) Large Red Diamond • (0.3%) <Freya's Dowry> • (1.5%) <Magma Carta>

dverge crackler [28] (57%) Heart of Fire • (70%) Necklace of Flames • (75% each) Fire Opal, Yellow Topaz • (80%) Blood Red Ruby • (0.3%) Hearthwood Branch, Shadowformed Ring **or** Lightbound Ring • (1.5%) <Magma Carta>

dverge fire-eater [30] (70% each) Heart of Fire, Fire Opal Earring, Crystalized Ball of Flame • (41%) Large Yellow Topaz • (45%) Large Red Diamond • (0.3%) <Freya's Dowry> • (1.5%) <Magma Carta>

dverge igniter [26] (70%) Glowing Ember • (75%) Piece of Obsidian • (57%) Necklace of Flames • (65% each) Fire Opal, Blood Red Ruby • (0.3%) <All Fired Up> • (1.5%) <Magma Carta>

dverge smith [28] *see dverge crackler [28]*

dverge sparker [24] (65%) Glowing Ember • (70%) Ball of Fire • (55%) Fire Opal • (60%) Piece of Obsidian • (40%) Blood Red Ruby • (0.3%) <All Fired Up> • (1.5%) <Magma Carta>

Eld [23] (80%) Fire Seeds • (75%) Flaming Root • (72%) Glowing Ember • (52%) Flower of Flame • (1.5%) <From the Caldera> • (0.3%) <Great Balls O' Fire>

Ember [30] (70% each) Flaming Chunk of Lava, Large Glowing Eye • (54%) Large Yellow Topaz • (80%) Pile of Glowing Cinders • (0.3%) <Freya's Dowry>

fire ant gatherer [21] (46%) Fire Ant Larva • (75%) Fire Ant Mandible • (70%) Fire Ant Leg • (80%) Sulphuric Rock • (1.5%) <Fiery Ants> • (10%) Warm Fire Ant Larva

fire ant scavenger [20] (75%) Chunk of Soot • (65% each) Fire Ant Mandible, Sulphuric Rock • (60%) Fire Ant Leg • (1.5%) <Fiery Ants>

fire ant worker [22] (75%) Fire Ant Larva • (60%) Fire Ant Mandible • (85%) Fire Ant Leg • (80%) Sulphuric Rock • (1.5%) <Fiery Ants>

fire flower [20] (80%) Fire Petal • (70%) Fiery Stem • (40%) Flaming Root • (50%) Fire Seeds • (1.5%) <From the Caldera> • (0.3%) <Thief's Nest Egg>

fire flower [22] (70%) Fire Petal • (60%) Glowing Ember • (75% each) Fire Seeds, Flaming Root • (1.5%) <From the Caldera> • (0.3%) <Great Balls O' Fire>

fire giant guard [30] (55%) Fire Giant Tooth • (56%) Fire Giant Scalp • (70%) Fire Giant Toes • (75%) Belt of Flames • (0.3%) <Freya's Dowry> • (1.5%) <Hot Goods>

fire giant lookout [27] (50%) Lookout's Spyglass • (70% each) Blood Red Ruby, Fire Giant Finger • (60%) Fire Giant Nosering • (0.3%) <All Fired Up> • (1.5%) <Hot Stuff>

fire giant scout [28] (45% each) Fire Giant Tooth, Scalp • (67%) Fire Giant Nosering • (70%) Fire Giant Finger • (0.3%) <All Fired Up> • (1.5%) <Hot Stuff>

fire giant spirit [40] (55%) Fire Giant Tooth • (50%) Fire Giant Scalp • (70%) Fire Giant Nosering • (65%) Belt of Flames • (0.3%) <Freya's Dowry> • (1.5%) <Hot Goods>

fire giant watchman [29] *see fire giant spirit [40]*

fire phantom [25] (80%) Blood Red Ruby • (70%) Red Carnelian • (65%) Piece of Polished Onyx • (45%) Red Diamond • (0.3%) <All Fired Up>

fire toad [27] (83%) Fire Toad Tongue • (45%) Flaming Wart • (70%) Fire Toad Leg • (80%) Red Carnelian

firecat [24/26] (70/80%) Firecat Pelt • (60/70%) Firecat Fang • (52/65%) Firecat Claw • (40/57%) Collar of Red Carnelians • (1.5%) Lava Forged Coif **or** Boots, Lava Etched Gloves **or** Sleeves **or** Blunted Fire Cat Tooth

flame spout [26] (85%) Blood Red Ruby • (62%) Red Diamond • (70%) Piece of Polished Onyx • (50%) Crystalized Ball of Flame

flame thrower [21,23] (60%) Glowing Ember • (70%) Ball of Fire • (55%) Piece of Obsidian • (40%) Blood Red Ruby • (1.5%) APOA: Flame Charred, Fiery Sword **or** Flame Wrought Bracer • (0.3%) <Great Balls O' Fire>

flaming raukomaz [30] (80% each) Flaming Chunk of Lava, Pile of Glowing Cinders • (57%) Red Diamond Necklace • (62%) Glowing Red Orb • (0.3%) <Freya's Dowry>

Gokstorm [25] *see fire giant scout [28]*

Hrodrek [25] (65%) Glowing Ember • (70%) Piece of Obsidian • (45%) Necklace of Flames • (60% each) Fire Opal, Blood Red Ruby • (0.3%) <All Fired Up> • (1.5%) <Magma Carta>

lava lizard [22] (80%) Lava Lizard Tongue • (70%) Lava Lizard Hide • (60%) Lizard Eye • (65%) Hardened Lava Stone

lava monster [28] (70%) Flaming Chunk of Lava • (60%) Large Red Diamond • (65%) Large Glowing Eye • (44%) Large Yellow Topaz

Lord Fire [31] (80%) Flaming Chunk of Lava • (50%) Circlet of Flames • (75% each) Red Diamond Necklace, Glowing Red Orb • (0.3%) <Freya's Dowry>

maghemoth [30] (60%) Glowing Red Orb • (80% each) Pile of Glowing Cinders, Flaming Chunk of Lava • (70%) Large Red Diamond • (0.3%) <Freya's Dowry>

magmatasm [29/31] (70%) Pile of Glowing Cinders • (66/73%) Large Yellow Topaz • (65/83%) Flaming Chunk of Lava • (40/70%) Red Diamond Necklace • (0.3%) <Freya's Dowry> • (1.5%) Vest **or** Gloves of Living Flame, **or** Flame of the Earth Pants **or** Boots

mephitic ghoul [26/28] (77/70%) Flask of Sulphuric Gas • (65/80%) Chunk of Ghoul Flesh • (70/75%) Yellow Topaz • (50/70%) Piece of Polished Onyx • (45/70%) Red Diamond • (0.3%) <All Fired Up> • (9%) Melted Ghoul Flesh

nocuous hound [29] (85%) Hound Pelt • (65%) Large Yellow Topaz • (83%) Glowing Hound Eye • (70%) Gaseous Pouch

noxious hound [24/26] (60/70%) Hound Pelt • (65/75%) Hound Paw • (70/80%) Hound Tail • (40/60%) Glowing Hound Eye

Olash [24] Pile of Ashes • (85%) Obsidian Bracelet • (80% each) Charred Leg Bone, Glowing Ember • (0.3%) <Great Balls O' Fire>

Ove Alfevson [21] (50% each) Thick Pristine Werewolf Pelt, Silver Moon Circlet • (40%) Silver Werewolf Fang • (1.4%) Noble Supple Jerkin, Leggings **or** Sleeves • (0.3%) <Great Balls O' Fire> • (1.4%) Noble Wanderer's Axe

plasmatasm [23/25] (65/70%) Blood Red Ruby • (75/80%) Fire Opal • (60/70%) Yellow Topaz • (45%) Large Garnet [23] • (60%) Red Carnelian [25] • (0.3%) <Great Balls O' Fire>/<All Fired Up>

pyrophantom [28/30] (60/72%) Large Red Diamond • (70/85%) Fire Opal Earring • (70/80%) Large Glowing Eye • (40/55%) Onyx and Carnelian Belt • (0.3%) <All Fired Up>/<Freya's Dowry>

pyrotasm [35,38,42] (65%) Blood Red Ruby • (75%) Fire Opal • (60%) Yellow Topaz • (45%) Large Garnet • (0.3%) <Great Balls O' Fire>

Santh [45] *see fire giant spirit [40]*

seared skeleton [27/29] (60/70% each) Charred Finger Bone, Onyx and Ruby Ring • (65%) Seared Skull • (45/70%) Seared Bone Nosering • (0.3%) <All Fired Up>/<Freya's Dowry> • (1.5%) Seared Axe

Seer of Ancient Dawning [28] *see vapor wraith [30]*

Sentry Incin [21] (40%) Burned Skull • (75%) Singed Wristband • (60%) Small Burned Satchel • (70%) Fire Opal • (0.3%) <Great Balls O' Fire>

Shade of Gunnar [26] *see charred skeletal commander [26]*

Sinyr [31] *see Duneyr [31]*

soot harvester [20] (60%) Harvester Carapace • (85%) Chunk of Soot • (62%) Soot Harvester Leg • (70%) Pile of Ashes • (1.5%; hi-lo) Soot Encrusted Gloves **or** Boots, **or** Runed Harvester Leg

soot harvester [22] (73%) Harvester Carapace • (80% each) Soot Harvester Leg, Pile of Ashes • (62%) Sooty Eye • (1.5%; hi-lo) Soot Encrusted Cap, Runed Harvester Leg, Soot Encrusted Gloves

Spirit of Flames [29] (58%) Large Red Diamond • (65%) Bracelet of Flames • (80%) Crystalized Ball of Flame • (75%) Fire Opal Earring • (0.3%) <Freya's Dowry>

Strykel [27] (70%) Blood Red Ruby • (81%) Yellow Topaz • (65% each) Large Garnet, Red Carnelian • (50%) Onyx and Ruby Ring • (0.3%) <All Fired Up>

Sulphine [22] (80%) Sulphur Crab Shell • (75%) Sulphur Crab Claw • (90%) Sulphur Crab Meat • (65%) Glowing Yellow Eye

sulphur crab [20/22] (70/80%) Sulphur Crab Shell • (60/75%) Sulphur Crab Claw • (80%) Sulphur Crab Meat • (45/65%) Glowing Yellow Eye

sulphuric ghoul [22] (80%) Sulphuric Rock • (60%) Flask of Sulphuric Gas • (70%) Yellowed Ghoul Skin • (45%) Yellow Topaz • (0.3%) <Great Balls O' Fire> • (1.5%; hi-lo) Acid Etched Leggings, Sleeves **or** Gauntlets

Svan Alfevson [90] (no loot)

vapor wraith [30] (70%) Pile of Glowing Cinders • (80%) Flaming Chunk of Lava • (60% each) Large Yellow Topaz, Bracelet of Hot Vapor • (0.3%) <Freya's Dowry> • (1.5%) Vaporous Sleeves **or** Crown

young fire wyrm [25/27] (70/80% each) Wyrm Hide, Red Carnelian • (60/70%) Piece of Polished Onyx • (45/70%) Fire Wyrm Fang

Young Wyrm Lord [30] (80% each) Wyrm Hide, Red Carnelian • (70% each) Piece of Polished Onyx, Fire Wyrm Fang

Myrkwood Forest

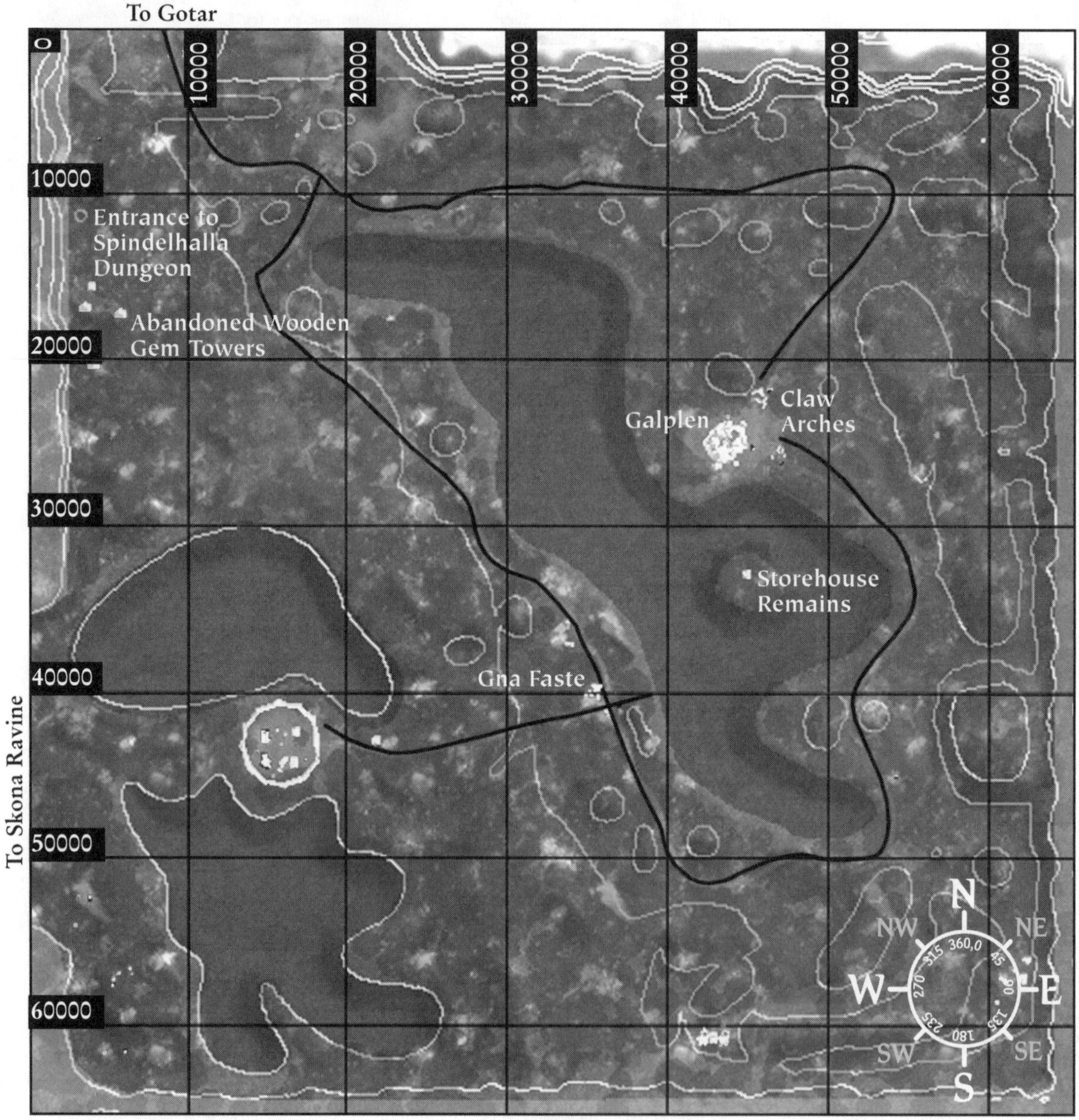

To Gotar

0
10000
20000
30000
40000
50000
60000

Entrance to Spindelhalla Dungeon

Abandoned Wooden Gem Towers

Claw Arches

Galplen

Storehouse Remains

Gna Faste

To Skona Ravine

N
NE
E
SE
S
SW
W
NW
360,0
45
90
135
180
225
270
315

Quest NPCs

Galplen	
Krek	Venture to Gotar (lvl 4)
Wariel	Trappers Pride (lvl 1)
Wariel	Trappers Joy (lvl 3)

Gna Faste Tower	
Sentry Dwarn	Morana's Tunic (lvl 18)

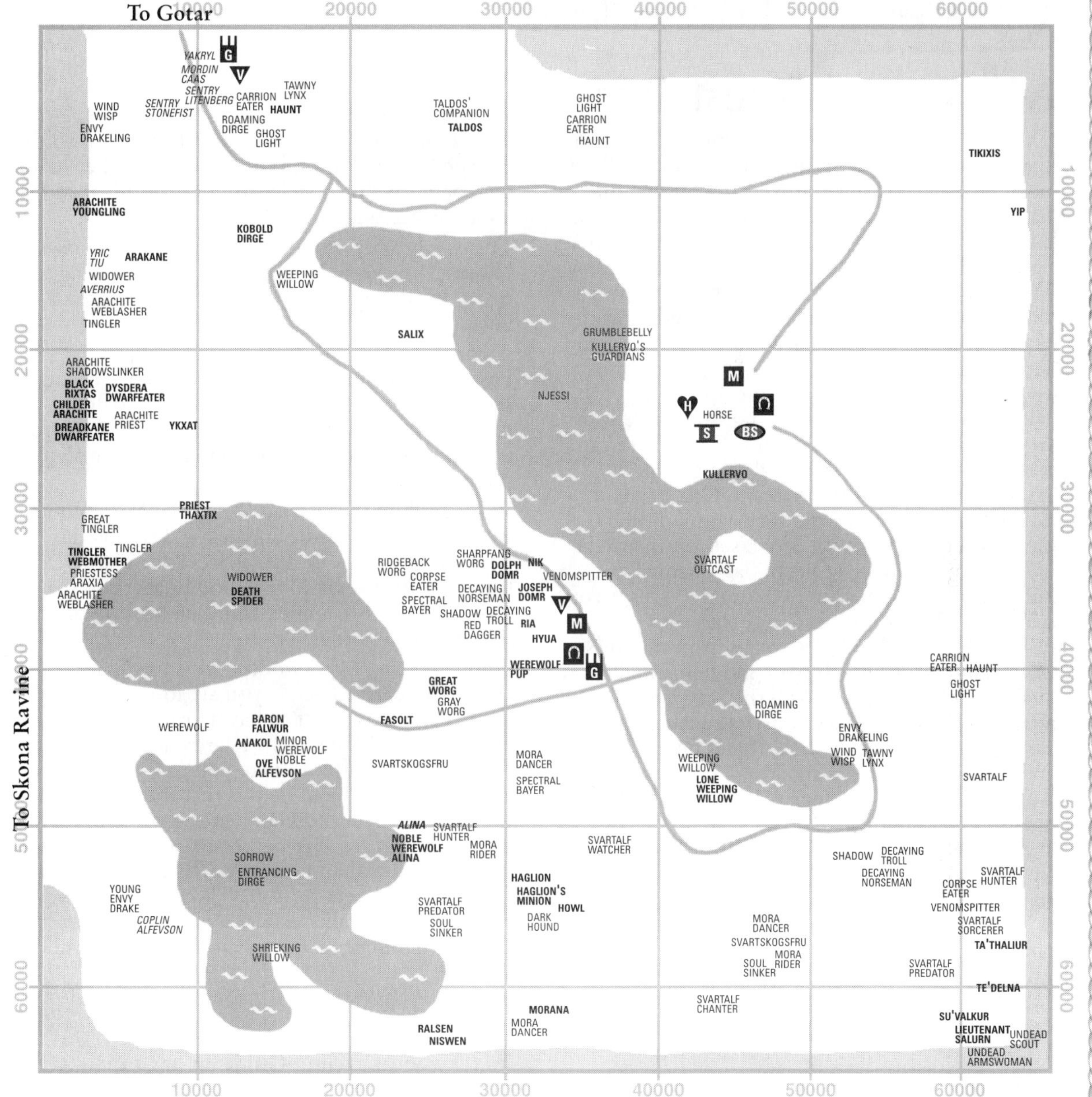

Lower-level monsters not shown on map:

Creature	Lvl	Location	Creature	Lvl	Location	Creature	Lvl	Location	Creature	Lvl	Location
arachite greensilk	5	NC,NE	giant bull frog	1	NC,C	myrkcat	3	NC,NE,EC	undead woodcarver	4	NC,NE,EC
arachite hatchling	1	NC,NE	green serpent	2	NC,EC	pine imp	6	NW,NC,EC	wayward ghoul	4	NC,NE,EC
black mauler cub	0	NC,EC	hbgbln. fish-catcher	0	C,EC	sapherd	5	NC,NE,EC	wild hog	2	NC,NE,EC
blk. mauler juvenile	5	NC,NE,EC	hobgoblin pincher	4	NC,NE,EC	scavenger	1	NC,EC	wood imp	5	NC,NE,EC
brittle skeleton	0	NC,EC	hobgoblin snagger	2	NC,NE,EC	spectral hog	2	NC,NE,EC	Yip	4	NE
carrion crawler	6	NW,NC,NE,EC	hbgbln. snake-finder	1	NC,C,EC	spook	6	NW,NC,NE,EC			
carrion lizard	3	NE,EC	hog-nose slither	0	NC,C,EC	tawny lynx cub	0	NC,EC			
fragile skeleton	3	NC,NE,EC	lupine snarler	2	NC,NE,EC	undead explorer	3	NC,NE,EC			

Myrkwood Forest Tips

This area is a good place to start and go through a good chunk of levels. When you hit level 5, head north east from Galplen toward the mountain base and fight the bugs. When they are low, head a bit more east between the mountain base and a couple hills. These hills have undead monsters to hunt. When level 8 I believe it is, head towards the north east corner of Mrykwood and fight the goblins that are standing around trees. At around level 10 head east up a mountain and fight the spiders and wisps you see at the top. Be careful of where you pull too as all the monsters here wander up and down the mountain. All of these can be done several levels earlier if in a group. At level 12, head across the water to Gna Faste. South and north along the road you will find three sets of trees. South is one set, north are the other two. The first set north has a named tree called Willy or something - I forget :(- that drops a Willow Heart to be used in the jewelry slot. When ~level 15, head west away from the trees you found on the north road and fight tinglers. A little known trick is to go all the way west until you find the north lake. Follow the lake north until you see where the lake comes up against the mountain. Watch for wandering arachites and huge spiders that will aggro! There are tinglers there - great hunting for a group. A soloer can do it, however a group will benefit from the group xp bonus given for BAF creatures. There is also a large spider that spawns with them and the group will be needed for them. I would suggest no more then two go unless they are low yellow or you are a class that can take multiple yellows (2 come for a single player).

-Monica "Seraphym" Hayes

This zone is well liked for its wide range of soloing spots, so much so folks starting in other newbie zones save up 5 silver for a horse ride to this zone for hunting.

This is a heavily wooded zone (thus the name "Forest") so keep on your toes when hunting there. It can be hard at times to see what lurks behind a tree.

A common way to get from Galphen to Gna Faste is to swim the lake, though beware if you are below level 20. There is a great envy drake named Nessie who patrols the waters looking for her next snack, so be on the lookout when swimming.

When pulling to the road to fight in Myrkwood, watch out for Guard Flintrock — he will take your kill. His guard route is from the guard tower on the Gotar-Myrkwood border to Gna Faste and on to Gaphlen and then back to the tower on the border.

Upon entering Myrkwood Forest from Gotar there is a guard tower, if you are lower level (1-12) you may want to pay a visit to the tower and speak with one of the guards inside the tower. He will offer to take you to Galphen. The reason this may be of help is that the road from the Gotar boarder to Gaphlen has wondering creatures that are very aggressive and would like nothing better than to kill you. The guard will kill these monsters for you. Though it must be said the guard walks very, very, slow…so use **/stick** or **/follow** on him, or just switch to walk speed.

(Myrkwood Leveling Guide on page 158.)

Loot

arachite greensilk [5] (25% each) Sticky Arachite Silk, Arachite Silk Gland • (40%) Arachite Egg Sac • (1%) <Har's Adornments>

arachite hatchling [1] (26% each) Weak Arachite Silk, Arachite Silk Gland • (1%) <Into the Woods>

arachite priest [15] (45%) Spider-Carved Jade • (57%) Strong Arachite Silk • (45%) Crystalized Amber • (0.3%) <Thief's Nest Egg> • (1.4%) Lashed Web Hauberk ***or*** Legs • (1.4%) Spined Spear

arachite priest [16] (60%) Jewels 40 • (60%) Strong Arachite Silk • (5%) Spider-Claw Arrows • (0.3%) <Thief's Nest Egg> • (1.4%) Lashed Web Gloves ***or*** Helm • (1.4%) Forgotten Svartalf Sword

arachite shadowslinker [13] (70% each) Arachite Egg Sac, Woven Silk Collar • (72%) Strong Arachite Silk • (4%) Spider-Claw Arrows • (0.3%) <Brendig's Gear> • (1.4%) Lashed Web Gloves ***or*** Helm • (1.4%) Spined Spear

arachite shadowslinker [15] (40%) Jewels 40 • (60%) Strong Arachite Silk • (35%) Woven Silk Collar • (4%) Spider-Claw Arrows • (0.3%) <Thief's Nest Egg> • (1.4%) Lashed Web Hauberk ***or*** Legs • (1.4%) Forgotten Svartalf Sword

arachite weblasher [14] (55%) Strong Arachite Silk • (60%) Spider-Carved Jade • (15%) Arachite Silk Cloak • (5%) Spider-Claw Arrows • (0.3%) <Brendig's Gear> • (1.4%) Lashed Web Sleeves ***or*** Boots • (1.4%) Spined Spear

arachite weblasher [16] *see arachite priest [16]*

Arakane [9] *see arachite shadowslinker [13]*

Baron Falwur [22] (40% each) Silver Moon Circlet, Jeweled Wolf's Head Necklace • (25% each) Thick Pristine Werewolf Pelt, Silver Full Moon Collar • (3%) APOA: Noble Supple

black mauler cub [0] (60%) Mauler Cub Teeth • (10%) Small Mauler Skin

black mauler juvenile [5] (51%) Small Mauler Skin • (25%) Mauler Claw

Black Rixtas [16] *see arachite priest [16]*

brittle skeleton [0] (25% each) Shattered Skull, Yellowed Bone Beads • (5% each piece) Tattered Padded and Mjuklaedar • (1%) <Into the Woods>

carrion crawler [6] (45% each) Lump of Carrion, Dead Rabbit, Tawny Lynx Meat, Chunk of Wolf Meat

carrion eater [7] (48% each) Lump of Carrion, Dead Rabbit • (70% each) Tawny Lynx Meat, Chunk of Wolf Meat

carrion lizard [3] (23%) Diseased Claw • (70%) Rotting Carrion

childer arachite [14] (no loot)

corpse eater [11,13] (50% each) Corpse Eater Leg, Chunk of Rotting Flesh, Death Mask • (1.5%) Decayed Bone Ring

dark hound [17/18] (60%) Dark Hound Pelt • (60/67%) Dark Hound Ear • (40/20%) Collar of Dark Mist • (60/70%) Chunk of Dark Hound Meat

death spider [18] (42%) Death Spider Head • (50%) Caustic Venom Gland • (30%) Multifaceted Eye

decaying norseman [11] (20%) Jewels 40 • (1.3%) APOA: Decaying • (0.3%) <Brendig's Gear> • (1.3% each) Noble Supple Helm *or* Decayed Bone Ring

decaying troll [10] (70% each) Troll Skull, Rotting Troll Hide • (30%) Decaying Troll Paw • (1.4% each) Decaying Hammer, Decayed Bone Ring • (0.5%) <Grimnir's Adornment>

Dolph Domr [13] (no loot)

Dreadkane Dwarfeater [21] *see arachite weblasher [14]*

Dysdera Dwarfeater [21] *see arachite weblasher [14]*

entrancing dirge [21] (20%) Shimmering Sapphire Bone Flute • (75% each) Silken Shroud, Crystal Teardrop Pendant • (0.3%) <Great Balls O' Fire> • (1.4%) APOA: Noble Supple • (1.4%) Noble Wanderer's Axe

envy drakeling [9] (68% each) Envy Drakeling Hide, Tail

fragile skeleton [3] (75%) Jewels 45 • (8% each piece) Tattered Padded and Mjuklaedar • (1%) <Into the Woods>

ghost light [7] (65%) Round Sapphire • (80% each) Square Aquamarine, Small Green Topaz

giant bull frog [1] (60%) Frog Legs

gray worg [10] (20%; hi-lo) Shredded, Bloodied *or* Pristine Worg Skin • (45%) Worg's Head

great tingler [16/18] (45/35%) Tingler Mandible • (45/40%) Chitin • (25/40%) Tingler Claw • (20/40%) Multifaceted Eye

Great Worg [16] (48%) Worg's Head • (25%; hi-lo) Shredded, Bloodied *or* Pristine Worg Skin

green serpent [2] (48%) Green Serpent Skin

Haglion [18] (50% each) Werewolf Hide, Paw, Silver Werewolf Fang • (25%) Silver Full Moon Collar • (3%) APOA: Noble Supple • (0.3%) <Thief's Nest Egg> • (1.4%) Noble Wanderer's Axe

Haglion's minion [16] (50%) Werewolf Hide • (35% each) Silver Full Moon Pin, Werewolf Paw • (1.4%) Noble Supple Boots, Gauntlets *or* Helm • (0.3%) <Thief's Nest Egg> • (1.4%) Noble Wanderer's Axe

haunt [7] (20% each) Rusty Slave's Collar, Obsidian Stone • (40%) Small Silver Nugget • (1%) <Har's Adornments>

hobgoblin fish-catcher [0] (55%) Dead Fish • (80% each) Fishing Pole, Fishing Hook

hobgoblin pincher [4] (80% each) a Hook Shaped Earring, Flat Round Rock • (60%) a Little Hobgoblin Finger • (65%) Garnet Chip • (1%) <Into the Woods>

hobgoblin snagger [2] (60%) Shiny Metal Pin • (80%) Little Hobgoblin Toe • (70%) Flat Round Rock • (50%) a Hook Shaped Earring • (1%) <Into the Woods>

hobgoblin snake-finder [1] (50%) Patched Old Sack • (5%) Jewels 45 • (1%) <Into the Woods>

hog-nose slither [0] (15%) Snake Meat • (40%) Snake's Head

horse [55] (75%) Horse Hair • (10%) Auburn Mane • (80%) Ruined Horse Skin • (35%) Horse Skin • (60%) Horse Hair

Howl [20] (40%) Pristine Dark Hound Pelt • (80%) Dark Hound Ear • (65%) Collar of Dark Mist • (90%) Chunk of Dark Hound Meat

Joseph Domr [14] (no loot)

Kobold Dirge [10] (no loot)

Lieutenant Salurn [16] (no loot)

Lone Weeping Willow [10] *see weeping willow [12]*

lupine snarler [2] (95%) Lupine Skin

minor werewolf noble [19] (50% each) Thick Pristine Werewolf Pelt, Silver Moon Circlet • (40%) Silver Werewolf Fang • (1.4%) Noble Supple Jerkin, Leggings *or* Sleeves • (0.3%) <Great Balls O' Fire> • (1.4%) Noble Wanderer's Axe

minor werewolf noble [21] (40% each) Silver Werewolf Fang, Silver Full Moon Collar • (20%) Thick Pristine Werewolf Pelt • (1.4%) Noble Supple Boots, Gauntlets *or* Helm • (0.3%) <Great Balls O' Fire> • (1.4%) Noble Wanderer's Axe

mora dancer [14/16] (35% each) Silken Veil, Bag of Dark Powder • (20% each) Dream Stone, Black Metal Choker • (1.4%) Ornate *or* Jeweled Bracer, *or* Ornate Studded Vest • (0.3%) <Thief's Nest Egg> • (1.4%) Lashed Web Hauberk *or* Legs/Gloves *or* Helm

mora rider [15] (35% each) Silken Veil, Bag of Dark Powder • (20% each) Dream Stone, Black Metal Choker • (1.4%) Ornate *or* Jeweled Bracer, *or* Ornate Studded Vest • (0.3%) <Thief's Nest Egg> • (1.4%) Lashed Web Sleeves *or* Boots

Morana [18] (35% each) Silken Veil, Bag of Dark Powder • (20% each) Dream Stone, Black Metal Choker • (1.4%) Ornate *or* Jeweled Bracer, *or* Ornate Studded Vest • (0.3%) <Thief's Nest Egg> • (1.4%) Lashed Web Gloves *or* Helm

myrkcat [3] (45%) Myrkcat Skin • (25%) Myrkcat Claw

Nik [20] (no loot)

Niswen [20] (no loot)

Njessi [22] (30%) Virulent Green Eye • (40%) Envy Stone • (50%) Spiteful Black Heart

Noble Werewolf Alina [21] *see minor werewolf noble [19]*

Ove Alfevson [21] *see minor werewolf noble [19]*

pine imp [6] (75%) Pine Talisman • (70%) Pine Cone • (50%) Knobby Root • (30%) Crystalized Pine Sap

Priest Thaxtix [18] (50% each) Crystalized Amber, Strong Arachite Silk • (10%) Spider-Claw Arrows • (40% each) Arachite Silk Cloak, Spider-Carved Jade • (0.3%) <Thief's Nest Egg> • (1.3%) Lashed Web Hauberk *or* Legs • (1.3%) Lashed Web Sleeves *or* Boots • (1.3%) Lashed Web Gloves *or* Helm

Ralsen [16] (no loot)

Red Dagger [14-15,19-20] (no loot)

Ria [13] (no loot)

ridgeback worg [11/13] (20/25%; hi-lo) Shredded, Bloodied *or* Pristine Worg Skin • (32/48% each) Worg's Paw, Tooth

roaming dirge [8] (84%) Dirge Scraps • (2.7%) APOA: of the Wanderer • (0.3%) APOA: of the Old Wanderer • (1.5%) Wanderer's Spirit Staff • (0.5%) <Har's Adornments>

Salix [14] (10%) Shimmering Am Willow Dirge Flute • (12%) Pulsing Rotwood Heart • (30%) Supple Willow Branch • (0.5%) <Brendig's Gear>

sapherd [5] (75%) Pile of Seeds

scavenger [1] (20%) Chunk of Meat • (60% each) Chewed Bone, Dead Bird

shadow [10-11] (40%) Globe of Black Mist • (20% each) Black Glass Earring, Bracelet of Black Mist, Black Glowing Crystal • (1.3%) APOA: Decaying • (1.3% each) Decaying Hammer, Decayed Bone Ring • (0.3%) <Grimnir's Adornment>

sharpfang worg [12/14] (20/30%; hi-lo) Shredded, Bloodied *or* Pristine Worg Skin • (43/50% each) Worg's Paw, Tooth

shrieking willow [18] (30%) Pulsing Rotwood Heart • (15%) Shimmering Willow Dirge Flute • (45%) Supple Willow Branch • (3%) Willow Branch Arrows • (0.3%) <Thief's Nest Egg> • (hi-lo) Shredded, Bloodied *or* Pristine Worg Skin

Sorrow [22] (25%) Shimmering Am Bone Flute • (50% each) Silken Shroud, Crystal Teardrop Pendant • (0.3%) <Great Balls O' Fire> • (3%) APOA: Noble Supple

soul sinker [16] (40% each) Black Soul Stone, Onyx Ring • (70%) Kobold Skull Cup • (1.4%) APOA: Svartalf Padded • (1.4%) Spined Spear • (0.3%) <Thief's Nest Egg>

spectral bayer [13] Gnawed-Upon Bone • (70% each) Bone Bayer Skull, Bayer Fang • (40%) Skeletal Paw

spectral hog [2] (26%) Frigid Hog's Tusk • (23%) Pallid Hog's Hoof

spook [6] *see haunt [7]*

Su'Valkur [18] (70% each) Worg-Hide Pouch, Pouch of Food • (30% each) Human Bone Necklace, Human-Hide Belt • (0.3%) <Thief's Nest Egg> • (1.4%) Svartalf Padded Vest *or* Pants • (1.4%) Forgotten Svartalf Sword

svartalf chanter [14] (40%) Amethyst • (41%) Carnelian • (70%) Chryoprase • (60%) Bloodstone • (0.3%) <Brendig's Gear>

svartalf hunter [14-15] *see svartalf chanter [14]*

svartalf outcast [8] (55%) Lynx Pelt Bag • (70%) Copper Amber Pin • (75%) Small Packet of Food • (0.5%) <Har's Adornments>

svartalf predator [16] (70% each) Worg-Hide Pouch, Pouch of Food • (30%) Human Bone Necklace • (0.3%) <Thief's Nest Egg> • (1.4%) Svartalf Padded Vest *or* Pants • (1.4%) Forgotten Svartalf Sword

svartalf sorcerer [15] (70%) Fiery Red Stone • (40%) Troll Tooth Earring • (75%) Troll-Hide Bag • (0.3%) <Brendig's Gear> • (1.4%) Svartalf Padded Sleeves *or* Gloves • (1.4%) Forgotten Svartalf Sword

svartalf watcher [13] (40%) Pouch of Food • (45%) Troll-Hide Bag • (60%) Scrying Mirror • (0.3%) <Brendig's Gear> • (1.4%) Svartalf Padded Cap *or* Boots • (1.4%) Forgotten Svartalf Sword

svartskogsfru [17] (85%) Wand of Twisted Wood • (30%) Leaf and Twig Crown • (80%) Bracelet of Bark • (0.3%) <Thief's Nest Egg>

Ta'Thaliur [17] (60%) Troll-Hide Bag • (50% each) Troll Tooth Earring, Fiery Red Stone • (40%) Troll Hide Bracelet • (0.3%) <Thief's Nest Egg> • (1.4%) Svartalf Padded Sleeves *or* Gloves • (1.4%) Forgotten Svartalf Sword

Taldos [11] (no loot)

Taldos' companion [11] (no loot)

tawny lynx [8] (33%) Tawny Pelt • (60% each) Lynx Claw, Tawny Lynx Meat • (40%) Lynx Skull

tawny lynx cub [0] (55%) Small Lynx Skin

Tikixis [6] (35% each) Sticky Arachite Silk, Arachite Silk Gland • (50%) Arachite Egg Sac • (1%) <Har's Adornments>

tingler [12] (45%) Tingler Mandible • (25% each) Tingler Chitin, Claw

tingler webmother [19] (50% each) Tingler Claw, Chitin • (27%) Multifaceted Eye (x2)

undead armswoman [13] (20%) Jewels 40 • (1.3%) APOA: Decaying • (0.3%) <Brendig's Gear> • (1.3% each) Decaying Hammer, Decayed Bone Ring

undead explorer [3] (25%) Obsidian Stone • (15%) Hand-Tooled Belt • (1%; all or none) a Suit of Tattered Shimmering Studded armor, Huntsman's Cloak, Pitted Shimmering Battle Axe

undead scout [10] (no loot)

undead woodcarver [4] (25%) Obsidian Stone • (15% each) Hand-Tooled Belt, Unfinished Carving • (1%) <Into the Woods>

venomspitter [11/13] (40/50% each) Venomspitter Skin, Tail • (55/75%) Venomspitter's Head

wayward ghoul [4] (40%) Patch of Decayed Hair • (20%) Jewels 45 • (1%) <Into the Woods>

weeping willow [12] (5%) Bright Stone Willow Dirge Flute • (10%) Pulsing Rotwood Heart • (30%) Supple Willow Branch • (0.5%) <Brendig's Gear>

werewolf [17] (50% each) Werewolf Hide, Paw • (40%) Silver Full Moon Pin • (1.4%) Noble Supple Boots, Gauntlets *or* Helm • (0.3%) <Thief's Nest Egg> • (1.4%) Noble Wanderer's Axe

Widower [20] (50% each) Caustic Venom Gland, Death Spider Head • (52%) Multifaceted Eye

wild hog [2] (35% each) Curly Hog Tail, Small Hog Hoof • (50% each) Small Hog Tusk, Hide

wind wisp [9] (80%) Round Sapphire (x2) • (70%) Clear Blue Orb

wood imp [5] (70%) Pine Branch • (50%) Pile of Seeds • (45%) Twisting Vine • (40%) Knobby Root • (1%) <Rig's Lament>

Yip [4] (no loot)

Ykkat [17] (64%) Spider-Carved Jade • (45%) Strong Arachite Silk • (70%) Arachite Silk Cloak • (8%) Spider-Claw Arrows • (0.3%) <Thief's Nest Egg> • (1.3%) Lashed Web Hauberk *or* Legs • (1.3%) Lashed Web Sleeves *or* Boots • (1.3%) Lashed Web Gloves *or* Helm

young envy drake [20/22] (45/30%) Virulent Green Eye • (35/40%) Envy Stone • (25/50%) Spiteful Black Heart

(Myrkwood Forest Leveling Guide, cont. from page 156)

Solo Levelling Tips

You can stay in Myrkwood Forest and go all the way to 20 without leaving your home zone.

1-5 Pretty much anything around Galplen. It's pretty well designed in that the closer you are to Galpaln, the easier the critters are. The farther away you get, the tougher the monsters are.

5-7 These levels are mostly in the south, near the road. The higher your level is, the farther south you go. At first, after you get your 5th level under your belt, take on the bears and wood imps. When that gets too easy, wander a little farther afield and try envy drakelings and tawny lynxes. After those, head farther south and look for shadows and undead trolls.

After a while, go for hill people, carrion crawlers or try hanging out at the Tomte camps.

8 Now you get a little more variety in your travel. Look around for Tomte camps, spooks, haunts, and ghost lights. For a little flesh-and-blood adventure, try carrion crawlers and eaters.

10 One place to start is with the Svartalfs on the island. They should be fine for a level 10. Also check out the wind wisps and envy drakelings. They don't take much, and they give good loot. Be careful, though. It's possible to get careless since most of the early-level monsters don't BAF. Now that you're level 10, BAF becomes a distinct possibility.

11-12 Around Gna Faste you can hunt grey worgs and undead trolls. Another alternative is trying a go-round with the weeping willows (nukers) and shadows.

Be sure to ask the guard in the tower for kill tasks ... even if they send you to seriously camped places, you'll still do level faster than normal.

13-14 At these levels you should try mora dancers. They have nice 1-time drops and don't take too much out of you. Extra nice is that they don't drop a lot of heavy stuff, so you can stay out longer between trips to the store.

16-17 At these levels, look at mora riders, they should con blue to level 17. Blues give nice xp, and yellows aren't bad, either.

18-21 Great tinglers and werewolves will finish off your journey to level 21.

Raumarik Tips

Solo Levelling Tips

It's possible to do lower-level advancement, but you've got to be careful and stay close to cities.

40-50 Bloodfelags and shrieking willows

40-50 Raumarik is good xp and fun, but it's tough. It's fun because it's a challenge, with plenty of scary stuff.

47-50 Icestrider Interceptors. Stick to the unlinked ones. Casters, low hp.

48-50 Low Wraiths. Added bonus, they drop cloth. I'm pretty sure wraithes don't drop cloth; you have to take out Liches. They con orange, red, and purple at 50, so I don't know how viable they are at 48/49.

Raumarik Loot

chillsome wight [51/52] (18%) Frozen Waterskin • (2%) Carved Ice Totem • (1%) Chillsome Icebound Gloves/Legs • (0.5%) Frozen Windswept Axe • (0.5%) Rigid Wight Claw/Band of Ice

dire wolverine [58] (18%) Snowy Wolverine Pelt • (2%) Pristine Snowy Wolverine Pelt

enhorning [50-51] (18%) Enhorning Hide • (2%) Pristine Enhorning Hide

frore lich [55/56/57] (18%) Frosty Bandages • (2%) Frost-Rimmed Silver Cup • (1.7%) Snow Crystal Boots ***or*** Gloves/Cap ***or*** Vest/Sleeves ***or*** Pants • (1.7%) Snow Crystal Runecarver's Staff [55-56], Snow Crystal Summoner's Staff [56-57] ***or*** Icebound Spellbook

frost stallion [54-55] (18%) Frosty Hide • (2%) Pristine Frosty Hide

fylgja [50-51] (18%) Fylgja Pelt • (2%) Pristine Fylgja Pelt

Hagall the Red Dagger [58] (no loot)

icestrider interceptor [47/48/49/50/51] (18%) Icestrider Leg • (2%) Icestrider Mandible • (10%) Jewels 36 [47-50]/Jewels 06 [51] • (1.7%) Twilight-Mail Boots ***or*** Gloves [47,50]/Coif ***or*** Leggings [48,51]/Hauberk ***or*** Sleeves [49] • (1.7%) Twilight Battle Crusher [47]/Cleaver [48]/Soul Searer [49]/Impaler [50]/Doombringer [51] ***or*** Shadowsteel Orb [47]/Lattice [48,50]/Twisted Lattice [49,51]

Major Terentius [52] (no loot)

mature wyvern [54-57] (18%) Mature Wyvern Hide • (2%) Pristine Mature Wyvern Hide

Oona [65] (no loot)

Raumarik Revenent [70] (10% each) Elder Staff of Iceshadow, Icy Sundering, Frozen Runes, Windy Calling

Red Dagger [46] (no loot)

Red Dagger lookout [41] (no loot)

Red Hagen [53] (no loot)

savage wyvern [45-47] (18%) Wyvern Hide • (2%) Pristine Wyvern Hide • (8%) Malefic Tooth

sleipneirsson [55-56] (18%) Sleipneirson Hide • (2%) Pristine Sleipneirson Hide

undead soldier [49] (no loot)

white wolf [28-29] (18%) White Wolf Pelt • (2%) Snowy White Wolf Pelt

white wolf [30-31] (18%) Large White Wolf Pelt • (2%) Pristine White Wolf Pelt

windswept wraith [50/51/52/53] (18%) Orb of Wind • (2%) Pulsing Orb of Wind • (1%) Chillsome Icebound Boots/Helm/Sleeves/Hauberk • (0.5%) Frozen Windswept Axe • (0.5%) Band of Ice

winter wolf [42-43] (18%) Winter Wolf Pelt • (2%) Perfect White Wolf Pelt • (8%) Malefic Tooth

winter wolf [44-45] (18%) Large Winter Wolf Pelt • (2%) Pristine Winter Wolf Pelt • (8%) Malefic Tooth

winter wolf [46] (18%) Icy Winter Wolf Pelt • (2%) Pristine Icy Wolf Pelt • (8%) Malefic Tooth

Wretch of Winter [70] (20%) Ring of Hoarfrost • (10% each) Frozen Tree Splitter ***or*** Double-Bladed Ice Razor

Wretch of Winter [71] (30%) Skrunken Ribcage • (15% each) Frozen, Great Ice Claw

Wretch of Winter [72] (30%) Belt of Glacial Might • (15% each) Ice Breaker, Great Ice Breaker

Wretch of Winter [73] (45%) Frozen Tundra Walker's Mantle • (23% each) Spirit of Prey, Ice Bone Prey Killer

Wretch of Winter [74] (30% each) Icebound Buckler, Jewel of Raumarik, Icebound Protector

Wretch of Winter [75] (45% each) Icebound Warshield, Necklace of Hoarfrost

Raumarik

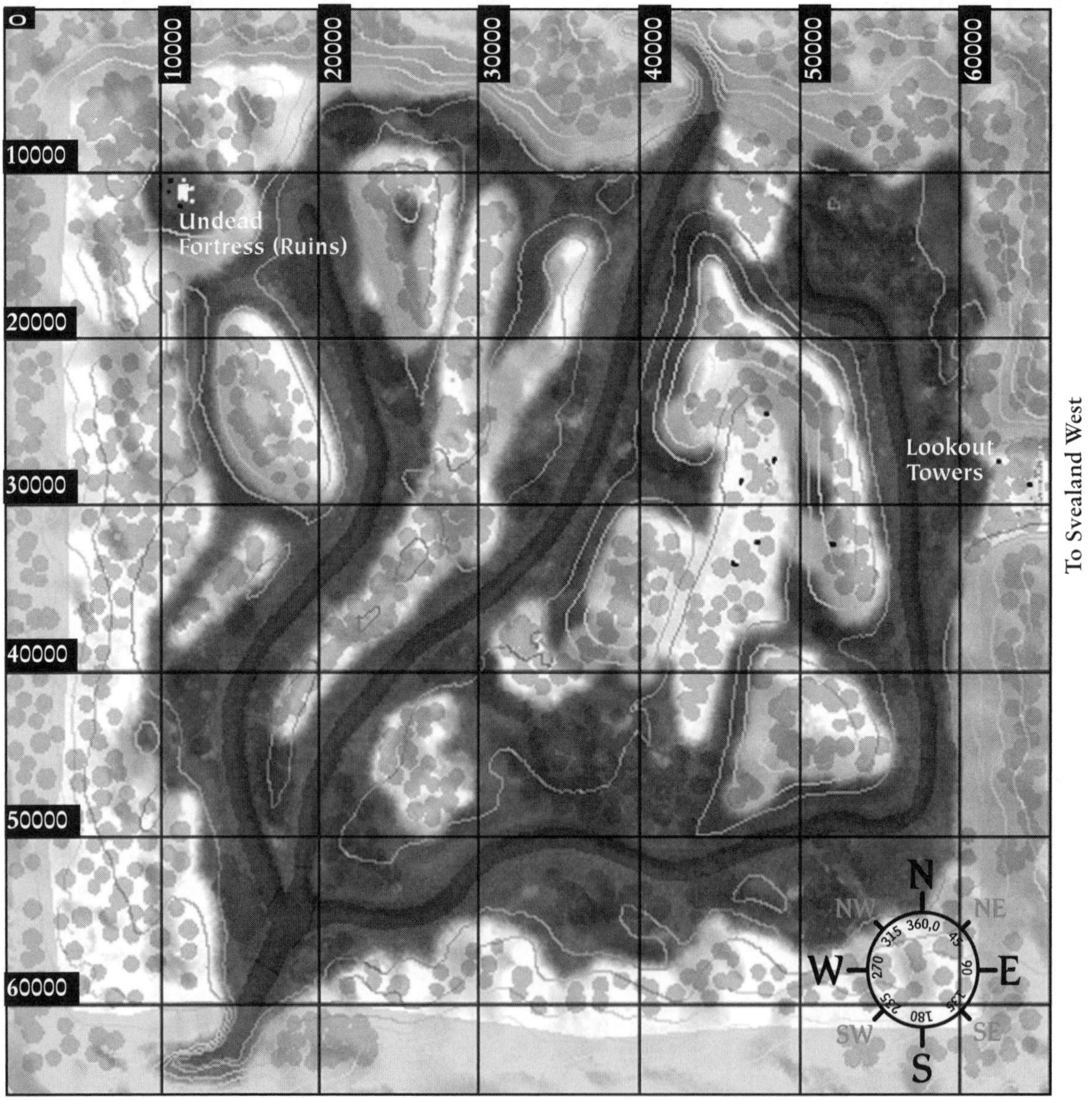

Undead Fortress (Ruins)

Lookout Towers

To Svealand West

Raumarik Tips and Loot on Page 159.

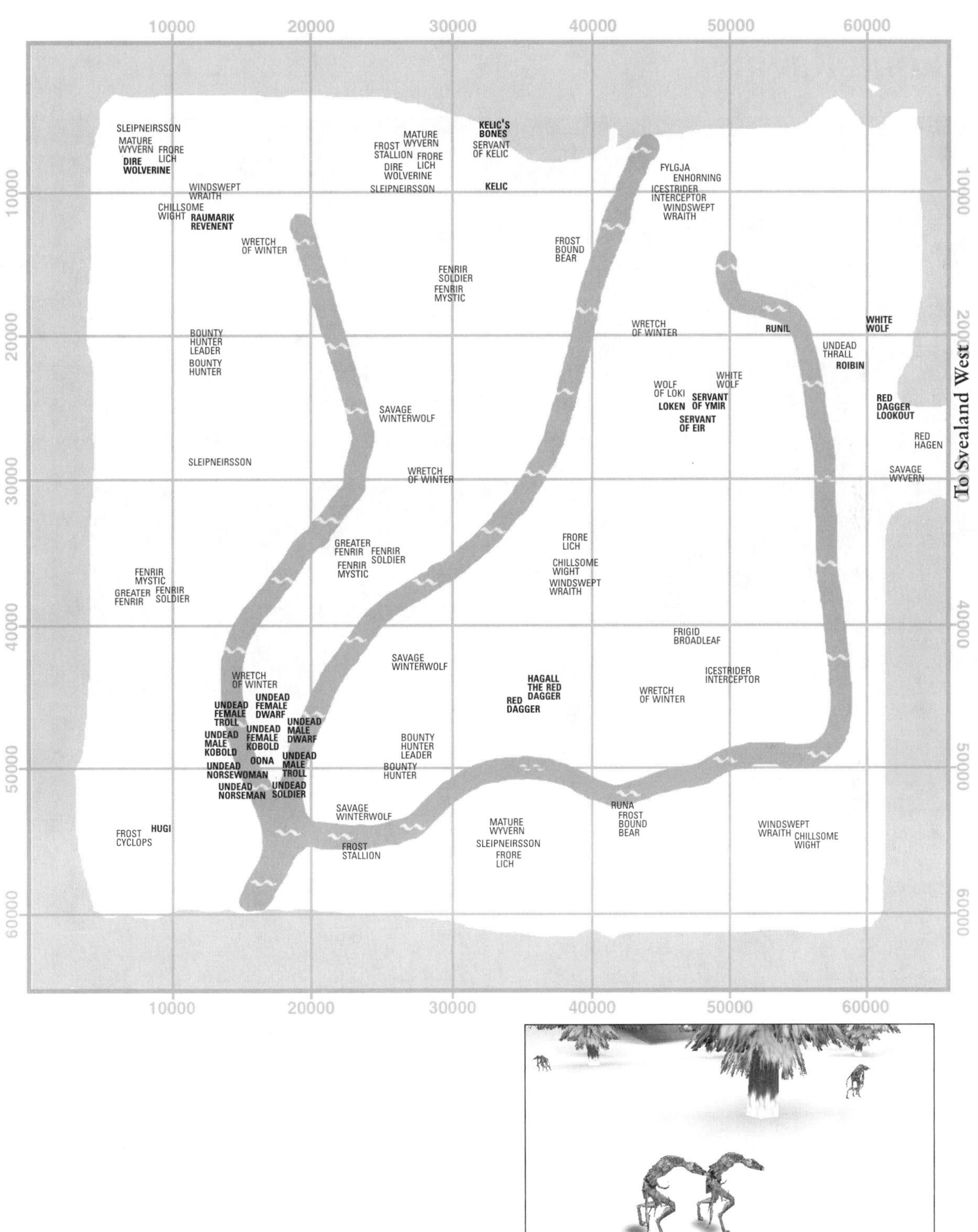

10000
20000
30000
40000
50000
60000
SLEIPNEIRSSON
MATURE WYVERN
FRORE LICH
DIRE WOLVERINE
MATURE WYVERN
FROST STALLION
FRORE LICH
DIRE WOLVERINE
KELIC'S BONES
SERVANT OF KELIC
SLEIPNEIRSSON
KELIC
WINDSWEPT WRAITH
CHILLSOME WIGHT
RAUMARIK REVENENT
FYLGJA
ENHORNING
ICESTRIDER INTERCEPTOR
WINDSWEPT WRAITH
WRETCH OF WINTER
FROST BOUND BEAR
FENRIR SOLDIER
FENRIR MYSTIC
BOUNTY HUNTER LEADER
BOUNTY HUNTER
WRETCH OF WINTER
RUNIL
WHITE WOLF
UNDEAD THRALL
ROIBIN
WHITE WOLF
WOLF OF LOKI
LOKEN
SERVANT OF YMIR
SERVANT OF EIR
SAVAGE WINTERWOLF
RED DAGGER LOOKOUT
RED HAGEN
SLEIPNEIRSSON
WRETCH OF WINTER
SAVAGE WYVERN
To Svealand West
GREATER FENRIR
FENRIR SOLDIER
FENRIR MYSTIC
FRORE LICH
CHILLSOME WIGHT
WINDSWEPT WRAITH
FENRIR MYSTIC
GREATER FENRIR
FENRIR SOLDIER
FRIGID BROADLEAF
SAVAGE WINTERWOLF
ICESTRIDER INTERCEPTOR
WRETCH OF WINTER
HAGALL THE RED DAGGER
RED DAGGER
WRETCH OF WINTER
UNDEAD FEMALE DWARF
UNDEAD FEMALE TROLL
UNDEAD MALE DWARF
UNDEAD FEMALE KOBOLD
UNDEAD MALE KOBOLD
BOUNTY HUNTER LEADER
OONA
UNDEAD MALE TROLL
UNDEAD NORSEWOMAN
BOUNTY HUNTER
UNDEAD NORSEMAN
UNDEAD SOLDIER
SAVAGE WINTERWOLF
RUNA
FROST BOUND BEAR
FROST CYCLOPS
HUGI
MATURE WYVERN
SLEIPNEIRSSON
FRORE LICH
FROST STALLION
WINDSWEPT WRAITH
CHILLSOME WIGHT

Skona Ravine

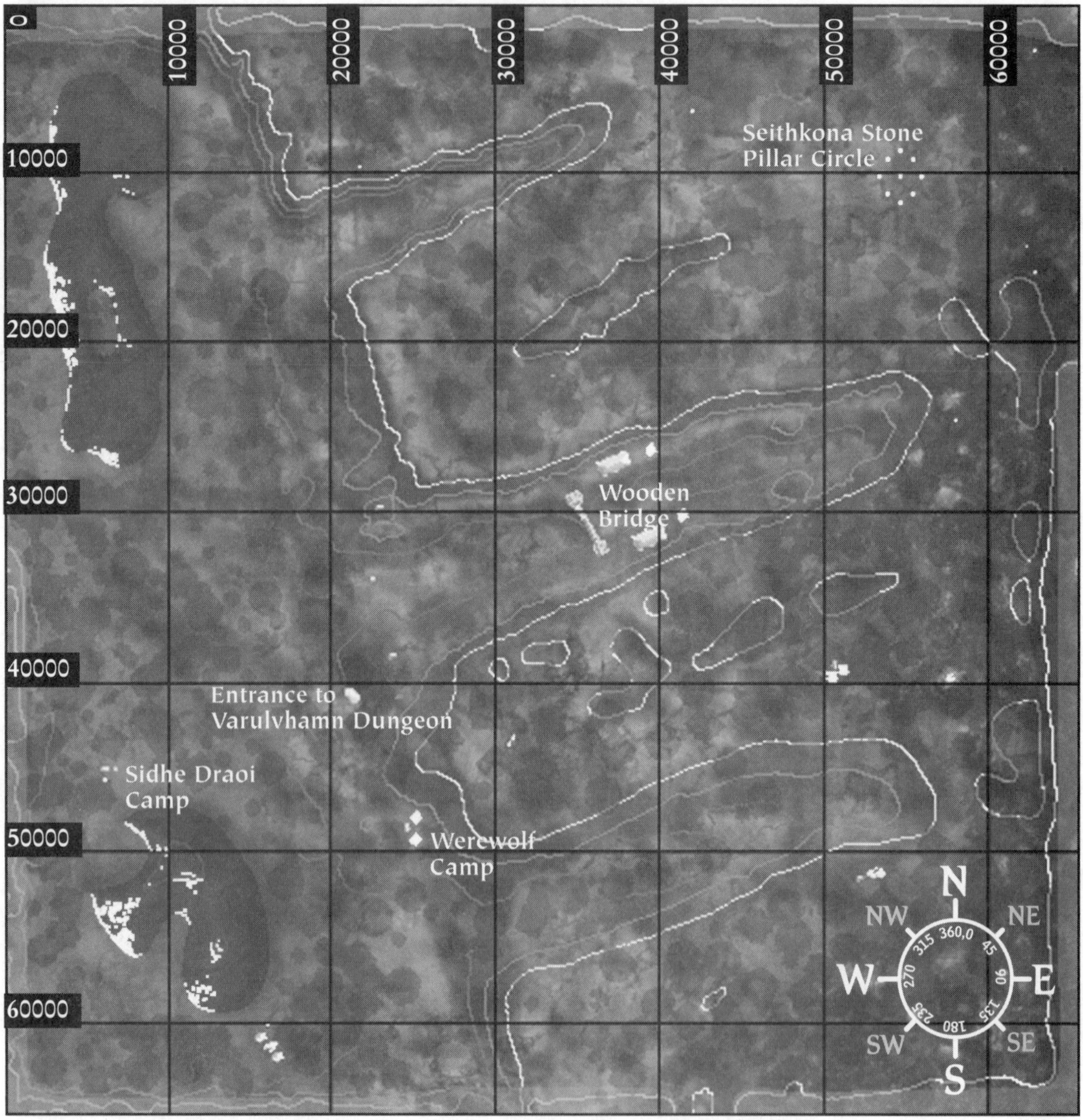
0
10000
20000
30000
40000
50000
60000
10000
20000
30000
40000
50000
60000
Seithkona Stone
Pillar Circle
Wooden
Bridge
Entrance to
Varulvhamn Dungeon
Sidhe Draoi
Camp
Werewolf
Camp
N
NE
E
SE
S
SW
W
NW
360,0
45
90
135
180
225
270
315

To Vanern Swamp

To Myrkwood Forest

To Malmohus

Lower-level monsters not shown on map:

Creature	Lvl	Location
Avund	22	SE
black mauler	14	NC,SC
dryad blossom	20	EC,SE
dryad greenthumb	21	SE
Elf of Gashir	20	NW
envy drakeling	9	EC
giant tree frog	20	NE,EC
giant tree frog	21	NC,NE,EC
gray worg	10	NE
great tingler	18	NC,NE,EC
invis mob for Q2044	0	NW
Korban	18	NE
Krrrck	22	NE
minor wwlf. noble	19	SE
minor wwlf. noble	21	SE
moss maiden	24	NW,NC,WC,SC
perfidious pook	10	NE,EC
Pfapfnur	22	SE
pine mephit	23	NW,NC,SC
Priestess of Gashir	20	NW
seithkona	14	NE
seithkona	15	NE
shrieking willow	18	NE
skogsfru	14	NC,SC

Creature	Lvl	Location	Creature	Lvl	Location	Creature	Lvl	Location	Creature	Lvl	Location
stordo werewolf	13	NE	werewolf	17	NE,EC	wood mephit	22	NC,SC,SE	young envy drake	20	SE
Stripe	24	SC	werewolf runner	21	NE,EC,SE	wood rat	24	NW,NC,WC,SC	young envy drake	22	SC,SE
Tradalva	21	SE	werewolf skulker	23	NC	woodland badger	22	NC,NE,EC, SC,SE	y. silverscale drake	22	SC,SE
Tradman	22	SE	werewolf skulker	24	NC,SC	woodland badger	23	NW,NC,NE,SC			
treekeep	22	SE	Witch	22	NW						

Skona Ravine Tips

Group Friendly? Yes

Don't tackle which creatures alone? Werewolf commanders in the huts/houses near the bridge that crosses the ravine.

Who hates this area? No one, there is something there for every class

Who loves this area? 21–40. Great for soloing, and very group-friendly.

Other Notes. Unlike Myrkwood Forest, this zone is more open; it's easier to see what's going on around you.

When soloing, keep an eye out for wandering werewolf warders. They're casters and easy to beat, but if you're caught off guard while soloing the outcome of the fight might be shaky.

If you're soloing or even in a group, keep on your toes while hunting the dryads. They are very social and will BAF, and they can be very swarmy in group situations. Crowd control is nice to have on hand when hunting these guys.

The creatures in this zone drop a lot of vendor items (hunks of meat, pelts, etc.). The closest place to sell your loot is Gna Faste in Myrkwood.

It start getting good around 28 with ww warders, then guards, and then willows.

These monsters con orange, move slowly (other than that they look just like wildings), and are nearly never camped. It's possible to score one million plus experience (with 250k of it from camp bonus). Location is good in case there is a group forming in Varul dungeon

Solo Levelling Tips

19-23 Shrieking willows are the best for this level, although RC or Supp nukes don't do the damage they normally do, due to a tree's resistance to energy attacks. You can find a bunch of them just south of Gna Faste.

21-23 There's a nest of envy drakes that you'll find are pretty easy to kill, sometimes even if it looks like it will be out of your range. You get there by taking the road that goes to the werewolf fort, then going behind the fort and going along the shore for a little ways. The only problem is that they spawn quickly, so you can wear out the camp bonus without trying. Also good for level 22 would be the treekeeps and dryad blossoms that live in the south east corner of Skona Ravine.

And, of course, more shrieking willows. There are three major places to find shrieking willows. One is near the log at the peninsula south of the WW fort. It's better if you stay close to the log, and don't let the dirges get you. Another is sort of northwest from the ww fort, near a hill with old stones on it. There's plenty there to keep you busy for a while. There's another one to the south, although it's difficult to get there because there are higher level dirges and moras in the way, but you can avoid those.

23-24 More trees! Look for the ra of pine and the ra of Oak at the top of the hill southwest of Varulvheim. You can also look to the north side of the northernmost ravine for some pine mephits, rats and wolverines. That will be enough to keep you busy for a while.

24-28 These are the levels when you want to hunt werewolves as much as you can. Not only is it good hunting (you can pull ww one at a time forever, practically) but it really helps your reputation with the local races. The more werewolves you kill, the easier it is for you to go adventuring in Midgard. Varulvheim and Spindelhalla are much easier to survive if you don't have the svartalfs, arachites and wolfaurs aggroing all over you every time you stick your head underground. Even if you don't care about reputation, and you should, it's still a source of good xp. Werewolf skulkers usually have good camp bonuses, as well.

Also good at these levels are tree spirits, cats, ratss, wolverines and certain mephits.

Werewolf warders have nice drops, and have the typical casters' low hp.

29-32 There's a small hill towards the center (a little north) of the zone that has a nice cluster of tree spirits. It's especially nice that there are two groups, so you can switch back and forth to keep the camp bonus up.

33-36 Werewolf Guards are good at this level. You can hunt around the dungeon entrance, near the tower, and also a little east of there. They are in a few different places: guarding the ravine above the bridge ... both sides ... and then near the tower in the west side. These are actually dangerous because there's a patrol that will come by eventually. However, there's a few more down the hill, and those are out of range of the patrol. Whatever you do, don't underestimate these guys. Keep your escape route in mind, and if you get an add, turn tail and run into the dungeon. However, as long as they are neutral or better, they won't add.

The farther east in the ravines you go, the tougher the guards. As you increase your level, look around for a ww or wolfaur gladiator, those give good xp.

Skona Ravine Loot on Page 166.

Quest NPCs

Audliten	
Aleaniver	A Deed of Old (lvl 7)
Dahn	The Red Dagger (lvl Guild Track - 25)
Gwaell	Tomte Jerkin (lvl 5)
Lefur	Ghoul Hair Belt (lvl 5)
Dvalin	
Aesirdia	Covet Wiley (lvl 11)
Vasudheim	
Alomali	Copious Striders (lvl 2)
Alomali	Klippa's Claw (lvl 11)
Arnlief	Krrrck's Torment (lvl 22)
Frimeth	Hole of the Dead (lvl 6)
Greidash	Sveabone Hilt Sword (lvl 1)
Kyba	Svartmoln's Appetite (lvl 6)
Saeunn	Letter to Sveck (lvl 3)
Tric	Tric's Lost List (lvl 4)
your trainer	Troubled Wild (lvl 1)
Outside Vasudheim	
Thrall Keeper	Brutal Chains (lvl 4)

Skona Rav. Loot

Ash Tree [33] (70%) Bloodstone • (80%) Green Jasper • (53%) Bloodstone Ring • (0.3%) <Freya's Dowry>

Askafroa [33] (70%) Bloodstone • (80%) Green Jasper • (53%) Bloodstone Ring • (0.3%) <Freya's Dowry>

Avund [22] (30%) Virulent Green Eye • (40%) Envy Stone • (50%) Spiteful Black Heart

battle-scarred mauler [34/35] (80%) Broken Mauler Fang • (70/72%) Scarred Mauler Paw • (50/68%) Scarred Mauler Pelt

Big Paw [36] (80%) Broken Mauler Fang • (72%) Scarred Mauler Paw • (68%) Scarred Mauler Pelt

black mauler [14] (41%) Mauler Skin • (4.5%) Pristine Mauler Skin • (72%) Mauler Claw(x2) • (1.5%) <Been Mauled>

brush cat [26] (80%) Brush Cat Paw • (69%) Cat Fang • (55%) Brush Cat Ear

brush cat [27] (83%) Cat Fang • (70%) Brush Cat Ear • (64%) Brush Cat Pelt

Caelis Manoi [39] (80%) Wand of Yarrow • (70% each) Sun Pendant, Round Diamond • (0.3%) <Freya's Dowry>

callow wolverine [30/31] (80%) Small Wolverine Paw [30] • (70/76%) Small Wolverine Pelt • (65/80%) Wolverine Meat • (60%) Small Wolverine Tail

Captain Gruff [38] (65%) Large Werewolf Pelt • (77%) Large Werewolf Paw • (60%) Golden Military Chain • (1.5%) <Howling at the Moon> • (0.3%) <Freya's Dowry>

Cargila [38] (70%) Timber Cat Paw • (60%) Timber Cat Meat • (80%) Timber Cat Pelt

dryad blossom [20] (70%) Silvery Petal • (50%) Wooden Totem • (80%) Flower Shaped Pin • (0.3%) <Thief's Nest Egg>

dryad greenthumb [21] (79%) Silvery Petal • (80%) Flower Shaped Pin • (60%) Wooden Totem • (0.3%) <Great Balls O' Fire>

elder skogsfru [32] (70%) Bloodstone • (80%) Green Jasper • (53%) Bloodstone Ring • (0.3%) <Freya's Dowry>

Elf of Gashir [20] (no loot)

envy drakeling [9] (68% each) Envy Drakeling Hide, Tail

Fjalar [37] (60%) Black Star Diopside • (70%) Jasper • (20%) Cat's Eye Opal • (30%) Zircon

Furf [28] (83%) Cat Fang • (70%) Brush Cat Ear • (64%) Brush Cat Pelt

Galar [36] (60%) Black Star Diopside • (70%) Jasper • (20%) Cat's Eye Opal • (30%) Zircon

Gashir [30] (55%) Pearl • (80%) Topaz • (50% each) Chrome Diopside, Green Tourmaline

giant tree frog [20/21] (80%) Giant Frog Legs [20] • (70/80%) Giant Frog Tongue • (55/75%) Giant Frog Eye • (54%) Frog Wart Ring [21]

gray worg [10] (20%; hi-lo) Shredded, Bloodied ***or*** Pristine Worg Skin • (45%) Worg's Head

great tingler [18] (35%) Tingler Mandible • (40% each) Multifaceted Eye, Tingler Chitin, Claw

green orm [38/39/40] (80%) Round Diamond • (69/75/75%) Green Orm Scale • (50/55/67%) Green Orm Fang

Headsman Yantu [37] (70% each) Headsman's Pendant, Iron Shackle • (60%) Headsman's Hood • (0.3%) <Freya's Dowry> • (1.5%) APOA: Claw Forged, ***or*** Wolftooth ***or*** Wolfsclaw Hauberk

Korban [18] (no loot)

Krrrck [22] (80%) Giant Frog Tongue • (54%) Frog Wart Ring • (75%) Giant Frog Eye

Lasaer [26] (50%) Small Werewolf Pelt • (80%) Werewolf Ear • (70%) Werewolf Tongue • (0.3%) <Great Balls O' Fire>

Leildolf [35] (no loot)

Listening Tree [34] (75%) Leafy Willow Branch • (57%) Willow-Carved Emerald • (80%) Heart of Wood • (70%) Willow Leaf Coronet

minor werewolf noble [19/21] (50/20%) Thick Pristine Werewolf Pelt • (50%) Silver Moon Circlet [19] • (40%) Silver Full Moon Collar [21] • (40%) Silver Werewolf Fang • (1.4%) Noble Supple Jerkin, Leggings ***or*** Sleeves/Boots, Gauntlets ***or*** Helm • (0.3%) <Great Balls O' Fire> • (1.4%) Noble Wanderer's Axe

moss maiden [24/25] (39%) Cloak of Moss • (1.2%) Glimmering Mantle • (80/85%) Bag of Moss • (75/85%) Moss-Covered Wand • (0.3%) <Great Balls O' Fire>

Nagoltooth [41] (80%) Wolverine Claw • (72%) Wolverine Tooth • (55%) Wolverine Pelt

Nimh [25] (80%) Rat Paw • (25%) Rat Pelt • (15%) Wood Rat Tail • (23%) Rat Whiskers

Pellinistra [27] (50% each) Thick Pristine Werewolf Pelt, Silver Moon Circlet • (40%) Silver Werewolf Fang • (1.4%) Noble Supple Jerkin, Leggings ***or*** Sleeves • (0.3%) <Great Balls O' Fire> • (1.4%) Noble Wanderer's Axe

perfidious pook [10] (80%) Smooth Blue Stone • (50% each) Clouded Beryl, Yellow Quartz • (85%) Round Sapphire • (0.5%) <Grimnir's Adornment>

Pfapfnur [22] (75%) Silvery Scale • (45%) Blue Topaz • (60%) Yellow Topaz

pine mephit [23] (80%) Wooden Totem • (70%) Leafy Branch • (66%) Leafy Bracelet • (0.3%) <Great Balls O' Fire>

Priestess of Gashir [20] (75%) Carnelian • (60%) Azurite • (40%) Garnet • (80%) Amethyst • (20%) Topaz

ra of oak [30] (80%) Branch of Oak • (70%) Belt of Oak Leaves • (53%) Oak Tree Pendant

ra of pine [29] (60%) Pine Tree Amulet • (62%) Silver Pine Cone Earring • (80%) Wand of Pine

ra of willow [31] (80%) Leafy Willow Branch • (65%) Willow Wood Bracelet • (55%) Willow Leaf Coronet

seithkona [14-15] (no loot)

shrieking willow [18] (30%) Pulsing Rotwood Heart • (15%) Shimmering Willow Dirge Flute • (45%) Supple Willow Branch • (3%) Willow Branch Arrows • (0.3%) <Thief's Nest Egg> • (hi-lo) Shredded, Bloodied ***or*** Pristine Worg Skin

sidhe draoi [36/37/38] (80%) Wand of Yarrow • (59/65/70% each) Sun Pendant, Round Diamond • (0.3%) <Freya's Dowry>

sidhe gaoite [35/36] (53/55%) Round Diamond • (60/70%) Clear Oval Stone • (80%) Cloudy White Gem • (0.3%) <Freya's Dowry>

skogsfru [14] (50%) Amethyst • (41%) Carnelian • (70%) Chryoprase • (60%) Bloodstone • (1.5%) <Strange Threshholds> • (0.3%) <Brendig's Gear>

stordo werewolf [13] (50% each) Werewolf Hide, Paw • (40%) Silver Full Moon Pin • (1.4%) Noble Supple Boots, Gauntlets ***or*** Helm • (0.3%) <Thief's Nest Egg> • (1.4%) Noble Wanderer's Axe

Stripe [24] (40%) Badger Claw • (80%) Badger Tooth • (60%) Ruined Badger Pelt • (41%) Badger Pelt

Thasior [31] (65%) Werewolf Tail • (70%) Medium Werewolf Pelt • (62%) Werewolf Meat • (0.3%) <All Fired Up> • (1.4%) <Alvis's Chest> • (1.4%) <Wolf Loot> • (15%) Warder's Ear

timber cat [36/37] (80%) Timber Cat Fang/Pelt • (65/70%) Timber Cat Paw • (56/60%) Timber Cat Meat

timberland badger [32/33] (80%) Timberland Badger Claw [32] • (65%) Timberland Badger Pelt [33] • (71/80%) Timberland Badger Fang • (50/71%) Timberland Badger Paw • (12%) Badger Stomach

Tradalva [21] (79%) Silvery Petal • (80%) Flower Shaped Pin • (60%) Wooden Totem • (0.3%) <Great Balls O' Fire>

Tradande [28] (60%) Glowing Green Seed • (80%) Seed Pod • (71%) Heart of Wood • (1.5%) <Greenman's Wares> • (0.3%) <All Fired Up>

Tradman [22] (73%) Leafy Branch • (50%) Spiral Twig Ring • (80%) Pouch of Seeds • (9%) Warm Tree Sap

tree spirit [26/27] (50%) Glowing Green Seed • (80%) Seed Pod • (60/71%) Heart of Wood • (1.5%) <Greenman's Wares> • (0.3%) <All Fired Up>

treekeep [22] (73%) Leafy Branch • (50%) Spiral Twig Ring • (80%) Pouch of Seeds • (9%) Warm Tree Sap

Vindvasen [29] (53%) Square-Cut Sapphire • (18%) Cat's Eye Apatite • (70%) Blue Topaz • (1.5%) Wind Swept Pants ***or*** Vest, ***or*** Wind Swept ***or*** Wrapped Staff • (0.3%) <All Fired Up>

werewolf [17] (50% each) Werewolf Hide, Paw • (40%) Silver Full Moon Pin • (1.4%) Noble Supple Boots, Gauntlets ***or*** Helm • (0.3%) <Thief's Nest Egg> • (1.4%) Noble Wanderer's Axe

werewolf captain [38] (65%) Large Werewolf Pelt • (77%) Large Werewolf Paw • (60%) Golden Military Chain • (1.5%) <Howling at the Moon> • (0.3%) <Freya's Dowry>

werewolf commander [36] (55%) Large Werewolf Pelt • (73%) Large Werewolf Paw • (43%) Golden Military Chain • (1.4%) <Howling at the Moon> • (1.4%) Garou Axe • (0.3%) <Freya's Dowry>

werewolf courier [26] (70%) Courier Pouch • (80%) Small Werewolf Pelt • (52%) Bundle of Coded Letters • (0.3%) <All Fired Up>

werewolf gladiator [36] (55%) Large Werewolf Pelt • (73%) Large Werewolf Paw • (43%) Golden Military Chain • (1.4%) <New-Moon Wear> • (1.4%) Garou Axe

werewolf guard [31/32/33] (65/70/0%) Werewolf Meat • (60%) Guard's Medal [33] • (63/65/70%) Guard's Wristband • (45/60/70%) Guard's Ration • (0.3%) <Freya's Dowry> • (1.4%) Garou Axe • (1.4%) <Wolf Loot>

werewolf lieutenant [33/34] (60/70%) Lieutenant's Pin • (55/60%) Lieutenant's Pouch • (45/47%) Lieutenant's Ration • (0.3%) <Freya's Dowry> • (1.4%) Garou Axe

werewolf runner [21] (40%) Bundle of Coded Letters • (85%) Illegible Map • (75%) Runner's Pouch • (0.3%) <Great Balls O' Fire>

werewolf skulker [23/24/25] (40/50/65%) Small Werewolf Pelt • (80%) Werewolf Ear • (67/70/75%) Werewolf Tongue • (0.3%) <Great Balls O' Fire>

werewolf warder [27/28/29/30] (70/74%) Warder's Pack [27/28] • (60/65%) Werewolf Tail [29/30] • (45/60/72/70%) Medium Werewolf Pelt • (57/70/75/0%) Werewolf Fang • (62%) Werewolf Meat [30] • (0.3%) <All Fired Up> • (1.4% each) <Alvis's Chest>, <Wolf Loot> [27,30] • (1.4%) <Fiery Ants>, <Forged in the Cauldron> [28,29] • (9/11/13/15%) Warder's Ear

whispering willow [33/34] (70/75%) Leafy Willow Branch • (45/57%) Willow-Carved Emerald • (80%) Heart of Wood • (65/70%) Willow Leaf Coronet

wind spirit [27/28] (50/53%) Square-Cut Sapphire • (16/18%) Cat's Eye Apatite • (60/70%) Blue Topaz • (1.5%) Wind Swept Pants ***or*** Vest, ***or*** Wind Swept ***or*** Wrapped Staff • (0.3%) <All Fired Up>

Witch [22] (50%) Laering Necklace • (80%) Bag of Blue Dust • (45%) Locked Spell Book • (70%) Crooked Wand • (0.5%) <Norseman Cache>

wolfaur gladiator [36] (80%) Headsman's Pendant • (60% each) Headsman's Hood, Iron Shackle • (0.3%) <Freya's Dowry> • (1.5%) <New-Moon Wear>

wolfaur headsman [33/34/35/36] (55/59/70/70%) Headsman's Pendant • [(64/70%) Human Head/(50/60%) Headsman's Hood] • [(60/70%) Bronze Shackle/(69/70%) Iron Shackle] • (0.3%) <Freya's Dowry> • (1.5%) APOA: Claw Forged, ***or*** Wolftooth ***or*** Wolfsclaw Hauberk

wolfaur shaman [36] (55%) Large Werewolf Pelt • (73%) Large Werewolf Paw • (43%) Golden Military Chain • (1.4%) <Howling at the Moon> • (1.4%) Garou Axe • (0.3%) <Freya's Dowry>

wolverine [39/40] (79%) Wolverine Paw [39] • (55/80%) Wolv. Claw • (65/72%) Wolv. Tooth • (55%) Wolv. Pelt [40]

wood mephit [22] (75%) Wooden Totem • (65%) Leafy Branch • (55%) Leafy Bracelet • (0.3%) <Great Balls O' Fire>

wood rat [24/25] (75/80%) Rat Paw • (20/25%) Rat Pelt • (10/15%) Wood Rat Tail • (20/23%) Rat Whiskers

woodland badger [(22)23] (40%) Badger Claw • (80%) Badger Tooth • (60%) Ruined Badger Pelt • (41%) Badger Pelt [level 22 currently has no loot]

Yecats [50] (no loot)

young envy drake [20/22] (45/30%) Virulent Green Eye • (35/40%) Envy Stone • (25/50%) Spiteful Black Heart

young silverscale drake [22] (75%) Silvery Scale • (45%) Blue Topaz • (60%) Yellow Topaz

young wolverine [28/29] (80%) Small Wolverine Claw [28] • (54%) Small Wolverine Pelt [29] • (70/80%) Small Wolverine Tooth • (50/75%) Small Wolverine Paw

Zrit-Zrit [34] (80%) Timberland Badger Fang • (71%) Timberland Badger Paw • (65%) Timberland Badger Pelt • (12%) Badger Stomach

Svealand East Tips

Levels 1 – 12 love this area. It's great for soloing, and group friendly for low level groups.

Norseman Vikings, Rogues, Mystics, and Dwarf Seers start in Vasudheim.

Its location near Jordheim makes it handy for taking up a trade and seeing your class trainer when you reach level 5.

Audliten (nearby town) is another great source for fed-ex and kill tasks.

If you're venturing to West Svealand (or beyond), take care when crossing the bridge. Rock crabs lurk below and will attack anyone under level 10 who is crossing.

Solo Levelling Tips

1 sveawolf cubs and lupine gnawers (near V.)

2 young sveawolves and lupine gnawers

3 young sveawolves and lupine snarlers

4 lupine snarlers, appropriate quests

6 Audliten neighborhood.

6-8 Wood-eaters, huldus, vein spiders. ant workers, Skeletal Oarsmen, and pretty much anything around or east of Dvalin.

The Tomtes' camps are pretty good, but the scouts make it dangerous … avoid them.

10 Galplen kill tasks are best. As far as monsters go, try silver drakelings and envy drakes between Auditlen to Dvalin *or* the first area in Nisse's Lair. Also try rock crabs on the beach or tawny lynxes.

Killing silverscale drakelings builds faction with envycell drakelings. Njessi is an envycell drake.

11 Grey wargs and rock crabs. By level 11 you can try perdificous pooks.

12 At 12 you're in line for perdificous pooks, but you're running out of leveling options.

Loot

army ant soldier [8] (50%) Army Ant Carapace • (23%) Army Ant Mandible • (50%) Army Ant Leg • (8%) Army Ant Leg

army ant worker [6] (33%) Army Ant Carapace • (45%) Army Ant Leg • (2%) Army Ant Leg • (3%) Army Ant Mandible

baby spider [2] (no loot)

black mauler juvenile [5] (51%) Small Mauler Skin • (25%) Mauler Claw

Breeze [7] (58%) Windblown Crystal • (1.5%) Windswept Cloak • (0.5%) <Har's Adornments>

Brut [9] (1.5%; hi-lo) Iron Skull Sword ***or*** Bracer • (2.7%) APOA: Tomte Leather • (0.3%) APOA: Supple Leather • (15%) Jewels 55 • (0.5%) <Grimnir's Adornment>

Darksong [9] (71%) Dirge Scraps • (40%) Dirge Scraps • (3.6%) APOA: of the Wanderer • (0.4%) APOA: of the Old Wanderer • (1.5%) Wanderer's Spirit Staff • (0.5%) <Grimnir's Adornment>

dwarf bone skeleton [5] (50%) Jewels 45 • (8% each piece) Tattered Padded and Mjuklaedar • (1%) <Into the Woods>

Edigo [9] (no loot)

Envy Drake Dorga [10] (68% each) Envy Drakeling Hide, Tail

envy drakeling [9] (68% each) Envy Drakeling Hide, Tail

escaped thrall [3] (45%) Broken Iron Shackle • (10%) Jewels 45 • (1%) <Into the Woods>

fragile skeleton [3] (75%) Jewels 45 • (8% each piece) Tattered Padded and Mjuklaedar • (1%) <Into the Woods>

Frigol [9] (no loot)

giant water strider [5] (no loot)

Gib [2] (no loot)

green serpent [2] (48%) Green Serpent Skin

harvestman [3] (60%) Harvest Silk • (10%) Harvestman Carapace

hill cat [10] (25%) Hill Cat Skin • (66%) Hill Cat Claw (x2) • (1.5%) Mystical Beast Eye

horse [55] (75%) Horse Hair • (10%) Auburn Mane • (80%) Ruined Horse Skin • (35%) Horse Skin • (60%) Horse Hair

Jabrylla [7] (no loot)

Klippa [8] (60%) Rock Crab Leg (x2) • (10%) Rock Crab Leg (x2) • (43%) Rock Crab Shell

little water goblin [2] (70%) Clump of Seaweed • (50%) String of Blue Beads • (60%) Dead Fish • (1%) <Into the Woods>

lupine gnawer [0] (70%) Lupine Skin

lupine snarler [2] (95%) Lupine Skin

Morra [6] (99%) Pristine Sveawolf Skin

Mourn [7] (69%) Dirge Scraps • (2.7%) APOA: of the Wanderer • (0.3%) APOA: of the Old Wanderer • (1.5%) Wanderer's Spirit Staff • (0.5%) <Har's Adornments>

mud snake [0] (10%) Snake Meat • (70%) Snake's Head

nordic dirge [6] (48%) Dirge Scraps • (1.5%) Runed Wanderer's Staff • (0.5%) <Har's Adornments>

Ocug [9] (no loot)

Olag [11] (1.5%; hi-lo) Iron Skull Sword ***or*** Bracer • (2.7%) APOA: Tomte Leather • (0.3%) APOA: Supple Leather • (20%) Jewels 55 • (0.5%) <Grimnir's Adornment>

phantom hound [3] (10%) Phosphorescent Pelt • (70%) Phosphorescent Claw

plague rat [6-7] (50%) Rat Tail • (10%) Rat Fur

plague rat scout [6] (50%) Rat Tail • (10%) Rat Fur

Queen Major [10] (75%) Army Ant Carapace • (63%) Army Ant Mandible • (20%) Army Ant Carapace

rattling skeleton [1] (50%) Jewels 45 • (8% each piece) Tattered Padded and Mjuklaedar • (1%) <Into the Woods>

Riv [10] (55%) Spindly Rock Crab Leg (x2) • (38%) Spindly Rock Crab Leg (x2) • (58%) Rock Crab Shell

roaming dirge [8] (84%) Dirge Scraps • (2.7%) APOA: of the Wanderer • (0.3%) APOA: of the Old Wanderer • (1.5%) Wanderer's Spirit Staff • (0.5%) <Har's Adornments>

roaming thrall [7] (35%) Dead Master's Jeweled Bracer • (1.4%) Dead Master's Signet Ring • (1.4%) Stolen Hunting Bow • (2.7%) APOA: of the Wanderer • (0.3%) APOA: of the Old Wanderer • (5%) Stolen Arrows

rock crab [7] (50%) Rock Crab Leg (x2) • (30%) Rock Crab Shell • (5%) Rock Crab Leg (x2)

Rognvald [35] (no loot)

rugged dwarven pony [4] (10%) Pony Hoof • (60%) Pony Hide

Scrip [0] (no loot)

silverscale drakeling [9] (60% each) Silver Drakeling Hide, Tail

Smack [9] (1.5%; hi-lo) Iron Skull Sword ***or*** Bracer • (2.7%) APOA: Tomte Leather • (0.3%) APOA: Supple Leather • (15%) Jewels 55 • (0.5%) <Grimnir's Adornment>

small hill cat [7] (10%) Small Hill Cat Skin • (35%) Small Hill Cat Claw • (70%) Small Hill Cat Claw

smiera-gatto [4] (no loot)

soft-shelled crab [1] (60%) Crab Leg • (20%) Crab Leg

spindly rock crab [9] (50%) Spindly Rock Crab Leg (x2) • (10%) Spindly Rock Crab Leg (x2) • (50%) Rock Crab Shell

Svartmoln [6] (50%) Small Mauler Skin • (40%) Mauler Claw

sveawolf [3] (71%) Sveawolf Skin

sveawolf cub [0] (65%) Small Sveawolf Skin

sveawolf mother [5] (73%) Pristine Sveawolf Skin

tawny lynx cub [0] (55%) Small Lynx Skin

tomte aggressor [9] (1.5%; hi-lo) Iron Skull Sword ***or*** Bracer • (2.7%) APOA: Tomte Leather • (0.3%) APOA: Supple Leather • (15%) Jewels 55 • (0.5%) <Grimnir's Adornment>

tomte pillager [8] (1.5%; hi-lo) Iron Skull Sword ***or*** Bracer • (2.7%) APOA: Tomte Leather • (0.3%) APOA: Supple Leather • (12%) Jewels 55 • (0.5%) <Har's Adornments>

tomte plunderer [10] (1.5%; hi-lo) Iron Skull Sword ***or*** Bracer • (2.7%) APOA: Tomte Leather • (0.3%) APOA: Supple Leather • (20%) Jewels 55 • (0.5%) <Grimnir's Adornment>

tomte skirmisher [7] (1.5%; hi-lo) Iron Skull Sword ***or*** Bracer • (2.7%) APOA: Tomte Leather • (0.3%) APOA: Supple Leather • (10%) Jewels 55 • (0.5%) <Har's Adornments>

tomte thug [5] (30%) Tomte Bracer • (20%) Jewels 45 • (1%) <Into the Woods> • (1.5%) Large Tomte Axe

vein spiderling [0] (80%) Spider Legs • (50%) Veined Mandible

water strider [1] (30%) Strider Carapace • (80%) Strider Eye • (70%) Strider Antenna

wayward ghoul [4] (40%) Patch of Decayed Hair • (20%) Jewels 45 • (1%) <Into the Woods>

whirlwind [6] (42%) Windblown Crystal • (1.5%) Windswept Cloak • (0.5%) <Har's Adornments>

wildling [0] (50%) Jewels 45 • (8% each piece) Tattered Padded and Mjuklaedar • (1%) <Into the Woods>

wood-eater hunter [5] Jewels 23

young lynx [2] (73%) Small Lynx Skin

young sveawolf [1] (70%) Small Sveawolf Skin

Svealand East

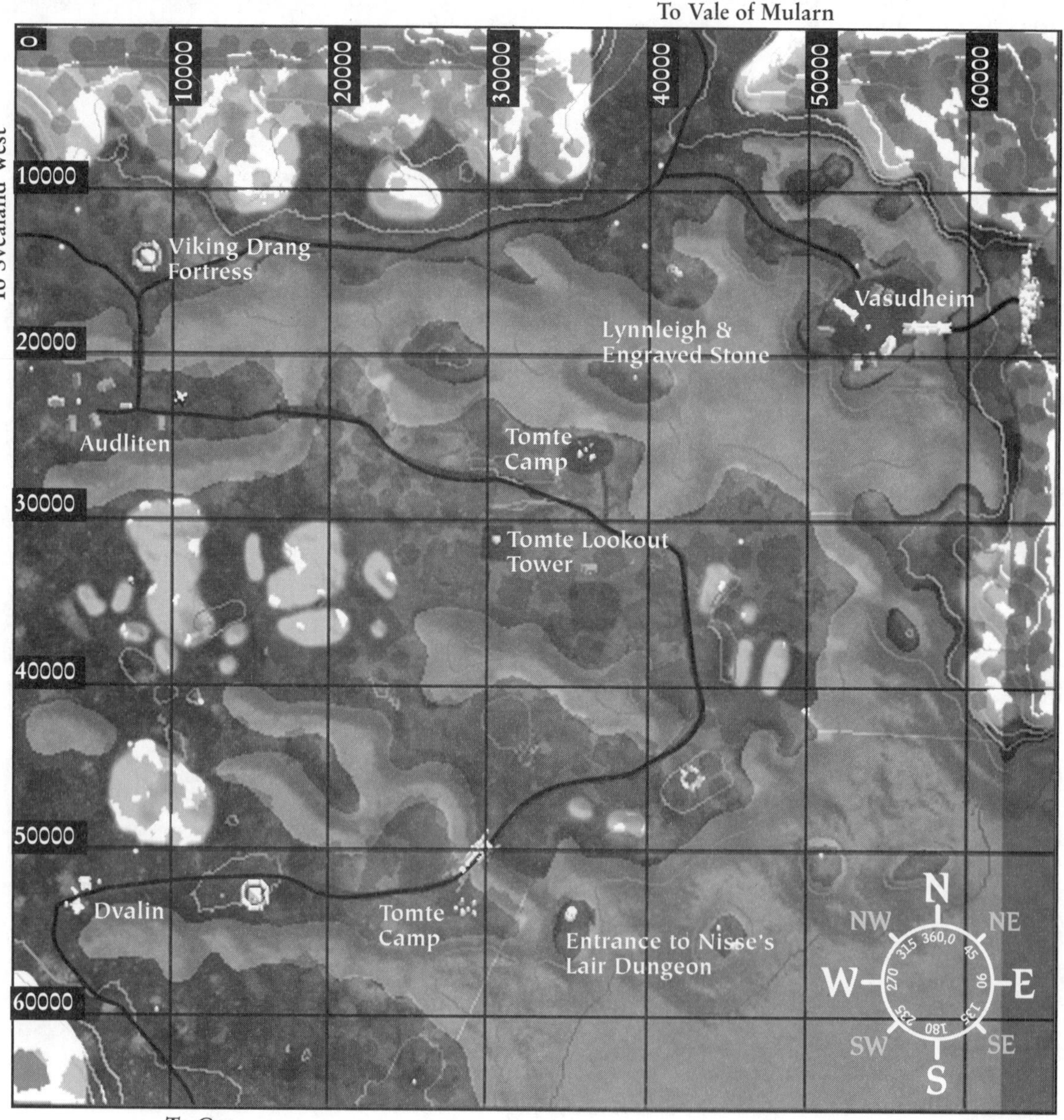

Svealand East Tips and Loot on Page 167.

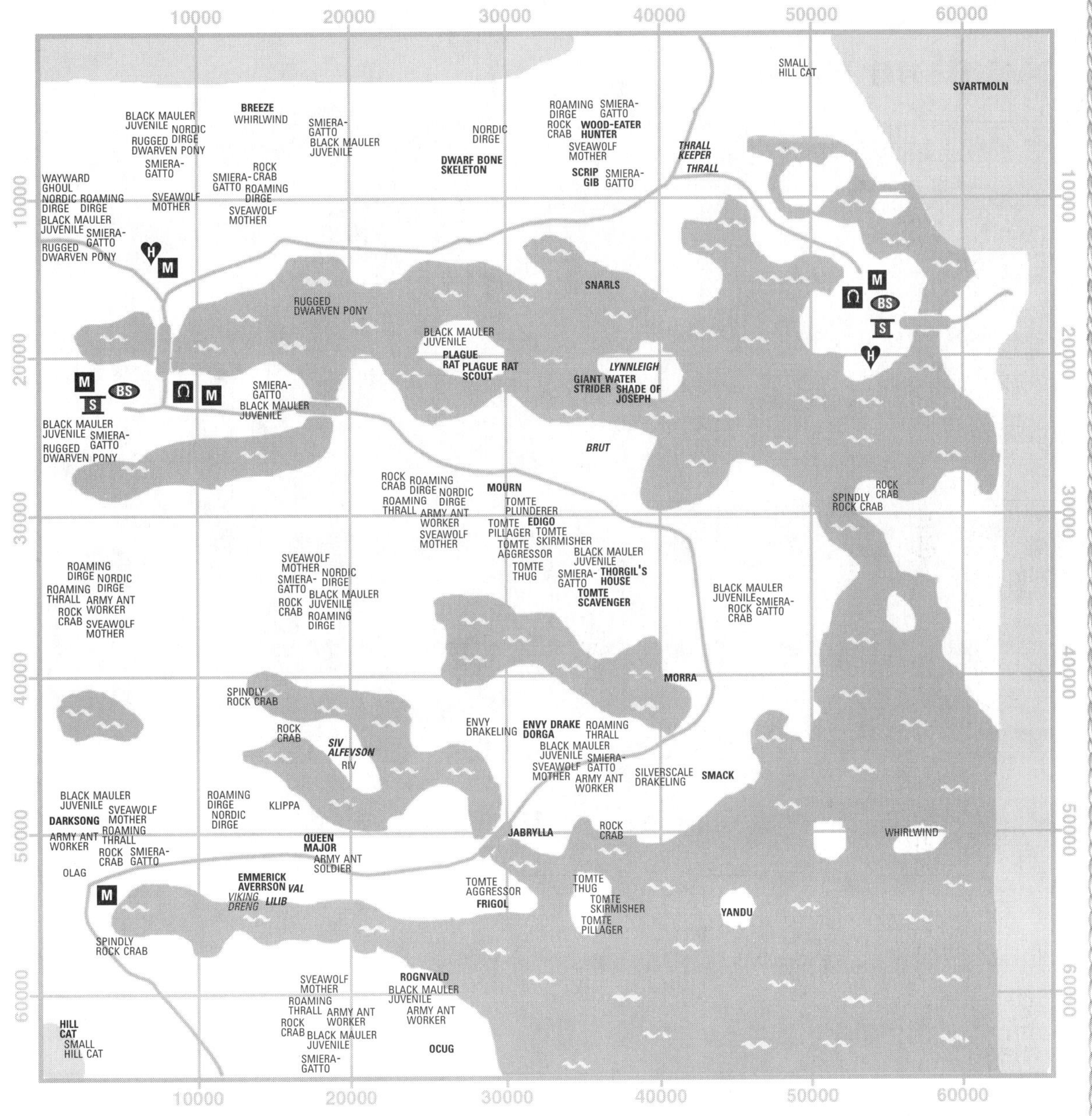

Lower-level monsters not shown on map:

Creature	Lvl	Location	Creature	Lvl	Location	Creature	Lvl	Location	Creature	Lvl	Location
baby spider	2	NC	little water goblin	2	NC	Scrip	0	NC	water strider	1	NC
escaped thrall	3	NW,NC,EC	lupine gnawer	0	NW,NC,NE,EC	soft-shelled crab	1	NE	wildling	0	NW,NC,NE,EC
fragile skeleton	3	NW,NC	lupine snarler	2	NW,NC,NE,EC	sveawolf	3	NW,NE	young lynx	2	NW,NC,NE,EC
Gib	2	NC	mud snake	0	NC,NE	sveawolf cub	0	NC,NE	young sveawolf	1	NW,NC,NE,C
green serpent	2	NW,NC,NE,EC	phantom hound	3	NC	tawny lynx cub	0	NW,NC,NE,EC			
harvestman	3	NC,WC	rattling skeleton	1	NW,NC,NE	vein spiderling	0	NC,NE			

Svealand West

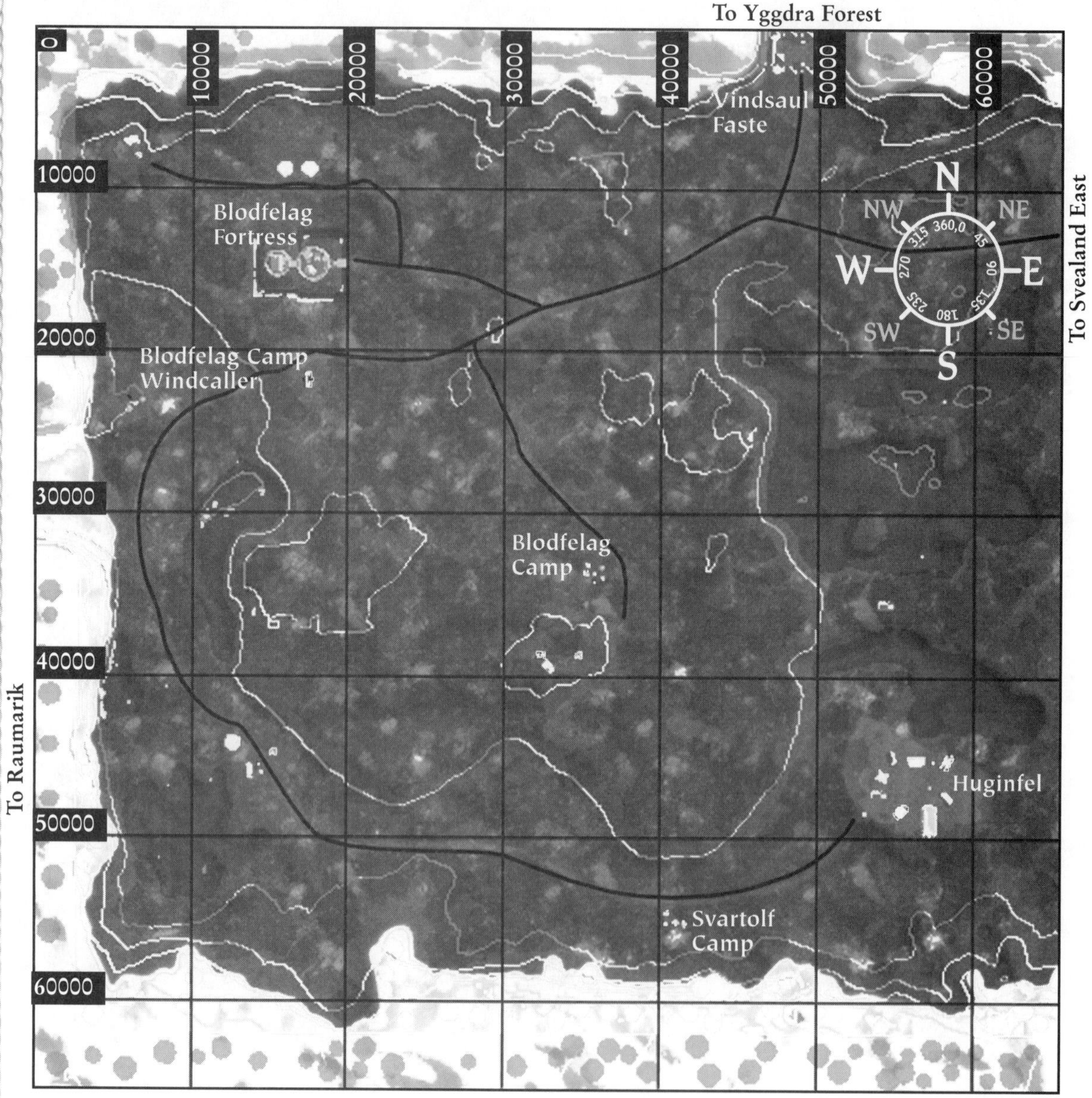

To Yggdra Forest

0 10000 20000 30000 40000 50000 60000

Vindsaul Faste

Blodfelag Fortress

Blodfelag Camp Windcaller

Blodfelag Camp

Huginfel

Svartolf Camp

N NE E SE S SW W NW

360,0 45 90 135 180 235 270 315

To Svealand East

To Raumarik

10000 20000 30000 40000 50000 60000

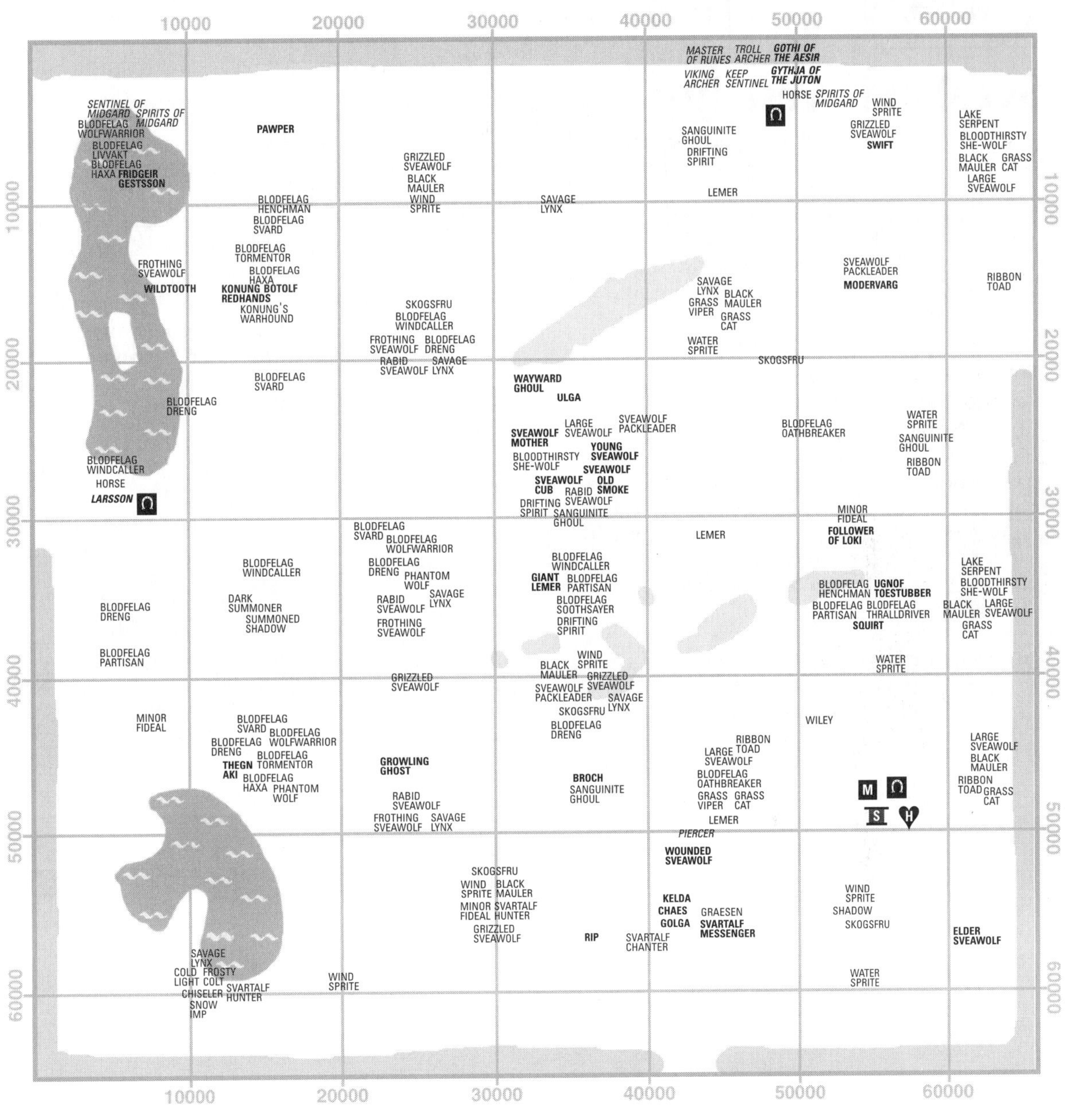

Quest NPCs

Huginfell	
Agnor Crusher	Paranoid guard (lvl 15)
Aylarn	Reach of the shadow (lvl 15)
Bork	Hunting party (lvl 12)
Bork	Silent death (lvl 23)
Gudlor	Protect Huginfel (lvl 16)
Gudlor	Living warning (lvl 21)
Hakon	Bowyer's Draw (lvl 20)
Halla	Stripe (lvl 25)

Huginfell (cont'd)	
Hurg	Minx Wiley (lvl 10)
Samlauf Kolsson	Protecting the Healer (lvl 17)
Saydyn	Waking of the fallen (lvl 16)
Sughnild	Lover's circle (lvl 15)
Sunghild	Sugnhild's revenge (lvl 22)
S.E. of Huginfell	
Elder Sveawolf	Sveawolf Guardian (lvl 8)
Elder Sveawolf	Fervent (lvl 18)

Svealand West Tips

Just outside of Huginfell is a great place to level. Not only are there multiple spawns of wolves, shadows and two named bosses, but there are two guards in town in case you get into trouble. Also, It seems like a place where a lot of people bind because I never have a problem finding a good party there, even at 4 in the morning. (group 8-10)

Group Friendly? Yes

Who loves this area? Levels 10-22. Great for soloing, and group friendly.

Other Notes. Take care when approaching the Huginfel town — there's a named Bloodfeng name Toestubber that patrols around the town with one or two cronies and a wolf. They are high aggro and will attack folks under level 16 (I think not 100% on that level). He is part of a quest that starts out in Vale of Mularn's Haggerfel.

Solo Levelling Tips

9-12 It's not too hard to find good hunting. For instance, if you start off on drakelings east of the bridge at Dvalin, you'll be set for a while. When you get too high for the drakelings, go to Huginfel ... it's got a good range of critters.

13-15 Around level 13 in Hugginfel you'll be looking for maulers, wolves, oathbreakers, shadows and things like that.

Slightly higher level would be to the west of Hugginfel. Skogsfru and water wisps are good, and wind spirits are good for cash, usually. Also the bears drop pelts that go for a good price back in town.

15-16 After a while in the west of Hugginfel, you'll want to put on your walking shoes and head north to Vindsaul Faste. (Fortunately there's a stable there, so you don't have to walk all the way back when you're done.) Once you get there, you should concentrate on wind sprites. They give decent xp and decent cash drops, which is a nice combination when you can find it ... and thus it's worth the journey.

16-20 This is when the zone comes into its own, as far as leveling goes.

Casters are windcallers (17-18) and haxa (19-20) are prime. The windcallers are on the hill NW of Hugginfel, which you follow all the way around to the Blodfelg Fort. They don't have high hp, obviously, and they tend to be loners that are yellow or orange. It's an excellent way of racking up xp.

Look around for good opportunities, but when in doubt stay with bloodfelgs, lynxes, etc. near Huginfel.

Loot

black mauler [12/13/14] (28/32/41%) Mauler Skin • (3.1/3.6/4.5%) Pristine Mauler Skin • (52/65/72%) Mauler Claw (x2) • (1.5%) <Been Mauled>

blodfelag captive [10] (80%) Rusty Shackles • (70% each) Rotting Ration, Half-Gnawed Bone • (50% each) Cracked Horn, Bottle of Dirty Water

blodfelag dreng [14/15/16] (5%) Golden Brooch • (10%) Amber Beaded Necklace • (21/11/11%) Polished Wooden Bowl • (20/10/10%) Valkyrie Figurine • (1.5%) Ring of Redhands • (40%) Soapstone Lamp • (6% each) Golden Horned Figurine, Silver Cup • (0.3%) <Brendig's Gear>/<Brendig's Gear>/<Full Moon Wear> • (1.5%) <Blodjeger Gear>

blodfelag haxa [19-20] (0.1% each) Golden Brooch, Amber Beaded Necklace, Polished Wooden Bowl, Valkyrie Figurine • (1.5%) Ring of Redhands • (10%) Soapstone Lamp • (23% each) Golden Horned Figurine, Silver Cup • (0.3%) <Thief's Nest Egg> • (1.5%) Blod Flekket Cloak ***or*** Jerkin, Blodstein Ring ***or*** Styring

blodfelag henchman [12/13] (15%) Golden Brooch • (20%) Amber Beaded Necklace • (31%) Polished Wooden Bowl • (5/7%) Valkyrie Figurine • (1.5%) Ring of Redhands • (4/8%) Soapstone Lamp • (0.2% each) Golden Horned Figurine, Silver Cup • (0.3%) <Grimnir's Adornment>/<Brendig's Gear> • (1.5%) <Blod Flekket Bounty>

blodfelag livvakt [20] (0.1% each) Golden Brooch, Amber Beaded Necklace, Polished Wooden Bowl, Valkyrie Figurine • (1.5%) Ring of Redhands • (10%) Soapstone Lamp • (23% each) Golden Horned Figurine, Silver Cup • (0.3%) <Thief's Nest Egg> • (1.5%) Bloddarlig Helm ***or*** Tjen Og Adlyd

blodfelag oathbreaker [10-12] (25%) Golden Brooch • (20%) Amber Beaded Necklace • (1%) Polished Wooden Bowl • (5%) Valkyrie Figurine • (1.5%) Ring of Redhands • (4%) Soapstone Lamp • (0.2% each) Golden Horned Figurine, Silver Cup • (0.5%) <Grimnir's Adornment> • (1.5%) APOA: Edbrottsjo, Edbrottsjo ***or*** Regnbrottsjo Shield, ***or*** Edskiver

blodfelag partisan [13] (5%) Golden Brooch • (20%) Amber Beaded Necklace • (31%) Polished Wooden Bowl • (27%) Valkyrie Figurine • (1.5%) Ring of Redhands • (8%) Soapstone Lamp • (0.5% each) Golden Horned Figurine, Silver Cup • (0.3%) <Brendig's Gear> • (1.5%; hi-lo) Wand of Twisted Wood, Bracelet of Bark, ***or*** Leaf and Twig Crown • (0.01%) <Thief's Nest Egg>

blodfelag partisan [14/15] (5%) Golden Brooch • (20/10%) Amber Beaded Necklace • (31/11%) Polished Wooden Bowl • (30/10%) Valkyrie Figurine • (1.5%) Ring of Redhands • (10/40%) Soapstone Lamp • (1% each) Golden Horned Figurine, Silver Cup • (0.3%) <Brendig's Gear> • (1.5%) <Blod Flekket Bounty>/<Blodjeger Gear>

blodfelag soothsayer [14] (5%) Golden Brooch • (10%) Amber Beaded Necklace • (21%) Polished Wooden Bowl • (20%) Valkyrie Figurine • (1.5%) Ring of Redhands • (40%) Soapstone Lamp • (1% each) Golden Horned Figurine, Silver Cup • (0.3%) <Brendig's Gear> • (1.5%) Helm of Future Visions ***or*** Soothsayer's Ring

blodfelag svard [16/17] (1/0.1%) Golden Brooch • (5% each) Amber Beaded Necklace, Valkyrie Figurine • (11/5%) Polished Wooden Bowl • (1.5%) Ring of Redhands • (40/60%) Soapstone Lamp • (8/10% each) Golden Horned Figurine, Silver Cup • (0.3%) <Thief's Nest Egg> • (1.5%; hi-lo) Blodbror Leggings, Boots ***or*** Necklace

blodfelag thralldriver [14] (5%) Golden Brooch • (10%) Amber Beaded Necklace • (21%) Polished Wooden Bowl • (20%) Valkyrie Figurine • (1.5%) Ring of Redhands • (40%) Soapstone Lamp • (1% each) Golden Horned Figurine, Silver Cup • (0.3%) <Brendig's Gear> • (1.5%; hi-lo) Blodbror Jerkin ***or*** Necklace, ***or*** Blodsverd

blodfelag tormentor [19-20] (0.1% each) Golden Brooch, Amber Beaded Necklace, Polished Wooden Bowl, Valkyrie Figurine • (1.5%) Ring of Redhands • (10%) Soapstone Lamp • (23% each) Golden Horned Figurine, Silver Cup • (0.3%) <Thief's Nest Egg> • (1.5%) Bloddarlig Helm ***or*** Tjen Og Adlyd

blodfelag warhound [10] (80%) Warhound Pelt • (70%) Warhound Tooth • (50%) Warhound Tail

blodfelag windcaller [17/18] (0.1%) Golden Brooch • (5/1% each) Amber Beaded Necklace, Polished Wooden Bowl, Valkyrie Figurine • (1.5%) Ring of Redhands • (60%) Soapstone Lamp • (10/11% each) Golden Horned Figurine, Silver Cup • (0.3%) <Thief's Nest Egg> • (1.5%) <Vind Kind>

blodfelag wolfwarrior [18/19] (0.1%) Golden Brooch • (1/0.1% each) Amber Beaded Necklace, Polished Wooden Bowl, Valkyrie Figurine • (1.5%) Ring of Redhands • (60%) Soapstone Lamp • (23%) Golden Horned Figurine • (13/23%) Silver Cup • (0.3%) <Thief's Nest Egg> • (1.5%; hi-lo) Wolftooth Studded Jerkin ***or*** Boots, ***or*** Blodsnitt

bloodthirsty she-wolf [12] (27%) Large Sveawolf Skin • (3%) Pristine Large Sveawolf Skin • (60%) Sveawolf Fang • (28%) Sveawolf Fang

Broch [15] (40%) Chunk of Ghoul Flesh • (0.3%) <Brendig's Gear>

Chaes [16] (40%) Amethyst • (41%) Carnelian • (70%) Chryoprase • (60%) Bloodstone • (0.3%) <Brendig's Gear>

chiseler [20] (no loot)

cold light [20] (no loot)

drifting spirit [12/13/14] (50/55/65%) Spirit Shreds • (0.3%) <Brendig's Gear>

elder sveawolf [13] (46%) Large Sveawolf Skin • (85%) Sveawolf Fang

follower of Loki [10] (60%) Spinel • (80%) Jade • (70%) Obsidian • (35%) Carnelian

Fridgeir Gestsson [21] (0.1% each) Golden Brooch, Amber Beaded Necklace, Polished Wooden Bowl, Valkyrie Figurine • (1.5%) Ring of Redhands • (10%) Soapstone Lamp • (23% each) Golden Horned Figurine, Silver Cup • (0.3%) <Thief's Nest Egg> • (1.5%) Bloddarlig Helm ***or*** Tjen Og Adlyd

frosty colt [20] (no loot)

frothing sveawolf [19] (90% each) Sveawolf Fang, Large Sveawolf Skin • (7%) Vial of Spittle

giant lemer [22] (80%) Giant Lemer Head • (30%) Giant Lemer Paw • (75%) Lemer Tail • (1.5%) Fanged Tooth

Golga [17] (40%) Amethyst • (41%) Carnelian • (70%) Chryoprase • (60%) Bloodstone • (0.3%) <Brendig's Gear>

grass cat [11/12] (66%) Grass Cat Skin • (42/57%) Grass Cat Fang

grass viper [12] (25%) Grass Viper Skin • (70%) Forked Snake Tongue • (1.5%) Grass Viper Fang

grizzled sveawolf [13] (46%) Large Sveawolf Skin • (85%) Sveawolf Fang

Growling Ghost [21] Wolf Skull

horse [55] (75%) Horse Hair • (10%) Auburn Mane • (80%) Ruined Horse Skin • (35%) Horse Skin • (60%) Horse Hair

Konung Botolf Redhands [22] (0.1% each) Golden Brooch, Amber Beaded Necklace, Polished Wooden Bowl, Valkyrie Figurine • (1.5%) Ring of Redhands • (10%) Soapstone Lamp • (23% each) Golden Horned Figurine, Silver Cup • (0.3%) <Thief's Nest Egg> • (1.5%) Bloddarlig Helm ***or*** Tjen Og Adlyd

konung's warhound [19] (50%) Studded Warhound Collar • (70%) Large Wolfhound Pelt • (55%) Large Warhound Paw

lake serpent [10/11] (80/90%) Lake Serpent Skin • (75/95%) Lake Serpent Fang

large sveawolf [11] (27%) Large Sveawolf Skin • (3%) Pristine Large Sveawolf Skin • (60%) Sveawolf Fang • (9%) Sveawolf Fang

lemer [15] (no loot)

mindless thrall [10] (80%) Rusty Shackles • (70% each) Rotting Ration, Half-Gnawed Bone • (50%) Bottle of Dirty Water • (20%) Brain

minor fideal [15-16] (50%) Amethyst • (51%) Carnelian • (70%) Chryoprase • (65%) Bloodstone • (1.5%) Vannsang Cloak, Sleeves, Axe ***or*** Belt • (0.3%) <Thief's Nest Egg>

Modervarg [13] (27%) Large Sveawolf Skin • (3%) Pristine Large Sveawolf Skin • (70%) Sveawolf Fang • (40%) Sveawolf Fang

Old Smoke [15] (86%) Large Sveawolf Skin • (80%) Sveawolf Fang

Pawper [19] (no loot)

phantom wolf [17/18/19] (78/90/100%) Wolf Skull

Piercer [16] (0.1%) Golden Brooch • (0.1% each) Amber Beaded Necklace, Polished Wooden Bowl, Valkyrie Figurine • (1.5%) Ring of Redhands • (10%) Soapstone Lamp • (23% each) Golden Horned Figurine, Silver Cup • (0.3%) <Thief's Nest Egg> • (1.5%; hi-lo) Wolftooth Studded Jerkin ***or*** Boots, ***or*** Blodsnitt

rabid sveawolf [18] (90% each) Sveawolf Fang, Large Sveawolf Skin • (5%) Vial of Spittle

ribbon toad [12/13] (60/72%) Ribbon Toad Leg

sanguinite ghoul [13-14] (40%) Chunk of Ghoul Flesh • (0.3%) <Brendig's Gear>

savage lynx [15/16] (60/70%) Lynx Skin • Lynx Claw

shadow [10-11] (40%) Globe of Black Mist • (20% each) Black Glass Earring, Bracelet of Black Mist, Black Glowing Crystal • (1.3%) APOA: Decaying • (1.3% each) Decaying Hammer, Decayed Bone Ring • (0.3%) <Grimnir's Adornment>

skogsfru [13/14] (47/50%) Amethyst • (80%) Spinel [13] • (41%) Carnelian [14] • (70%) Chryoprase • (60%) Bloodstone • (1.5%) <Strange Threshholds> • (0.3%) <Brendig's Gear>

snow imp [20] (no loot)

Squirt [15] (60%) Amethyst • (51%) Carnelian • (75%) Chryoprase • (60%) Bloodstone • (1.5%) <Water Rings> • (0.3%) <Brendig's Gear>

svartalf chanter [14-15] (40%) Amethyst • (41%) Carnelian • (70%) Chryoprase • (60%) Bloodstone • (0.3%) <Brendig's Gear>

svartalf hunter [14-15] (40%) Amethyst • (41%) Carnelian • (70%) Chryoprase • (60%) Bloodstone • (0.3%) <Brendig's Gear>

sveawolf [3] (71%) Sveawolf Skin

sveawolf cub [0] (65%) Small Sveawolf Skin

sveawolf mother [5] (73%) Pristine Sveawolf Skin

sveawolf packleader [14] (66%) Large Sveawolf Skin • (80%) Sveawolf Fang

Swift [16] (60%) Amethyst • (51%) Carnelian • (75%) Chryoprase • (65%) Bloodstone • (0.3%) <Brendig's Gear>

Thegn Aki [16] (5%) Golden Brooch • (10% each) Amber Beaded Necklace, Valkyrie Figurine • (11%) Polished Wooden Bowl • (1.5%) Ring of Redhands • (40%) Soapstone Lamp • (6% each) Golden Horned Figurine, Silver Cup • (0.3%) <Brendig's Gear> • (1.5%; hi-lo) Blodbror Jerkin ***or*** Necklace, ***or*** Blodsverd

Ugnof Toestubber [16] (5%) Golden Brooch • (20%) Amber Beaded Necklace • (31%) Polished Wooden Bowl • (30%) Valkyrie Figurine • (1.5%) Ring of Redhands • (10%) Soapstone Lamp • (1% each) Golden Horned Figurine, Silver Cup • (0.3%) <Brendig's Gear> • (1.5%) <Blod Flekket Bounty>

Ulga [13] (65%) Spirit Shreds • (0.3%) <Brendig's Gear>

water sprite [13/14] (47/40%) Amethyst • (70%) Spinel [13] • (41%) Carnelian [14] • (60% each) Chryoprase, Bloodstone • (1.5%) <Water Rings> • (0.3%) <Brendig's Gear>

wayward ghoul [4] (40%) Patch of Decayed Hair • (20%) Jewels 45 • (1%) <Into the Woods>

Wildtooth [20] (90% each) Sveawolf Fang, Large Sveawolf Skin • (10%) Vial of Spittle

Wiley [10] (60%) Spinel • (80%) Jade • (70%) Obsidian • (35%) Carnelian

wind sprite [14/15] (50/60%) Amethyst • (41/51%) Carnelian • (70/75%) Chryoprase • (50/65%) Bloodstone • (0.3%) <Brendig's Gear>

wind wisp [9] (80%) Round Sapphire (x2) • (70%) Clear Blue Orb

wounded sveawolf [11] (27%) Large Sveawolf Skin • (3%) Pristine Large Sveawolf Skin • (60%) Sveawolf Fang • (9%) Sveawolf Fang

young sveawolf [1] (70%) Small Sveawolf Skin

Vale of Mularn

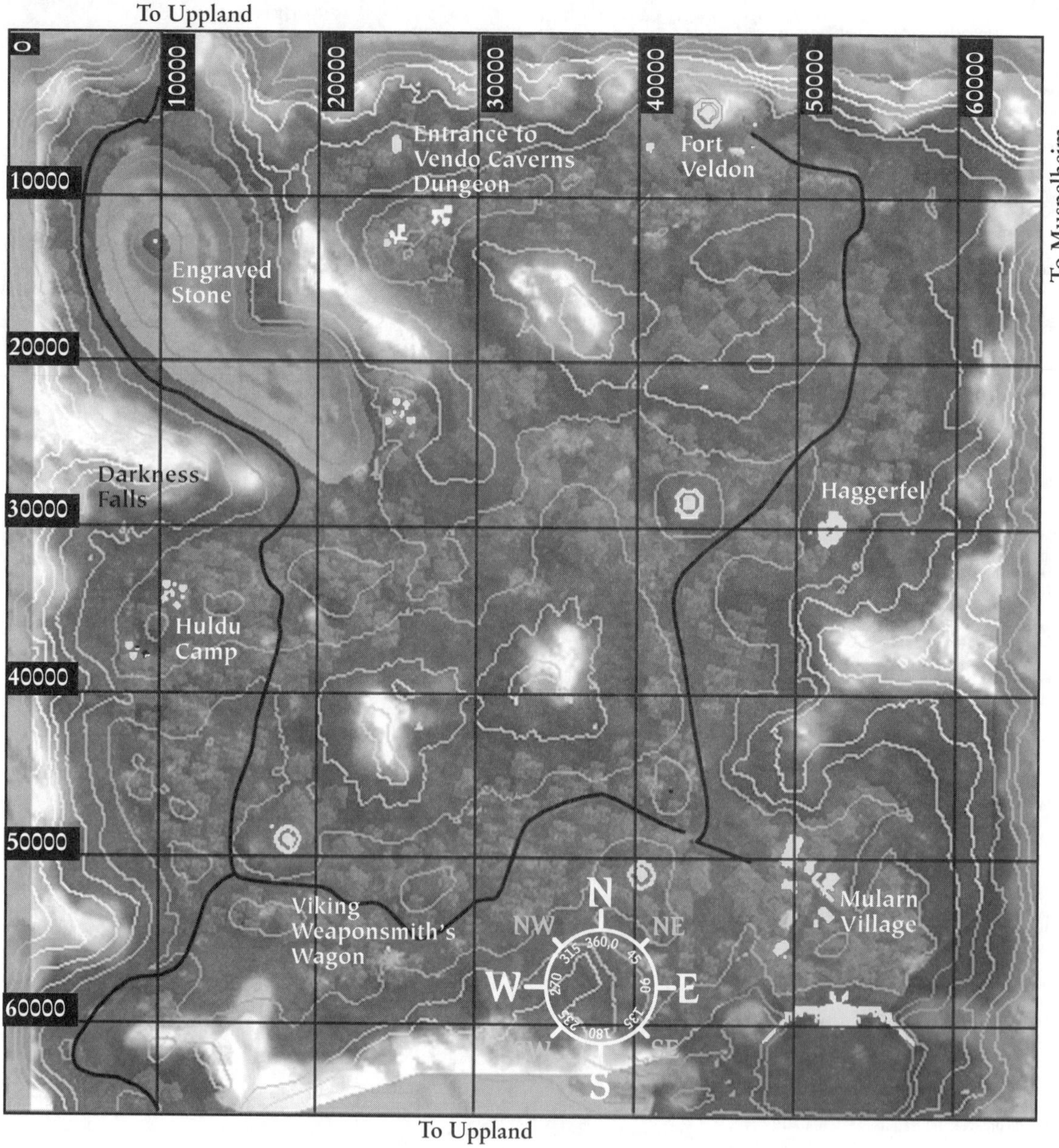

To Uppland

0 10000 20000 30000 40000 50000 60000

Entrance to Vendo Caverns Dungeon

Fort Veldon

Engraved Stone

Darkness Falls

Haggerfel

Huldu Camp

Viking Weaponsmith's Wagon

Mularn Village

N NE E S W NW

360,0 45 90 135 180 225 270 315

To Muspelheim

To Uppland

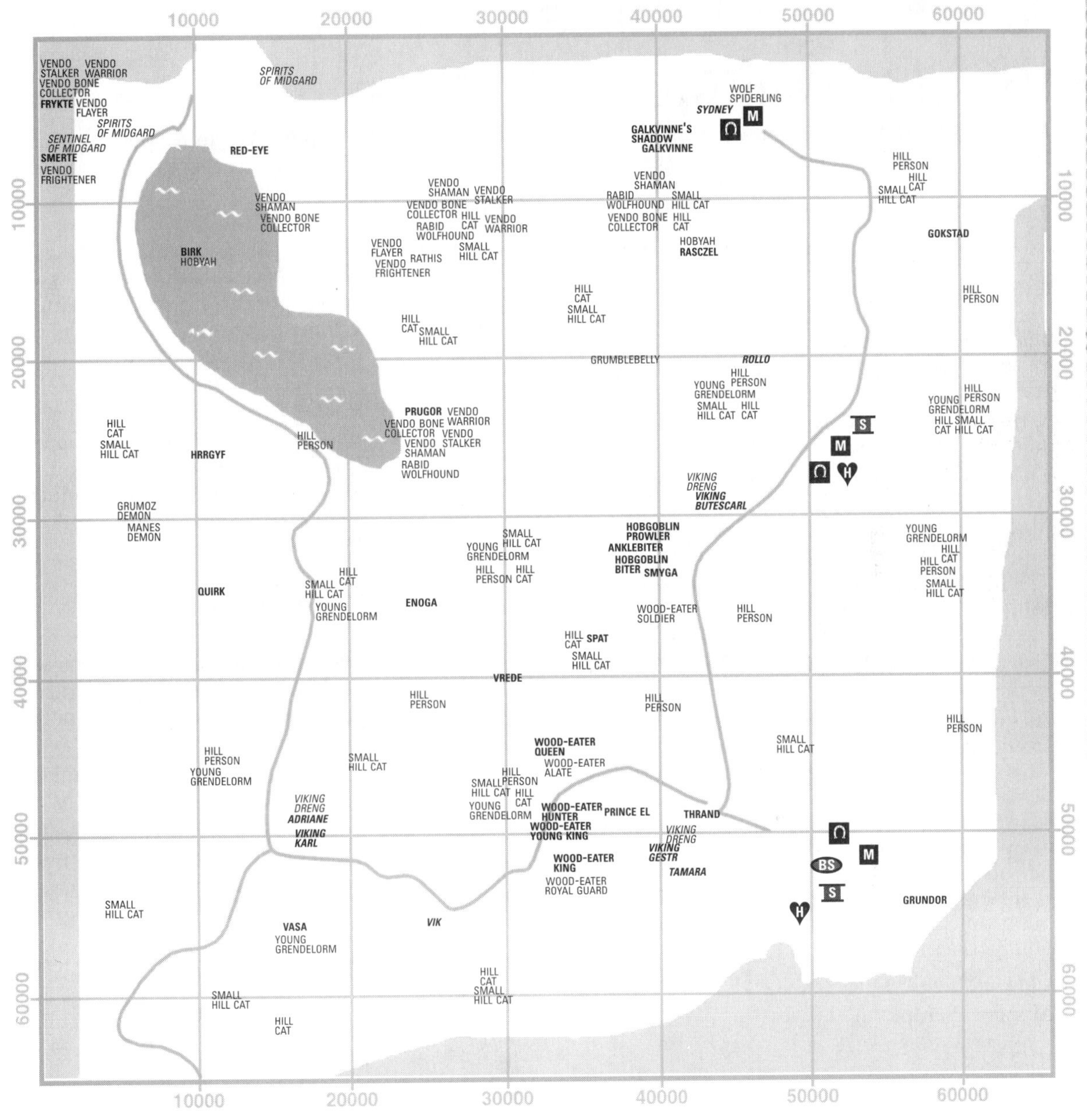

Lower-level monsters not shown on map:

Creature	Lvl	Location
black mauler cub	0	NE,C,EC,SE
carrion lizard	3	SC,SE
hobgoblin prankster	3	NE,C,EC,SC
hbgbln. snake-finder	1	NE,C,EC
huldu hunter	4	NE,WC,C,EC, SW,SC
huldu lurker	2	WC,SW,SC,SE
huldu outcast	1	SE
huldu stalker	5	NE,WC,C,EC, SW,SC
little water goblin	2	NE,C,EC,SC,SE
meandering spirit	1	NE,EC,SC
mud snake	0	NE,EC,SE
phantom hound	3	NE,WC,C,EC, SW,SC
rattling skeleton	1	SC,SE
vein spider	5	NE,WC,C,EC, SW,SC
vein spiderling	0	NE,EC,SE
wayward ghoul	4	SC
wild hog	2	NE,C
wood-eater	3	NE,C,EC,SC
wood-eater hunter	5	SC
wood-eater worker	4	SC
young lynx	2	NE,C,EC

Vale of Mularn Tips

Group Friendly? Yes. The area has a high spawn rate in it, since it's home to a couple of starting areas. Since the zone is mostly under level 25, It's a good spot for lower-level groups of tanks.

There are two Vendo camps. These are best with groups. A small group will do well with the valley camp, a large group is better for the lakeside one. The vendos cast and heal/buff each other and they BAF. These are good for 13-17. The vendos in the dungeon drop good leather and studded armor. You can also find staffs.

Who loves this area? Anyone 1-12. It's great for soloing, and friendly for low-level groups.

Other Notes. Dwarf Viking, Dwarf Mystic, and Kobold Seer starting place is Mularn in Vale of Mularn. The Dwarf Rogue begins at Haggerfil in the Vale of Mularn.

The newbie city Mularn is near the Midgard capitol Jordheim, handy for taking up a trade and seeing your class trainer when you achieve level 5.

The portal to the RvR dungeon Darkness Falls is in this zone.

As you go farther out, the monsters get progressively harder and there are a few wandering monsters that are too high. (e.g., Ant King, Vrede, a demon that wanders through). At night, there are spawns of orms near Vix's cart. Vix can be used to draw a monster to you if you're going to die — he will protect you. The vein spiderlings are good monsters to hunt for loot and xp. Watch for the hill people and the wandering hill cats wherever you go there.

- Marc "Biggs" Quesnel,
Monica "Seraphym" Hayes

Solo Levelling Tips

There are spots that can be soloed without fear of getting jumped. Outside the cities (Mularn Village, Haggerfel), the monsters are not aggressive.

1-5 Near Mularn Village is good for newbies.

5-8 Outside Haggerfel on the other side of the fort, there's a hill. There's decent pickings for a solid lowbie soloist.

The monsters above the fort near Mularn don't aggro, so it's a good place for a soloist to go without too much trouble.

Worker ants are an excellent choice. Near the Mularn fort is a sweet spot that doesn't get many wandering ants passing too close, and isn't close enough to the guards that they "rescue" you against your will.

Wood-eaters, huldus, vein spiders, and Tomte camps are also good. Skeletal oarsmen and pretty much any critter around or east of Dvalin works well.

9-11 The hill people west of Mularn Village are good targets.

12-15 This is when the vendo camps that are to the west of Ft. Veldon are best. South of the vendo camps, near Fort Veldon, are some good rabid sveawolves.

Also, you can get some useful kill tasks at Haggerfel.

15-16 Try the Vendo bone collectors along the road heading south from Svasud Faste. It doesn't take much to knock them out, and they give nice xp.

Loot

Anklebiter [7] (60%) Beaded Hobgoblin Belt • (30%) Clan Crest • (1.5%) Crusty Old Bracer • (40%) Jewels 45 • (0.5%) <Har's Adornments>

Birk [13] (no loot)

black mauler cub [0] (60%) Mauler Cub Teeth • (10%) Small Mauler Skin

carrion lizard [3] (23%) Diseased Claw • (70%) Rotting Carrion

enoga [25] (no loot)

Frykte [13] (no loot)

Gokstad [16] (no loot)

hill cat [10] (25%) Hill Cat Skin • (66%) Hill Cat Claw (x2) • (1.5%) Mystical Beast Eye

hill person [6] (75%) Moonstone • (15%) Jade • (25%) Small Copper Bracelet • (0.5%) <Into the Woods>

hobgoblin biter [6] (50%) Beaded Hobgoblin Belt • (20%) Clan Crest • (1.5%) Crusty Old Bracer • (0.5%) <Har's Adornments> • (20%) Jewels 45

hobgoblin prankster [3] (50%) Patched Old Sack • (10%) Beaded Hobgoblin Belt • (1.5%) Hobgoblin Hammer • (1%) <Into the Woods> • (20%) Jewels 45

hobgoblin prowler [8] (80%) Beaded Hobgoblin Belt • (40%) Clan Crest • (1.5%) Crusty Old Bracer • (40%) Jewels 45 • (0.5%) <Har's Adornments>

hobgoblin snake-finder [1] (50%) Patched Old Sack • (5%) Jewels 45 • (1%) <Into the Woods>

hobyah [10,12] (no loot)

horse [55] (75%) Horse Hair • (10%) Auburn Mane • (80%) Ruined Horse Skin • (35%) Horse Skin • (60%) Horse Hair

Hrrgyf [10] (50%) Hill Cat Claw (x2) • (45%) Hill Cat Skin

huldu hunter [4] (35%) Carved Wood Norseman • (25%) Carved Wood Troll • (15%) Carved Wood Kobold • (5%) Carved Wood Dwarf • (10%) Old Carving Tool • (1%) <Into the Woods> • (1.4%) Huldu Axe • (1.4%) Huldu Mantle of Obscurity

huldu lurker [2] (10%) Carved Wood Norseman • (7.5%) Carved Wood Troll • (5%) Carved Wood Kobold • (2.5%) Carved Wood Dwarf • (10%) Old Carving Tool • (1%) <Into the Woods> • (7.5% each piece) Tattered Padded and Mjuklaedar

huldu outcast [1] (10%) Carved Wood Norseman • (7.5%) Carved Wood Troll • (5%) Carved Wood Kobold • (2.5%) Carved Wood Dwarf • (10%) Old Carving Tool • (1%) <Into the Woods> • (7.5% each piece) Tattered Padded and Mjuklaedar

huldu stalker [5] (35%) Carved Wood Norseman • (25%) Carved Wood Troll • (15%) Carved Wood Kobold • (5%) Carved Wood Dwarf • (10%) Old Carving Tool • (1%) <Into the Woods> • (1.4%) Huldu Axe • (1.4%) Huldu Mantle of Obscurity

little water goblin [2] (70%) Clump of Seaweed • (50%) String of Blue Beads • (60%) Dead Fish • (1%) <Into the Woods>

meandering spirit [1] (50%) Jewels 45 • (8% each piece) Tattered Padded and Mjuklaedar • (1%) <Into the Woods>

mud snake [0] (10%) Snake Meat • (70%) Snake's Head

phantom hound [3] (10%) Phosphorescent Pelt • (70%) Phosphorescent Claw

Prugor [11] (25%) Mother Totem • (15%) Jewels 23 • (0.5%) <Grimnir's Adornment> • (2.7%) APOA: Vendo Bone Studded • (0.3%) APOA: Jagged Bone • (1.5%) Vendo Flesh-Flayer ***or*** Bone-Splitter • (3%) Vendo Bone Ring

Quirk [6] (no loot)

rabid wolfhound [11] (70%) Wolfhound's Ear • (38%) Wolfhound's Ear • (10%) Wolfhound Hide • (1.5%) Mystical Beast Eye

Rasczel [10] (no loot)

Rathis [13] (30%) Mother Totem • (15%) Jewels 23 • (0.5%) <Brendig's Gear> • (2.7%) APOA: Vendo Bone Studded • (0.3%) APOA: Jagged Bone • (1.5%) Vendo Flesh-Flayer ***or*** Bone-Splitter • (3%) Vendo Bone Ring

rattling skeleton [1] (50%) Jewels 45 • (8% each piece) Tattered Padded and Mjuklaedar • (1%) <Into the Woods>

Red-eye [13] (68%) Wolfhound's Ear (x2) • (20%) Wolfhound Hide

small hill cat [7] (10%) Small Hill Cat Skin • (35%) Small Hill Cat Claw • (70%) Small Hill Cat Claw

Smerte [13] (no loot)

Smyga [9] (80%) Beaded Hobgoblin Belt • (40%) Clan Crest • (1.5%) Crusty Old Bracer • (60%) Jewels 45 • (0.5%) <Har's Adornments>

Spat [8] (10%) Small Hill Cat Skin • (35%) Small Hill Cat Claw • (70%) Small Hill Cat Claw

Vasa [9] (60%) Scrap of Grendelorm Hide • (80%) Hunk of Gooey Flesh

vein spider [5] (26%) Veined Carapace • (70%) Bulbous Spider Eye

vein spiderling [0] (80%) Spider Legs • (50%) Veined Mandible

vendo bone-collector [13] (30%) Mother Totem • (15%) Jewels 23 • (0.5%) <Brendig's Gear> • (2.7%) APOA: Vendo Bone Studded • (0.3%) APOA: Jagged Bone • (1.5%) Vendo Flesh-Flayer ***or*** Bone-Splitter • (3%) Vendo Bone Ring

vendo flayer [15] (35%) Mother Totem • (20%) Jewels 23 • (0.5%) <Thief's Nest Egg> • (2.7%) APOA: Vendo Bone Studded • (0.3%) APOA: Jagged Bone • (1.5%) Vendo Flesh-Flayer ***or*** Bone-Splitter • (3%) Vendo Bone Ring

vendo frightener [14] (30%) Mother Totem • (15%) Jewels 23 • (0.5%) <Brendig's Gear> • (2.7%) APOA: Vendo Bone Studded • (0.3%) APOA: Jagged Bone • (1.5%) Vendo Flesh-Flayer ***or*** Bone-Splitter • (3%) Vendo Bone Ring

vendo shaman [10] (25%) Mother Totem • (10%) Jewels 23 • (0.5%) <Grimnir's Adornment> • (2.7%) APOA: Vendo Bone Studded • (0.3%) APOA: Jagged Bone • (1.5%) Vendo Flesh-Flayer ***or*** Bone-Splitter • (3%) Vendo Bone Ring

vendo stalker [12] (30%) Mother Totem • (15%) Jewels 23 • (0.5%) <Grimnir's Adornment> • (2.7%) APOA: Vendo Bone Studded • (0.3%) APOA: Jagged Bone • (1.5%) Vendo Flesh-Flayer ***or*** Bone-Splitter • (3%) Vendo Bone Ring

vendo warrior [11] (25%) Mother Totem • (15%) Jewels 23 • (0.5%) <Grimnir's Adornment> • (2.7%) APOA: Vendo Bone Studded • (0.3%) APOA: Jagged Bone • (1.5%) Vendo Flesh-Flayer ***or*** Bone-Splitter • (3%) Vendo Bone Ring

Vrede [11] (no loot)

wayward ghoul [4] (40%) Patch of Decayed Hair • (20%) Jewels 45 • (1%) <Into the Woods>

wild hog [2] (35% each) Curly Hog Tail, Small Hog Hoof • (50% each) Small Hog Tusk, Hide

wolf spiderling [7] (99%) Spider Silk

wood-eater [3] (60%) Small Woodeater Leg • (8%) Small Woodeater Leg • (1%) Digestive Sac • (1%) <Rig's Lament> • (1.5%) Spined Woodeater Leg

wood-eater alate [7] (65%) Large Woodeater Leg • (10%) Large Woodeater Leg • (3%) Digestive Sac • (0.5%) <Wood-Eaten Wonders> • (1.5%) Piece of Amber

wood-eater hunter [5] Jewels 23

wood-eater king [15] (70%) Large Woodeater Leg (x2) • (27%) Digestive Sac • (1.5%) Piece of Amber • (0.5%) <Khertik's Wares>

wood-eater queen [8] (70%) Large Woodeater Leg • (25%) Large Woodeater Leg • (7%) Digestive Sac • (0.5%) <Wood-Eaten Wonders> • (1.5%) Piece of Amber

wood-eater royal guard [16] (65%) Large Woodeater Leg • (10%) Large Woodeater Leg • (3%) Digestive Sac • (0.5%) <Wood-Eaten Wonders> • (1.5%) Piece of Amber

wood-eater soldier [6] (70%) Woodeater Leg • (28%) Woodeater Leg • (3%) Digestive Sac • (1%) <Wood-Eaten Wonders> • (1.5%) Piece of Amber

wood-eater worker [4] (70%) Small Woodeater Leg • (15%) Small Woodeater Leg • (2%) Digestive Sac • (1%) <Rig's Lament> • (1.5%) Spined Woodeater Leg

wood-eater young king [10] (70%) Large Woodeater Leg (x2) • (27%) Digestive Sac • (1.5%) Piece of Amber • (0.5%) <Khertik's Wares>

young grendelorm [7] (20%) Scrap of Grendelorm Hide • (72%) Hunk of Gooey Flesh

young lynx [2] (73%) Small Lynx Skin

Quest NPCs

Ft. Veldon	
Cornelis	Foolish Dancers (lvl 24)
Haggerfel	
Genlu Edrill	The Red Dagger (lvl Guild Track - 20)
Helen	Bear skins (lvl 1)
Hilde	Simple Misgivings (lvl 7)
Hilde	Brack - Rollo's story (lvl 16)
Inaksha	Mimir's Protection (lvl Guild Track - 40)
Inaksha	Visions of Darkness (lvl Guild Track - 20)
Inaksha	Decoding the Map (lvl Guild Track - 25)
Inaksha	Gashir (lvl Guild Track - 30)
Macalena	Sulphine's Demise (lvl 23)
Trustan	Mystic Trainer (lvl 4)
Trustan	Trustan's Belongings (lvl 12)
Yver	Widower Hunt (lvl 21)
Yver Tiu	Mucking through the Ick (lvl 8)

Mularn	
Aegan	Aegan's letter to Helen (lvl 3)
Mularn	
Aegan	Evenings Empty Blessing (lvl 15)
Bolli	Young Fire Wyrm Lord (lvl 30)
Carr	Smyga's Raid (lvl 10)
Elizabeth	Blessed Enchantments (lvl Guild Track - 40)
Carr	Defeat the Hobgoblin Anklebiter (lvl 8)
Thrand	Family Business (lvl 18)
Vic	Monsterous Beast (lvl 10)
Vic	Spat the Wild Cat (lvl 10)

Vanern Swamp

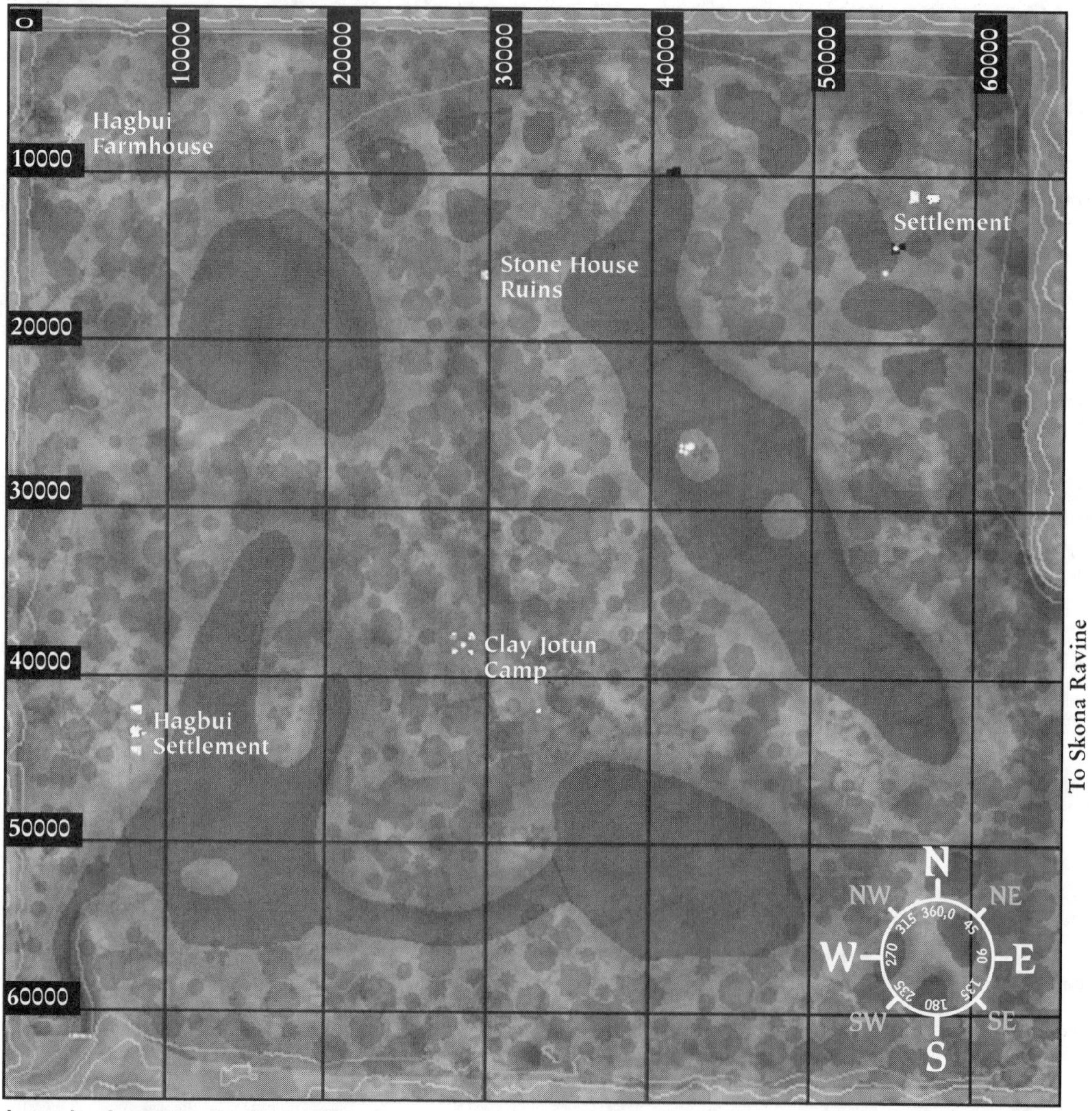

Hagbui Farmhouse

Settlement

Stone House Ruins

Clay Jotun Camp

Hagbui Settlement

Lower-level monsters not shown on map:

Creature	Lvl	Location
black orm	36	NC,NE,EC
black orm	37	NC,NE,EC
black orm	38	NC,NE,EC
clay jotun	40	C
clay jotun	42	C
enslaved orm	40	WC,SW
enslaved orm runner	42	WC,SW
forest viper	40	C,EC,SW,SC,SE
forest viper	42	C,EC,SW,SC,SE
hagbui forge tender	37	NW
hagbui guard	40	NW
hagbui guard	42	NW
hagbui herald	38	NW
hagbui page	36	NW
hagbui runemaster	42	NW
hagbui shaman	40	NW
hagbui spiritmaster	43	NW
hagbui squire	39	NW
hagbui swordbearer	35	NW
mud crab	35	C,EC,SC,SE

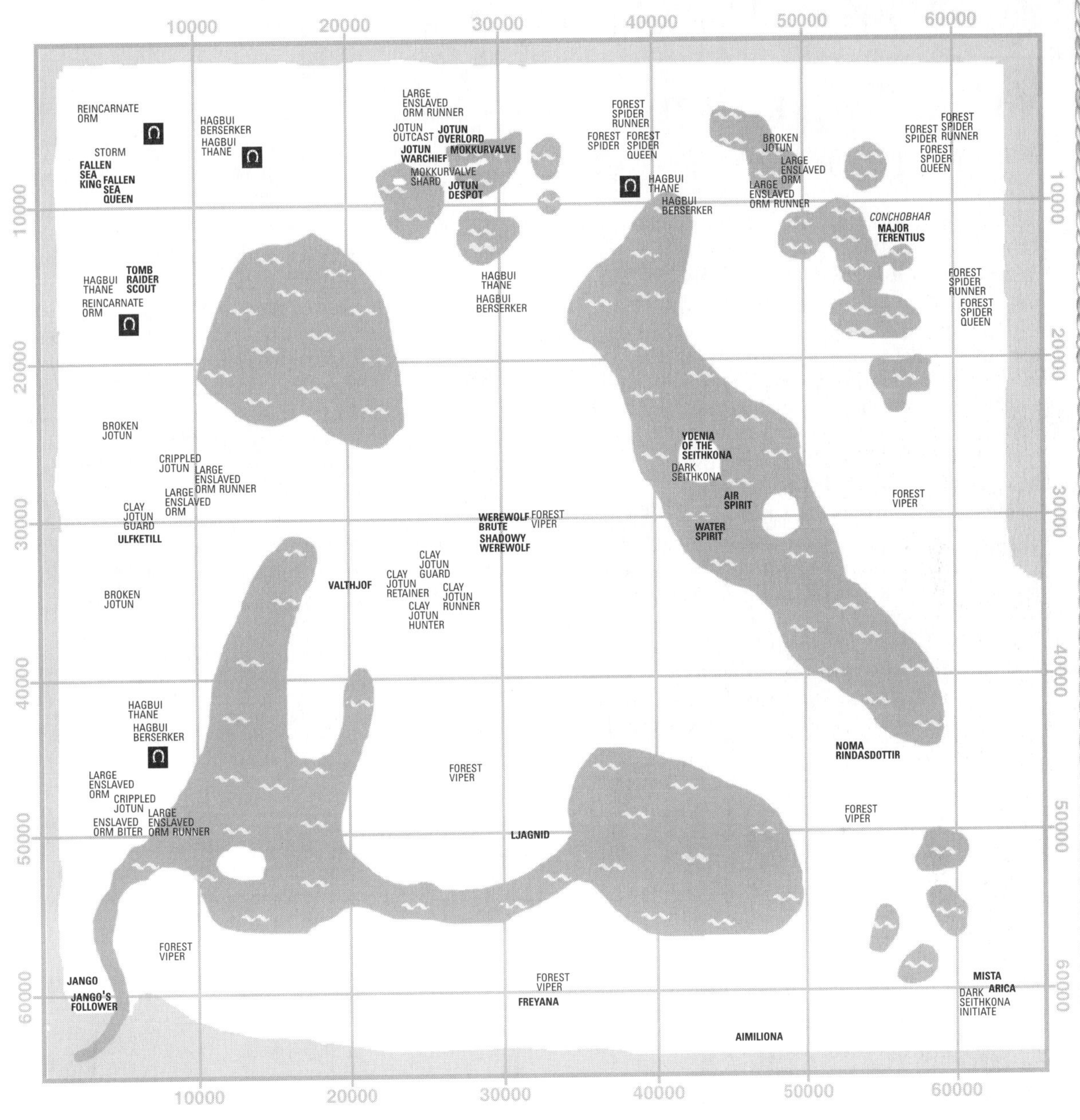

Creature	Lvl	Location
mud crab warrior	36	C,EC,SC,SE
mud frog	30	NW,NC,WC,C,EC,SW,SC,SE
mud frog	32	NW,NC,WC,C,EC,SW,SC,SE
mud frog	34	NW,NC,WC,C,EC,SW,SC,SE
mud frog	36	NW,NC,WC,C,EC,SW,SC,SE
Noma Rindasdottir	35	EC
shadowy werewolf	40	C
small black orm	35	NC,NE,C,EC,SC,SE
tomb raider scout	15	NW

Vanern Swamp Tips

Group Friendly? Yes, very much so for a group of level 30+.

Who hates this area? No one, there is something there for every class

Who loves this area? Anyone levels 35 – 50, great for soloing, and very group friendly.

Other Notes. A fun zone, but keep your eye out for viper snakes. They're small and blend in well in the grass, and they are very aggressive and have a nasty poison. They are mainly near the Skona Ravine and Vanern Swamp border.

Solo Levelling Tips

35-38 In general a good place to play would be in the southeast of the zone. The mud crabs there are yellow at 35, and give around 6mil xp. Mud frogs nearby are also good at this level or a little higher. In fact, it works out rather well, because crabs have a slow spawn, and you can kill frogs while you wait for crabs to spawn.

37-38 At this level you're looking for sidhe, and you'll find them over near the border between Skona Ravine and Vanern swamp, near the ww lair. (Okay, that's in Skona Ravine, but it's all part of the same experience of leveling in this area.) There are casters and sidhe, and between them you can really rake in the xp. It doesn't take much effort at all to take them out, and they give glorious xp. At level 37 you can get almost 7 mil for yellows, and nearly 8 for oranges. The drawback is that it's tough to control them. They BAF if they're close to camp, and if you let them get close to each other while you're pulling them.

When it comes to cold hard cash, you want to explore the sidhe gaoites. Yes, they're still in Skona, but if you want to level up to 43 in Vanern Swamp, you have to do some vacationing in the Ravine. Anyway, take the sidhe gaoites, followed by the elf gaoites. They drop gems, and you can usually sell those off for about 2 gold per stack of ten. When the camp bonus gets low, wander back over the border for a while and try your hand at orms.

38-40 Orms a great, especially for darkness Runies. They have some interesting drops too. Keep an eye out for the forest spiders ....

40-43 Now is when you want to start working the hagbui guards who hang out in the northwest part of the zone. The xp is okay, but the loot is even better. At 42 you can start taking on the runners for staves ... groups can tend to land you an orm spine staff. Try tackling an orange reincarnate orm.

Loot

black orm [36-37/38] (19/24%) Black Orm Tooth • (1/1.2%) Serrated Black Tooth • (18/20%) Black Orm Hide • (2/2.2%) Touched Black Orm Hide • (1.3/1.6% each) Crystalized Jotun Hand, Giant Green Sapphire Ring • (11%) Black Orm Gland

broken jotun [54-55] (25%) Worked Viper Skin • (15%) Horn of Fire Grog • (25%) Jewels 13 • (1.5%) APOA: Jotun Black Orm ***or*** Shrunken Orm Skull • (1.5%) Reincarnate Femur War Maul, Runic Manslayer, ***or*** Death Whisper • (1.5%) <Bogged Down>

broken jotun [56-57] (25%) Jotun Jeweled Chest • (20%) Horn of Fire Grog • (20%) Jewels 13 • (1.5%) APOA: Jotun Black Orm ***or*** Shrunken Orm Skull • (1.5%) Orm Skullcap Shield • (1.5%) <Bogged Down>

clay jotun [40,42] (20%) Magic Saturated Clay • (16%) Magic Enriched Clay • (1.6%) Hardened Clay Heart • (1.6%) Runed Clay War-Shield ***or*** Runic Clay Axe

clay jotun guard [44] (20%) Magic Saturated Clay • (17%) Magic Enriched Clay • (2%) Hardened Clay Heart • (1.6%) Runed Clay Battle-Shield ***or*** Runic Clay War Hammer • (1.6%) APOA: Runed Hollow Clay

clay jotun hunter [50] (25% each) Magic Saturated Clay, Magic Enriched Clay • (5%) Hardened Clay Heart • (1.6%) Runed Clay Buckler ***or*** Runic Clay Spear • (1.6%) APOA: Runed Hollow Clay

clay jotun retainer [46] (20% each) Magic Saturated Clay, Magic Enriched Clay • (3%) Hardened Clay Heart • (1.6%) Runed Clay Battle-Shield ***or*** Runic Clay War Hammer • (1.6%) APOA: Runed Hollow Clay

clay jotun runner [48] (25%) Magic Saturated Clay • (20%) Magic Enriched Clay • (5%) Hardened Clay Heart • (1.6%) Runed Clay Buckler ***or*** Runic Clay Spear • (1.6%) APOA: Runed Hollow Clay

crippled jotun [50-51/52-53] (25%) Worked Frog Skin/Worked Crab Chitin • (15/20%) Golden Drinking Horn • (15/20%) Jewels 13 • (1.5%) APOA: Studded Ormhide • (1.5%) Carved Orm Fang Sword/<From Mjoes Depths> • (1.5%) <Bogged Down>

dark seithkona [48] (no loot)

enslaved orm [40] (19%) Shadowy Orm Eye • (1.1%) Glowing Black Eye • (18%) Touched Black Orm Hide • (2%) Enriched Black Orm Hide • (1.6%) Enslaved Orm's Collar

enslaved orm biter [44] (21%) Shadowy Orm Eye • (1.2%) Glowing Black Eye • (20%) Touched Black Orm Hide • (2.2%) Enriched Black Orm Hide • (1.5% each) Crystalized Jotun Hand, Giant Pink Sapphire Ring • (1.5%) Enslaved Biter's Muzzle Wrap

enslaved orm runner [42] (24%) Shadowy Orm Eye • (1.2%) Glowing Black Eye • (18%) Touched Black Orm Hide • (2%) Enriched Black Orm Hide • (1.5% each) Crystalized Jotun Hand, Giant Pink Sapphire Ring • (1.5%) Enslaved Orm's Collar

fallen sea king [60] (5% each) Spiked Coral Crown, Heavy Coral Crown

fallen sea queen [60] (5% each) Light Coral Crown, Coral Crown

forest spider [50/52] (3%) Forest Spider Poison Sac • (31/35%) Forest Spider Carapace • (1.7%) Jewel of Venom

forest spider queen [55] (5%) Forest Spider Poison Sac • (41%) Forest Spider Carapace • (1.7% each) Huge Silken Cocoon, Crystalized Troll Remains, Fate Stealer

forest spider runner [53] (4%) Forest Spider Poison Sac • (37%) Forest Spider Carapace • (1.7% each) Huge Silken Cocoon, Crystalized Troll Remains, Fate Stealer

forest viper [40/42/44] (21/23/23%) Forest Viper Skin • (2.3/2.5/2.6%) Crystalized Viper Skin • (24%) Forest Viper Fang/Eye/Spine • (1.4%) Forest Viper Fang/Crystalized Viper Eye Necklace/Viper Spine Wrist Wrap • (12%) Forest Viper Venom

hagbui berserker [50-51] (30%) Berserker's Jeweled Insignia • (10%) Sunstone Bearclaw Necklace • (10%) Jewels 13 • (1.6%) APOA: Supple Serpent-Hide • (1.6%) Ebony Axe of Mindless Rage

hagbui forge tender [37] (30%) Beaded Sinew Bracelet • (5%) Jewels 13 • (1.5%) <Voluspa Adornments> • (1.5%) APOA: Serpent-Hide • (1.5%) Forge Tender's Hammer ***or*** Tunic

hagbui guard [40,42] (25%) Royal Guard's Beaded Insignia • (10%) Gilded Ornamental Bracer • (5%) Jewels 13 • (1.5%) APOA: Blood Crystal • (1.5% each) Embossed Hagbui Bracelet, Seafarer's Trident

hagbui herald [38] (30%) Herald's Beaded Insignia • (5%) Jewels 13 • (1.5%) APOA: Serpent-Hide • (1.5%) <Voluspa Adornments> • (1.5%) Herald's Furlined Cloak

hagbui page [36] (30%) Retainer's Beaded Insignia • (20%) Beaded Sinew Bracelet • (1.5%) APOA: Serpent-Hide • (1.5%) <Voluspa Adornments> • (1.5%) Bloodied Coral Sword

hagbui runemaster [42] (20%) Carved Elemental Idol • (5%) Sea Serpent Totem • (20%) Jewels 13 • (1.5% each) Elder Runed Scroll, Hagbui Runecarver's Staff • (1.5%) APOA: Supple Frog Skin

hagbui shaman [40] (20%) Carved Elemental Idol • (5%) Sea Serpent Totem • (20%) Jewels 13 • (1.4%) APOA: Blood Crystal • (1.3% each) Embossed ***or*** Etched Hagbui Bracelet, Serpent Bone Ring

hagbui spiritmaster [43] (20%) Carved Elemental Idol • (5%) Sea Serpent Totem • (20%) Jewels 13 • (1.5% each) Elder Runed Scroll, Hagbui Spiritmaster's Staff • (1.5%) APOA: Supple Frog Skin

hagbui squire [39] (25%) Squire's Beaded Insignia • (5%) Beaded Sinew Bracelet • (5%) Jewels 13 • (1.5%) APOA: Serpent-Hide • (1.5%) <Voluspa Adornments> • (1.5%) Squire's Practice Spear

hagbui swordbearer [35] (30%) Retainer's Beaded Insignia • (15%) Beaded Sinew Bracelet • (1.5%) APOA: Serpent-Hide • (1.5%) <Voluspa Adornments> • (1.5%) Bloodied Coral Sword

hagbui thane [53] (30%) Thane's Jeweled Insignia • (15%) Statue of Thor • (20%) Jewels 13 • (1.5%) APOA: Jotun Black Orm ***or*** Shrunken Orm Skull • (1.5% each) Thunder Embossed Sleeves, Celestial Storm Caller

jotun despot [61] (20%) Black Opal • (15%) Black Sapphire • (10%) Violet Diamond • (25%) Jewels 13 • (1.5%) APOA: Jotun Black Orm ***or*** Shrunken Orm Skull • (1.5%) <Last Stand Arms> • (1.5%) <Bogged Down>

jotun outcast [58-59] (20%) Precious Jasper Necklace • (15%) Horn of Fire Grog • (10%) Jotun Jeweled Chest • (25%) Jewels 13 • (1.5%) APOA: Jotun Black Orm ***or*** Shrunken Orm Skull • (1.5%) <Last Stand Arms> • (1.5%) <Bogged Down>

jotun overlord [62] (20%) Black Opal • (15%) Black Sapphire • (10%) Violet Diamond • (25%) Jewels 13 • (1.5%) APOA: Jotun Black Orm ***or*** Shrunken Orm Skull • (1.5%) <Last Stand Arms> • (1.5%) <Bogged Down>

jotun warchief [60] (20%) Black Opal • (15%) Black Sapphire • (10%) Violet Diamond • (25%) Jewels 13 • (1.5%) APOA: Jotun Black Orm ***or*** Shrunken Orm Skull • (1.5%) <Last Stand Arms> • (1.5%) <Bogged Down>

large enslaved orm [48/50] (24/23%) Black Orm Claw • (1.4%) Hooked Orm Claw • (23/27%) Enriched Black Orm Hide • (2.5/3%) Saturated Black Orm Hide • (1.6/1.3% each) Crystalized Jotun Hand, Giant [Alexandrite/Black Sapphire] Ring

large enslaved orm runner [48] (24%) Black Orm Claw • (1.4%) Hooked Orm Claw • (23%) Enriched Black Orm Hide • (2.5%) Saturated Black Orm Hide • (1.6% each) Crystalized Jotun Hand, Giant Alexandrite Ring

Major Terentius [52] (no loot)

mud crab [35] (27%) Mud Crab Chitin Shell • (3%) Crystalized Crab Chitin Shell • (1.7%) Hollowed Chitin Sleeves • (12%) Mud Crab Claw

mud crab warrior [36] (29%) Mud Crab Chitin Shell • (3%) Crystalized Crab Chitin Shell • (1.7%) Hollowed Chitin Sleeves

mud frog [30/32/34/36] (18/23/25/30%) Mud Frog Skin • (2/2.5/2.8/3.3%) Glistening Mud Frog Skin • (1.7%) Crystalized Kobold [30,32]/Dwarven [34,36] Remains • (1.7%) Poor Sod's Belt [30,32]/Hardened Viper Skin Bracer (x2) [34,36] • (8/10/12/15%) Mud Frog Tongue

Noma Rindasdottir [35] (no loot)

reincarnate orm [45,47/49,51/53,55] (10%) Black Orm Tooth (x2) • (75/10/10%) Shadowy Orm Eye • (5/7.5/10%) Saturated Orm Scales • (1/7.5/10%) Enriched Orm Scales • (1.3%) Reincarnate Orm Eye • (1.3%) Runic ***or*** Wispy Rigid Orm Spine • (1.3% each) Crystalized Jotun Hand, Giant [Alexandrite/Black Sapphire/Black Sapphire] Ring

shadowy werewolf [40] (65%) Large Werewolf Pelt • (70%) Large Werewolf Paw • (54%) Golden Military Chain • (1.5%) <Howling at the Moon> • (0.3%) <Freya's Dowry>

small black orm [35] (19%) Black Orm Tooth • (1%) Serrated Black Tooth • (18%) Black Orm Hide • (2%) Touched Black Orm Hide • (1.3% each) Crystalized Jotun Hand, Giant Green Sapphire Ring • (11%) Black Orm Gland

tomb raider scout [15] (25% each) Dried Pork, Canteen of Water • (40%) Carnelian • (10%) Agate • (1%) Garnet • (1.4%) <Mounds of Salisbury> • (3%) APOA: Faded • (0.3%) <Grave Goods> • (0.3%) Chain Sleeves of Disparity • (0.2%) Chain Gloves of Disparity • (0.2%) Chain Hauberk of Disparity • (0.1%) Deathscent Mace • (0.1%) Spirit Crafted Shield

werewolf brute [45] (65%) Large Werewolf Pelt • (70%) Large Werewolf Paw • (54%) Golden Military Chain • (1.5%) <Howling at the Moon> • (0.3%) <Freya's Dowry>

Ydenia of the Seithkona [65] (no loot)

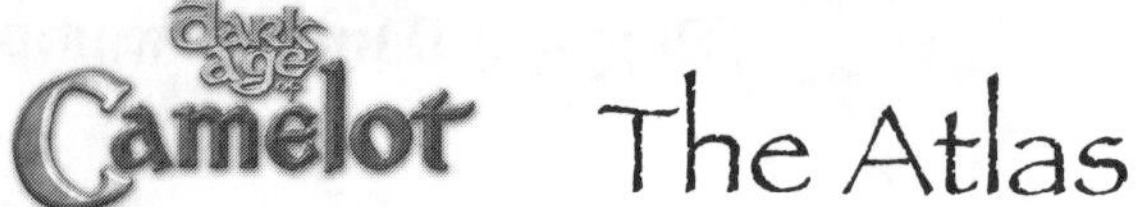

Jordheim

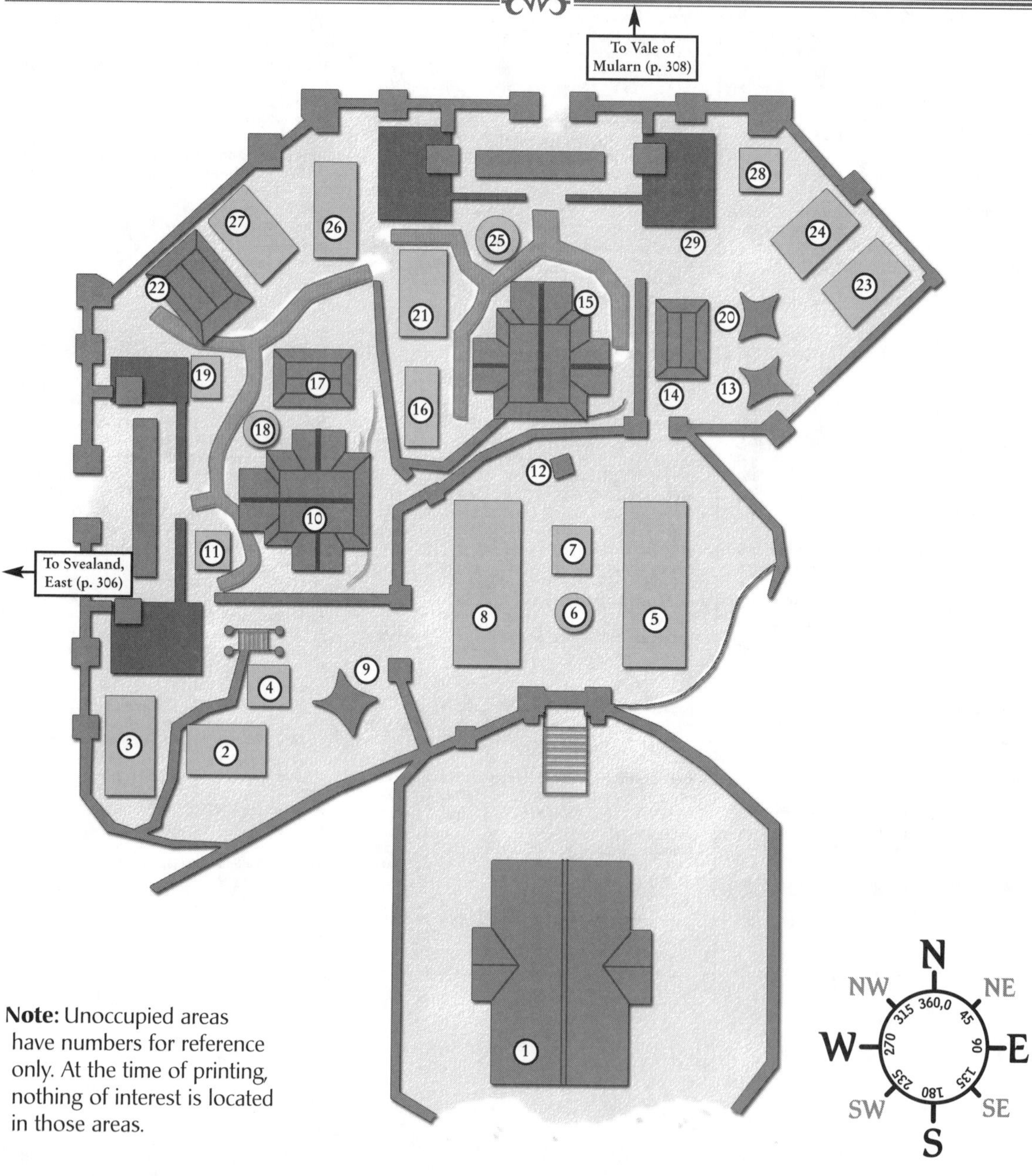

To Vale of Mularn (p. 308)
To Svealand, East (p. 306)
1
2
3
4
5
6
7
8
9
10
11
12
13
14
15
16
17
18
19
20
21
22
23
24
25
26
27
28
29
N
NE
E
SE
S
SW
W
NW
360,0
45
90
135
180
235
270
315

Note: Unoccupied areas have numbers for reference only. At the time of printing, nothing of interest is located in those areas.

1 **Tora** Bounty Store - Crystals
1 **Aesa**
1 **Karis** Guild Emblemeer
1 **Jarl Uffenlong** Name Registrar
1 **Jarl Yuliwyf** Vault Keeper
1 **Brit** Guild Registrar
2 **Tait** Mithril chain armor
2 **Hakan** Mithril studded armor
2 **Flosi** Blades
2 **Ema** Axes
2 **Signy** Hammers
2 **Ole** Bows
2 **Aric** Shields
2 **Hedin** Spears
2 **Fiora** Embossed leather armor
4 **Nanna** Healer
4 **Anya** Runemaster staves
4 **Magna** Spiritmaster staves
5 **Per** Healer Trainer
5 **Solveig** Green/brown/grey/orange/ yellow enamel dye
5 **Grimma** Shaman Trainer
5 **Falla** Tailoring Equipment
5 **Miri**
6 **Gungir** Healer
7 **Gest** Armorcraft Master
7 **Aase** Weaponscraft Master
8 **Dane** Shaman Trainer
8 **Greip** Blue/turq/teal/red/purple enamel dye
8 **Rana** Healer Trainer
8 **Om** Smithing equipment
9 **Tove** Mithril large weapons
9 **Kalf** Large weapons
9 **Harry** Throwing weapons
9 **Asra** Arrows
9 **Morgen** Starklaedar leather armor
10 **Elli** Bounty Store - Crystals
11 **Ander** Poison
11 **Oilibhear** Poison
12 **Kiarr** Smith
13 **Im** Mjuklaeder leather armor
13 **Keki** Stelskodd studded armor
13 **Njal** Pansarkedja chain armor
14 **Leif** Skald Trainer
15 **Royd** Bounty Store - Crystals
16 **Gris** Smith
16 **Morlin Caan** Smith
18 **Amma** Enchanter
19 **Uli** Sylvan padded armor
19 **Ozur** Green/brown/grey/orange/ yellow leather dye
19 **Ella** Blue/turquoise/teal/red/purple leather dye
20 **Gerd** Arrows
20 **Synna** Spears
20 **Saga** Large weapons
20 **Canute** Throwing weapons
20 **Hodern** Svarlaeder leather armor
20 **Frode** Thane Trainer
20 **Hrapp** Blades
20 **Borg** Staff
20 **Digby** Shields
20 **Thir** Bows
20 **Gymir** Axes
21 **Barkeep Prugar**
21 **Barkeep Banak**
21 **Anrid**
22 **Hauk** Hunter Trainer
22 **Singrid** Hunter Trainer
22 **Hreidar** Shadowblade Trainer
22 **Elin** Shadowblade Trainer
23 **Eskil** Tailoring Master
23 **Sven** Skald Trainer
23 **Osten** Warrior Trainer
23 **Katla** Thane Trainer
23 **Hodr** Berserker Trainer
25 **Arve** Enchanter
25 **Ottar** Woodworking equipment
26 **Dyre** Spiritmaster Trainer
26 **Signa** Runemaster Trainer
26 **Bera** Runemaster Trainer
26 **Galn** Spiritmaster Trainer
27 **Darg** Fletching equipment (feathers)
27 **Gils** Fletching Master
27 **Dala** Mithril weapons
28 **Thordia** Warrior Trainer
28 **Torrad** Padded armor
28 **Gro** Tailoring equipment
28 **Alleca** Blue/turq/teal/red/purple cloth dye
28 **Hyndla** Green/brown/grey/orange/ yellow cloth dye
29 **Haaken** Berserker Trainer

Quest NPCs

Jordheim	
Anrid	The Three Sisters (lvl Guild Track - 40)
Anrid	Coplin's Spirit (lvl Guild Track - 20)
Anrid	Fallen Warrior (lvl Guild Track - 25)
Anrid	Forgotten journey (lvl Guild Track - 30)
Gythja of Bragi	Thane's Blood (lvl Guild Track - 30)
Morlin Caan	A War of Old (lvl Guild Track - 20)
Morlin Caan	A War of Old (lvl Guild Track - 25)
Morlin Caan	A War of Old (lvl Guild Track - 30)
Singrid	Gokstad's Jewel (lvl 18)
Thordia	Hill Cat Hunt (lvl 11)
your trainer	Traveler's Way (lvl 7)
your trainer	Darksong's Dirge (lvl 11)
your trainer	Prove Kobold Helen's innocence (lvl 11)
your trainer	Rasczel's bane (lvl 11)
your trainer	Runes of Darkness (lvl 11)
your trainer	Taldos' Amulet (lvl 11)
your trainer	The War Continues (lvl Guild Track - 40)
your trainer	A War of Old (lvl Guild Track - 15)
your trainer	Grenlock Clan (lvl Guild Track - 15)
your trainer	The Red Dagger (lvl Guild Track - 15)
your trainer	The Rod and the Scholars (lvl Guild Track - 15)
your trainer	Wisdom of Time (lvl Guild Track - 15)

Audliten (Svealand East)

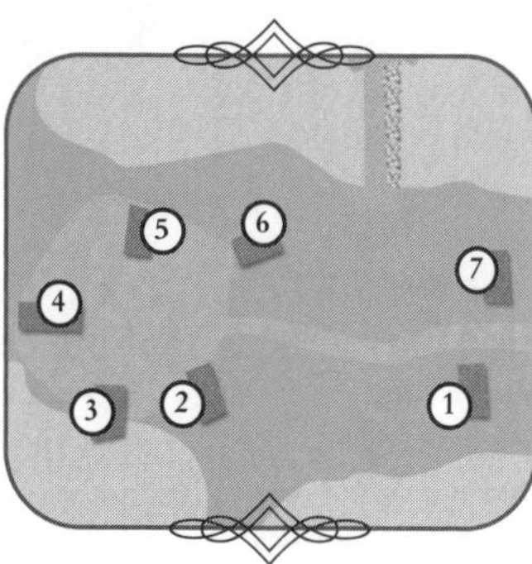

1 **Gwaell** *Poison*
1 **Serath** *Leather dye*
1 **Tozur** *Padded cloth A.*
1 **Eirik** *Staff*
2 **Hulda** *Shields*
3 **Dahn** *Smith*
3 **Garon**
3 **Lefur**
3 **Osk** *Poison (1)*
3 **Jolgeir** *Poisons (2)*
4 **May**
4 **Jordan** *Svarlaedar leather A.*
4 **Pireda** *Starklaedar leather A.*
4 **Ragnar** *Svarskodd studded A.*
4 **Leim** *Starkaskodd studded A.*
5 **Rhomali**
5 **Thorgil**
5 **Olav** *Mjuklaedar leather A.*
5 **Eigil** *Stelskodd studded A.*
5 **Gruth** *Svarkedja chain A.*
5 **Deilf** *Starkakedja chain A.*
6 **Aleaniver**
6 **Cnute**
6 **Gorne**
6 **Brede** *Bows*
6 **Inga** *Arrows*
7 **Trapper Jora**
7 **Geirrid** *Pansarkedja chain A.*
7 **Pater** *Sword W.*
7 **Armond** *Axe W.*
7 **Frey** *Hammer*
7 **Josli** *Spear W.*
7 **Delg** *Throwing W.*
7 **Ostein** *Drums*
7 **Fraglock** *Stable*
Dwarven Guard Eske
Viking Dreng

Dvalin (Svealand East)

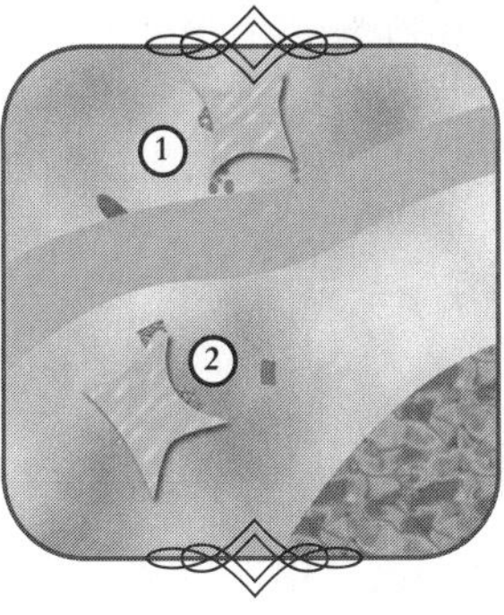

1 ***Flayer Fali***
1 ***Rae*** *Svarlaedar leather A.*
1 ***Marianne*** *Svarskodd studded A.*
1 ***Vordn*** *Sword W.*
1 ***Svard*** *Axe W.*
1 ***Laran*** *Hammer*
1 ***Alfrig*** *Starkakedja chain A.*
2 ***Tyrn*** *Starkalaedar leather A.*
2 ***Laed*** *Starkaskodd studded A.*
2 ***Brok*** *Bows*
2 ***Aesirdia*** *Shields*

Fort Atla (Gotar)

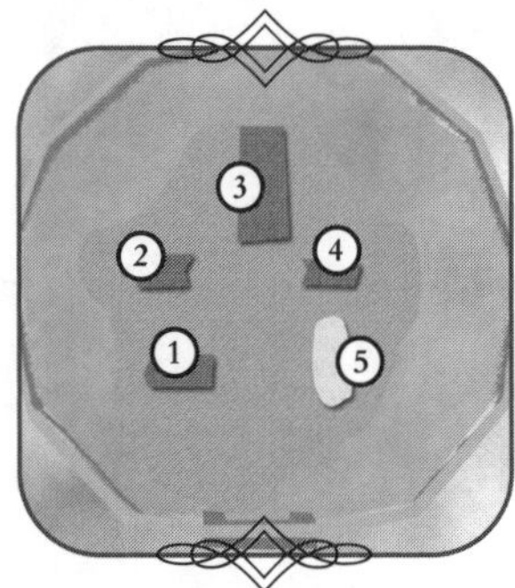

1 ***Finna***
1 ***Hyndia*** *Seer Tr.*
1 ***Jucla*** *Rogue Tr.*
1 ***Korgan*** *Shaman Tr.*
1 ***Hrin*** *Cloth dye*
1 ***Ullaria*** *Cloth dye*
1 ***Og*** *Mjuklaedar leather A.*
1 ***Ruk*** *Staff*
1 ***Sillis*** *Arrow*
2 ***Amora***
2 ***Budo*** *Hunter Tr.*
2 ***Halker*** *Warrior Tr.*
2 ***Lalida*** *Skald Tr.*
2 ***Magnild***
2 ***Trunk*** *Svarskodd studded A.*
2 ***Isleif*** *Large W.*
3 ***Barkeep Tesin***
3 ***Kari*** *Healer*
3 ***Lycla*** *Mystic Tr.*
3 ***Masrim***
3 ***Onund*** *Enchanter*
3 ***Thetus*** *Runemaster Tr.*
3 ***Welgen*** *Healer Tr.*
3 ***Helja*** *Poison (1)*
3 ***Bersi*** *Poisons (2)*
3 ***Lagg*** *Stelskodd studded A.*
3 ***Ugg*** *Pansarkedja chain A.*
3 ***Vifil*** *Sword W.*
3 ***Niniver*** *Runemaster staff*
3 ***Rundorik*** *Stable*
4 ***Boidoc*** *Shadowblade Tr.*
4 ***Finni***
4 ***Kalli*** *Berserker Tr.*
4 ***Sarry*** *Spiritmaster Tr.*
4 ***Merarka*** *Spiritmaster staff*
5 ***Eindridi*** *Smith*
5 ***Salma*** *Thane Tr.*
5 ***Harald*** *Sword W.*
5 ***Yop*** *Axe W.*
5 ***Stap*** *Hammer W.*
5 ***Krak*** *Bows*
5 ***Klag*** *Shields*
5 ***Freydis*** *Spear W.*
5 ***Carl*** *Throwing W.*
1 ***Arni***
3 ***Darrius***
5 ***Dissa***
3 ***Lyngheid***
3 ***Salevia***
1 ***Troll Digby***
3 ***Looga*** *Spear W.*
2 ***Meeka*** *Padded cloth A.*
5 ***Flayer Kegnar***
5 ***Estrilith*** *Drums*

Fort Veldon (Vale of Mularn)

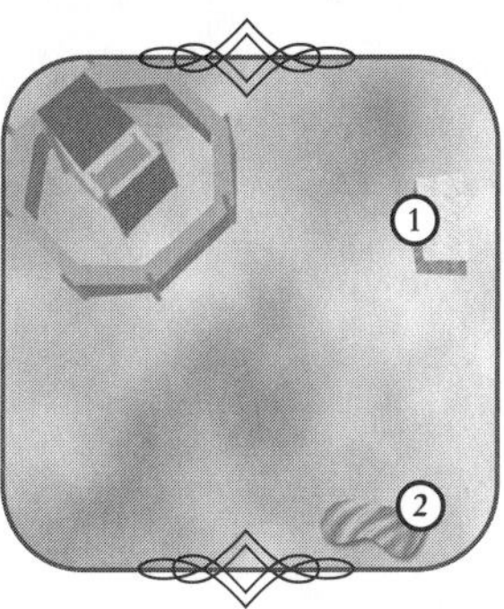

1 ***Cornelis***

1 ***Rulongja*** *Enamel dye*

1 ***Seiml*** *Enamel dye*

1 ***Idona Tiu*** *Starklaedar leather A.*

1 ***Darby*** *Starkaskodd studded A.*

1 ***Liv*** *Sword W.*

1 ***Hlif*** *Axe W.*

1 ***Olof*** *Hammer W.*

2 ***Gerda*** *Starklaedar leather A.*

2 ***Connor*** *Starkaskodd studded A.*

2 ***Bitta*** *Bows*

2 ***Avar*** *Shields*

2 ***Kell*** *Starkakedja chain A.*

2 ***Arskar*** *Stable*

Galplen (Myrkwood Forest)

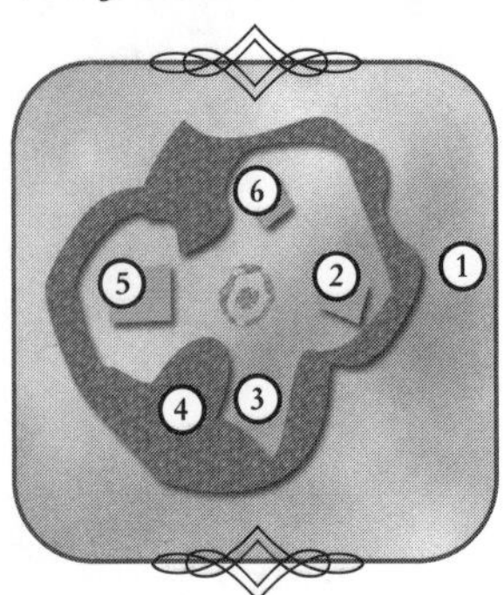

1 **Bec** *Shaman Tr.*
1 **Kelcea**
1 **Kullervo**
1 **Vanah** *Skald Tr.*
1 **Wariel**
1 **Ohar** *Enamel dye*
1 **Tallya** *Enamel dye*
1 **Nikgor** *Svarskodd studded A.*
1 **Kaiti** *Padded cloth A.*
1 **Galena** *Large W.*
1 **Ysunoic** *Runemaster staff*
1 **Curka** *Spiritmaster staff*
1 **Treflun** *Stable*
2 **Otkel** *Shields*
2 **Serilyna** *Staff*
3 **Krek** *Viking Tr.*
3 **Seph**
3 **Stein** *Sword W.*
3 **Gestod** *Axe W.*
3 **Helga** *Hammer W.*
4 **Gord** *Smith*
4 **Gudrid** *Spear W.*
4 **Aki** *Throwing W.*
5 **Barkeep Yseniver**
5 **Hord** *Healer*
6 **Canan** *Seer Tr.*
6 **Toli**
6 **Nyden** *Svarskodd studded A.*
6 **Thyra** *Pansarkedja chain A.*
6 **Ola** *Drums*
Guard Flintrock
Sentry Gaaruun
Sentry Stenbjorn

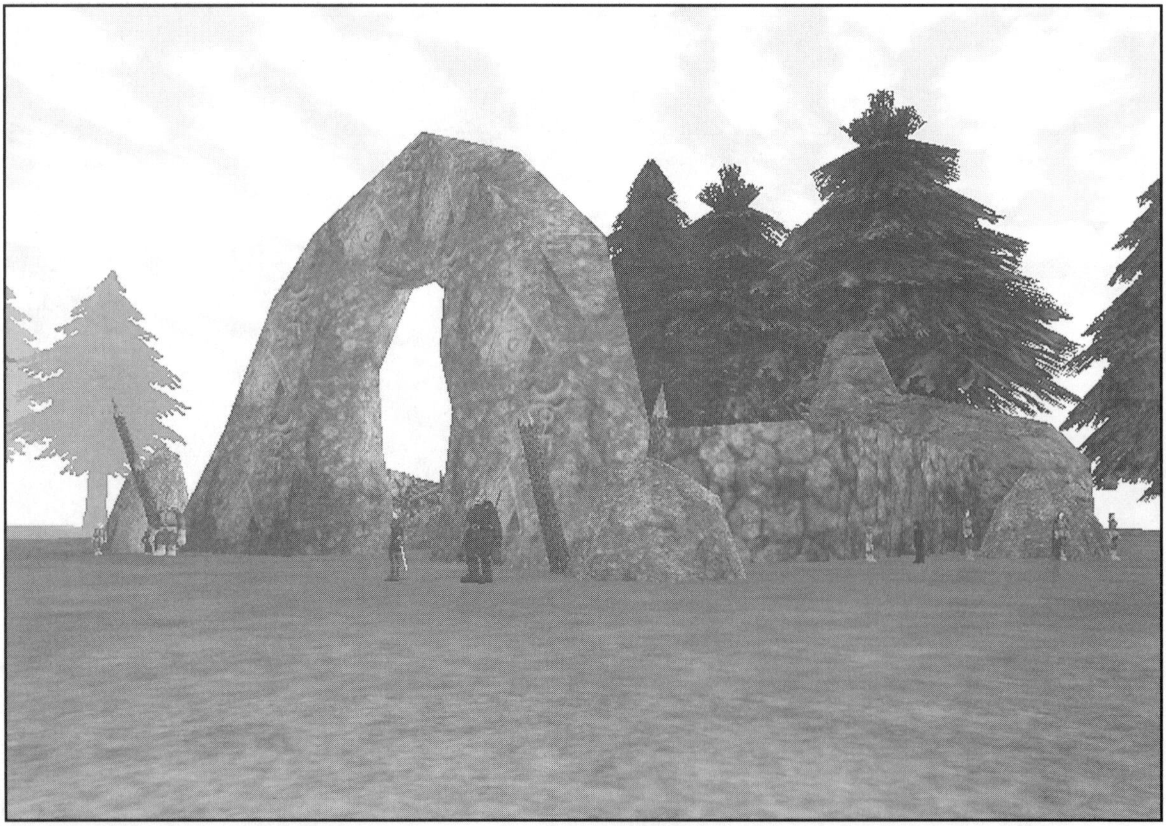

Gna Faste (Myrkwood Forest)

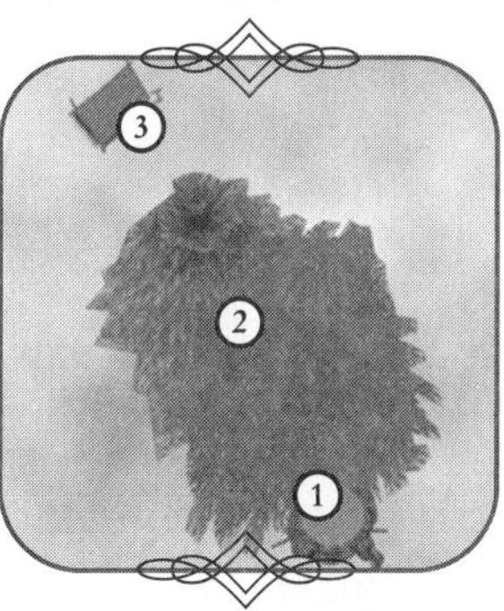

1 ***Atzar***
1 ***Halldis*** *Enchanter*
1 ***Khelad*** *Warrior Tr.*
2 ***Alrik***
2 ***Aphriodora*** *Thane Tr.*
2 ***Idonna*** *Vault*
2 ***Itesta*** *Healer Tr.*
2 ***Magnor***
2 ***Valgerd***
2 ***Zalerik*** *Berserker Tr.*
2 ***Ulwatyl*** *Smith/Tailoring Supplies*
2 ***Jytal*** *Fletching/Tailoring Supplies*
3 ***Kedin*** *Bows*
3 ***Ingrid*** *Arrow*
3 ***Wolgrun*** *Stable*

Haggerfel (Vale of Mularn)

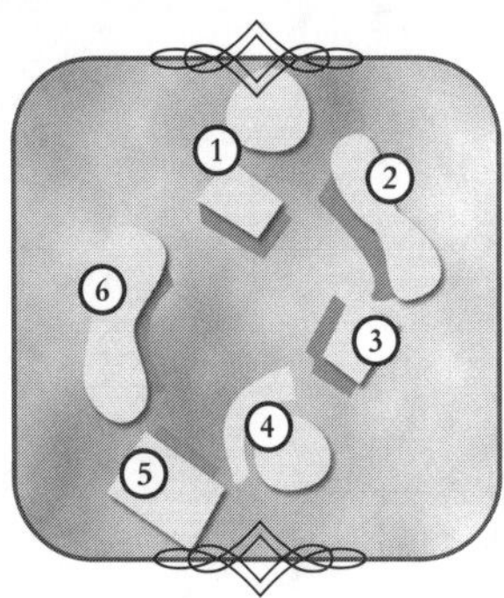

1 ***Genlu Edrill*** *Smith*
1 ***Groa*** *Seer Tr.*
1 ***Helen***
1 ***Culben*** *Padded cloth A.*
1 ***Yolafson*** *Stable*
2 ***Hilde*** *Smith*
2 ***Burr*** *Axe W.*
2 ***Ime*** *Shields*
2 ***Fuiren*** *Spear W.*
2 ***Frikk*** *Woodworking skill item*
3 ***Arnkatla***
3 ***Armund*** *Sword W.*
3 ***Cort*** *Hammer W.*
3 ***Mattie*** *Bows*
3 ***Takker*** *Arrows*
4 ***Glum*** *Rogue Tr.*
4 ***Gustav*** *Healer*
4 ***Inaksha***
4 ***Macalena***
5 ***Dritsa*** *Svarlaedar leather A.*
5 ***Erik*** *Svarskodd studded A.*
5 ***Den*** *Pansarkedja chain A.*
5 ***Eda*** *Staff*
5 ***Bodil*** *Throwing W.*
6 ***Kran***
6 ***Yver Tiu***
6 ***Belyria*** *Leather dye*
6 ***Gale*** *Enamel dye*
6 ***Sinmora*** *Large W.*
Dwarven Guard
Dwarven Guard Rinda
Dwarven Thegn
Marveth
Mildrid
Pavar *Enchanter*
Borghilda *Drums*

Huginfel (Svealand West)

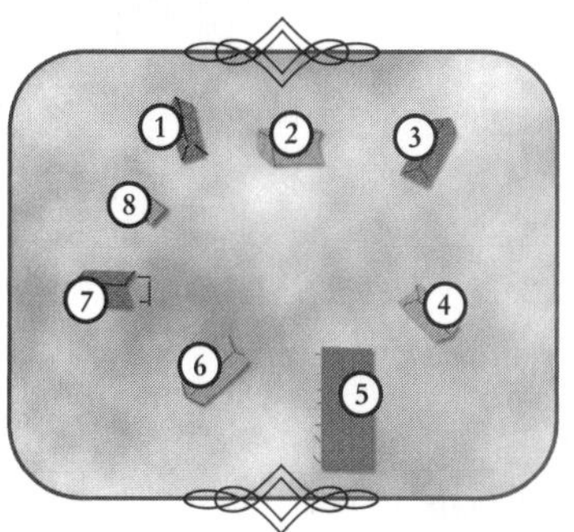

1 ***Linnea***
1 ***Liot***
1 ***Ljufa***
1 ***Olgara***
1 ***Samlauf Kolsson***
1 ***Svala*** *Staff*
1 ***Rorik*** *Drums*
2 ***Hrut***
2 ***Kol Smithir*** *Smith*
2 ***Arnlaug*** *Enamel dye*
2 ***Ruloia*** *Enamel dye*
2 ***Radgar*** *Pansarkedja chain A.*
2 ***Orm*** *Sword W.*
2 ***Auda*** *Axe W.*
2 ***Lodin*** *Hammer W.*
2 ***Hakon*** *Bows*
2 ***Ivara*** *Spear W.*
2 ***Dana*** *Arrow*
2 ***Ryden*** *Throwing W.*
3 ***Hurg***
4 ***Besje***
4 ***Bork***
4 ***Gudlor***
4 ***Thora***
5 ***Agnor Crusher***
5 ***Barkeep Alaka***
5 ***Corath***
5 ***Halla***
5 ***Ljot***
5 ***Sugnhild***
5 ***Valgard***
5 ***Prulgar*** *Stable*
6 ***Virge***
7 ***Raker*** *Enchanter*
7 ***Saydyn*** *Healer*
7 ***Trustan***
7 ***Elengwen*** *Runemaster staff*
7 ***Alyllyra*** *Spiritmaster staff*
8 ***Dail***
8 ***Dvaln***
8 ***Wulfwer*** *Starklaedar leather A.*
8 ***Enir*** *Starkaskodd studded A.*
8 ***Runolf*** *Shields*
8 ***Aylarn*** *Padded cloth A.*

Mularn Village (Vale of Mularn)

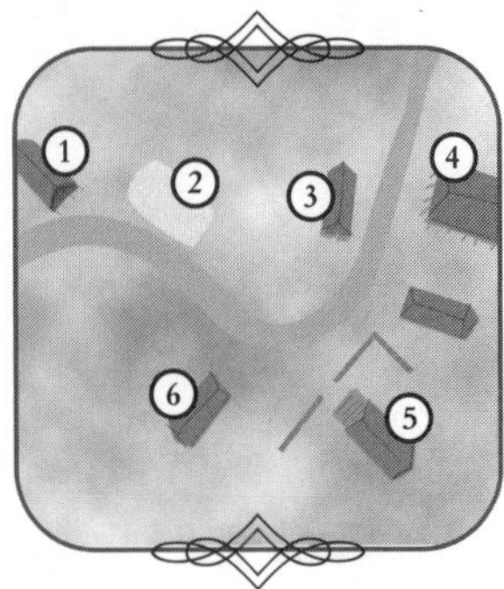

1 **Elizabeth** *Enchanter*
1 **Kalbin** *Healer*
1 **Vigdis** *Mystic Tr.*
1 **Hild** *Throwing W.*
1 **Oken** *Drums*
2 **Diego**
2 **Vahn** *Smith*
2 **Finn** *Leather dye*
2 **Cale** *Leather dye*
2 **Lene** *Mjuklaedar leather A.*
2 **Blyn** *Stelskodd studded A.*
2 **Bein** *Pansarkedja chain A.*
2 **Aren** *Sword W.*
2 **Hrolf** *Axe W.*
2 **Gram** *Hammer W.*
2 **Linna** *Bows*
2 **Marie** *Shields*
2 **Grenlyr** *Spear W.*
2 **Geir** *Arrows*
3 **Aegan**
3 **Danica**
3 **Oslin**
3 **Vers** *Svarkedja chain A.*
3 **Raelyan** *Runemaster staff*
3 **Lyna** *Spiritmaster staff*
4 **Arnljot**
4 **Barkeep Nognar**
4 **Bolli**
4 **Denise**
4 **Gnup**
4 **Brik** *Staff*
4 **Gularg** *Stable*
5 **Gordin Tuhan** *Smith*
5 **Skapi** *Viking Tr.*
5 **Viking Kreimhilde**
6 **Asta** *Padded cloth A.*
Chieftain Guard

Nalliten (Gotar)

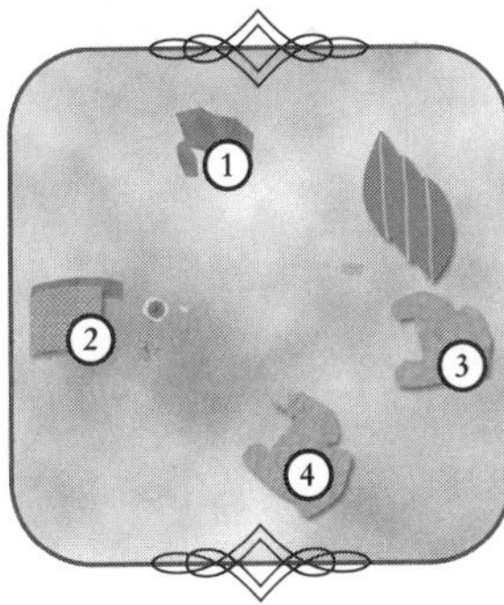

1 ***Flayer Jicq***
1 ***Dink*** *Svarskodd studded A.*
2 ***Geiri***
2 ***Grungir*** *Pansarkedja chain A.*
2 ***Moona*** *Padded cloth A.*
2 ***Eryklan*** *Stable*
3 ***Dunfjall***
3 ***Gautr***
3 ***Rooka*** *Leather dye*
3 ***Hallaya*** *Leather dye*
3 ***Tig*** *Svarlaedar leather A.*
4 ***Cragg*** *Arrow*

Vasudheim (Svealand East)

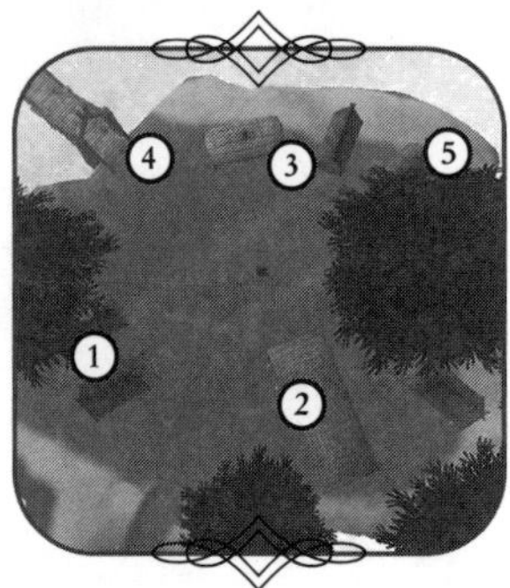

1 **Daga**
1 **Frimeth**
1 **Garu**
1 **Ragna** *Mystic Tr.*
1 **Saeunn** *Viking Tr.*
1 **Tric**
1 **Kerr** *Bows*
1 **Krisst** *Arrow*
2 **Barkeep Kanar**
2 **Geoffrey Krath**
2 **Gridash**
2 **Kristen**
2 **Sijur Halfdan**
2 **Tosti** *Seer Tr.*
2 **Viking Dreng**
2 **Yosef Angor**
2 **Thord** *Cloth dye*
2 **Gregor** *Cloth dye*
2 **Krip** *Svarkedja chain A.*
2 **Harlfug** *Stable*
3 **Alomali**
3 **Aud** *Healer*
3 **Hrut** *Rogue Tr.*
3 **Kjell**
3 **Kyba**
3 **Ulf** *Enchanter*
3 **Gunnar** *Padded cloth A.*
3 **Merwdda** *Runemaster staff*
3 **Clena** *Spiritmaster staff*
3 **Wyborn** *Drums*
4 **Arnfinn** *Smith*
4 **Karl Gat**
4 **Fianna** *Mjuklaedar leather A.*
4 **Baldus** *Stelskodd studded A.*
4 **Vidar** *Pansarkedja chain A.*
4 **Gyda** *Sword W.*
4 **Leik** *Axe W.*
4 **Burl** *Hammer W.*
4 **Galagore** *Spear W.*
4 **Mildri** *Staff*
4 **Hallfred** *Throwing W.*
4 **Ingerd** *Tailoring equipment*
5 **Arnleif**
5 **Erekith**
5 **Finn**
5 **Jana**
5 **Bothe** *Shields*

Vindsaul Faste (Svealand West)

Audney *Shaman Tr.*
Var *Runemaster Tr.*
Dain *Spiritmaster Tr.*
Eryk *Skald Tr.*
Gunnolf *Shadowblade Tr.*
Ingemur *Berserker Tr.*
Mar *Thane Tr.*
Rika *Warrior Tr.*
Lin *Hunter Tr.*
Ari *Healer Tr.*
Beni *Various Skill Items*
Ulufgar *Stable*
Gothi of Aesir
Gothi of Juton
Gythja of Aesir
Gythja of Juton
Master of Runes
Viking Huscarl

Cursed Tomb

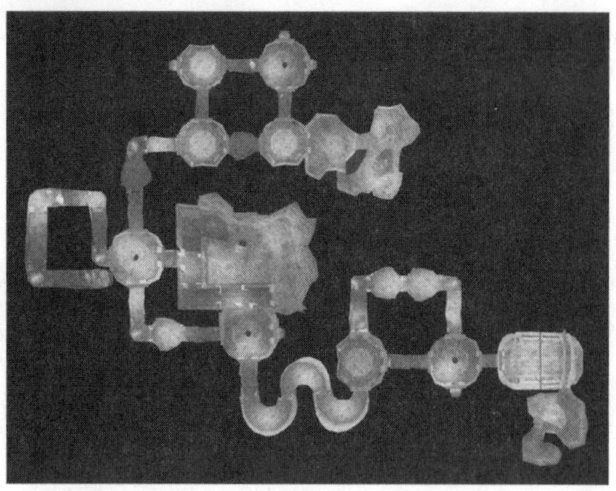

Loot

Bevard [24] (35%) <Really Ghouled Loot> • (17%) Jewels 41 • (1.7%) Bevard's Ghostly *or* Ghastly Chain

cave crab [19-20/21] (15/18%) Tomb Crab Leg (x2) • (15/18%) Cracked Crab Carapace (x2) • (15/18%) Pristine Crab Carapace (x2)

corpse crawler [21/22-23] *see dungeon chitin [22/23]*

cursed mora [23/24] (30%) <Really Ghouled Loot> • (15%) Jewels 41 • (1.6%) Mora Staff of Runecarving/Summoning *or* Accursed Shield/Tower Shield • (1.6%) Cursed *or* Baneful Mora Ring • (9/11%) Scroll of Eternal Sorrow

cursed mora dancer [25] (30%)<Really Ghouled Loot> • (20%) Jewels 41 • (1.6%) Mora Staff of Darkness *or* Accursed Hammer • (1.6%) Cursed *or* Baneful Mora Ring • (13%) Scroll of Eternal Sorrow

cursed mora weeper [25] (30%)<Really Ghouled Loot> • (17%) Jewels 41 • (1.6%) Mora Staff of Suppression *or* Accursed Great Hammer • (1.6%) Cursed *or* Baneful Mora Ring • (13%) Scroll of Eternal Sorrow

cursed spirit [19/20] (25/30%) <Really Ghouled Loot> • (15%) Jewels 41 • (1.6%) Moldy Tombdweller Sleeves *or* Cap/Pants *or* Boots • (1.6%) Cursed *or* Trapped Spirit Shackle

dishonored hagbui [23/24] (30%) <Really Ghouled Loot> • (17/20%) Jewels 41 • (1.6%) Flayed Hagbui Gloves, Sleeves, Boots *or* Leggings/Helm *or* Jerkin • (1.6%) Shrouded Hagbui Mantle *or* Pall

Draugr Commander [25] (35%) <Really Ghouled Loot> • (20%) Jewels 41 • (1.7%) Rusty Draugr Commander Medal *or* Draugr Commander Axe

draugr hound [23-24] (25%) Draugr Hound Pelt (x2) • (25%) Mangled Toe (x2) • (25%) Gnawed Bone (x2)

draugr warrior [21/22/23] (30%) <Really Ghouled Loot> • (15/15/17%) Jewels 41 • (1.6%) Putrescent Boots *or* Bowyer's Gloves/Leggings *or* Parrying Gloves/Sleeves, Helm *or* Jerkin • (1.6%) Ghostly *or* Ghastly Gem

Dread Lichess [26] (30%) <Really Ghouled Loot> • (25%) Jewels 41 • (1.7%) Dread Lichess Demolisher *or* Belt

dungeon chitin [22/23] (20/25%) Spider Poison Gland (x2) • (20/25%) Tomb Spider Leg (x2) • (20/25%) Gnawed Insect Wing (x2)

dungeon crab [20-22] (18%) Tomb Crab Leg (x2) • (18%) Cracked Crab Carapace (x2) • (18%) Pristine Crab Carapace (x2)

Haggert [25] (30%) <Really Ghouled Loot> • (25%) Jewels 41 • (1.7%) Haggert's Shroud of Death *or* Haggert's Bane

lost spirit [19] (30%) <Really Ghouled Loot> • (15%) Jewels 41 • (1.7%) Evanescent Long Spear *or* Kite Shield

mad rat [22] (25%) Bloodied Rat Fur (x2) • (20%) Mangled Rat's Paw (x2) • (20%) Flayed Rat Tail (x2)

poisonous cave spider [23-24] (25%) Spider Poison Gland (x2) • (25%) Tomb Spider Leg (x2) • (25%) Gnawed Insect Wing (x2)

roaming corpse [19/20/21] (30%) <Really Ghouled Loot> • (15/15/17%) Jewels 41 • (1.6%) Woeful Melody Gloves *or* Woeful Chain Boots/Woeful Chain Coif *or* Gloves/Stormcaller Woeful Gloves *or* Woeful Chain Sleeves • (1.6%) Ghostly *or* Ghastly Chain

Rotting corpse [24] (30%) <Really Ghouled Loot> • (17%) Jewels 41 • (1.6%) Woeful Chain Hauberk *or* Leggings • (1.6%) Ghostly *or* Ghastly Chain

Tomb Priestess [23] (30%) <Really Ghouled Loot> • (20%) Jewels 41 • (1.7%) Cursed Spirit Spear *or* Tomb Priestess Bracelet

tomb sentry [19/20] (25%) <Really Ghouled Loot> • (15%) Jewels 41 • (1.6%) Blighted Chain Sleeves, Leggings *or* Coif [19] *or* Blighted Chain Hauberk [20] *or* Bone-Handle Great Axe • (1.6%) Mildewed *or* Moldy Leather Belt

trapped thrall [19/20] (25/30%) <Really Ghouled Loot> • (15%) Jewels 41 • (1.6%) Moldy Summoner *or* Runecarving Gloves/Moldy Tombdweller's Bow *or* Vest • (1.6%) Cursed *or* Trapped Spirit Shackle

Troika [24] (30%) <Really Ghouled Loot> • (20%) Jewels 41 • (1.7%) Troika's Cursed Axe *or* Enchanted Ring

vengeful ghoul [23/24] (30%) <Really Ghouled Loot> • (20/25%) Jewels 41 • (1.7%) Vengeful Sword, Great Sword *or* Shield/Vengeful War Hammer *or* Great Hammer

way keeper [19/20] (25%) <Really Ghouled Loot> • (15%) Jewels 41 • (1.6%) Blighted Keeper Chain Gloves *or* Blighted Chain Gloves/Bone-Handle Axe *or* Blighted Chain Boots • (1.6%) Mildewed *or* Moldy Leather Belt

Nisse's Lair

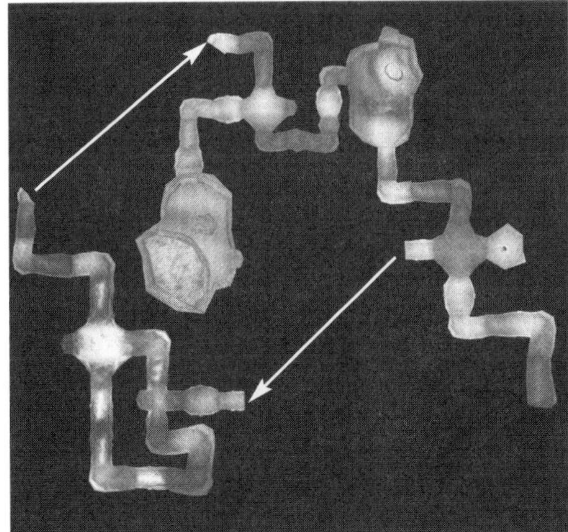

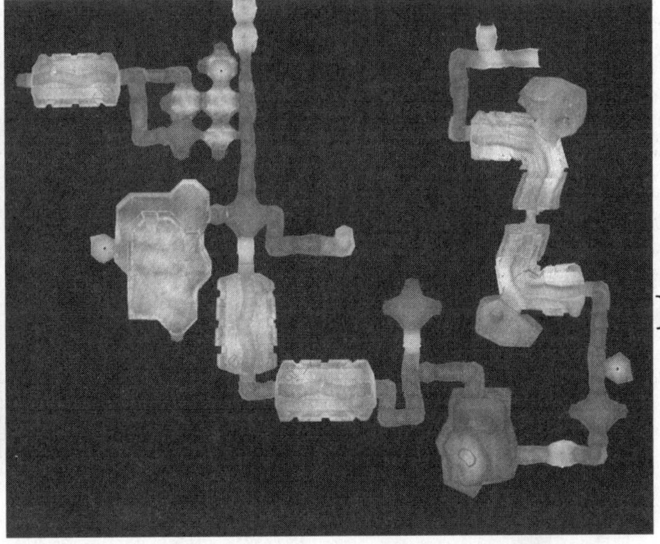

N

Loot

Callilepis Nocturna [19] (26%) Cave Spider Leg • (13%) Cave Spider Leg • (19%) Cave Spider Leg Tip • (9.6% each) Cave Spider Leg Tip, Carapace • (10%) Cave Spider Silk • (6.4%) Poison Sac • (40%) Chitin-Tipped Arrows, Crystallized Spider Eye, ***or*** Tomte Throwing Hammers

cave spider [13-14] (80%) Cave Spider Leg • (40%) Cave Spider Leg • (15%) Cave Spider Carapace • (60%) Cave Spider Leg Tip • (30%) Cave Spider Leg Tip • (5%) Cave Spider Silk

Executioner [13] (25%) <Tomte Treasures> • (25%) Jewels 12 • (5%) Light Blue, Light Red ***or*** Light Green Colors • (1.5%) APOA: Mephitic Leather, Malignant, Malefic Studded ***or*** Miscreant's • (1.5%) <Nisse's Nest Egg 1> • (1.5%) <Nisse's Nest Egg 2> • (0.5%) <Brendig's Gear>

Haunt [17] (60%) <Blood and Ice> • (40%) Jewels 55 • (5%) Light Blue, Light Red ***or*** Light Green Colors • (1.5%) APOA: Mephitic Leather, Malignant, Malefic Studded ***or*** Miscreant's • (1.5%) <Nisse's Nest Egg 2> • (1.5%) <Nisse's Nest Egg 1> • (0.5%) <Thief's Nest Egg>

Hnaki [20] (40%) <Blood and Ice> • (30%) Jewels 55 • (5%) Light Blue, Light Red, ***or*** Light Green Colors • (0.5%) Gold Stitched Boots ***or*** Gloves, Blazing Sleeves, Pilllager's Boots, Ancient Engraved Maul, Small Warrior Figurine, Boar's Head Ring, Huntsman's ***or*** Blackened Leather Jerkin, ***or*** Driftwood Staff • (1.7%) Malevolent Shield ***or*** Chain

lair guard [10-11] (30%) <Tomte Treasures> • (20%) Jewels 12 • (5%) Light Blue, Light Red ***or*** Light Green Colors • (4%) APOA: Tomte Padded, Leather, Studded ***or*** Chain • (1.7%) <Angry Dwarf> • (0.5%) <Grimnir's Adornment>

lair patrol [9] (20%) <Tomte Treasures> • (20%) Jewels 12 • (5%) Light Blue, Light Red ***or*** Light Green Colors • (4%) APOA: Tomte Padded, Leather, Studded ***or*** Chain • (1.7%) <Angry Dwarf> • (0.5%) <Har's Adornments>

mature sand lizard [16] (44% each) Sand Lizard Leg, Tail

Nioll [10] *see tomte handler [10]*

Nisse [19] *see Haunt [17]*

poisonous cave spider [15,17] (80%) Cave Spider Leg • (40%) Cave Spider Leg • (60%) Cave Spider Leg Tip • (30%) Cave Spider Leg Tip • (15%) Cave Spider Carapace • (20%) Cave Spider Silk • (10%) Poison Sac

prisoner [0] (3.5%) Pulsing Ruby • (3%) Rotting Robes • (0.3%) <Pilfered Prizes>

Rygnol [12] *see tomte captor [12]*

sand lizard hatchling [11] (21% each) Sand Lizard Leg, Tail

Skirr [22] (40%) <Blood and Ice> • (30%) Jewels 55 • (5%) Light Blue, Light Red, ***or*** Light Green Colors • (0.5%) Gold Stitched Boots ***or*** Gloves, Blazing Sleeves, Pilllager's Boots, Ancient Engraved Maul, Small Warrior Figurine, Boar's Head Ring, Huntsman's ***or*** Blackened Leather Jerkin, ***or*** Driftwood Staff • (40%) Malefic Shield ***or*** Cloak

Thorhalla [6] (no loot)

tomte apprentice [13] *see tomte hoodoo [13]*

tomte caitiff [17] (30%) <Blood and Ice> • (20%) Jewels 55 • (5%) Light Blue, Light Red ***or*** Light Green Colors • (1.5%) APOA: Mephitic Leather, Malignant, Malefic Studded ***or*** Miscreant's • (1.5%) <Nisse's Nest Egg 2> • (1.5%) <Nisse's Nest Egg 1> • (0.5%) <Thief's Nest Egg>

tomte captor [12] (30%) <Tomte Treasures> • (20%) Jewels 12 • (5%) Light Blue, Light Red ***or*** Light Green Colors • (4%) APOA: Tomte Padded, Leather, Studded ***or*** Chain • (1.7%) <Angry Dwarf> • (0.5%) <Brendig's Gear>

tomte cutthroat [8] (35%) <Tomte Treasures> • (5%) Light Blue, Light Red ***or*** Light Green Colors • (3%) APOA: Tomte Padded, Leather, Studded ***or*** Chain • (0.5%) <Har's Adornments>

tomte elder [16] (40%) <Blood and Ice> • (30%) Jewels 55 • (5%) Light Blue, Light Red, ***or*** Light Green Colors • (0.5%) Traitors Bane, Gold Stitched Tunic ***or*** Pants, Pillager's Gauntlets, Ring of the Stalwart Soul, Bracer of Valor, Necklace of Solid Darkness, Jewel of Augmentation, Blazing Boots, ***or*** Pitted Firesteel • (1.7%) Tomte Axe ***or*** Throwing Knives, ***or*** Jewel of Adroitness

tomte guard [16-17] *see tomte seer [18]*

tomte handler [10] (20%) <Tomte Treasures> • (15%) Jewels 12 • (5%) Light Blue, Light Red ***or*** Light Green Colors • (4%) APOA: Tomte Padded, Leather, Studded ***or*** Chain • (1.7%) <Angry Dwarf> • (0.5%) <Grimnir's Adornment>

tomte hoodoo [13] (30%) <Tomte Treasures> • (20%) Jewels 12 • (5%) Light Blue, Light Red ***or*** Light Green Colors • (1.5%) APOA: Mephitic Leather, Malignant, Malefic Studded ***or*** Miscreant's • (1.5%) <Nisse's Nest Egg 2> • (1.5%) <Nisse's Nest Egg 1> • (0.5%) <Brendig's Gear>

tomte jager [15] *see tomte caitiff [17]*

tomte lookout [14] *see tomte caitiff [17]*

tomte protector [13] *see tomte hoodoo [13]*

tomte runner [13] *see tomte hoodoo [13]*

tomte seer [18] (40%) <Blood and Ice> • (30%) Jewels 55 • (5%) Light Blue, Light Red ***or*** Light Green Colors • (1.5%) APOA: Mephitic Leather, Malignant, Malefic Studded ***or*** Miscreant's • (1.5%) <Nisse's Nest Egg 2> • (1.5%) <Nisse's Nest Egg 1> • (0.5%) <Thief's Nest Egg>

tomte sentinel [17] *see tomte seer [18]*

tomte shaman [10] (5%) Shaman's Totem • (30%) <Tomte Treasures> • (20%) Jewels 12 • (5%) Light Blue, Light Red ***or*** Light Green Colors • (4%) APOA: Tomte Padded, Leather, Studded ***or*** Chain • (1.7%) <Angry Dwarf> • (0.5%) <Grimnir's Adornment>

tomte trainer [13] *see tomte hoodoo [13]*

tomte warhound [9] (20%) Warhound Hide • (80%) Warhound Claw (x2)

tomte warlord [18] (40%) <Blood and Ice> • (30%) Jewels 55 • (5%) Light Blue, Light Red, ***or*** Light Green Colors • (0.5%) Traitors Bane, Gold Stitched Tunic ***or*** Pants, Pillager's Gauntlets, Ring of the Stalwart Soul, Bracer of Valor, Necklace of Solid Darkness, Jewel of Augmentation, Blazing Boots, ***or*** Pitted Firesteel • (40%) Tomte Throwing Axes, Runic Necklace ***or*** Chain of Suppression

tomte witch doctor [15] *see tomte seer [18]*

tomte zealot [16] (40%) <Blood and Ice> • (20%) Jewels 55 • (5%) Light Blue, Light Red ***or*** Light Green Colors • (1.5%) APOA: Mephitic Leather, Malignant, Malefic Studded ***or*** Miscreant's • (1.5%) <Nisse's Nest Egg 2> • (1.5%) <Nisse's Nest Egg 1> • (0.5%) <Thief's Nest Egg>

Spindelhalla

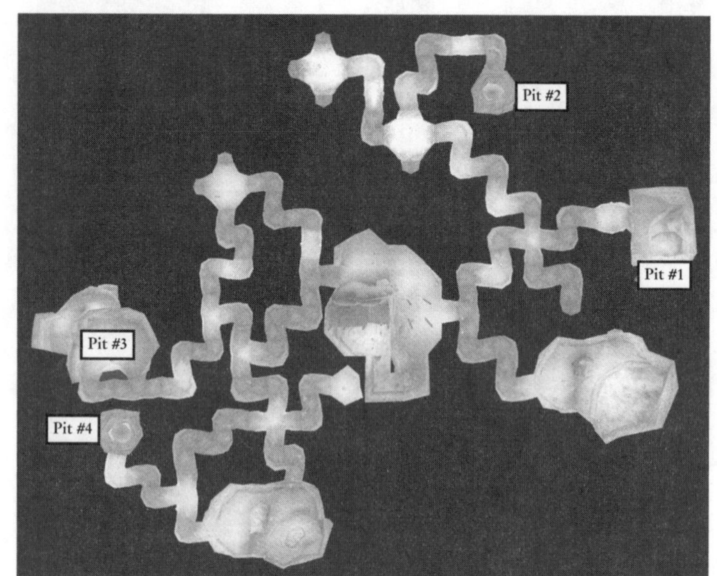

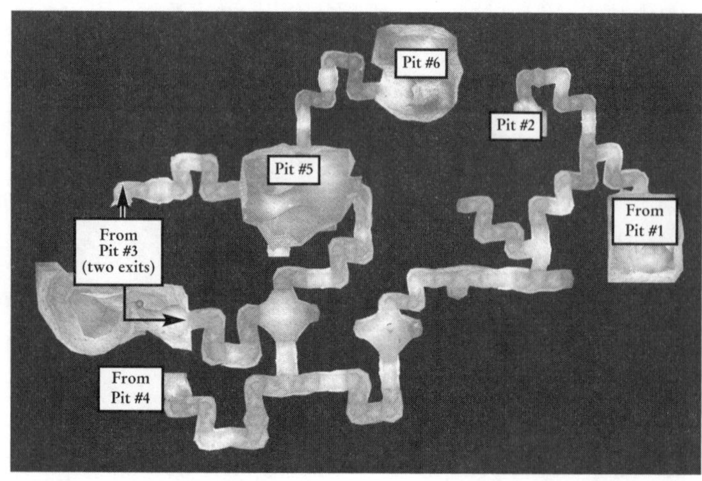

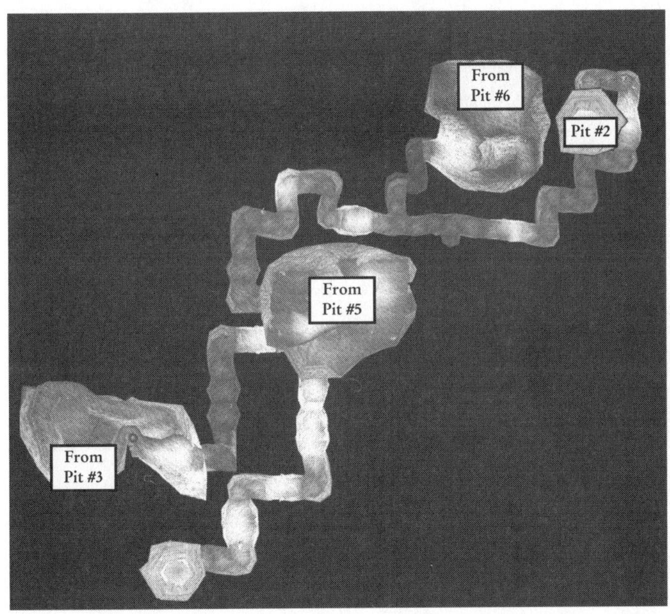

Loot

arachite grymherre [42] (20%) Blood Stained Carapace • (50%) Jewels 35 • (0.5%) Jewels 28 • (4%) Light Purple, Dark Gray ***or*** Light Turquoise Colors • (1%) Purple, Charcoal ***or*** Turquoise Colors • (2%) APOA: Woven, Braided, Crafted ***or*** Ringed Darksteel • (2%) <Svipdag's Love> • (2%) Darksteel ***or*** Twisted Darksteel Bracer ***or*** Ring, ***or*** Darksteel Necklace

arachite husker [38-39] (35%) Husker's Silksteel Cutters • (10%) Arachite Carapace • (50%) Jewels 32 • (1%) Jewels 15 • (4.2%) Blue ***or*** Red Colors • (0.8%) Teal, Light Turquoise ***or*** Light Purple Colors • (6%; hi-lo) APOA: Faded, Faded Bound, Woven ***or*** Braided Silksteel • (5.1%) <Edgeless Armaments> • (0.9%) <Razor-Sharp Armaments> • (2%) Svartalf Crafted Bracer, Ring, Necklace ***or*** Belt

arachite impaler [37-38/39] (10%) Arachite Carapace • (30/35%) Impaler's Barbed Leg • (45/60%) Jewels 32 • (0.9/1.2%) Jewels 15 • (4.2%) Blue ***or*** Red Colors • (0.8%) Teal, Light Turquoise ***or*** Light Purple Colors • (6%; hi-lo) APOA: Faded, Faded Bound, Woven ***or*** Braided Silksteel • (5.1%) <Edgeless Armaments> • (0.9%) <Razor-Sharp Armaments> • (2%) Svartalf Crafted Bracer, Ring, Necklace ***or*** Belt

arachite krigare [40] (30%) Blood Rune Krigare Carapace • (50%) Jewels 32 • (1%) Jewels 15 • (4.2%) Blue ***or*** Red Colors • (0.8%) Teal, Light Turquoise ***or*** Light Purple Colors • (6%; hi-lo) APOA: Faded, Faded Bound, Woven ***or*** Braided Silksteel • (5.1%) <Edgeless Armaments> • (0.9%) <Razor-Sharp Armaments> • (2%) Svartalf Crafted Bracer, Ring, Necklace ***or*** Belt

arachite prelate [39-40] (25%) Polished Blood Runed Tablets • (10%) Prelate's Polished Carapace • (50%) Jewels 32 • (1%) Jewels 15 • (4.2%) Blue ***or*** Red Colors • (0.8%) Teal, Light Turquoise ***or*** Light Purple Colors • (6%; hi-lo) APOA: Faded, Faded Bound, Woven ***or*** Braided Silksteel • (5.1%) <Edgeless Armaments> • (0.9%) <Razor-Sharp Armaments> • (2%) Svartalf Crafted Bracer, Ring, Necklace ***or*** Belt

arachite tunnelhost [36-37] *see arachite vakt [37-38]*

arachite vakt [37-38] (35%) Small Arachite Chitin Plates • (10%) Arachite Carapace • (50%) Jewels 32 • (1%) Jewels 15 • (4.2%) Blue ***or*** Red Colors • (0.8%) Teal, Light Turquoise ***or*** Light Purple Colors • (6%; hi-lo) APOA: Faded, Faded Bound, Woven ***or*** Braided Silksteel • (5.1%) <Edgeless Armaments> • (0.9%) <Razor-Sharp Armaments> • (2%) Svartalf Crafted Bracer, Ring, Necklace ***or*** Belt

blindsnake [37-38] (23%) Blindsnake Skin • (2.5%) Pristine Blindsnake Skin • (80%) Blindsnake Fang • (1.5%) Long Gnarled Tooth • (0.5%) Black Gnarled Tooth

cave trow [47] (45%) Cursed Ekyps Control Orb • (20%) Jewels 15 • (0.4%) Jewels 65 • (4.5%) Rust, Purple ***or*** Charcoal Colors • (0.5%) Crimson, Royal Purple ***or*** Black Colors • (2%) APOA: Webbed Shadow ***or*** Latticed Shadow • (2%) <Freya's Doom> • (2%) <Skirnir's Gift>

cave trow trollkarl [48] (45%) Cursed Ekyps Control Orb • (25%) Jewels 15 • (0.5%) Jewels 65 • (4.5%) Rust, Purple ***or*** Charcoal Colors • (0.5%) Crimson, Royal Purple ***or*** Black Colors • (2%) APOA: Webbed Shadow ***or*** Latticed Shadow • (2%) <Freya's Doom> • (2%) <Skirnir's Gift>

crusher [48,50] (98%) Jewels 15 • (2%) Jewels 65 • (2%) <Freya's Doom> • (2%) APOA: Webbed Shadow ***or*** Latticed Shadow

cursed thulian [47] (40%) Cursed Ekyps Control Orb • (25%) Jewels 15 • (0.5%) Jewels 65 • (4.5%) Rust, Purple ***or*** Charcoal Colors • (0.5%) Crimson, Royal Purple ***or*** Black Colors • (2%) APOA: Webbed Shadow ***or*** Latticed Shadow • (2%) <Freya's Doom> • (2%) <Skirnir's Gift>

Danin [39] (30%) Black Duegar Satchel • (15%) Stolen Book of Blood Magic • (50%) Jewels 32 • (1%) Jewels 15 • (4.2%) Blue ***or*** Red Colors • (0.8%) Teal, Light Turquoise ***or*** Light Purple Colors • (6%; hi-lo) APOA: Faded Studded, Faded Chain, Crafted ***or*** Ringed Silksteel • (5.1%) <Edgeless Armaments> • (0.9%) <Razor-Sharp Armaments> • (2%) <Smooth as Silk, Hard as Steel>

deeplurk dissembler [47-48/49] (18/20%) Spined Chitin Plates • (10/12%) Savage Arachite Claw • (7/8%) Spined Carapace • (3.5/4%) Blood Rune Paint • (15/20%) Jewels 15 • (0.3/0.4%) Jewels 65 • (4.5%) Rust, Purple ***or*** Charcoal Colors • (0.5%) Crimson, Royal Purple ***or*** Black Colors • (2%) APOA: Twilight ***or*** Twilight-Mail • (2%) <Freya's Doom> • (2%) <Skirnir's Gift>

deeplurk feeder [47] (18%) Spined Chitin Plates • (10%) Savage Arachite Claw • (7%) Spined Carapace • (3.5%) Blood Rune Paint • (15%) Jewels 15 • (0.3%) Jewels 65 • (4.5%) Rust, Purple ***or*** Charcoal Colors • (0.5%) Crimson, Royal Purple ***or*** Black Colors • (2%) APOA: Twilight ***or*** Twilight-Mail • (2%) <Freya's Doom> • (2%) <Skirnir's Gift>

deeplurk manslayer [47-48] *see deeplurk feeder [47]*

djupt odjur [49] (20%) Spined Chitin Plates • (12%) Savage Arachite Claw • (8%) Spined Carapace • (4%) Blood Rune Paint • (20%) Jewels 15 • (0.4%) Jewels 65 • (4.5%) Rust, Purple ***or*** Charcoal Colors • (0.5%) Crimson, Royal Purple ***or*** Black Colors • (2%) APOA: Twilight ***or*** Twilight-Mail • (2%) <Freya's Doom> • (2%) <Skirnir's Gift>

djupt usling [48] (18%) Spined Chitin Plates • (10%) Savage Arachite Claw • (7%) Spined Carapace • (3.5%) Blood Rune Paint • (20%) Jewels 15 • (0.4%) Jewels 65 • (4.5%) Rust, Purple ***or*** Charcoal Colors • (0.5%) Crimson, Royal Purple ***or*** Black Colors • (2%) APOA: Twilight ***or*** Twilight-Mail • (2%) <Freya's Doom> • (2%) <Skirnir's Gift>

djupt vivunder [50] (23%) Spined Chitin Plates • (13.5%) Savage Arachite Claw • (9%) Spined Carapace • (4.5%) Blood Rune Paint • (20%) Jewels 15 • (0.4%) Jewels 65 • (4.5%) Rust, Purple ***or*** Charcoal Colors • (0.5%) Crimson, Royal Purple ***or*** Black Colors • (2%) APOA: Twilight ***or*** Twilight-Mail • (2%) <Freya's Doom> • (2%) <Skirnir's Gift>

duegar tjuv [37] (30%) Black Duegar Satchel • (10%) Stolen Book of Blood Magic • (50%) Jewels 32 • (1%) Jewels 15 • (4.2%) Blue ***or*** Red Colors • (0.8%) Teal, Light Turquoise ***or*** Light Purple Colors • (6%; hi-lo) APOA: Faded Studded, Faded Chain, Crafted ***or*** Ringed Silksteel • (5.1%) <Edgeless Armaments> • (0.9%) <Razor-Sharp Armaments> • (2%) <Smooth as Silk, Hard as Steel>

duegarhunter [36] (25%) Phosphorescent Carapace • (50%) Jewels 32 • (1%) Jewels 15 • (4.2%) Blue ***or*** Red Colors • (0.8%) Teal, Light Turquoise ***or*** Light Purple Colors • (6%; hi-lo) APOA: Faded, Faded Bound, Woven ***or*** Braided Silksteel • (5.1%) <Edgeless Armaments> • (0.9%) <Razor-Sharp Armaments> • (2%) Svartalf Crafted Bracer, Ring, Necklace ***or*** Belt

ekyps gunstling [45] (30%) Poisonous Fungus • (20%) Phosphorescent Fungus • (10%) Ekyps Orb of Command • (45%) Jewels 35 • (0.9%) Jewels 28 • (4%) Light Purple, Dark Gray ***or*** Light Turquoise Colors • (1%) Purple, Charcoal ***or*** Turquoise Colors • (19%) Purple, Charcoal ***or*** Turquoise Colors • (2%) APOA: Woven, Braided, Crafted ***or*** Ringed Darksteel • (2%) <Svipdag's Love> • (2%) Darksteel ***or*** Twisted Darksteel Bracer ***or*** Ring, ***or*** Darksteel Necklace

ekyps scavenger [42] (25%) Poisonous Fungus • (10%) Phosphorescent Fungus • (50%) Jewels 35 • (0.5%) Jewels 28 • (4%) Light Purple, Dark Gray ***or*** Light Turquoise Colors • (1%) Purple, Charcoal ***or*** Turquoise Colors • (2%) APOA: Woven, Braided, Crafted ***or*** Ringed Darksteel • (2%) <Svipdag's Love> • (2%) Darksteel ***or*** Twisted Darksteel Bracer ***or*** Ring, ***or*** Darksteel Necklace

Fas [52] (25%) Spined Chitin Plates • (15%) Savage Arachite Claw • (10%) Spined Carapace • (5%) Blood Rune Paint • (25%) Jewels 15 • (0.5%) Jewels 65 • (4.5%) Rust, Purple ***or*** Charcoal Colors • (0.5%) Crimson, Royal Purple ***or*** Black Colors • (2%) APOA: Twilight ***or*** Twilight-Mail • (2%) <Freya's Doom> • (2%) <Skirnir's Gift>

fell cat [45] (55%) Fell Cat's Tooth • (27%) Sheer Black Pelt • (3%) Pristine Sheer Black Pelt • (1.5%) Fell Cat's Razor Tooth • (0.3%) Shadow Razor • (0.2%) Dark Frozen Eviscerator

hallaratta [36-37/38] (15/18%) Hallaratta Pelt • (1.7/2%) Pristine Hallaratta Pelt • (33/36%) Phosphorescent Tooth (x2) • (1.5%) Long Gnarled Tooth • (0.5%) Black Gnarled Tooth

husk [10] (8.5%) Husk Carapace

Igo [49] (45%) Cursed Ekyps Control Orb • (30%) Jewels 15 • (0.6%) Jewels 65 • (4.5%) Rust, Purple ***or*** Charcoal Colors • (0.5%) Crimson, Royal Purple ***or*** Black Colors • (2%) APOA: Webbed Shadow ***or*** Latticed Shadow • (2%) <Freya's Doom> • (2%) <Skirnir's Gift>

Kalf [47] *see cave trow [47]*

kopparorm [49] (80%) Jewels 15 • (1.6%) Jewels 65 • (10%) Fiery Diamond Orb

lost hagbui [42] (35%) Gilded Ornamental Bracer • (35%) Royal Guard's Beaded Insignia • (2%) APOA: Woven, Braided, Crafted ***or*** Ringed Darksteel • (2%) <Voluspa Adornments> • (70%) Jewels 35 • (0.7%) Jewels 28 • (81%) Light Purple, Dark Gray ***or*** Light Turquoise Colors • (19%) Purple, Charcoal ***or*** Turquoise Colors • (2%) <Svipdag's Love>

mad kobold [42] (30%) Cursed Ekyps Control Orb • (55%) Jewels 35 • (1.1%) Jewels 28 • (4%) Light Purple, Dark Gray ***or*** Light Turquoise Colors • (1%) Purple, Charcoal ***or*** Turquoise Colors • (19%) Purple, Charcoal ***or*** Turquoise Colors • (2%) APOA: Woven, Braided, Crafted ***or*** Ringed Darksteel • (2%) <Geirrod's Hoard> • (2%) Darksteel ***or*** Twisted Darksteel Bracer ***or*** Ring, ***or*** Darksteel Necklace

Ond [53] (35%) Fiery Diamond Orb • (20%) Jewels 15 • (0.4%) Jewels 65 • (4.5%) Rust, Purple ***or*** Charcoal Colors • (0.5%) Crimson, Royal Purple ***or*** Black Colors • (2%) APOA: Webbed Shadow ***or*** Latticed Shadow • (2%) <Freya's Doom> • (2%) <Skirnir's Gift>

Smarta [36] (30%) Glowing Chainless Shackle • (60%) Jewels 32 • (1.2%) Jewels 15 • (4.2%) Blue ***or*** Red Colors • (0.8%) Teal, Light Turquoise ***or*** Light Purple Colors • (6%; hi-lo) APOA: Faded Studded ***or*** Chain Silksteel, ***or*** Crafted ***or*** Ring Silksteel • (5.1%) <Edgeless Armaments> • (0.9%) <Razor-Sharp Armaments> • (2%) <Smooth as Silk, Hard as Steel>

spindel [37] (70%) Chitin Leg • (35%) Chitin Leg • (20%) Spindel Silk • (40%) Chitin Poison • (18%) Chitin Carapace • (2%) Pristine Chitin Carapace • (2%) <Beetle's Shell>

spindel layer [41] (50%) Chitin Leg (x2) • (50% each) Spindel Silk, Chitin Poison • (18%) Chitin Carapace • (2%) Pristine Chitin Carapace • (2%) <Beetle's Shell>

spindel silkster [39] (75%) Chitin Leg • (50%) Chitin Leg • (30%) Spindel Silk • (50%) Chitin Poison • (18%) Chitin Carapace • (2%) Pristine Chitin Carapace • (2%) <Beetle's Shell>

stinger [37-38/39] (23%) Chitin Carapace • (2.5%) Pristine Chitin Carapace • (60/65%) Chitin Tail • (30/50%) Chitin Poison • (20%) Chitin Claw (x2) • (2%) <Beetle's Shell>

stor ekyps [47] (10%) Ekyps Orb of Command • (40%) Phosphorescent Fungus • (20%) Jewels 15 • (0.4%) Jewels 65 • (4.5%) Rust, Purple ***or*** Charcoal Colors • (0.5%) Crimson, Royal Purple ***or*** Black Colors • (2%) APOA: Twilight ***or*** Twilight-Mail • (2%) <Freya's Doom> • (2%) <Skirnir's Gift>

svartalf arbetare [37] (25%) Glowing Gold Key • (75%) Jewels 32 • (1.5%) Jewels 15 • (4.2%) Blue ***or*** Red Colors • (0.8%) Teal, Light Turquoise ***or*** Light Purple Colors • (6%; hi-lo) APOA: Faded Studded ***or*** Chain Silksteel, ***or*** Crafted ***or*** Ring Silksteel • (5.1%) <Edgeless Armaments> • (0.9%) <Razor-Sharp Armaments> • (2%) <Smooth as Silk, Hard as Steel>

svartalf foreman [39] (25%) Foreman's Plans • (75%) Jewels 32 • (1.5%) Jewels 15 • (4.2%) Blue ***or*** Red Colors • (0.8%) Teal, Light Turquoise ***or*** Light Purple Colors • (6%; hi-lo) APOA: Faded Studded ***or*** Chain Silksteel, ***or*** Crafted ***or*** Ring Silksteel • (5.1%) <Edgeless Armaments> • (0.9%) <Razor-Sharp Armaments> • (2%) <Smooth as Silk, Hard as Steel>

svartalf thrall [36] (30%) Glowing Chainless Shackle • (60%) Jewels 32 • (1.2%) Jewels 15 • (4.2%) Blue ***or*** Red Colors • (0.8%) Teal, Light Turquoise ***or*** Light Purple Colors • (6%; hi-lo) APOA: Faded Studded Silksteel, Faded Chain Silksteel, Crafted Silksteel, ***or*** Ringed Silksteel • (5.1%) <Edgeless Armaments> • (0.9%) <Razor-Sharp Armaments> • (2%) <Smooth as Silk, Hard as Steel>

Grjotgard [23] *see cave bear [22-23]*

vendo snake charmer [22] APOA: Cave Lurker's ***or*** Cave Prowler's

Te'Bui [35] *see svartalf thrall [36]*

terra crab [38-39/40] (60/72%) Chitin Claw • (30/35%) Chitin Claw • (27%) Chitin Carapace • (3%) Pristine Chitin Carapace • (2%) <Beetle's Shell> • (12%) Terra Crab Claw

undead troll warrior [47] *see cave trow [47]*

Vixitr [39] (45%) Small Arachite Chitin Plates • (10%) Arachite Carapace • (60%) Jewels 32 • (1.2%) Jewels 15 • (4.2%) Blue ***or*** Red Colors • (0.8%) Teal, Light Turquoise ***or*** Light Purple Colors • (6%; hi-lo) APOA: Faded, Faded Bound, Woven ***or*** Braided Silksteel • (5.1%) <Edgeless Armaments> • (0.9%) <Razor-Sharp Armaments> • (2%) Svartalf Crafted Bracer, Ring, Necklace ***or*** Belt

Yleg [45] (40%) Gilded Ornamental Bracer • (40%) Royal Guard's Beaded Insignia • (2%) APOA: Woven, Braided, Crafted ***or*** Ringed Darksteel • (2%) <Voluspa Adornments> • (80%) Jewels 35 • (1.3%) Jewels 28 • (4%) Light Purple, Dark Gray ***or*** Light Turquoise Colors • (1%) Purple, Charcoal ***or*** Turquoise Colors • (19%) Purple, Charcoal ***or*** Turquoise Colors • (2%) <Svipdag's Love>

Varulvhamn

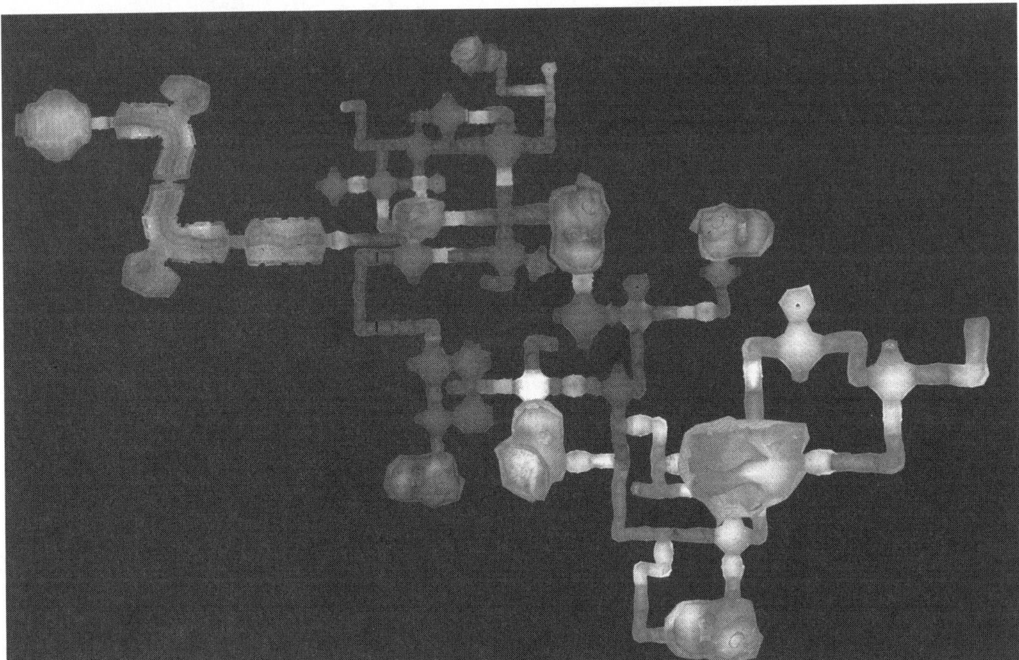

N →

Loot

crazed lycantic [34] (10%) <Werewolves of Midgard> • (1.5%) <Once Bitten ...> • (1.5%) <Lycanthropic Loot> • (1.5%) APOA: Lupine Lunatic ***or*** Feral Wulf • (10%) Jewels 29 • (12%) Lost Pearl

Faz [35] (10%) <Werewolves of Midgard> • (10%) Jewels 29 • (1.5%) APOA: Lupine Lunatic ***or*** Feral Wulf • (1.5%) Feral Fiery Axe ***or*** Wicked Wulf Chain • (1.5%) <Once Bitten ...>

frenetic wolfspider [38] (4%) Large Venomous Spider Gland • (16%) Large Wolfspider Leg

forodande warg [37] (35%) Tattered Warg Pelt • (25%) Pristine Warg Pelt • (20%) Ivory Warg Tooth

frukta warg [39] (35%) Tattered Warg Pelt • (25%) Pristine Warg Pelt • (20%) Ivory Warg Tooth

Grimnought Ejnar [45] (1.7%) Royal Lupine Necklace, Gem, ***or*** Ring • (30%) Jewels 29 • (35%) <Werewolves of Midgard>

High Lord Athulf [44] (30%) Regal Lupine Staff ***or*** Lupine Chain of Criticality • (30%) <Werewolves of Midgard> • (30%) Jewels 29

High Lord Tarnkappe [44] (30%) Regal Lupine War Hammer ***or*** Lupine Chain of Restoration • (30%) <Werewolves of Midgard> • (30%) Jewels 29

High Lord Modolfr [44] (30%) Royal Lupine Staff ***or*** Shadowy Regal Cloak • (30%) <Werewolves of Midgard> • (30%) Jewels 29

Hresvelgr [46] *see werewolf elite guard [41]*

King Hresvelgr [46] (20% each) Regal Lupine Shield, Hammer, Noxious Lupine Gem • (30%) <Werewolves of Midgard> • (30%) Jewels 29

large wolfspider [28] (3.8%) Venomous Spider Gland • (16.2%) Wolfspider Leg

Lord Bete [38] *see werewolf noble [38]*

Lord Brumma [38] *see werewolf noble [38]*

Lord Gifttand [38] *see werewolf noble [38]*

Lord Grym [38] *see werewolf noble [38]*

Lord Huggtand [38] *see werewolf noble [38]*

Lord Ungar [39] *see werewolf noble [38]*

Lord Vild [38] *see werewolf noble [38]*

Manstrale [39] (10%) <Werewolves of Midgard> • (10%) Jewels 29 • (1.5%) Varulv Icy Spear ***or*** Wicked Wulf Belt • (1.5%) <Full Moon Wear> • (1.5%) APOA: Vicious Varulv ***or*** Growling Garou

Ridder [39] (10%) <Werewolves of Midgard> • (10%) Jewels 29 • (1.5%) Ominous Moonstruck Hammer ***or*** Wicked Wulf Gem • (1.5%) <Full Moon Wear> • (1.5%) APOA: Vicious Varulv ***or*** Growling Garou

Thelod [36] (10%) <Werewolves of Midgard> • (10%) Jewels 29 • (1.5%) Lupine Lumen Longsword ***or*** Wicked Wulf Cloak • (1.5%) <Lycanthropic Loot> • (1.5%) APOA: Lupine Lunatic ***or*** Feral Wulf

werewolf advisor [41] *see werewolf elite guard [41]*

werewolf bodyguard [37] *see werewolf noble [38]*

werewolf churl [34] *see crazed lycantic [34]*

werewolf elite guard [41] (0.5%) APOA: Lupine Lunatic • (0.3% each) APOA: Feral Wulf, Vicious Varulv • (0.5%) Gnarling Garou Coif, ***or*** APOA: Growling Garou • (1.5%) Lupine, Gnarling Lupine, ***or*** Giant Garou Axe, Garou Sword, Great Hammer ***or*** Defender, Growling Garou Warhammer, Feral Protector, Varulvhamn Bow ***or*** Spear, Varulv Staff of Runecarving, Darkness, Suppression ***or*** Spirit Magic, Gigantic Garou Sword, ***or*** Varulv Shield • (1.5%) Wild Wulf ***or*** Lunatic Lupine Cloak, Carved ***or*** Werewolf Bone Ring, Flayed Wolfskin Belt ***or*** Bracer, Lycanthropic ***or*** Lycanthrope's Necklace, Wolfskin Belt ***or*** Bracer, ***or*** Varulvhamn ***or*** Wulf Gem • (50%) <Werewolves of Midgard> • (20%) Jewels 29

werewolf grimnought [39] *see werewolf noble [38]*

werewolf noble [38] (10%) <Werewolves of Midgard> • (10%) Jewels 29 • (1.5%) <Full Moon Wear> • (1.5%) <Lordly Loot> • (1.5%) APOA: Vicious Varulv ***or*** Growling Garou

werewolf prowler [41] *see werewolf elite guard [41]*

werewolf royal guard [42] *see werewolf elite guard [41]*

werewolf scavenger [39] *see werewolf elite guard [41]*

werewolf scruff [35] (10%) <Werewolves of Midgard> • (1.5%) <Once Bitten ...> • (1.5%) <Lycanthropic Loot> • (1.5%) APOA: Lupine Lunatic ***or*** Feral Wulf • (10%) Jewels 29

wolfaur lunarian [39] *see werewolf noble [38]*

wolfaur pragmatic [35] *see werewolf scruff [35]*

wolfaur quixot [37] *see werewolf noble [38]*

wolfspider [25] (2.8%) Venomous Spider Gland • (11%) Wolfspider Leg

Vendo Caverns

Loot

albino cave mauler [25] (80%) Cave Bear Meat • (75%) Large Mauler Tooth • (45%) Large Mauler Claw • (14%) Large Cave Mauler Skin • (1.5%) Pristine Cave Mauler Skin

cave bear [20-21/22-23] (75% each) Cave Bear Meat, Tooth • (40/50%) Cave Bear Claw • (9/18%) Cave Bear Skin • (1/2%) Pristine Cave Bear Skin

cave crawler [16-17/18-19/20-21/22] (70/75/75/75%) Crawler Meat (x2) • (4.5/4.5/18/27%) Crawler Skin • (0.5/0.5/2/3%) Pristine Cave Crawler Skin • (10/30/40/50%) Crawler Fang

cave mauler [20-21/22] (70/75%) Cave Bear Meat (x2) • (40/45%) Cave Bear Tooth • (14/20%) Cave Bear Skin • (1.5/2.2%) Pristine Cave Bear Skin

cave ogre [29-30] (75%) Ogre's Food Catcher • (45%) <Death's Delight> • (75%) Jewels 10 • (1.5%) Jewels 25 • (4.5%) Light Turquoise, Light Purple ***or*** Dark Gray Colors • (0.5%) Turquoise, Rust ***or*** Charcoal Colors • (1.5%) <Darkling's Delight> • (1.5%) <Gone Berzerk> • (1.5%) APOA: Cave Lurker's ***or*** Cave Prowler's

cave viper [25] (22%) Cave Viper Skin • (2.5%) Pristine Cave Viper Skin • (75% each) Cave Viper Meat, Tooth

goblin advisor [29] (80%) Twisted Mithril Nose Ring • (40%) <Death's Delight> • (80%) Jewels 10 • (1.6%) Jewels 25 • (4.5%) Blue, Red ***or*** Green Colors • (0.5%) Light Turquoise, Light Purple ***or*** Dark Gray Colors • (1.5%) <Darkling's Delight> • (1.5%) <Gone Berzerk> • (1.5%) APOA: Cave Lurker's ***or*** Cave Prowler's

goblin guard [26-27] (80%) Guard's Gold Nose Ring • (25%) <Death's Delight> • (80%) Jewels 10 • (1.6%) Jewels 25 • (4.5%) Blue, Red ***or*** Green Colors • (0.5%) Light Turquoise, Light Purple ***or*** Dark Gray Colors • (1.6%) <Darkling's Delight> • (1.6%) <Voluspa Gear> • (4%) APOA: Crusty Fur ***or*** Rusted Ringmail

Grjotgard [23] *see cave bear [22-23]*

small cave mauler [18] (65%) Cave Bear Meat (x2) • (20%) Cave Bear Tooth • (9%) Cave Bear Skin • (1%) Pristine Cave Bear Skin

spider [25-26/27-28] (80%) Spider Leg • (20%) Spider Leg • (70/80%) Chitin Leg Tip • (20%) Chitin Leg Tip • (10/20%) Spider Silk • (9/18%) Spider Carapace • (1/2%) Pristine Spider Carapace

svendo [31-32/33-34] (75/80%) Golden Bear-Blood Basin • (10/20%) <Inspired by a Curmudgeon> • (50/60%) Jewels 48 • (1/1.2%) Jewels 53 • (4.5%) Light Turquoise, Light Purple ***or*** Dark Gray Colors • (0.5%) Turquoise, Rust ***or*** Charcoal Colors • (1.5%) <Den Dressings> • (1.5%) <Ode to Yorik> [33-34] • (1.5%) APOA: Grizzled Bear Fur [33-34] • (1.5%) Skull-Bone Hammer, Axe, Shield ***or*** Spear, ***or*** Rune [31-32]

vendo guard [22-23/24-25/26] (70/80/80%) Mantle of Bear-Like Visage • (15/20/40%) <Death's Delight> • (70/80/90%) Jewels 10 • (1.4/1.6/1.8%) Jewels 25 • (4.5%) Blue, Red ***or*** Green Colors • (0.5%) Light Turquoise, Light Purple ***or*** Dark Gray Colors • (1.6%) <Bear Hide> [22-25]/<Darkling's Delight> [26] • (1.6%) <Voluspa Gear> • (4%) APOA: Muddied Hide ***or*** Bone Shard [22-25]/APOA: Crusty Fur ***or*** Rusted Ringmail [26]

vendo reaver [24-25/26-27/28-29/30] (70/75/85/85%) Reavers Bear Claw Bracer • (10/20/30%) <Death's Delight>/(10%) <Inspired by a Curmudgeon> [30] • (70/75/85/85%) Jewels 10 • (1.4/1.5/1.7/1.7%) Jewels 25 • (4.5%) Blue, Red ***or*** Green Colors [24-29] • (0.5%) Light Turquoise, Light Purple ***or*** Dark Gray Colors [4.5% for level 30] • (0.5%) Turquoise, Rust ***or*** Charcaol Colors [30 only] • (1.6%) <Darkling's Delight> • (1.6%) <Voluspa Gear> [24-25] • (1.6%) <Bear Hide> [26-27] • (1.6%) <Gone Berzerk> [28-30] • (4%) APOA: Crusty Fur ***or*** Rusted Ringmail [24-27] • (1.5%) APOA: Cave Lurker's ***or*** Cave Prowler's [28-30]

vendo snake charmer [22] APOA: Cave Lurker's ***or*** Cave Prowler's

vendo savager [32/34-35] (75%) Savager's Ivory Drinking Horn • (10/25%) <Inspired by a Curmudgeon> • (60/75%) Jewels 48 • (1.2/1.5%) Jewels 53 • (4.5%) Light Turquoise, Light Purple ***or*** Dark Gray Colors • (0.5%) Turquoise, Rust ***or*** Charcoal Colors • (1.5%) <Den Dressings> • (1.5%) <Ode to Yorik> • (1.5%) APOA: Grizzled Bear Fur

vendo yowler [29] (75%) Yowler's Blood Runed Bear-Skin • (45%) <Death's Delight> • (75%) Jewels 10 • (1.5%) Jewels 25 • (4.5%) Blue, Red ***or*** Green Colors • (0.5%) Light Turquoise, Light Purple ***or*** Dark Gray Colors • (1.5%) <Darkling's Delight> • (1.5%) <Gone Berzerk> • (1.5%) APOA: Cave Lurker's ***or*** Cave Prowler's

vendo yowler [30-31] (75%) Yowler's Blood Runed Bear-Skin • (10%) <Inspired by a Curmudgeon> • (50%) Jewels 48 • (1%) Jewels 53 • (4.5%) Light Turquoise, Light Purple ***or*** Dark Gray Colors • (0.5%) Turquoise, Rust ***or*** Charcoal Colors • (1.5%) <Den Dressings> • (1.5%) <Gone Berzerk> • (1.5%) APOA: Cave Lurker's ***or*** Cave Prowler's

Realm vs. Realm

Forest Sauvage

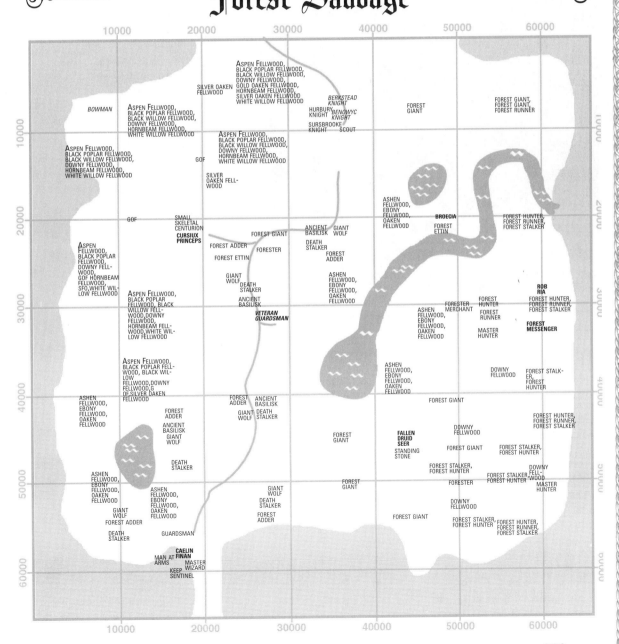

10000 20000 30000 40000 50000 60000

Aspen Fellwood, Black Poplar Fellwood, Black Willow Fellwood, Downy Fellwood, Gold Oaken Fellwood, Hornbeam Fellwood, Silver Oaken Fellwood White Willow Fellwood

Silver Oaken Fellwood

Berkstead Knight

Hurbury Knight

Benowyc Knight

Sursbrooke Knight

Scout

Forest Giant

Forest Giant, Forest Giant, Forest Runner

Bowman

Aspen Fellwood, Black Poplar Fellwood, Black Willow Fellwood, Downy Fellwood, Hornbeam Fellwood, White Willow Fellwood

Aspen Fellwood, Black Poplar Fellwood, Black Willow Fellwood, Downy Fellwood, Hornbeam Fellwood, White Willow Fellwood

Aspen Fellwood, Black Poplar Fellwood, Black Willow Fellwood, Downy Fellwood, Hornbeam Fellwood, White Willow Fellwood

GOF

Silver Oaken Fell-wood

Ashen Fellwood, Ebony Fellwood, Oaken Fellwood

Broecia

Forest Ettin

Forest Hunter, Forest Runner, Forest Stalker

GOF

Small Skeletal Centurion

Cursiux Princeps

Forest Giant

Ancient Basilisk

Giant Wolf

Forest Adder

Forester

Death Stalker

Forest Adder

Forest Ettin

Aspen Fellwood, Black Poplar Fellwood, Downy Fell-wood, GOF Hornbeam Fellwood, SFO, White Wil-low Fellwood

Giant Wolf

Death Stalker

Ancient Basilisk

Ashen Fellwood, Ebony Fellwood, Oaken Fellwood

Rob Ria

Aspen Fellwood, Black Poplar Fellwood, Black Willow Fell-wood, Downy Fellwood, Hornbeam Fell-wood, White Wil-low Fellwood

Veteran Guardsman

Ashen Fellwood, Ebony Fellwood, Oaken Fellwood

Forester Merchant

Forest Hunter

Forest Runner

Master Hunter

Forest Hunter, Forest Runner, Forest Stalker

Forest Messenger

Aspen Fellwood, Black Poplar Fell-wood, Black Wil-low Fellwood, Downy Fellwood, G of, Silver Oaken Fellwood

Ashen Fellwood, Ebony Fellwood, Oaken Fellwood

Downy Fellwood

Forest Stalk-er, Forest Hunter

Ashen Fellwood, Ebony Fellwood, Oaken Fellwood

Forest Adder

Ancient Basilisk

Giant Wolf

Death Stalker

Forest Giant

Forest Adder

Ancient Basilisk

Giant Wolf

Forest Hunter, Forest Runner, Forest Stalker

Forest Giant

Fallen Druid Seer

Standing Stone

Downy Fellwood

Forest Giant

Forest Stalker, Forest Hunter

Death Stalker

Forest Stalker, Forest Hunter

Downy Fell-wood

Forest Stalker, Forest Hunter

Ashen Fellwood, Ebony Fellwood, Oaken Fellwood

Forest Giant

Forester

Master Hunter

Ashen Fellwood, Ebony Fellwood, Oaken Fellwood

Giant Wolf

Death Stalker

Downy Fellwood

Giant Wolf

Forest Adder

Forest Adder

Forest Giant

Forest Stalker, Forest Hunter

Forest Hunter, Forest Runner, Forest Stalker

Death Stalker

Guardsman

Caelin Finan

Man at Arms

Master Wizard

Keep Sentinel

10000 20000 30000 40000 50000 60000

Special thanks go to Ethan "Esis" Kidhardt for risking life, limb and sanity in the investigation of the most dangerous realms in the game!

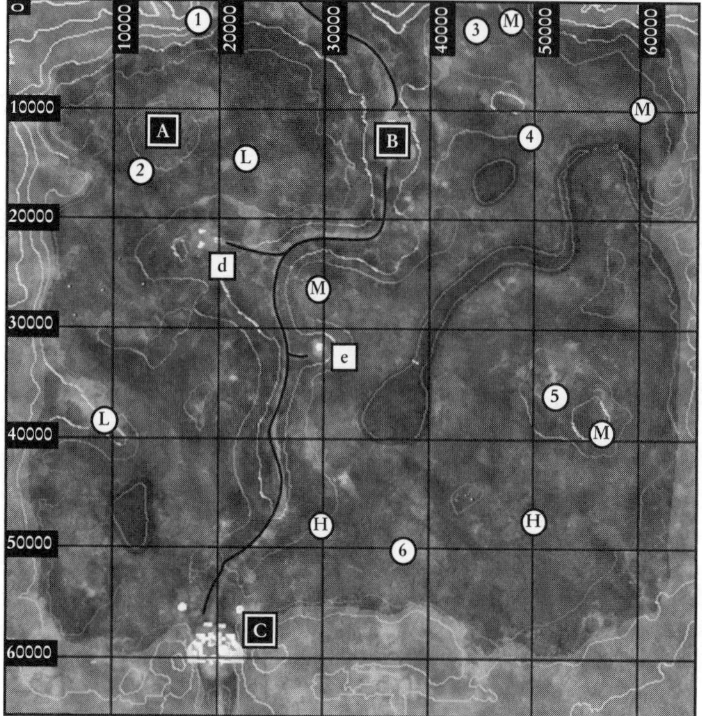

Map Key

A. Caer Renaris
B. Castle Excalibur & Scabbard Relic
C. Castle Sauvage
d. Skeletons
e. Guard Tower
(L) Low Invader Risk
(M) Medium Invader Risk
(H) High Invader Risk

Forest Sauvage is truly a forest of as many trees that move as don't move. This zone takes the cake as the most friendly realm zone where monsters are concerned due to the wide-open forests with sporadic friendly creatures. Relic Fort Excaliber sits at the northern end along friendly roads where the only worry is from invaders. Along the eastern side the woods become slightly swampy and there seems to be a misty haze covering the lowest areas. Small lakes and rivers wind through the eastern side, but the western area is virtually empty of creature variety and is mostly just a foggy woodland. The average creature level here is around 27 with highs in the 30's and lows in the 20's. In the daylight, Forest Sauvage is one of the most beautiful and scenic places in the world.

1. Knotted Fellwood Grove

These are probably Sauvage's most formidable creatures, likely because they're near the Pennine Mountains. Sitting right on the border, these are gigantic gray Trees with an appetite for travelers. These creatures don't move at all and there are no wandering creatures nearby, making this a decent spot.

Location 20, 1
Invader Risk 3 Slim
Quantity 10-15
Terrain Type Aside from some Trees, a barren rocky hillside. No wandering creatures. These don't move.

2. Roaming Fellwoods (Aspen/Downy/Hornbeam)

This spot encompasses virtually the entire western area of Sauvage. For a massive area, there are only groups of Trees blindly wandering around. Occasionally there are some snakes and large cats, but it's otherwise a simple flat expanse of wandering Fellwoods.

Location 8, 11
Invader Risk 2 Very Slim
Quantity 40-50 Spread over massive area.
Terrain Type Dense woods/swamp. These Trees wander constantly and are spread out. Otherwise, no other creatures.

3. Forest Giant Woods

These are some of the more powerful creatures in Sauvage, yet there aren't enough of them to constitute a serious warning. However, consider it your civic duty to rid the world of these enormous and green creatures. They wander a great deal, but there is nothing else to worry about in the vicinity.

Location 45, 3
Invader Risk 4 Slim
Quantity 5-8
Terrain Type A generally flat, almost swampy area, these guys wander a lot. No other wandering dangers, though.

4. Forest Ettin Woods

Forest Ettins take the cake as the strangest creatures to walk the land in Albion territory. They look like a bad genetic experiment, a green two-headed Frankenstein creature with ripped pants. They seem to move frequently in small groups of 2 or 3, with one parent figure followed by a couple of younger ones. The area around is very safe with only a slight risk of invaders.

Location 50, 18
Invader Risk 5 Small
Quantity 20+
Terrain Type In groups of 3-4, spread out over a misty woods. They wander frequently, but there are no other wandering creatures.

5. Ashen/Oaken Fellwood Grove

These are another strange group of creatures. They're similar to their cousins to the western part of Sauvage; they are small trees that congregate and move like small flocks of birds. Looks like good hunting material, and the area is very safe with a medium risk of invaders.

Location 46, 31
Invader Risk 6 Medium
Quantity 15-30
Terrain Type Open, misty woods. They move in packs of 3-4 over a large area.

6. Forest Giant Woods

This spot is a popular Albion attraction for a variety of players. They are huge green Giants with one eye, but not quite a Cyclops. They are located close to the realm gate for easy access, but invader probability is likely. A very safe area for any player.

Location 39, 50
Invader Risk 6 Medium
Quantity 10-20
Terrain Type Misty wooden area, almost swamp on zone border. Huge wandering giants.

Loot

ancient basilisk [21] (85%) Ancient Basilisk Skin • (24%) Clouded Basilisk Eye

ashen fellwood [16-17] (90%) Ashen Fellwood Branch • (50%) Pitted Ashen Fellwood Staff • (7%) Fellwood Heartwood • (10%) Endearment Dagger ***or*** Ashen Spirit Staff

aspen fellwood [23] (85%) Aspen Branch • (3%) Fellwood Heartwood

black poplar fellwood [26] (85%) Black Poplar Branch • (4%) Fellwood Heartwood

black willow fellwood [20] (80%) Black Willow Branch • (1.6%) Fellwood Heartwood

Broecia [16] (20% each) Hide Sack, Topaz, Forest Ettin Head

Cursiux princeps [24] (60%) Roman Commanders Seal • (30%) Small Silver Statue • (50%) Jewels 26 • (1.4%) APOA: Bloodied Leather • (1.4%) Decorated Roman Dagger ***or*** Stiletto, ***or*** Roman Tactician Bracer • (0.3%) <Salisbury Stock 1>

death stalker [16-17] (80%) Death Stalker Hide • (24%) Death Stalker Fang

downy fellwood [24] (85%) Downy Branch • (3.5%) Fellwood Heartwood

ebony fellwood [13-14] (80%) Ebony Fellwood Branch (x2)

forest adder [16-17] (80%) Adder Meat • (30%) Adder Skin

forest ettin [12-13/14-15/16] (15/15/20%) Hide Sack • (17%) Lapis Lazuli/Azurite/Topaz • (10/15/20%) Forest Ettin Head

forest giant [18-21] (30% each) Berry Wine, Cooked Deer, Torn Leather Sack • (1%) APOA: Forester's • (1%) Green Tourmaline • (0.3%) Salisbury Dagger, Giants Toothpick ***or*** Majestical Ring

forest hunter [21/23-24] (75% each) Berry Wine, Cooked Deer • (35%) Leather Sack • (15%) Pouch of Seeds • (5%) Topaz • (0.9) Natures Charm ***or*** Natures Blessing • (0.1%) Flight Bodkin Arrows • (1%) APOA: Forester's • (0.3%) <Arthurian Artifacts 3> • (10%) Blood Red Berry Wine

forest messenger [15] (no loot)

forest runner [20] *see forest hunter [21/23-24]*

forest stalker [27] *see forest hunter [21/23-24]*

forester [31] (no loot)

forester merchant [26] *see forest hunter [21/23-24]*

giant wolf [15-17] (75%) Giant Wolf Skin • (20%) Giant Wolf Fang

gold oaken fellwood [33] (80%) Golden Oak Branch • (5%) Fellwood Heartwood

hornbeam fellwood [27] (85%) Hornbeam Branch • (4%) Fellwood Heartwood

horse [10] (75%) Horse Hair • (10%) Auburn Mane • (80%) Ruined Horse Skin • (35%) Horse Skin • (60%) Horse Hair

master hunter [33] (no loot)

oaken fellwood [18] (5%) Pitted Fellwood Cudgel • (50%) Oaken Fellwood Branch • (6%) Fellwood Heartwood

Rob Ria [40] (no loot)

silver oaken fellwood [31] (90%) Silver Oak Branch • (5%) Fellwood Heartwood

small skeletal centurion [17] (1%) Tattered Leather Jerkin • (15% each) Pitted Tower Shield, Short Sword, Topaz • (30%) Azurite • (2.7%) Ancient Body Shield, Ancient Battle Bracer, Battleworn Gladius, ***or*** Shimmering Etheric Helm • (0.3%) Blade of Etheric Mist • (1%) Pearl

small skeletal legionnaire [14] (1%) Tattered Leather Jerkin • (15% each) Pitted Tower Shield, Pitted Short Sword, Agate • (30%) Carnelian • (2.7%) Ancient Body Shield, Ancient Battle Bracer, Battleworn Gladius, ***or*** Shimmering Etheric Helm • (0.3%) Blade of Etheric Mist • (1%) Garnet

white willow fellwood [21] (80%) White Willow Branch • (2.4%) Fellwood Heartwood

young forest runner [10] (no loot)

Hadrian's Wall

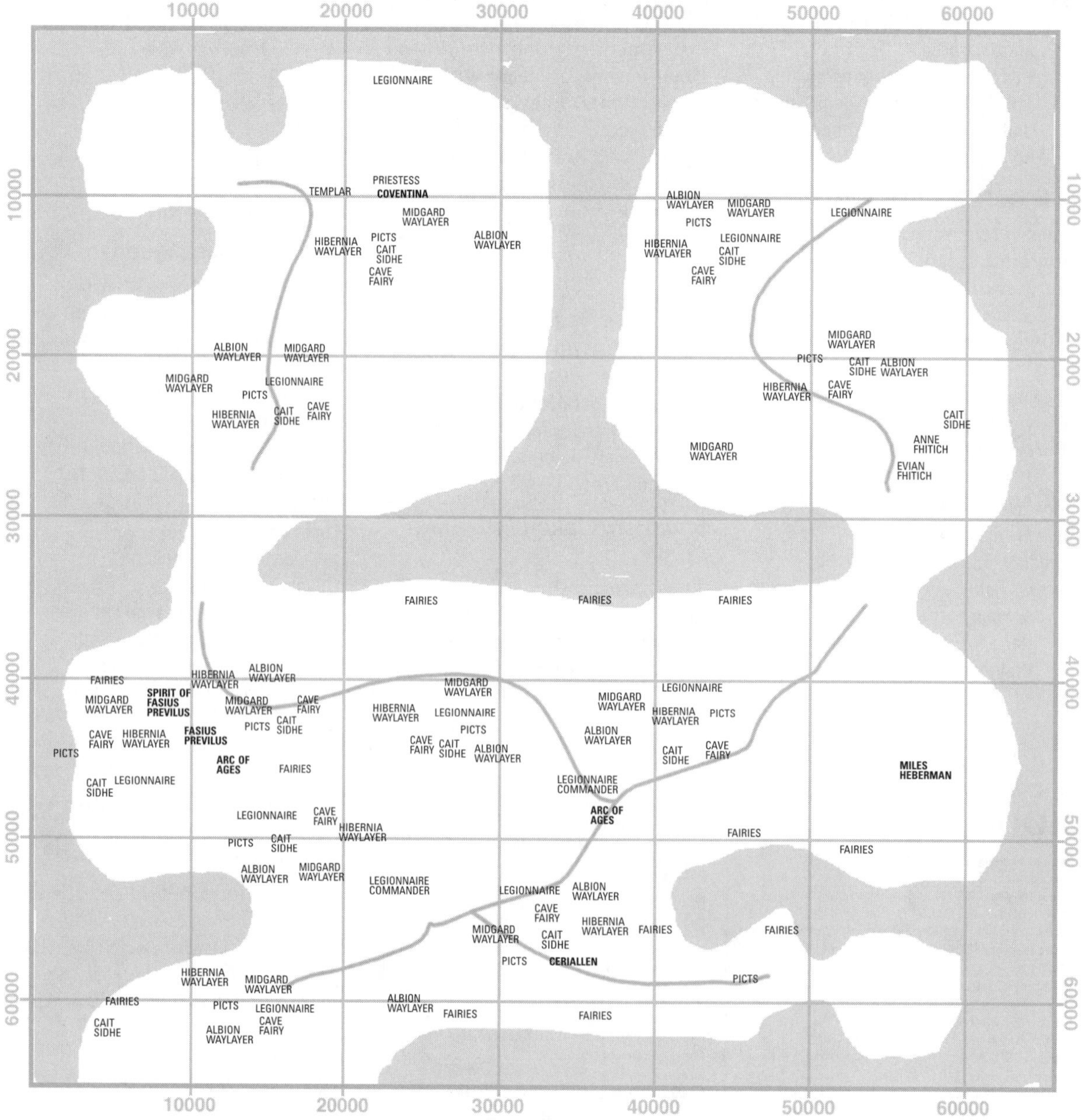

10000 20000 30000 40000 50000 60000

LEGIONNAIRE

PRIESTESS
COVENTINA
TEMPLAR
MIDGARD WAYLAYER
HIBERNIA WAYLAYER
PICTS
CAIT SIDHE
CAVE FAIRY
ALBION WAYLAYER

ALBION WAYLAYER
MIDGARD WAYLAYER
PICTS
LEGIONNAIRE
HIBERNIA WAYLAYER
LEGIONNAIRE
CAIT SIDHE
CAVE FAIRY

ALBION WAYLAYER
MIDGARD WAYLAYER
MIDGARD WAYLAYER
LEGIONNAIRE
PICTS
HIBERNIA WAYLAYER
CAIT SIDHE
CAVE FAIRY

MIDGARD WAYLAYER
PICTS
CAIT SIDHE
ALBION WAYLAYER
HIBERNIA WAYLAYER
CAVE FAIRY
CAIT SIDHE
ANNE FHITICH
MIDGARD WAYLAYER
EVIAN FHITICH

FAIRIES
FAIRIES
FAIRIES

FAIRIES
HIBERNIA WAYLAYER
ALBION WAYLAYER
MIDGARD WAYLAYER
SPIRIT OF FASIUS PREVILUS
MIDGARD WAYLAYER
CAVE FAIRY
CAVE FAIRY
HIBERNIA WAYLAYER
FASIUS PREVILUS
PICTS
CAIT SIDHE
PICTS
ARC OF AGES
FAIRIES
CAIT SIDHE
LEGIONNAIRE

MIDGARD WAYLAYER
HIBERNIA WAYLAYER
LEGIONNAIRE
PICTS
CAVE FAIRY
CAIT SIDHE
ALBION WAYLAYER

MIDGARD WAYLAYER
LEGIONNAIRE
HIBERNIA WAYLAYER
PICTS
ALBION WAYLAYER
CAIT SIDHE
CAVE FAIRY
LEGIONNAIRE COMMANDER
ARC OF AGES
MILES HEBERMAN

LEGIONNAIRE
CAVE FAIRY
HIBERNIA WAYLAYER
PICTS
CAIT SIDHE
FAIRIES
FAIRIES
ALBION WAYLAYER
MIDGARD WAYLAYER
LEGIONNAIRE COMMANDER

LEGIONNAIRE
ALBION WAYLAYER
CAVE FAIRY
HIBERNIA WAYLAYER
FAIRIES
FAIRIES
MIDGARD WAYLAYER
CAIT SIDHE
PICTS
CERIALLEN

HIBERNIA WAYLAYER
MIDGARD WAYLAYER
PICTS
FAIRIES
PICTS
LEGIONNAIRE
ALBION WAYLAYER
FAIRIES
FAIRIES
CAIT SIDHE
ALBION WAYLAYER
CAVE FAIRY

10000 20000 30000 40000 50000 60000

Monsters with levels lower than 8 are not marked on map.

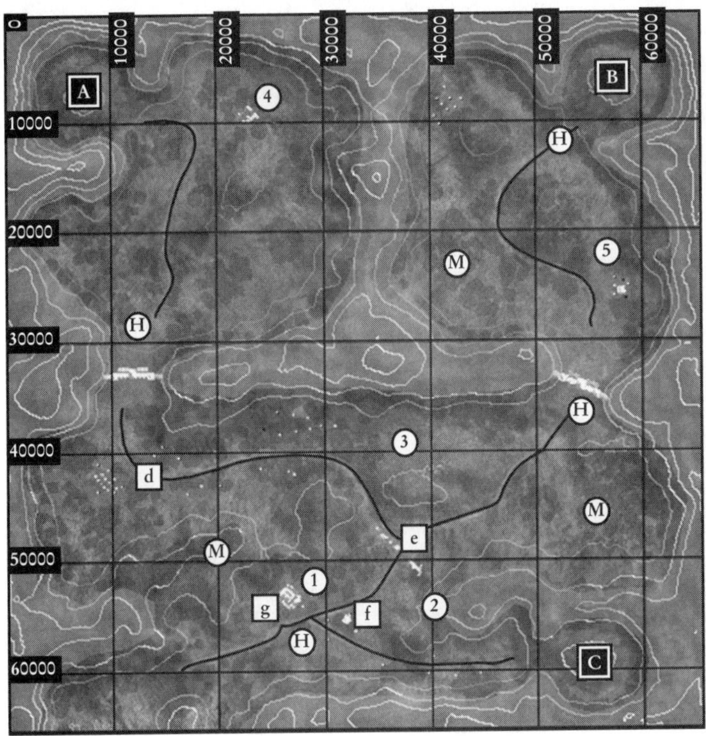

Map Key

A. Hibernia Outpost
B. Midgard Outpost
C. Caer Benowyc
d. Colonnade Ruins
e. Ruined Aqueduct
f. Tower Ruins
g. Legionnaires

(L) Low Invader Risk
(M) Medium Invader Risk
(H) High Invader Risk

Hadrian's Wall is where Hibernians and the Midgard armies come to invade Albion territory. The terrain is a mostly grassy knoll with some rugged hills among a variety of trees. It's often sunny and rather picturesque, and except for the massive amount of bloodshed here, it's a generally pleasant place to visit. There aren't too many hunting spots, but there are a variety of places to ambush other players from. Hadrian's Wall is home to an occasional strong group of creatures, but is mostly filled with monsters that are there to pester people. Where exactly is the 'wall' for which this zone was named? Well, no one is really sure ....

1. Legionnaire's Camp

The Legionnaire's Camp is one of the most dangerous areas you can enter due to the RvR traffic. It sits at a common intersection heading towards the dangerous Pennine Mountains, but one might be able to sneak a few kills here and there, Notably, there is a named spawn here. Some candidly refer to this spot as "Taco Bell" because it almost looks like a typical Bell building.

Location 27, 54
Invader Risk 8 High
Quantity 5-8, one named "Legionnaire Commander"
Terrain Type Destroyed building harboring Undead Legionnaires. No wandering monster risk.

2. Cave Fairy Corner

Cave Fairies are nothing to scoff at. They're small and really mean. Don't get too close, they do bite. The area around them is benign, and for those who own the castle nearby, it's a bit more safe than if you didn't. This is a very high RvR risk area, and not a place to dally.

Location 48, 55
Invader Risk 8 Very High
Quantity 5-6

Terrain Type Side of a hill beside a road leading to a castle. Close to guards, but high danger from invaders.

3. Waylayer Knoll

Between the Midgard and Hibernian roads, there is a hill. And for anyone who wishes to cut across this hill to get at the other, they will run smack into Midgard and Hibernian Waylayers. This isn't exactly a hunting spot, but it's a spot of interest to avoid, and maybe if you're in the mood for a little danger, you can bring a group here. They wander frequently but there is little else here of interest.

Location 39, 41
Invader Risk 8 High
Quantity 6-10
Terrain Type A knoll! They're spread out, they wander, and they're not friendly.

4. Templar's Ruins

These "Templars" look like fallen warriors. They have shiny armor and appear well prepared for an onslaught. If someone is actually looking to gain experience in this zone, this is one of the better spots. Other than the wandering they do themselves, the area is relatively safe.

Location 22, 9
Invader Risk 6 Medium
Quantity 13
Terrain Type Near zone wall at a ruin with open treed fields on all sides but one. Templars wander slightly, but no other wandering enemies nearby.

5. Cait Sidhe Ruins

This is a dangerous spot due to the RvR risks; however, there is a decent quantity of these creatures and there is little danger other than this, so if you have a group who wants to stick in the action but still gain experience while you are waiting, this is not a bad spot.

Location 58, 26
Invader Risk 8 Very High
Quantity 10
Terrain Type Near a road in an open area. They are translucent, no wandering creatures nearby.

Loot

Albion waylayer [35] (no loot)
Anne Fhitich [60] (no loot)
Arc of Ages [0] (no loot)
arch [0] (no loot)
cait sidhe [48,50,52,54,56] (no loot)
cave fairy [40,42,44,46] (no loot)
Ceriallen [40] (29%) Celtic Bracelet • (24%) Ornamental Necklace • (19%) Keltoi Crafted Belt • (14%) Traveling Backpack • (9.5%) Thick Rope • (20%) <The Spy's Satchel> • (95%) Jewels 09 • (20%) Jewels 60 • (5%) Blue, Red ***or*** Light Teal Colors • (1.5%) APOA: Insurgent's, Observer's, ***or*** Prey-Stalker's, ***or*** Keltoi Infiltrators Disguise • (1.5%) <To Hang My Sporran> • (1.5%) <Celtic Wonders> • (0.5%) <Arthurian Artifacts 2>
Coventina [70] (no loot)
Evian Fhitich [59] (no loot)
Fasius Previlus [42] (no loot)
Hibernian waylayer [35] (no loot)
legionnaire [30,32,34,36] (no loot)
Legionnaire Commander [42] (no loot)
Midgard waylayer [35] (no loot)
Miles Heberman [50] (no loot)
Pictish druid [40,42] (no loot)
Pictish warrior [40,42,44] (no loot)
piper fairy [52,54,56] (no loot)
Priestess [40,44] (no loot)
Spirit of Fasius Previlus [0] (no loot)
Templar [50,52,54] (no loot)
temple [0] (no loot

Pennine Mountains

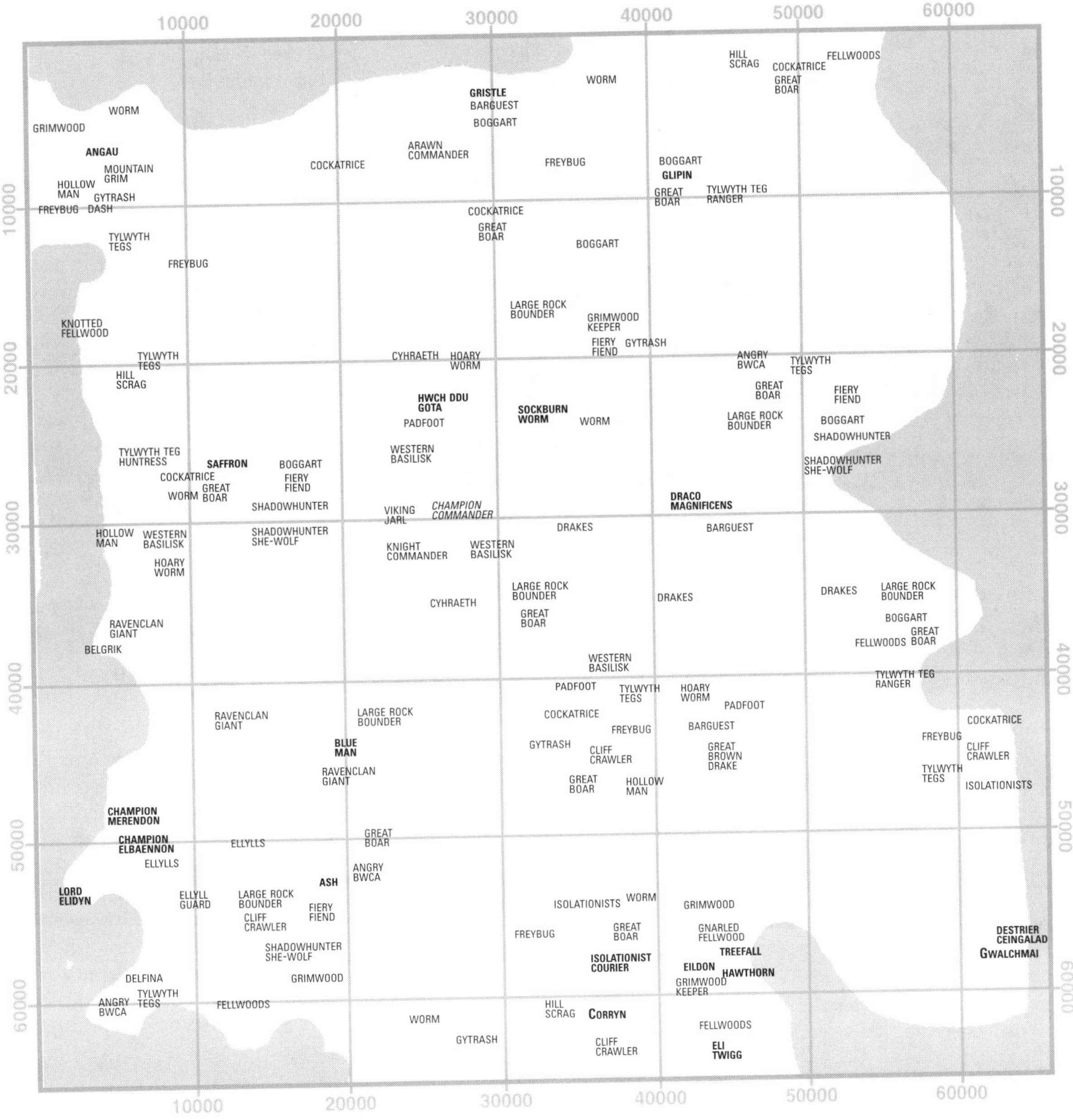

10000 20000 30000 40000 50000 60000

HILL SCRAG
COCKATRICE
FELLWOODS
GREAT BOAR
WORM
GRISTLE
BARGUEST
BOGGART
WORM
GRIMWOOD
ANGAU
ARAWN COMMANDER
COCKATRICE
FREYBUG
BOGGART
GLIPIN
MOUNTAIN GRIM
HOLLOW MAN
GYTRASH
FREYBUG
DASH
GREAT BOAR
TYLWYTH TEG RANGER
COCKATRICE
GREAT BOAR
TYLWYTH TEGS
BOGGART
FREYBUG
LARGE ROCK BOUNDER
GRIMWOOD KEEPER
KNOTTED FELLWOOD
FIERY FIEND
GYTRASH
TYLWYTH TEGS
CYHRAETH
HOARY WORM
ANGRY BWCA
TYLWYTH TEGS
HILL SCRAG
GREAT BOAR
FIERY FIEND
HWCH DDU GOTA
SOCKBURN WORM
WORM
LARGE ROCK BOUNDER
BOGGART
PADFOOT
SHADOWHUNTER
WESTERN BASILISK
TYLWYTH TEG HUNTRESS
SAFFRON
BOGGART
SHADOWHUNTER SHE-WOLF
COCKATRICE
FIERY FIEND
WORM
GREAT BOAR
DRACO MAGNIFICENS
SHADOWHUNTER
VIKING JARL
CHAMPION COMMANDER
HOLLOW MAN
WESTERN BASILISK
SHADOWHUNTER SHE-WOLF
DRAKES
BARGUEST
KNIGHT COMMANDER
WESTERN BASILISK
HOARY WORM
LARGE ROCK BOUNDER
DRAKES
LARGE ROCK BOUNDER
DRAKES
CYHRAETH
GREAT BOAR
BOGGART
RAVENCLAN GIANT
GREAT BOAR
FELLWOODS
BELGRIK
WESTERN BASILISK
TYLWYTH TEG RANGER
PADFOOT
TYLWYTH TEGS
HOARY WORM
PADFOOT
RAVENCLAN GIANT
LARGE ROCK BOUNDER
COCKATRICE
COCKATRICE
FREYBUG
BARGUEST
FREYBUG
GYTRASH
CLIFF CRAWLER
CLIFF CRAWLER
BLUE MAN
GREAT BROWN DRAKE
TYLWYTH TEGS
RAVENCLAN GIANT
GREAT BOAR
HOLLOW MAN
ISOLATIONISTS
CHAMPION MERENDON
CHAMPION ELBAENNON
ELLYLLS
GREAT BOAR
ELLYLLS
ANGRY BWCA
ASH
LORD ELIDYN
ELLYLL GUARD
LARGE ROCK BOUNDER
FIERY FIEND
ISOLATIONISTS
WORM
GRIMWOOD
CLIFF CRAWLER
DESTRIER CEINGALAD
FREYBUG
GREAT BOAR
GNARLED FELLWOOD
GWALCHMAI
SHADOWHUNTER SHE-WOLF
TREEFALL
ISOLATIONIST COURIER
EILDON
HAWTHORN
DELFINA
GRIMWOOD
GRIMWOOD KEEPER
TYLWYTH TEGS
ANGRY BWCA
FELLWOODS
HILL SCRAG
CORRYN
WORM
FELLWOODS
GYTRASH
CLIFF CRAWLER
ELI TWIGG

10000 20000 30000 40000 50000 60000

Monsters with levels lower than 30 are not marked on map.

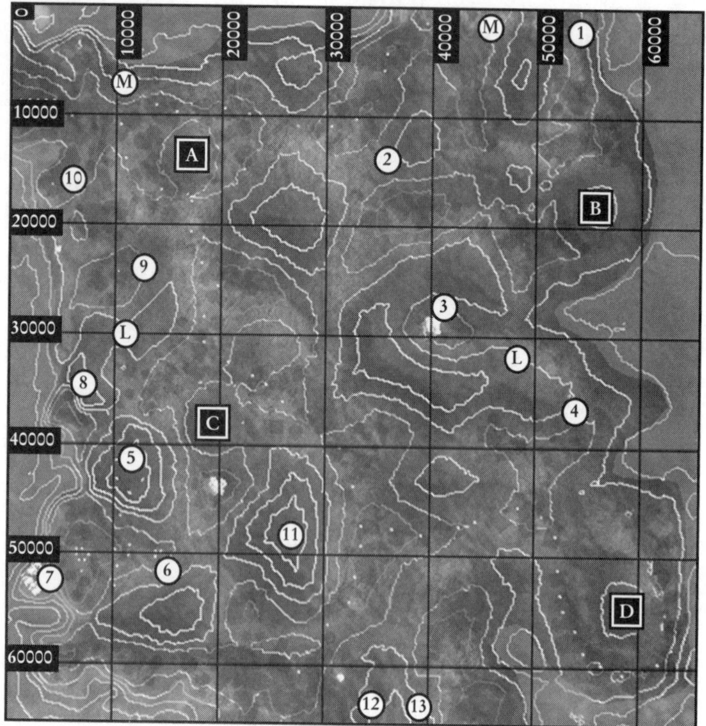

Map Key

A. Caer Sursbrook
B. Caer Erasleigh
C. Caer Berkstead
D. Caer Boldiam
(L) Low Invader Risk
(M) Medium Invader Risk
(H) High Invader Risk

No single zone in the entire world even remotely compares to the dangers that the Pennine Mountains hold. This zone is laced with extremely high level and aggressive creatures; it's a death trap for any explorer. The Pennine Mountains, as the name implies, is a zone full of sharp rocky peaks and very deep ravines, all of which are covered with horrible monsters of every sort. For a large group, this place may be heaven as the creature spots are endless, and there are named spawns all over the place. The average creature level here is around 50, or possibly higher.

1. Gnarled Fellwood Grove

These Trees are situated very near to Hadrian Wall border and are densely packed together. They're gigantic gray Trees with gaping maws; not the sort of tree you'd make a lean-to out of. The area is surprisingly safe in the local vicinity; although, the Invader Risk factor is relatively high. Great spot for archers.

Location 53, 3
Invader Risk 7 Medium
Quantity 10-14
Terrain Type Hillside near Road; sedentary; no roaming creatures.

2. Tylwyth Teg Ranger Valley

These Rangers seem to be the 'filler' for every spot in Pennine that doesn't contain some outrageously powerful creature. Be warned that they shoot from a long distance, and they have scouts that you may not see, which could bring the entire group running at you. One of the safer spots; by safer I mean safer than sitting inside a dragon's mouth.

Location 36, 18
Invader Risk 4 Slim
Quantity 9-12
Terrain Type Steep hills, creatures spread over large area with large detection range, some wandering creatures.

3. Draco's Pit (Draco Magnificens)

This big guy looks like a house-sized chameleon inside a massive stone structure. He resides in a pit that is surrounded by lesser powerful, but by no means weak, creatures. On the hills surrounding him, you'll find Young Brown Drakes and larger and meaner versions. This is not a place to set up camp; it's not even a good place to visit unless you're looking to slay this giant.

Location 41, 29
Invader Risk 3 Slim
Quantity 1 Draco, 4-5 Young Brown Drakes
Terrain Type This guy sits in a huge stone hut in a large barren pit surrounded by mountains. Tons of drakes

4. Knotted/Gnarled Fellwood Grove

Luckily, these mean old trees don't have territorial instincts. They're all in close proximity to each other and don't move at all, unless provoked. Like their cousins, they're large gray trees with pulsing red eyes. If you get to this spot alive, you're lucky; there are wandering creatures everywhere.

Location 54, 38
Invader Risk 4 Slim
Quantity 8-13
Terrain Type Rocky hillside, few normal trees around. Many wandering creatures.

5. Ravenclan Giant Peak

Beside an Albion keep lies this enormous mountain where on top sits a large group of Ravenclan Giants. Amidst them is what looks to be their boss, named "Belgrik." They really are giants too. They run fast, they hit hard, and they don't like visitors. There is virtually no Invader Risk here due to the monsters and close proximity of a castle.

One named "Belgrik" is here.

Location 10,42
Invader Risk 3 Very Slim
Quantity 8-12
Terrain Type Top of a huge mountain! Wandering creatures everywhere. Unsafe

6. Ellyll Village

In the broadest and deepest valley of Pennine sits an array of miniature folk. The Ellyll may look like little munchkins, but they're all around Level 50 and they're social deviants. On the outskirts of their castle is this spot, small huts and mushrooms are their homes, and they move slowly in groups of 3-4. There is one little fella named "Champion Merendon".

Location 14, 50
Invader Risk 3 extremely low
Quantity 20-30 Spread out, one named "Champion Merendon."
Terrain Type Large rocky barren hills around, some wandering creatures. These wander only slightly.

7. Ellyll Castle

If somehow you make it through the Ellyll Village, you'll come upon the ruined castle of the Ellylls. No spot in the entire world has more high-level creatures densely packed together. In two broken down rooms, there are roughly 40 of these little guys all vying for breathing room. Don't be fooled, they're all extremely powerful, and have some pets as allies to boot. If you make it through this small city of them, their boss, "Lord Elidyn" awaits you in one of the back rooms. Good luck.

Location 3, 52
Invader Risk 2 Extremely Low
Quantity 40+
Terrain Type Castle ruins with a massive amount of these wandering around. One named Lord Elidyn at the bottom of an enormous pit.

8. Ravenclan Giant Ravine

It looks as though most of the Ravenclan Giants have fallen into this pit. They don't move, but they're highly aggressive. If you fall into this pit, it's mostly likely the end of the road for you. There are many ways in, but one way out — and it's past those giants. It may be a great spot for ranged attackers.

Location 5, 37
Invader Risk 4 Low
Quantity 10+
Terrain Type Bottom of a deep pit. They're close together and wander little. Castle guards frequent the area.

9. Saffron, named Cockatrice

What wonders this armored chicken may hold is a mystery. The area is rife with violent and ugly creatures, so be careful where you step.

Location 11, 26
Invader Risk 4 Low
Quantity 1
Terrain Type Mountainside near Rangers, wandering creatures everywhere.

10. Hill Scrag Lair

If for you're still alive and looking for a decent hunting spot, here you'll find a large group of Hill Scrags for the picking; this is one of the few spots where there aren't wandering creatures. If you live to make it here, it might be a lucrative endeavor.

Location 4, 21
Invader Risk 5 Small
Quantity 10-20
Terrain Type Zone border on barren hill, no trees and no wandering enemies.

11. Cyhraeth Mountain

If Hill Giants, Armored Chickens, Brown Drakes, and Ellylls aren't enough, there is a mighty mountain peak covered with Cyraeths. Not only are they spread out and aggressive, but they're virtually invisible. They look like ghosts, and if you're not paying complete attention, you'll run right into them. Avoid this place if you can.

Location 28, 46
Invader Risk 2 Slim
Quantity 20-30 Spread out and translucent.
Terrain Type Spread out over a huge hill. Extremely Dangerous.

12. Cliff Crawler Mountain

Every mountain in Pennine has inhabitants. This particular one is covered with lots of gigantic spiders. They move frequently and cover an enormous amount of territory. Tread carefully. This may be a great spot, if you can find a safe place for your party to sit.

Location 36, 62
Invader Risk 6 Medium
Quantity 10-20
Terrain Type Huge barren hill covered with these huge spiders.

13. Corryn

Corryn is the named Cliff Crawler. He's big, ugly and meaner than the others, but he may drop something nice.

Location 36, 62
Invader Risk 6 Medium
Quantity 1
Terrain Type Spider-covered barren hill. This is a named Cliff Crawler.

Loot

Angau [43] (no loot)

angry bwca [45-47] (75%) Cat's Eye Apatite/Blue Spinel • (7.5%) Fell Creature's Tooth • (1.5%) Bwcan Colored Beads

Arawn Commander [55] (50% each) Carved Bone Key, Red Crystal Flagon, Gold Plated Gaming Dice, Pouch of Food • (20%) Golden Belt Buckle • (10%) Cat's Eye Apatite • (1.4%) APOA: Arawnite • (1.4%) Arawnite Longsword ***or*** Serrated Halberd, Deathward, Morbid Mantle, ***or*** Wristband of the Eye • (0.3%) <Cuisinart>

Ash [45] (no loot)

barguest [57-58] (no loot)

behind a rock [0] (no loot)

Blue Man [53] (no loot)

boggart [45-47,49] (no loot)

brown drakeling [34] (no loot)

cliff crawler [42-43,45] (no loot)

cockatrice [42-43] (no loot)

Corryn [46] (no loot)

cyhraeth [50-51] (30%) Cyhraeth Hair • (50%) Cyhraeth Medallion • (1.2%) <Pennine Prizes> • (1.2%) APOA: Woven Elemental • (1.2%) APOA: Woven Spirit • (1.2%) Robes of Celerity ***or*** Pillar of Might

Dash [39-40] (no loot)

Destrier Ceingalad [31] (no loot)

Draco Magnificens [61] (no loot)

Eildon [53] (no loot)

Eli Twigg [49] (no loot)

Ellyll champion [53-55] (50% each) Gold Threaded Sash, Silver Lined Pack, Ellyll Silken Hair • (25%) Champion Royal Guardian Chevron • (20%) Yellow Diamond/Pink Sapphire • (10%) Alexandrite/Jacinth • (1.3%) <Ellyll's Lair> • (1.3%) APOA: Kraggon Worm ***or*** Sword • (1.3%) <Ellyll's Enchantments>

Ellyll champion [57] (75% each) Gold Threaded Sash, Ellyll Silken Hair, Champion Royal Guardian Chevron • (30%) Featureless Kunzite Statuette • (20%) Precious Jasper • (10%) Chrysoberyl • (1.3%) <Ellyll's Lair> • (1.3%) APOA: Kraggon Worm ***or*** Sword • (1.3%) <Ellyll's Enchantments>

Ellyll froglord [51/54] (50% each) Frogrider Cavalry Chevron, Ellyll Silken Hair • (25%) Silver Lined Pack • (22%) Aquamarine Beryl/Kornerupine • (10%) Pink Sapphire/Precious Jasper • (1.3%) <Ellyll's Lair> • (1.3%) APOA: Kraggon Worm ***or*** Sword • (1.3%) <Ellyll's Enchantments>

Ellyll guard [49/51] (50% each) Ellyll Silken Hair, Silver Lined Pack • (40%) Gold Threaded Sash • (20%) Violet Sapphire/Yellow Tourmaline • (10%) Kornerupine/Yellow Diamond • (1.3%) <Ellyll's Lair> • (1.3%) APOA: Kraggon Worm ***or*** Sword • (1.3%) <Ellyll's Enchantments>

Ellyll sage [53] (50% each) Ellyll Silken Hair, Medicinal Herbs, Glittering Dust • (25% each) Mortar and Pestle, Gnarled Fellwood Dust • (10%) Heliodor • (7.5%) Black Sapphire • (1.4%) <Ellyll's Enchantments> • (1.4%) Emerald, Ruby, Sapphire ***or*** Diamond Dusted Robe, ***or*** Sage's Rune Stitched Cloak

Ellyll villager [45] (50% each) Bottle of Ellyll Wine, Ellyll Silken Hair, Gem Studded Stein • (20%) Red Spinel • (10%) Green Sapphire • (1.5%) Ellyll Lute, Drum ***or*** Flute

Ellyll windchaser [47/50] (50% each) Gold Threaded Sash, Silver Lined Pack • (20%) Heliodor • (10%) Aquamarine Beryl/Kornerupine • (1.3%) <Ellyll's Lair> • (1.3%) APOA: Kraggon Worm ***or*** Sword • (1.3%) <Ellyll's Enchantments>

faerie frog [28,30] (55%) Faerie Frog Legs (x2) • (70%) Harness • (10% each) Faerie Frog Skin, Eye

fiery fiend [41-43] (no loot)

freybug [35-36,38] (12%) Decorative Arrow

Glipin [49] (no loot)

gnarled fellwood [45-47,49] (no loot)

great boar [42-43,45-46] (no loot)

great brown drake [55,57-59] (no loot)

grimwood [46-47,49-50] (no loot)

grimwood keeper [43,45-47] (no loot)

Gristle [61] (no loot)

Gwalchmai [42] (no loot)

gytrash [35-36,38] (no loot)

Hawthorn [53] (no loot)

hill scrag [39,41] (25%) Chisled Stone Statue • (50%) Small Chisled Statue • (7.5%) Hide Cloak • (1.3%) Staff of the North, South, East ***or*** West • (1.3%) APOA: Bounder Fur • (1.3%) Ghost Wolf Hide Cloak, Jewel of Dark Beauty, ***or*** Human Tooth Necklace

hoary worm [53-55] (no loot)

hollow man [39,41] (50% each) Hollow Bone Totem, Necklace • (1.3%) Staff of the North, South, East ***or*** West • (1.3%) APOA: Hollow • (1.3%) Ghost Wolf Hide Cloak, Jewel of Dark Beauty, ***or*** Human Tooth Necklace

Hwch Ddu Gota [55] (no loot)

isolationist armsman [47] (no loot)

isolationist cleric [46,48] (no loot)

isolationist mercenary [46] (no loot)

isolationist paladin [48] (no loot)

isolationist scout [47] (no loot)

isolationist sorcerer [46] (no loot)

isolationist wizardess [47] (no loot)

knotted fellwood [43,45-46] (no loot)

large rock bounder [45-46] (60%) Large Bounder Pelt • (80%) Large Rock Bounder Tooth • (7.5%) Fell Creature's Tooth

Lord Elidyn [59] (50% each) Chevron of the Royal Lord, Ellyll Silken Hair, Gold Threaded Sash • (15% each) Water Opal Circlet, Alexandrite, Black Opal • (1.3%) <Ellyll's Lair> • (2%) APOA: Kraggon Worm ***or*** Sword • (1.3%) <Ellyll's Enchantments>

mountain grim [35-36,38-39] (no loot)

padfoot [51,53-54] (no loot)

ravenclan giant [50-51] (5%) Jacinth • (4%) Chrysoberyl • (3%) Black Opal • (2%) Black Sapphire • (1.4%) Raven Clan Meat Cleaver, Battle Sword ***or*** Skewer, ***or*** Darkened Sledge • (1.4%) Robes of Celerity ***or*** Pillar of Might

Saffron [45] (no loot)

shadowhunter [39,41] (40%) Shadowhunter Pelt • (80%) Shadowhunter Teeth • (7.5%) Fell Creature's Tooth • (1.5%) Dead Warrior's Pike

shadowhunter she-wolf [42-43] (40%) Shadowhunter Pelt • (80%) Shadowhunter Teeth • (7.5%) Fell Creature's Tooth • (1%) Dead Warrior's Pike

Sockburn Worm [59] (no loot)

Treefall [49] (no loot)

Tylwyth Teg huntress [43/45] (7.5%) Elven Arrows (x2) • (40% each) Dried Bear Meat, Dried Venison, Rovers Pack • (20%) Blue Spinel/Water Opal • (1.3%) Fire Asterite Ring, Chitin Ring, Oaken Girdle, Girdle of Cat-Like Movement • (1.3%) APOA: Studded Fae • (1.3%) <Teg's Hoard>

Tylwyth Teg ranger [46-47] (7.5%) Elven Arrows (x2) • (40%) Dried Bear Meat (x2) • (40%) Rovers Pack • (25%) Rhodolite • (1.3%) Fire Asterite Ring, Chitin Ring, Oaken Girdle, Girdle of Cat-Like Movement • (1.3%) APOA: Studded Fae • (1.3%) <Teg's Hoard>

Tylwyth Teg rover [41-42] (10%) Elven Arrows • (40% each) Dried Bear Meat, Dried Venison, Rovers Pack • (20%) Cat's Eye Apatite • (1.3%) <Teg's Hoard> • (1.3%) Fire Asterite Ring, Chitin Ring, Oaken Girdle, ***or*** Girdle of Cat-Like Movement • (1.3%) APOA: Studded Fae

western basilisk [49-50] (70%) Western Basilisk Skin • (7.5%) Fell Creature's Tooth

worm [39,41-42] (no loot)

young brown drake [47] (no loot)

Snowdonia

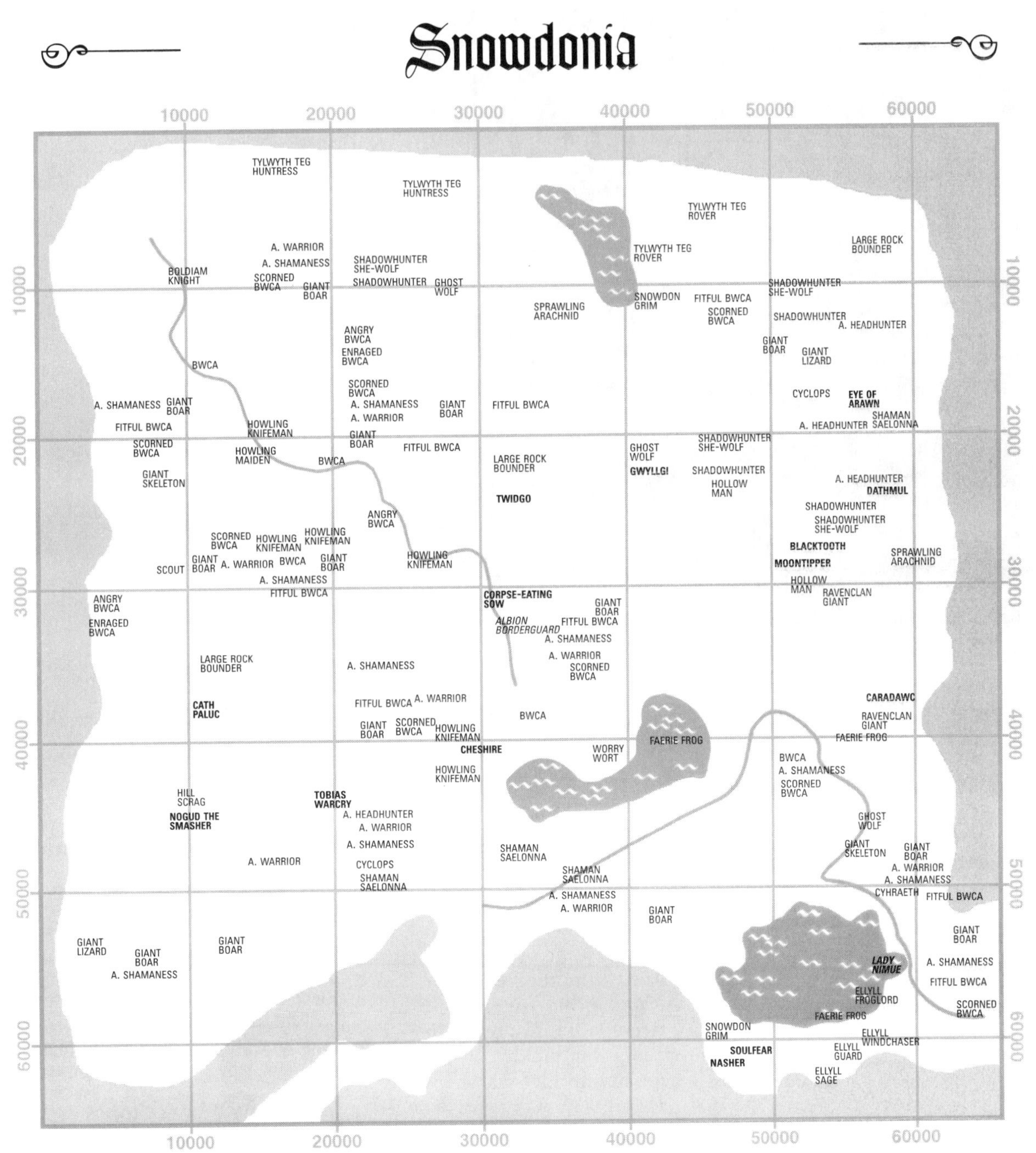

Monsters with levels lower than 24 are not marked on map.

A = Arawnite

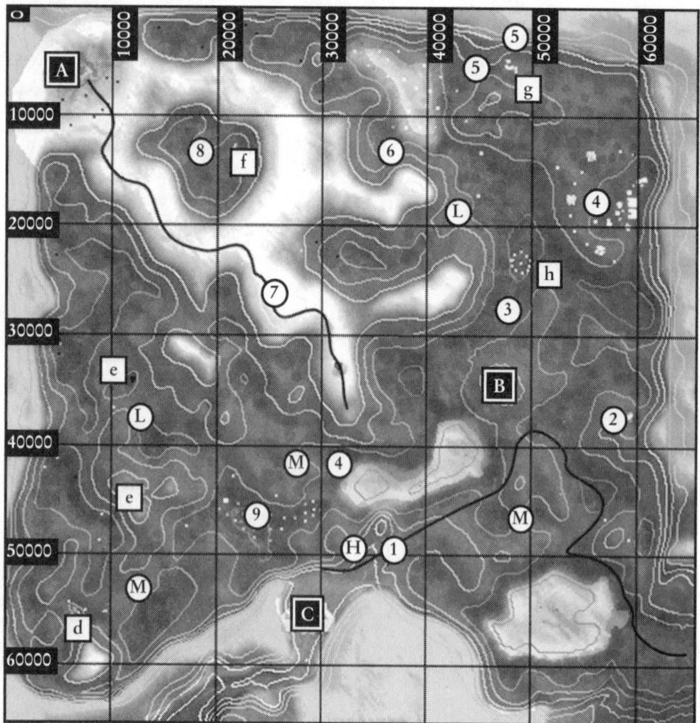

Map Key

A. Castle Myrddin
B. Caer Hurbury
C. Snowdonia Fortress
d. Arawnites
e. Stone Hut
f. Bwcas
g. Tylwyths
h. Hollow Men Stones
(L) Low Invader Risk
(M) Medium Invader Risk
(H) High Invader Risk

Snowdonia, despite what the name says, is mostly snow free. Only in the northwestern regions will one find snow at higher altitudes. Otherwise, it's a zone comprised of steep rocky barren hills with valleys of dense trees and an occasional vicious creature. Realm invaders here near the gate are a constant risk, but farther to the north, it is generally safe. There are few wandering creatures here intent on the traveler's doom, but there is a unique quantity of small fortifications by large groups of rogue creatures. Snowdonia is an impressive realm of the world's highest peaks and lowest rocky valleys.

1. Arawnite Camp

Due to the close proximity of the Snowdonia border fortress, this spot is generally popular. However, due to its easy access and low danger, invaders will certainly stop here to check if Albions are hunting. The creatures here don't move much and there are no wandering threats.

Location 36, 50
Invader Risk 8 High
Quantity 8
Terrain Type Side of a steep hill right beside Snowdonia border gate.

2. Ravenclan Giants

It seems some of the Ravenclan Giants from the Pennine Mountains have moved north! Here you'll find a medium-sized group looking to intercept any invader that might pass his way. As the name suggests, they're huge and can crush you pretty quickly. Fortunately, they are spread out, allowing an attacker to take them down one at a time.

Location 59, 37
Invader Risk 6 Medium
Quantity 5-8
Terrain Type Spread over a wide area of rocky sparsely treed terrain, they do not wander far.

3. Hollow Man's Stones

These Hollow Men are ugly

creatures near the heart of Snowdonia. There is a small Invader Risk here and they wander occasionally without any other wandering threats nearby. There are enough that a small group could make some good experience while staying relatively safe.

Location 48, 23
Invader Risk 5, Low
Quantity 8-10
Terrain Type Open rolling hills with occasional trees, they wander slightly, but not far.

4. Arawnite Headhunter/Cyclops Stronghold

It seems that each realm has allowed a single large stronghold to exist of enemy creatures. This one is in a bit more shambles than the other realms'; there is an effective combination of Cyclops and Arawnites that comb a large area of land. The Arawnites look like they've employed the Cyclops as mean scouts. Those looking to hunt here will find plenty to fight; just be wary of getting in over your head.

Location 56, 18
Invader Risk 5 Low
Quantity 15-25
Terrain Type Many large rock and wooden outposts over a substantial area; wandering Cyclops.

5. Tylwyth Teg Rover Camps

These rangers seem to be the aggressive space fillers for the entire Albion frontier. They look like friendly Scouts dressed in green, but don't be fooled, they often stand behind trees to mask their presence, and by the time they attack, you're going to be in bad shape due to their longbow range.

Location 47, 5 and at 42, 7
Invader Risk 4 Slim
Quantity 5
Terrain Type Open area beside a hill with occasional trees. Most don't move, with the exception of a couple scouts.

6. Sprawling Arachnid Pit

Albion gets to claim the largest quantity of spiders in the entire world. Not only are there many of them, but they're huge! These aren't the kinds that make pretty webs in your barn; these are the kinds that eat the horses. There are enough here for a full group. They don't move much and they move only slowly. It seems they've claimed a pit all to themselves.

Location 35, 12
Invader Risk 4 Slim
Quantity 10
Terrain Type Beside a lake in a barren pit with no trees around. Wandering guards for protection; no other wandering creatures. These move only slightly and slowly.

7. Tylwyth Teg Rover Camp

Similar to the other camps, these Rangers populate areas that might catch travelers off-guard. However, if you're looking to attack some creatures that use ranged attack, this is a good place.

Location 26, 29
Invader Risk 3 Slim
Quantity 6-8
Terrain Type Small unmoving group in a wooded valley with scouts wandering around them.

8. Angry Bwca Pit

And boy are they angry! They'll chase you all around if you're not careful. Located in a small recess from the snowy portion of Snowdonia, the Bwca are little rodent-looking fellas that walk on two legs. The only risk is that they travel a lot and cover a great deal of land.

Location 19, 13
Invader Risk 3 Slim
Quantity 5-10
Terrain Type A wide recess in the snow which is filled by Angry Bwcas wandering around randomly. Very spread out.

9. Arawnite Camp

The Arawnite have made quite a home of Snowdonia. This is one of their camps that might be a safer bet than the larger one to the northeast. There seem to be many sedentary Arawnites with the occasional Cyclops, but not nearly as many as their other larger camp/stronghold. Aside from the ugly Cyclops, there are no wandering threats.

Location 20, 44
Invader Risk 4 Slim
Quantity 10-12
Terrain Type Open hilly area with wandering Cyclops, otherwise clear from wandering aggros.

Loot

angry bwca [45-46/47] (75%) Cat's Eye Apatite/Blue Spinel • (7.5%) Fell Creature's Tooth • (1.5%) Bwcan Colored Beads

Arawnite Assassin [28] (no loot)

Arawnite headhunter [36,38] (50% each) Carved Bone Key, Red Crystal Flagon, Gold Plated Gaming Dice, Pouch of Food • (20%) Golden Belt Buckle • (10%) Cat's Eye Apatite • (1.4%) APOA: Arawnite • (1.4%) Arawnite Longsword ***or*** Serrated Halberd, Deathward, Morbid Mantle, ***or*** Wristband of the Eye • (0.3%) <Cuisinart>

Arawnite shamaness [34-35] *see Arawnite warrior [34-35]*

Arawnite warrior [34-35] (50% each) Red Crystal Flagon, Gold Plated Gaming Dice, Carved Bone Key • (15%) Golden Belt Buckle • (10%) Cat's Eye Apatite • (1.4%) APOA: Arawnite • (1.4%) Arawnite Longsword ***or*** Serrated Halberd, Deathward, Morbid Mantle, ***or*** Wristband of the Eye • (0.3%) <Cuisinart>

Blacktooth [45] (70%) Shadowhunter Pelt • (80%) Shadowhunter Teeth • (7.5%) Fell Creature's Tooth • (1.5%) Dead Warrior's Pike

bwca [24,26] (80% each) Topaz, Citrine • (0.3%) Manaweave Ring • (0.6% each) Smoldering, Netherworldly Robes • (0.3%) <Arthurian Artifacts 4> • (9%) Silver Mirror

Caradawc [54] (6%) Jacinth • (5%) Chrysoberyl • (4%) Black Opal • (3%) Black Sapphire • (2%) Violet Diamond • (1.4%) Raven Clan Meat Cleaver, Battle Sword ***or*** Skewer, ***or*** Darkened Sledge • (1.4%) Robes of Celerity ***or*** Pillar of Might

Cath Paluc [49] *see large rock bounder [45-46]*

Cheshire [24] (15%) Small Bounder Pelt • (75%) Small Rock Bounder Tooth (x2)

corpse-eating sow [36] *see giant boar [34-35]*

cyclops [41-42] (5%) Ring of Arawn • (1.5%) Cyclops Headsman's Axe, Cyclops Eye, ***or*** Ghost Wolf Hide Cloak • (4%) Yellow Tourmaline • (3%) Aquamarine Beryl • (2%) Kornerupine

cyhraeth [50-51] (30%) Cyhraeth Hair • (50%) Cyhraeth Medallion • (1.2%) <Pennine Prizes> • (1.2%) APOA: Woven Elemental • (1.2%) APOA: Woven Spirit • (1.2%) Robes of Celerity ***or*** Pillar of Might

Dathmul [47] *see hollow man [39,41]*

Ellyll froglord [51/54] (50% each) Frogrider Cavalry Chevron, Ellyll Silken Hair • (25%) Silver Lined Pack • (22%) Aquamarine Beryl/Kornerupine • (10%) Pink Sapphire/Precious Jasper • (1.3%) <Ellyll's Lair> • (1.3%) APOA: Kraggon Worm ***or*** Sword • (1.3%) <Ellyll's Enchantments>

Ellyll guard [49/51] (50% each) Ellyll Silken Hair, Silver Lined Pack • (40%) Gold Threaded Sash • (20%) Violet Sapphire/Yellow Tourmaline • (10%) Kornerupine/Yellow Diamond • (1.3%) <Ellyll's Lair> • (1.3%) APOA: Kraggon Worm ***or*** Sword • (1.3%) <Ellyll's Enchantments>

Ellyll sage [53] (50% each) Ellyll Silken Hair, Medicinal Herbs, Glittering Dust • (25% each) Mortar and Pestle, Gnarled Fellwood Dust • (10%) Heliodor • (7.5%) Black Sapphire • (1.4%) <Ellyll's Enchantments> • (1.4%) Emerald, Ruby, Sapphire ***or*** Diamond Dusted Robe, ***or*** Sage's Rune Stitched Cloak

Ellyll windchaser [47/50] (50% each) Gold Threaded Sash, Silver Lined Pack • (20%) Heliodor • (10%) [Aquamarine Beryl/Kornerupine] • (1.3%) <Ellyll's Lair> • (1.3%) APOA: Kraggon Worm ***or*** Sword • (1.3%) <Ellyll's Enchantments>

Eye of Arawn [45] (5%) Ring of Arawn • (1.5%) Cyclops Headsman's Axe, Cyclops Eye, ***or*** Ghost Wolf Hide Cloak • (5%) Yellow Tourmaline • (4%) Aquamarine Beryl • (3%) Kornerupine

faerie frog [28,30] (55%) Faerie Frog Legs (x2) • (70%) Harness • (10% each) Faerie Frog Skin, Eye

faint grim [20-21] (75% each) Grim Shreds, Carnelian • (15%) Grim Scraps • (1.5%) APOA: of the Resolute • (0.3%) Shadowhands Gloves ***or*** Cloak, Silver Oak Longbow, ***or*** Crypt Robbers Bracer

fitful bwca [35-36] (75%) Sphene • (7.5%) Fell Creature's Tooth • (1.5%) Bwcan Beads

ghost wolf [32,34] (50%) Ghost Wolf Hide • (80%) Ghost Wolf Teeth • (7.5%) Fell Creature's Tooth • (0.5%) Dead Warrior's Pike

giant boar [34-35] (50%) Giant Boar Hide • (80%) Giant Boar Tusk • (7.5%) Fell Creature's Tooth • (0.5%) Dead Warrior's Pike • (12%) Giant Boar Claw

giant lizard [36,38] (70%) Giant Lizard Hide • (7.5%) Fell Creature's Tooth • (11%) Giant Lizard Sinew

giant skeleton [27-28] (50% each) Skeleton Skull, Large Bleached Bone • (0.3%) Manaweave Ring • (0.6% each) Smoldering ***or*** Netherworldly Robes • (1.4%) Jeweled Left ***or*** Right Eye • (0.3%) <Cuisinart>

Grunge [36] *see giant boar [34-35]*

Gwyllgi [36] *see ghost wolf [32,34]*

Haegan McLeary [45] (10% each) Water Opal, Rhodolite, Peridot, Yellow Tourmaline, Kornerupine, Pink Sapphire, Alexandrite, Chrysoberyl, Black Sapphire ***or*** Precious Heliodor

hill scrag [39,41] (25%) Chisled Stone Statue • (50%) Small Chisled Statue • (7.5%) Hide Cloak • (1.3%) Staff of the North, South, East ***or*** West • (1.3%) APOA: Bounder Fur • (1.3%) Ghost Wolf Hide Cloak, Jewel of Dark Beauty, ***or*** Human Tooth Necklace

hollow man [39,41] (50% each) Hollow Bone Totem, Necklace • (1.3%) Staff of the North, South, East ***or*** West • (1.3%) APOA: Hollow • (1.3%) Ghost Wolf Hide Cloak, Jewel of Dark Beauty, ***or*** Human Tooth Necklace

horse [10] (75%) Horse Hair • (10%) Auburn Mane • (80%) Ruined Horse Skin • (35%) Horse Skin • (60%) Horse Hair

howling knifeman [26-27] *see howling maiden [24,26]*

howling maiden [24,26] (50% each) Warm Patched Hide Blanket, Flask of Fire Wine, Small Silver Statue • (10% each) Agate, Garnet • (5% each) Citrine, APOA: Mithril Chain • (1.5%) Knifeman's Gold, Crystal ***or*** Silver Dagger, Snowdonian Bandit Bow, Frosted Scimitar, Furlined Cloak, Snowdonian Bandit Warmer • (0.3%) <Arthurian Artifacts 4>

juggernaut [32] (20%) Jewels 18 • (1.5%) APOA: Woebegone Miner • (1.5%) <Mined from the Deep> • (1.5%) <Goblin' It Up>

large rock bounder [45-46] (60%) Large Bounder Pelt • (80%) Large Rock Bounder Tooth • (7.5%) Fell Creature's Tooth

Moontipper [46] *see Blacktooth [45]*

Nasher [39] *see snowdon grim [36,38]*

Nogud the Smasher [43] *see hill scrag [39,41]*

ravenclan giant [50-51] (5%) Jacinth • (4%) Chrysoberyl • (3%) Black Opal • (2%) Black Sapphire • (1.4%) Raven Clan Meat Cleaver, Battle Sword ***or*** Skewer, ***or*** Darkened Sledge • (1.4%) Robes of Celerity ***or*** Pillar of Might

scorned bwca [32,34] (75%) Black Star Diopside • (7.5%) Fell Creature's Tooth • (1.5%) Bwcan Beads

shadowhunter [39,41] (40%) Shadowhunter Pelt • (80%) Shadowhunter Teeth • (7.5%) Fell Creature's Tooth • (1.5%) Dead Warrior's Pike

shadowhunter she-wolf [42-43] (40%) Shadowhunter Pelt • (80%) Shadowhunter Teeth • (7.5%) Fell Creature's Tooth • (1%) Dead Warrior's Pike

small rock bounder [22-23] (15%) Small Bounder Pelt • (75%) Small Rock Bounder Tooth (x2)

snowdon grim [36,38] (25%) Grim Shreds • (50%) Grim Scraps • (30%) Green Sapphire • (1.3%) APOA: Glittering Netherite • (1.3%) APOA: Glittering Arcanite • (0.2%) Jewel of Dark Beauty • (0.2%) Deathly Lochaber Axe • (0.5%) Whirling Defender • (0.4%) Robe of Deft Movement

Soulfear [54] (80% each) Cyhraeth Hair, Cyhraeth Medallion • (1.3%) <Pennine Prizes> • (1.3%) APOA: Woven Elemental • (1.3%) APOA: Woven Spirit

sprawling arachnid [34-35] (70%) Arachnid Leg (x2) • (50%) Sprawling Arachnid Carapace • (1.5%) Dead Warrior's Pike

Tobias Warcry [41] (no loot)

Twidgo [35] *see ghost wolf [32,34]*

Tylwyth Teg huntress [43/45] (7.5%) Elven Arrows (x2) • (40% each) Dried Bear Meat, Dried Venison, Rovers Pack • (20%) [Blue Spinel/Water Opal] • (1.3%) Fire Asterite Ring, Chitin Ring, Oaken Girdle, Girdle of Cat-Like Movement • (1.3%) APOA: Studded Fae • (1.3%) <Teg's Hoard>

Tylwyth Teg ranger [46] (7.5%) Elven Arrows (x2) • (40%) Dried Bear Meat (x2) • (40%) Rovers Pack • (25%) Rhodolite • (1.3%) Fire Asterite Ring, Chitin Ring, Oaken Girdle, Girdle of Cat-Like Movement • (1.3%) APOA: Studded Fae • (1.3%) <Teg's Hoard>

Tylwyth Teg rover [41-42] (10%) Elven Arrows • (40% each) Dried Bear Meat, Dried Venison, Rovers Pack • (20%) Cat's Eye Apatite • (1.3%) <Teg's Hoard> • (1.3%) Fire Asterite Ring, Chitin Ring, Oaken Girdle, ***or*** Girdle of Cat-Like Movement • (1.3%) APOA: Studded Fae

Worry Wort [32] (70% each) Faerie Frog Legs, Harness • (45%) Faerie Frog Legs

Briefine

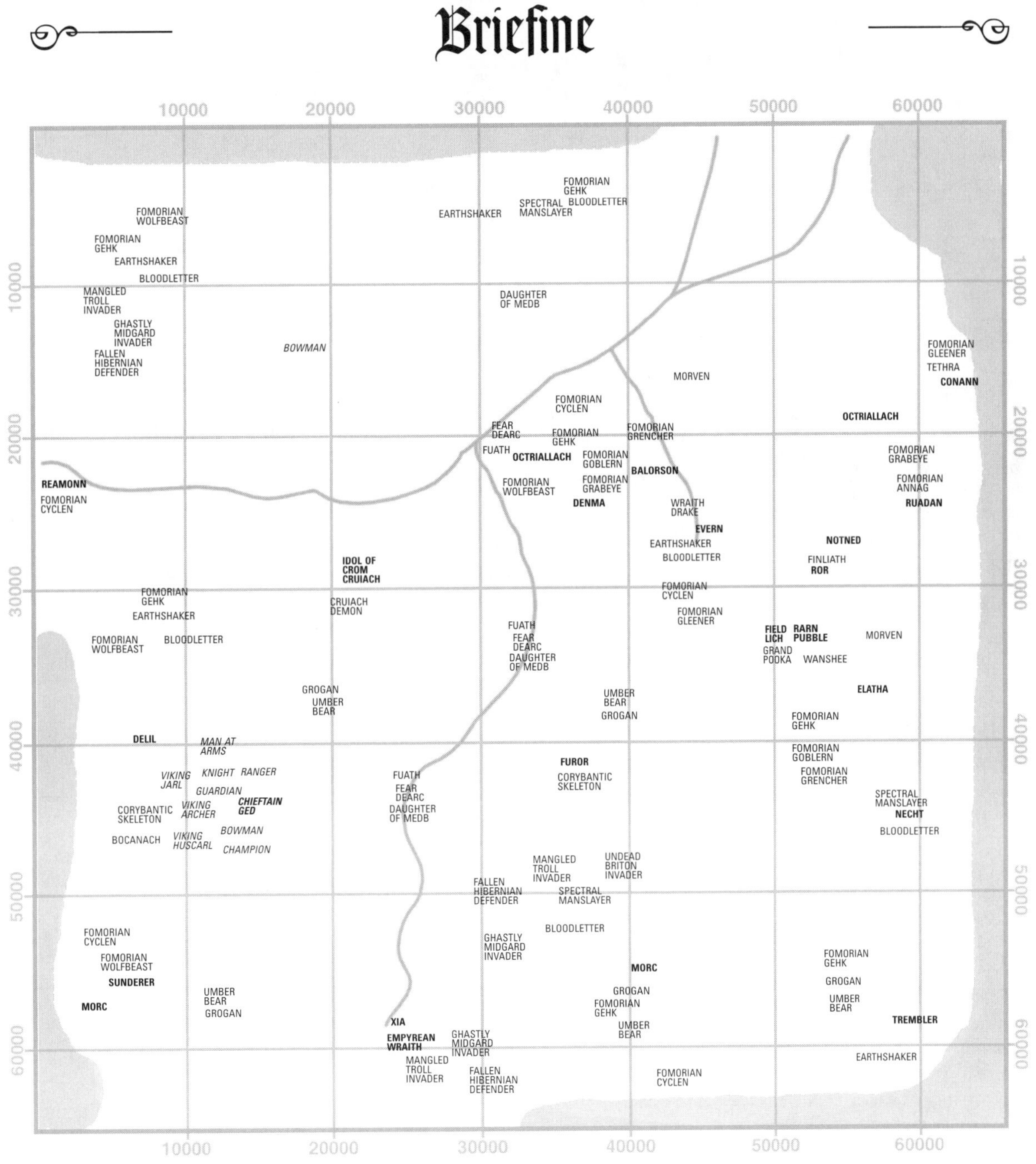
10000
20000
30000
40000
50000
60000
FOMORIAN GEHK
SPECTRAL MANSLAYER
BLOODLETTER
EARTHSHAKER
FOMORIAN WOLFBEAST
FOMORIAN GEHK
EARTHSHAKER
BLOODLETTER
MANGLED TROLL INVADER
GHASTLY MIDGARD INVADER
FALLEN HIBERNIAN DEFENDER
DAUGHTER OF MEDB
BOWMAN
MORVEN
FOMORIAN GLEENER
TETHRA
CONANN
FOMORIAN CYCLEN
OCTRIALLACH
FEAR DEARC
FOMORIAN GEHK
FOMORIAN GRENCHER
FUATH
OCTRIALLACH
FOMORIAN GOBLERN
FOMORIAN GRABEYE
BALORSON
FOMORIAN ANNAG
RUADAN
REAMONN
FOMORIAN CYCLEN
FOMORIAN WOLFBEAST
FOMORIAN GRABEYE
DENMA
WRAITH DRAKE
EVERN
NOTNED
EARTHSHAKER
BLOODLETTER
FINLIATH
ROR
IDOL OF CROM CRUIACH
FOMORIAN GEHK
EARTHSHAKER
CRUIACH DEMON
FOMORIAN CYCLEN
FOMORIAN GLEENER
FOMORIAN WOLFBEAST
BLOODLETTER
FUATH
FEAR DEARC
DAUGHTER OF MEDB
FIELD LICH
RARN PUBBLE
MORVEN
GRAND POOKA
WANSHEE
GROGAN
UMBER BEAR
UMBER BEAR
GROGAN
ELATHA
FOMORIAN GEHK
DELIL
MAN AT ARMS
FOMORIAN GOBLERN
FURIOR
FOMORIAN GRENCHER
VIKING JARL
KNIGHT
RANGER
GUARDIAN
FUATH
FEAR DEARC
DAUGHTER OF MEDB
CORYBANTIC SKELETON
CORYBANTIC SKELETON
VIKING ARCHER
CHIEFTAIN GED
SPECTRAL MANSLAYER
NECHT
BOWMAN
BLOODLETTER
BOCANACH
VIKING HUSCARL
CHAMPION
MANGLED TROLL INVADER
UNDEAD BRITON INVADER
FALLEN HIBERNIAN DEFENDER
SPECTRAL MANSLAYER
BLOODLETTER
FOMORIAN CYCLEN
GHASTLY MIDGARD INVADER
FOMORIAN WOLFBEAST
MORC
FOMORIAN GEHK
SUNDERER
GROGAN
GROGAN
UMBER BEAR
FOMORIAN GEHK
UMBER BEAR
GROGAN
MORC
UMBER BEAR
TREMBLER
XIA
EMPYREAN WRAITH
GHASTLY MIDGARD INVADER
MANGLED TROLL INVADER
FALLEN HIBERNIAN DEFENDER
EARTHSHAKER
FOMORIAN CYCLEN

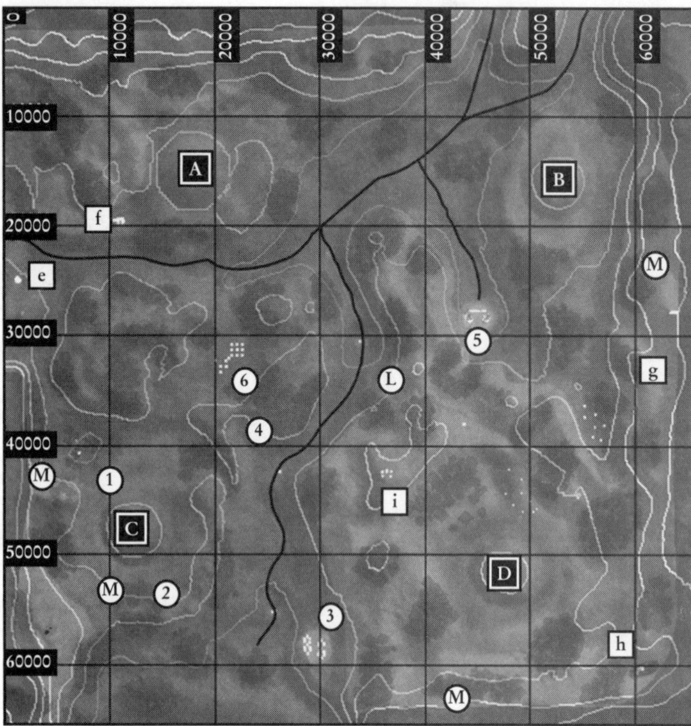

Map Key

A. Dun Bolg
B. Dun Crimthainn
C. Dun na nGed
D. Dun da Behnn
e. Stone Tower
f. Ruins
g. Formorian Stones
h. Earthshaker Quarry
i. Corybantic Stones
(L) Low Invader Risk
(M) Medium Invader Risk
(H) High Invader Risk

Breifine is hardly a friendly retreat; you'll find no vacationers here. Other than in one of the nearby castles, there is virtually no safe spot; even the roads are spotted with highly aggressive creatures. The average creature level is around 45 with creatures that go down to 35 or so, and up to 65. The landscape is similar to the rest of the Hibernian RvR areas, rolling hills, spotted with forests and even the occasional lake. For the brave and foolish alike, Breifine is home to what are perhaps Hibernia's most powerful denizens.

1. Bocanach

Though few travelers come here for business, this spot is rather decent if you want to avoid the crowd. They're humanoid and have lots of hit points, but they're beside a castle with a good amount of space. Find a group and pay a visit, the Invader Risk is fairly low.

Location 7.5, 39
Invader Risk 3 Low
Quantity Roughly 13
Terrain Type bottom of a bowl surrounded by hills. Plenty of safe spots with occasional other wandering creatures.

2. Formorian Camp

These one-eyed creatures don't like visitors. There aren't too many of them, but they pack a wallop. Other than their gigantic single eye, the other notable attribute is the jet thrusters they must have installed somewhere in their boots, because you'll not outrun these guys without a bard!

Location 4, 56
Invader Risk 3Low
Quantity 4 + One named "Morc"
Personality Very aggressive. They run faster than you can sprint, so stay away unless you're ready for them.
Terrain Type Top of a knoll. Fairly safe surrounding area though.

3. Empyrean's Stones

These are generally pleasant ghostly folk who have made these standing stones their home. They don't move a whole lot, and they've been known to drop some magic loot. There are plenty of them here if you bring a group, but beware the wandering Undead. They are faction based, so if you kill them and ruin your faction, go kill some Siabra to raise it again.

Location 29, 58
Invader Risk 2 Very Low
Level Range 34-48
Quantity 10-15
Personality Faction based. They're in a medium sized area and stand still frequently.
Terrain Type Open field with hill on one side, frequented by wandering higher-level creatures.

4. Corybantic Skeletons

These guys are just giant skeletons that sit between two castles. The area is decent for hunting, but supplies are hard to come by if needed and the nearest shop is a long run. If you want a spot that is unlikely to be camped, head over this way. Just be careful of the horrible monsters en route to the spot.

Location 38, 21
Invader Risk 5 Mid/Low
Quantity Roughly 8
Terrain Type Top of a knoll with an occasional wandering creature; not a bad spot!

5. Wraith Drakes

These Wraith Drakes look like gigantic evil chameleons. These guys are *tough*, as in level 65 (yes, that's 65). This basically means 'look but don't touch' — unless you're looking for a quick trip back to town. I would imagine they're worth a whole lot of experience, but not many living have ever killed one.

Location 44, 28
Invader Risk 4 Low
Quantity Around 4
Terrain Type Bottom of a small valley surrounded by other level 50'ish creatures.

6. Cruiach Demon Stones

These demons are as strong as they are ugly. This is an obviously dangerous spot with wandering high-level creatures ambling by frequently. If you're in the area, take a look. They're impressive, with one 'boss' demon towering above the rest; don't try to feed them though.

Location 20, 31
Invader Risk 3 Very Low
Level Range 55-57
Quantity 8-10
Terrain Type Open fields with lots of wandering aggro. Avoid!

Loot

Balorson [52] (no loot)
bananach [40-41] (no loot)
bloodletter [48-49] (no loot)
bocanach [46-48] (no loot)
boogie man [34] (no loot)
Briton woodcutter [37] *see Celtic brehon [37]*
Celtic brehon [37] (70%) Eagle Head Brooch • (60%) Jeweled Scabard • (2%) Siabrian Raider's Head • (10%) Cat's Eye Opal • (1.2%) APOA: Raider's Chitin • (1.2%) Left ***or*** Right Bracer of Skill, Siabrian Belt, Mystic Shield ***or*** Crusher, ***or*** Crescent Razor • (1.5%) <Rogue Pendants (Highest)> • (1.2%) Cath Drum ***or*** APOA: Cath
Conann [63] (no loot)
corybantic skeleton [46] (no loot)
cruiach demon [55-57] (no loot)
Daughter of Medb [44-45] (no loot)
Delil [48] (no loot)
Denma [55] (no loot)
earthshaker [47-49] (no loot)
Elatha [53] (no loot)
empyrean guardian [34-35/36-37(38)] (15/25%) Drakescale Venom • (10%) Empyrean Wine • (20/15%) Cat's Eye Apatite • (1.5%) Empyreal Leggings ***or*** Sleeves, Empyreal Ranger Gauntlets ***or*** Boots, ***or*** Spectral Flight Arrows [34-35] • (1.8%; hi-lo) Empyreal Vest ***or*** Helm, Spectral Flight Arrows, Spectral Flight, ***or*** Sentinel's Ring [36-37]
Evern [70] (no loot)
fallen Hibernian defender [45] (no loot)
fear dearc [46-47] (no loot)
field lich [58] (no loot)
finliath [58-60] (10%) Jewels 61 • (3.5%) Translucent Finliath Tooth • (1.5%) Pouch of Fettered Screams • (2%) Box of Childrens Toys • (3%) Bloodstained Golden Splinter • (1.5%) Finliath Firebrand • (0.5%) <Valor's Heart>
Fomorian annag [55/56] (10%) Jewels 05 • (1.5%) Small Annag Head • (1%) Large Annag Head • (3.5%) Rune Etched Seashell • (0.5%) <Valor's Heart> • (4%) Glowing Ultramarine Stone • (1.5%) Diabolical Fomorian Pants/vest ***or*** Robe
Fomorian cyclen [46-47] (10%) Jewels 04 • (4%) Punctured Cyclen Eye • (2.5%) Undamaged Cyclen Eye • (2%) Painted Elven Skull • (1.5%) Shrunken Elven Head • (1.5%) Fomorian Protector • (0.5%) <Granny's Basket>
Fomorian gehk [47] *see Fomorian cyclen [46-47]*
Fomorian gehk [48/49] (10%) Jewels 04 • (4.5/3%) Stone Wolfbeast Figurine • (7.5/1.5%) Cask of Fomorian Swill • (3/2%) Gehk Hoof • (1.5%) Fomorian Protector/Gehk Gouger • (0.5%) <Granny's Basket>
Fomorian gleener [61-62] (no loot)
Fomorian goblern [49/50] (10%) Jewels 04 • (4.5%) Cask of Fomorian Swill • (1%) Orb of the Sea • (3.5%) Glowing Ultramarine Stone • (0.5%) Polished and Painted Seashell • (0.5%) Rune Etched Seashell • (1.5%) Fomorian Staff of Light/Mana • (0.5%) <Granny's Basket>
Fomorian grabeye [53-54/55] (10%) Jewels 05 • (1.5/2.3%) Orb of the Sea • (5.5/7.8%) Polished and Painted Seashell • (3.5/5.3%) Golden Statuette • (1.5%) Diabolical Fomorian Gloves [53]/Sleeves [54]/Cap [55] • (0.5%) <Granny's Basket>
Fomorian grencher [50/51/52] (10%) Jewels 04 • (2.5%) Cask of Fomorian Swill • (1%) Orb of the Sea • (2.5%) Glowing Ultramarine Stone • (2%) Polished and Painted Seashell • (2%) Rune Etched Seashell • (1.5%) Diabolical Mentalist/Enchanter/Eldritch Boots • (0.5%) <Granny's Basket>
Fomorian Guard [40] (no loot)
Fomorian underling [37-38] (no loot)
Fomorian wolfbeast [46-47/48/49] (20/25/26%) <Wolfbeast Adornments> • (30/27/30%) <Wolfbeast Gear> • (8%) Dangerous Tooth
fuath [46] (no loot)
Furor [48] (no loot)
ghastly Midgard invader [44] (no loot)
ghostly Midgard invader [43] (no loot)
grand pooka [61-62/63-64] (7.5%) Jewels 61 • (0.8%) Fuliginous Mane Hairs • (2%) Pooka's Luminous Horseshoe • (4%) Broken Carved Music Box • (3%) Grand Pooka Hoof • (1.5%) Pooka's Broken Horn • (0.5%) <Valor's Heart> [currently no loot for level 63-64]
grogan [46] (no loot)
hillock changeling [36-37] (no loot)
Idol of Crom Cruiach [60] (no loot)
juvenile megafelid [36] (8%) Dangerous Tooth
mangled troll invader [45] (no loot)
Morc [46] (no loot)
Morven [46] (no loot)
moss monster [40-41] (no loot)
Necht [51] (no loot)
Norseman chopper [37] *see Celtic brehon [37]*
Notned [62] (no loot)
Octriallach [50] (no loot)
Rarn Pubble [65] (no loot)
Reamonn [44] (no loot)
Ror [61] (no loot)
Ruadan [56] (no loot)
sett dweller [31] (8%) Sett Fur
skeletal dwarf invader [43] (no loot)
spectral Briton invader [43-44] (no loot)
spectral manslayer [50/(51)/52/53] (2.4%) Runed Pitcher of Ashes • (5%) Gold Embossed Parchment • (3.9%) Ash and Gold Dust Mix • (10%) Jewels 04 • (1.6%) Spectral Impaler [50]/Spectral Crusher [52]/Finliath Firebrand [53] • (0.4%) <Granny's Basket> [level 51 currently has no loot]
Sunderer [52] (no loot)
Tethra [62] (no loot)
torcan [31] (no loot)
Trembler [50] (no loot)
umber bear [42-45] (8%) Dangerous Tooth
undead Briton invader [43-44] (no loot)
wanshee [61-64] (no loot)
wraith drake [65] (no loot)

Cruachan Gorge

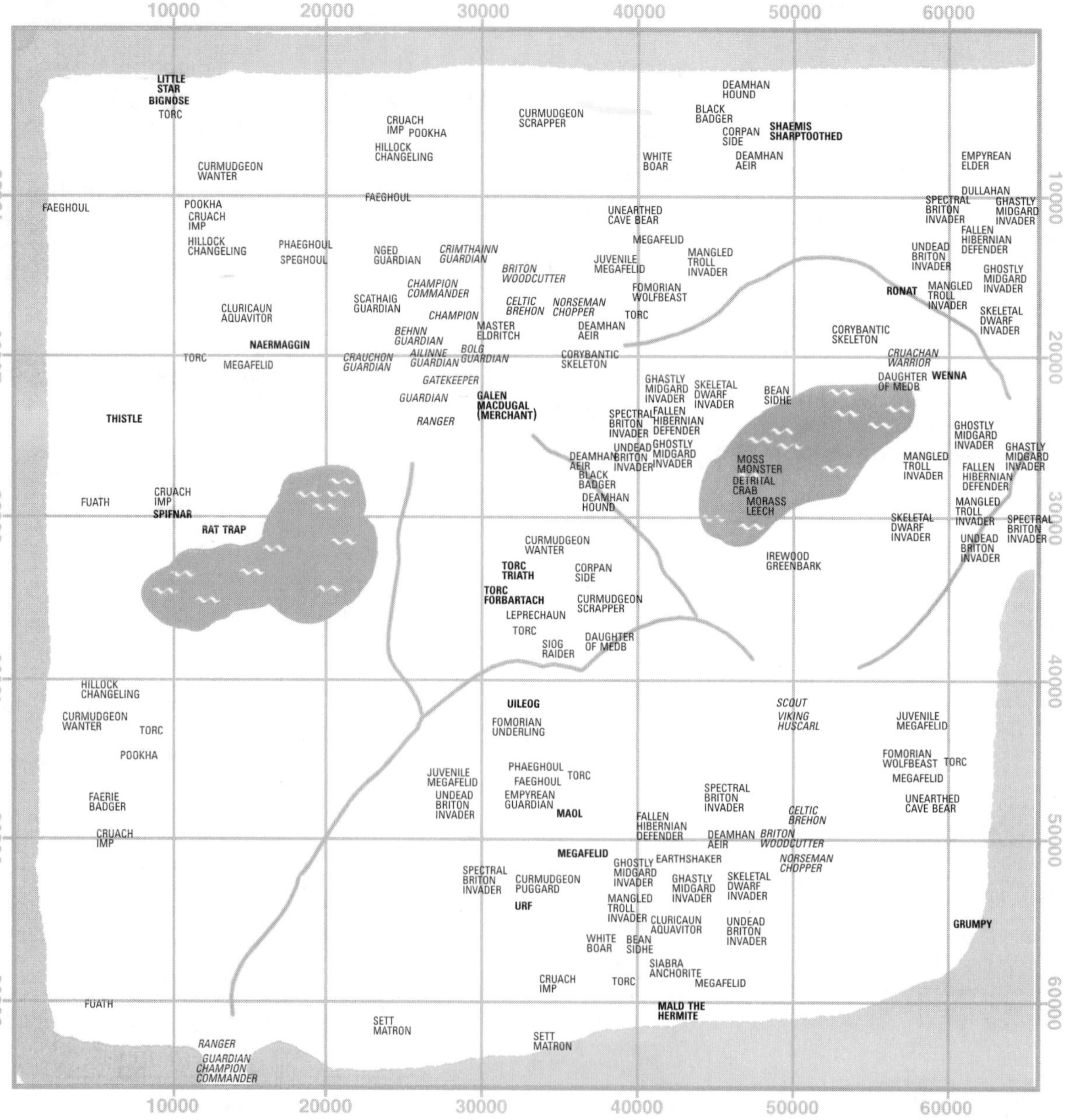

10000 20000 30000 40000 50000 60000

LITTLE STAR
BIGNOSE
TORC
CRUACH IMP POOKHA
HILLOCK CHANGELING
CURMUDGEON SCRAPPER
DEAMHAN HOUND
BLACK BADGER
CORPAN SIDE
SHAEMIS SHARPTOOTHED
DEAMHAN AEIR
WHITE BOAR
EMPYREAN ELDER
CURMUDGEON WANTER
FAEGHOUL
FAEGHOUL
POOKHA
CRUACH IMP
HILLOCK CHANGELING
PHAEGHOUL
SPEGHOUL
NGED GUARDIAN
CRIMTHAINN GUARDIAN
BRITON WOODCUTTER
UNEARTHED CAVE BEAR
MEGAFELID
JUVENILE MEGAFELID
MANGLED TROLL INVADER
DULLAHAN
SPECTRAL BRITON INVADER
GHASTLY MIDGARD INVADER
FALLEN HIBERNIAN DEFENDER
UNDEAD BRITON INVADER
GHOSTLY MIDGARD INVADER
CHAMPION COMMANDER
SCATHAIG GUARDIAN
CHAMPION
CELTIC BREHON
NORSEMAN CHOPPER
FOMORIAN WOLFBEAST
TORC
RONAT
MANGLED TROLL INVADER
SKELETAL DWARF INVADER
CLURICAUN AQUAVITOR
BEHNN GUARDIAN
MASTER ELDRITCH
DEAMHAN AEIR
CORYBANTIC SKELETON
NAERMAGGIN
TORC
MEGAFELID
CRAUCHON GUARDIAN
AILINNE GUARDIAN
BOLG GUARDIAN
CORYBANTIC SKELETON
CRUACHAN WARRIOR
DAUGHTER OF MEDB
WENNA
GATEKEEPER
GUARDIAN
GALEN MACDUGAL (MERCHANT)
RANGER
GHASTLY MIDGARD INVADER
SKELETAL DWARF INVADER
BEAN SIDHE
THISTLE
SPECTRAL BRITON INVADER
FALLEN HIBERNIAN DEFENDER
GHOSTLY MIDGARD INVADER
UNDEAD BRITON INVADER
GHOSTLY MIDGARD INVADER
DEAMHAN AEIR
BLACK BADGER
MOSS MONSTER
DETRITAL CRAB
MORASS LEECH
MANGLED TROLL INVADER
GHASTLY MIDGARD INVADER
FALLEN HIBERNIAN DEFENDER
FUATH
CRUACH IMP
SPIFNAR
DEAMHAN HOUND
MANGLED TROLL INVADER
SKELETAL DWARF INVADER
SPECTRAL BRITON INVADER
UNDEAD BRITON INVADER
RAT TRAP
CURMUDGEON WANTER
IREWOOD GREENBARK
TORC TRIATH
CORPAN SIDE
TORC FORBARTACH
CURMUDGEON SCRAPPER
LEPRECHAUN
TORC
SIOG RAIDER
DAUGHTER OF MEDB
HILLOCK CHANGELING
UILEOG
SCOUT
VIKING HUSCARL
CURMUDGEON WANTER
TORC
FOMORIAN UNDERLING
JUVENILE MEGAFELID
POOKHA
FOMORIAN WOLFBEAST
TORC
PHAEGHOUL
TORC
FAEGHOUL
JUVENILE MEGAFELID
MEGAFELID
UNDEAD BRITON INVADER
EMPYREAN GUARDIAN
MAOL
SPECTRAL BRITON INVADER
UNEARTHED CAVE BEAR
FAERIE BADGER
FALLEN HIBERNIAN DEFENDER
CELTIC BREHON
CRUACH IMP
DEAMHAN AEIR
BRITON WOODCUTTER
MEGAFELID
GHOSTLY MIDGARD INVADER
EARTHSHAKER
NORSEMAN CHOPPER
SPECTRAL BRITON INVADER
CURMUDGEON PUGGARD
GHASTLY MIDGARD INVADER
SKELETAL DWARF INVADER
URF
MANGLED TROLL INVADER
CLURICAUN AQUAVITOR
UNDEAD BRITON INVADER
GRUMPY
WHITE BOAR
BEAN SIDHE
SIABRA ANCHORITE
CRUACH IMP
TORC
MEGAFELID
FUATH
MALD THE HERMITE
SETT MATRON
SETT MATRON
RANGER
GUARDIAN CHAMPION COMMANDER

10000 20000 30000 40000 50000 60000

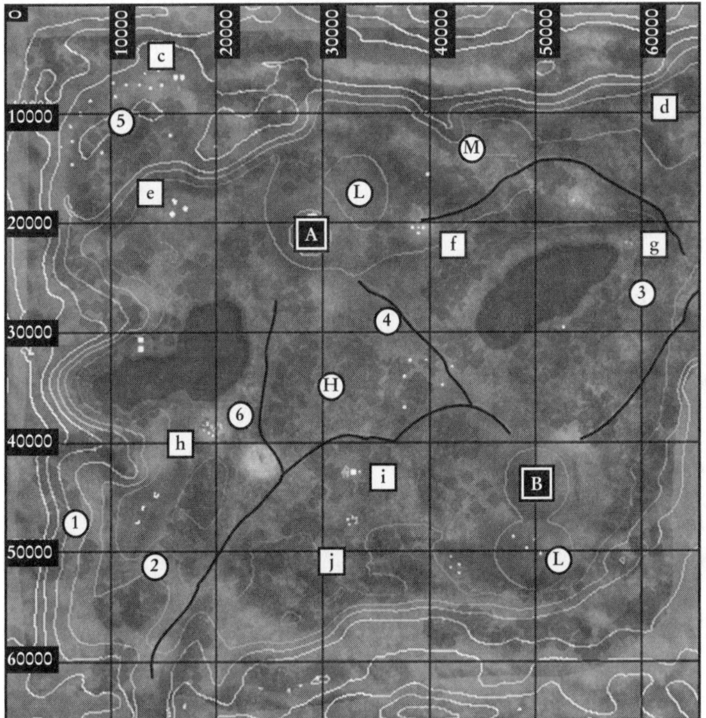

Key Explanation

A Keep or Outpost

e Significant Feature

(L) Invader risk

(4) Tip Reference (see tips for each map)

Map Key

A. Dun Lamfhota & Spear Relic
B. Dun Ailinne
c. Curmudgeon Stones
d. Empyrean Elder Stones
e. Cluricaun Fairy Rings
f. Stones
g. Daughters of Medb & Cruachan Warriors
h. Mist Wraith Stones
i. Formorians
j. Empyrean Guardian Stones

(L) Low Invader Risk

(M) Medium Invader Risk

(H) High Invader Risk

At the northern tip of Hibernia lies Druim Ligen, Hibernia's most active realm gate. Directly outside the doors is Cruachan Gorge, which is constantly under siege by invaders. Cruachan Gorge comprises rolling hills and grassy valleys with the occasional lake harboring gigantic crabs. The "Gorge" as it's known, sports a variety of creatures, the lowest of which is around 20, and the highest in the high 40's ; however, generally speaking it's almost entirely populated by Level 20-35 creatures. Although some of the creatures might be fierce, the real worry here is invaders. The hunting spots can be lucrative, but with the likelihood of invaders, most of this zone falls into a "High Risk" category.

1. Ant Valley

Virtually dead north from the Ligen gate lies Ant Valley. The pit that these Ants sit in makes them natural targets for archers; just watch out when they call for friends.

Location 12, 47
Invader Risk 8
Terrain Type These Ants are situated in a deep valley, great for ranged attackers.
Level Range 21-24
Behaviors Generally docile, they are non aggro but call on friends when in trouble.

2. Gray Specters Woods

These Gray Specters cast spells and have decent melee to boot. Word has it that they drop some magical items too. Save invaders, this is a decent hunting spot. For low 20th levels.

Location 8, 45
Invader Risk 8 High
Level Range 22-24
Quantity Roughly 10
Personality Aggressive, they rarely stop moving so you have to pick your target quickly to keep it in range
Terrain Type Woods and sloping hill

3. Greenbark Grove

Greenbark Grove is usually

hunted thoroughly by solo Rangers, but often a large group can be found here gaining experience. While the loot isn't so wonderful, recently they have been dropping magical cloth armor frequently. Pretty dangerous unless you're in a group: for Levels 35+. Perfect for archers from 38-48!

Location 51, 32
Invader Risk 7 High
Level Range 40-44
Quantity 20+
Terrain Type Sloping hill for increased range
Magic Drop Level 30'ish Hardened Cloth Armor

4. Corybantic Skeletons

These skinny fellas aren't too friendly, but thankfully they're not on any public road. They don't cast spells, and make for pretty good hunting if you have a group in the low 40's — at the time this book printed — cash drop!

Location 38, 21
Invader Risk 5 Mid/Low
Level Range 46
Quantity Roughly 8
Personality Aggressive, but no BAF
Terrain Type Top of a knoll

5. Curmudgeon Valley

These wandering oafs may be aggressive depending on your faction with them. In this particular spot, they wander along a valley, and since they're spread out, you don't have to worry about pulling too many at once. If you're looking for a spot most people haven't been to, this is the place. It is particularly good for solo archers.

Location 8, 8
Invader Risk 8 High
Level Range 34
Quantity 12-15
Personality Faction based, these guys rarely stop to smell the flowers but archers can take advantage of the terrain. They are often grouped and may come in pairs.
Terrain Type These Curmudgeons patrol a valley near the border. No other enemies to worry about nearby.

6. Beetle Log

One can always find a group of newbies beating up beetles at this spot. However, due to that specific reason, invaders always stop here. So, if you plan on hunting, expect to be killed. The beetles are dense and there's plenty of them, so dive in!

Location 24, 41
Invader Risk 8.5 Very High
Level Range 20-21
Quantity 5-10*Personality* Slow moving in a concentrated area. Wide-open fields would make this a great spot if not for the danger of invaders.
Terrain Type Wide open field on all sides, no threat of other creatures nearby.

7. Mist Wraiths

They spawn only at night, but it's a popular spot for a group in their low 20's. These Wraiths are known to drop some valuable magic items. The spot is decent, but beware invaders!

Location 20, 39
Invader Risk 8.5 Very High
Level Range 27-28
Quantity 5-10
Personality Nighttime spawn only. Aggressive.
Terrain Type Open field without anything dangerous nearby.

Loot

alp luachra [29] (25%) Alp Luachra Hand (x2) • (25%) Alp Luachra Eye • (8%) Alp Luachra Head

amadan touched [29-30/32] (1.5%) Ring of the Amadan ***or*** Ring of Undead Might • (40%) Worn Carnielian Studded Belt • (8/12%) Forgotten Silver Jasper Locket • (80% each) Well Crafted Lantern, Flint • (60%) Copper Amethyst Bracelet • (10/20%) Small Silver Laden Box • (0.3%) <The Four Elements>

aughisky [33] (85%) Patch of Aughisky Hide • (70%) Pristine Aughisky Hide • (45%) Aughisky Mane

bean sidhe [39-41] (12%) Medicinal Herbs

Bignose [37] (no loot)

bird-eating frog [20-22] (no loot)

black badger [36] (75%) Black Badger Tooth (x2) • (65%) Black Badger Claw (x2) • (35%) Black Badger Meat (x2) • (15%) Pristine Black Badger Pelt • (1.5%) Badger Pelt Shield

bocaidhe [27-29] (no loot)

bodach [32] (no loot)

Briton woodcutter [37] *see Celtic brehon [37]*

Celtic brehon [37] (70%) Eagle Head Brooch • (60%) Jeweled Scabard • (2%) Siabrian Raider's Head • (10%) Cat's Eye Opal • (1.2%) APOA: Raider's Chitin • (1.2%) Left ***or*** Right Bracer of Skill, Siabrian Belt, Mystic Shield ***or*** Crusher, ***or*** Crescent Razor • (1.5%) <Rogue Pendants (Highest)> • (1.2%) Cath Drum ***or*** APOA: Cath

cluricaun [22] (5%) Silver Goblet • (75% each) Pouch of Ill Gotten Gain, Forgetful Dust • (1.3%) <Hedge Clippers> • (1.3%) APOA: Woven Hedge Weed • (0.3%) <Muire's Riches 3> • (0.8%) Lucky Lauean, Lucky Muinneelyn ***or*** Lucky Failm • (0.5%) Mollachd Coin

cluricaun aquavitor [40] (no loot)

corpan side [39] (80% each) Changeling Hair, Changeling Skin • (20% each) Jasper Beetle Chitin Necklace, Changeling Blood • (1.5%) Giant Gutter ***or*** Spine Splitter

corybantic skeleton [46] (no loot)

cruach imp [33-35] (12%) Red Cruach Wings

Cruachan warrior [46-47] (no loot)

curmudgeon puggard [39-40] (no loot)

curmudgeon ratoner [31-33] (no loot)

curmudgeon scrapper [40-43] (no loot)

curmudgeon wanter [34-35] (no loot)

Daughter of Medb [44-48] (no loot)

deamhan aeir [37] (70%) Deamhan Wing (x2) • (70%) Deamhan Claw (x2) • (30%) Cat's Eye Opal • (5%) Green Sapphire • (1.4%) Deamhan Circlet of Speed • (1.4%) Ether Staff, Ether Staff of Thought ***or*** Light, ***or*** Abrasive Necklace • (12%) Essence of Deamhan Aeir

deamhan hound [40] (68%) Deamhan Hound Tooth (x2) • (72%) Deamhan Hound Claw • (40%) Deamhan Hound Claw • (20%) Deamhan Hound Pelt • (1.2%) Infernal Edge ***or*** Flute • (0.3%) Infernal Cloak

detrital crab [42] (25% each) Chunk of Clay (x2), Glob of Mud (x2) • (40%) Detrital Crab Claw (x2) • (49%) Detrital Crab Meat (x2)

dullahan [48-49,51] (80%) Dullahan's Skin • (70%) Dullahan's Blackened Heart • (60%) Blood Stained Bag • (1.4%) Harvester of Malign Doom ***or*** Dullahan's Luminescent Head • (1.4%) Dread Blackscale

earthshaker [47] (no loot)

empyrean elder [44] (20%) Silken Sash • (25%) Empyreal Mist Orb • (5%) Otherworldly Wine • (1.5%) <Ancient Wisdom>

empyrean guardian [36-37] (10%) Empyrean Wine • (25%) Drakescale Venom • (1.4%) Empyreal Vest ***or*** Helm • (0.1%) Spectral Flight • (0.2%) Spectral Flight Arrows • (0.1%) Sentinel's Ring • (15%) Cat's Eye Apatite

empyrean sentinel [27/28] (35%) Orb of Viewing • (5/7%) Empyrean Wine • (15%) Red Spinel • (1.5%) APOA: Twined, ***or*** Twined Piercer/Twined Hauberk ***or*** Sleeves, ***or*** Twined Sentinel

faeghoul [34-36] (no loot)

faerie badger [32] (75%) Faerie Badger Tooth (x2) • (60%) Faerie Badger Claw (x2) • (90%) Faerie Badger Meat • (25%) Faerie Badger Pelt

fallen Hibernian defender [45] (no loot)

fee lion [25-27] (90%) Fee Lion Meat • (70% each) Fee Lion Tooth, Fee Lion Claw [25-26] • (75%) Fee Lion Tooth (x2) [27] • (50%) Fee Lion Claw (x2) [27] • (20%) Fee Lion Pelt • (1.5%) Blackened Feelion Paw ***or*** Feelion Razor [25-26]

Fomorian underling [37-38] (no loot)

Fomorian wolfbeast [47] (20%) <Wolfbeast Adornments> • (30%) <Wolfbeast Gear> • (8%) Dangerous Tooth

fuath [46] (no loot)

ghastly Midgard invader [44] (no loot)

ghostly Midgard invader [43] (no loot)

ghoulie [20/22] (1.5%) Ghoulish Shackle • (80%) Ghoul Skin • (80%) Carnelian/Agate • (40%) Ghoul Skin • (20/30%) Azurite • (5% each) Forgotten Silk Coth, Citrine • (0.3%) <Muire's Riches 3>

giant ant [21-22/24] (70/80%) Giant Ant Legs (x2) • (40/55%) Giant Ant Mandible • (5/10%) Giant Ant Carapace

giant beetle [20-21] (60%) Giant Beetle Leg (x2) • (40%) Giant Beetle Leg Tip (x2) • (18%) Giant Beetle Mandible (x2) • (5%) Giant Beetle Carapace

gorge rat [30-31] (no loot)

graugach [32-33] (12%) Glowing Red Eye

gray spectre [22-23/24] (1.5%) Spectral Shroud • (40/60%) Spectral Essence • (80%) Spirit Shackles • (5%) Green Tourmaline/Chrome Diopside • (0.3%) <Muire's Riches 3> • (1.5%) Orb of Resistance [22-23] • **[remainder is 24 only]** (1.1%) Malicious Black Heart • (1.1%) Black Clawed Hand • (0.05%) Parthanan Head • (0.05%) Pearl • (0.2%) Lapis Lazuli • (0.01%) <Muire's Riches 2> • (0.02%) Parthanon Fist ***or*** Ether Ring

Grumpy [52] (no loot)

hill hound [20] (85%) Hill Hound Canine (x2) • (48%) Pristine Hill Hound Pelt

hillock changeling [35] (no loot)

ire wolf [25] (75%) Ire Wolf Tooth (x3) • (25%) Ire Wolf Pelt • (10%) Ire Wolf Claw

irewood greenbark [40] (80%) Irewood Greenbark Branch (x2) • (30%) Glowing Irewood Greenbark Sap • (20%) Bundle of Greenbark Branches • (1.4%) APOA: Hardened Cloth • (1.4%) Bardic Wonder, ***or*** Staff of Thought, Destruction ***or*** Enchantments (All Petrified)

juvenile megafelid [36,38] (8%) Dangerous Tooth

leprechaun [50] (1.7%) Forest Green ***or*** Royal Green Enamel • (0.3%) Black, Royal Purple ***or*** Dark Purple Enamel • (2%) <Lucky Charms> • (15%) Jewels 49 • (1.5%) Leprechaun's Staff of the Void • (0.5%) <Granny's Basket>

Little Star [34] (no loot)

luch catcher [28] (55%) Luch Tooth • (68%) Luch Meat (x2) • (35%) Luch Claw • (22%) Pristine Luch Hide • (1.5%) Missing Caster's Cap, Gloves ***or*** Belt, ***or*** Caster's Missing Eye

lugradan [25] (1.5%) Odd Ball • (80% each) Copper Spinel Bracelet, Silver Amethyst Ring • (20%) Green Tourmaline • (5% each) Black Star Diopside, Pitted Dirk • (0.3%) <De'velyn's Delights>

lugradan [28] (75% each) Silver Goblet, Pouch of Ill Gotten Gain • (10%) Golden Clover Brooch • (1.4%) Nearahd Sleeves, Gloves, Coif ***or*** Cloak, ***or*** Pluc • (1.3%) APOA: Woven Hedge Weed • (0.3%) <De'velyn's Delights>

mad changeling [26/28] (35% each) Changeling Ear, Changeling Tongue, Bleached Leg Bone • (1.5%) Madder Earring/Wrathfully Righteous Beads • (5/15%) Topaz

Mald the Hermite [41] (no loot)

mangled troll invader [45] (no loot)

Maol [38] (no loot)

megafelid [39-42] (8%) Dangerous Tooth

merman [25] (80% each) Seal Skin Bag, 50ft of Kelp Rope • (25% each) Silver Pearl Ring, Necklace • (1.4%) APOA: Coral • (20%) Azurite • (1.4%) Coral Spear • (0.3%) <De'velyn's Delights>

merman [36] (75% each) Merman Scales, Green Tourmaline • (50%) Orb of Swirling Sea Water • (5%) Red Spinel • (1.4%) APOA: Algae Covered Coral ***or*** Sidhe Spine Barbed Spear • (1.4%) Braided Kelp Belt, Bracelet ***or*** Necklace, ***or*** Coral Ring

mist wraith [27-28] (80%) Dark Heart of the Vindictive Spirit • (10%) Mist Wraith Essence • (1.5%) Wraith Necklace, Mist Necklace ***or*** Etheric Bludgeoner • (0.3%) <De'velyn's Delights>

morass leech [42] (59%) Worn Leech Skin • (1.7%) Leech Husk Bracer • (25%) Pristine Leech Skin • (59%) Worn Leech Skin

moss monster [40] (no loot)

mountain mephit [20-21] (80%) Mephit Wing • (40%) Mephit Wing • (80%) Poisonous Mephit Fang • (50%) Poisonous Mephit Fang • (10%) Silvered Bracer • (1.5%) Splintered Mephit Femur • (0.3%) <Muire's Riches 3> • (1.5%) Aeiry Belt ***or*** Forked Mephit Tail

Naermaggin [40] (no loot)

Norseman chopper [37] *see Celtic brehon [37]*

phaeghoul [37-39] (12%) Phaeghoul Red Hand

pookha [34] (20%) Pooka Skin • (70%) Pooka Hair (x2) • (1.5%) Horse, Goblin, Boogieman, Eagle ***or*** Goatman Mantle • (0.3%) <The Four Elements>

rage sprite [20] (45%) Pouch of Magic Dust • (45%) Jewels 59 • (0.3%) <Muire's Riches 2> • (1.5%) Rage Sprite Belt ***or*** Club, ***or*** Chain of Rage

rage wolf [32] (70%) Rage Wolf Fang (x2) • (70%) Rage Wolf Claw (x2) • (20%) Rage Wolf Pelt • (8%) Dangerous Tooth

Rat Trap [33] (no loot)

roan stepper [29-32] (no loot)

Ronat [43] (no loot)

sett dweller [30-31] (8%) Sett Fur

sett matron [36] (8%) Sett Fur

sett protector [32-33] (8%) Sett Fur

sett youngling [24] (no loot)

Shaemis [43] (no loot)

siabra anchorite [41] (no loot)

siog raider [37] *see Celtic brehon [37]*

siog seeker [28-29] (30%) Tattered Scroll • (30%) Luminescent Orb • (30%) Orb of Viewing • (10%) Primrose Eye • (1.5%) Spectral Legs, Gloves, Arms ***or*** Boots, Thumper, ***or*** Slicer • (50%) Bolt of Soft Gossamer

siog waylayer [26-27] (1.5%) <Rogue Pendants (Higher)> • (1.2%) Siabrian Bandit Helm • (70%) Bandit Mask • (10%) Siabra Waylayer Sash • (1.2%) Waylayer Short Sword, Great Sword, Shillelagh, Spiked Mace, Hammer, Rapier ***or*** Dirk • (40%) Silver Gaming Dice • (20%) Green Tourmaline • (0.3%) <De'velyn's Delights> • (2%) Siabrian Waylayer's Head • (1.2%) Cath Lute, Shield, Spear, Cloak ***or*** Charms

skeletal dwarf invader [43] (no loot)

spectral Briton invader [43-44] (no loot)

speghoul [40] (no loot)

Spifnar [35] (no loot)

spraggonale [22] (15%) Copper Moonstone Flagon • (80% each) Bottle of Grog, Copper Cryoprase Earring • (40%) Topaz • (3%) Pitted Falcata • (0.3%) <Muire's Riches 3> • (1.5%) Dusty Leggings ***or*** Silvermined Blade

squabbler [28-30] (no loot)

streaming wisp [21] (80%) Streaming Wisp Essence • (65%) Streaming Wisp Gem • (10%) Streaming Wisp Husk

Thistle [32] (no loot)

torc [34-37] (8%) Dangerous Tooth

Torc Forbartach [47] (no loot)

Torc Triath [53] (no loot)

torcan [31] (no loot)

Uileog [40] (no loot)

undead Briton invader [43-44] (no loot)

unearthed cave bear [49-51] (6.6%) Bloodstained Bear Claw • (4.3%) Gnarled Bear Tooth • (1.2%) Bloody Broken Bear Trap • (5%) Slashed Bear Pelt • (3.6%) Fine Bear Pelt • (1.2%) Supple Bear Pelt

Urf [40] (no loot)

vindictive bocan [20] (1% each piece) Tattered Stone Cailiocht • (80%) Agate • (40%) Topaz • (5%) Green Tourmaline • (0.3%) <Muire's Riches 3>

Wenna [50] (no loot)

white boar [40-41] (70%) Long White Boar Tusk [41 only]

wrath sprite [28] (80%) Bleached Leg Bone • (60%) Softly Glowing Orb • (50%) Red Spinel • (1.5%) Spritely Stiletto ***or*** Shield

Emain Macha

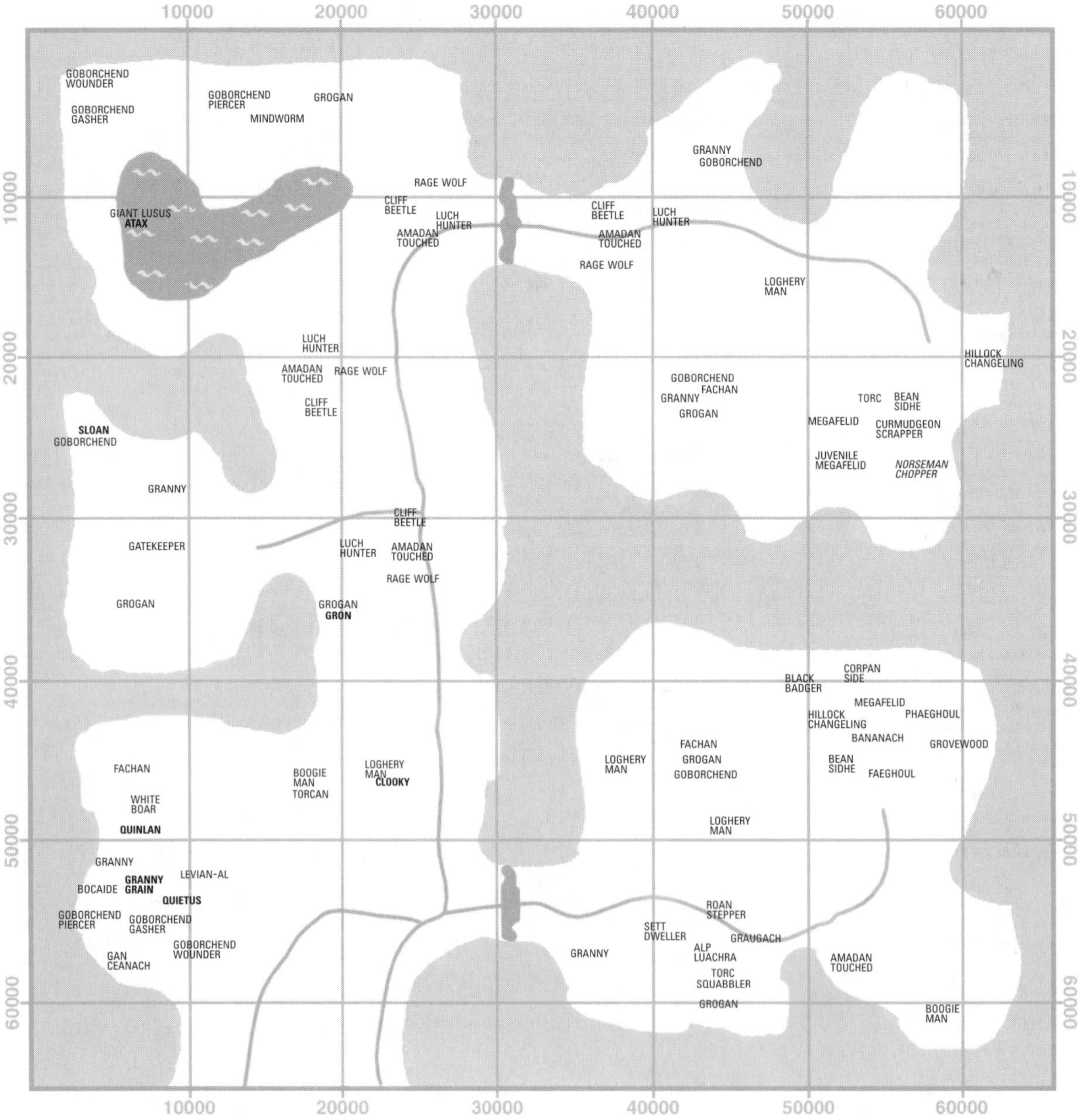

10000 20000 30000 40000 50000 60000

GOBORCHEND WOUNDER
GOBORCHEND GASHER
GOBORCHEND PIERCER
GROGAN
MINDWORM
GRANNY
GOBORCHEND
RAGE WOLF
GIANT LUSUS
ATAX
CLIFF BEETLE
LUCH HUNTER
AMADAN TOUCHED
CLIFF BEETLE
LUCH HUNTER
AMADAN TOUCHED
RAGE WOLF
LOGHERY MAN
LUCH HUNTER
AMADAN TOUCHED
RAGE WOLF
CLIFF BEETLE
HILLOCK CHANGELING
GOBORCHEND
FACHAN
GRANNY
GROGAN
TORC
BEAN SIDHE
MEGAFELID
CURMUDGEON SCRAPPER
SLOAN
GOBORCHEND
JUVENILE MEGAFELID
NORSEMAN CHOPPER
GRANNY
CLIFF BEETLE
GATEKEEPER
LUCH HUNTER
AMADAN TOUCHED
RAGE WOLF
GROGAN
GROGAN
GRON
BLACK BADGER
CORPAN SIDE
MEGAFELID
HILLOCK CHANGELING
PHAEGHOUL
BANANACH
GROVEWOOD
FACHAN
GROGAN
GOBORCHEND
LOGHERY MAN
FACHAN
BOOGIE MAN
TORCAN
LOGHERY MAN
CLOOKY
BEAN SIDHE
FAEGHOUL
WHITE BOAR
QUINLAN
LOGHERY MAN
GRANNY
GRANNY GRAIN
LEVIAN-AL
BOCAIDE
QUIETUS
GOBORCHEND PIERCER
GOBORCHEND GASHER
GOBORCHEND WOUNDER
GAN CEANACH
ROAN STEPPER
SETT DWELLER
GRAUGACH
GRANNY
ALP LUACHRA
AMADAN TOUCHED
TORC SQUABBLER
GROGAN
BOOGIE MAN

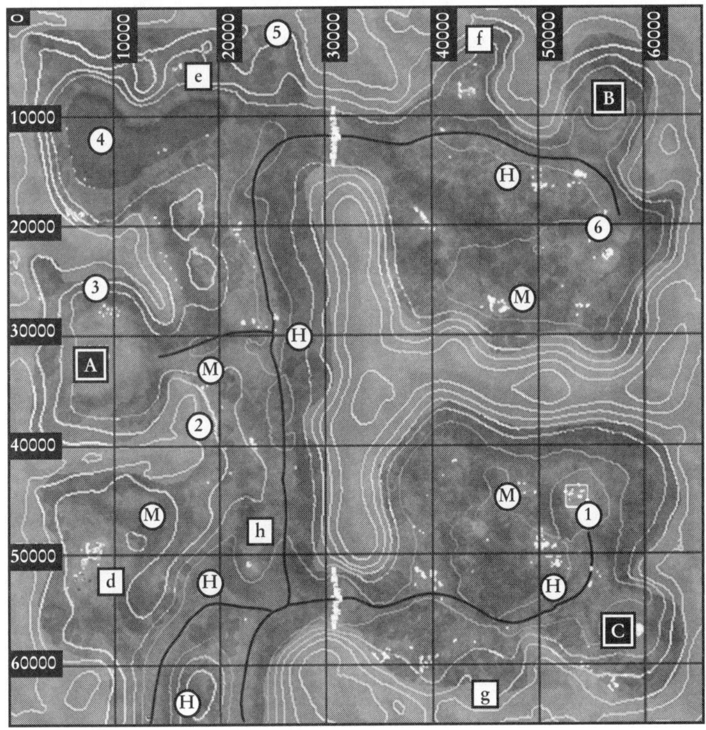

Map Key

A. Dun Cruachon
B. Midgard Outpost
C. Albion Outpost
d. Granny Stones & Ruins
e. Mindworm Holes
f. Ruins & Granny Stones
g. Ruins
h. Stone Tower
Ⓛ Low Invader Risk
Ⓜ Medium Invader Risk
Ⓗ High Invader Risk

Emain Macha is the world's most active RvR area. In all the realms, there is no single other zone that rivals the massive battles that continually happen here. Hunting for experience is not the most lucrative venture; however, if you want to be where the action is, and still get experience, this isn't a bad spot—that is, if you're willing to take the risk. The average creature level is around 35 ranging from high 20's to high 50's. Generally speaking, due to the RvR traffic, there are few to no wandering creaturse to hassle those looking to find some RvR action.

1. Faeghoul Graveyard

This is perhaps where some fallen invaders make their home. This graveyard sits beside the Albion Portal Fort, and it is not a bad spot for hunting, other than that Hibernian defenders regularly scour the area.

Location 54, 44
Invader Risk 10 Highest
Quantity 8-12
Terrain Type Small graveyard, various Undead creatures.

2. Grogan Grove

This spot is near a crossroad that marks perhaps the world's most busy RvR spot. The XP is great, but the risk is tremendous. For those interested in RvR and XP at the same time, here's your spot.

Location 19, 34
Invader Risk 10 Highest
Quantity 8-12
Terrain Type On a flat near a zone wall, massive RVR risk.

3. Granny Stones

For whoever owns Castle Cruachan, this spot is great for any high level group. Its right beside a castle and in guards range. Only a foolish few would tangle with someone here.

Location 9, 27
Invader Risk 4 Low

Quantity 8-12
Terrain Type Right beside a castle at the bottom of a hill. Great spot.

4. Giant Lusus Lake

If you've never seen a Lusus, they've evidently been beaten with the ugly stick. They're ugly, they're strong and don't like visitors. On the other hand, few RvR's wander to this spot, so it's a decent mix of RvR and XP.

Location 7, 10
Invader Risk 5 Average
Quantity 8-10 spread out over a lake
Terrain Type Lake with hills on one side, near a border. No wandering creatures.

5. Grogan Grove

Near the Midgard Milefort gate, this group of Grogans is generally unknown to most players. It's situated on a depression on a hill at a zone side with trees blocking the view from any wandering RvR'ers. Great place and unknown to most.

Location 19, 4
Invader Risk 6
Quantity 12-15
Terrain Type Side of a zone hill. Remote, relatively unknown spot.

6. Bean Sidhe Cemetery

Occasionally you'll see some players out here contending with the undead Bean Sidhe, but more often than not, it's empty. For a solo or duo group, it's a great spot that keeps you near the action.

Location 56, 22
Invader Risk 6
Quantity 6
Terrain Type Open area surrounded by fields, densely packed.

Loot

goborchend gasher [52(53-54)] [currently only level 52 has loot] (10%) Jewels 05 • (3%) Preserved Human Heart • (2.5%) Viscous Fragrant Fluid • (1%) Restless Ethereal Eye • (3.5%) Goborchend Hoof • (1.6%) Shagreen Fighter's Coif or Shagreen Coif • (0.4%) <Granny's Basket>

graugach [32-33] (12%) Glowing Red Eye

grovewood [38-40] (12%) Grovewood Bark

bean sidhe [39-41] (12%) Medicinal Herbs

phaeghoul [37,39] (12%) Phaeghoul Red Hand

alp luachra [30] (25%) Alp Luachra Hand (x2) • (25%) Alp Luachra Eye • (8%) Alp Luachra Head

cliff beetle [31] (65%) Cliff Beetle Leg (x2) • (48%) Cliff Beetle Leg Tip (x2) • (15%) Cliff Beetle Mandible • (5%) Cliff Beetle Carapace

luch hunter [34] (68%) Luch Tooth (x2) • (75%) Luch Meat (x2) • (80%) Luch Claw • (40%) Luch Claw • (30%) Pristine Luch Hide • (0.5%) Ranger's Last Flight • (0.8%) Silvered Arrow • (0.3%) Aotrom Pearls

mindworm [57/58/59] (7.5/8/8.5%) Translucent Mindworm Fang • (6/6.4/6.8%) Mindworm Poison Gland • (1.5/1.6/1.7%) Renitent Mindworm Skin

Norseman chopper [37] (70%) Eagle Head Brooch • (60%) Jeweled Scabard • (2%) Siabrian Raider's Head • (10%) Cat's Eye Opal • (1.2%) APOA: Raider's Chitin • (1.2%) Left or Right Bracer of Skill, Siabrian Belt, Mystic Shield or Crusher, or Crescent Razor • (1.5%) <Highest Rogue Pendants> • (1.2%) Cath Drum or APOA: Cath

white boar [41] (70%) Long White Boar Tusk

rage wolf [32] (70%) Rage Wolf Fang (x2) • (70%) Rage Wolf Claw (x2) • (20%) Rage Wolf Pelt • (8%) Dangerous Tooth

black badger [36] (75%) Black Badger Tooth (x2) • (65%) Black Badger Claw (x2) • (35%) Black Badger Meat (x2) • (15%) Pristine Black Badger Pelt • (1.5%) Badger Pelt Shield

juvenile megafelid [38] (8%) Dangerous Tooth

megafelid [40-41] (8%) Dangerous Tooth

torc [35-36] (8%) Dangerous Tooth

sett dweller [30] (8%) Sett Fur

corpan side [39] (80% each) Changeling Hair, Changeling Skin • (20% each) Jasper Beetle Chitin Necklace, Changeling Blood • (1.5%) Giant Gutter or Spine Splitter

Agorn [56] (no loot)

Atax [61] (no loot)

bananach [40-41] (no loot)

bocaide [51] (no loot)

boogie man [34] (no loot)

Clooky [46] (no loot)

curmudgeon scrapper [41] (no loot)

fachan [47-49] (no loot)

faeghoul [36] (no loot)

gan ceanach [53] (no loot)

goborchend [46-48] (no loot)

Granny Grain [50] (no loot)

grogan [46-47] (no loot)

Gron [47] (no loot)

hillock changeling [36-37] (no loot)

levian [60-62] (no loot)

loghery man [46] (no loot)

Quietus [53] (no loot)

Quinlan [53] (no loot)

roan stepper [32] (no loot)

Sloan [48] (no loot)

squabbler [30] (no loot)

Taman [62] (no loot)

torcan [31] (no loot)

Yrial [51] (no loot)

amadan touched [30] (1.5%) Ring of the Amadan or Ring of Undead Might • (40%) Worn Carnielian Studded Belt • (8%) Forgotten Silver Jasper Locket • (80% each) Well Crafted Lantern, Flint • (60%) Copper Amethyst Bracelet • (10%) Small Silver Laden Box • (0.3%) <The Four Elements>

granny [(48-49)50] [currently only level 50 has loot] (2.3%) Bag of Glowing Seeds • (5.3%) Leafy Silver Stemmed Vine • (6%) Luminous Golden Flower • (1.5%) Exotic Herbs • (2%) Granny's Shawl, Kettle or Needle

levian-al [50->54] (9->12%) Cracked Levian-Al Fang • (6->7.8%) Levian-Al Fang • (9->12%) Broken Levian-Al Claw • (6->8%) Levian-Al Claw • (16->20%) Slashed Levian-Al Pelt • (12->16%) Flayed Levian-Al Pelt • (3.1->3.9%) August Levian-Al Pelt

giant lusus [58-60/61] (9/10%) Jewels 61 • (9/10%) <Lusus Lootus> • (1.6%) Twisted Melody Boots or Twisted Lusus Boots [58]/Twisted Melody Helm or Twisted Lusus Sleeves [59]/Twisted Lusus Helm or Gauntlets [60]/Twisted Lusus Vest or Leggings, or Twisted Forestdweller Boots [61] • (0.4/0.2%) <Valor's Heart>

goborchend wounder [54/56] (10/15%) Jewels 05 • (2/2.4%) Preserved Human Heart • (2.4/2.9%) Viscous Fragrant Fluid • (3/3.6%) Restless Ethereal Eye • (2.6/3.1%) Goborchend Hoof • (1.6%) Shagreen Gloves/Hauberk • (0.4%) <Valor's Heart>

goborchend piercer [50/51/52-53] (10/12/14%) Jewels 04 • (3/3.6/4.2%) Preserved Human Heart • (2.5/3/3.5%) Viscous Fragrant Fluid • (1/1.2/1.4%) Restless Ethereal Eye • (3.5/4.2/5.5%) Goborchend Hoof • (1.6%) Shagreen Champion/Hero/Druid/Warden Boots • (0.4%) <Granny's Basket>

Mt. Collory

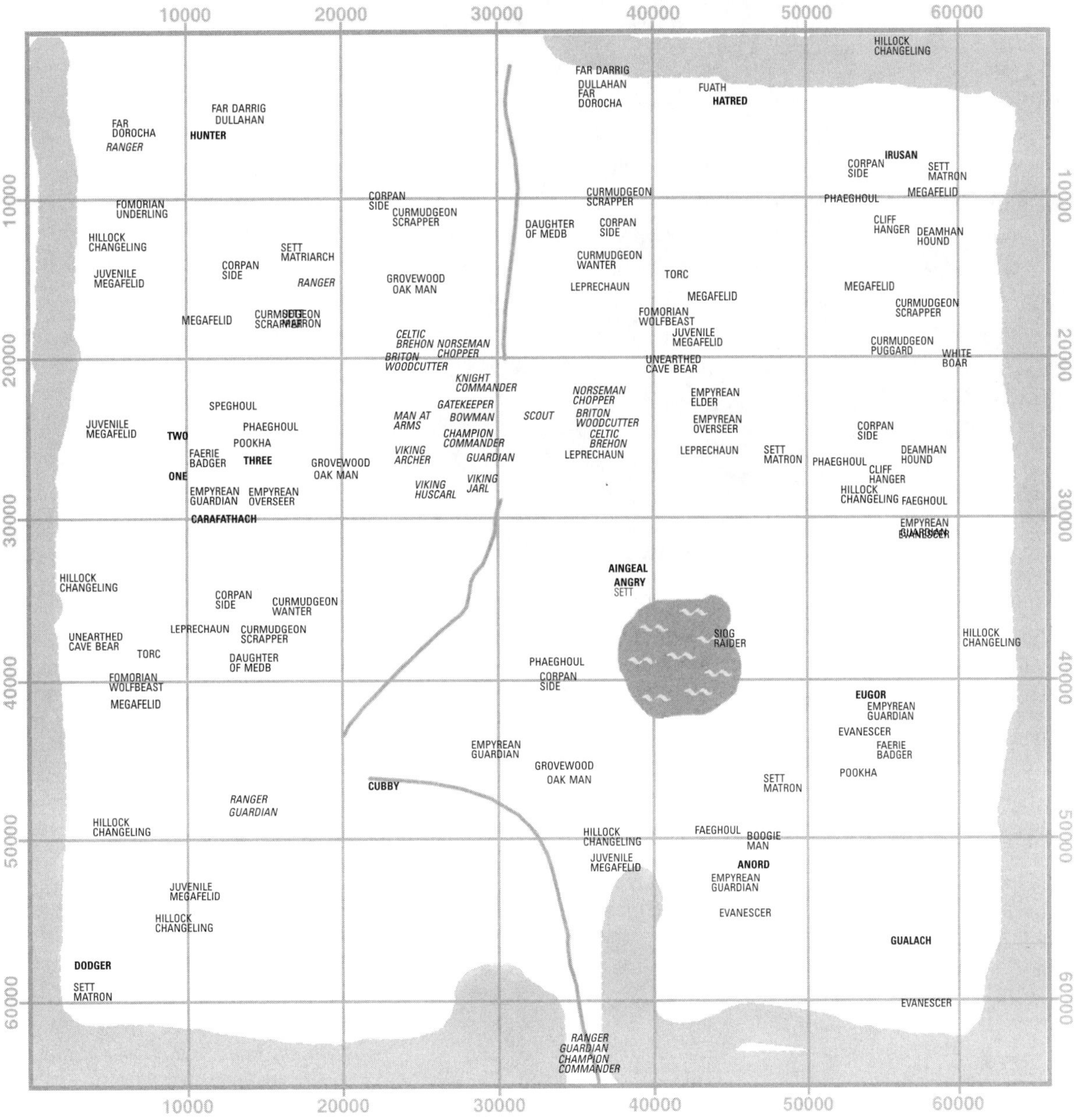

10000 20000 30000 40000 50000 60000

HILLOCK CHANGELING
FAR DARRIG
DULLAHAN
FAR DOROCHA
FUATH
HATRED
FAR DARRIG
DULLAHAN
FAR DOROCHA
HUNTER
RANGER
IRUSAN
CORPAN SIDE
SETT MATRON
10000
CORPAN SIDE
CURMUDGEON SCRAPPER
MEGAFELID
PHAEGHOUL
FOMORIAN UNDERLING
CURMUDGEON SCRAPPER
DAUGHTER OF MEDB
CORPAN SIDE
CLIFF HANGER
DEAMHAN HOUND
HILLOCK CHANGELING
SETT MATRIARCH
CURMUDGEON WANTER
JUVENILE MEGAFELID
CORPAN SIDE
RANGER
GROVEWOOD OAK MAN
TORC
LEPRECHAUN
MEGAFELID
MEGAFELID
CURMUDGEON SCRAPPER
FOMORIAN WOLFBEAST
MEGAFELID
CURMUDGEON SCRAPPER
SETT MATRON
CELTIC BREHON
NORSEMAN CHOPPER
JUVENILE MEGAFELID
CURMUDGEON PUGGARD
20000
BRITON WOODCUTTER
UNEARTHED CAVE BEAR
WHITE BOAR
KNIGHT COMMANDER
NORSEMAN CHOPPER
EMPYREAN ELDER
SPEGHOUL
GATEKEEPER
MAN AT ARMS
BOWMAN
SCOUT
BRITON WOODCUTTER
EMPYREAN OVERSEER
JUVENILE MEGAFELID
TWO
PHAEGHOUL
CHAMPION COMMANDER
CELTIC BREHON
CORPAN SIDE
POOKHA
FAERIE BADGER
THREE
GROVEWOOD OAK MAN
VIKING ARCHER
GUARDIAN
LEPRECHAUN
LEPRECHAUN
SETT MATRON
PHAEGHOUL
DEAMHAN HOUND
ONE
VIKING HUSCARL
VIKING JARL
CLIFF HANGER
EMPYREAN GUARDIAN
EMPYREAN OVERSEER
HILLOCK CHANGELING
FAEGHOUL
CARAFATHACH
30000
EMPYREAN GUARDIAN
EVANESCER
AINGEAL
ANGRY
SETT
HILLOCK CHANGELING
CORPAN SIDE
CURMUDGEON WANTER
LEPRECHAUN
CURMUDGEON SCRAPPER
SIOG RAIDER
HILLOCK CHANGELING
UNEARTHED CAVE BEAR
TORC
DAUGHTER OF MEDB
PHAEGHOUL
FOMORIAN WOLFBEAST
CORPAN SIDE
40000
MEGAFELID
EUGOR
EMPYREAN GUARDIAN
EVANESCER
EMPYREAN GUARDIAN
FAERIE BADGER
GROVEWOOD OAK MAN
CUBBY
SETT MATRON
POOKHA
RANGER
GUARDIAN
HILLOCK CHANGELING
HILLOCK CHANGELING
FAEGHOUL
BOOGIE MAN
50000
JUVENILE MEGAFELID
ANORD
EMPYREAN GUARDIAN
JUVENILE MEGAFELID
EVANESCER
HILLOCK CHANGELING
GUALACH
DODGER
SETT MATRON
EVANESCER
60000
RANGER
GUARDIAN
CHAMPION
COMMANDER

10000 20000 30000 40000 50000 60000

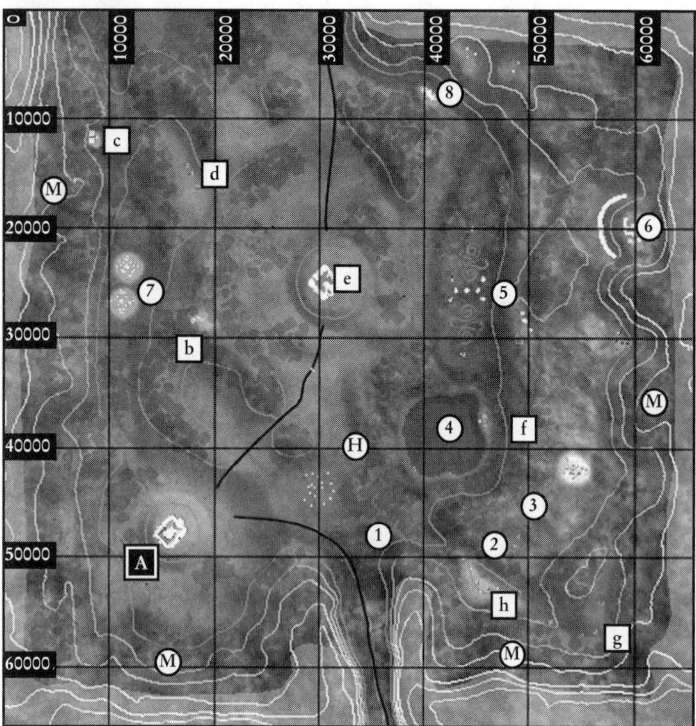

Map Key

A. Dun Dagda & Cauldron relic
b. Curmudgeons
c. Underlings
d. Sett Stones
e. Don Scathaig
f. Siabra
g. Sett Stones
h. Empyrean Stones
Ⓛ Low Invader Risk
Ⓜ Medium Invader Risk
Ⓗ High Invader Risk

Wide open, grassy plains with occasional dense woods characterize Mt. Collory. For Hibernia, Mt. Collory holds many experience opportunities due to the quantity of camps. To invaders, the wide-open fields make finding someone relatively easy. The zone itself is relatively safe with a typical setup of monsters; the farther away you wander from the entrance, the more difficult and aggressive they become. Overall though, this zone would almost be considered friendly if it weren't for the quantity of medium-level aggressive creatures.

1. Grovewoods

These Grovewoods are easy to find, they don't move, and there are plenty of them. That, however, doesn't mean they're easy. They cast Root spells and bring friends. A small group might find this spot perfect for them, but the looming presence of invaders may be a deterrent.

Location 36,46
Invader Risk 7
Quantity 10-15
Terrain Type Open field on one side, mountains & lake on the other, no wandering creatures.

2. Irewoods

There is no shortage of evil Trees in Mt. Collory. These Trees look just like normal trees, except that they have gaping maws and they want to eat you. These Trees make an excellent hunt spot for virtually anyone. Wandering creatures and invaders are the biggest risk here.

Location 42, 46
Invader Risk 7
Quantity 15-25
Terrain Type These Trees line a small mountain ridge.

3. Sett Dwellers

A duo might find this spot to be beneficial due to the quantity and personality of these creatures. They wander enough so a group wouldn't pull the entire camp, and only some of them are naturally aggressive.

Location 49, 46
Invader Risk 7
Quantity 10-15
Terrain Type Small dip in a field, no wandering enemies. Fairly safe.

4. Aughisky Shores

This may be the most popular spot in Mt. Collory. Groups have taken a fancy to these black stallions. Few horses can swim, but these swim like fish and the area around the lake is clear from wandering creatures, making it a popular spot for a couple of groups at a time.

Location 40, 41
Invader Risk 7
Quantity 8-12
Terrain Type spread out along the shores of a lake.

5. Empyrean Elders

These Empyrean Elders don't move much, but are in tight groups standing on top of strange crop formations in the grass. They're not very personable and there are some evil leprechauns nearby to deter visitors.

Location 43, 30
Invader Risk 4
Quantity 6
Terrain Type Large open field, hill on one side. No wandering enemies. Two groups of 6 spread out

6. Curmudgeon Bastion

Somehow, the forces of Hibernia have allowed these Curmudgeons to set up a stronghold in the northeastern corner of Mt. Collory. There are a good quantity of these here inside buildings, and when attacked, they generally respond as one force. It's a bit far away from home, but other than that, there's a variety of them here that need to be exterminated!

Location 59, 20
Invader Risk 4
Quantity 8-12
Terrain Type Top of a hill with wooden spikes. Various Curmudgeons, mostly Scrappers and Puggards.

7. Phaeghoul Stones

Two large areas of standing stones seem to attract the undead variety of housing applicants. These Phaeghouls don't move much and when they do, they amble slowly. There is a slight Invader Risk here, but otherwise there are many clear angles to sit a party or two.

Location 10, 26
Invader Risk 6
Quantity 20+
Personality Slowly wandering, spread out.
Terrain Type These guys are at the bottom of a small valley, like the bottom of a hot-dog bun, hills on two sides.

8. Fuath Camp

These Fuaths are densely packed and rarely move around. There is a slight risk of invaders but otherwise this is a safe spot with plenty of areas to camp around them. The only drawback is the distance it takes to get here, although you can be sure this is an un-camped and relatively unknown spot.

Location 44, 6
Invader Risk 5
Quantity 7-10
Terrain Type On the side of a hill in a small pit. They don't wander much; very safe spot.

Loot

amadan touched [30/32] (1.5%) Ring of the Amadan ***or*** Ring of Undead Might • (%) Worn Carnielian Studded Belt • (8/12%) Forgotten Silver Jasper Locket • (80% each) Well Crafted Lantern, Flint • (60%) Copper Amethyst Bracelet • (10/20%) Small Silver Laden Box • (0.3%) <The Four Elements>

Anord [31] (no loot)

aughisky [31-33] (85%) Patch of Aughisky Hide • (70%) Pristine Aughisky Hide • (45%) Aughisky Mane

bird-eating frog [22] (no loot)

bocaidhe [27] (no loot)

bodach [31-32] (no loot)

boogie man [34] (no loot)

Briton woodcutter [37] *see Celtic brehon [37]*

Carafathach [35] (no loot)

Celtic brehon [37] (70%) Eagle Head Brooch • (60%) Jeweled Scabard • (2%) Siabrian Raider's Head • (10%) Cat's Eye Opal • (1.2%) APOA: Raider's Chitin • (1.2%) Left ***or*** Right Bracer of Skill, Siabrian Belt, Mystic Shield ***or*** Crusher, ***or*** Crescent Razor • (1.5%) <Rogue Pendants (Highest)> • (1.2%) Cath Drum ***or*** APOA: Cath

cliff hanger [39] (60%) Cliff Hanger Leg (x2) • (50%) Cliff Hanger Leg Tip (x2) • (37%) Cliff Hanger Mandible • (15%) Cliff Hanger Carapace

cluricaun [22] (5%) Silver Goblet • (75% each) Pouch of Ill Gotten Gain, Forgetful Dust • (1.3%) <Hedge Clippers> • (1.3%) APOA: Woven Hedge Weed • (0.3%) <Muire's Riches 3> • (0.8%) Lucky Lauean, Lucky Muinneelyn ***or*** Lucky Failm • (0.5%) Mollachd Coin

corpan side [39-40/41] (80% each) Changeling Hair, Changeling Skin • (20/30% each) Jasper Beetle Chitin Necklace, Changeling Blood • (1.5%) Giant Gutter ***or*** Spine Splitter

Cubby [24] (no loot)

curmudgeon puggard [39-40] (no loot)

curmudgeon scrapper [40-43] (no loot)

curmudgeon wanter [34-35] (no loot)

Daughter of Medb [46] (no loot)

deamhan hound [40-41/42] (68/72%) Deamhan Hound Tooth (x2) • (72/65%) Deamhan Hound Claw • (40/55%) Deamhan Hound Claw • (20%) Deamhan Hound Pelt • (1.2%) Infernal Edge, Flute ***or*** Cloak/Infernal Bane ***or*** Bracer

Dodger [33] (no loot)

dullahan [48-49,51] (80%) Dullahan's Skin • (70%) Dullahan's Blackened Heart • (60%) Blood Stained Bag • (1.4%) Harvester of Malign Doom ***or*** Dullahan's Luminescent Head • (1.4%) Dread Blackscale

empyrean elder [41/42-44] (20%) Silken Sash • (20/25%) Empyreal Mist Orb • (1.5%) Ring of the Elder [41] • (5%) Otherworldly Wine [42-44] • (1.5%) <Ancient Wisdom> [42-44]

empyrean guardian [34-35/36-37(38)] (15/25%) Drakescale Venom • (10%) Empyrean Wine • (20/15%) Cat's Eye Apatite • (1.5%) Empyreal Leggings ***or*** Sleeves, Empyreal Ranger Gauntlets ***or*** Boots, ***or*** Spectral Flight Arrows [34-35] • (1.8%; hi-lo) Empyreal Vest ***or*** Helm, Spectral Flight Arrows, Spectral Flight, ***or*** Sentinel's Ring [36-37] [level 38 currently has no loot]

empyrean overseer [37-39] (20%) Guardian Veil Ring • (25%) Drakescale Venom • (1.5%) Gossamer Voided, Enchanter ***or*** Mentalist Robe

empyrean sentinel [26-27/28-29] (35%) Orb of Viewing • (5/7%) Empyrean Wine • (15%) Red Spinel • (1.5%) APOA: Twined, ***or*** Twined Piercer/Twined Hauberk ***or*** Sleeves, ***or*** Twined Sentinel

Eugor [36] (no loot)

evanescer [33-35] (no loot)

faeghoul [34-36] (no loot)

faerie badger [33] (75%) Faerie Badger Tooth (x2) • (60%) Faerie Badger Claw (x2) • (90%) Faerie Badger Meat • (25%) Faerie Badger Pelt

far darrig [46-47/48] (80%) Briar Horror Mask • (40/60%) Thorny Green Sapphire Bracelet • (1.4%) APOA: Mischievious Greenbriar • (1.4%) Wicked Thorn

far dorocha [53,56,59,62] [some have no loot] (15%) Jewels 05 • (5%) <Mementoes> • (1.5%) Far Dorocha Devastator • (0.5%) <Valor's Heart>

far liath [32] (1.5%) Fog Bound Cape • (80% each) Far Liath Essense, Green Tourmaline • (10%) Black Star Diopside • (0.3%) <The Four Elements>

fee lion [25-27] (90%) Fee Lion Meat • (70% each) Fee Lion Tooth, Fee Lion Claw [25-26] • (75%) Fee Lion Tooth (x2) [27] • (50%) Fee Lion Claw (x2) [27] • (20%) Fee Lion Pelt • (1.5%) Blackened Feelion Paw ***or*** Feelion Razor [25-26]

Fomorian underling [37-38] (no loot)

Fomorian wolfbeast [47] (20%) <Wolfbeast Adornments> • (30%) <Wolfbeast Gear> • (8%) Dangerous Tooth

fuath [46-47] (no loot)

ghoulie [20-21] (1.5%) Ghoulish Shackle • (80% each) Ghoul Skin, Carnelian • (40%) Ghoul Skin • (20%) Azurite • (5% each) Forgotten Silk Coth, Citrine • (0.3%) <Muire's Riches 3>

giant ant [21] (70%) Giant Ant Legs (x2) • (40%) Giant Ant Mandible • (5%) Giant Ant Carapace

giant beetle [20-21] (60%) Giant Beetle Leg (x2) • (40%) Giant Beetle Leg Tip (x2) • (18%) Giant Beetle Mandible (x2) • (5%) Giant Beetle Carapace

graugach [32-33] (12%) Glowing Red Eye

greater luch [25] (55%) Luch Tooth • (75%) Luch Meat • (60%) Luch Meat • (45%) Luch Claw • (10%) Pristine Luch Hide • (1.5%) Puinesean Fang ***or*** Eucail Eye

greater zephyr [33] (70% each) Zephyr's Windy Essence, Expended Commanding Stone • (1.4%) Zephyr's Commanding Stone • (20%) Sphene • (5%) Cat's Eye Apatite • (0.3%) <The Four Elements> • (1.4%) APOA: Eluvium

grovewood [38-40] (12%) Grovewood Bark

Gualach [34] (no loot)

Hatred [50] (no loot)

hillock changeling [35-37] (no loot)

Hunter [65] (no loot)

ire wolf [25-26/27] (75/80%) Ire Wolf Tooth (x3) • (25/33%) Ire Wolf Pelt • (10%) Ire Wolf Claw [25-26]

irewood [29-31] (no loot)

irewood sapling [21-22] (75%) Ire Wood Sapling Branch (x2) • (55%) Bundle of Sapling Branches (x2) • (5%) Pitted Glowing Ng Kit Ire Wood Sapling Staff

Irusan [49] (no loot)

juvenile megafelid [35-38] (8%) Dangerous Tooth

leprechaun [48/49-50] (0.9/1.7%) Forest Green ***or*** Royal Green Leather Dye/Enamel • (0.1/0.3%) Black, Royal Purple ***or*** Dark Purple Leather Dye/Enamel • (2%) <Lucky Charms> • (15%) Jewels 49 • (1.5%) Leprechaun's Staff of the Void • (0.5%) <Granny's Basket>

luch catcher [28] (55%) Luch Tooth • (68%) Luch Meat (x2) • (35%) Luch Claw • (22%) Pristine Luch Hide • (1.5%) Missing Caster's Cap, Gloves ***or*** Belt, ***or*** Caster's Missing Eye

lugradan [27-28] (75% each) Silver Goblet, Pouch of Ill Gotten Gain • (10%) Golden Clover Brooch • (1.4%) Nearahd Sleeves, Gloves, Coif ***or*** Cloak, ***or*** Pluc • (1.3%) APOA: Woven Hedge Weed • (0.3%) <De'velyn's Delights>

lugradan [30] (80% each) Silver Goblet, Pouch of Ill Gotten Gain • (15%) Golden Clover Brooch • (1.4%) <Hedge Clippers> • (1.4%) Nearahd Hauberk, Leggings ***or*** Boots, Lucky Striker, ***or*** Fainne Necklace • (0.3%) <The Four Elements>

mad changeling [26/28] (35% each) Changeling Ear, Changeling Tongue, Bleached Leg Bone • (1.5%) Madder Earring/Wrathfully Righteous Beads • (5/15%) Topaz

Mathair [46] (no loot)

megafelid [40-42] (8%) Dangerous Tooth

morghoul [33] (no loot)

mountain mephit [20-22/23] Mephit Eye, Aeiry Belt ***or*** Mephit Wing

Norseman chopper [37] *see Celtic brehon [37]*

Oak Man [43] (no loot)

One [39] (no loot)

phaeghoul [37-39] (12%) Phaeghoul Red Hand

pookha [33] (20%) Pooka Skin • (70%) Pooka Hair (x2) • (1.5%) Horse, Goblin, Boogieman, Eagle ***or*** Goatman Mantle • (0.3%) <The Four Elements>

rage wolf [31-32] (70% each) Rage Wolf Fang (x2), Claw (x2) • (20%) Rage Wolf Pelt • (8%) Dangerous Tooth

rock guardian [21-22] (5%) Pitted Short Sword • (20% each) Unworked Stone, Fine Unworked Stone • (1.3% each) Bloodstone Left, Right Eye • (0.3%) <Muire's Riches 3> • (1.3%) Perfect ***or*** Flawed Gem

Scuab [38] (no loot)

sett dweller [27-31] (8%) Sett Fur

sett matriarch [41] (no loot)

sett matron [35-38] (8%) Sett Fur

sett protector [32-33] (8%) Sett Fur

sett youngling [20-24] (no loot)

siog raider [37] *see Celtic brehon [37]*

siog seeker [30] (30%) Tattered Scroll • (30%) Luminescent Orb • (30%) Orb of Viewing • (10%) Primrose Eye • (1.5%) Spectral Legs, Gloves, Arms ***or*** Boots, Thumper, ***or*** Slicer • (50%) Bolt of Soft Gossamer

siog seeker [31] (35%) Primrose Eye • (35%) Siog Brandy • (35%) Topaz • (1.3%) Spectral Tunic, Helm ***or*** Shadow, ***or*** Bracer of Might • (1.3%) Smiter's Belt, Smiter, ***or*** Siog's Might • (50%) Bolt of Soft Gossamer • (1.3%) Cath Lute, Shield, Spear, Cloak ***or*** Charms

siog waylayer [26-27] (1.5%) <Rogue Pendants (Higher)> • (1.2%) Siabrian Bandit Helm • (70%) Bandit Mask • (10%) Siabra Waylayer Sash • (1.2%) Waylayer Short Sword, Great Sword, Shillelagh, Spiked Mace, Hammer, Rapier ***or*** Dirk • (40%) Silver Gaming Dice • (20%) Green Tourmaline • (0.3%) <De'velyn's Delights> • (2%) Siabrian Waylayer's Head • (1.2%) Cath Lute, Shield, Spear, Cloak ***or*** Charms

speghoul [40-41] (no loot)

spraggonale [21-22/23] (15/20%) Copper Moonstone Flagon • (80/70%) Bottle of Grog • (80/90%) Copper Cryoprase Earring • (40%) Topaz [21-22] • (30%) Pearl [23] • (3%) Pitted Falcata • (5%) Jasper [23] • (0.3%) <Muire's Riches 3> • (1.5%) Dusty Leggings [21-22 only] ***or*** Silvermined Blade

squabbler [28] (no loot)

streaming wisp [22/23-24] (80/85%) Streaming Wisp Essence • (65%) Streaming Wisp Gem • (10/20%) Streaming Wisp Husk

Three [42] (no loot)

torc [34] (8%) Dangerous Tooth

torcan [31] (no loot)

Two [41] (no loot)

unearthed cave bear [50] (6.6%) Bloodstained Bear Claw • (4.3%) Gnarled Bear Tooth • (1.2%) Bloody Broken Bear Trap • (5%) Slashed Bear Pelt • (3.6%) Fine Bear Pelt • (1.2%) Supple Bear Pelt

vanisher [26-29] (no loot)

walking rock [24] (5% each) Smooth Sling Stones, Chunk of Silver • (25%) Fine Unworked Stone • (45%) Unworked Stone • (50%) Malachite • (60% each) Silver Nugget, Chunk of Copper • (0.3%) <De'velyn's Delights> • (1.5%) Mineralized Ring

white boar [40] (no loot)

wrath sprite [28] (80%) Bleached Leg Bone • (60%) Softly Glowing Orb • (50%) Red Spinel • (1.5%) Spritely Stiletto ***or*** Shield

zephyr wraith [29] (80%) Dark Heart of the Vindictive Spirit • (20%) Zeypher Wraith Essence • (1.5%) Zephyr Belt, Eluvium Belt, Crystalline Band of Wind, ***or*** Windy Crusher • (5%) Black Star Diopside • (0.3%) <The Four Elements>

Jamtland Mountains

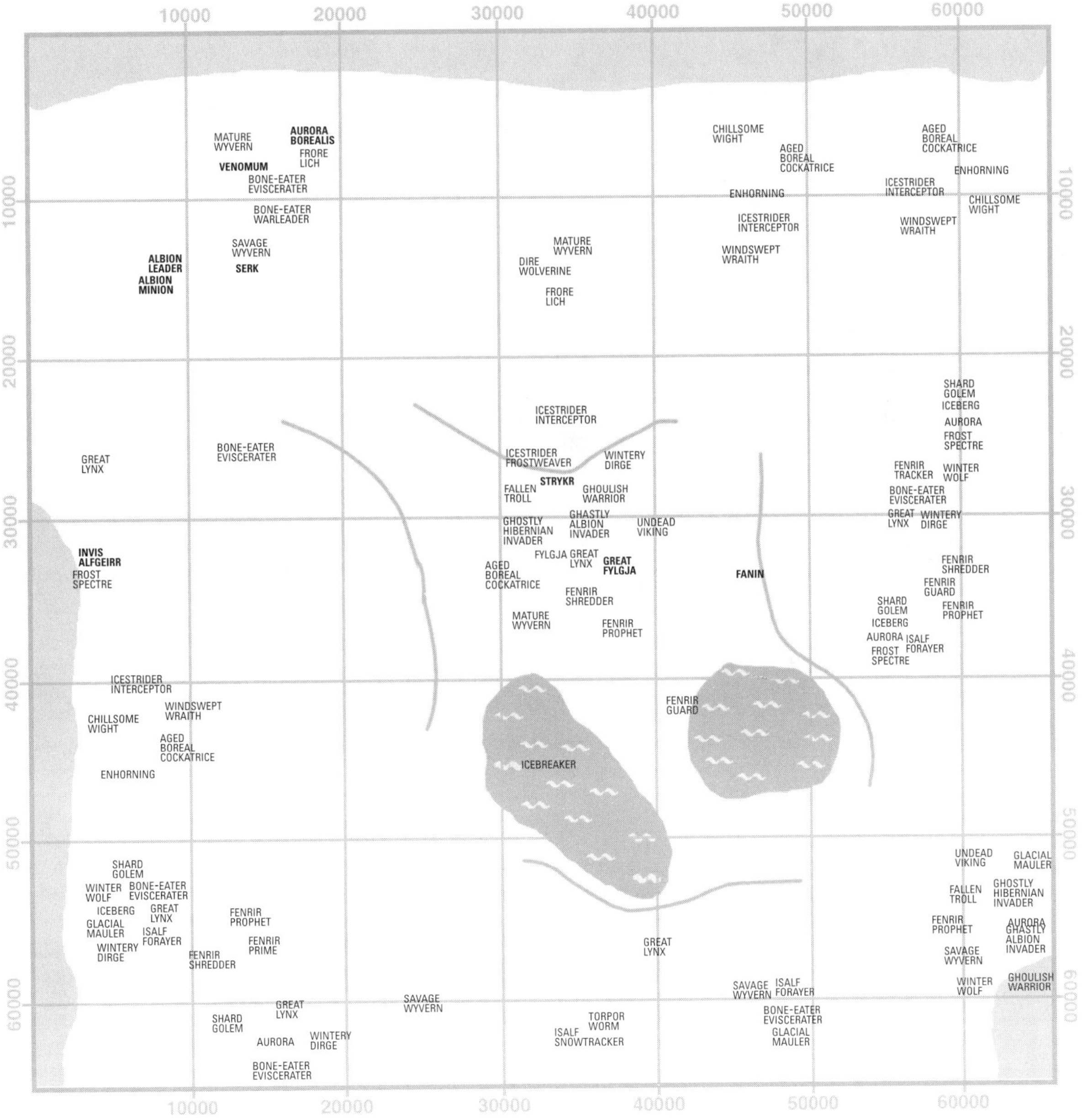

10000 20000 30000 40000 50000 60000

MATURE WYVERN
AURORA BOREALIS
FRORE LICH
VENOMUM
BONE-EATER EVISCERATER
BONE-EATER WARLEADER
SAVAGE WYVERN
SERK
ALBION LEADER
ALBION MINION
CHILLSOME WIGHT
AGED BOREAL COCKATRICE
ENHORNING
ICESTRIDER INTERCEPTOR
WINDSWEPT WRAITH
AGED BOREAL COCKATRICE
ENHORNING
ICESTRIDER INTERCEPTOR
CHILLSOME WIGHT
WINDSWEPT WRAITH
MATURE WYVERN
DIRE WOLVERINE
FRORE LICH
10000
20000
SHARD GOLEM
ICEBERG
AURORA
FROST SPECTRE
ICESTRIDER INTERCEPTOR
GREAT LYNX
BONE-EATER EVISCERATER
ICESTRIDER FROSTWEAVER
WINTERY DIRGE
FENRIR TRACKER
WINTER WOLF
STRYKR
FALLEN TROLL
GHOULISH WARRIOR
BONE-EATER EVISCERATER
GREAT LYNX
WINTERY DIRGE
GHOSTLY HIBERNIAN INVADER
GHASTLY ALBION INVADER
UNDEAD VIKING
30000
INVIS ALFGEIRR
FROST SPECTRE
FYLGJA
GREAT LYNX
GREAT FYLGJA
AGED BOREAL COCKATRICE
FANIN
FENRIR SHREDDER
FENRIR GUARD
FENRIR SHREDDER
SHARD GOLEM
FENRIR PROPHET
MATURE WYVERN
FENRIR PROPHET
ICEBERG
AURORA
ISALF FORAYER
FROST SPECTRE
40000
ICESTRIDER INTERCEPTOR
WINDSWEPT WRAITH
CHILLSOME WIGHT
FENRIR GUARD
AGED BOREAL COCKATRICE
ENHORNING
ICEBREAKER
50000
UNDEAD VIKING
GLACIAL MAULER
SHARD GOLEM
WINTER WOLF
BONE-EATER EVISCERATER
FALLEN TROLL
GHOSTLY HIBERNIAN INVADER
ICEBERG
GREAT LYNX
GLACIAL MAULER
FENRIR PROPHET
FENRIR PROPHET
AURORA
GHASTLY ALBION INVADER
ISALF FORAYER
WINTERY DIRGE
FENRIR PRIME
FENRIR SHREDDER
GREAT LYNX
SAVAGE WYVERN
WINTER WOLF
GHOULISH WARRIOR
60000
SAVAGE WYVERN
ISALF FORAYER
SAVAGE WYVERN
GREAT LYNX
BONE-EATER EVISCERATER
SHARD GOLEM
TORPOR WORM
AURORA
WINTERY DIRGE
ISALF SNOWTRACKER
GLACIAL MAULER
BONE-EATER EVISCERATER

10000 20000 30000 40000 50000 60000

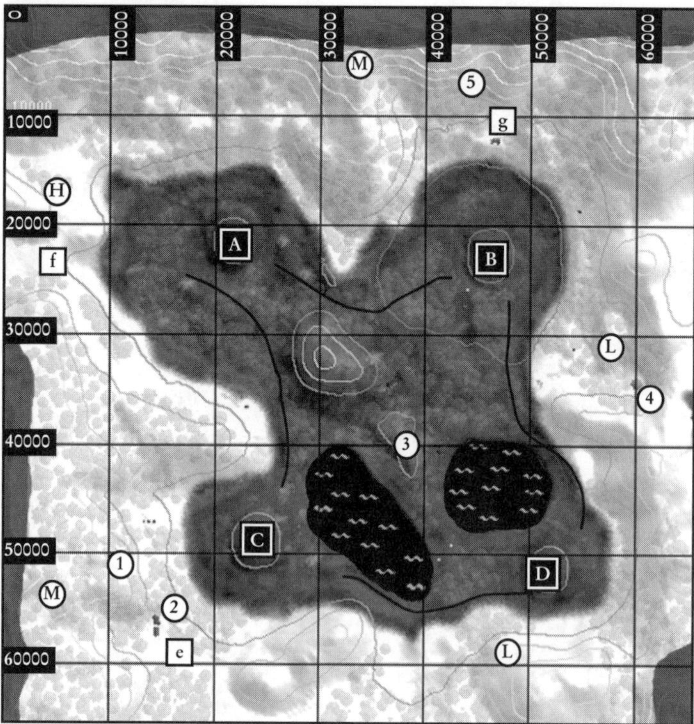

Map Key

A. Nottmoor Faste
B. Blendrake Faste
C. Hledskiaff Faste
D. Glenlock Faste
e. Fenrir
f. Stones
g. Wraiths
Ⓛ Low Invader Risk
Ⓜ Medium Invader Risk
Ⓗ High Invader Risk

The Jamtland Mountains are probably the least mountainous of all the Midgard zones and make claim to the largest snow-free spots of the entire Midgard frontier. There are four large castles in the corners of this zone and it's mostly flat with occasional rolling hills and mountains that meet the zone borders. The creatures here are relatively tame with few exceptions, the highest being around Level 48 and the lowest in the low 30's. Roads connect the castles, and large dirt swaths ensure someone won't likely get lost. With so many castles around, a Midgard player is protected by guards virtually all the time.

1. Wraith Stones

These Wraiths are near the zone border and are a good run from the nearest realm gate, so if you're looking for solitude and likely a monst likely un-camped spot, this might be a decent place to hunt.

Location 13, 46
Invader Risk 6 Medium
Quantity 6
Terrain Type Bottom end of a hill with a castle in sight. They move occasionally with no wandering creatures around.

2. Fenrir Shredder Cabins

The Fenrir have set up shop and are waiting to be hunted. The area around this spot is relatively flat with no wandering creatures to hassle you. Good spot for a solo or duo, although it's a bit far from home.

Location 13, 57
Invader Risk 6 Medium
Quantity 10
Terrain Type Snowy, woodsy, wide-open, flat area with no wandering creatures.

3. Fenrir Guard/Prophet Camp

The Fenrir here have constructed a lean-to log cabin for some reason, yet it's the only area around without snow. Situated beside a lake and near four castles, this spot is very safe from invaders.

Location 41, 40
Invader Risk 4 Slim
Quantity 6
Terrain Type Snow free! Beside a lake with plenty of guard protection from nearby castles.

4. Fenrir Hide Out

Now this place is a little more impressive than the Fenrir lean-to. They managed to construct a circular log cabin with all the amenities. There are a good amount of them here, with a variety of types including Fenrir Prophets. There are protective castles in plain view.

Location 59, 34
Invader Risk 4 Slim
Quantity 10
Terrain Type Mostly inside a medium-sized building with some outside on a hill; no wandering creatures.

5. Windswept Wraith Outpost

These ugly invisible folk are towards the northern border of this zone and are in a good spot to intercept invaders. A friendly castle is in direct sight, and there are plenty of these to go around. Unfortunately, they help define the word 'ugly' and they have a personality to match their looks. They like to move a good deal, and there are some aggressive wandering creatures nearby.

Location 45, 12
Invader Risk 6 Medium
Quantity 9
Personality They like to move frequently.
Terrain Type Snowy hillside near a castle; wandering creatures around them.

Loot

aged boreal cockatrice [49] (no loot)
alpine cockatrice [33] (no loot)
aurora [41-45] (no loot)
Aurora Borealis [55] (no loot)
biting wind [31] (no loot)
bone-eater eviscerater [41-42] (no loot)
bone-eater oracle [39-41] (8%) Thick White Pelt
bone-eater slayer [37-38] (no loot)
bone-eater spine-ripper [39-40] (no loot)
bone-eater warleader [45] (no loot)
chattering skeleton [32] (no loot)
chillsome wight [51/52] (18%) Frozen Waterskin • (2%) Carved Ice Totem • (1%) Chillsome Icebound Gloves/Legs • (0.5%) Frozen Windswept Axe • (0.5%) Rigid Wight Claw/Band of Ice
dire wolverine [58] (18%) Snowy Wolverine Pelt • (2%) Pristine Snowy Wolverine Pelt
enhorning [49] (18%) Enhorning Hide • (2%) Pristine Enhorning Hide
fallen troll [44-45] (no loot)
Fanin [36] (8%) Malefic Tooth
fenrir guard [45] (no loot)
fenrir prime [49] (no loot)
fenrir prophet [44-45] (no loot)
fenrir shredder [45-46] (no loot)
fenrir tracker [42] (no loot)
frore lich [55/56/57] (18%) Frosty Bandages • (2%) Frost-Rimmed Silver Cup • (1.7%) Snow Crystal [Boots ***or*** Gloves/Cap ***or*** Vest/Sleeves ***or*** Pants] • (1.7%) Snow Crystal Runecarver's Staff [55-56], Snow Crystal Summoner's Staff [56-57] ***or*** Icebound Spellbook
frost spectre [45-46] (no loot)
fylgja [50-52] (18%) Fylgja Pelt • (2%) Pristine Fylgja Pelt
ghastly Albion invader [42-43] (no loot)
ghostly Hibernian invader [42-43] (no loot)
ghoulish warrior [44] (no loot)
giant snowcrab [34] (12%) Giant Snow Crab Claw
glacial mauler [44-45] (8%) Malefic Tooth
Great Fylgja [53] (18%) Fylgja Pelt • (2%) Pristine Fylgja Pelt
great lynx [40-42] (8%) Malefic Tooth
ice lizard [32] (no loot)
ice scrag [34] (no loot)
iceberg [42] (no loot)
icebreaker [48] (no loot)
icestrider frostweaver [44] (18%) Frosty Leg • (2%) Frostweaver Web • (10%) Jewels 36 • (1.7%) Latticed Shadow Boots ***or*** Gauntlets • (1.7%) Runic Ember ***or*** Twisted Darksteel Bracer
icestrider interceptor [47/48/49/50/51] (18%) Icestrider Leg • (2%) Icestrider Mandible • (10%) Jewels 36 [47-50]/Jewels 06 [51] • (1.7%) Twilight-Mail Boots ***or*** Gloves [47,50]/Coif ***or*** Leggings [48,51]/Hauberk ***or*** Sleeves [49] • (1.7%) Twilight Battle Crusher [47]/Cleaver [48]/Soul Searer [49]/Impaler [50]/Doombringer [51] ***or*** Shadowsteel Orb [47]/Lattice [48, 50]/Twisted Lattice [49, 51]
icy wisp [31] (no loot)
isalf snowtracker [35] (no loot)
mature wyvern [54-57] (18%) Mature Wyvern Hide • (2%) Pristine Mature Wyvern Hide
miserable zombie [30] (no loot)
nordic yeti [36] (8%) Thick White Pelt
northern light [30] (no loot)
savage wyvern [45-46] (18%) Wyvern Hide • (2%) Pristine Wyvern Hide • (8%) Malefic Tooth
shard golem [42] (70%) Ice Shard
shivering presence [32] (no loot)
snowshoe bandit [34-35] (8%) Malefic Tooth
snowshoe bandit mage [33] (8%) Malefic Tooth
stromkarl [38-40] (no loot)
Strykr [52] (18%) Icestrider Leg • (2%) Icestrider Mandible • (10%) Jewels 06 • (1.7%) Twilight-Mail Hauberk ***or*** Sleeves • (1.7%) Twilight Blade-Stopper ***or*** Shadowsteel Necklace
taiga cat [32-33] (no loot)
torpor worm [37] (no loot)
undead viking [44-45] (no loot)
Venomum [59] (18%) Mature Wyvern Hide • (2%) Pristine Mature Wyvern Hide
white wolf [30-31] (18%) Large White Wolf Pelt • (2%) Pristine White Wolf Pelt
windswept wraith [50/51/52/53] (18%) Orb of Wind • (2%) Pulsing Orb of Wind • (1%) Chillsome Icebound Boots/Helm/Sleeves/Hauberk • (0.5%) Frozen Windswept Axe • (0.5%) Band of Ice
winter wolf [42-43] (18%) Winter Wolf Pelt • (2%) Perfect White Wolf Pelt • (8%) Malefic Tooth
wintery dirge [42] (70%) Frozen Teardrop

Midgard Frontier Tips

Group Friendly? Somewhat — keep an eye out for Hibernian and Albion PCs, since these are frontier zones.

Who hates these areas? Solo'ers hell-bent on EXP camping

Who loves these areas? Hiberians and Albions looking for Midgard players to kill for realm points. Seems casting classes and classes with a ranged ability like these zones for soloing (mid 20s and up for Ygg and Uppland; mid 40s and up for Jamtland and Odin's Gate).

Other Notes. At all times, soloing or grouped, you should keep your eye out for invaders from other realms. Also keep an eye out for patrolling guards near keeps. If the enemy (Albion or Hibernia) claims a keep, the patrolling guards will reflect that, and you will be seen as the enemy.

Odin's Gate Notes. Odin's Gate contains portal keeps for Albion and Hibernians to zone into for RvR combat. This zone sees the highest amount of enemy traffic, making hunting for experience a little riskier than in the other three Midgard frontier zones.

The largest monster in the game resides in this zone, the Glacier Giant. He is quite the sight and thankfully con's neutral so you can approach him without being squished. Though be warned — stealth classes like to lurk about him and snipe the tourists.

Uppland Notes. Unlike Jamtland Mountains and Odin's Gate, this zone is placed next to a PvE zone, so you have a guard fort running in between PvE and RvR. This makes hunting near the gates more solo friendly. Monsters near the gate are great for soloing during your mid 20s. Even though there is a permanent friendly fort nearby, you still need to be on the lookout for Albion and Hibernian invaders.

The Fort that runs between Vale of Mularn and Uppland, Svasud Faste, is the fort where medallions are purchased and porting to the enemy frontier is made possible.

Uppland hosts one of the two relic keeps in Midgard. The strength relic (Thor's hammer) is located at Mjollner Faste.

Yggdra Forest Notes. Similar to Uppland, Yggdra Forest is located next to a PvE zone, so you have a guard fort in between PvE and RvR. This makes hunting near the gates more solo-friendly. Monsters near the gate are great for soloing during your high 20s. Even though there is a permanent friendly fort nearby, you still need to be on the lookout for Albion and Hibernian invaders.

The Fort that runs between West Svealand and Yggdra Forest is called Vindsaul Faste.

Yggdra Forest hosts one of the two relic keeps in Midgard. The power relic (Horn) is located at Grallarhorn Faste.

Solo Levelling Tips

33-35 (Yggdra) Soloing can be tricky. On the one hand it's nice and inviting, with blues to oranges in the undead camps, good xp and some good loot/cash to be had. The downside? This is still a little young to be playing with the big boys. Don't be macho ... avoid invaders.

41-46 Bone-eater oracles are pretty decent for ranged attackers.

42-43 In the frontiers at this level you're looking for dirges. It's actually not too dangerous, except that you're really putting your neck out to grab the loot. Getting that close makes you a mez target! Dirges will be yellow with tendancies to orange. Bolt, bolt dd and you've got it (as long as you don't miss, and you probably won't). Camp bonus can add a cool 2-4 million to a decent 10-16 million. The frontiers are close enough so that you can run over for a break when your camp bonus dwindles.

44-46 At this level, your native targets are Frostweaver Icestriders. These roam all over the frontiers. Look for the unlinked casters before you target and attack … they have low hp, and you'll rack up xp faster.

You can also hunt Fernir in the frontiers, and like the F. Icestriders, you'll want to shop around for the unlinked casters. Keep an eye out for the prophets, because not only do they have guard buddies, but they've got a wicked Stun that'll take all the fun out your day.

46-47 For a full camp bonus and a yellow to 46 experience, check out the Yggdra shard golems that live to the northwest of the horn relic. It's good because by the time you get into your stride and your camp bonus goes away, you can just move over one campsite and presto, there's a brand-new camp with a new bonus. It's kind of out of the way, so it's almost always got the full bonus, but there are a lot of guards around so you don't have to worry too much about invaders bopping you on the back of the head for fun. Runemasters in particular do especially well.

47-50 At this point, in the frontiers, it's back to the Icestriders … only this time, it's the Icestrder Interceptors. Once again, the name of the game is stick to the unlinked casters for the highest return of xp to energy.

50 In Odin's Gate (and Raumarik, too, for that matter) Windswept Wraiths are good. They have nice loot, although they may be a little tougher than some people want to try.

Odin's Gate

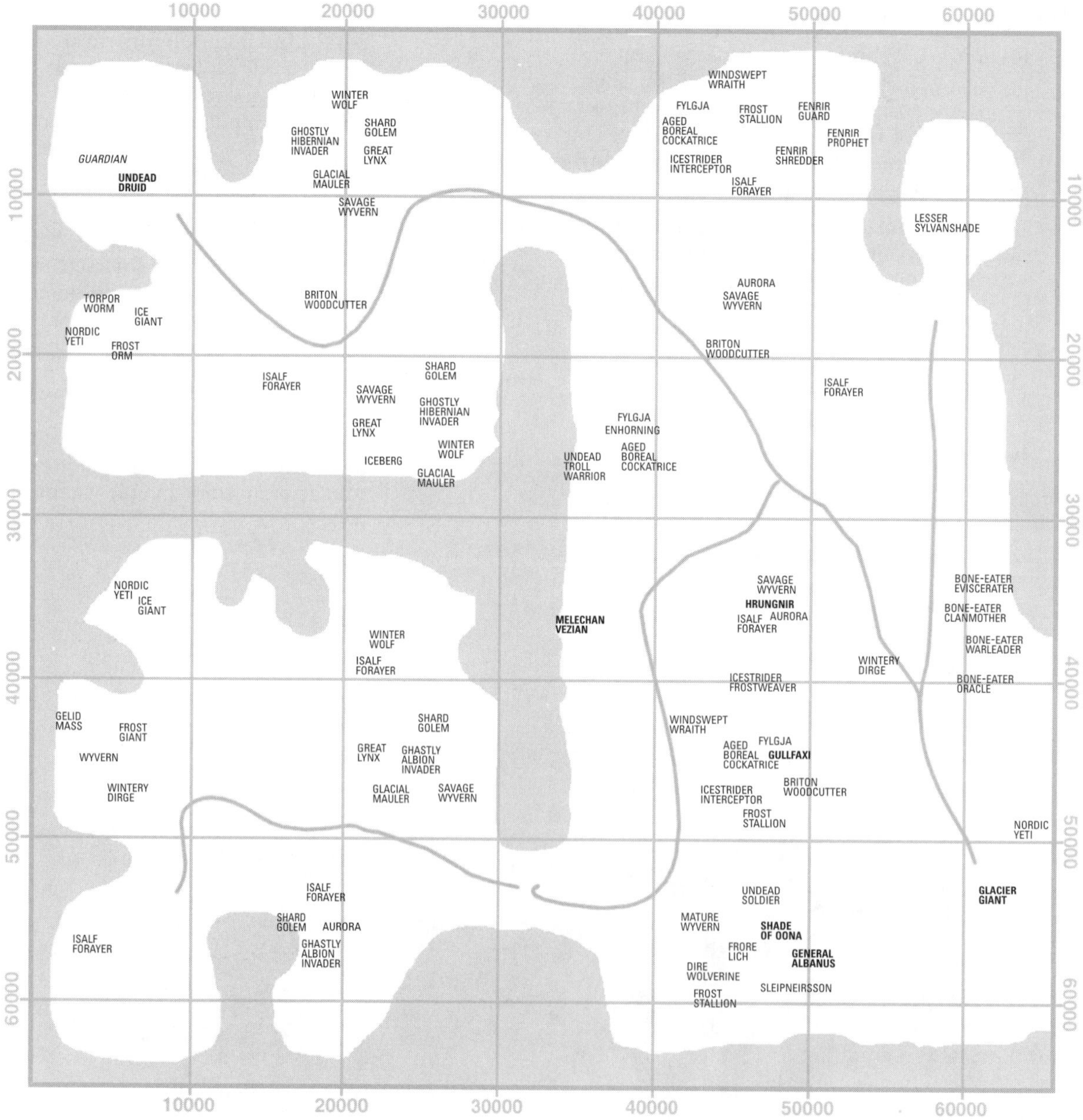

10000 20000 30000 40000 50000 60000

WINDSWEPT WRAITH
WINTER WOLF
FYLGJA
FROST STALLION
FENRIR GUARD
SHARD GOLEM
GHOSTLY HIBERNIAN INVADER
AGED BOREAL COCKATRICE
FENRIR PROPHET
GREAT LYNX
FENRIR SHREDDER
GUARDIAN
ICESTRIDER INTERCEPTOR
UNDEAD DRUID
GLACIAL MAULER
ISALF FORAYER
SAVAGE WYVERN
LESSER SYLVANSHADE
AURORA
TORPOR WORM
BRITON WOODCUTTER
SAVAGE WYVERN
ICE GIANT
NORDIC YETI
BRITON WOODCUTTER
FROST ORM
SHARD GOLEM
ISALF FORAYER
ISALF FORAYER
SAVAGE WYVERN
GHOSTLY HIBERNIAN INVADER
FYLGJA ENHORNING
GREAT LYNX
WINTER WOLF
AGED BOREAL COCKATRICE
UNDEAD TROLL WARRIOR
ICEBERG
GLACIAL MAULER
SAVAGE WYVERN
BONE-EATER EVISCERATER
NORDIC YETI
HRUNGNIR
ICE GIANT
MELECHAN VEZIAN
ISALF FORAYER
AURORA
BONE-EATER CLANMOTHER
WINTER WOLF
BONE-EATER WARLEADER
ISALF FORAYER
WINTERY DIRGE
ICESTRIDER FROSTWEAVER
BONE-EATER ORACLE
SHARD GOLEM
GELID MASS
FROST GIANT
WINDSWEPT WRAITH
FYLGJA
WYVERN
GREAT LYNX
GHASTLY ALBION INVADER
AGED BOREAL COCKATRICE
GULLFAXI
BRITON WOODCUTTER
WINTERY DIRGE
GLACIAL MAULER
SAVAGE WYVERN
ICESTRIDER INTERCEPTOR
FROST STALLION
NORDIC YETI
ISALF FORAYER
UNDEAD SOLDIER
GLACIER GIANT
SHARD GOLEM
AURORA
MATURE WYVERN
SHADE OF OONA
ISALF FORAYER
GHASTLY ALBION INVADER
FRORE LICH
GENERAL ALBANUS
DIRE WOLVERINE
SLEIPNEIRSSON
FROST STALLION

10000 20000 30000 40000 50000 60000

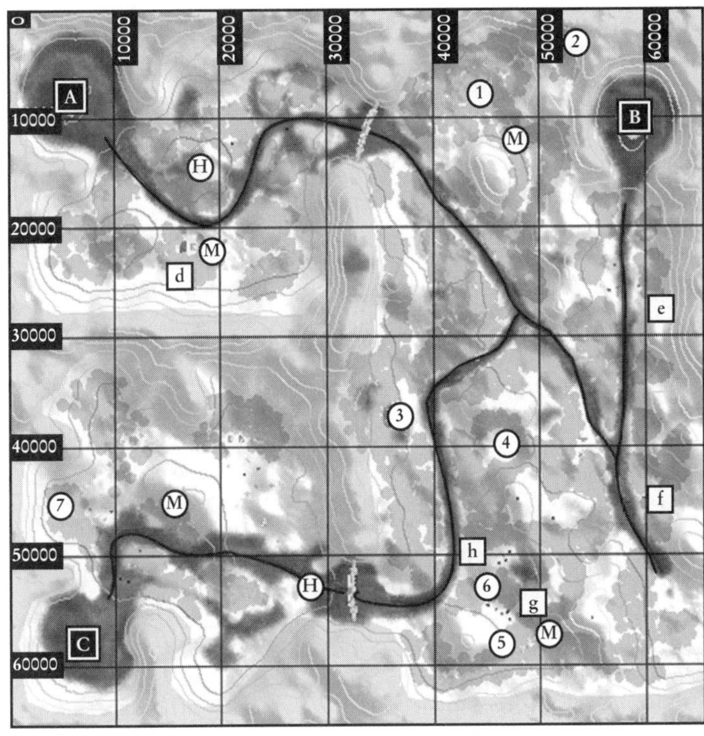

Map Key

A. Hibernia Outpost
B. Bledmeer Faste
C. Albion Outpost
d. Isalfs
e. Wooden Tower
f. Giant
v. Undead Soldiers
h. Icestrider Stones
Ⓛ Low Invader Risk
Ⓜ Medium Invader Risk
Ⓗ High Invader Risk

Odin's Gate is the entry point for Albion and Hibernia to invade Midgard frontier areas. It is generally considered unsafe to do anything but hunt enemy forces, although, for those who wish to spice up their lives with danger, this is a good place to do it. Odin's Gate is covered entirely with snow, large mountains, and occasionally dense forest. There aren't many decent hunting spots here, but there are plenty of creatures close to the roads which are rather powerful. Creature levels here range from low 30's to high 60's.

1. Isalf Forayer Hut

The Isalf apparently have some decent construction workers among them because they've made themselves a rather large and comfortable-looking log cabin. This is out of the way for any invader, so it may be a decent spot to find some experience–no wandering creatures to hassle you.

Location 44, 8
Invader Risk 5 Low
Quantity 8
Terrain Type Small hut in the middle of a snowy flat. No wandering creatures; these are sedentary.

2. Fenrir Guard Post

The Fenrir must have worked hard to stake claim to this remote and mostly useless portion of land. It's on a hill at the zone border, but they seem to like it plenty. Invader Risk is low due to its locale, and there are a good amount here for a solo, duo or group looking to find some experience.

Location 50, 4
Invader Risk 4 Low
Quantity 8
Terrain Type Near zone border on side of mountain. Guards and Prophets inside two buildings.

3. Snowshoe Bandit Camp

A small hillside camp by the path of Albion invaders, it is noteworthy for the named spawn "Melechan Vezian." This spot is dangerous to camp and easily visible from the road; no wandering creatures.

Location 35, 37
Invader Risk 5 Low
Quantity 4, named spawn "Melechan Vezian"
Terrain Type Near road on the side of a small hill, a couple of tents and a fireplace.

4. Icestrider Frostweaver Stone

They're strong ugly and mean. This group of monsters is placed to prevent Albions from crossing through the woods safely. This isn't a particularly good hunting spot, but definitely one to avoid; wandering creatures abound!

Location 46 39
Invader Risk 7 High
Quantity 5
Terrain Type On a flat in a small depression with a single stone in the middle.

5. Undead Soldiers

Some poor soldiers became Undead and now haunt a single stone. The important part here is that a named soldier, "General Albanus" makes this spot home. While this spot may not be wonderful for experience, the General might give you something nice.

Location 47, 56
Invader Risk Low
Quantity 2 regular, one named "General Albanus".
Terrain Type They stand still, with dangerous wandering creatures in a snowy plain with trees.

6. Icestrider Interceptor Totem

As their name implies, they're 'interceptors.' They're less hunting fodder than they are to keep people on the road. They're hidden on top of a snowy peak, ready to descend upon an errant traveler. They move only slightly, but there are plenty of other creatures in the local vicinity to cause worry.

Location 46, 50
Invader Risk 5, low
Quantity 5
Terrain Type Top of a snowy hill. They slowly wander over a short distance, with few other wandering creatures.

7. Wintery Dirge Outpost

This is located within sight of the Albion portal fort. It's not a bad spot by any means, and the only real drawback is the Invader Risk. They sit in an open area around a small fort and slowly wander around.

Location 6, 45
Invader Risk 8 Very High
Quantity 6
Terrain Type Near Albion Portal Fort, open area with no wandering creatures. Dirges move slowly.

Loot

aged boreal cockatrice [49] (no loot)
aurora [43,46] (no loot)
bone-eater clanmother [42] (8%) Thick White Pelt
bone-eater eviscerater [42] (no loot)
bone-eater oracle [41] (8%) Thick White Pelt
bone-eater warleader [45] (no loot)
dire wolverine [58] (18%) Snowy Wolverine Pelt • (2%) Pristine Snowy Wolverine Pelt
enhorning [50] (18%) Enhorning Hide • (2%) Pristine Enhorning Hide
fenrir guard [45] (no loot)
fenrir prophet [45] (no loot)
fenrir shredder [46] (no loot)
frore lich [55/56/57] (18%) Frosty Bandages • (2%) Frost-Rimmed Silver Cup • (1.7%) Snow Crystal [Boots ***or*** Gloves/Cap ***or*** Vest/Sleeves ***or*** Pants] • (1.7%) Snow Crystal Runecarver's Staff [55-56], Snow Crystal Summoner's Staff [56-57] ***or*** Icebound Spellbook
frost giant [37] (12%) Ice Cold Giant Blood
frost orm [35] (no loot)
frost stallion [54-55] (18%) Frosty Hide • (2%) Pristine Frosty Hide
fylgja [50-51] (18%) Fylgja Pelt • (2%) Pristine Fylgja Pelt
gelid mass [35] (no loot)
General Albanus [62] (no loot)
ghastly Albion invader [43] (no loot)
ghostly Hibernian invader [43] (no loot)
glacial mauler [44] (8%) Malefic Tooth
glacier giant [76] (5%) Gold Lined Rock (x4) • (40%) Snow Diamond • (20%) Frigid Glacier Skin (x4)
great lynx [42] (8%) Malefic Tooth
Gullfaxi [57] (18%) Frosty Hide • (2%) Pristine Frosty Hide
Hrungnir [61] (12%) Ice Cold Giant Blood
ice giant [35-36] (no loot)
ice lizard [32] (no loot)
ice scrag [33] (no loot)
iceberg [42] (no loot)
icestrider frostweaver [46] (18%) Frosty Leg • (2%) Frostweaver Web • (10%) Jewels 36 • (1.7%) Latticed Shadow Vest ***or*** Sleeves • (0.9%) Forged Darksteel Runic ***or*** Spirit Staff • (0.9%) Hollow Chitin
icestrider interceptor [47,49] (18%) Icestrider Leg • (2%) Icestrider Mandible • (10%) Jewels 36 • (1.7%) Twilight-Mail Boots ***or*** Gloves/Hauberk ***or*** Sleeves • (1.7%) Twilight Battle Crasher ***or*** Shadowsteel Orb/Twilight Soul Shearer ***or*** Shadowsteel Twisted Lattice
isalf forayer [44] (no loot)
mature wyvern [55-57] (18%) Mature Wyvern Hide • (2%) Pristine Mature Wyvern Hide
Melechan Vezian [41] (no loot)
miserable zombie [31] (no loot)
nordic yeti [35-36] (8%) Thick White Pelt
savage wyvern [45] (18%) Wyvern Hide • (2%) Pristine Wyvern Hide • (8%) Malefic Tooth
Shade of Oona [65] (no loot)
shard golem [42] (70%) Ice Shard
sleipneirsson [55-56] (18%) Sleipneirson Hide • (2%) Pristine Sleipneirson Hide
snowshoe bandit [30-31,34] (8%) Malefic Tooth
snowshoe bandit mage [32] (8%) Malefic Tooth
torpor worm [37] (no loot)
undead soldier [49] (no loot)
undead troll warrior [31] (45%) Cursed Ekyps Control Orb • (20%) Jewels 15 • (0.4%) Jewels 65 • (4.5%) Rust, Purple ***or*** Charcoal Colors • (0.5%) Crimson, Royal Purple ***or*** Black Colors • (2%) APOA: Webbed Shadow ***or*** Latticed Shadow • (2%) <Freya's Doom> • (2%) <Skirnir's Gift>
white wolf [30] (18%) Large White Wolf Pelt • (2%) Pristine White Wolf Pelt
windswept wraith [50] (18%) Orb of Wind • (2%) Pulsing Orb of Wind • (1%) Chillsome Icebound Boots • (0.5%) Frozen Windswept Axe • (0.5%) Band of Ice
winter wolf [44-45] (18%) Large Winter Wolf Pelt • (2%) Pristine Winter Wolf Pelt • (8%) Malefic Tooth
wintery dirge [40-41] (70%) Frozen Teardrop [no loot for level 40]
wyvern [38] (8%) Malefic Tooth

Uppland

10000 20000 30000 40000 50000 60000

MATURE WYVERN
VIKING ARCHER
ICESTRIDER FROSTWEAVER
FROST SPECTRE
SHYF
SNOWSHOE BANDIT
FROST ORM
ISALF FORAYER
ICESTRIDER INTERCEPTOR
GIANT SNOWCRAB
NORDIC YETI
ICESTRIDER CHILLER
AGED BOREAL COCKATRICE
AURORA
ISALF SNOWTRACKER
GELID MASS
10000
SNOWSHOE BANDIT MAGE
SIGUM
BONE-EATER EVISCERATER
BONE-EATER ORACLE
ISALF ICEMAGE
EIBHILIN
SNOWSHOE BANDIT
GHASTLY ALBION INVADER
GHOULISH WARRIOR
BONE-EATER CLANMOTHER
ISALF BLINDER
BONE-EATER SPINE-RIPPER
ISALF WARRIOR
GHOSTLY HIBERNIAN INVADER
FALLEN TROLL
NIOCLAS
MISERABLE ZOMBIE
ISALF SNOWTRACKER
STROMKARL
FROST HOUND
FROST SPECTRE
UNDEAD VIKING
FOSSEGRIM
SHIVERING PRESENCE
FENRIR SNOWSCOUT
20000
ICY WISP
SNOW GIANT
FENRIR TRACKER
BAUGI
ICE LIZARD
BITING WIND
FENRIR PROPHET
ICE SCRAG
ISALF BLINDER
FROST ORM
FENRIR GUARD
ICE GIANT
ISALF WARRIOR
ISALF ICEMAGE
ISALF SNOWTRACKER
NORDIC YETI
SNOW GIANT
FROST HOUND
WINTERY DIRGE
GREAT LYNX
BONE-EATER SPINE-RIPPER
BITING WIND
GHOSTLY HIBERNIAN INVADER
FENRIR TRACKER
BONE-EATER ORACLE
FENRIR SNOWSCOUT
GIANT SNOWCRAB
MISERABLE ZOMBIE
BITING WIND
30000
TAIGA CAT
AURORA
ICY WISP
FROST ORM
GELID MASS
SHIVERING PRESENCE
NORDIC YETI
SNOWSHOE BANDIT
ISALF SCRYER
ISALF WARRIOR
ISALF BLINDER
ALPINE COCKATRICE
ISALF SNOWTRACKER
ISALF SURVEYOR
MISERABLE ZOMBIE
40000
THORKATLA
SAVAGE WYVERN
SNOW GIANT
ISALF FORAYER
ICY WISP
ENTHRALLED ZOMBIE
GLACIAL MAULER
GHOSTLY HIBERNIAN INVADER
WINTER WOLF
MISERABLE ZOMBIE
SHIVERING PRESENCE
ICY WISP
BITING WIND
FENRIR PROPHET
AURORA
FROST HOUND
UNDEAD VIKING
FALLEN TROLL
50000
GHOULISH WARRIOR
ICE GIANT
ICE LIZARD
BALLE
ICE GIANT
GELID MASS
ICE SCRAG
GHASTLY ALBION INVADER
GIANT SNOWCRAB
NORDIC YETI
SNOWSHOE BANDIT
ASDIS
SNOW GIANT
WINTERY DIRGE
GAGNRAD
TORPOR WORM
FENRIR SNOWSCOUT
SENTINEL OF RUNES
60000
ICEBERG
BLOCK OF ICE
SHARD GOLEM
GREAT LYNX
AURORA
WYVERN

10000 20000 30000 40000 50000 60000

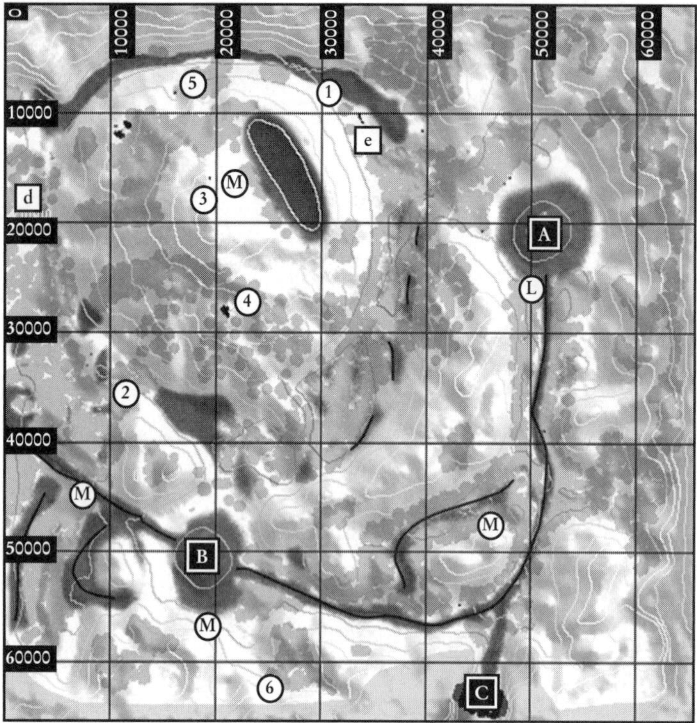

Map Key

A. Mjollner Faste & Hammer Relic
B. Fensalir Faste
C. Svasud Faste
d. Fenrir Camp
e. Snowshoe Bandits
(L) Low Invader Risk
(M) Medium Invader Risk
(H) High Invader Risk

Typical of Midgard territory, Uppland is a snowy mountainous region with gigantic pine trees everywhere. The creatures here are mostly mid to low level and hunting spots are spread out well with few wandering creatures to hassle explorers. To the northern end of this zone, the creatures become more powerful, but generally speaking, along the roads you can find a decent variet. Just beware invaders. Be sure to bring a hat! It gets cold.

1. Snowshoe Bandit Camp

This Snowshoe Bandit camp is in the northern reaches of Uppland. There is a relatively low risk of invaders, and other than a few wandering scouts, this hunting spot is a good choice if you're looking to get away from the crowds.

Location 33, 11
Invader Risk 5 Medium
Quantity 12-15
Terrain Type In a small ravine, plenty of room for a party here.

2. Isalf Camp

This is another good spot for a group of adventurers with an eye for something different. Most of the Isalfs stay within their camp area, but beware the scouts! They wander about freely and will hightail it back to their friends when they see you.

Location 9, 37
Invader Risk 5 Medium
Quantity 6-8
Terrain Type A dense wood, many wandering scouts.

3. Fenrir Camp

This is a decent hunting spot for anyone in their level range. There are few wandering creatures to hassle a party, including invaders, and there are large flat open areas around the camp to keep an eye on anything.

Location 17, 21
Invader Risk 4 Low
Quantity 7-12
Terrain Type Snowy flat area with large open areas. Few/No wandering creatures.

4. Bone-Eater Camp

As is usually the case, these Bone-Eaters have made a camp on the sloping side of a hill and are simply waiting to be attacked. Other than a couple of scouts that they send out, it's a relatively safe area with few other creatures to interfere, low risk of RvR encounters to boot.

Location 21,28
Invader Risk 4, Low
Quantity 8-12
Personality They stand still, with a couple scouts.
Terrain Type Side of a hill with trees. Very good spot.

5. Icestrider Frostweaver Pit

Every realm has their "Ugly" creature; this is perhaps Midgard's most ugly. It happens to be that the most scary creatures are often the most powerful as well, and this is the case with these Icestriders. They're situated along a broken road that goes through a valley. Think of a hot dog bun–these guys sit where the hot dog would be.

Location 17, 5
Invader Risk 6 Medium
Quantity 11
Terrain Type They line the bottom of a valley and up two sides. Very good spot for the brave!

6. Young Wyvern Mountain

Not far off the road from a castle, these Wyverns don't move very much and allow archers to have a good range on them. Unfortunately, many invaders follow the Zone wall to reach the gates at Uppland, and this is where they lay. Other than the Invader Risk, this is a decent spot for those looking to duo, or solo.

Location 21, 62
Invader Risk 7 High
Quantity 8
Personality They move, but not very far.
Terrain Type Zone side, Mountainside.

Loot

abominable snowman [26-30] (8%) Thick White Pelt
aged boreal cockatrice [49] (no loot)
alpine cockatrice [33] (no loot)
aurora [41-44] (no loot)
Baugi [34] (no loot)
biting wind [29,31] (no loot)
block of ice [36] (7%) Ice Creature Corpse
bone-eater clanmother [42] (8%) Thick White Pelt
bone-eater eviscerater [41] (no loot)
bone-eater oracle [39-41] (8%) Thick White Pelt
bone-eater slayer [37-38] (no loot)
bone-eater spine-ripper [39-40] (no loot)
boreal cockatrice [24-26] (no loot)
chattering skeleton [32] (no loot)
chiseler [20-24] (no loot)
cold light [20,22] (no loot)
Eibhilin [36] (no loot)
Eteki [27] (no loot)
fallen troll [44-45] (no loot)
fenrir guard [45] (no loot)
fenrir prophet [44-45] (no loot)
fenrir snowscout [37-38] (no loot)
fenrir tracker [40-41] (no loot)
flurry [23] (no loot)
fossegrim [29-31] (no loot)
frost hound [31] (8%) Malefic Tooth
frost orm [35] (no loot)
frost spectre [45-46] (no loot)
frostbite wildling [27-28] (no loot)
frosty colt [20] (no loot)
frosty scuttlebug [23-24] (no loot)
Gagnrad [33] (no loot)
gelid mass [35] (no loot)
ghastly Albion invader [43] (no loot)
ghostly Hibernian invader [42-43] (no loot)
ghoulish warrior [44-45] (no loot)
giant snowcrab [33-34] (12%) Giant Snow Crab Claw
glacial mauler [44] (8%) Malefic Tooth
great lynx [39-40,42] (8%) Malefic Tooth
hailer [28] (no loot)
hailstone [20] (no loot)
half-frozen madman [25] (no loot)
horse [55] (75%) Horse Hair • (10%) Auburn Mane • (80%) Ruined Horse Skin • (35%) Horse Skin • (60%) Horse Hair
ice giant [34,36] (no loot)
ice lizard [34] (no loot)
ice scrag [34] (no loot)
iceberg [42] (no loot)
icemuncher [28] (no loot)
icestrider chiller [43] (18%) Frosty Leg • (2%) Chiller Head • (10%) Jewels 36
icestrider frostweaver [46] (18%) Frosty Leg • (2%) Frostweaver Web • (10%) Jewels 36 • (1.7%) Latticed Shadow Vest ***or*** Sleeves • (0.9%) Forged Darksteel Runic ***or*** Spirit Staff • (0.9%) Hollow Chitin
icestrider interceptor [49] (18%) Icestrider Leg • (2%) Icestrider Mandible • (10%) Jewels 36 • (1.7%) Twilight-Mail Hauberk ***or*** Sleeves • (1.7%) Twilight Soul Searer ***or*** Twisted Shadowsteel Lattice
icy skeleton [25] (no loot)
icy wisp [31,33] (no loot)
isalf blinder [34-35] (no loot)
isalf icemage [34] (no loot)
isalf scryer [33] (no loot)
isalf snowtracker [35] (no loot)
isalf surveyor [33] (no loot)
isalf warrior [35] (no loot)
Jakr [23] (no loot)
mature wyvern [54] (18%) Mature Wyvern Hide • (2%) Pristine Mature Wyvern Hide
miserable zombie [28,31-32] (no loot)
Moira the Quiet [44] (no loot)
nip mephit [23-25] (no loot)
nordic yeti [33-36] (8%) Thick White Pelt
northern ettin [25-27] (no loot)
northern light [25-30] (no loot)
savage wyvern [45] (18%) Wyvern Hide • (2%) Pristine Wyvern Hide • (8%) Malefic Tooth
shard golem [42] (70%) Ice Shard
shivering presence [32] (no loot)
Shyf [46] (no loot)
Sigum [32] (8%) Malefic Tooth
sleigh horse [30] (no loot)
snow giant [30-33] (no loot)
snow imp [20,22] (no loot)
snowshoe bandit [30-31,34-35] (8%) Malefic Tooth
stromkarl [40] (no loot)
taiga cat [32] (no loot)
thawing corpse [31] (no loot)
torpor worm [37] (no loot)
undead minion [20] (no loot)
undead viking [44-45] (no loot)
white wolf [27-29] (18%) White Wolf Pelt • (2%) Snowy White Wolf Pelt [no loot on level 27]
white wolf [30-31] (18%) Large White Wolf Pelt • (2%) Pristine White Wolf Pelt
winter wolf [43] (18%) Winter Wolf Pelt • (2%) Perfect White Wolf Pelt • (8%) Malefic Tooth
wintery dirge [40-42] (70%) Frozen Teardrop [no loot on level 40]
wyvern [36-37,39] (8%) Malefic Tooth
young wyvern [28-30] (no loot)

Yggdra Forest

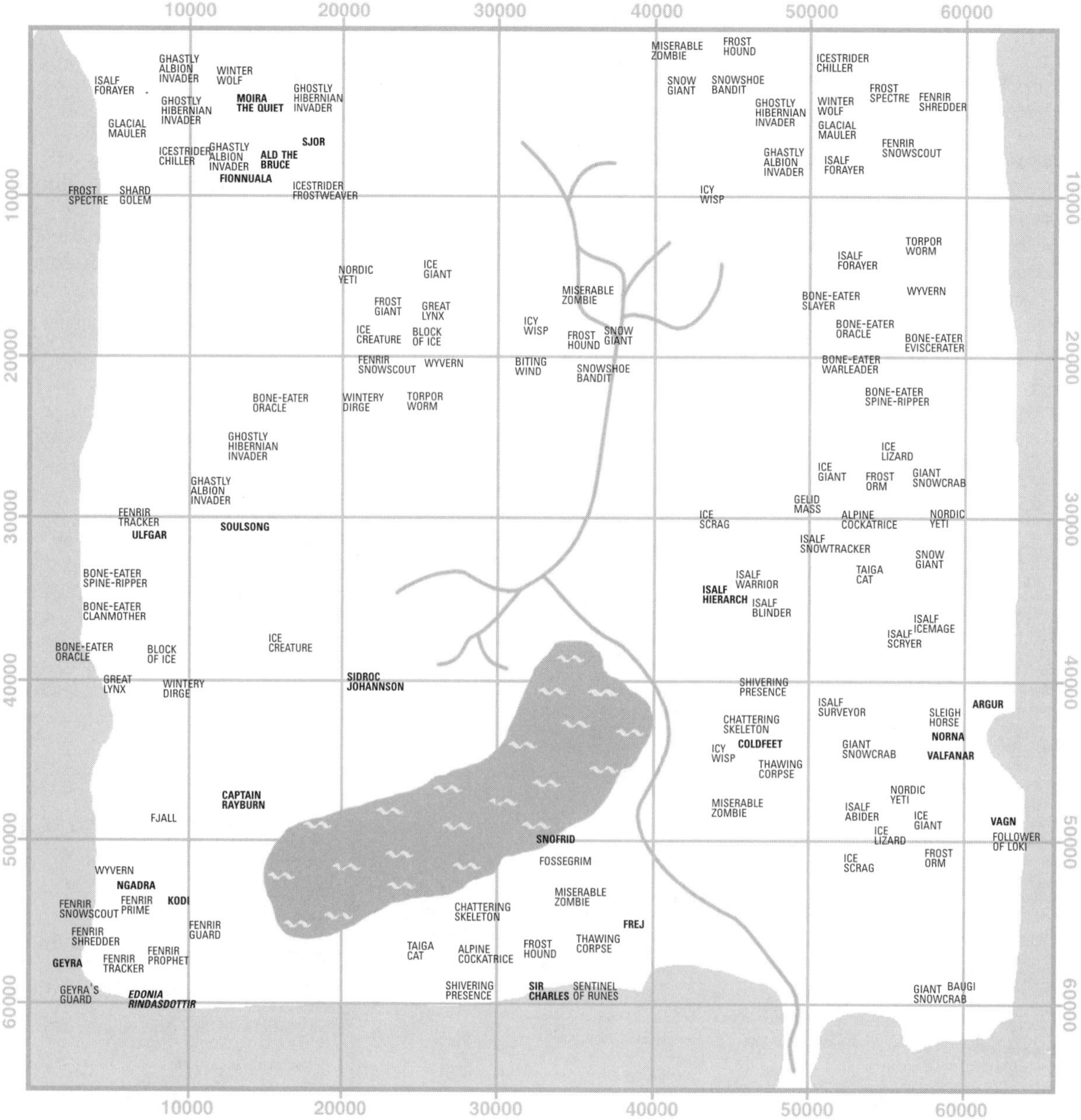

10000 20000 30000 40000 50000 60000

MISERABLE ZOMBIE
FROST HOUND
ICESTRIDER CHILLER
GHASTLY ALBION INVADER
WINTER WOLF
ISALF FORAYER
SNOW GIANT
SNOWSHOE BANDIT
FROST SPECTRE
FENRIR SHREDDER
GHOSTLY HIBERNIAN INVADER
MOIRA THE QUIET
GHOSTLY HIBERNIAN INVADER
GHOSTLY HIBERNIAN INVADER
WINTER WOLF
GLACIAL MAULER
GLACIAL MAULER
SJOR
FENRIR SNOWSCOUT
ICESTRIDER CHILLER
GHASTLY ALBION INVADER
ALD THE BRUCE
GHASTLY ALBION INVADER
ISALF FORAYER
FIONNUALA
10000
FROST SPECTRE
SHARD GOLEM
ICESTRIDER FROSTWEAVER
ICY WISP
10000
TORPOR WORM
ISALF FORAYER
NORDIC YETI
ICE GIANT
MISERABLE ZOMBIE
WYVERN
BONE-EATER SLAYER
FROST GIANT
GREAT LYNX
ICY WISP
BONE-EATER ORACLE
ICE CREATURE
BLOCK OF ICE
FROST HOUND
SNOW GIANT
BONE-EATER EVISCERATER
20000
BONE-EATER WARLEADER
20000
FENRIR SNOWSCOUT
WYVERN
BITING WIND
SNOWSHOE BANDIT
BONE-EATER ORACLE
WINTERY DIRGE
TORPOR WORM
BONE-EATER SPINE-RIPPER
GHOSTLY HIBERNIAN INVADER
ICE LIZARD
ICE GIANT
FROST ORM
GIANT SNOWCRAB
GHASTLY ALBION INVADER
GELID MASS
30000
FENRIR TRACKER
ICE SCRAG
ALPINE COCKATRICE
NORDIC YETI
30000
ULFGAR
SOULSONG
ISALF SNOWTRACKER
SNOW GIANT
BONE-EATER SPINE-RIPPER
TAIGA CAT
ISALF WARRIOR
ISALF HIERARCH
ISALF BLINDER
BONE-EATER CLANMOTHER
ISALF ICEMAGE
ISALF SCRYER
BONE-EATER ORACLE
BLOCK OF ICE
ICE CREATURE
40000
GREAT LYNX
WINTERY DIRGE
SIDROC JOHANNSON
SHIVERING PRESENCE
40000
ISALF SURVEYOR
SLEIGH HORSE
ARGUR
CHATTERING SKELETON
NORNA
ICY WISP
COLDFEET
GIANT SNOWCRAB
VALFANAR
THAWING CORPSE
CAPTAIN RAYBURN
NORDIC YETI
MISERABLE ZOMBIE
ISALF ABIDER
ICE GIANT
FJALL
VAGN
50000
ICE LIZARD
SNOFRID
FOLLOWER OF LOKI
50000
FOSSEGRIM
ICE SCRAG
FROST ORM
WYVERN
NGADRA
MISERABLE ZOMBIE
FENRIR SNOWSCOUT
FENRIR PRIME
KODI
CHATTERING SKELETON
FENRIR SHREDDER
FENRIR GUARD
FREJ
FENRIR PROPHET
TAIGA CAT
ALPINE COCKATRICE
FROST HOUND
THAWING CORPSE
GEYRA
FENRIR TRACKER
60000
GEYRA'S GUARD
EDONIA RINDASDOTTIR
SHIVERING PRESENCE
SIR CHARLES
SENTINEL OF RUNES
GIANT SNOWCRAB
BAUGI
60000

10000 20000 30000 40000 50000 60000

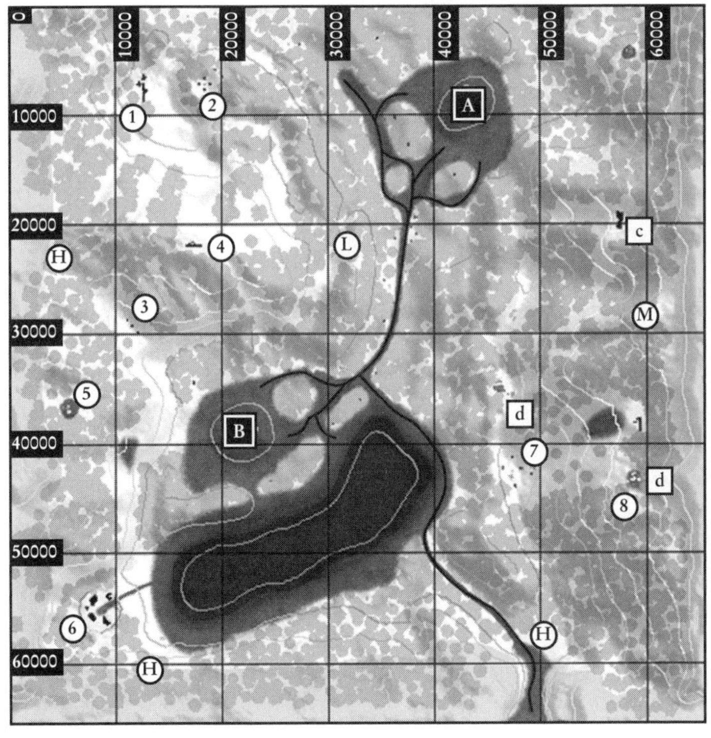

Map Key

A. Arvakr
B. Grallarhorn Faste & Horn relic
c. Bone Eaters
d. Isalfs
(L) Low Invader Risk
(M) Medium Invader Risk
(H) High Invader Risk

This is one of the most popular, and thus dangerous, RvR zones. It's a dense and often deadly forest, with plenty of mountains. There are two castles here, but due to the lack of manpower, there aren't enough guards to prevent all the invaders from terrorizing the locals. Yggdra Forest has many excellent hunting spots, but with its known history for invaders, it is a high-risk area. The creatures here are generally unfriendly once you step off the road, and there are a surprising amount of mid-level aggressive and scout-type creatures to harry explorers; the creatures range from the low 20's to the high 40's.

Quest NPCs

Yggdra Forest	
Drunken Dwarf	Price of Excellence (lvl 44)

1. Ghastly Albion Invader Wall

It appears that finding good real estate is hard to find in the underworld, and so these Ghastly Invaders have relocated. There are a plenty of them here for a medium- sized group, and they don't move a whole lot. The area is flat around them for good positioning and there is no threat from wandering creatures.

Location 12,8
Invader Risk 6, Medium
Quantity 9
Personality They move only slightly.
Terrain Type Flat area around this wall; no wandering creatures.

2. Icestrider Chiller Pit

These Chillers keep the same good looks as their cousins over in Uppland. They're packed in one sunken area, which would make them a good target if not for the wandering creatures waiting to assault you.

Location 18, 7
Invader Risk 4 Low
Quantity 10-12
Terrain Type Dip on top of a hill; they don't move, but wandering creatures are around.

3. Wintery Dirge Stones

These ugly folks are near a zone border on a hillside. The risk of invaders is average, but there are plenty of these to go around; they move only small distances, grouped together with few other wandering creatures to bother you.

Location 11,29
Invader Risk 7 High
Quantity 10
Personality They wander small distances.
Terrain Type Steep hills on two sides.

4. BoneEater Oracle Camp

The Bone Eater Oracle Camp is near the zone border where invaders frequently travel by; they're packed together tightly and only wander slightly. A short distance away are some mean aggressive creatures, but otherwise this is a popular archer spot to gain experience.

Location 16, 21
Invader Risk 8 High
Quantity 12
Personality They wander slightly.
Terrain Type Flat hilltop clearing.

5. Bone Eater Camp

Only the brave hunt her;, the cautious need not apply. This camp has a variety of Bone Eaters, and as the name suggests, they're not friendly and want to eat your bones. While the variety here is dangerous, the real danger is that it lies in the path of every invader coming into Yggdra Forest. The benefit here is that you'll never find people camping, but on the other side, you won't be alive very long.

Location 5, 36
Invader Risk 8 High
Quantity 10
Personality Sedentary.
Terrain Type Dense trees on a hillside, zone wall.

6. Fenrir Fort

How the armies of Midgard missed this spot is unknown. The Fenrir have made this their stronghold and it has become the size of a small town. There are guards, there are scouts and there are some mean individuals inside if you manage to make it past the first two. It's an easy-to-reach destination with few interruptions along the way, but the risk of invaders is very high.

Location 9, 55
Invader Risk 8 High
Quantity 20+
Personality Scouts.
Terrain Type Inside an open fort, various Fenrir types.

7. Undead Camp

This area is widely hunted for experience because it's close to the realm gate. However, it's also popular for invaders. This is a typical high risk area—great experience and lots of creatures, but at the price of safety.

Location 47, 42
Invader Risk 8 Very High
Quantity 20+
Personality Miserable Zombies, Shivering Presences, Thawing Corpses—all in a dense area.
Terrain Type Broad depression, woods on all sides.

8. Isalf Camp

Many have met their doom while wandering these slopes. The Isalf are legendary for their aggravating scouts, which can shoot you from a disturbing distance. However, once you get by the scouts, there's good hunting here, with only a relatively small risk of invasion.

Location 58, 43
Invader Risk 5 Low
Quantity 10
Personality Scouts, with majority being sedentary.
Terrain Type Side of a slowly sloping mountain in a wooded area.

Loot

abominable snowman [26-30] (8%) Thick White Pelt
Ald the Bruce [44] (no loot)
alpine cockatrice [33] (no loot)
Argur [34] (no loot)
Baugi [34] (no loot)
biting wind [29] (no loot)
block of ice [36-37] (7%) Ice Creature Corpse
bone-eater clanmother [42] (8%) Thick White Pelt
bone-eater eviscerater [41-42] (no loot)
bone-eater oracle [39,41] (8%) Thick White Pelt
bone-eater slayer [37], spine-ripper [39-40], warleader [45] (no loot)
boreal cockatrice [24-27] (no loot)
Captain Rayburn [36] (no loot)
chattering skeleton [32] (no loot)
chiseler [20-24] (no loot)
cold light [20-21,23-25] (no loot)
Coldfeet [33] (no loot)
fenrir guard [45], prime [49], prophet [44-45], shredder [45-46], snowscout [36,38], tracker [40,42] (no loot)
flurry [23] (no loot)
fossegrim [29-31] (no loot)
Frej [27] (no loot)
frost giant [37] (12%) Ice Cold Giant Blood
frost hound [30-31] (8%) Malefic Tooth
frost orm [35], frost spectre [46] (no loot)
frostbite wildling [27-29] (no loot)
frosty colt [20] (no loot)
frosty scuttlebug [23-24] (no loot)
gelid mass [35] (no loot)
ghastly Albion, Hlbernian invader [42-43] (no loot)
giant snowcrab [33-34] (12%) Giant Snow Crab Claw
glacial mauler [44] (8%) Malefic Tooth
great lynx [39] (8%) Malefic Tooth
hailer [28], hailstone [20] (no loot)
half-frozen madman [25] (no loot)
ice creature [39] (12%) Ice Creature Corpse
ice giant [33-36], ice lizard [34], ice scrag [33-34] (no loot)
icemuncher [28] (no loot)
icestrider chiller [43-45] (18%) Frosty Leg • (2%) Chiller Head • (10%) Jewels 36
icestrider frostweaver [44] (18%) Frosty Leg • (2%) Frostweaver Web • (10%) Jewels 36 • (1.7%) Latticed Shadow Boots ***or*** Gauntlets • (1.7%) Runic Ember ***or*** Twisted Darksteel Bracer
icy skeleton [25] (no loot)
icy wisp [28,30-33] (no loot)
isalf abider [30], blinder [35], hierarch [38], icemage [33], scryer [33], snowtracker [35], surveyor [32-33], warrior [35-36] (no loot)
Jakr [23] (no loot)
Kodi [51] (no loot)
miserable zombie [28-32] (no loot)
Moira the Quiet [44] (no loot)
Ngadra [47] (no loot)
nip mephit [23-25] (no loot)
nordic yeti [33-36] (8%) Thick White Pelt
Norna [34] (no loot)
northern ettin [25-27], northern light [26-28,30] (no loot)
shard golem [42] (70%) Ice Shard
shivering presence [32-33] (no loot)
Sir Charles [30] (no loot)
Sjor [46] (18%) Frosty Leg • (2%) Chiller Head • (10%) Jewels 36
sleigh horse [30] (no loot)
Snofrid [35] (no loot)
snow giant [30,33], snow imp [20-22] (no loot)
snowshoe bandit [30] (8%) Malefic Tooth
Soulsong [43] (no loot)
taiga cat [32-33] (no loot)
thawing corpse [31] (no loot)
torpor worm [37] (no loot)
twister [29] (no loot)
Ulfgar [44] (no loot)
undead soldier [26] (no loot)
Valfanar [30] (no loot)
white wolf [(27)28-29/30-31] (18%) White/Large White Wolf Pelt • (2%) Snowy/Pristine White Wolf Pelt [no loot on level 27]
winter wolf [43/44] (18%) Winter/Large Winter Wolf Pelt • (2%) Perfect White/Pristine Winter Wolf Pelt • (8%) Malefic Tooth
wintery dirge [(40)41-42] (70%) Frozen Teardrop [no loot on level 40]
wyvern [36-37] (8%) Malefic Tooth
young wyvern [28-30] (no loot)

Battleground

Topographic Map for All Three Zones

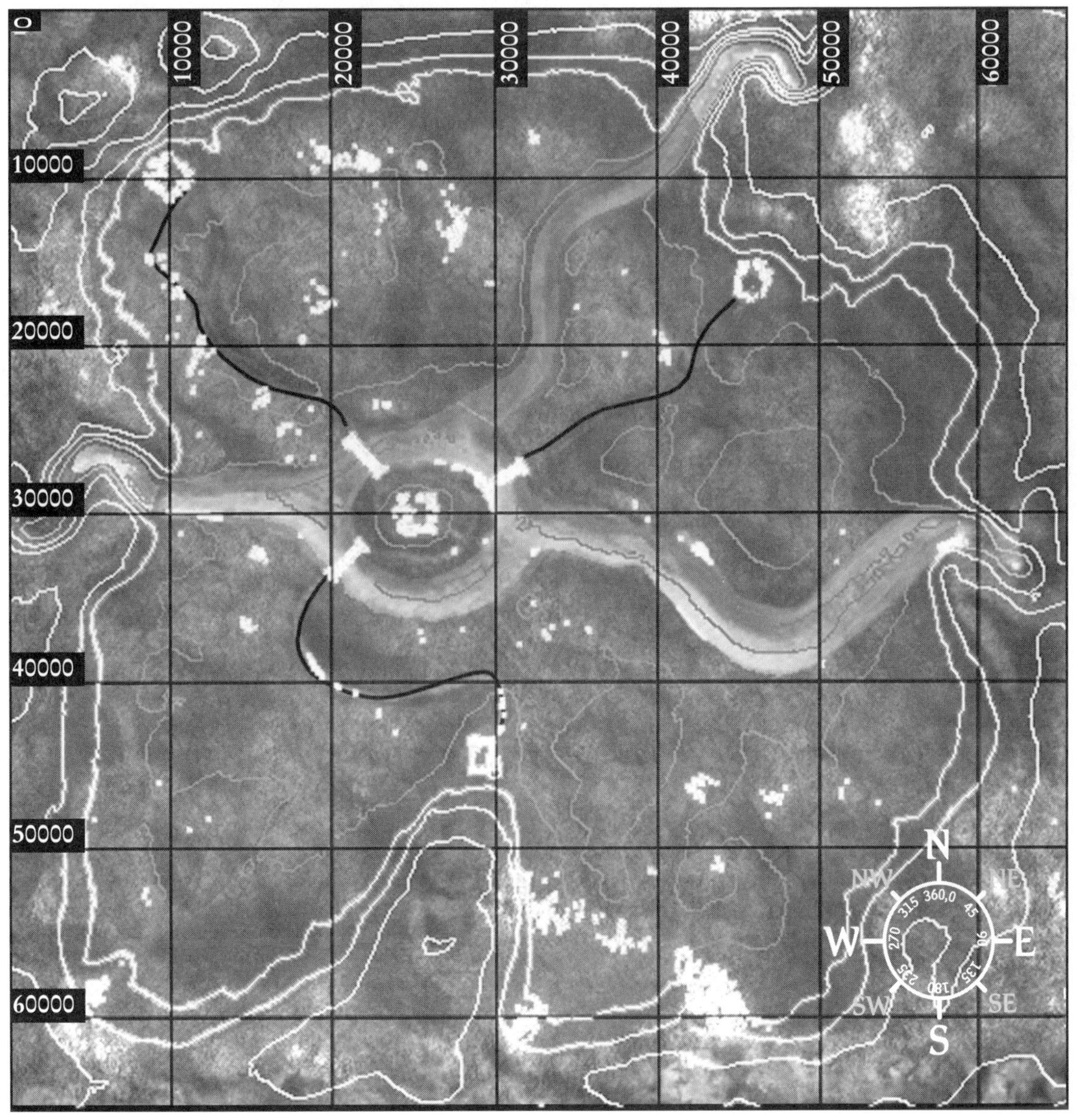

Thidranki (max level 24)

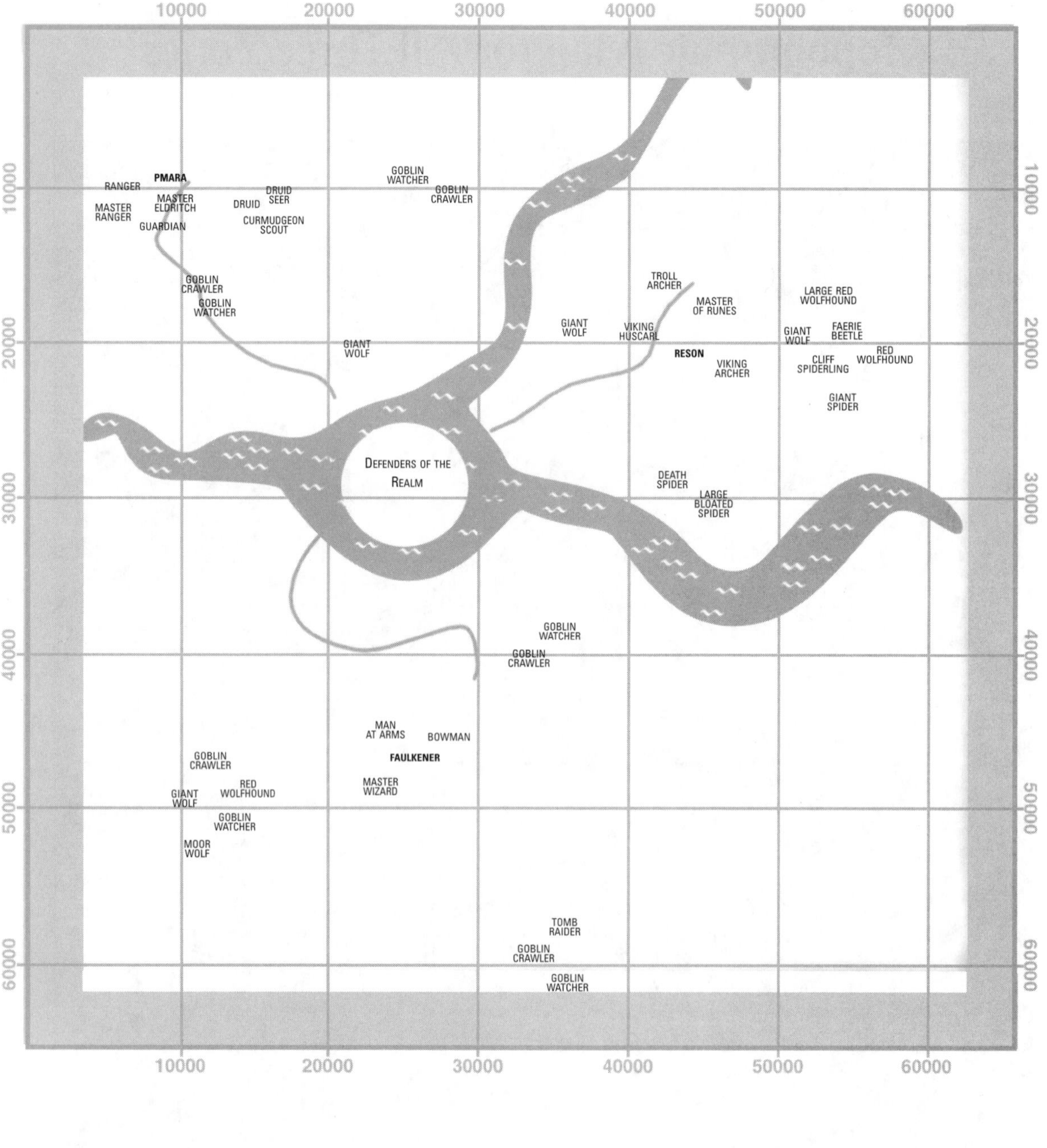

10000 20000 30000 40000 50000 60000

RANGER
PMARA
MASTER RANGER
MASTER ELDRITCH
GUARDIAN
DRUID
DRUID SEER
CURMUDGEON SCOUT
GOBLIN WATCHER
GOBLIN CRAWLER
GOBLIN CRAWLER
GOBLIN WATCHER
GIANT WOLF
TROLL ARCHER
MASTER OF RUNES
GIANT WOLF
VIKING HUSCARL
RESON
VIKING ARCHER
LARGE RED WOLFHOUND
GIANT WOLF
FAERIE BEETLE
RED WOLFHOUND
CLIFF SPIDERLING
GIANT SPIDER
DEFENDERS OF THE REALM
DEATH SPIDER
LARGE BLOATED SPIDER
GOBLIN WATCHER
GOBLIN CRAWLER
MAN AT ARMS
BOWMAN
FAULKENER
MASTER WIZARD
GOBLIN CRAWLER
GIANT WOLF
RED WOLFHOUND
GOBLIN WATCHER
MOOR WOLF
TOMB RAIDER
GOBLIN CRAWLER
GOBLIN WATCHER

Murdaigean (max level 29)

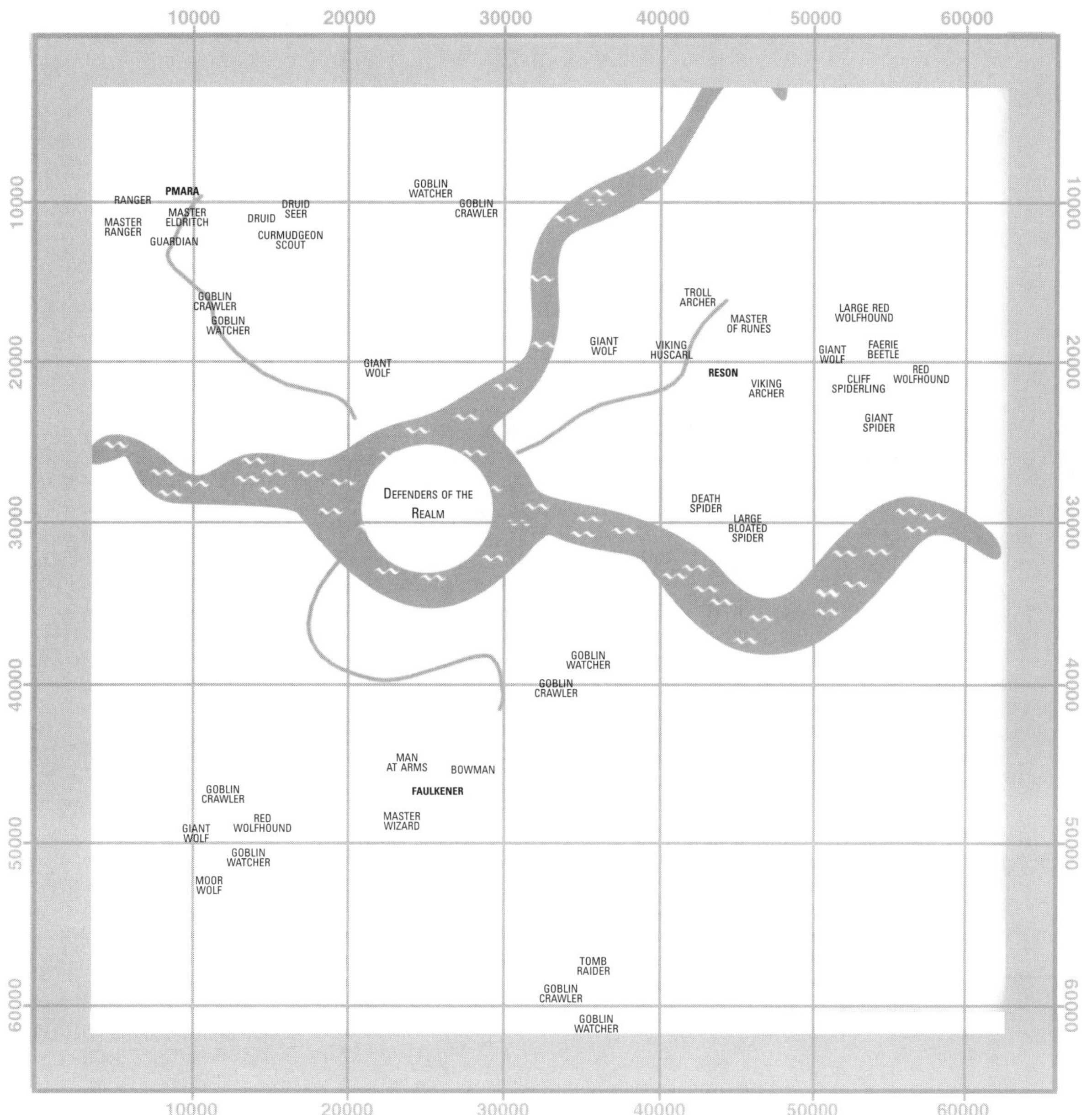
10000
20000
30000
40000
50000
60000
RANGER
PMARA
MASTER RANGER
MASTER ELDRITCH
GUARDIAN
DRUID
DRUID SEER
CURMUDGEON SCOUT
GOBLIN WATCHER
GOBLIN CRAWLER
GOBLIN CRAWLER
GOBLIN WATCHER
GIANT WOLF
TROLL ARCHER
MASTER OF RUNES
GIANT WOLF
VIKING HUSCARL
RESON
VIKING ARCHER
LARGE RED WOLFHOUND
GIANT WOLF
FAERIE BEETLE
RED WOLFHOUND
CLIFF SPIDERLING
GIANT SPIDER
DEFENDERS OF THE REALM
DEATH SPIDER
LARGE BLOATED SPIDER
GOBLIN WATCHER
GOBLIN CRAWLER
MAN AT ARMS
BOWMAN
FAULKENER
MASTER WIZARD
GOBLIN CRAWLER
RED WOLFHOUND
GIANT WOLF
GOBLIN WATCHER
MOOR WOLF
TOMB RAIDER
GOBLIN CRAWLER
GOBLIN WATCHER

Caledonia (max level 35)

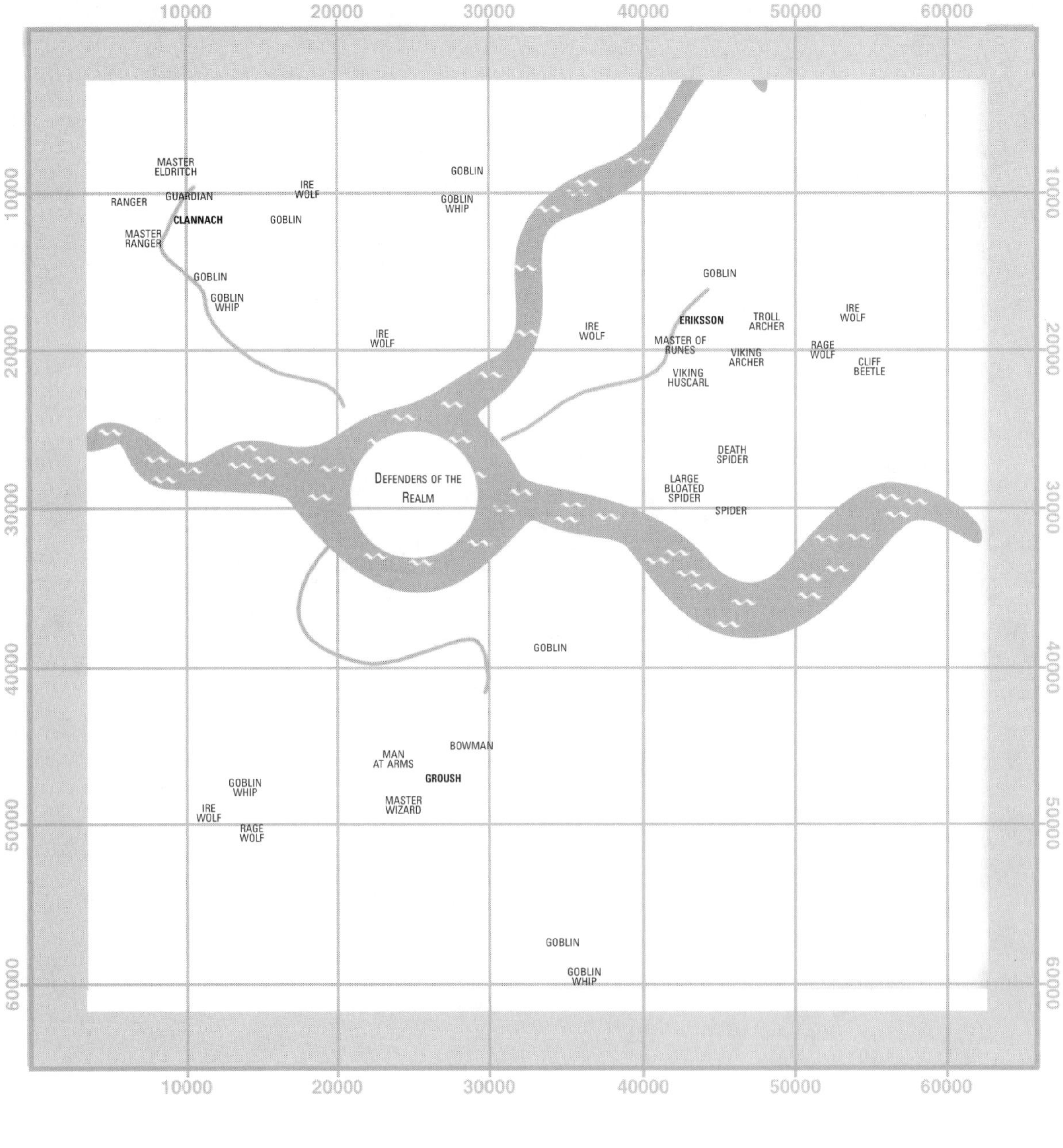

10000 20000 30000 40000 50000 60000

MASTER ELDRITCH
RANGER
GUARDIAN
CLANNACH
MASTER RANGER
IRE WOLF
GOBLIN
GOBLIN
GOBLIN WHIP
GOBLIN
GOBLIN WHIP
IRE WOLF
GOBLIN
IRE WOLF
ERIKSSON
TROLL ARCHER
IRE WOLF
MASTER OF RUNES
VIKING ARCHER
RAGE WOLF
CLIFF BEETLE
VIKING HUSCARL
DEATH SPIDER
DEFENDERS OF THE REALM
LARGE BLOATED SPIDER
SPIDER
GOBLIN
BOWMAN
MAN AT ARMS
GROUSH
GOBLIN WHIP
MASTER WIZARD
IRE WOLF
RAGE WOLF
GOBLIN
GOBLIN WHIP

Thidranki Loot

Baron Protector [35] (no loot)
Baron Stoddard [1] (no loot)
Baron Thidranki [1] (no loot)
Bowman [24,45,90] (no loot)
Champion [27,40] (no loot)
Champion Commander [50] (no loot)
Chieftain Marzhin [33] (no loot)
cliff spiderling [14] (no loot)
curmudgeon scout [15-17] (no loot)
death spider [18] (no loot)
druid [18-19] (no loot)
druid seer [20] (no loot)
faerie beetle [17] (no loot)
Faulkener [8] (no loot)
Gatekeeper [1] (no loot)
giant spider [6-8] (no loot)
giant wolf [15-16] (no loot)
goblin crawler [23-24] (no loot)
goblin watcher [20-22] [one (level 20) has this; the rest have no loot] (8%) <Miner Midden> • (8%) Jewels 33 • (1.5%) APOA: Fire-Forged • (1.5%) <Tepok Treasures 1> • (1.5%) <Tepok Treasures 2>
Guardian [24,45,90] (no loot)
Jarl Gunnulf [33] (no loot)
Knight Commander [27,40,50] (no loot)
Lady Bromley [33] (no loot)
large bloated spider [13-14] (no loot)
large red wolfhound [17] (no loot)
Lord Weathers [50] (no loot)
Man at Arms [24,45,90] (no loot)
Master Eldritch [95] (no loot)
Master of Runes [95] (no loot)
Master Ranger [95] (no loot)
Master Wizard [95] (no loot)
moor wolf [14] (no loot)
Pmara [35] (no loot)
Ranger [24,45,90] (no loot)
red wolfhound [10-13] (no loot)
Reson [41] (no loot)
Stoddard Archer [35] (no loot)
Stoddard Warder [40] (no loot)
tomb raider [16-17] (no loot)
Troll Archer [90] (no loot)
Viking Archer [24,45,90] (no loot)
Viking Huscarl [24,45,90] (no loot)
Viking Jarl [27,40,50] (no loot)

Murdaigean Loot

Baron Murdaigean [1] (no loot)
Baron Protector [35] (no loot)
Baron Stoddard [1] (no loot)
Bowman [30,45,90] (no loot)
Champion [33,40] (no loot)
Champion Commander [50] (no loot)
Chieftain Sgoith-Gleigeil [40] (no loot)
corpse crawler [22-23] (no loot)
death spider [18] (no loot)
Gatekeeper [1] (no loot)
goblin [25-26,29] (no loot)
goblin crawler [23-24] (no loot)
goblin watcher [20-22] (no loot)
Guardian [30,45,90] (no loot)
ire wolf [25-27] (no loot)
Jarl Kollsvein [40] (no loot)
Knight Commander [33,40,50] (no loot)
large bloated spider [13-14] (no loot)
Lord Halward [40] (no loot)
Lord Weathers [50] (no loot)
Man at Arms [30,45,90] (no loot)
Master Eldritch [95] (no loot)
Master of Runes [95] (no loot)
Master Ranger [95] (no loot)
Master Wizard [95] (no loot)
Neprac [41] (no loot)
rage wolf [31-32] (70%) Rage Wolf Fang (x2) • (70%) Rage Wolf Claw (x2) • (20%) Rage Wolf Pelt • (8%) Dangerous Tooth
Ranger [30,45,90] (no loot)
Sourg [8] (no loot)
spider [25-27] (no loot)
Stoddard Archer [35] (no loot)
Stoddard Warder [40] (no loot)
Teegra [35] (no loot)
Troll Archer [90] (no loot)
Viking Archer [30,45,95] (no loot)
Viking Huscarl [30,35,45,90] (no loot)
Viking Jarl [33,40,50] (no loot)
water badger [21] (no loot)

Caledonia Loot

Baron Protector [35] (no loot)
Baron Stoddard [1] (no loot)
black mauler [12-14] (41%) Mauler Skin • (4.5%) Pristine Mauler Skin • (72%) Mauler Claw (x2) • (1.5%) <Been Mauled>
dark hound [17-18] (60% each) Dark Hound Pelt, Ear • (60%) Chunk of Dark Hound Meat • (40%) Collar of Dark Mist
giant wolf [15-17] (75%) Giant Wolf Skin • (20%) Giant Wolf Fang
huge boar [18-19] (50% each) Huge Boar Hide, Huge Cloven Hoof • (20% each) Bloody Boar Tusk, Large Pig Tail • (15%) Huge Boar Tusk
lone wolf [20] (50%) Lone Wolf Fang (x2) • (23%) Lone Wolf Pelt • (2.5%) Pristine Lone Wolf Pelt • (1.5%) Long Animal Fang
savage lynx [15-16] (70%) Lynx Skin • Lynx Claw
spriggarn ambusher [15] (50%) Agate • (20%) Garnet • (2%) APOA: Tattered Hard Leather • (2%) APOA: Footman's Chain ***or*** Kite Shield • (0.3%) <Grave Goods> • (1.5%) Bushwack Mace ***or*** Heart Piercer
spriggarn howler [16] (40%) Agate • (10%) Garnet • (2%) APOA: Tattered Hard Leather ***or*** Shield • (2%) APOA: Footman's Chain ***or*** Shield • (0.3%) <Out of the Woods>
spriggarn waylayer [14] *see spriggarn ambusher [15]*
Welsh hobgoblin [17-19] (25% each) Bloody Hobgoblin Eyeball (x2), Severed Hobgoblin Toe (x2) • (1%) Mutilated Hobgoblin Hand • (0.3%) <Out of the Woods> • (1.5%) APOA: Bloodied Leather
Welsh hobgoblin chief [20] (30%) Bloody Hobgoblin Eyeball (x2) • (25%) Severed Hobgoblin Toe (x2) • (10%) Mutilated Hobgoblin Hand • (0.3%) <Out of the Woods> • (1.5%) APOA: Bloodied Leather

Darkness Falls Dungeon

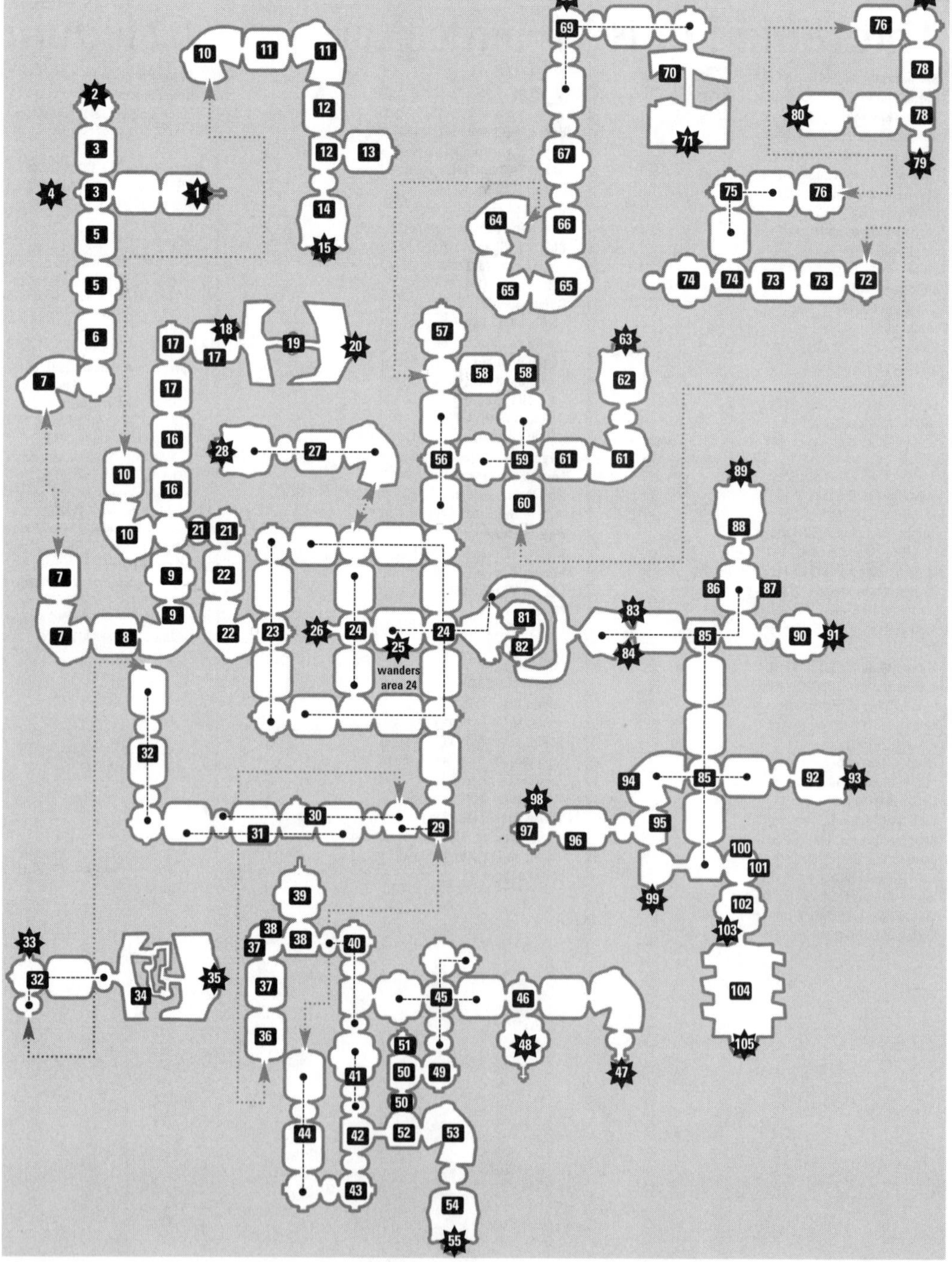

Key

1 Midgard Entrance (M)
2 Midgard Stores
3 Demoniac Familiar (rat)
4 Portal (P)
5 Plated Fiend
6 Apprentice Necyomancer, Plated Fiend
7 Demoniac Familar (scorpion), Soultorn, Avernal Quasit
8 Demoniac Familiar (boar), Young Necyomancer, Soultorn
9 Lilispawn, Demoniac Familiar (spider, scorpion)
10 Deamhaness, Demoniac Familiar (wolf)
11 Soultorn
12 Rocot
13 Experienced Necyomancer, Demoniac Familiar (cat, scorpion, boar)
14 Soultorn, Molochian Tempter
15 Lecherous Gress
16 Umbrood Warrior
17 Chthonic Knights
18 Commander Abgar, Lieutenant Persun
19 Chthonic Knights, Pale Guardian, Umbral Aegis, Chaosian, Umbrood Warrior, Essence Shredder (in pit), Earl Glassalab
20 Prince Abdin
21 Molochian Tempter, Naburite Drinker, Cursed Necyomancer
22 Cambion, Soultorn, Demoniac Familiar (scorpion, boar, wolf, lynx), Naburite Drinker, Cursed Necyomancer
23 Essence Shredder, Condemned Necyomancer, Tormented Necyomancer
24Mahr, Succubus, Nightmare, Chthonian Crawler
25 Director Kobil (wanders)
26 Portal (P)
27 Succubus, Nightmare
28 Princess Nahemah
29 Cambion
30 Mahr, Cursed Necyomancer, Condemned Necyomancer, Tormented Necyomancer
31 Essence Shredder
32 Mutilator
33 Portal (P)
34 Mutilator, Chaosian, Umbral Aegis, Pale Guardian, Earl Ipostian, Essence Shredder (in pit)
35 Prince Asmoien
36 Rocot
37 Apprentice Necyomancer, Demoniac Familiar (lynx, wolf, spider)
38 Soultorn, Demoniac Familiar (lynx)
39 Rocot
40 Avernal Quasit, Soultorn, Young Necyomancer
41 Young Necyomancer, Avernal Quasit, Demoniac Familiar (cat, scorpion, boar)
42 Necyomancer, Young Necyomancer, Soultorn
43 Experienced Necyomancer, Cursed Necyomancer, Molochian Tempter
44 Naburite Drinker
45 Apprentice Necyomancer, Demoniac Familiar, Plated Fiend, Soultorn
46 Demoniac Familiar (rat)
47 Hibernia Entrance (H)
48 Hibernia Stores
49 Lilispawn
50 Soultorn
51 Deamhaness, Necyomancer
52 Ricot
53 Experienced Necyomancer, Soultorn, Rocot
54 Molochian Tempter, Soultorn
55 Archivist Borath
56 Essence Shredder, Tormented Necyomancer, Condemned Necyomancer
57 Rocot, Deamhaness
58 Soultorn, Experienced Necyomancer, Demoniac Familiar (lynx), Rocot
59 Deamhaness, Lilispawn, Necyomancer, Soultorn
60 Lilispawn, Soultorn, Young Necyomancer
61 Rocot, Experienced Necyomancer, Soultorn
62 Molochian Tempter, Soultorn
63 Malroch the Cook
64 Cursed Necyomancer, Molochian Tempter
65 Cursed Necyomancer, Naburite Drinker, Soultorn, Demoniac Familiar (wolf, lynx)
66 Cursed Necyomancer, Condemned Necyomancer, Demoniac Familiar (lynx)
67 Tormented Necyomancer, Condemned Necyomancer, Essence Shredder, Cambion, Demoniac Familiar (spider, wolf, lynx)
68 Portal (P)
69 Inquisitors
70 Umbrood Warrior, Pale Guardian, Inquisitor, Earl Mermer, Chaosian, Essence Shredder (in pit), Umbral Aegis (in pit)
71 Prince Ba'alorien
72 Lilispawn, Soultorn, Young Necyomancer
73 Young Necyomancer, Plated Fiend, Deamhaness, Avernal Quasit, Demoniac Familiar (boar)
74 Avernal Quasit, Young Necyomancer, Demoniac Familiar (cat, scorpion), Soultorn
75 Plated Fiends, Apprentice Necyomancer, Demoniac Familiar (ant, cat)
76 Plated Fiend, Apprentice Necyomancer, Demoniac Familiar (ant)
77 Albion Stores
78 Demoniac Familiar (rat)
79 Portal (P)
80 Albion Entrance (A)
81 Center
82 Umbral Hulk
83 Gate Room
84 Gatekeeper Dommel
85 Umbral Aegis, Succubus, Inquisitors, Mutilators, Chthonic Knights, Chthonian Crawler, Nightmare
86 Duke Bimure
87 Marquis Scottiax
88 Duke Sallis, Marquis Sabonach, Earl Mercur
89 High Lord Oro
90 Marquis Focallaste, Duke Harboris, Earl Fenex
91 High Lord Baelerdoth
92 Duke Zepor, Marquis Almen, Earl Oraxus
93 High Lord Saeor
94 Duke Eligar
95 Marquis Dortaleon
96 Duke Aypol
97 Marquis Chaosmar, Duke Alloc, Earl Amagin
98 High Lord Baln
99 Portal
100 Duke Satori
101 Marquis Valupa
102 Chthonic Knights, Mutilators, Inquisitors, Earl Vone
103 Grand Chancellor Adremal
104 The Chamberlain, Pale Guardian, Chaosian, Marquis Haurian, Inquisitors, Mutilators, Chthonic Knights, Umbrood Warrior, Behemoth
105 Legion

Special Loot

Lecherous Gress [40] (30%) Lecherous Gress Skin

Gatekeeper Dommel [58] (60%) Dommel's Incendiary Seal ***or*** Fiery Gauntlets

Malroch the Cook [40] (30%) Malroch's Tenderizer, Cleaver ***or*** Flaying Knife

Archivist Borath [40] (30%) Book of Chaos

Director Kobil [50] Kobil's Fiery Seal ***or*** Fiery Gauntlets

High Lord Loot (99%) Dommel's Incendiary Seal ***or*** Fiery Gauntlets • (99%) Kobil's Fiery Seal ***or*** Fiery Gauntlets

High Lord Saeor [77] [A/H/M] *High Lord Loot, plus* • (99%) Saeor's Sword, Fiery Hammer ***or*** Impaler [A]/ Saeor's Fiery Sword, Rod of Balefire ***or*** Sleeves of Balefire [H]/ Saeor's Fiery Sword, Barbed Hammer ***or*** Serrated Cleaver [M]

High Lord Baelerdoth [77] [A/H/M] *High Lord Loot, plus* • (99%) Vambraces, Rod/Hammer/Rod of the Soulshade ***or*** Stiletto/Dagger/Sword of the Soulshade

High Lord Oro [77] [A/H/M] *High Lord Loot, plus* • (99%) Oro's Helm of Fiery Might, Sleeves of Balefire [A,M]/Stiletto of Night [H] ***or*** Shield of the Forsaken

High Lord Baln [77] [A/H/M] *High Lord Loot, plus* • (99%) Baln's Mephitic Bludgeoner, Sulfuric Slicer, ***or*** [Fuliginous Crusher ***or*** Fiery Chest Splitter]/Black Diamond Rapier/Cleaver

Princess Nahemah [71] [A/H/M] (5%) Dommel's Incendiary Seal ***or*** Fiery Gauntlets • (5%) Kobil's Fiery Seal ***or*** Fiery Gauntlets • Princess Nahemah [A/H/M] Special Loot: (80%) Gauntlets/Sleeves/Gauntlets of Nightfire, Fuliginous Tiara ***or*** Smoldering Ember

Prince Loot [A] (99%) Saeor's Sword, Fiery Hammer ***or*** Impaler • (99%) Vambraces, Rod ***or*** Stiletto of the Soulshade • (99%) Oro's Helm of Fiery Might, Sleeves of Balefire ***or*** Shield of the Forsaken • (99%) Baln's Mephitic Bludgeoner, Sulfuric Slicer, Fuliginous Crusher ***or*** Fiery Chest Splitter

Prince Loot [H] (99%) Saeor's Fiery Sword, Rod of Balefire ***or*** Sleeves of Balefire • (99%) Vambraces, Hammer ***or*** Dagger of Soulshade • (99%) Oro's Helm of Fiery Might, Stiletto of Night ***or*** Shield of the Forsaken • (99%) Baln's Mephitic Bludgeoner, Sulfuric Slicer ***or*** Black Diamond Rapier

Prince Loot [M] (99%) Saeor's Fiery Sword, Barbed Hammer ***or*** Serrated Cleaver • (99%) Vambraces, Rod ***or*** Sword of the Soulshade • (99%) Oro's Helm of Fiery Might, Sleeves of Balefire ***or*** Shield of the Forsaken • (99%) Baln's Mephitic Bludgeoner, Sulfuric Slicer ***or*** Fuliginous Cleaver

Prince Abdin [78] [A] *Prince Loot [A], plus Abdin [A] Special Loot:* (99%) Twisted Evil Emerald Scepter, Wretched Skin Robe ***or*** Ring of Malice

Prince Abdin [78] [H] *Prince Loot [H], plus Abdin [H] Special Loot:* (99%) Twisted Evil Emerald Scepter, Daemon Fire-forged Bow ***or*** Spear of Malice

Prince Abdin [78] [M] *Prince Loot [M], plus Abdin [M] Special Loot:* (99%) Twisted Evil Emerald Scepter, Daemon Fire-forged Bow ***or*** Smoldering Ruby Spear

Prince Asmoien [78] [A]*Prince Loot [A], plus Asmoien [A] Special Loot:* (99%) Twisted Evil Sapphire Scepter, Daemon Fire Ring ***or*** Necklace, ***or*** Daemon Fire-forged Bow

Prince Asmoien [78] [H] *Prince Loot [H], plus Asmoien [H] Special Loot:* (99%) Twisted Evil Sapphire Scepter, Black Sapphire Ring ***or*** Sapphire of the Dread Glow

Prince Asmoien [78] [M] *Prince Loot [M], plus Asmoien [M] Special Loot:* (99%) Twisted Evil Sapphire Scepter, ***or*** Daemon Fire Ring ***or*** Jewel

Prince Ba'alorien [78] [A/H/M] *Prince Loot [A/H/M], plus Ba'alorien [A/H/M] Special Loot:* (99%) Twisted Evil Ruby Scepter, Soul-forged Bracer ***or*** Belt/Cloak/Cloak of Barbed Scales

Grand Chancellor Adremal [79] [A] *Abdin, Asmoien, Ba'alorien and Nahemah [A] Special Loot, plus* • (99%) Twisted Evil Diamond Scepter, Black Sapphire Bracer, Sapphire of the Dread Glow, ***or*** Adremel's Avernal Hammer ***or*** Impaler

Grand Chancellor Adremal [79] [H] *Abdin, Asmoien, Ba'alorien and Nahemah [H] Special Loot, plus* • (99%) Twisted Evil Diamond Scepter, Twisted Dark Jeweled Scepter, Adremel's Daemon Fire Spear, ***or*** Black Sapphire Bracer ***or*** Belt

Grand Chancellor Adremal [79] [M] *Abdin, Asmoien, Ba'alorien and Nahemah [M] Special Loot, plus* • (99%) Twisted Evil Diamond Scepter, Black Sapphire Bracer ***or*** Belt of the Dread Glow

Legion [83] [A]*Abdin, Asmoien, Ba'alorien and Nahemah [A] Special Loot, plus* • (99%) Breastplate of Forlorn Souls, Hauberk of the Wretched, Vest of the Vile Dominion, Ancient Daemon Jerkin ***or*** Robes of the Diabolic • (99%) Ring ***or*** Bracer of Dire Omen, Ensorcelled Blade of Power, Flute of Balefire, Towering Avernal Defender ***or*** Legion's Soul Splitter • (99%) Twisted Evil Diamond Scepter, Black Sapphire Bracer, Sapphire of the Dread Glow, ***or*** Adremel's Avernal Hammer ***or*** Impaler (x2)

Legion [83] [H] *Abdin, Asmoien, Ba'alorien and Nahemah [H] Special Loot, plus* • (99%) Hauberk of Forlorn Souls ***or*** the Wretched, Vest of the Vile Dominion ***or*** Hateful Deceit, Ancient Daemon Jerkin ***or*** Robes of the Diabolic • (99%) Ring ***or*** Bracer of Dire Omen, Legion's Soul Crusher, Ensorcelled Blade of Power, Flute of Balefire, Towering Avernal Defender ***or*** Fiery Revenger • (99%) Twisted Evil Diamond Scepter, Twisted Dark Jeweled Scepter, Adremel's Daemon Fire Spear, ***or*** Black Sapphire Bracer ***or*** Belt (x2)

Legion [83] [M] *Abdin, Asmoien, Ba'alorien and Nahemah [M] Special Loot, plus* • (99%) Hauberk of Forlorn Souls ***or*** the Wretched, Vest of the Vile Dominion, Ancient Daemon Jerkin ***or*** Vest of the Diabolic • (99%) Ring ***or*** Bracer of Dire Omen, Ensorcelled Blade of Power, Axe of Balefire, Dreaded Soul Splitter ***or*** Legion's Soul Crusher • (99%) Twisted Evil Diamond Scepter, Black Sapphire Bracer ***or*** Belt of the Dread Glow (x2)

Beliathan [A/H/M] *see Legion [] [A/H/M]*

Abdin's Fury [65] (no loot)
Abdin's Rage [65] (no loot)
Aindreas [40] (no loot)
aleax of Albion [99] (no loot)
aleax of Hibernia [99] (no loot)
aleax of Midgard [99] (no loot)
Ambassador Mannam [65] (48%) Daemon Diamond Seal (x4)
angelic visage [99] (no loot)
Anwar [40] (no loot)
Aodh [40] (no loot)
Archived Souls [40] (no loot)
Archivist Borath [40] Fiery Emerald Seal (3 chances: 40%, 20%, 10%)
Asmoien's Wrath [50] (no loot)
avernal quasit [32] (12%) Shimmering Stone Daemon Emerald Seal (x3)
avernal quasit [33] (40%) Daemon Emerald Seal (x2) • (15%) Daemon Emerald Seal (x2)
avernal quasit [34] (16%) Shimmering Sapphire Daemon Emerald Seal (x4)
Ba'alorien's Wrath [50,61] (no loot)
Baln Fanatic [99] (no loot)
Beelo [36] (no loot)
Behemoth [99] (no loot)
Beliathan [99] * (10%) Arrows of Slaying • (30%) Wormskin Wrap (x3) • (98%) Seal of the Master Daemon (X10)
Blathnaid [40] (no loot)
Bolo [36] (no loot)
Breeda [40] (no loot)
Brother Ethelbald [50] (no loot)
Brother Maynard [27] (no loot)
cambion [52-53] (20%) Am Daemon Sapphire Seal (x5)
cambion [54] (20%) Flawless Daemon Sapphire Seal (x5)
Captain Alphin [50] (no loot)
Chamberlain [79] (50%) Fiery Diamond Seal (x8)
chaosian [55] (20%) Daemon Sapphire Seal (x5)
chthonian crawler [60] (32%) Daemon Diamond Seal (x3)
CHTHONIC KNIGHTS
Exte, Ibeko, Obarus [60], Aciel, Ain, Babyzu [62] (32%) Daemon Diamond Seal (x3)
Carnivon,Prosel, Zafan [64], Ezpeth, Ronoro, Ukobat [66], Exal, Marbos, Zaeber [68] (48%) Daemon Diamond Seal (x4)
Absax, Azea, Zagal [70], Gaapoler, Haag, Vosoes [72], Fonath, Olov, Tamuel [74] (64%) Daemon Diamond Seal (x5)
clinging soul [42] (no loot)
Commander Abgar [69] (64%) Daemon Diamond Seal (x5)
Cordelia [40] (no loot)
Damhnait [40] (no loot)
Dane [50] (no loot)
Dano [36] (no loot)
Darbo [36] (no loot)
Daro [36] (no loot)
deamhaness [32] (16%) Shimmering Stone Daemon Emerald Seal (x3)
deamhaness [33] (40%) Daemon Emerald Seal (x2) • (15%) Daemon Emerald Seal (x2)
deamhaness [34] (16%) Shimmering Am Daemon Emerald Seal (x4)
Debo [36] (no loot)
DEMONIAC FAMILIARS
rat, ant [15,18] (no loot)
cat, scorpion, boar, spider [21,24,27,30] (some have no loot) (16%) Daemon Emerald Seal (x2)
dog [33] (some have no loot) (16%) Daemon Emerald Seal (x4)
lynx [36] (some have no loot) (16%) Daemon Emerald Seal (x5)
Director Kobil [50] * (50%) Fiery Sapphire Seal (x4)
DUKES Alloc, Aypol, Bimure, Eligar, Harboris, Sallis, Satori, Zepor [75] (64%) Daemon Diamond Seal (x5)
EARLS Fenex,Glassalab, Ipostian, Mercur, Mermer, Oraxus, Vone [71] (64%) Daemon Diamond Seal (x5)
Ebo [36] (no loot)
Empo [36] (no loot)
escaping souls [99] (no loot)
essence shredder [54-55] (20%) Daemon Sapphire Seal (x5)
essence shredder [56] (20%) Stone Daemon Sapphire Seal (x5)
Etain [40] (no loot)
Etho [36] (no loot)
Field Marshal Nebir [70] (64%) Daemon Diamond Seal (x5)
Flannery [40] (no loot)
Frode [50] (no loot)
Galn [50] (no loot)
Gatekeeper Dommel [58] * (50%) Fiery Sapphire Seal (x4)
Glum [50] (no loot)
Godo [36] (no loot)
Grand Chancellor Adremal [79] * (50%) Fiery Diamond Seal (x8)
Haaken [50] (no loot)
HIGH LORDS * Oro [65] (35%) Fiery Diamond Seal (x3)
Baelerdoth, Baln, Oro, Saeor [77] (50%) Fiery Diamond Seal (x5)
Hopeless Soul [50] (no loot)
Horto [36] (no loot)
Hreidar [50] (no loot)
Hulo [36] (no loot)
Iago [36] (no loot)
INQUISITORS
Irawn, Lokis, Medebo [60], Hellos, Morg, Morrian [62] (32%) Daemon Diamond Seal (x3)
Hadis, Mucifen, Nifil [64], Asil, Eciraum, Niloc [66] Haimir, Nej, Yor [68] (48%) Daemon Diamond Seal (x4)
Bor, Factol, Tlaw [70], Haap, Zaviben, Zazinol [72], Famuel, Kireasil, Yonzael [74] (64%) Daemon Diamond Seal (x5)
Ionhar [35] (no loot)
Iono [36] (no loot)
Kalbin [20] (no loot)
Kiernan [40] (no loot)
Kodo [36] (no loot)
Kulo [36] (no loot)
Labhras [40] (no loot)
Lady Winchell [50] (no loot)
Lecherous Gress [40] * Fiery Emerald Seal (3 chances: 40%, 20%, 10%)
Legion [83] * (99%) Seal of the Master Daemon (x10)
Legion's Will [0] (no loot)
Leif [50] (no loot)
Lieutenant Rydderac [50] (no loot)
LIEUTENANTS
Gargantan, Loran, Persun [68] (48%) Daemon Diamond Seal (x4)
lilispawn [29-30] (16%) Glowing Diamond Daemon Emerald Seal (x2)
lilispawn [31] (16%) Shimmering Daemon Emerald Seal (x3)
Lord Prydwen [50] (no loot)
lost soul [99] (no loot)
Lucifo [36] (no loot)
Luighseach [40] (no loot)
Lulo [36] (no loot)
Magus Aldred [25] (no loot)
Magus Cormac [50] (no loot)
Magus Isen [50] (no loot)
mahr [55] (20%) Daemon Sapphire Seal (x5)
Malroch the Cook [40] * Fiery Emerald Seal (3 chances: 40%, 20%, 10%)
Marbo [36] (no loot)
MARQUISES Almen, Chaosmar, Dortaleon, Focalleste, Haurian, Sabonach, Scottiax, Valupa [73] (64%) Daemon Diamond Seal (x5)
Master Arenis [50] (no loot)
Master Dubri [50] (no loot)
Master Edric [50] (no loot)
Master Grundelth [50] (no loot)
Master Odon [50] (no loot)
Master Stearn [25] (no loot)
Master Torr [25] (no loot)
Meppo [36] (no loot)
Mistress Welss [50] (no loot)
molochian tempter [40-41] (12%) Stone Daemon Sapphire Seal (x3) [some have no loot]
molochian tempter [45] (12%) Sapphire Daemon Sapphire Seal (x3)
MUTILATORS
Axtanax, Okabi, Zurabo [60], Laicanroth, Nianax, Uxybab [62] (32%) Daemon Diamond Seal (x3)
Lazorous, Novinrac, Xakanos [64], Oronor, Phaxazis, Taboku [66], Axalnam, Marbozer, Xaabaro [68] (48%) Daemon Diamond Seal (x4)
Axa'al, Xagalith, Xazbalor [70], Vorazax, Vozoaz, Yooginroth [72], Konapher, Oprionach, Samiol [74] (64%) Daemon Diamond Seal (x5)
naburite drinker [47] (16%) Polished Daemon Sapphire Seal (x4)
naburite drinker [49] (16%) Daemon Sapphire Seal (x4)
naburite drinker [51] (20%) Stone Daemon Sapphire Seal (x5)
NECYOMANCERS
apprentice necyomancer [18] (no loot)
apprentice necyomancer [21] (18%) Daemon Emerald Seal (x2)
young necyomancer [24,27] (18%) Daemon Emerald Seal (x2)
necyomancer [30] (18%) Daemon Emerald Seal (x2)
necyomancer [33] (20%) Daemon Emerald Seal (x3) ***or*** (16%) Daemon Emerald Seal (x4)
experienced necyomancer [36,39] (18%) Daemon Emerald Seal (x5)
cursed necyomancer [42] (15%) Daemon Sapphire Seal (x3)
cursed necyomancer [45] (16%) Daemon Sapphire Seal (x4)
condemned necyomancer [48] (16%) Daemon Sapphire Seal (x4)
tormented necyomancer [50] (16%) Daemon Sapphire Seal (x4)
Neno [36] (no loot)
nightmare [61] (32%) Daemon Diamond Seal (x3)
Olo [36] (no loot)
Orto [36] (no loot)
pale guardian [72] (64%) Daemon Diamond Seal (x5)
Pico [36] (no loot)
plated fiend [25-27] (16%) Daemon Emerald Seal (x2)
PRINCES *
Abdin, Asmoien, Ba'alorien [78] (50%) Fiery Diamond Seal (x5)
Princess Nahemah [71] * (50%) Fiery Diamond Seal (x5)
Ragna [50] (no loot)
Rana [50] (no loot)
Riofach [40] (no loot)
rocot [36-37] (16%) Glowing Uncut Daemon Emerald Seal (x5)
rocot [38] (16%) Daemon Emerald Seal (x5)
Signa [43] (no loot)
Sile [40] (no loot)
Singrid [50] (no loot)
Sister Gwendolyn [25] (no loot)
Skapi [40] (no loot)
SOULTORN
hibernian wayfarer [25], hibernian savant [28] (16%) Glowing Daemon Emerald Seal (x2)
albion protector [25], norse vakten [25], albion guardian [28], norse skiltvakten [28], albion warder [30], norse isen vakten [30] (16%) Daemon Emerald Seal (x2)
hibernian cosantoir [30] (16%) Shimmering Daemon Emerald Seal (x2)
hibernian brehon [33] (16%) Shimmering Daemon Emerald Seal (x4)
albion myrmidon [33], norse flammen vakten [33], albion gryphon knight [35], norse elding vakten [35] (16%) Daemon Emerald Seal (x4)
hibernian grove protecter [35] (16%) Shimmering Sapphire Daemon Emerald Seal (x4)
hibernian raven ardent [38] (16%) Glowing Duskwood Daemon Emerald Seal (x5)
norse stormur vakten [38] (16%) Shimmering Daemon Emerald Seal (x5)
albion eagle knight [38] (16%) Daemon Emerald Seal (x5)
albion phoenix knight [40], albion alerion knight [43] (12%) Daemon Sapphire Seal (x3)
hibernian silver hand [40], norse isen herra [40], norse flammen herra [43] (12%) Shimmering Daemon Sapphire Seal (x3)
hibernian thunderer [43] (12%) Shimmering Stone Daemon Sapphire Seal (x3)
albion unicorn knight [45], albion lion knight [48], albion dragon knight [50] (16%) Daemon Sapphire Seal (x4)
hibernian tiarna [48] (16%) Glowing Crystalized Daemon Sapphire Seal (x4)
norse elding herra [45], norse einherjar [50] (16%) Glowing Daemon Sapphire Seal (x4)
hibernian gilded spear [45] (16%) Shimmering Am Daemon Sapphire Seal (x4)
norse stormur herra [48] (16%) Shimmering Daemon Sapphire Seal (x4)
succubus [57] (32%) Daemon Diamond Seal (x3)
Suno [36] (no loot)
Thago [36] (no loot)
The Dark [50] (no loot)
The Faction Maker [35] (no loot)
Thordia [60] (no loot)
Torrance [40] (no loot)
Tosti [40] (no loot)
Tulo [36] (no loot)
Ulo [36] (no loot)
umbral aegis [63] (32%) Daemon Diamond Seal (x3)
umbral hulk [65] (48%) Daemon Diamond Seal (x4)
umbrood warrior [59] (32%) Daemon Diamond Seal (x3) (some have no loot)
Uvo [36] (no loot)
Wovo [36] (no loot)
Yojo [36] (no loot)

** All monsters with an asterisk also have **Special Loot**, listed on page 251.*

Appendix A: Caches & Jewels

Loot Notes

There's a *lot* of loot in this game, and a lot of the time, there are a wide variety of items that a monster *might* drop. The loot lists for each zone note everything each monster might drop; a few abbreviations along the way helped make sure that all the lists would fit. Here are a few examples of what we say in the lists, and what we mean by it.

Level(s)

After each monster's name in a loot list is the level (or levels) that can be found.

[12] The monster only appears at level 12 in the zone.

[12-14] The monster appears at level 12, 13 and 14. All three levels use the same loot list.

[12,14] The monster appears at level 12 and 14, but not 13. Both levels 12 and 14 use the same loot list.

[12/14] The monster appears at level 12 and 14, but the loot lists for level 12 are slightly different from the loot lists for level 14. In the loot list, each time a percentage or item appears before a slash, that percentage or item applies to the level 12 monster. Each percentage or item that appears after a slash applies to the level 14 monster.

[12-13/14] The monster appears at levels 12, 13 and 14. Levels 12 and 13 use one loot list, while the loot list for level 14 is slightly different.

[12-13/14,16/18-20] The monster appears at levels 12, 13, 14, 16, 18, 19 and 20. There are three slightly different loot lists — everything before the first slash applies to levels 12 and 13. Everything between the two slashes applies to levels 14 and 16. Everything after the second slash applies to levels 18, 19 and 20.

[12-13(14)] The monster appears at levels 12, 13 and 14, but the level 14 monster doesn't have any loot. The loot list only applies to levels 12 and 13.

Occasionally, the loot lists for a single type of monster at two different levels are not similar enough to combine. In that case, the two loot lists are in separate paragraphs; be careful you find the right list when checking on a monster that can appear at multiple levels in the zone.

Percentages

In most cases, there is a chance, but not a certainty, that a monster will drop something. The percentage in parentheses before an item gives the percentage chance that that item will be dropped.

(25%) Agate There's a 25 percent chance that the monster will drop an Agate.

(25%) Agate *or* Carnelian There's a 25% chance that the monster will drop either an Agate or a Carnelian. That is, a percentage check is made. If the result is less than 25%, the monster will drop a jewel. A second check is made to see whether the jewel dropped is an Agate or is a Carnelian.

(25% each) Agate, Carnelian There is a 25% chance that an Agate will drop, and another 25% chance that a Carnelian will drop. If a separate check is made for each item, the word **each** appears next to the percentage. If the percentage applies to the entire list, so that only one item from the list will be dropped if the percentage check is successful, the word ***or*** appears in the list.

(25/30%) Agate or Carnelian This loot list is actually the combination of two similar loot lists. The first percentage (25%) is the chance that the item (an Agate or a Carnelian) will be found on the first loot list (for a lower-level monster). The second percentage (30%) is the chance that one of the jewels will be found on the higher-level version of the monster.

(25/30/35%) Agate or Carnelian Just as the previous entry was the combination of two loot lists, this is the combination of three loot lists, for a monster found at three different levels in the zone.

(25%) Agate *or* Ruby/Carnelian *or* Malachite. This time, it isn't the percentages that vary, it's the item itself. The lower-level monster has a 25% chance of dropping an Agate or a Ruby. The higher-level monster has a 25% chance of dropping a Carnelian or a Malachite.

(25%; hi-lo) Agate, Ruby *or* Carnelian In general, if the percentage check is successful, there are even odds as to which item is randomly selected from the list. However, in several cases, some items are likelier to be picked than others. This is indicated by hi-lo (meaning high to low chances). In this case, assuming the first percentage check is successful and one of the three jewels will be dropped, an Agate is the most likely jewel to drop. A Carnelian is the least likely jewel to drop.

Other Abbreviations

There are a few other abbreviations used in the loot lists.

(25%) Agate (x2) There are two 25% checks made. If either one is successful, the monster drops an Agate. If *both* are successful, it drops *two* Agates.

(25%) APOA: Footman's Chain APOA stands for "a piece of armor." In this case, the loot list gives a 25% chance that the monster will drop a single piece of Footman's Chain armor — helm, hauberk, sleeves, gauntlets, legs ***or*** boots.

see horse [10] The loot list for this monster is identical to the loot list for the horse. (These cross-references never send you to another zone.)

Colors This always refers to a combination of cloth dyes, leather dyes and enamels. For instance, **Turquoise, Royal Teal *or* Purple Colors** is a much shorter way of saying that you might find one of: Turquoise Cloth Dye, Turquoise Leather Dye, Turquoise Enamel, Royal Teal Cloth Dye, Royal Teal Leather Dye, Royal Teal Enamel, Purple Cloth Dye, Purple Leather Dye, or Purple Enamel.

Combinations and Complications

You may have already noticed that not all loot lists are as simple as the examples given above. Let's look at some of the combinations that occur.

(15%) Magmas Imbued Helm *or* Gloves, *or* Helm *or* Gloves of Opposition
If this check is successful, the monster will drop one (and only one) of the following four items: Magmas Imbued Helm, Magmas Imbued Gloves, Helm of Opposition, or Gloves of Opposition.

(1.7%) Stonecrush Leggings *or* Helm/Vest *or* Boots/Arms *or* Gauntlets
This is the combination of three loot lists. For each loot list, there's a 1.7% chance that *one* of the items will drop. For the lower-level monster, the item will be either Stonecrush Leggings or Stonecrush Helm. For the mid-level monster, it'll be Stonecrush Vest or Stonecrush Boots. For the higher-level monster, it'll be Stonecrush Arms or Stonecrush Gauntlets.

(1.5%) APOA: Loyalist Scalemail, *or* Jewel Spiked, Rigid *or* Dusted This means there is a 1.5% chance to find a single piece of armor: either a piece of Loyalist Scalemail armor, Jewel Spiked armor, Jeweled Rigid armor, or Jewel Dusted armor.

(2%; hi-lo) Gloves/Leggings/Boots of the Stoneharvest, Fiery Pious Bludgeoner *or* Polished Granite Pin [51]/Rift Sealer *or* Feather Light Granite Hammer [53]/Polished Hammer of Eldspar *or* Polished Granite Pin [55]
This is the combination of three loot lists, for a monster found at level 51, 53 and 55. In each case, there's a 2% chance that *one* of these items will drop. In each case, the items listed first are more likely than the items listed last (indicated by the **hi-lo**).
At level 51, the monster might drop Gloves of the Stoneharvest, Fiery Pious Bludgeoner ***or*** Polished Granite Pin.
At level 53, the monster might drop Leggings of the Stoneharvest, Rift Sealer ***or*** Feather Light Granite Hammer.
At level 55, the monster might drop Boots of the Stoneharvest, Polished Hammer of Eldspar ***or*** Polished Granite Pin.

<Caches>

For many monsters, there is a very small chance that one of several items will drop. Rather than repeat every one of those items for every monster (which would have made the lists too small to read or too long to fit in this book), we've abbreviated the lists by giving each one a name, and then listed all of the caches, alphabetically by name, in this appendix (just below the explanation you're reading right now). A cache is always indicated by the "<" and ">" at each end of its name; when you find those brackets, you'll find the cache in the list below. For a more detailed description, see **Caches and Jewels**, on the next page.

Caches and Jewels

The loot lists for the monsters in each zone include the following caches. For example, King Vian, in Treibh Caillte (p. 202), has a 1.5% chance of dropping an item from the <Aganar's Arms> cache (the first cache listed) — a Caustic Slicer, *or* a Ceremonial Black Dirk, *or* a Darkened Battle Shield, etc. (Note that a monster will never drop more than one item from any particular cache.) All caches are listed here alphabetically. (Some are found in more than one realm, so they aren't divided by realm.) The number in parentheses following the cache name shows how many different types of monsters in different zones might drop an item from that cache.

Jewels. After the general caches, the jewel caches are listed. They are numbered, not named (e.g., Jewels 02, Jewels 54), and are listed in numerical order. (The numerical order follows the alphabetical order of the most likely jewels in each cache.)

(hi-lo). The jewels in each jewel cache are listed in descending order of likelihood that they will drop. For example, if you get a jewel from Jewels 01, you're most likely to get an Agate. Azurite is next most likely, followed by Garnet, Topaz and (least likely) Citrine.

Caches

Agnar's Arms (7) Caustic Slicer, Ceremonial Black Dirk, Darkened Battle Shield, Ursine Great Recurve Bow & Finely Crafted Ursine, *or* Mentalist, Enchanter *or* Eldritch Staff of Magic

All Fired Up (22) Rager's Axe, Svart-alfar Forged Sword, Serrated Bone Spear, Hammer of the Wildcrusher, pitted Hardened Stone Axe, Hearthwood Branch, Shadowformed Ring, Lightbound Ring, Svart-alfar Battlebracer, *or* Trollish Stone Bracer

Alvis's Chest (2) Werewolf Paws, Wolf Fur Leggings, Wolf Skull Helm, Scapula Bone Axe *or* Fur Edged Cloak

Ancient Wisdom (5) Elder's Staff of the Voided Land, of Thought, of the Mind, of Mana, of Light; Elder's Pearl Strand, *or* Jewel of Intensity

... And Carry a Big Stick (4) Big Shillelagh, Rock Sword *or* Dagger, Hollow Root, Eldritch, Mentalist *or* Enchanter Stone Staff, Round Slate Shield, *or* Cracked Stone Mace

Angry Dwarf (5) Ring of Hatred, Bracer of Malevolence, Pulsing Jewel of Anger, Tomte Necklace of Agitation, *or* Dwarf-skin Cloak

Arcane Artifacts (3) Book of Arcane Dealings, Siabrian Arcane Methods, Ring of Delightful Deception, Ring of Enchanting Emanations, Necklace of Combat, Necklace of the Arcane, Bracer of Zo'arkat, Belt of Resilience, *or* Void Formed Ring

Arch-Mage Artifacts (1) Staff of the Arch-Eldritch, Arch-Mentalist *or* Arch-Enchanter, Ruby Weave Robes, *or* Belt of Arcane Power

Arctic Articles (9) (hi-lo) Glowing Crystal, Dirty Gold Lined Belt, Glowing Crystal Dust, Gold Veined Rock,Ttrue Silver Nugget, *or* True Silver Chisel

Arthurian Artifacts 1 (12) Bowmasters Bracer, Corpsecleaver, Cythrian Baldric, Shadow-slicer, Magus Battlestaff, Lion Faced Shield, Gauntlets of Celerity, Shadowhunter's Vest, Spellhurler's Vest, *or* Breastplate of the Depths

Arthurian Artifacts 2 (7) Bowmasters Bracer, Corpsecleaver, Cythrian Baldric, Shadow-slicer, Magus Battlestaff, Lion Faced Shield, Gauntlets of Celerity, Shadow-slinkers Blade, Sleeves of Deflection, *or* Prismatic Jewel

Arthurian Artifacts 3 (4) (hi-lo) Bowmasters Bracer, Silver Oak Longbow, Majestical Ring, Singed Fellwood Shield, Shadow-slicer, *or* Sphene

Arthurian Artifacts 4 (5) (hi-lo) Magus Battlestaff, Deathrune Robes,Bowmasters Bracer, Corpsecleaver, Cythrian Baldric, Shadow-slicer, Lion Faced Shield, *or* Gauntlets of Celerity

Ashes to Ashes (3) Ash Stained Boots *or* Jerkin, Cinder Stained Vest, Cinder Encrusted Spear, Ashmonger Eye Earring, *or* Lavastone Ring *or* Collar

Asterite Attic (11) Great Asterite Shod Staff, Slender Asterite Wizard, Theurgist, Cabalist *or* Sorcerer Staff, *or* Fine Asterite Lute, Flute *or* Drum

Bear Hide (2) Kobold Bone Ring, Bear-hide Bracer, Bear-hide Belt, *or* Bear-totem Necklace

Been Mauled (3) Mauler Claw Sleeves, Gloves, Boots *or* Axe, *or* Sangsbrottsjo Shield

Beetle's Shell (5) Hollow Chitin, Singed Hollow Chitin, Band of Chitin, *or* Facetted Insect Eye

Bio 101: Dissection (3) Chitinous Worm Round, Slimy Chitinous Worm Round, Clouded White Eye, *or* Slimy Clouded White Eye

Blod Flekket Bounty (3) (hi-lo) Blod Flekket Sleeves, Berolig, *or* Blod Flekket Hammer

Blodjeger Gear (2) Blodjeger Hammer, Bracer, Leggings *or* Gloves, *or* Bow of the Blodjeger

Blood and Ice (7) (hi-lo) Sturdy Tomte Belt, Frigid Tundra Wine, Pulsing Red Orb, Book on Nifleheim, *or* Crown of Bone

Blue Fire Gear (1) Azure Swathe Cutter, Fine Steel Long Sword, Azure Soul Quencher, Bloodfire Battle Spear, Great Shadowed Impaler, *or* Runed Asgardian Vest

Bogged Down (7) Glowing Vial of Swamp Water, Vial of Brackish Water, Vial of Fetid Bog Water, *or* Giant Black Sapphire Ring

Bogman's Bundle (4) Alluvion Club *or* Great Hammer, Sinister Alluvion Club, *or* Rubigo Round Shield

Bone Up On Your Loot (24) Bone Ring, Bone Necklace, Bone Studded Belt, Bone Studded Bracer, *or* Molded Cloak

Braided Beauties (54) Ivy Ring *or* Quartz Ring, Banded Reed *or* Woven Grass Bracer, Braided Silver Necklace, Sparrow Pendant, Resilient Oak Shield, Wavy Piercer, Granite Longsword, *or* Thorny Club

Brendig's Gear (46) Brendig's Belt, Silverleaf Bow, Spiritist Amulet, Fiery Jewel, Golden Swathcutter, War Rager's Axe, Hammer of Atonement, Blazing Hauberk, Blazing Gauntlets, *or* Wolfhead Totem Staff

Carved from Coral (1) Shaped Watery Staff, Twisted Coral Staff, Deluged Carved Staff, Water Opal Staff, *or* Imperial Staff of the Depths

Celtic Knots (17) Hollowed Fingerbone Ring, Mystical Metal Band, Sturdy Leather Belt, Heart of Oak, Sturdy Woven Vest, Leggings of the Deft, Imbued Sleeves, Well-balanced Celtic Spear *or* Great Sword, *or* Spine-breaker

Celtic Wonders (10) Carved Keltoi Bow, Heraldic Keltoi Shield, Dark Embossed Crossbow, Keen Dark Gladius, Dark Lucerne Hammer, Dark Sheer Great Sword, *or* Wizard, Sorcerer, Cabalist *or* Theurgist Staff of the Imposter

Craftsman Pendants (14) (hi-lo) Apprentice Craftsman Pendant, Neophyte Craftsman Pendant, Journeyman Craftsman Pendant, Adept Craftsman Pendant, *or* Master Craftsman Pendant

Crystal Clear (5) (hi-lo) Small Crystal Chest, Gold Flecked Water Crystal, Crystal Serpent Figureine, *or* Crystal Shell Sea Crown

Crystal Visions (10) Focus Stone, Headband of Focus, Staff of Winds, Shield of Uln, Helm of Vision, Robe of Chance, Gornax Bracers, Harping Pin, ***or*** Pitted Parrying Falchion

Cuisinart (7) Corpsecleaver, Shadow-slicer, Lion Faced Shield, Golden Oak Bow, Battlesword of Command, Staff of the Blazing Inferno, Gauntlets of Celerity, Spiderweave Leggings ***or*** Jerkin, ***or*** Windbound Cloak

Danaoin Delights (2) (hi-lo) Danaoin Bladeblocker, Blessed Planter's Necklace, ***or*** Jewel of Elemental Biding

Dark Knight Wear (14) Cloak of the Blackheart, Ghastly Ring of Bone, Necklace of the Dark Soul, ***or*** Bracer of Shaved Bone

Darkling's Delight (6) Incandescent Black Jewel, Bear-skin Mantle, Bear-Shaman's Ring, Troll-skin Bracer, ***or*** Dwarf-skin Belt

De'velyn's Delights (25) De'velyn's Fine Robes, Sturdy Woven Cap, Vest of Dislocation, Imbued Leggings, Smoldering Scale Sleeves, Void Rifter, Mind Rifter, Dweomer Rifter, Cruanach Crusher, ***or*** Deathly Vindicator

Death's Delight (6) (hi-lo) Viper-hide Belt, Bear Tooth Ring, Jeweled Bear Skull, Viper-Hide Pouch, ***or*** Runic Hardened Hide

Death's Door (14) Bracer of Shaved Bone, Belt of Deathly Might, Jewel of Insight into Undeath, Ring of Forgotten Arcane Words, ***or*** Necklace of Glowing Ebony

Den Dressings (3) Bear-tooth necklace, Shrunken Bear Skull, Grizzly Skin Cloak, Ancient Bear Shaped Ring, ***or*** Skin-flayer's Bracer

Drako's Droppings (6) Branded Keltoi Shield, Dark Mace, Dark Spine-breaker, Dark Short Sword, Keltoi Honed Halberd, Dark Scimitar, Keltoi Defender, ***or*** Dark Shod Staff

Ebony and Ivory (19) Crackling Ebony Sunderer, Wizardly, Theurgist, Cabalist ***or*** Sorcerer Slender Ebony Staff, Lute of Haunting Melody, Flute of Dementia ***or*** Drum of Fading Valor

Edgeless Armaments (14) Dull Asterite Axe, Large Axe, Hammer, Large Hammer, Sword, Great Sword, Spear, Runed Staff, ***or*** Spirit Staff

Ellyll's Enchantments (11) Mantle of the Champion, Etheric Ring, Ring of Sturdy Warding, Woven Reed Bracelet, Bracelet of the Arctic, Runic Troll-hide Belt

Ellyll's Lair (9) Gladius of the Battlelord, Ellyll Round Shield, Rapier, Sword ***or*** Hammer, Defender's Crossbow, ***or*** Radiant Moonclipper

Engraved Enchantments (32) Etched ***or*** Embossed Crystal Bracer, Changeling Skin Belt, Crystal-threaded Necklace, Sturdy Woven Pants, Sleeves of Might, Imbued Gloves, ***or*** Eldritch, Mentalist ***or*** Enchanter Staff of Channeling

Fathoms Below (8) Water Opal Ring, Polished Coral Ring, Banded Coral Bracer, Opal Studded Bracer, Deepscale Belt, ***or*** Fathomless Coral Wrap

Fiery Ants (4) Ant Skull Helm, Mandible Headed Axe, Bow of Flames, ***or*** Flaming Shield

Filled with Radiance (11) Razor Edged Asterite Falcata, Etched Drum, Runic Recurve Bow, ***or*** Balanced Asterite Mace, Hammer, Dirk ***or*** Shield (Round, Kite ***or*** Tower)

Fire and Ice (14) Frosted Silverblade, Shadow Crystal Slicer, Mace ***or*** Rapier, Fire Heatstone Stalagmite, Small Heatstone Protector, Earthen Protector, Tower of the Mind Fortress, Drum of the Hollow Heart ***or*** Shadow Walkers Great Bow

Fire and Rain (4) Charred Skull Hammer, Scorched Bone Shield, Razor-Edged Leg Bone, Charred Rib Cage Shield, ***or*** Charred Bone Shield

Flash of Wonders (5) Mantle of Unseelie Skill, Heatstone Band, Twisted Truesilver Ring, Crystal Flecked Belt, ***or*** Shadow Crystal Orb

Flecks O' Gold (9) (hi-lo) Gold Flecked Shell Necklace, Gold Flecked Shell Armband, Bound Coral Signet Ring, ***or*** Gold Flecked Shell Horn

Forged in the Cauldron (2) Flame Charred Boots ***or*** Sleeves, Fire Charred Leggings, Jerkin, Gloves ***or*** Mask, Fiery Sword, ***or*** Flame Wrought Bracer

Freedon's Gift (16) Worn Asterite Blade, Main Gauche, Hammer ***or*** Shield (Round, Kite ***or*** Tower), ***or*** Shod Bow

Freya's Doom (17) Twilight Battle Crasher, Cleaver, Soul Searer, Impaler, Doombringer ***or*** Blade-stopper, Runic Ember, ***or*** Frozen Soul-shatterer

Freya's Dowry (35) Sleeves of the Dauntless, Boots of the Frenzied Bear, Gauntlets of Stormrage, Note-spun Tunic, Gloves of Precision, Skadi's Blessed Huntsman's Bow, Rune Embroidered Tunic, Cap of the Wisened Dead, Eir Blessed Tunic, ***or*** Primordial Skull Helm

Frigg's Gift (11) Keen Asterite Blade ***or*** Main Gauche, Light Asterite Hammer, ***or*** Fine Asterite Shield (Round, Kite ***or*** Tower) ***or*** Shod Bow

From Mjoes Depths (1) Runed Orm Bone Staff, Carved Orm Bone Staff, ***or*** Death Whisper

From the Caldera (3) Fire Petal Sleeves, Vest ***or*** Leggings, Fire Flower Stalk, ***or*** Crystalized Fire Flower Pin

Full Moon Wear (15) Lunatic Lupine Cloak, Werewolf Bone Ring, Wolfskin Belt, Lycanthrope's Necklace, Flayed Wolfskin Bracer, ***or*** Wulf Gem

Gaudy Jewelry (3) Gaudy Silver Ring, Gaudy Silver-lined Bracer, Bauble Studded Belt, Summoned Jewel, Gaudy Thin Necklace, ***or*** Ceremonial Cloak

Gaudy *or* Gorgeous (2) Richly Designed Round ***or*** Kite Shield, Richly Designed Broadsword, Spiked Club, Rapier, Short Spear ***or*** Sword, Adorned Recurve Bow, Gaudy Void Caster's Staff, Gaudy Enchantment Staff, ***or*** Gaudy Staff of Mentalism

Geirrod's Arms (3) (hi-lo) Sludge Covered Mace, Virulent Darkened Spear, Darkened Defender, ***or*** Caustic Slicer

Geirrod's Hoard (1) Keen Asterite Axe, Large Axe, Sword, Great Sword orSpear, Weighted Asterite Hammer, Large Hammer, Runed Staff ***or*** Spirit Staff, ***or*** Reinforced Chitin Shield

Geirrod's Wish (7) Ursine Battle Bracer, Bracer of Tracelessness, Ceremonial Robe, ***or*** Spider Silk Robe

Glimmer Gear (11) Light Asterite Mattock, Lucerne Hammer ***or*** Great Hammer, Broad Asterite War Axe, Keen Asterite Pike ***or*** Lochaber Axe, ***or*** Fine Asterite Shod Crossbow ***or*** Shod Short Bow

Glint of Brilliance (13) Gem Flecked Ring, Ring of the Mental Fortress, Gem Covered Belt, ***or*** Truesilver Laced Jewel

Glittering Goodies 1 (8) Coruscating Truesilver Blade, Mace, Dagger ***or*** Drum, Coruscating Spiked Club, Truesilver Round, Kite ***or*** Heater Shield, ***or*** Truesilver Recurve Bow

Glittering Goodies 2 (8) Coruscating Truesilver Sword, Hammer, Spear, Flute ***or*** Lute, Truesilver Staff of the Veil, Mind ***or*** Magic, ***or*** Truesilver Short Bow

Goblin' It Up (8) Goblin Mine Cloak, Goblinskin Belt ***or*** Bracer, Hob Hunter Gem

Goblin's Cellar (16) (hi-lo) Goblinskin Backpack, Pile of Glimmering Metallic Dust, Bottle of Fine Goblin Wine, ***or*** Golden Goblin Totem

Goblin's Forge (13) Goblin-forged Bracer of Speed ***or*** Gem of Resistance, ***or*** Hob Hunter Necklace ***or*** Ring

Gone Berzerk (5) Vendo Berzerker Axe, Flesh Reaver, Blade Blocker ***or*** Impaler, ***or*** Bone ***or*** Great Bone Heart-finder

Gone Fishin' (6) (hi-lo) Gold Embossed Ivory Fish, Jeweled Golden Fishing Hook, Jewel Filled Driftwood Box, History of Danaoa, ***or*** Silvery Shifting Orb

Granny's Basket (17) (hi-lo) Granny's Shawl, Ring of Protection, ***or*** Acid-Etched Bracer

Grave Goods (42) Drakescale Gauntlets, Ebony Staff, Ancient Body Shield, Ancient Battle Bracer, Battleworn Gladius, Wisp Heart Amulet, Shimmering Etheric Helm, Blade of Etheric Mist, Belt of Acuity, ***or*** Ancient Red Steel Hauberk

Great Balls O' Fire (33) Gold Stitched Boots ***or*** Gloves, Blazing Sleeves, Pillager's Boots, Ancient Engraved Maul, Small Warrior Figurine, Boar's Head Ring, Blackened Leather Jerkin, Huntsman's Jerkin, ***or*** Driftwood Staff

Greenman's Wares (2) Leaf-Embossed Gloves ***or*** Sleeves, Acorn Cap, Bark Edged Boots, Leaf Wrapped Staff, ***or*** Leaf Carved Staff

Grimnir's Adornment (22) (hi-lo) Huntsman's Cloak, Pillager's Vest, Icebound Bracer, Bracer of the Lost Soul, Pillager's Sleeves, Oiled Leather Leggings, Conditioned Leather Vest, Thickened Cloth Pants, Thickened Cloth Boots, ***or*** Valorbound Spear

Hand of Darkness (19) Ancient Ebony Mattock, Fiery Headsman's Axe, Solemn Destroyer, Grim Impaler, Hammer of the Yearning Soul, Halberd of the Covetous, ***or*** Crossbow ***or*** Short Bow of the Blackheart

Har's Adornments (25) Ring of the Quickening ***or*** of Surefooting, Necklace of Purification, Treecutter, Gleaming Axe, Khertik's Staff, Thickened Cloth Tunic, Fishgutter's Gloves, Old Smithy Hammer, ***or*** Brendig's Kneebiter

Heart of Darkness (20) Ancient Ebony Scimitar, Smoldering Sable Mace, Frozen Heart-piercer, Runed Bow of Ill Omen, Jet Bone Shield, Smoking Sable Protector ***or*** Crimson Blade-stopper

Hearts of the North (1) Ensorcelled Robes ***or*** Staff of Celerity, Ring of Arcane Gestures, Heart of the North, Archaic Assassin's Vest, ***or*** Cloth Cap

Heavy Handed (1) (hi-lo) Heavy Bastard Sword, Heavy Curved Dagger, Heavy Great Sword, ***or*** Thrall's Short Recurve Bow & Ursine Fletched Arrows

Hedge Clippers (8) Gold Coin, Hedge Chopper, Briar Club, Oaken Impaler, ***or*** Oaken Mallet

Hi Ho, Hi Ho, It's … (6) (hi-lo) Earth Digging Tool, Irewood Root, Special Trinket Pouch, Rock Cracking Tool, Small Well Crafted Lantern, ***or*** Dingy Mining Pick

Hot Goods (4) Giant Skull Helm, Singed Gloves, Smoldering Sleeves, Flaming Boots, Obsidian Hauberk, Ring of Fire, ***or*** Dancing Flame Necklace

Hot Stuff (3) Fiery Giant Bone, Inferno Sword, Blazing Giant Axe, ***or*** Smoldering, Scorched ***or*** Flaming Leggings

Howling at the Moon (6) Crazed Lupine Gloves, Hauberk ***or*** Coif, Dark Moon Lupine Sleeves, Howl of the Moon, Hammer of the Moon, Strength of the Wolf, ***or*** Wolf-Headed Hammer

Impenetrable Arms (4) Fathomless Great Sword, Great Hammer, Spear, Short Sword, Mace ***or*** Stiletto, Flute of Shaped Shells, Fathomless Lute, ***or*** Shaped Coral Drum

In a Spider's Web (3) Werewolf Tooth Necklace, Staff of Winter, Golden Oak Bow, Spiderweave Leggings, Spiderweave Jerkin, Staff of the Blazing Inferno, Windbound Cloak, Battlesword of Command, Band of Pious Might, ***or*** Belt of Arcane Protection

Inspired by a Curmudgeon (4) (hi-lo) Statue of the Angry Bear, Crown of Claws, Jewel Studded Bear Totem, ***or*** Runic Bear Mask

Into the Woods (48) Oiled Leather Boots, Wooden Band, Engraved Bracer, Kobold Forged Sword, Twisted Wood, Wood Choppers Axe, Bone Studded Jerkin, Red Crystal Eye, Thickened Cloth Sleeves, ***or*** Oiled Leather Belt

It's a Mad, Mad World (9) Ring of the Maddened, Bracer of the Paranoid, Belt of the Deranged, Jewel of Madness, Lavish Necklace, ***or*** Marvelous Cloak

It's Golden (10) Golden Mithrian Ring ***or*** Necklace, Gilded Golden Belt, Golden Bracer, ***or*** Regal Mithrian Cloak

Khertik's Wares (2) Wooden Band, Khertik's Staff, Huntsman's Cloak, Icebound Bracer ***or*** Bracer of the Lost Soul

King's Ransom (2) Ancient Oak Bow, Finely Crafted Crossbow, Scepter of Intellect, Lightfoot boots, Golden Inlaid Sword, Bounder Fur Mantle, Spear of the Legions, Skullcracker, ***or*** Jeweled Rapier

Last Stand Arms (4) Reincarnate Femur War Maul, Runic Manslayer, Carved Orm Fang Sword, Runed ***or*** Carved Orm Bone Staff, Black Orm Scaled Shield, Orm Skullcap Shield, ***or*** Death Whisper

Lordly Loot (12) Giant Garou Axe, Gnarling Lupine Axe, Gigantic Garou Sword, Varulvhamn Spear, Garou Great Hammer, Varulv Shield, ***or*** Varulv Staff of Darkness ***or*** Suppression

Lucky Charms (3) (hi-lo) Burnished Rabit's Foot, Glowing Cos-a-phooka, Humming Luminous Coin, Animate Four Leaf Clover, ***or*** Jewel of Captured Starlight

Luminescence (11) Razor Edged Asterite Sword, Runic Shillelagh, Balanced Asterite Spear, Void Walkers Staff, Mind Walkers Staff, Staff of the Underhill, Carved Flute, Embossed Lute ***or*** Runic Bow

Lusus Lootus (2) (hi-lo) Giant Lusus Eye, Giant Lusus Tooth, Giant Lusus Tail Spine, ***or*** Giant Lusus Egg

Lycanthropic Loot (5) Wild Wulf Cloak, Carved Bone Ring, Flayed Wolfskin Belt, Lycanthropic Necklace, Wolfskin Bracer, ***or*** Varulvhamn Gem

Magi Pendants (3) (hi-lo) Fledgling Magi Pendant, Apprentice Magi Pendant, Learned Magi Pendant, ***or*** Skillful Magi Pendant

Magi Pendants (Higher) (1) (hi-lo) Adroit Magi Pendant, Masterful Magi Pendant, Arch Magi Pendant, ***or*** Arch Magi Overlord Pendant

Magma Carta (9) Lava Forged Gloves ***or*** Leggings, Lava Etched Hauberk, Lava Scorched Hammer, ***or*** Burnt ***or*** Glowing Ember Shield

Mantles of Magic (20) Necklace of Glowing Ebony, Bracer of Dauntless Courage, Runic Belt of Arcane Might, Belt of Etheric Mist, Majestic Mantle of the Eternal, ***or*** Stone of Evil Emanations

Mementoes (2) (hi-lo) Scrap of a Doll's Golden Dress, Collection of Lost Mementos, ***or*** Eerily Lifelike Statuette

Merlin's Closet (16) Worn Asterite Shod Staff, Wizard, Theurgist, Cabalist ***or*** Sorcerer Staff, Lute, Flute ***or*** Drum

Military Pendants (4) (hi-lo) Footman Pendant, Infantryman Pendant, Captain Pendant, ***or*** Battlemaster Pendant

Mined from the Deep (8) Goblin Demolisher, Great Hammer, War Mattock, Lochaber Axe, Tower Shield, Excavator's Lute ***or*** Archer Crossbow, ***or*** Goblin Staff of Mind Twisting, Spirit Animation ***or*** Fire Magic

Miner Midden (9) (hi-lo) Miner's Golden Flask, Bottle of Goblin Wine, Golden Goblin Totem, ***or*** Miner's Gold Gambling Dice

Mists of Lyonesse (9) (hi-lo) Bent Golden Key, Small Crafted Chest, Ancient Banner, Jeweled Cloak Pin, ***or*** Bag of Netherium Dust

Mounds of Salisbury (6) Lightbringer, Stinging Gauche, Michaelian Staff, Ring of Inspiration, Velvet Lined Cloak, Ruby Encrusted Ring, spirit stone, ***or*** Hammer of the Plains

Muire's Riches 1 (10) Bloodstone Studded Falcata, Adorned Stiletto, Finely Crafted Spear, Gold Embossed Mace, Silver Rune Hammer, Great Silver Rune Bow, ***or*** Eldritch, Enchanter ***or*** Mentalist Staff of Grandeur, ***or*** Shield of the Decadent ***or*** Gold Embossed Shield

Muire's Riches 2 (53) Rough Hide Bracer, Beaded Silk Bracelet, Belt of Misdirection, Sturdy Woven Gloves, Boots of Agile Movement, Imbued Helm, Smoldering Scale Hauberk, pitted Fire Hardened Irewood Spear, Ancient Granite Mace, ***or*** Long Thorned Tree Knot

Muire's Riches 3 (39) Ring of Blades, Ring of Blunts, Mantle of Regalia, Sturdy Woven Boots, Helm of Shadow Melding, Imbued Vest, Smoldering Scale Leggings, Stoic Defender, Silver Blade, ***or*** Crystal Shard

New-Moon Wear (2) Moon-struck Lupine Sleeves, New Moon Lupine Sleeves, Crazed Lupine Boots ***or*** Legs, Wolfpaw Sword, ***or*** Wolf's Fang

Nisse's Nest Egg 1 (11) Carved Hollow Bone Ring, Runed Hollow Bone Bracer, Blood Stained Bead Necklace, Wretched Cloak, ***or*** Shrunken Jeweled Skull

Nisse's Nest Egg 2 (11) Brittle-bone Bow, Trident, Great Axe, War Axe, Great Sword, Bastard Sword, Round Shield ***or*** Tower Shield, ***or*** Rigid Runed ***or*** Embossed Spine

No Such Thing as the Bogeyman (4) Eagle Talon Amulet, Horse Mane Bracelet, Goblin Skin Tunic, Bogeyman Crystalized Eye, ***or*** Goat Fur Leggings

Nobody's Perfect (10) (all flawed) Asterite Sword ***or*** Spear, Runic Shillelagh ***or*** Bow, Void ***or*** Mind Walkers Staff, Staff of the Underhill, Carved Flute, ***or*** Embossed Lute

Norseman Cache (3) Huntsman's Cloak, Icebound Bracer, Bracer of the Lost Soul, ***or*** Thickened Cloth Pants ***or*** Boots

Ode to Yorik (2) Skull-bone Hammer, Axe, Shield ***or*** Spear, ***or*** Rune ***or*** Spirit Skull-bone Staff

Odin's Wish (10) Worked Stone Bracer, Etched Stone Bracer, Carved Red Spinel Ring, Carved Sphene Ring, Polished Fire Opal Necklace, ***or*** Well Crafted Work Belt

Of a Sylvan Glade (95) Forest Runners Boots, Elven Ring, Melodic Lute, Netherworld Bracelet, Gem Studded Dagger, Gem Studded Long Sword, Pilfered Jerkin, Hammer of Smiting, Ring of Longevity ***or*** Preserved Studded Vest

Ogre Skins (7) Thick Hide Belt ***or*** Bracer, garnet, ***or*** Ogre Forged Cutter, Impaler, Cleaver ***or*** Slicer

Older than Dirt (4) Dried Earth Bracer, Cracked Earth Bracer, Carved Sunstone Ring, Carved Crome Diopside Ring, Polished Stone Necklace, ***or*** Crusty Old Work Belt

Once Bitten … (5) Lupine Axe, Garou Sword ***or*** Defender, Growling Garou Warhammer, Feral Protector, Varulvhamn Bow, Varulv Staff of Runecarving ***or*** Spirit Magic

Only Just Begun (74) Bonecharm Amulet, Petrified Branch, Faithbound Ring, Bark Shield, Scaled Belt, Aged Leather Baldric, Farmers Gloves, Mildewed Sleeves, Fencer's Rapier ***or*** Supple Hide Jerkin

Out of the Sea (8) Cloak of the Oceanic Predator, Ageless Turquioise, Water Bound Gem, Gem of the Watery Depths, ***or*** Luminescent Water Opal

Out of the Woods (38) Golden Inlaid Sword, Ancient Oak Bow, Bounder Fur Mantle, Lightfoot boots, Scepter of Intellect, Spear of the Legions, Skullcracker, Jeweled Rapier, Robes of Battle, ***or*** Alloy Shod Staff

Pennine Prizes (3) Etheric Ring, Ring of Sturdy Warding, Shaped Bone Bracelet, Bracelet of Bonded Matter, Netherite Dusted Belt, ***or*** Jewel of Enticement

Pilfered Prizes (77) Signet Ring, Mildewed Tunic, Sureflight Arrows, Fey Jewelry, Faerie Charm Necklace, Pilfered Leather Leggings, Spined Fish-sticker, Raiders Blade, Great Iron Sword, ***or*** Cloak of the Old Defender

Quoth the Raven (4) (hi-lo) Symbol of Loyalty in Death, Jeweled Bone Comb, Stuffed Raven, Exquisite Wine Decanter, Essence of Madness, Advisor's Skull, ***or*** Bottle of Poisoned Wine

Razor-Sharp Armaments (14) Keen Asterite Spear, Axe ***or*** Large Axe, Weighted Asterite Hammer ***or*** Large Hammer, Keen Asterite Sword ***or*** Great Sword, Weighted Asterite Runed ***or*** Spirit Staff, ***or*** Reinforced Chitin Shield

Really Ghouled Loot (19) (hi-lo) Putrid Bone, Chunk of Rotting Flesh, Scroll of Death Rites, Withered Flower, ***or*** Gem Encrusted Broach

Rig's Lament (4) Wooden Band, Engraved Bracer, Twisted Wood ***or*** Red Crystal Eye

Rogue Pendants (Higher) (8) (hi-lo) Rogue Infiltrator Pendant, Rogue Captain Pendant, Master Rogue Pendant, Rogue Assassin Pendant, ***or*** Pendant of the Nightblade

Rogue Pendants (Highest) (14) (hi-lo) Master Rogue Pendant, Rogue Assassin Pendant, Rogue Assassin Pendant, Master Assassin Pendant, Rogue Overlord Pendant, Pendant of the Nightblade, Pendant of the Nightblade Overseer, ***or*** Nightblade Overlord Pendant

Rogue Pendants (Low) (5) (hi-lo) Rogue Petitioneer Pendant, Rogue Pendant, Rogue Infiltrator Pendant, ***or*** Rogue Captain Pendant

Rogue Pendants (Mid) (6) (hi-lo) Rogue Lord Pendant, Master Assassin Pendant, Rogue Overlord Pendant, Pendant of the Nightblade Overseer, ***or*** Nightblade Overlord Pendant

Rogue's Clothes (1) (hi-lo) Shadowhands Gloves ***or*** Cloak, Crypt Robbers Bracer, Singed Fellwood Shield, Majestical Ring, Salisbury Dagger, Giants Toothpick, ***or*** Silver Oak Longbow

Sacred Jewelry (6) Keltoi Forester's Ring, Insurgent's Ring, Bracer of Arms, Bracer of Magic, Necklace of the Pious, ***or*** Necklace of Brilliance

Salisbury Stock 1 (27) Crypt Robbers Bracer, Singed Fellwood Shield, Majestical Ring, Salisbury Dagger, Giants Toothpick, Silver Oak Longbow, Shadowhands Gloves ***or*** Cloak, Deathrune Robes, ***or*** Hauberk of the Valiant

Salisbury Stock 2 (9) Crypt Robbers Bracer, Singed Fellwood Shield, Majestical Ring, Salisbury Dagger, Giants Toothpick, Silver Oak Longbow, Shadowhands Gloves ***or*** Cloak, Deathrune Robes, ***or*** Ring of Insane Might

Salisbury Stock 4 (7) Staff of Melting, Cold Clay Idol, Wight-scarred Breastplate, Runed Elm Staff, Troll Bone Necklace, Rotting Robes, Resilient Sleeves, Resilient Gloves, ***or*** Skull of Aer'Ambor

Salvaged Goods (2) Fine Opal Pendant, Strung Shell Necklace, Watery Kelp Cloak, ***or*** Manta Skin Cloak

Seconds of the Best (10) (all flawed) Asterite Falcata, Mace, Hammer ***or*** Dirk, Round, Kite ***or*** Tower Shield, ***or*** Etched Drum ***or*** Runic Recurve Bow

Sepulchral Secrets (24) Worn Mithiran Bow, Ceremonial Scimitar, Ornamental Rapier, Old Sledge, Old Headsman's, Old Lucerne Hammer, Old Quarterstaff, Old Banded Shield, Old Staff of Elements, ***or*** Old Otherworldly Staff

Silverhand's Hoard (17) Crystal Flecked Belt, Shadow Crystal Orb, Bracer of the Silverhand, Bracer of the Triumvirate, ***or*** Cloak of the Silverhand

Skirnir's Gift (16) Shadowsteel Belt, Orb ***or*** Lattice, ***or*** Twisted Shadowsteel Lattice

Skirnir's Promise (10) Giant Femur Cracker, Worm Tipper, Rib Tickler, Earthen Defender, Worm Round Drum, Eldritch, Mentalist ***or*** Enchanter Etched Stone Staff, Earth Crafted Shield, ***or*** Spined Granite Mace

Smooth as Silk, Hard as Steel (6) (hi-lo) Silksteel Lattice, Horned Silksteel Ring, Twisted Silksteel Necklace, ***or*** Black Silksteel Cloak

Strange Threshholds (2) Mask of the Skogfru, Shield of the Forest Spirit, Spirit of the Wood Sleeves, ***or*** Skogfru Skin Bracer

Svipdag's Love (5) Forged Darksteel Pick Hammer, Spiked Axe, Bastard Sword, Kite Shield, Composite Bow, ***or*** Runic ***or*** Spirit Staff

Tanks for the Loot (16) Worn Asterite Mattock, Great Hammer, War Axe, Pike, Lucerne Hammer, Lochaber Axe, Shod Crossbow ***or*** Shod Short Bow

Teg's Hoard (6) Prey Seeker, Timber Walker's Slicer ***or*** Defender, Ivory Handled Stiletto ***or*** Rapier, ***or*** Barbed Elven Arrows

Tepok Treasures 1 (5) Goblin Reaver, War Hammer, Rapier, Defender, Excavator's Flute, Quarterstaff ***or*** Archer Short Bow, Goblin Staff of Matter ***or*** Body Magic, ***or*** Hob Hunter Hammer

Tepok Treasures 2 (5) Goblin-forged Ring of Health ***or*** Chain of Strength, ***or*** Hob Hunter Belt ***or*** Cloak

The Four Elements (25) Feverish Runner, Gilded Dark Bow, Petrified Wisened Oak Shield, Robes of Regalia, Smoldering Scale Gloves, Cloak of Concealment, Ring of Ice, Ring of Earth, Bracer of the Honored Warrior, Archer's Bracer

The Spy's Satchel (16) (hi-lo) Guide to Infiltration, Map Case, Map of Known Albion, ***or*** Small Silver Lined Chest

Thief's Nest Egg (43) Traitors Bane, Gold Stitched Tunic ***or*** Pants, Pillager's Gauntlets, Ring of the Stalwart Soul, Bracer of Valor, Necklace of Solid Darkness, Jewel of Augmentation, Blazing Boots, ***or*** Pitted Firesteel

Thrym's Dream (13) Goblin Cleaver, Crusher, Gauche, Protector, Excavator's Drum ***or*** Archer Long Bow, Goblin Staff of Cold, Earth ***or*** Wind Magic, ***or*** Fire-forged Pike

Thrym's Gift (14) Shadow Crystal Great Sword, Great Mace ***or*** Great Spear, Dark, Tali ***or*** Dweomer Shard of the Triumvirate, Flute of the Hollow Wind, Lute of the Hollow Soul, ***or*** Bow of the Silver Talon

Timeless Treasures (1) Fine Steel Long Sword, Bloodstained War Hammer, Virulent Soul Sapper, Robes of the Magus, Ageless Fluted Protector, ***or*** Timeless Indigo Mail

To Hang My Sporran (9) Jewel of the Prowler, Jewel of the Resilient, Resplendent Mantle, Keltoi Mantle of Insight, Wanderer's Belt, ***or*** Keltoi Belt of Agility

Tomte Treasures (10) (hi-lo) Tomte Key Ring, Vial of Caustic Liquid, Dingy Copper Bracer, Ivory Horn, ***or*** Bone Necklace

Treasures of the Fey (38) Twisted Silver Band, Sprite Ring, Fey Jewel, Melodic Flute, Sturdy Woven Sleeves, Gloves of Quickness, Imbued Boots, Crystal Bleeder, Jagged Bastard Sword, ***or*** Oaken Recurve Bow

Treasures of the Magi (1) Book of Arcane Dealings, Ring of Enchanting Emanations, Necklace of the Arcane, Belt of Resilience, ***or*** Void Formed Ring

Twinkling Treasures (4) Truesilver Laced Jewel, Encrusted Truesilver Necklace, Bracer of the Unseelie, Loyalist Observer's Bracer, ***or*** Mantle of Unseelie Skill

Vafprudnir's Adornment (2) Huntsman's Cloak, Pillager's Vest, Icebound Bracer, Bracer of the Lost Soul, Pillager's Sleeves, Oiled Leather Leggings, Conditioned Leather Vest, ***or*** Valorbound Spear

Valor's Heart (13) (hi-lo) Pearlescent Necklace, Medal of Valor ***or*** Stout Leather Belt

Vaulted Weaponry (10) Mithrian Longsword, Gladius, Mace, Great Hammer, Barbed Pike, Staff of Elements ***or*** Otherworldly Staff, Shield of the Abandoned, Staff of Forgotten Ways, ***or*** Ancient Mithrian Bow

Vind Kind (1) Vind Kalte Vest, Sleeves ***or*** Pants, ***or*** Vind Etset ***or*** Vind Pakket Staff

Voluspa Adornments (7) Ceremonial Belt, Retainers Signet Ring, Retainer's Ceremonial Ring, Jewel of Venern Swamp, ***or*** Seafarer's Death Shroud

Voluspa Gear (3) Longsword, Hammer, Shield, Spear, Rune Staff ***or*** Spirit Staff of the Indomitable

Water Rings (2) Water Stained Boots, Staff ***or*** Gloves, ***or*** Watery Ring

Wealth of an Empire (9) Imperial Sword, Hammer ***or*** Rapier of the Depths, Imperial Shield (Small, Kite ***or*** Great), Water-logged Short Bow, ***or*** Abandoned Recurve Bow

Werewolves of Midgard (20) (hi-lo) Bloodied Werewolf Paw, Werewolf Blood Wine, Chunk of Pure Silver, ***or*** Vial of Werewolf Blood

Wine Shine (6) (hi-lo) Gem Encrusted Bone Comb, Pewter Wine Decanter, Essence of Insanity, or Bottle of Envenomed Wine

Wolf Loot (3) Wolf Fur Sleeves, Boots ***or*** Jerkin, Engraved Wolf Blade, Wolf Bone Blade, ***or*** Wolf Engraved Shield

Wolfbeast Adornments (3) (hi-lo) Wolfbeast Claw, Wolfbeast Tooth, Wolfbeast Ear, ***or*** Large Wolfbeast Fang

Wolfbeast Gear (3) (hi-lo) Sullied Wolfbeast Pelt, Wolfbeast Pelt, ***or*** Fine Wolfbeast Pelt

Wood-Eaten Wonders (4) Ring of the Quickening, Ring of Surefooting, Necklace of Purification, Khertik's Staff ***or*** Wooden Band

Jewel Caches

Jewels 01 (hi-lo) agate, azurite, garnet, topaz, citrine

Jewels 02 (hi-lo) alexandrite, jacinth, chrysoberyl, black opal, black sapphire, violet diamond

Jewels 03 (hi-lo) amethyst, carnelian, lapis lazuli, agate, azurite

Jewels 04 (hi-lo) aquamarine beryl, alexandrite, black opal, black sapphire, violet diamond, green diamond

Jewels 05 (hi-lo) black opal, black sapphire, violet diamond, precious heliodor, blue diamond

Jewels 06 (hi-lo) black sapphire, violet diamond, precious heliodor, green diamond, emerald, blue diamond

Jewels 07 (hi-lo) black star diopside, sphene, cat's eye opal, cat's eye apatite, blue spinel

Jewels 08 (hi-lo) bloodstone, amethyst, carnelian, lapis lazuli, agate

Jewels 09 (hi-lo) bloodstone, carnelian, agate, garnet, citrine

Jewels 10 (hi-lo) carnelian, agate, garnet, citrine, malachite

Jewels 11 (hi-lo) carnelian, agate, garnet, citrine, malachite, green tourmaline

Jewels 12 (hi-lo) carnelian, lapis lazuli, agate, azurite

Jewels 13 (hi-lo) cat's eye apatite, water opal, peridot, kornerupine, alexandrite, jacinth, chrysoberyl, black opal, black sapphire

Jewels 14 (hi-lo) cat's eye apatite, blue spinel, water opal, rhodolite, peridot, yellow tourmaline

Jewels 15 (hi-lo) cat's eye apatite, blue spinel, water opal, rhodolite, peridot

Jewels 16 (hi-lo) cat's eye apatite, orange tourmaline, blue spinel, kunzite

Jewels 17 (hi-lo) cat's eye apatite, orange tourmaline, blue spinel, kunzite, water opal, green sapphire, rhodolite

Jewels 18 (hi-lo) cat's eye opal, cat's eye apatite, blue spinel, water opal

Jewels 19 (hi-lo) cat's eye opal, cat's eye apatite, blue spinel, water opal, rhodolite

Jewels 20 (hi-lo) cat's eye tourmaline, cat's eye opal, zircon, cat's eye apatite

Jewels 21 (hi-lo) chrome diopside, sphene, cat's eye apatite, water opal, peridot

Jewels 22 (hi-lo) chryoprase, amethyst, lapis lazuli, azurite, topaz

Jewels 23 (hi-lo) chryoprase, bloodstone, amethyst, carnelian

Jewels 24 (hi-lo) chryoprase, bloodstone, amethyst, carnelian, lapis lazuli

Jewels 25 (hi-lo) fire opal, green tourmaline, sunstone, chrome diopside, jasper

Jewels 26 (hi-lo) garnet, citrine, malachite, green tourmaline

Jewels 27 (hi-lo) green sapphire, heliodor, violet sapphire, aquamarine beryl, yellow diamond, precious jasper

Jewels 28 (hi-lo) green sapphire, heliodor, violet sapphire, aquamarine beryl, yellow diamond

Jewels 29 (hi-lo) green sapphire, rhodolite, heliodor, peridot

Jewels 30 (hi-lo) green sapphire, yellow tourmaline, precious jasper, black sapphire

Jewels 31 (hi-lo) green tourmaline, chrome diopside, black star diopside, sphene, cat's eye opal, cat's eye apatite

Jewels 32 (hi-lo) green tourmaline, chrome diopside, black star diopside, sphene, cat's eye opal

Jewels 33 (hi-lo) green tourmaline, chrome diopside, black star diopside, sphene

Jewels 34 (hi-lo) jasper, fire opal, black star diopside

Jewels 35 (hi-lo) jasper, red spinel, zircon, orange tourmaline, kunzite

Jewels 36 (hi-lo) kornerupine, pink sapphire, alexandrite, chrysoberyl

Jewels 37 (hi-lo) kunzite, water opal, green sapphire, rhodolite

Jewels 38 (hi-lo) lapis lazuli, agate, azurite, garnet, topaz

Jewels 39 (hi-lo) lapis lazuli, agate, azurite, garnet, topaz, citrine, pearl, malachite, fire opal

Jewels 40 (hi-lo) lapis lazuli, azurite, topaz, pearl, fire opal

Jewels 41 (hi-lo) malachite, fire opal, green tourmaline, sunstone

Jewels 42 (hi-lo) malachite, green tourmaline, chrome diopside, black star diopside, sphene

Jewels 43 (hi-lo) moonstone, jade, obsidian, spinel, chryoprase

Jewels 44 (hi-lo) obsidian, spinel, chryoprase, bloodstone, amethyst

Jewels 45 (hi-lo) onyx, aventurine, moonstone, jade

Jewels 46 (hi-lo) onyx, aventurine, moonstone, jade, obsidian, spinel, chryoprase, bloodstone, amethyst

Jewels 47 (hi-lo) orange tourmaline, blue spinel, kunzite, water opal

Jewels 48 (hi-lo) pearl, fire opal, sunstone, jasper, red spinel

Jewels 49 (hi-lo) precious jasper, chrysoberyl, emerald, blue diamond

Jewels 50 (hi-lo) red spinel, cat's eye tourmaline, zircon, orange tourmaline, kunzite, green sapphire

Jewels 51 (hi-lo) red spinel, sphene, cat's eye tourmaline, cat's eye opal

Jewels 52 (hi-lo) rhodolite, peridot, yellow tourmaline, kornerupine, pink sapphire

Jewels 53 (hi-lo) sphene, cat's eye tourmaline, cat's eye opal, zircon, cat's eye apatite

Jewels 54 (hi-lo) sphene, cat's eye tourmaline, cat's eye opal, zircon

Jewels 55 (hi-lo) spinel, chryoprase, bloodstone, amethyst, carnelian

Jewels 56 (hi-lo) sunstone, chrome diopside, jasper, black star diopside

Jewels 57 (hi-lo) sunstone, chrome diopside, jasper, black star diopside, red spinel, sphene, cat's eye tourmaline, cat's eye opal, zircon

Jewels 58 (hi-lo) sunstone, jasper, red spinel, cat's eye tourmaline, zircon

Jewels 59 (hi-lo) topaz, citrine, pearl, malachite

Jewels 60 (hi-lo) topaz, pearl, fire opal, sunstone, jasper

Jewels 61 (hi-lo) violet diamond, green diamond, blue diamond

Jewels 62 (hi-lo) water opal, green sapphire, rhodolite

Jewels 63 (hi-lo) yellow tourmaline, alexandrite, black sapphire, emerald

Jewels 64 (hi-lo) yellow tourmaline, aquamarine beryl, kornerupine, yellow diamond, pink sapphire, precious jasper, alexandrite, jacinth, chrysoberyl

Jewels 65 (hi-lo) yellow tourmaline, kornerupine, pink sapphire, alexandrite, chrysoberyl

Appendix B: Monster Stats

This atlas lists most of the monsters in *Dark Age of Camelot*. Note that even as you read this book more monsters are being added to the game, so there's always a chance that you'll run into something you don't find listed here. However, this appendix includes nearly anything you'll find, and gives you a good idea of the different kinds of monsters you might encounter in your adventures. In particular, Quest or special "named" monsters are not included in this list.

Type. Each monster is part of a general category. A monster's type generally determines which charming classes can charm it (for example, some classes can charm "animals") or if it is vulnerable to certain weapon types (for example, a "Giant" monster is vulnerable to the Sword of Giant Slaying). The types are as follows:

Animal	Giant	Reptile
Demon	Human-like	Tree or Plant
Dragon	Insect (& spider)	Undead
Elemental	Magical	

Within each realm, the monster list is organized by type of monster. (For example, all of each realm's Giants are listed together, as are all of the Reptiles, and so forth.)

Name. Obvious.

Zones. Where you can find the monster:

Albion Zones		Hibernia Zones	
AvM	Avalon Marsh	**BoC**	Bog of Cullen
BMN	Black Mountains North	**CoM**	Cliffs of Moher
BMS	Black Mountains South	**Con**	Connacht
CmH	Camelot Hills	**CuF**	Cursed Forest
Cmp	Campacorentin Forest	**LoD**	Lough Derg
Cor	Cornwall	**LoG**	Lough Gur
Dar	Dartmoor	**ShE**	Shannon Estuary
Lly	Llyn Barfog	**ShH**	Sheeroe Hills
Lyo	Lyonesse	**SmM**	Silvermine Mountains
Sal	Salisbury Plains	**VBL**	Valley of Bri Leith

Albion Dungeons		Hibernia Dungeons	
DCC	Catacombs of Cardova	**DCM**	Coruscating Mine
DKF	Keltoi Fogou	**DKC**	Koalinth Caverns
DSB	Stonehenge Barrows	**DMT**	Muire Tomb
DTe	Tepok's Mine	**DSD**	Spraggon Den
DTo	Tomb of Mithra	**DTC**	Treibh Caillte

Midgard Zones		Realm vs. Realm Frontiers	
Got	Gotar	**FFS**	Forest Sauvage (Albion)
Mal	Malmohus	**FHW**	Hadrian's Wall (Albion)
Mus	Muspelheim	**FPM**	Pennine Mountains (Albion)
Myr	Myrkwood	**FSn**	Snowdonia (Albion)
Rau	Raumarik	**FBr**	Breifine (Hibernia)
SkR	Skona Ravine	**FCG**	Cruachan Gorge (Hibernia)
SvE	Svealand (East)	**FEM**	Emain Macha (Hlbernia)
SvW	Svealand (West)	**FMC**	Mount Collory (Hibernia)
VMu	Vale of Mularn	**FJM**	Jamtland Mountains (Midgard)
VnS	Vanern Swamp	**FOG**	Odin's Gate (Midgard)
		FUp	Uppland (Midgard)
		FYF	Yggdra Forest (Midgard)

Midgard Dungeons		RvR Battlezones & Dungeons	
DCT	Cursed Tomb	**RCa**	Caledonia (Battlezone)
DNL	Nisse's Lair	**RMu**	Murdaigean (Battlezone)
DSp	Spindelhalla	**RTh**	Thidranki (Battlezone)
DVa	Varulvhamn	**RDF**	Darkness Falls (Dungeon)
DVC	Vendo Caverns		

Level. A monster's level determines its Hit Points, Strength, experience and other typical combat stats. This column lists each monster's base level. However, any monster over Level 5 has a 25% chance to gain a level when it spawns, and the stats for any monster may vary from the base values by up to 5%.

Body. This indicates the monster's skin (or whatever ...). For example, a lion is a "furry animal" ("FA"). Common sense suggests that a "furry animal" is vulnerable to fire but resistant to cold. Some creatures (especially Human-likes) wear armor, in which case the type of armor is also listed, after a slash. (For example, a Moor Boogey (Albion Human-like) has "Tr/Ch," which means it has a troll-like skin, protected by chain armor.) The body types are:

BU	Bony Undead	**EW**	Elemental Water	**Pl**	Plate
Ch	Chain	**FM**	Feeble-Minded	**Rp**	Reptile (Scaled)
Cl	Cloth	**FU**	Fleshy Undead	**Sh**	Shell (Chitin)
DV	Darkness/Void	**FA**	Furry Animal	**Soft**	Soft
EA	Elemental Air	**IU**	Incorporeal Undead	**St**	Studded Leather
EE	Elemental Earth	**Lr**	Leather	**TP**	Tree/Plant
EF	Elemental Fire	**LE**	Light Energy	**Tr**	Troll-like
EI	Elemental Ice	**ME**	Magical Energy		

Speed. The speed at which the monster runs: **S**low, **M**edium, **F**ast, **2x**, **3x** or **4x** (two, three and four times faster than the average PC). For perspective, an unenhanced player character runs at speed 192. (The number in parentheses is the actual speed, in world units.)

Aggression (Aggr). **L**ow, **M**edium, **H**igh. (The number in parentheses is the actual percent chance that a monster will attack you if you're within its aggression radius.)

Attack Speed (Atk Sp). How often a monster can attack (in seconds).

Attack. Up to three stats are included in the next column:

Primary Attack. The type of damage that a monster's primary melee attack inflicts: **C**rush, **S**lash or **T**hrust

Secondary Attack. If a monster can make a second attack in the same attack round, the secondary attack determines the type of melee damage that this second attack inflicts.

Secondary Attack Chance. This is the percent chance (per round) that a monster will make two attacks. A monster's level may increase its chance to make two attacks.

Evade. This is the base percent chance that the monster can evade your attack. A monster's chance to evade may increase as its level increases.

Social. This is where it gets a little tricky, unfortunately. If a monster is Social, it may be found with other monsters, and it might respond to another monster's "Bring a Friend" or "Call for Help." Some Social monsters might Call for Help if their Health drops below 50%; if within hearing range, other monsters of the attacked monster's group may come to help. However, since only Social monsters might Call for Help, this column lists "**C**" (monsters that are Social and might Call for Help), "**S**" (monsters that are Social but won't Call for Help) or "**–**" (monsters that aren't Social).

Vulnerabilities and Resistances

An observant person will notice early on that some types of weapons or spells work especially well against certain types of creatures. Usually it makes sense. Stabbing a skeleton, for instance, does less damage than hitting it with a hammer. That's because of its body type.

You can usually tell what kind of body type a creature has just by looking at it. However, in the monster list — starting on the next page — every monster has its body type listed. If the creature always wears a certain kind of armor, then that counts as part of its body type, too.

Some body types are more vulnerable to certain kinds of attacks, so an attack by that weapon or spell will do a certain percent more damage. The extra percent of damage is listed as a positive number in the list below. Some body types are resistant to certain kinds of attacks, and the percent less damage a weapon or spell will give is listed as a negative number.

Abbreviations: Crush / **Sl**ash / **Thr**ust / **Mat**ter / **Sp**irit / **En**ergy.

Attack Type:	**Cr**	**Sl**	**Thr**	**Heat**	**Cold**	**Mat**	**Body**	**Sp**	**En**
Body Type									
Bony Undead	20	–	-20	5	-15	–	–	30	–
Chain	–	-15	15	-10	–	–	–	–	10
Cloth	–	–	–	–	–	–	–	–	–
Darkness/Void	–	–	–	–	–	-20	–	10	–
Drakulv (Furry Animal)	–	-5	15	–	15	–	–	–	–
Elemental: Air	-10	-10	-10	10	-10	–	–	30	-5
Elemental: Earth	15	-10	-15	-10	10	–	–	30	–
Elemental: Fire	-10	-10	-10	-20	20	–	–	30	–
Elemental: Ice	10	-10	10	20	-20	–	–	30	10
Elemental: Water	-15	-10	-10	15	10	–	–	–	10
Feeble-Minded	–	–	–	–	–	–	–	–	–
Fleshy Undead	-10	15	15	10	-10	–	–	30	–
Furry Animal	–	10	10	15	-5	–	5	–	–
Incorporeal Undead	-15	-15	-15	10	10	–	-20	30	–
Leather	–	15	-15	15	-10	–	–	–	–
Light Energy	-15	-15	-15	–	–	-20	–	–	–
Magical Energy	-15	-15	-15	–	–	–	–	10	–
Plate	10	-5	–	-10	10	–	–	–	10
Reptile (Scaled)	–	-15	15	–	15	–	–	–	–
Shell (Chitin)	15	–	–	-10	10	–	–	–	–
Soft	–	–	–	–	–	–	–	–	–
Studded Leather	10	–	-10	-10	5	–	–	–	5
Tree/Plant	–	20	-15	20	–	–	-15	–	-10
Troll-like	-15	10	10	25	-15	–	-5	–	15

Albion

ANIMAL

Name	Zones	Lvl	Body Type	Spd	Agg	Atk Spd	Atk Type	Ev %	S/C
Bear	BMN,BMS,CmH,Sal	8	FA	M/195	–	4.2	C	-	-
Bear Cub	BMS	2	FA	M/192	–	4.8	C	-	-
Black Bear	AvM,Cor,Lly	16-21	FA	M/200	L/10	3.4	C	-	-
Black Dog	Sal	9-10	FA	M/205	M/50	4.1	T	-	S
Black Lion	Cmp	30	FA	M/205	L/20	2.6	S/S3	1	S
Black Lioness	Cmp	30	FA	M/205	L/20	2.6	S/S3	1	S
Black Wolf	BMS,CmH	3	FA	M/197	–	4.7	S	-	S
Black Wolf Pup	BMS	1	FA	S/150	–	4.9	S	-	S
Boar Piglet	BMS,CmH	1	FA	S/150	–	4.9	S	-	-
Brown Bear	Cor	15	FA	M/200	L/3	3.8	C	-	-
Cart Horse	Sal	10	FA	F/270	–	4.0	C	-	-
Cave Bear	DTe	24	FA	M/192	L/10	3.8	S/S5	-	S
Cave Bear Cub	DTe	16-18	FA	M/192	L/10	3.8	S	-	S
Cave Hound	DSB	38	FA	M/200	H/80	3.7	T	-	S
Cave Lion	DTe	24-26	FA	M/192	L/10	3.8	S/S5	-	S
Cornish Frog	Cor	13	Soft	S/150	–	4.6	C	-	-
Corpse-Eating Sow	FSn	36	FA	M/200	L/20	3.7	S	-	-
Cwn Annwn	Lly	20-22	FA	M/200	L/10	3.5	S	-	-
Dappled Lynx	Cmp	2-3	FA	M/195	–	3.8	S	-	-
Dappled Lynx Cub	Cmp	0	FA	S/160	–	4.0	S	-	-
Dartmoor Pony	Dar	34-36	FA	M/188	–	3.8	C	-	S
Death Stalker	Cor,FFS	16-27	FA	M/210	M/30	3.4	S	-	-
Diamondback Toad	Lly	51-55	Rp	F/250	–	4.0	C	-	-
Diseased Rat	DSB	38	FA	M/200	H/80	3.5	T	2	-
Eel	BMS	2	Soft	S/150	–	4.8	S	-	-
Faerie Frog	Sal,FPM,FSn	28-30	Soft	F/235	–	4.0	C	-	-
Forest Bear	Cmp	7-9	FA	M/192	L/10	4.1	C	-	-
Forest Bear Cub	Cmp	3	FA	M/180	–	4.3	C	-	-
Forest Cat	Cor	16	FA	M/195	L/20	3.6	S/S1	1	-
Forest Lion	BMN,BMS,Cmp	6	FA	M/195	L/20	3.7	S	-	-
Giant Boar	FSn	34-35	FA	M/200	L/20	3.5	S	-	-
Giant Frog	AvM,BMS,CmH,Cmp	3-4	Soft	S/150	–	4.3	C	-	-
Giant Rooter	Cor	30-34	FA	M/210	L/20	3.0	T/S5	-	-
Giant Water Leaper	AvM	15	Soft	M/188	M/50	3.7	S	-	-
Giant Wolf	AvM,FFS	15-17	FA	F/220	H/75	3.5	S	-	-
Gray Warg	BMN,Sal	9-11	FA	M/192	M/50	3.7	S	-	S
Gray Wolf	CmH,Cmp	4	FA	M/190	–	3.6	S	-	-
Gray Wolf Pup	CmH,Cmp	1	FA	S/150	–	3.9	S	-	-
Great Boar	FPM	42-46	FA	M/200	–	3.8	S	-	-
Huge Boar	Lly,Sal	18-19	FA	F/220	H/80	3.2	S	-	S
Keltoi Familiar	DKF	23-25	FA	M/200	–	3.5	S/S1	1	S
Large Rock Bounder	FPM,FSn	45-46	FA	F/230	H/90	3.5	S/S5	3	S
Lone Wolf	Cor	20	FA	F/300	H/90	3.0	S	-	-
Marrow Leech	DSB	38	Soft	M/170	H/80	3.5	T	-	-
Marsh Worm	AvM	9-11	Soft	M/175	M/40	3.7	S	-	-
Moor Den Mother	Cor	17	FA	M/205	M/50	3.7	S	-	S
Moor Pack Leader	Cor	15	FA	M/205	M/33	3.6	S	-	S
Moor Wolf	Cor	14	FA	M/205	L/13	3.6	S	-	S
Mud Worm	AvM	0	Soft	S/150	–	3.8	C	-	-
Red Lion	BMS,CmH,Cmp	3	FA	M/198	–	4.7	S	-	-
Rot Worm	AvM,Cmp	5	Soft	S/165	–	3.8	S	-	-
Scrawny Red Lion	Cmp	3	FA	M/205	–	4.1	S	-	-
Scum Toad	AvM	0	Soft	S/160	–	3.8	C	-	-
Shadowhunter	FPM,FSn	39-41	FA	F/220	H/70	3.5	T/T1	4	C
Shadowh. She-Wolf	FPM,FSn	42-43	FA	F/220	H/70	3.5	T/T1	4	C
Small Bear	BMN,BMS,CmH,Cmp	4	FA	M/188	–	4.6	C	-	-
Small Gray Wolf	CmH,Cmp	3	FA	M/188	–	3.8	S	-	-
Small Rock Bounder	FSn	22-23	FA	M/210	L/1	3.6	S/S2	3	S
Spiny Eel	AvM	3	Rp	S/155	–	4.7	T	-	-
Swamp Rat	AvM,Cmp	4	FA	M/200	H/99	1.0	T	-	C
Water Leaper	AvM	8-10	Soft	M/185	L/2	3.7	C	2	-
Wild Boar	Cmp,Sal	10	FA	F/220	M/30	4.0	S	-	-
Wild Mare	Sal	9	FA	F/270	–	4.1	C	-	S
Wild Sow	BMS,CmH	2	FA	S/150	–	4.8	S	-	-
Wild Stallion	Sal	10	FA	F/270	–	4.0	C	-	S
Woodeworm	Lyo	55	Rp	M/175	L/20	3.8	C	-	S
Yell Hound	Sal	15-16	FA	F/220	H/75	3.5	T	3	C
Young Boar	CmH,Cmp	6	FA	S/150	H/90	4.4	S	-	-
Young Brown Bear	Cor,Sal	13	FA	M/195	L/20	4.0	C	-	-

DEMON

Name	Zones	Lvl	Body Type	Spd	Agg	Atk Spd	Atk Type	Ev %	S/C
Boulder Imp	BMS	7	EE	M/188	L/20	4.1	C	-	-
Fiery Fiend	FPM	41-43	EF	M/170	H/80	3.8	S	-	-
Gabriel Hound	Lyo	40-48	EA	F/230	H/80	2.7	S	-	-
Grumoz Demon	CmH	10-11	EF	M/192	H/90	3.7	S	-	S
Impling	AvM	0	Soft	M/170	–	3.8	C	-	-
Manes Demon	CmH	8-7	EF	M/180	H/80	4.2	C	-	S
Rock Imp	BMS,Sal	3-5	EE	M/188	–	4.0	C	-	-
Scaled Fiend	DSB	42	Rp	F/240	H/80	3.2	T/S8	5	S
Wind Mephit	Sal	14	EA	F/270	M/60	3.6	S	2	C

DRAGON

Name	Zones	Lvl	Body Type	Spd	Agg	Atk Spd	Atk Type	Ev %	S/C
Brown Drakeling	FPM	34	Rp	F/240	–	3.8	S	-	C
Carrion Drake	Sal	8-9	Rp	M/180	–	4.2	T	-	C
Cornwall Drake	Cor	40-44	Rp	M/192	L/20	2.4	S	-	S
Draconic Ancilla	Dar	50	Rp	2x/350	M/50	2.0	S	8	-
Great Brown Drake	FPM	55-59	Rp	2x/500	H/70	3.9	C	-	S
River Drake Hatchl.	AvM,CmH,Cmp	3	Rp	S/150	–	4.7	T	-	S
River Drakeling	AvM,CmH,Cmp	5	Rp	S/160	L/5	4.5	T	-	S
Young Brown Drake	FPM	47	Rp	F/260	M/50	3.8	S	-	C

ELEMENTAL

Name	Zones	Lvl	Body Type	Spd	Agg	Atk Spd	Atk Type	Ev %	S/C
Boulderling	CmH	9	EE	M/192	H/100	4.1	C	-	-
Dryad	AvM,BMN,Cmp	7-9	Soft	M/188	M/50	3.7	C	-	S
Dryad Invert	BMN	9	Soft	S/150	M/50	4.1	C	-	S
Dryad Twig	Cmp	1	Soft	M/170	–	3.8	S	-	S
Faerie Bell-Wether	CmH,Cmp	5	Cl	M/185	–	4.5	S	-	C
Faerie Mischief-Maker	CmH	3	Cl	M/180	–	4.7	S	-	C
Faerie Wolf-Crier	CmH,Cmp	4	Cl	M/185	–	4.6	S	-	C
Large Boulderling	BMN	11-12	EE	M/192	H/100	3.9	C	-	C
Mist Monster	AvM	16	EW	M/195	H/80	3.6	C	-	-
Mist Sprite	AvM	6	EW	M/170	M/30	3.5	C	-	C
Mud Golem	AvM	14	EE	S/160	M/50	3.6	C	-	-
Pixie	AvM,BMN,Cmp	6-7	Soft	M/170	M/30	4.3	C	-	S
Pixie Imp	Cmp	0	Soft	S/150	–	4.1	T	-	S
Pixie Scout	BMN,Cmp	8	Soft	M/180	M/50	3.7	T	-	S
Quicksand	AvM	16	EE	F/230	M/50	3.4	C/C2	-	-
River Sprite	AvM,CmH,Cmp	6	EW	M/170	L/5	4.4	C	-	C
River Spriteling	AvM,CmH,Cmp	3-4	EW	S/150	–	4.6	C	-	C
Rock Elemental	BMN	11-12	EE	M/192	H/100	3.9	C	-	C
Spriggarn	BMS,CmH,Cmp	2	FA	M/175	–	4.8	C	-	S
Spriggarn Ambusher	Sal	15	FA	F/220	H/99	3.5	S	1	S
Spriggarn Elder	CmH,Cmp	3	FA	M/185	L/1	4.7	C	-	C
Spriggarn Howler	Sal	16	FA	F/220	H/99	3.4	S	1	S
Spriggarn Waylayer	Sal	14	FA	F/220	H/99	3.6	S	1	S
Stone Sentinel	DSB	48-50	EE	S/150	H/80	4.1	C	-	S

Name	Zones	Lvl	Body Type	Spd	Agg	Atk Spd	Atk Type	Ev %	S/C
GIANT									
Cornish Giant	Cor	40	Lr	F/250	H/99	5.0	C	-	-
Cyclops	FSn	41-42	FM	M/175	H/90	3.9	C/C1	-	S
Cyclops Scout	Lly	32	FM	M/175	H/90	3.9	C/C1	-	-
Forest Ettin	FFS	12-16	Cl	M/192	H/80	3.8	C	-	C
Forest Giant	FFS	18-21	FM/Cl	F/230	H/99	4.0	C	-	-
Granite Giant	Dar	36-40	EE	F/250	H/80	4.0	C	-	C
GG Earthmagi	Dar	65	EE	3x/600	H/99	3.8	C	-	S
GG Elder	Dar	62-64	EE	F/250	H/80	5.4	C/C5	-	C
GG Gatherer	Dar	42-46	EE	F/250	H/80	4.4	C	-	C
GG Herdsman	Dar	39-43	EE	F/250	H/80	4.2	C	-	C
GG Oracle	Dar	62-64	EE	F/250	H/80	5.2	C	-	C
GG Outlooker	Dar	51-55	EE	F/250	H/80	4.8	C	-	S
GG Pounder	Dar	54-58	EE	F/250	H/80	5.0	C/C4	-	S
GG Reinforcer	Dar	65	EE	3x/600	H/99	3.8	C	-	S
GG Stonecaller	Dar	45-49	EE	F/250	H/80	4.4	C	-	C
GG Stonelord	Dar	57-61	EE	F/250	H/80	5.2	C	8	S
GG Stonemender	Dar	65	EE	3x/600	H/99	3.8	C	-	S
GG Stoneshaper	Dar	48-52	EE	F/250	H/80	4.6	C	-	S
Marsh Scrag	AvM	11	Tr	M/180	H/80	3.6	C	-	C
Pogson	Lyo	42	FM	M/175	H/90	3.9	C/C1	25	-
Pygmy Goblin Bombardier	Lyo	42	FM	M/200	H/90	4.2	C/C1	-	S
Ravenclan Giant	FPM,FSn	50-51	St	M/175	H/70	4.1	C/C6	-	C
Salisbury Giant	Sal	18-21	FM	F/220	H/99	3.2	C	-	C
Scrag	AvM	8	Tr	M/170	H/70	3.7	C	-	C
Scragling	AvM	6	Tr	S/160	M/60	3.8	C	-	C
Stonecrush Demolisher	Dar	51-55	FM/Cl	F/220	H/80	3.4	C/C5	-	S
Stonecrush Excavator	Dar	45-49	FM/Cl	F/220	H/80	3.8	C	-	S
Stonecrush Rockgrinder	Dar	48-52	FM/Cl	F/220	H/80	3.6	C/C1	-	S
Wood Ogre Berserker	AvM,Cmp	14-15	FM/Cl	M/192	H/100	3.5	C	-	C
Wood Ogre Lord	Cmp	16	FM/Cl	M/192	H/70	3.4	C	-	C
Wood Ogre Mystic	Cmp	11	FM/Cl	M/192	H/80	3.9	C	-	C
Wood Ogre Scourge	AvM,Cmp	12-13	FM/Cl	M/192	H/80	3.6	C	-	C
Wood Ogre Seer	AvM,Cmp	14	FM/Cl	M/192	M/50	3.8	C	-	C
HUMAN-LIKE									
Albion Waylayer	FHW	35	Lr	M/192	M/30	3.0	S	-	S
Angry Bwca	FPM,FSn	45-47	FA	M/175	H/70	3.5	C	-	-
Apprent. Beastmaster	DTe	31	St	M/192	L/10	3.6	C	-	S
Arawnite Headhunter	FSn	36-38	Lr	M/175	H/90	3.6	T	-	C
Arawnite Shamaness	FSn	34-35	Lr	M/175	H/90	4.0	C	-	C
Arawnite Warrior	FSn	34-35	Lr	M/175	H/90	3.7	S/S4	-	S
Bandit	BMS,CmH,Cmp,Sal	5-6	Lr	M/188	H/100	3.8	S	-	C
Bandit Henchman	CmH,Sal	9	St	M/188	H/100	3.4	S	-	C
Bandit Leader	CmH,Sal	11	St	M/188	H/100	3.7	C	-	C
Bandit Lieutenant	CmH,Sal	9	St	M/188	H/100	3.8	S	-	C
Bandit Messenger	CmH	9	Lr	M/200	–	4.1	S	-	C
Bandit Thaumaturge	CmH,Sal	8	Cl	M/185	H/100	4.2	C	-	C
Boggart	FPM	45-49	Lr	M/170	–	3.8	S	-	C
Bogman	AvM	3-4	Cl	S/160	M/45	4.1	S	-	C
Bogman Fisher	AvM	9	Cl	S/150	M/40	3.8	T	-	C
Bogman Gatherer	AvM	8	Cl	S/160	M/45	3.8	S	-	C
Bogman Grappler	AvM	5	Cl	S/150	M/55	4.5	C	-	C
Bogman Hunter	AvM	11	Cl	S/150	M/55	3.7	C	-	C
Bogman Trapper	AvM	10	Cl	S/165	M/50	3.7	T	-	C
Brownie	CmH,Cmp	0	FA	M/170	–	5.0	C	-	S
Brownie Grassrunner	Sal	7	FA	M/195	L/5	4.3	T	-	C
Brownie Nomad	CmH,Cmp,Sal	8-9	FA	M/188	L/15	4.2	T	-	C
Brownie Rover	Cmp,Sal	12	FA	M/188	H/70	3.8	T	-	C
Bucca	Cor	23-24	FA	M/175	–	3.8	C	-	-
Bullyboy	BMS	5-6	Cl	M/188	M/50	3.8	S	-	S
Bwca	FSn	24	FA	M/175	–	3.8	C	-	-
Bwgan	Lly	22-23	Cl	M/188	L/20	3.8	S	-	S
Bwgan Elder	Lly	24	Cl	M/188	L/20	3.8	S	-	S
Bwgan Fisherman	Lly	27-29	Cl	M/192	–	3.8	S	-	S
Bwgan Horde	Lly	23	Cl	M/188	L/20	3.8	S	-	S
Bwgan Horde Leader	Lly	24	Cl	M/188	L/20	3.8	S	-	S
Bwgan Hunter	Lly	22-23	Cl	M/192	L/20	3.7	T	-	S
Cornwall Hunter	Cor	23-25	Lr	M/192	L/25	2.7	S	-	S
Cornwall Leader	Cor	25	Lr	M/192	L/25	2.7	S	-	S
Cutpurse	BMS,CmH	4	Lr	M/188	L/5	4.6	T	-	C
Deep Goblin	DSB	42	Lr	M/188	H/80	3.6	T/T1	4	C
Deep Goblin Blighter	DSB	43	Lr	M/188	H/80	3.6	T/T1	4	C
Devout Filidh	BMN,BMS, CmH,Cmp,Sal	8-9	Cl	M/188	H/90	4.2	C	-	C
Druid	Cmp,Sal	18-19	Cl	M/192	H/90	4.3	C	-	C
Druid	Cmp,Sal	7-8	Cl	M/200	H/90	4.3	T	-	C
Druid Sacrificer	Cmp,Sal	20-21	Cl	M/192	H/90	4.1	C	-	C
Druid Sacrificer	Cmp,Sal	9	Cl	M/200	H/90	4.1	S	-	C
Druid Seer	Cmp,Sal	8	Cl	M/192	H/90	4.2	C	-	C
Druid Seer	Cmp,Sal	15	Cl	M/192	H/90	4.1	C	-	C
Druid Seer	Cmp,Sal	19-21	Cl	M/192	H/90	4.2	C	-	C
Dwarf Brawler	BMS	3-4	Lr	M/170	L/2	3.6	S	-	C
Dwarf Pillager	BMS	4-5	Lr	M/170	L/20	3.6	S	-	C
Dwarf Raider	BMS	5-6	Lr	M/170	L/20	3.6	S	-	C
Ellyll Champion	FPM	53-57	Pl	M/215	H/90	3.8	S/S4	-	C
Ellyll Froglord	FPM,FSn	51-54	Pl	F/235	H/90	3.3	S/S4	2	C
Ellyll Guard	FPM,FSn	49-51	Ch	M/215	H/90	3.4	S/S2	2	C
Ellyll Sage	FPM,FSn	53	Cl	M/200	H/90	4.0	C	-	C
Ellyll Seer	FPM	59	Cl	M/200	H/90	4.0	C	-	S
Ellyll Villager	FPM	45	Cl	M/180	M/40	3.9	C	-	C
Ellyll Windchaser	FPM,FSn	47-50	Lr	F/220	H/90	3.9	C	5	C
Escaped Bandit	Sal	18	Lr	M/192	H/100	4.5	S	-	S
Escaped Bandit Leader	Sal	19	Ch	M/200	H/100	3.9	C	-	C
Filidh	BMN,BMS,CmH,Cmp,Sal	7-8	Cl	M/188	H/90	4.3	C	-	C
Filidh Sacrif.	BMN,BMS,Cmp,Sal	9-10	Cl	M/188	H/90	4.1	C	-	C
Fitful Bwca	FSn	38-36	FA	M/175	M/50	3.6	C	-	-
Forest Chief	BMN	19	Lr	M/192	M/50	3.5	S/S3	2	-
Forest Hunter	FFS	21-24	St	M/192	–	2.9	S	3	S
Forest Messenger	FFS	15	Cl	M/192	–	3.5	S	-	S
Forest Runner	FFS	20	St	M/192	–	3.5	T	-	S
Forest Smuggler	BMN	17	Lr	M/192	M/50	3.5	S/S2	2	-
Forest Stalker	FFS	27	St	M/192	–	2.9	T	4	S
Forest Tracker	BMN	15	Lr	M/192	M/50	3.5	S	-	-
Forester	FFS	31	St	M/192	–	3.0	S	4	S
Forester Merchant	FFS	24	St	M/192	–	2.9	S	3	S
Freybug	Lyo,FPM	35-38	Lr	M/170	–	3.8	S	1	-
Goblin	BMN,BMS,DTe	25-29	Lr	M/192	L/10	3.8	S	-	S
Goblin	BMN,BMS,DTe	8-10	Cl	M/188	L/20	3.8	S	-	C
Goblin Apprentice	DTe	24-27	St	M/192	H/90	3.7	S	-	S
Goblin Beastmaster	DTe	31	St	M/192	L/10	3.8	S	-	S
Goblin Cleaner	DTe	30	Lr	M/192	L/10	3.8	C	-	S
Goblin Crawler	DTe	23-24	Lr	M/192	L/10	3.5	S/S5	-	S
Goblin Fisherman	BMS,Sal	4-6	Cl	M/188	L/20	4.2	S	-	C
Goblin Imperator	DTe	31	St	M/192	H/90	3.7	S	-	S
Goblin Lookout	BMS	8	Lr	M/188	L/20	3.8	S	-	C
Goblin Lord	BMN	11	Lr	M/188	L/20	4.2	S	-	C
Goblin Monitor	DTe	33	St	M/192	H/90	3.7	S	-	S
Goblin Patrol Leader	DTe	27	St	M/192	H/90	3.7	S/T5	-	S
Goblin Scout	BMN,BMS	7	Lr	M/188	L/20	3.8	T	-	C
Goblin Shaman	BMN,BMS	9-10	Lr	M/188	L/20	4.4	C	-	C

Monster	Zones	Lvl	Body Type	Spd	Agg	Atk Spd	Atk Type	Ev %	S/C
Goblin Snatcher	DTe	31	St	F/220	H/90	3.7	S	-	S
Goblin Warrior	BMN	8	Lr	M/188	M/50	3.8	S	-	S
Goblin Watcher	DTe	20-22	Lr	M/192	L/10	3.8	S	-	S
Goblin Whip	DTe	30-32	St	M/192	H/90	3.8	S	-	S
Granite Knocker	Dar	47	Lr	M/188	H/80	2.8	T	-	-
Grave Goblin	DSB	40	Lr	M/188	H/80	3.6	T/T1	1	C
Grave Goblin Shaman	DSB	38	Lr	M/188	H/80	3.6	T/T1	-	C
Grave Goblin Whelp	DSB	28-32	Lr	M/188	L/1	3.6	T/T1	1	C
Greater Boogey	Cor	35-41	Tr	M/180	L/20	2.4	T/T5	-	S
Greenhorn Poacher	Dar	25-31	St	M/188	H/80	3.3	T/T1	1	-
Gremlin	DKF	20-21	Cl	M/188	M/50	3.8	C	-	-
Grove Nymph	Sal	10-18	Cl	M/192	H/90	3.8	S	3	C
Heretical Hermit	Cmp	20	Cl	M/170	H/80	3.0	C	-	C
Hibernian Waylayer	FHW	35	St	M/192	M/30	3.0	S	-	S
Highwayman	BMS	7	Cl	M/188	H/75	3.8	S	-	S
Hill Avenger	BMN	12	St	M/192	H/75	3.5	S/S5	-	C
Hill Chief	BMN	14	St	M/192	H/75	3.5	S/S5	3	C
Hill Guard	BMN	11	St	M/192	M/50	3.5	S/S2	2	C
Hill Scrag	FPM,FSn	39-41	St	M/175	H/90	3.9	C/C3	-	C
Hill Shaman	BMN	12	Cl	S/150	M/50	4.4	C	-	C
Hill Warrior	BMN	10	St	M/192	M/50	3.5	S/S1	2	C
Hollow Man	FPM,FSn	39-41	Lr	M/175	H/70	3.7	C	-	C
Howling Knifeman	FSn	26-27	Cl	M/180	H/90	3.6	S/S1	1	S
Howling Maiden	BMN,FSn	24-26	Cl	M/180	H/90	3.6	S	1	S
Isolationist Armsman	FPM	47	Pl	M/180	L/20	3.3	S/S5	-	C
Isolationist Cleric	FPM	46-48	Ch	M/180	L/20	3.7	C	-	C
Isolationist Courier	FPM	46	Ch	M/180	L/20	3.3	S/S8	2	C
Isolationist Mercenary	FPM	46	Ch	M/180	L/20	3.3	S/S8	2	C
Isolationist Paladin	FPM	48	Pl	M/180	L/20	3.3	S/S1	-	C
Isolationist Scout	FPM	47	St	M/180	L/20	3.3	T/T1	4	C
Isolationist Sorcerer	FPM	46	Cl	M/180	L/20	4.0	C	-	C
Isolationist Wizardess	FPM	47	Cl	M/180	L/20	4.0	C	-	C
Keltoi Banisher	DKF	22-23	Cl	M/188	M/50	3.6	S/T1	4	S
Keltoi Eremite	DKF	21	Cl	M/188	–	4.2	C	-	S
Keltoi Initiate	DKF	20	Cl	M/188	–	4.0	C	-	C
Keltoi Recluse	DKF	22	Cl	M/188	–	4.3	C	-	S
Keltoi Ritualist	DKF	23	Cl	M/188	L/5	3.8	C	-	S
Keltoi Spiritualist	DKF	25	Cl	M/188	L/5	3.8	C	-	S
Keltoi Visionary	DKF	21-22	Cl	M/188	–	3.8	C	-	S
Master Hunter	FFS	33	St	M/192	–	2.7	S	6	S
Mercenary Tomb Raider	Sal	26-28	St	M/195	H/99	3.0	T	6	C
Midgard Waylayer	FHW	35	Ch	M/192	M/30	3.0	S	-	S
Mindless Minion	Cmp	8-10	Cl	S/165	H/95	4.1	C	-	S
Moor Boogey	Cor,Sal	25-30	Tr	M/180	L/20	3.0	C/C5	-	S
Nain Dwarf	BMS	9	St	M/170	L/20	3.6	S	-	C
Outcast Rogue	AvM	1	Lr	M/188	–	3.8	T	-	-
Peallaidh	Lyo	35-41	Lr	M/192	H/80	3.5	S	3	S
Pictish Druid	FHW	40-42	Cl	M/188	M/30	4.0	C	-	S
Pictish Warrior	FHW	40-44	Cl	M/188	M/30	3.7	S/S2	-	S
Poacher	BMN,BMS,CmH,Cmp	4	Lr	M/188	L/5	4.6	S	-	C
Poacher Leader	BMN,BMS	5	Lr	M/188	L/20	4.5	S	-	C
Priestess	FHW	40-44	Ch	S/165	–	4.0	C	-	S
Pygmy Goblin	Lyo	43	Lr	M/192	H/99	3.0	T	4	C
Pygmy Goblin Tangler	Lyo	45	Lr	M/192	H/99	2.5	T	8	C
Red Dwarf Bandit	BMS	6-8	Lr	M/180	L/20	3.7	S	1	C
Red Dwarf Chief	BMS	10	St	M/180	L/10	3.6	S/S1	-	C
Red Dwarf Matron	BMN,BMS	6-8	Lr	M/180	L/20	3.6	C	-	C
Red Dwarf Thief	BMS	5-7	Lr	M/180	L/20	3.8	T	1	C
Red Dwarf Youth (F)	BMS,DTe	25	Ch	M/192	L/10	3.6	S	-	S
Red Dwarf Youth (M)	BMS,DTe	5	Cl	M/180	L/20	3.8	S	-	C
Renegade Guard	Lly	19-20	Pl	M/192	L/25	3.1	S	-	S
Ruthless Brigand	Dar	39-43	St	M/188	H/80	3.3	S/S3	4	-
Scorned Bwca	FSn	32-34	FA	M/175	L/1	3.7	C	-	-
Scrawny Bogman	AvM	2	Cl	S/165	–	4.2	T	-	C
Slave	Sal	11	Cl	M/180	–	3.9	S	-	S
Slave Master	Sal	13-15	St	M/188	–	3.7	S	-	C
Slave Master Bodyguard	Sal	15	Ch	M/192	H/99	3.5	S	-	S
Slaver	Sal	12-15	St	M/192	H/90	3.8	S	-	S
Sylvan Goblin	Cmp	5	Cl	S/165	M/50	4.5	C	-	S
Sylvan Goblin Chief	Cmp	16-17	Ch	M/185	H/75	3.4	S/T4	-	S
Sylvan Goblin Hunter	Cmp	6-8	Lr	M/190	M/50	3.7	T	1	S
Sylvan Goblin Magician	Cmp	10	Cl	S/150	H/75	4.0	C	-	S
Sylvan Goblin Warrior	Cmp	9-12	St	M/180	M/50	3.7	S/S2	-	S
Sylvan Goblin Whelp	Cmp	3	Cl	S/150	–	4.0	C	-	S
Templar	FHW	50-54	Pl	M/192	M/30	3.2	S/S3	-	S
Tomb Raider	Sal	16-17	St	M/188	H/99	3.4	S	4	C
Tomb Raider Comm.	Sal	18-20	Ch	M/192	H/99	3.2	S	5	C
Tomb Raider Digger	Sal	10-13	Lr	M/188	H/99	4.0	S	-	C
Tomb Raider Scout	Sal	13-15	St	M/188	H/99	3.7	T	3	C
Tylwyth Teg Huntress	FPM,FSn	43-45	St	M/190	M/50	3.6	S	4	C
Tylwyth Teg Ranger	FPM,FSn	46-47	St	M/190	M/50	3.5	S	4	C
Tylwyth Teg Rover	FPM,FSn	41-42	St	M/190	M/50	3.7	S	4	C
Welsh Hobgoblin	BMS,Lly	17-19	Cl	M/192	L/20	3.2	S	-	S
Welsh Hobgoblin Chief	Lly	20	Ch	M/192	L/25	3.0	S	-	S
Young Cutpurse	BMS,CmH	3	Lr	M/188	L/5	4.7	S	-	C
Young Forest Runner	FFS	10	Cl	M/192	–	4.0	S	-	S
Young Poacher	BMS,CmH	3	Lr	M/188	L/3	4.7	S	-	C

INSECT

Monster	Zones	Lvl	Body Type	Spd	Agg	Atk Spd	Atk Type	Ev %	S/C
Angler	DTe	28	Sh	M/192	L/10	3.8	S/T20	-	S
Ant Drone	BMS,Cmp	2	Sh	S/150	–	3.0	T	-	S
Bloated Spider	Cmp	10-11	Sh	M/170	H/75	4.0	T	-	S
Bone Snapper	Lyo	63	Sh	F/300	H/99	3.3	S/S4	-	-
Carrion Crab	AvM	2	Sh	S/150	–	4.8	S	-	-
Cave Fisher	DTe	22-24	Sh	M/192	L/10	3.6	S/T20	-	S
Cliff Crawler	FPM	42-45	Sh	F/240	–	3.7	T	-	C
Cliff Spider	Cor	18	Sh	M/198	M/60	3.1	T	-	S
Cliff Spiderling	Cor	14	Sh	M/180	M/40	3.2	T	-	C
Dragon Ant Drone	BMN,CmH	8	Sh	M/192	L/20	4.2	T	-	C
Dragon Ant Queen	BMN,CmH	10	Sh	M/200	L/20	4.0	T	-	C
Dragon Ant Soldier	BMN,CmH	7	Sh	M/192	L/20	4.3	T	-	C
Dragon Ant Worker	BMN,CmH	5	Sh	M/192	L/2	4.5	T	-	C
Fisher Hatchling	DTe	15-17	Sh	M/192	L/10	3.7	S	-	S
Giant Spider	BMN,BMS,Cmp	6-8	Sh	M/180	–	4.0	T	-	-
Large Ant	BMS,CmH	1	Sh	S/150	–	3.9	T	-	S
Plague Spider	CmH	0	Sh	S/165	–	5.0	T	-	-
Sprawling Arachnid	FSn	34-35	Sh	F/240	H/90	3.6	T	-	-
Stalker	DTe	18-21	Sh	M/192	L/10	3.8	S	-	-
Tree Spider	Cmp	2	Sh	S/150	–	4.8	T	-	S
Worker Ant	BMS	0	Sh	S/150	–	5.0	T	-	S

MAGICAL

Monster	Zones	Lvl	Body Type	Spd	Agg	Atk Spd	Atk Type	Ev %	S/C
Bearded Gorger	Lly	55	Rp	F/230	H/99	3.0	T/T5	5	-
Cailleach Guard	Lyo	60-66	Pl	M/192	H/80	3.0	S/T3	-	S
Cailleach Priest	Lyo	64-67	Pl	M/192	H/80	3.9	C	-	S
Cave Fairy	FHW	40-46	EE	M/188	M/30	3.8	C	-	S
Frenzied Feeder	Lly	57	Rp	F/230	H/99	2.0	T/T5	5	-
Greater Telamon	Lyo	54	Pl	2x/450	H/99	4.2	S/S5	-	S
Lesser Telamon	Lyo	44	Pl	F/300	H/99	3.5	S/S5	-	S
Medial Telamon	Lyo	49	Pl	2x/375	H/99	3.8	S/S5	-	S
Muryan	Cor	18-20	Sh	M/188	–	3.8	T	-	S
Muryan Emmisary	DKF	25	Sh	M/188	–	3.8	T	-	S
Muryan Trickster	Cor	20-21	Sh	M/188	–	3.8	T	-	S

Name	Zones	Lvl	Body Type	Spd	Agg	Atk Spd	Atk Type	Ev %	S/C
Needletooth Devourer	Lly	59	Rp	F/230	H/99	4.0	T/T5	5	-
Piper Fairy	FHW	52-56	EE	M/188	M/30	3.6	C	-	S
Will O' Wisp	AvM,Cmp	9-11	LE	M/180	–	3.7	S	3	S

REPTILE

Name	Zones	Lvl	Body Type	Spd	Agg	Atk Spd	Atk Type	Ev %	S/C
Adder	CmH	7	Rp	M/200	–	4.3	T	-	-
Afanc Hatchling	Lly	25	Rp	M/192	L/25	2.5	S/C2	-	-
Aged Basilisk	Sal	19	Rp	S/150	M/50	3.1	T	-	-
Ancient Basilisk	FFS	21	Rp	S/150	M/50	3.1	T	-	-
Basilisk	Sal	15	Rp	S/150	M/50	3.5	T	-	-
Cockatrice	FPM	42-43	Rp	M/180	H/99	3.3	T	-	-
Cornish Hen	Cor	24	Rp	M/188	L/5	3.5	S	-	-
Emerald Snake	BMN,CmH,Cmp	5	Rp	M/185	–	4.5	T	-	-
Enraged Cockatrice	BMN	12	Rp	F/230	H/99	3.3	T	-	-
Forest Adder	FFS	16-17	Rp	M/192	M/50	3.4	T	2	-
Forest Snake	BMS,CmH	3	Rp	S/150	–	4.7	T	-	-
Giant Lizard	Lyo,FSn	36-38	Rp	M/210	–	3.9	T	-	-
Grass Snake	CmH,Sal	5	Rp	M/188	–	4.5	T	-	-
Green Snake	BMS	0	Rp	S/150	–	5.0	T	-	-
Hoary Worm	FPM	53-55	Rp	M/210	M/40	3.9	C	-	-
Lake Adder	Lly	10	Rp	M/185	L/5	4.0	T	-	-
Muck Snake	AvM	1	Rp	S/150	–	3.8	T	-	-
Pseudo Basilisk	Sal	12	Rp	S/150	M/50	3.8	T	-	-
Red Adder	Sal	10	Rp	M/205	L/10	4.0	T	5	-
River Racer	AvM,Cmp,Sal	7	Rp	M/188	–	4.3	T	-	-
Slime Lizard	AvM	1	Rp	S/160	–	3.8	T	-	-
Slith Broodling	BMS	0	Rp	S/150	–	5.0	T	-	-
Slough Serpent	AvM	0	Rp	S/160	–	3.8	T	-	-
Small Snake	CmH,Cmp	0	Rp	S/165	–	5.0	T	-	-
Snake	BMS,CmH,Cmp	3	Rp	S/150	–	4.7	T	-	-
Tree Snake	Cmp	0	Rp	S/160	–	4.9	T	-	-
Trimbeak	BMN	15	Rp	F/230	H/99	3.3	T	-	-
Tunneler	DSB	37	Rp	M/175	L/5	3.7	T	-	-
Water Snake	BMS	0	Rp	S/150	–	5.0	S	-	-
Western Basilisk	FPM	49-50	Rp	M/200	M/40	3.8	T	-	-
Worm	FPM	39-42	Rp	M/210	–	3.8	C	-	-

TREE OR PLANT

Name	Zones	Lvl	Body Type	Spd	Agg	Atk Spd	Atk Type	Ev %	S/C
Ashen Fellwood	Cmp,FFS	16-17	TP	M/192	M/50	3.4	C	-	S
Aspen Fellwood	FFS	23	TP	M/192	M/50	4.3	C	-	S
Black Poplar Fellwood	FFS	24	TP	M/192	M/50	4.3	C	-	S
Black Willow Fellwood	FFS	20	TP	M/192	M/50	3.8	C	-	S
Creeping Crud	AvM	2	TP	S/140	–	3.8	S	-	-
Death Grip Vines	AvM	7	TP	S/130	H/80	3.7	S	-	S
Downy Fellwood	FFS	24	TP	M/192	M/50	4.3	C	-	S
Ebony Fellwood	Cmp,FFS	13-14	TP	M/192	M/50	3.7	C	-	S
Elder Beech	Cor	23-28	TP	M/200	L/20	4.0	C	-	S
Gnarled Fellwood	FPM	45-49	TP	M/180	M/50	4.1	C/C1	-	C
Gold Oaken Fellwood	FFS	33	TP	M/192	M/50	4.3	C	-	S
Grimwood	FPM	46-50	TP	M/174	H/70	4.2	C/C1	-	S
Hamadryad	Lyo	30-38	TP	M/185	H/80	4.0	C	-	-
Hornbeam Fellwood	FFS	27	TP	M/192	M/50	4.3	C	-	S
Knotted Fellwood	FPM	43-46	TP	M/180	M/30	4.0	C/C1	-	C
Oak Man	Cmp	7-9	TP	M/192	M/30	4.3	C	-	-
Oaken Fellwood	Cmp,FFS	18	TP	M/192	M/50	3.2	C	-	S
Shambler	AvM	12-13	TP	S/140	M/60	3.5	C	-	S
Silver Oaken Fellwood	FFS	31	TP	M/192	M/50	4.3	C	-	S
Swamp Slime	AvM,Cmp	3	TP	S/125	–	3.8	S	-	-
White Willow Fellwood	FFS	21	TP	M/192	M/50	4.3	C	-	S
Witherwoode	Lyo	57	TP	2x/350	H/99	3.8	C/S6	-	S

UNDEAD

Name	Zones	Lvl	Body Type	Spd	Agg	Atk Spd	Atk Type	Ev %	S/C
Actarius	DCC	31	IU	M/188	L/5	4.0	C	-	S
Aquilifer	DCC	31	IU	M/188	L/5	3.9	T/T1	-	S
Archer	Lyo	45	IU/Pl	M/192	H/80	3.0	S	-	S
Barguest	FPM	57-58	FA	M/180	M/40	3.5	T	1	S
Barrow Wight	DSB	43-44	BU	M/190	H/80	3.8	S/S4	-	S
Bean-Nighe	Lyo	50-54	IU	M/195	H/80	3.3	S	-	S
Bleeder	DTo	10	FU	F/220	–	3.0	S	-	-
Bloody-Bones	AvM	7	Tr	M/188	L/25	3.7	S	-	-
Botched Sacrifice	DTo	11	FU/Cl	M/188	H/75	3.8	S	-	S
Bwgwl	Lly,Sal	28-29	BU	M/188	L/20	3.3	S	-	S
Cait Sidhe	FHW	48-56	IU	M/200	M/30	3.0	S	-	S
Celtic Lich	DSB	50	FU	M/188	H/80	3.8	C	-	S
Celtic Sepulchre Chieft.	DSB	52	FU	M/188	H/80	3.4	S/S6	3	S
Celtic Sepulchre Warr.	DSB	47	FU	M/188	H/80	3.5	S/S2	1	S
Centurio Manipularis	DCC	31	IU	M/188	L/5	3.3	T/T4	-	S
Centurio Pilus Posterior	DCC	31	IU	M/188	L/5	3.1	T/T5	-	S
Centurio Primus Ordines	DCC	31	IU	M/188	L/5	3.1	T/T5	-	S
Centurio Primus Pilus	DCC	32	IU	M/188	L/5	3.1	T/T6	-	S
Chilled Presence	DTo	10	BU/St	M/188	H/100	3.8	C	-	S
Clergyman	Lyo	36	IU/Cl	M/192	H/80	3.0	S	-	S
Cohorstalis	DCC	30	IU	M/188	L/5	3.4	T/T2	-	S
Creeping Ooze	DSB	42	FU	S/140	–	4.0	C	-	-
Cursed Believer	DTo	13	IU/Ch	M/188	H/85	2.9	C	-	S
Cyhraeth	FPM,FSn	50-51	IU	M/188	H/70	3.3	S	1	-
Cythraul	Lly	20-21	BU	M/192	L/25	3.0	S	-	-
Danaoin Clerk	Lyo	35-39	IU/Lr	M/192	H/80	3.9	C	-	S
Danaoin Commander	Lyo	60	IU/Ch	M/192	H/80	2.8	S/T5	-	S
Danaoin Farmer	Lyo	44-46	IU/Cl	M/192	H/80	3.0	S	-	S
Danaoin Fisherman	Lyo	40-42	IU/Cl	M/192	H/80	3.0	S	-	S
Danaoin Priest	Lyo	42-44	IU/Lr	M/192	H/80	3.7	C	-	S
Danaoin Sailor	Lyo	44-46	IU/Cl	M/192	H/80	3.0	S	-	S
Danaoin Soldier	Lyo	50-54	IU/Ch	M/192	H/80	3.0	S	-	S
Dark Fire	DSB	42	DV	M/188	H/80	3.8	C	-	-
Decayed Barbarian	DSB	40	FU	M/175	H/80	3.8	C/C1	-	S
Decayed Barb. Chieftain	DSB	42	FU	M/175	H/80	3.8	C/C3	-	S
Decayed Zombie	AvM,BMS, CmH,Cmp	3	FU	M/175	L/1	4.7	C	-	S
Decaying Spirit	DTo	8	BU	M/188	M/65	4.2	C	-	S
Decaying Tomb Raider	DSB	36	FU	M/175	H/80	3.8	S	-	S
Decurion	DCC	31	IU	M/188	L/5	3.5	T/T3	-	S
Devout Follower	DTo	9	IU/Cl	M/188	M/65	4.2	S	-	S
Disturbed Presence	BMN,Cmp,Sal	12-14	IU	M/175	H/75	3.8	S	-	-
Doomed Minion	DTo	12	IU/St	M/188	H/85	2.9	C	-	S
Draconarius	DCC	31	IU	M/188	L/5	3.9	T/T1	-	S
Dreadful Cadaver	DTo	8	FU/Cl	M/188	M/65	4.2	S	-	S
Druidic Spirit	Sal	21	IU/Cl	M/192	H/90	4.0	C	-	C
Dunter	Lyo	30-34	FU	M/180	H/80	3.8	S/S1	-	-
Dux	DCC	32	IU	M/188	L/5	3.3	T/T3	-	S
Echo Of Life	DSB	41	IU	M/188	H/80	3.8	C	-	-
Ectoplasm	DSB	41	FU	M/170	L/1	3.9	C	-	-
Eternal Scream	DTo	14	BU/St	M/188	H/70	2.9	S	-	S
Fading Spirit	AvM,CmH,Cmp,Sal	7-8	IU	M/175	M/50	4.3	S	-	S
Faint Grim	FSn	20-21	IU	M/188	–	3.8	S	-	S
Fallen Cleric	DTo	10	IU/St	M/188	H/75	3.8	C	-	S
Fallen Paladin	DTo	11	IU/St	M/188	H/75	3.8	S	-	S
Fallen Warrior	DSB	41	Pl	M/188	H/80	3.7	S/S5	2	S
Footman	Lyo	45	IU/Pl	M/192	H/80	3.0	S	-	S
Forgotten Emperor	DCC	35	IU	M/188	L/5	3.8	T	-	S
Forgotten Promise	DTo	9	IU/Cl	M/188	M/65	4.2	C	-	C
Ghost Miner	BMN	11-12	IU/Lr	M/192	H/75	3.8	C	-	C

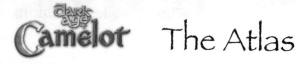

Monster	Zones	Lvl	Body Type	Spd	Agg	Atk Spd	Atk Type	Ev %	S/C
Ghost Wolf	FSn	32-34	IU	M/205	H/70	3.1	T	1	-
Ghostly Cleric	Cor	12	IU/Ch	M/190	L/20	3.8	C	-	-
Ghostly Knight	AvM,Cmp	8-10	IU/Pl	S/150	H/100	3.7	S	3	S
Ghostly Paladin	Cor	12-13	IU/Ch	M/190	L/25	3.8	S	-	-
Ghoul Footman	AvM	17	FU	M/188	H/70	3.4	S/S3	2	S
Ghoul Knight	AvM	18	FU	M/188	H/70	3.3	S/S4	3	S
Ghoul Lord	AvM	19	FU	M/188	H/70	3.2	S/S5	4	S
Ghoulic Viper	DSB	42	Rp	M/200	H/80	3.5	T	2	-
Giant Skeleton	Cor,Sal,FSn	27-28	BU	S/160	H/90	3.8	S	-	-
Glowing Goo	DSB	36	FU	S/160	–	3.9	C	-	-
Green Ghast	Sal	12-14	IU	M/175	H/80	3.8	S	-	-
Grimwood Keeper	FPM	43-47	FU	M/174	H/70	3.5	S/S3	-	C
Guardsman	BMN,BMS,CmC, CmH,Lyo,FFS	45	IU/Pl	M/192	H/80	3.0	S	-	S
Gwr-Drwgiaid	Lly,Sal	15-17	IU	M/180	L/20	3.5	S	-	-
Gytrash	FPM	35-38	FA	M/180	M/50	3.8	C	-	-
Haunting Gloom	DTo	8	IU/Ch	M/188	M/65	4.2	C	-	S
Imaginifer	DCC	31	IU	M/188	L/5	3.9	T/T1	-	S
Immunis	DCC	29	IU	M/188	L/5	3.4	T/T2	-	S
Insidious Whisper	DTo	14	BU/St	M/188	H/70	2.9	S	-	S
King'S Wight	DSB	50	FU	M/190	H/80	3.1	S/S10	5	S
Knight	Lyo,FFS,FHW,FPM,FSn	49	IU/Pl	M/192	H/80	3.0	S	-	S
Large Skeleton	AvM,CmH,Cmp	5	BU	M/188	L/10	4.5	C	-	S
Last Breath	DTo	15	BU/St	M/188	H/90	2.9	C	-	S
Legatio	DCC	33	IU	M/188	L/5	2.9	T/T3	2	S
Legionarius	Cor,DCC	29	IU	M/188	L/5	3.5	T/T1	-	S
Legionnaire	FHW	30-36	BU	S/160	M/30	3.0	S	-	S
Lingering Shade	DTo	11	IU/Cl	M/188	H/75	3.8	C	-	S
Living Entombed	DTo	11	FU/Cl	M/188	H/75	3.8	S	-	S
Magister	DCC	32	IU	M/188	L/5	3.8	T	-	S
Malefic Phantom	DSB	47	IU	M/188	H/80	3.8	C	-	S
Malevolent Disciple	DTo	13	IU/Cl	M/188	H/85	2.9	C	-	S
Manipularis	DCC	30	IU	M/188	L/5	3.3	T/T3	-	S
Megalith Wight	DSB	46	BU	M/190	H/80	3.8	S/S6	-	S
Megalithic Terror	DSB	49	FU	M/190	H/80	3.2	S/S8	5	S
Menacing Presence	DTo	8	BU/St	M/188	H/100	4.2	C	-	S
Moldy Skeleton	BMS,Cmp	2	BU	S/150	–	4.8	S	-	S
Moorlich	Lyo	48	FU	F/300	H/80	3.8	C	-	-
Mountain Grim	FPM	35-39	IU	M/174	H/70	3.8	S	-	-
Optio	DCC	31	IU	M/188	L/5	3.2	T/T4	-	S
Ossuary Guardian	DSB	48	FU	M/188	H/80	3.5	C/S4	1	S
Padfoot	FPM	51-54	FA	M/195	M/50	3.6	T	-	-
Pendragon Ardent	DSB	48	Pl	M/188	H/80	3.5	S/S5	1	S
Pendrake	DSB	48	Rp	M/199	H/80	3.5	T/S2	-	S
Petrified Grovewood	DSB	43	EE	S/160	–	3.8	C	-	-
Phantom	DTe	2	FU/Cl	M/192	–	3.6	S	-	S
Phantom Page	AvM,Cmp	4-5	IU/Cl	S/160	H/80	4.6	C	-	C
Phantom Squire	AvM	6-7	IU/Cl	M/170	H/80	3.8	T	-	S
Pikeman	Lyo	45	IU/Pl	M/192	H/80	3.0	S	-	S
Praefectus	DCC	32	IU	M/188	L/5	3.3	T/T3	-	S
Praetor	DCC	31	IU	M/188	L/5	3.3	T/T4	-	S
Praetorian Guard	DCC	33	IU	M/188	L/5	3.5	T/T3	2	S
Princep	DCC	32	IU	M/188	L/5	3.2	T/T4	-	S
Puny Skeleton	AvM,BMS,CmH	1	BU	S/160	–	5.0	C	-	-
Putrid Sacrificer	DTo	9	FU/Cl	M/188	M/65	4.2	S	-	S
Putrid Zombie	AvM,CmH,Cmp	4	FU/Cl	M/180	L/2	4.6	S	-	S
Reanimated Foe	DSB	37-38	BU	M/188	H/80	3.8	S/S2	-	S
Redbone Skeleton	DSB	37	FU	M/188	H/80	3.7	S	3	-
Repentant Follower	DSB	37	Pl	M/188	H/80	3.7	S/S2	-	S
Rotting Skeleton	AvM,Cmp	1	BU	S/150	–	5.0	C	-	S
Rotting Tombraider	DTo	9	IU/Cl	M/188	M/65	4.2	C	-	S
Rotting Zombie	AvM,CmH,Cmp	5-6	FU/Cl	M/180	H/70	4.4	C	-	S
Sacrificed Slave	DTo	10	IU/Cl	M/188	H/75	3.8	C	-	S
Sacrificial Soul	DSB	43	IU	M/188	H/80	3.8	S	-	-
Saxonbone Skeleton	DSB	40	BU	M/188	H/80	3.7	S	-	S
Shepherd	Lyo	34	IU/Cl	M/192	H/80	3.0	S	-	S
Signifier	DCC	31	IU	M/188	L/5	3.9	T/T1	-	S
Singular	DCC	33	IU	M/188	M/50	2.7	T/T5	7	S
Skeletal Centurion	Cor,Sal	21	BU/Pl	M/198	H/70	3.5	T/S2	-	S
Skeletal Druid	DSB	44	BU	M/188	H/80	3.8	S	-	S
Skeletal Druidess	DSB	44	BU	M/188	H/80	3.8	S	-	S
Skeletal High Priestess	DSB	46	BU	M/188	H/80	3.8	S	-	S
Skeletal Legionnaire	Cor,Sal	18	BU/Pl	M/198	M/50	3.5	S/S1	-	S
Skeleton	AvM,BMS,CmH,Cmp	2	BU	M/180	–	4.8	C	-	S
Small Skeletal Centurion	Cor,FFS	17	BU/Pl	M/198	H/70	3.4	T/S1	-	S
Small Skel. Legionnaire	FFS	14	BU/Pl	M/198	M/50	3.8	S/S1	-	S
Snowdon Grim	FSn	36-38	IU	M/188	H/70	3.8	S	-	-
Soul Harvester	DSB	41	IU	M/188	H/80	3.4	T/S2	-	-
Spectral Essence	DSB	46-47	IU	M/188	H/80	3.8	C	-	S
Spectral Wizard	DSB	47	IU	M/188	H/80	3.8	C	-	S
Spirit	CmH,Sal	6	IU	M/175	M/40	4.4	S	-	S
Spirit Hound	BMS,CmH	0	IU	S/150	–	5.0	S	-	-
Spiritual Advisor	DSB	48	IU	M/188	H/80	3.8	C	-	S
Spiteful Wraith	DTo	10	BU/St	M/188	H/100	3.8	C	-	S
Suffering Apparition	DTo	12	BU/St	M/188	H/100	2.9	C	-	S
Tomb Keeper	DSB	41	IU	M/188	H/80	3.8	T	-	-
Tomb Wight	DSB	42	FU	M/190	H/80	3.5	C/S2	5	S
Tortured Soul	DTo	9	IU/Cl	M/188	M/65	4.2	C	-	S
Townsman	Lyo	30	IU/Cl	M/192	H/80	3.0	S	-	S
Tree Spirit	Cmp	6	IU	M/175	M/40	4.4	C	-	S
Tribune	DCC	32	IU	M/188	L/5	3.0	T/T5	-	S
Tribunus Laticlavicus	DCC	33	IU	M/188	L/5	3.0	T/T6	-	S
Undead Builder	DTo	9	IU/Cl	M/188	M/65	4.2	C	-	S
Undead Druid	BMN,CmH, Cmp,Sal,FHW	8-10	FU	M/178	H/90	4.2	C	-	S
Undead Filidh	BMN,CmH,Cmp,Sal	5-7	FU	M/178	H/90	4.5	C	-	-
Undead Goblin Chief	BMS	6	Lr	M/192	H/85	3.7	C	-	C
Undead Goblin Fisherman	BMS	4	BU	M/180	M/50	4.6	S	-	S
Undead Goblin Warrior	BMS,Cmp	5	Rp	M/192	H/85	3.7	C	-	S
Undead Guardsman	DTo	9	IU/Pl	M/188	M/65	4.2	C	-	C
Undead Miner	DTe	20-23	FU/Cl	M/192	L/20	3.7	S	-	S
Undead Monk	Lly	29-30	BU	M/192	L/20	3.8	S	-	S
Undead Poacher	DTo	9	IU/Cl	M/188	M/65	4.2	C	-	S
Undead Retainer	DSB	36-37	FU	M/175	H/80	3.8	C	-	S
Unfortunate Pragmatic	DTo	9	BU	M/188	M/65	4.2	S	-	S
Vigilant Soul	DSB	46	IU	M/188	H/80	3.5	S	-	-
Vigilis	DCC	29	IU	M/188	M/50	3.8	T	1	S
Wandering Spirit	AvM,Cmp,Sal	9-11	IU	M/175	M/55	4.1	S	-	-
Weak Skeleton	BMS,Cmp	1	BU	S/150	–	4.9	S	-	S
Wicked Cythraul	BMN,Lly	26-27	BU	M/192	L/25	3.0	S	-	-
Wight	DTe	23	FU/Cl	M/192	–	3.7	S	-	S
Wisp Ghoul	AvM	0	FU	M/188	–	3.8	S	-	-
Zombie Boar	CmH	5	FU	M/185	M/50	4.5	S	-	C
Zombie Farmer	CmH	7	FU	M/188	–	4.3	C	-	C
Zombie Sow	CmH	4	FU/Cl	M/170	L/4	4.6	S	-	C

Hibernia

ANIMAL

Name	Zones	Lvl	Body Type	Spd	Agg	Atk Spd	Atk Type	Ev %	S/C
Aqueous Slug	DKC	23	Soft	S/145	H/99	3.8	S	-	S
Badger	LoD	9-11	FA	M/170	L/5	3.5	S	-	S
Badger Cub	Con,LoD,ShE,SmM	0	FA	S/160	–	3.8	S	-	S
Beach Rat	ShE	1-2	FA	S/150	–	3.8	T	-	-
Bird-Eating Frog	FCG,FMC	20-22	Soft	M/175	–	3.8	C	-	-
Black Badger	BoC,LoG,FCG,FEM	36-40	FA	M/188	–	3.6	S	-	-
Bog Frog	BoC	47-50	Soft	M/195	–	3.8	C	-	-
Bog Worm	BoC	30	Rp	M/188	–	3.8	S	-	-
Cave Toad	DKC	22	Soft	M/175	–	3.8	C	-	S
Death Worm	DMT	14	Soft	S/165	H/99	3.8	S	-	-
Derg Monster	LoD	5	Rp	M/188	–	3.8	T	-	-
Faerie Badger	FCG,FMC	32-34	FA	M/188	–	3.8	S	-	-
Faerie Horse	LoG,VBL	18-23	FA	F/220	–	3.7	C	-	C
Faerie Steed	VBL	19-24	FA	F/225	–	3.7	C	-	C
Fee Lion	VBL,FCG,FMC	25-27	FA	M/190	M/30	3.5	S/S5	3	-
Fishing Bear	BoC,Con,LoG	18-20	FA	M/180	–	3.8	T	1	C
Fishing Bear Cub	LoD,SmM	11-12	FA	M/188	L/5	3.7	T	-	S
Fishing Bear Forager	Con,LoD,LoG	13-14	FA	M/175	–	3.8	T	1	C
Fomorian Wolfbeast	CuF,FBr, FCG,FMC	46-49	FA	F/230	H/80	3.8	T/T1	-	S
Glow Worm	DCM	36	LE	M/188	–	3.8	C	-	-
Gorge Rat	FCG	30-31	FA	M/190	L/5	3.6	T	-	-
Greater Luch	LoG,FMC	24-27	FA	M/190	–	3.8	T	3	-
Hill Hound	LoD,LoG,SmM,FCG	18-20	FA	M/195	–	3.5	T	1	-
Hill Toad	Con,LoD,ShE,SmM	5-7	Soft	M/175	–	3.8	C	-	-
Horned Cave Toad	DKC	23	Soft	M/175	–	3.8	T/T2	-	S
Horse	CoM,Con,LoD,LoG, ShE,SmM,VBL	55	FA	3x/600	–	4.0	C	-	-
Ick Worm	DSD	17	Rp	S/165	–	3.8	S	-	S
Ire Wolf	LoG,ShE,FCG,FMC	25-27	FA	M/210	M/50	3.5	T	1	S
Juvenile Megafelid	CoM,FBr, FCG,FEM,FMC	35-38	FA	M/200	–	3.7	S/S1	-	-
Lair Worm	DTC	31-35	Rp	M/188	–	3.8	T	-	-
Large Frog	Con,LoD,ShE,SmM	0-1	Soft	S/150	–	3.8	C	-	-
Large Luch	LoG	18-21	FA	M/190	–	3.8	T	1	-
Large Red Wolfhound	LoD,LoG	17-19	FA	M/200	–	3.7	T/S5	1	-
Levian	FEM	60-62	FA	M/200	M/30	3.8	S	-	-
Levian-Al	CuF,FEM	50-54	FA	M/200	M/30	3.8	S	-	-
Lough Wolf	LoD,LoG	7-9	FA	M/200	–	3.8	T	-	-
Lough Wolf Cadger	LoD	2-3	FA	M/200	–	3.8	T	-	-
Luch Catcher	LoG,FCG,FMC	25-28	FA	M/200	L/1	3.7	S/S3	1	-
Luch Hunter	LoG,FEM	31-34	FA	M/200	L/1	3.6	S/S8	1	-
Megafelid	FCG,FEM,FMC	39-42	FA	M/215	M/60	3.5	S/S5	-	-
Mindworm	CuF,FEM	57-59	Rp	M/175	M/30	3.8	C	-	-
Morass Leech	BoC,FCG	41-43	Rp	M/175	L/10	3.8	S	-	-
Poisonous Cave Toad	DKC	22	Soft	M/175	–	3.8	C	-	S
Rage Wolf	LoG,VBL,FCG, FEM,FMC	31-32	FA	F/220	H/80	3.5	T	1	S
Red Wolfhound	LoD,LoG	10-13	FA	M/200	–	3.7	T/S5	1	-
Roan Stepper	FCG,FEM	29-32	FA	M/210	–	4.0	C	-	-
Root Worm	DSD	18-21	Rp	S/165	–	3.8	S	-	S
Savage Fishing Bear	BoC,CuF,LoG	52-53	FA	M/188	H/80	3.3	T	3	-
Scourge Rat	LoG	10-23	FA	M/188	L/5	3.6	T	-	S
Sett Dweller	FBr,FCG,FEM,FMC	27-31	FA	M/175	–	3.8	S	-	C
Sett Matron	FCG,FMC	35-38	FA	M/178	–	3.7	S	-	C
Sett Protector	FCG,FMC	32-33	FA	M/180	M/60	3.6	S/S3	-	S
Sett Youngling	FCG,FMC	20-24	FA	M/172	–	3.8	S	-	C
Shaft Rat	DCM	36	FA	M/188	L/5	3.3	T	-	-
Shock Aqueous Slug	DKC	24	Soft	S/145	H/99	3.8	S	-	S
Silvermine Badger	SmM	22-23	FA	M/180	L/5	3.3	S/S4	-	-
Squabbler	FCG,FEM,FMC	28-30	FA	M/188	–	3.7	T	1	-
Swamp Hopper	BoC	43-44	Soft	M/188	–	3.8	C	-	-
Torc	FCG,FEM,FMC	34-37	FA	M/195	–	3.8	S	-	-
Torcan	FBr,FCG,FEM,FMC	31	FA	M/195	–	3.8	S	-	-
Umber Bear	FBr	42-45	FA	M/205	–	3.3	C/S1	-	-
Unearth. Cave Bear	CuF,FCG,FMC	49-51	FA	M/210	–	3.8	C/S4	-	-
Water Badger	ShE	21-23	FA	M/175	L/5	3.8	S	-	-
White Boar	FCG,FEM,FMC	40-41	FA	M/195	–	3.8	S	-	-
Wiggle Worm	BoC,LoD,ShE,SmM	0	Soft	S/150	–	3.8	C	-	-
Young Badger	LoD	7	FA	M/170	L/5	3.5	S	-	S

DEMON

Name	Zones	Lvl	Body Type	Spd	Agg	Atk Spd	Atk Type	Ev %	S/C
Abysmal	DCM	50	DV	M/188	H/80	2.9	S	-	-
Cruach Imp	FCG	33-35	ME	M/188	L/20	3.8	T	1	-
Cruiach Demon	FBr	55-57	DV	M/188	H/80	3.5	S/S5	-	S
Deamhan Aeir	LoG,SmM,FCG	34-37	EA	M/200	H/80	3.5	S/S7	5	-
Deamhan Creig	SmM	17-18	EE	M/188	L/10	3.8	C	-	-
Deamh. Hound	BoC,LoG,FCG,FMC	40-42	FA	M/205	M/50	3.3	T	-	S
Mountain Mephit	SmM,FCG,FMC	20-23	EE	M/188	M/30	3.8	C/C5	1	-
Parthanan	Con,LoD,LoG	17-18	EE	M/205	M/60	3.6	S	-	-
Tunnel Imp	DCM	38	DV	M/188	M/30	3.0	S	2	-

DRAGON

Name	Zones	Lvl	Body Type	Spd	Agg	Atk Spd	Atk Type	Ev %	S/C
Faerie Drake	VBL	20-22	Rp	M/188	–	3.5	T	1	S

ELEMENTAL

Name	Zones	Lvl	Body Type	Spd	Agg	Atk Spd	Atk Type	Ev %	S/C
Bodachan Sabhaill	Con,ShE,SmM	2-4	CI	M/188	–	3.8	S	-	-
Chipstone Sheerie	LoG	21	EE	M/198	M/50	3.7	C	-	C
Clubmoss Sheerie	LoD	11	TP	M/188	H/80	3.8	S	1	S
Dew Sheerie	LoD,LoG,SmM	16-19	EW	M/188	H/70	3.8	S	-	S
Earth Sprite	DSD	24-26	EE	M/192	M/30	3.6	C	-	S
Earthshaker	FBr,FCG	47-49	EE	M/179	L/1	3.9	C	-	-
Gale	CoM	16-18	EA	M/215	M/30	3.5	S	2	S
Grass Sheerie	CoM,LoD,VBL	13-15	TP	M/188	H/80	3.8	S	1	S
Greater Zephyr	CoM,FMC	31-33	EA	M/205	L/1	3.7	S	2	S
Lesser Zephyr	ShE	23-24	EA	M/180	–	3.4	S	-	-
Lode Protector	DCM	47-48	EE	M/188	H/80	4.2	C	-	-
Mist Sheerie	LoD	20-21	EW	M/188	H/70	3.8	S	-	S
Moss Monster	FBr,FCG	40-41	TP	M/179	–	3.9	C	-	-
Moss Sheerie	Con,LoD,ShE,VBL	9-12	TP	M/188	H/80	3.8	S	1	S
Mudman	Con,LoD,ShE,SmM	2-4	EE	M/170	–	3.8	C	-	-
Pit Boss	DSD	23-24	FA	M/188	L/10	3.8	S	-	S
Pit Spraggon	DSD	20-22	FA	M/188	–	3.8	S	-	S
Rock Golem	DTC	35-37	EE	M/180	–	3.8	C	-	S
Rock Guardian	FMC	21-22	EE	M/188	–	3.8	C	-	-
Rock Sheerie	CoM,LoD,SmM	18-21	EE	M/198	M/50	3.7	C	-	C
Rock Sprite	DSD	21-23	EE	M/175	–	4.0	S	-	S
Rockbiter	DCM	37	EE	M/188	–	3.6	C	-	-
Sandman	ShE	2-4	EE	M/170	–	3.8	C	-	-
Scragger	DTC	30-32	Tr	M/180	L/5	3.8	C	-	S
Small Walking Rock	ShE,SmM	2-3	EE	M/188	–	3.8	C	-	-
Spraggon	Con,LoD,ShE,SmM	3-5	CI	M/188	–	3.8	S	-	C
Spraggon Cutter	DSD	23-25	FA	M/188	L/10	3.8	S	-	S
Spraggon Runner	DSD	21-23	FA	M/188	L/10	3.7	S	-	-

Monster	Zones	Lvl	Body Type	Spd	Agg	Atk Spd	Atk Type	Ev %	S/C
Spraggon Springer	DSD	22-24	FA	M/188	M/30	3.7	S	-	S
Spraggonale	SmM,FCG,FMC,DSD	21-23	Cl	M/188	L/10	3.7	S	-	C
Spraggonite	Con,LoD,ShE,SmM	5-6	Cl	M/188	L/10	3.8	S	-	C
Spraggonix	DSD	25-26	FA	M/188	H/80	3.7	C	-	S
Spraggonoll	Con,LoD,SmM	7-9	Cl	M/188	L/10	3.8	S	-	C
Spraggonote	DSD	24-25	FA	M/188	M/40	3.7	S	-	S
Stone Sheerie	LoG,SmM	19-22	EE	M/198	M/50	3.7	C	-	C
Streaming Wisp	Con,FCG,FMC	21-24	EA	M/200	–	3.8	S	4	S
Tidal Sheerie	CoM	35-39	EW	M/188	M/50	3.8	S	-	C
Vein Golem	DCM	49	EE	M/188	–	4.3	C	-	-
Walking Rock	Con,SmM,FMC	24	EE	M/188	–	3.8	C	-	-

GIANT

Monster	Zones	Lvl	Body Type	Spd	Agg	Atk Spd	Atk Type	Ev %	S/C
Fomorian Annag	CuF,FBr	55-56	FM	F/220	H/99	4.2	C	-	C
Fomorian Cyclen	CuF,FBr	46-47	FM	F/220	H/99	3.9	C	-	C
Fomorian Gehk	CuF,FBr	47-49	FA	F/220	H/99	3.9	C	-	C
Fomorian Gleener	CuF,FBr	61-62	Sh	F/220	H/99	4.2	C	-	C
Fomorian Goblern	CuF,FBr	49-50	FM	F/220	H/99	4.0	C	-	C
Fomorian Grabeye	CuF,FBr	53-55	FM	F/220	H/99	4.1	C	-	C
Fomorian Grencher	CuF,FBr	50-52	FU	F/220	H/99	4.1	C	-	C
Fomorian Underling	FBr,FCG,FMC	37-38	FM	M/188	H/70	3.8	C	-	S
Giant Lusus	CuF,FEM	58-61	Soft	M/179	M/30	3.8	C	-	-

HUMAN-LIKE

Monster	Zones	Lvl	Body Type	Spd	Agg	Atk Spd	Atk Type	Ev %	S/C
Amadan Touched	BoC,Con,LoG, FCG,FEM,FMC	29-34	Cl	M/178	H/70	3.9	S	-	-
Annoying Lucradan	Con,LoD, ShE,SmM	0	Cl	M/188	–	3.8	S	-	-
Azure Avenger	ShH	51-55	Cl	F/250	H/80	3.4	S/S5	-	C
Azure Banisher	ShH	48-52	Cl	F/250	H/80	3.6	T/T1	-	C
Azure Cleanser	ShH	45-49	Cl	F/250	H/80	3.8	C	-	C
Azure Idolater	Con	24-25	Cl	F/250	–	3.5	S/S5	-	C
Bodach	FCG,FMC	31-32	Cl	M/188	H/80	3.8	C	-	C
Boogie Man	FBr,FEM,FMC	34	Cl	M/188	M/30	3.8	C	-	-
Cliff Dweller	CoM	36-38	Cl	M/188	–	3.8	S	-	C
Cliff Dweller Hunter	CoM	37-38	Pl	M/200	L/2	3.5	T/T2	1	C
Cliff Dweller Spearman	CoM	38-40	Pl	M/188	L/10	3.5	T/T3	1	C
Cluricaun	Con,LoG,FCG,FMC	22-24	Cl	M/188	L/1	3.8	C	-	-
Cluricaun Aquavitor	FCG	40	Cl	M/188	L/1	3.6	C	-	-
Cluricaun Trip	LoD,ShE,SmM	7-9	Cl	M/188	L/5	3.8	C	1	-
Coerced Groover	DCM	45	Cl	M/188	–	3.8	C	-	S
Collared Gemgetter	DCM	38-39	Cl	M/188	–	3.8	C	-	S
Corpan Side	BoC,LoG,FCG, FEM,FMC	39-41	Cl	M/188	M/60	3.8	T	-	-
Curm. Crab-Catcher	LoD	11	Lr	M/188	H/70	3.7	S	-	C
Curmudgeon Fighter	LoD,LoG	16-18	St	M/188	H/70	3.6	S/T4	-	C
Curmudgeon Harvester	LoD	9-11	Lr	M/188	H/70	3.7	S	-	C
Curmudgeon Poacher	LoD,LoG	15	Lr	M/188	H/70	3.7	T	2	C
Curmudgeon Puggard	FCG,FMC	39-40	Lr	M/188	H/80	3.8	T	2	C
Curmudgeon Ratoner	FCG	31-33	Lr	M/188	H/80	3.8	T	-	C
Curmudgeon Scout	LoG	15-17	St	M/188	M/60	3.5	S/T2	2	C
Curmudg. Scrapper	FCG,FEM,FMC	40-43	St	M/188	H/80	3.7	T	3	C
Curmudgeon Skinner	LoD	10-11	Lr	M/188	H/70	3.7	S	-	C
Curmudgeon Trapper	LoD	11-12	Lr	M/188	H/70	3.7	S	2	C
Curmudgeon Wanter	FCG,FMC	34-35	Lr	M/188	H/80	3.8	T	-	C
Dergan Enchanter	LoD	12	Cl	M/188	H/70	3.8	T	-	C
Dergan Fury	LoD	13-15	Cl	M/188	H/70	3.4	S/S3	-	C
Dergan Tussler	LoD	14	St	M/188	M/60	3.6	T/S3	2	C
Elfshot Madman	ShH	34-36	Cl	M/188	–	3.8	C	-	-
Enthralled Silvier	DCM	36-37	Cl	M/188	L/1	3.8	C	-	S
Eriu Ambusher	ShE	19	Lr	M/188	H/80	3.7	T/S1	2	S
Eriu Fiscere	ShE	13-15	Cl	M/188	L/5	3.8	T	-	C
Eriu Henter	ShE	19-22	Cl	M/188	L/5	3.8	T	-	C
Eriu Kedger	ShE	16-18	Cl	M/188	L/5	3.8	T	-	C
Eriu Waylayer	ShE	26-27	Lr	M/188	H/80	3.7	T/S1	2	S
Fachan	FEM	47-49	Cl	M/172	H/80	3.8	C	-	-
Feckless Lucragan	Con,LoD,SmM	4	Cl	M/188	–	3.8	S	-	-
Forest Poacher	CuF	53-55	St	M/188	–	3.5	T	3	S
Gan Ceanach	CuF,FEM	50-53	St	M/188	H/80	3.8	S	-	-
Geas-Bound Hewer	DCM	39	Cl	M/188	L/1	3.8	C	-	S
Goborchend	FEM	46-49	Ch	M/195	H/80	3.8	C/C4	4	C
Goborchend Gasher	CuF,FEM	52-55	Ch	M/195	H/80	3.8	S/S4	4	C
Goborchend Piercer	CuF,FEM	50-53	Ch	M/195	H/80	3.8	T/T4	4	C
Goborchend Wounder	CuF,FEM	54-56	Ch	M/195	H/80	3.6	T/T4	4	C
Grogan	FBr,FEM	46-47	Cl	M/188	–	3.8	C	-	C
Gurite Ambusher	LoG	19	Lr	M/188	H/80	3.7	T/S1	2	S
Gurite Assailer	LoG	23-24	St	M/188	H/80	3.7	T/S2	-	C
Gurite Footpad	LoG	16	St	M/188	H/80	3.7	T/T2	2	S
Gurite Lookout	LoG	37	St	–	H/80	3.7	T	2	C
Gurite Raider	LoG	37-39	St	M/188	H/80	3.4	T/S5	-	C
Gurite Seeker	LoG	31	St	M/188	H/80	3.6	S/S4	4	C
Gurite Tempriar	LoG	24	Ch	M/188	H/80	3.7	S/S2	-	C
Gurite Waylayer	LoG	26-27	Lr	M/188	H/80	3.7	T/S1	2	S
Koalinth Bouncer	DKC	20	EW	M/192	H/99	4.4	S	5	S
Koalinth Castellan	DKC	26	EW	M/188	H/80	4.4	C	5	S
Koalinth Elder	DKC	27	EW	M/188	H/80	4.4	C	-	S
Koalinth Envoy	DKC	23-25	EW	M/192	H/99	4.4	S	5	-
Koalinth Guardian	DKC	24	EW	M/192	H/99	4.4	S	5	S
Koalinth Sentinel	CoM,DKC	18-22	EW	M/192	H/99	4.4	S	5	S
Koalinth Slinker	CoM	34-38	Rp	M/188	M/50	3.6	T/S1	-	S
Koalinth Spectator	DKC	19	EW	M/192	H/99	4.4	S	5	-
Koalinth Warden	DKC	19	EW	M/192	H/99	4.4	S	5	S
Koalinth Warder	DKC	20	EW	M/192	H/99	4.4	S	5	S
Koalinth Wrestler	DKC	20	EW	M/192	H/99	4.4	S	5	-
Leprechaun	CuF,FCG,FMC	48-50	Cl	M/188	M/60	3.8	C	-	-
Loghery Man	FEM	46	Cl	M/188	–	3.8	C	-	-
Lugradan	LoG,FCG,FMC	25-30	Cl	M/188	M/30	3.8	S	5	-
Lugr. Whelp	Con,LoD,ShE,SmM	4-6	Cl	M/188	–	3.8	T	-	-
Luricaduane	SmM	6-8	Cl	M/188	L/5	3.8	S	1	-
Merrow	ShE	20-22	Rp/Cl	M/180	–	3.8	C	-	C
Moheran Distorter	CoM	17-19	Cl	M/188	H/80	3.8	S	-	C
Orchard Nipper	Con,LoD	5-6	Cl	M/188	L/5	3.8	C	-	-
Primrose	VBL	10	Cl	M/188	–	3.8	S	-	-
Raging Subverter	ShH	39-43	Lr	M/188	H/80	3.3	T/T3	-	-
Roane Maiden	LoD	12-13	Cl	M/188	–	3.8	C	-	C
Rowdy	Con,LoD,ShE,SmM	5-8	Lr	M/188	H/100	3.8	C	-	-
Sheevra Archer	SmM	14	St	M/188	M/60	3.5	T	2	C
Sheevra Chieftain	SmM	15-16	St	M/188	M/60	3.5	S/S6	-	C
Sheevra Miner	SmM	13-14	Lr	M/188	L/10	3.8	T	-	C
Sheevra Skirmisher	SmM	13-15	St	M/188	M/60	3.6	T/S3	2	C
Sheevra Swordsman	SmM	12-13	Lr	M/188	M/60	3.5	S	-	C
Siabra Anchorite	FCG	41	Cl	M/188	H/80	3.8	S	-	C
Siabra Archmagi	BoC	57-65	Cl	M/188	H/80	4.0	C	-	C
Siabra Guardian	BoC	56-64	Pl	M/188	H/80	3.2	S/T4	4	C
Siabra Lookout	BoC	47	St	–	H/80	3.7	T	2	C
Siabra Mireguard	BoC	38	St	M/188	H/80	3.6	S	2	C
Siabra Raider	BoC	37-39	St	M/188	H/80	3.4	T/S5	-	C
Siabra Seeker	BoC	30-13	St	M/188	H/80	3.6	S/S4	4	C
Siabra Venator	BoC	46-48	Ch	M/188	H/80	3.4	T	4	C
Siabra Waterwalker	BoC	49-52	Lr	M/188	H/80	4.0	C	-	C

Name	Zones	Lvl	Body Type	Spd	Agg	Atk Spd	Atk Type	Ev %	S/C
Siabra Wayguard	BoC	43-44	St	M/188	H/80	3.5	S	2	C
Silvermine Guard	DCM	45	St	M/188	H/80	3.2	S/S5	2	S
Silvermine Knocker	DCM	36-37	Cl	M/188	L/1	3.8	C	2	-
Silvermine Sentry	DCM	39	St	M/188	H/80	3.2	S/S5	2	S
Siog Footpad	VBL	15-16	St	M/188	H/80	3.7	T/T2	2	S
Siog Piller	VBL	18-19	St	M/188	H/80	3.7	T/T3	2	C
Siog Raider	FCG,FMC	37	St	M/188	H/80	3.4	T/S5	-	C
Siog Seeker	VBL,FCG,FMC	28-31	St	M/188	H/80	3.6	S/S4	4	C
Siog Waylayer	FCG,FMC	19	Lr	M/188	H/80	3.7	T/S1	2	S
Tomb Creeper	DMT	9-16	Cl	M/188	H/99	3.7	S/T1	-	S
Trammer	DCM	36	Cl	M/188	–	3.8	C	-	S
Troglodyte	DCM,DTC	36-37	Rp	M/180	L/25	3.8	C	-	S
Unseelie Overman	DCM	49	Ch	M/188	H/80	3.3	S	-	C
Unseelie Underviewer	DCM	42	Lr	M/188	H/80	3.5	S/S1	2	C
Unseelie Viewer	DCM	48	Ch	M/188	H/80	3.3	S	-	C
Ursine Dweller	DTC	36	FA	M/205	M/50	3.8	S	-	S
Ursine Patrol	DTC	37	FA	M/205	M/50	3.8	S	-	S
Ursine Shaman	DTC	38	FA	M/205	M/50	3.8	S	-	S
Ursine Sorcerer	DTC	39	FA	M/205	M/50	3.8	C	-	S
Ursine Thrall	DTC	33-36	Cl	M/188	L/1	3.8	C	-	S
Ursine Warrior	DTC	37	FA	M/205	M/50	3.8	C	-	S
Villain. Youth	Con,LoD,ShE,SmM	3-4	Lr	M/188	H/100	3.8	S	-	C
Watery Escort	DKC	18	EW	M/192	H/99	4.4	S	5	S
Wild Lucradan	Con,LoD,LoG	9-10	Cl	M/188	L/20	3.6	S	-	-

INSECT

Name	Zones	Lvl	Body Type	Spd	Agg	Atk Spd	Atk Type	Ev %	S/C
Arachnid	DTC	37-39	Sh	M/200	M/50	3.8	T	-	S
Arachnite	DTC	28-30	Sh	M/200	L/25	3.8	T	-	S
Bloodletter	FBr	48-49	Sh	F/220	M/50	3.4	T/T5	-	-
Bog Crawler	BoC	46-47	Sh	M/188	–	3.8	T	-	-
Bog Creeper	BoC	42-44	Sh	M/188	–	3.8	T	-	-
Carrion Scorpionida	DMT	15	Sh	S/165	H/99	3.8	S	-	S
Cliff Beetle	CoM,FEM	31-37	Sh	M/188	L/5	3.8	T	-	-
Cliff Hanger	CoM,FMC	36-39	Sh	M/188	–	3.8	T	-	-
Crypt Spider	DMT	10-12	Sh	M/192	H/99	3.6	S	-	-
Dampwood Mite	LoG	22	Sh	M/188	L/10	3.6	T	-	S
Detrital Crab	BoC,FCG	42	Sh	M/188	L/10	3.6	S/S3	-	-
Eirebug	Con,LoD,SmM	4-5	Sh	S/165	–	3.9	T	-	-
Faerie Beetle	Con,LoG	17	Sh	M/188	–	3.8	T	-	-
Forest Scourge Scorpion	CuF	57	Sh	M/190	–	3.5	C/T4	3	S
Gemclicker	DCM	37-39	Sh	M/188	–	3.8	T	-	-
Gemclicker Horder	DCM	40	Sh	M/188	–	3.8	T	-	-
Giant Ant	LoG,ShE,FCG,FMC	21-24	Sh	M/180	–	3.8	T	-	C
Giant Beetle	CoM,LoG,FCG,FMC	20-21	Sh	M/188	L/5	3.8	T	-	-
Large Eirebug	Con,LoD,LoG,SmM	9-11	Sh	M/185	–	3.8	T	-	-
Larval Predator	DCM	36	Sh	M/188	M/65	2.1	T/S50	-	-
Malefic Forest Scorpion	CuF	61	Sh	M/190	–	3.5	C/T4	3	S
Malevolent Forest Scorp.	CuF	59	Sh	M/190	–	3.5	C/T4	3	S
Pelagian Alliant	DKC	28	Sh	M/192	H/99	4.4	S	5	S
Pelagian Crab	DKC	25-26	Sh	M/192	H/99	4.4	S	5	S
Pelagian Guard	DKC	28	Sh	M/192	H/99	4.4	S	5	S
Rock Clipper	SmM	21-23	Sh	M/185	–	3.8	T	-	-
Sand Crab	ShE	0-1	Sh	S/150	–	3.8	S	-	-
Small Freshwater Crab	LoD	4	Sh	S/165	–	3.8	T	-	-
Water Beetle	Con,LoD,ShE,SmM	6-8	Sh	S/165	–	3.8	T	-	S
Water Beetle Collectorr	Con,LoD, ShE,SmM	4-5	Sh	S/165	–	3.8	T	-	C
Water Beetle Larva	Con,LoD,SmM	0-1	Sh	S/145	–	3.8	C	-	S

MAGICAL

Name	Zones	Lvl	Body Type	Spd	Agg	Atk Spd	Atk Type	Ev %	S/C
Alp Luachra	BoC,Con,LoG, FCG,FEM	29-31	Cl	M/188	H/70	3.5	T	-	-
Anger Sprite	Con,LoD	11-13	Cl	M/192	H/90	3.7	S/S3	-	S
Aughisky	BoC,CoM,FCG,FMC	31-33	FA	M/188	M/50	3.8	S	-	-
Barca	VBL	10-12	Cl	M/188	H/80	3.8	C	-	-
Bocaidhe	FCG,FMC	27-29	Cl	M/188	–	3.8	S	-	-
Breaker Roane Comp.	CoM	46-47	Rp	M/188	–	3.8	S	-	C
Changeling	Con	11	Cl	M/188	M/50	3.8	C	-	-
Empyrean Elder	VBL,FCG,FMC	41-44	St	M/188	–	3.9	C	-	C
Empyr. Guardian	VBL,FBr,FCG,FMC	34-38	St	M/188	–	3.5	S/S9	6	C
Empyrean Keeper	VBL	23-25	St	M/188	–	3.9	C	-	C
Empyrean Orb	VBL	10	Cl	M/188	–	3.8	T	-	-
Empyrean Overseer	VBL,FMC	37-39	St	M/188	–	3.4	S/S10	8	C
Empyrean Sentinel	VBL,FCG,FMC	25-29	St	M/188	–	3.9	C	-	C
Empyrean Watcher	VBL	16-18	St	M/188	–	3.7	T/S3	2	C
Empyrean Wisp	VBL	13-15	TP	M/190	–	3.8	T	-	-
Evanescer	FMC	33-35	FA	M/188	M/30	3.6	T	-	-
Far Darrig	BoC,LoG,FMC	46-48	Cl	M/188	M/60	3.8	C	-	-
Far Dorocha	BoC,CuF,FMC	50-55	Ch	M/210	H/80	3.1	T/T8	-	S
Far Dorocha	BoC,CuF,FMC	53-62	IU/Ch	M/210	H/80	3.8	T/T8	-	-
Fear Dearc	FBr	46-47	Cl	M/188	M/60	3.8	S	-	-
Feccan	Con,ShE,SmM	1-3	Cl	M/188	–	3.8	C	-	-
Fetch	CoM	15	Cl	M/188	M/30	3.8	C	-	-
Fury Sprite	CoM,VBL	14-16	Cl	M/188	H/80	3.5	T/S2	-	S
Glimmer Ardent	ShH	45-49	FU	F/250	H/80	3.8	S	-	C
Glimmer Avenger	ShH	65	Pl	3x/600	H/99	3.8	S	-	S
Glimmer Deathwatcher	ShH	57-61	Pl	F/250	H/80	3.5	S	-	S
Glimmer Geist	ShH	60-62	FU	F/250	H/80	3.8	S	-	C
Glimmer Ghoul	ShH	39-43	FU	F/250	H/80	3.8	T	4	C
Glimmer Griever	ShH	48-52	FU	F/250	H/80	4.0	S	6	S
Glimmer Jinn	ShH	65	Pl	3x/600	H/99	3.8	S	-	S
Glimmer Knight	ShH	60-62	Pl	F/250	H/80	5.5	S/S3	-	S
Glimmer Messenger	ShH	50	Pl	2x/350	–	2.0	S	8	S
Glimmer Prophet	ShH	65	Pl	3x/600	H/99	3.8	S	-	S
Glimmer Striker	ShH	51-55	Pl	F/250	H/80	3.0	T	-	S
Glimmer Ward	ShH	42-46	Pl	F/250	H/80	3.6	C	-	C
Glimmer Warshade	ShH	54-58	Pl	F/250	H/80	5.0	C/C4	-	S
Glimmerling	ShH	36-40	FU	F/250	H/80	3.8	T	2	C
Grand Pooka	CuF,FBr	61-64	ME	M/210	M/50	3.4	C	-	-
Graugach	FCG,FEM,FMC	32-33	FA/Cl	M/188	–	3.8	C	-	-
Hillock Changeling	CoM,FBr, FCG,FEM,FMC	35-37	Cl	M/188	M/30	3.8	C	-	-
Lhiannan-Sidhe	BoC,LoG	49	Cl	M/188	H/90	3.8	S	-	-
Lunantishee	Con,LoD,ShE	8-9	Cl	M/188	L/5	3.8	C	-	C
Mad Changeling	VBL,FCG,FMC	27-29	St	M/188	–	3.6	C/S5	4	S
Merman	BoC,LoG,ShE,FCG	23-36	Rp	M/180	–	3.7	S/S1	-	S
Minor Changeling	LoD	1-2	Soft	M/188	–	3.8	C	-	-
Pooka	BoC,CuF,LoG	52-57	FA	M/195	H/80	3.8	C/C2	5	-
Pookha	Con,FCG,FMC	33-35	FA	M/195	M/50	3.7	C	3	-
Rage Sprite	FCG	18-20	Cl	M/188	H/80	3.5	T/S3	-	S
Rat Boy	LoD,ShE,SmM	3	Soft	M/188	L/5	3.8	S	-	-
Roane Companion	LoD,ShE	12-13	Soft	M/188	–	3.8	S	-	C
Silver-Mad. Werewolf	DCM	47	FA/Cl	M/188	H/80	2.3	S/S5	-	-
Vanisher	FMC	27-32	Cl	M/188	H/80	3.8	C	-	C
Veil Wisp	VBL	11-13	Cl	M/190	–	3.8	T	-	-
Weewere	DCM	48-49	FA	M/188	L/20	3.0	S/S5	3	-
Wild Crouch	Con,LoD,SmM	5-6	Cl	M/188	L/5	3.6	C	-	-
Wrath Sprite	CoM,VBL,FCG,FMC	27-28	Cl	M/188	H/80	3.4	T/S7	-	S

REPTILE

Monster	Zones	Lvl	Body Type	Spd	Agg	Atk Spd	Atk Type	Ev %	S/C
Ollipheist	ShE	34-37	Rp	M/195	H/80	3.8	S/C6	-	-
Sinach	CoM	49-51	Rp	M/188	H/70	3.8	S	-	-

TREE OR PLANT

Monster	Zones	Lvl	Body Type	Spd	Agg	Atk Spd	Atk Type	Ev %	S/C
Blackthorn	LoD	8-9	TP	M/180	L/5	4.2	C	-	C
Grovewood	CoM,FEM,FMC	38-40	TP	M/180	–	3.8	C	-	C
Haunted Driftwood	ShE	1	TP	S/150	–	3.8	C	-	-
Irewood	FMC	29-31	TP	M/180	H/80	3.8	C	-	S
Irewood Greenbark	BoC,LoG,FCG	40	TP	M/172	–	3.7	C/T5	-	S
Irewood Sapling	BoC,Con, LoG,FMC	21-22	TP	M/172	M/30	3.8	C/T5	-	S

UNDEAD

Monster	Zones	Lvl	Body Type	Spd	Agg	Atk Spd	Atk Type	Ev %	S/C
Badh	BoC	46-47	IU/Cl	M/180	M/50	3.5	S	3	S
Bananach	FBr,FEM	40-41	IU	M/188	H/80	3.8	S	-	-
Banshee	BoC,CuF	55-59	IU/Cl	M/195	H/70	3.7	S	1	S
Bantam Spectre	CoM,Con	15	IU	M/188	H/70	3.8	C	-	-
Bean Sidhe	FCG,FEM	39-41	IU/Cl	M/195	H/90	3.7	S	1	-
Black Wraith	BoC,CuF,LoG	52-55	IU	M/200	M/60	3.3	T/S3	5	S
Bocan	CoM	15	IU	M/188	H/70	3.8	C	-	-
Bocanach	CuF,FBr	46-48	IU	M/188	H/80	3.8	S	-	-
Corybantic Skeleton	FBr,FCG	46	BU	M/188	H/99	2.8	S/S3	-	-
Dullahan	LoG,FCG,FMC	48-51	IU/Ch	F/230	M/50	3.2	T/S4	3	-
Eidolon	BoC	58-64	IU/Cl	M/200	H/80	3.8	C	-	S
Faeghoul	FCG,FEM,FMC	34-36	FU	M/177	M/60	4.0	S	-	S
Fallen Hib. Defender	FBr,FCG	45	IU	M/188	L/20	3.8	S	-	-
Far Liath	LoG,ShE,FMC	31-32	IU	M/180	H/80	3.2	C	-	-
Finliath	CuF,FBr	58-60	FU	M/188	M/50	3.8	S	-	-
Fog Phantom	CoM	21-23	IU	M/188	L/3	3.7	C	2	-
Fog Wraith	BoC,CoM	28-30	IU	M/188	M/60	3.7	T	2	-
Fuath	FBr,FCG,FMC	46-47	IU	M/188	H/80	3.8	S	-	-
Gem-Dusted Skeleton	DCM	37	BU	M/188	L/10	3.5	S	-	-
Ghastly Siabra	LoD	13-15	IU	M/188	H/80	3.8	S	-	-
Ghostly Midgard Invader	FBr,FCG	43	IU	F/240	L/20	3.8	S	-	-
Ghostly Siabra	Con,LoD	11-12	IU	M/188	H/80	3.8	S	-	-
Ghoulie	CoM,LoG,FCG,FMC	20-22	FU/Cl	M/188	H/70	3.7	S/S5	-	S
Granny	CuF,FEM	48-50	IU	M/188	L/5	3.8	S	-	-
Grass Spirit	LoD	1	IU	M/188	–	3.8	S	-	-
Gray Spectre	LoG,SmM,FCG	22-24	IU	M/205	H/90	3.3	S/S5	-	-
Haunting Draft	DCM	49	EA	M/188	H/80	3.0	S	1	-
Lesser Banshee	BoC	36-37	IU/Cl	M/175	M/40	3.8	S	1	S
Mangled Troll Invader	FBr,FCG	45	IU	F/240	L/20	3.8	S	-	-
Mist Wraith	CoM,LoG,FCG	27-28	IU	M/188	M/30	3.7	T	2	-
Morghoul	FMC	33	FU	M/177	M/60	4.0	S	-	S
Mummy Hag	DMT	11-13	BU	M/210	H/99	3.0	T	3	S
Murkman	DMT	15-16	FU	S/165	H/99	3.8	S	-	S
Pale Horse	ShH	50	IU	F/250	H/80	2.8	C	-	-
Phaeghoul	CoM,FCG,FEM,FMC	37-39	FU	M/177	M/60	4.0	S	-	S
Phantom Miner	DCM	47	IU	M/188	H/80	3.8	C	-	-
Phantom Wickerman	Con,LoG	28	IU	M/188	H/80	3.7	T	-	-
Raven Wraith	BoC	58-64	IU	F/220	H/90	3.1	T/S7	8	S
Shrieking Wraith	BoC	41-43	IU	F/220	H/90	3.1	T/S7	8	C
Silver-Flecked Skeleton	DCM	47	BU	M/188	L/10	3.8	S	-	-
Skeletal Dwarf Invader	FBr,FCG	43	IU	M/188	L/20	3.8	S	-	-
Skeletal Minion	Con,LoD, ShE,SmM	3-4	BU	M/180	–	3.8	S	-	-
Skeletal Pawn	Con,LoD,ShE,SmM	1-2	BU	M/180	–	3.8	S	-	-
Spectral Briton Invader	FBr,FCG	43	IU	F/240	L/20	3.8	S	-	-
Spectral Manslayer	CuF,FBr	50-53	IU	M/188	H/99	3.8	T	2	-
Spectral Wickerman	ShE	14-17	IU	M/188	H/80	3.7	S/S1	-	-
Speghoul	FCG,FMC	40-41	FU	M/177	M/60	4.0	S	-	S
Suitor Spirit	DMT	14-15	IU	S/165	H/99	3.8	S	-	S
Undead Briton Invader	FBr,FCG	44	IU	M/188	L/20	3.8	S	-	-
Undead Drudger	DCM	38-39	FU/Cl	M/188	H/80	3.8	C	-	-
Vindictive Bocan	CoM,LoG,FCG	20-22	IU	M/188	H/99	3.7	C/S1	-	S
Wanshee	FBr	61-64	IU	M/188	H/80	3.8	S	-	-
Wind Ghoul	Con,ShE	7	IU	M/200	L/5	3.8	C	1	-
Zephyr Wraith	CoM,FMC	29-32	IU	F/225	M/60	3.3	T/S3	8	-

Midgard

ANIMAL

Name	Zones	Lvl	Body Type	Spd	Agg	Atk Spd	Atk Type	Ev %	S/C
Albino Cave Mauler	DVC	25	FA	M/192	H/70	3.7	S	-	-
Battle-Scarred Mauler	SkR	34-35	FA	M/200	M/40	3.6	C/C6	-	-
Black Mauler	SkR,SvW	12-14	FA	F/225	L/10	3.6	C/C5	-	-
Black Mauler Cub	Myr,VMu	0	FA	S/160	–	4.1	C	-	-
Black Maul. Juvenile	Got,Myr,SvE	5	FA	M/180	–	3.7	C	-	-
Blodfelag Warhound	SvW	10	FA	M/200	H/85	3.3	T	1	S
Bloodthirsty She-Wolf	SvW	12	FA	M/210	L/20	3.3	T	2	S
Brush Cat	SkR	25-27	FA	M/188	M/30	3.6	T	2	-
Callow Wolverine	SkR	30-31	FA	M/178	H/80	3.3	S/S6	-	C
Cave Bear	DVC	20-23	FA	M/192	H/70	3.8	S	-	-
Cave Mauler	DVC	20-22	FA	M/192	H/70	3.7	S	-	-
Coastal Wolf	Got	3	FA	M/190	–	3.8	T	-	-
Dark Hound	Myr	17-18	FA	M/215	H/90	3.3	T	2	-
Dire Wolverine	Rau,FJM,FOG	58	FA	M/195	H/80	2.1	S/S4	-	-
Draugr Hound	DCT	22-24	FA	M/188	L/15	3.8	T	-	S
Elder Sveawolf	SvW	13	FA	M/210	–	3.3	S	2	-
Enhorning	Rau,FJM,FOG	48-51	FA	F/230	L/1	4.0	C/T1	-	S
Fell Cat	DSp	45	FA	M/200	M/50	3.8	S	-	-
Fire Toad	Mus	27	Rp	M/188	–	3.8	C	-	-
Firecat	Mus	24	Rp	F/220	H/80	3.5	S/S2	2	-
Frost Bound Bear	Rau	47-50	FA	M/200	H/80	3.8	C	-	-
Frost Hound	FUp,FYF	30-31	FA	M/205	L/5	3.7	T	-	-
Frost Stallion	Rau,FOG	54-55	FA	F/230	L/25	4.0	C	-	S
Frosty Colt	SvW,FUp,FYF	20	FA	F/230	–	4.0	C	-	S
Frothing Sveawolf	SvW	19	FA	M/210	H/99	3.2	T	-	S
Fylgja	Rau,FJM,FOG	50-52	IU	F/230	–	3.5	S/S3	-	-
Giant Bull Frog	Myr	1	Soft	M/175	–	3.8	T	-	-
Giant Tree Frog	SkR	20-21	Soft	M/175	–	3.8	C	-	-
Glacial Mauler	FJM,FOG,FUp,FYF	44-45	FA	M/200	H/80	3.8	C	-	-
Grass Cat	SvW	11-12	FA	F/230	–	3.5	S/S1	3	-
Gray Worg	Myr,SkR	10	FA	M/210	M/50	3.6	T/S5	3	S
Great Lynx	FJM,FOG,FUp,FYF	39-42	FA	M/210	–	3.5	S/S3	-	-
Grizzled Sveawolf	SvW	13	FA	M/210	M/50	3.3	T	2	S
Hallaratta	DSp	36-38	FA	M/195	L/10	3.8	T	-	-
Hill Cat	SvE,VMu	10	FA	M/200	L/20	3.7	S	2	-
Icebreaker	FJM	48	Rp	M/177	–	3.9	C	-	-
Icemuncher	FUp,FYF	28	Rp	M/177	–	3.9	C	-	-
Kopparorm	DSp	49	Rp	M/183	–	3.8	T	-	-
Large Sveawolf	SvW	11	FA	M/210	M/50	3.3	T	2	S
Lupine Gnawer	SvE	0	FA	M/200	–	3.8	T	-	-
Lupine Snarler	Myr,SvE	2	FA	M/200	–	3.8	T	-	-
Mad Rat	DCT	20-22	FA	M/188	L/13	3.8	T	-	-
Mud Frog	VnS	30-36	Soft	M/192	–	3.5	C	-	-
Myrkcat	Myr	3	FA	M/180	–	3.7	S	-	-
Nocuous Hound	Mus	29	Rp	F/225	H/80	3.3	T	3	-
Noxious Hound	Mus	24	Rp	M/210	H/80	3.5	T	1	S
Rabid Sveawolf	SvW	18	FA	M/210	H/99	3.2	T	-	-
Rabid Wolfhound	VMu	11	FA	M/200	H/99	3.7	T/S5	-	-
Ribbon Toad	SvW	12-13	Soft	M/170	–	3.8	C	-	-
Ridgeback Worg	Myr	11-13	FA	M/210	H/70	3.6	T/S5	3	S
Rugged Dwarven Pony	Got,SvE	4	FA	M/210	–	3.8	C	-	-
Savage Lynx	SvW	15-16	FA	M/210	H/99	3.0	S/S5	7	-
Savage Winterwolf	Rau	51-55	FA	F/225	L/1	3.4	T	-	S
Scaled Retriever	Mal	50	FA-Rp	2x/350	M/50	2.0	S	8	-
Scaled Varg Snarler	Mal	34-36	FA-Rp	F/224	H/80	3.8	C	-	-
Scaled Varg Yearling	Mal	25-31	FA-Rp	F/220	H/80	3.3	T/T1	1	-
Scavenger	Got,Myr	1	FA	S/150	–	3.8	T	-	-
Sharpfang Worg	Myr	12-14	FA	M/210	H/90	3.5	T/S5	3	S
Sleigh Horse	FUp,FYF	30	FA	F/270	–	4.0	C	-	-
Sleipneirsson	Rau,FOG	55-56	FA	F/230	–	4.0	C	-	-
Small Cave Mauler	DVC	18-19	FA	M/192	H/70	3.8	S	-	-
Small Hill Cat	SvE,VMu	7	FA	M/210	H/70	3.0	S/S3	10	-
Smiera-Gatto	Got,SvE	4	FA	F/220	L/1	3.8	S	2	-
Sveawolf	SvE,SvW	3	FA	M/200	–	3.8	T	-	S
Sveawolf Cub	SvE,SvW	0	FA	S/140	–	3.8	T	-	S
Sveawolf Mother	SvE,SvW	5	FA	M/200	–	3.8	T	-	S
Sveawolf Packleader	SvW	14	FA	M/210	M/50	3.3	T	2	S
Taiga Cat	FJM,FUp,FYF	32-33	FA	M/200	–	3.6	S/S3	-	-
Tawny Lynx	Got,Myr	8	FA	M/205	L/5	3.6	S/S1	5	-
Tawny Lynx Cub	Myr,SvE	0	FA	F/220	–	3.8	S	1	-
Timber Cat	SkR	36-37	FA	M/201	–	3.5	S/S9	3	-
Timberland Badger	SkR	32-33	FA	M/180	L/10	3.7	S/T3	-	-
Tomte Warhound	DNL	9	FA	M/200	H/85	3.3	T	1	S
Torpor Worm	FJM,FOG,FUp,FYF	37	Rp	M/177	L/2	3.9	C	-	-
Wee Wolf	Got	5	FA	M/200	L/10	3.5	T	1	-
White Wolf	Rau,FJM,FOG,FUp,FYF	27-31	FA	M/215	–	3.6	T	-	S
Wild Hog	Got,Myr,VMu	2	FA	M/188	–	3.8	S	-	-
Winter Wolf	Rau,FJM,FOG, FUp,FYF	42-46	FA	F/225	L/1	3.4	T	-	S
Wolf Nipper	Got	0	FA	S/150	–	3.8	T	-	-
Wolfhound	Got	6	FA	M/205	L/10	3.8	T	2	S
Wolverine	SkR	39-40	FA	M/190	H/90	3.0	S/S2	2	S
Wood Rat	SkR	24-25	FA	M/188	M/30	3.7	T	2	-
Woodland Badger	SkR	22-23	FA	M/175	L/1	3.7	S/T2	-	-
Wounded Sveawolf	SvW	11	FA	M/210	–	3.3	S	2	-
Young Lynx	Got,SvE,VMu	2	FA	F/220	–	3.8	S	1	-
Young Sveawolf	SvE,SvW	1	FA	S/160	–	3.8	T	-	S
Young Wolverine	SkR	28-29	FA	M/170	H/70	3.3	S/S4	-	C

DEMON

Name	Zones	Lvl	Body Type	Spd	Agg	Atk Spd	Atk Type	Ev %	S/C
Flaming Raukomaz	Mus	30	EF	M/200	H/80	3.1	S/S5	6	C
Nip Mephit	FUp,FYF	23-25	EI	M/188	L/1	3.8	S	-	-
Pine Imp	Got,Myr	6	TP	M/190	M/50	3.6	C/T2	1	-
Pine Mephit	SkR	23	TP	M/188	M/50	3.6	C/T5	5	-
Snow Imp	SvW,FUp,FYF	20-22	EI	M/188	L/1	3.8	S	-	-
Wood Imp	Got,Myr	5	TP	M/190	M/50	3.6	C/T5	1	-
Wood Mephit	SkR	22	TP	M/188	M/50	3.6	C/T5	5	-

DRAGON

Name	Zones	Lvl	Body Type	Spd	Agg	Atk Spd	Atk Type	Ev %	S/C
Cinder Drake	Mus	28	Rp	F/220	–	3.2	S/S1	2	-
Envy Drakeling	Got,Myr,SkR,SvE	9	Rp	F/240	M/50	3.6	T/S2	-	C
Mature Wyvern	Rau,FJM, FOG,FUp	54-57	Rp	M/188	L/5	3.3	T	-	S
Savage Wyvern	Rau,FJM, FOG,FUp	45-48	Rp	M/188	H/90	3.1	T	-	S
Silverscale Drakeling	SvE	9	Rp	F/240	–	3.6	T	12	C
Spawn Of Gjalpinulva	Mal	37	FA-Rp	F/275	H/100	3.0	T/S4	-	S
Wyvern	FOG,FUp,FYF	36-39	Rp	M/188	L/15	3.5	T	-	S
Young Envy Drake	Myr,SkR	20-22	Rp	F/240	H/90	3.6	T/S5	5	S
Young Silverscale Drake	SkR	22	Rp	F/240	–	3.7	T	12	C
Young Wyvern	FUp,FYF	28-30	Rp	M/188	L/2	3.6	T	-	S

The Atlas

Monster	Zones	Lvl	Body Type	Spd	Agg	Atk Spd	Atk Type	Ev %	S/C
ELEMENTAL									
Biting Wind	FJM,FUp,FYF	29-33	EA	M/188	L/20	3.2	S/S1	-	-
Block Of Ice	FUp,FYF	36-37	EI	M/188	–	4.3	C	-	-
Crusher	DSp	48-50	EE	M/175	L/1	4.0	C	-	-
Dryad Blossom	SkR	20	Cl	M/188	M/50	3.8	T	-	C
Dryad Greenthumb	SkR	21	Cl	M/188	M/50	3.8	T	-	C
Dryad Sprig	Got	4	Soft	M/188	–	3.8	T	-	C
Dryad Sprout	Got	3	Soft	M/188	–	3.8	T	-	C
Flame Spout	Mus	25	EF	M/188	H/80	3.7	S	-	-
Flame Thrower	Mus	21-23	EF	M/188	M/30	3.8	S	-	S
Flurry	FUp,FYF	23	EA	M/188	L/20	3.3	S	-	-
Gelid Mass	FOG,FUp,FYF	35	EI	M/188	–	4.1	C	-	-
Hailer	FUp,FYF	28	EI	M/188	M/50	3.8	C	-	S
Hailstone	FUp,FYF	20	EI	M/188	–	3.0	C	-	S
Host Of The Earth	Got	6	EE	F/220	–	4.3	C/C5	-	S
Host Of The Wind	Got	7	EA	F/220	–	3.5	S	4	S
Iceberg	FJM,FOG,FUp	41-42	EI	M/188	–	3.9	C	-	-
Lava Monster	Mus	28	EF	M/188	H/80	4.0	C	-	-
Maghemoth	Mus	30	EF	M/188	H/80	4.2	C	-	-
Nacken	Got	8	EI	M/188	H/80	3.8	S	-	-
Ra Of Oak	SkR	30	Cl	M/188	L/20	3.8	T	-	S
Ra Of Pine	SkR	29	Cl	M/188	L/20	3.8	T	-	S
Ra Of Willow	SkR	31	Cl	M/188	L/20	3.8	T	-	S
Shard Golem	FJM,FOG,FUp,FYF	42	EI	M/188	L/5	3.8	C	-	-
Sidhe Gaoite	SkR	35-36	EA	M/188	–	3.8	C	-	S
Tree Spirit	SkR	27	TP	M/188	–	3.8	C	-	C
Twister	FYF	29	EA	M/188	L/20	3.3	S	-	-
Water Sprite	SvW	13-14	EW	M/188	M/30	3.8	C	-	S
Whirlwind	SvE	6	EA	M/210	L/10	4.0	S	7	-
Wind Spirit	SkR	27-28	EA	M/188	–	3.8	C	-	C
Wind Sprite	SvW	14-15	EA	M/188	M/30	3.8	S	-	S
Wind Wisp	Got,Myr,SvW	9	EA	F/220	–	3.5	S/S2	6	S
GIANT									
Broken Jotun	VnS	54-57	St	M/192	L/20	3.4	C/S15	-	S
Clay Jotun	VnS	40-42	St	M/200	L/20	2.5	C/S15	-	S
Clay Jotun Guard	VnS	44	St	M/200	L/20	2.5	C/S15	-	S
Clay Jotun Hunter	VnS	50	St	M/200	L/20	3.4	C/S15	-	S
Clay Jotun Retainer	VnS	46	St	M/200	L/20	2.5	C/S15	-	S
Clay Jotun Runner	VnS	48	St	F/250	L/20	2.5	C/S15	-	S
Crippled Jotun	VnS	50-53	St	S/100	L/20	3.4	C/S15	-	S
Fire Giant Guard	Mus	30	St	M/200	H/80	4.2	C	-	C
Fire Giant Lookout	Mus	27	St	M/200	H/80	4.2	C	-	C
Fire Giant Scout	Mus	28	St	M/200	H/80	4.2	C	-	C
Fire Giant Spirit	Mus	40	IU	M/200	H/80	4.2	C/C20	-	-
Fire Giant Watchman	Mus	29	St	M/200	H/80	4.2	C	-	C
Frost Cyclops	Rau	61-62	EI/Cl	F/260	H/70	4.5	C	-	S
Frost Giant	FOG,FYF	37-39	EI/Cl	F/260	L/10	4.4	C	-	-
Ice Giant	FOG,FUp,FYF	33-36	EI/Cl	F/230	L/10	4.2	C	-	-
Ice Scrag	FJM,FOG,FUp,FYF	33-34	EI	M/178	H/80	3.7	C	-	-
Jotun Despot	VnS	61	St	F/250	L/20	2.1	C/S15	-	S
Jotun Outcast	VnS	58-59	St	M/192	L/20	3.4	C/S15	-	S
Jotun Overlord	VnS	62	St	F/250	L/20	2.1	C/S15	-	S
Jotun Warchief	VnS	60	St	F/250	L/20	2.1	C/S15	-	S
Snow Giant	FUp,FYF	30-33	EI/Cl	M/200	L/10	4.0	C	-	-

Monster	Zones	Lvl	Body Type	Spd	Agg	Atk Spd	Atk Type	Ev %	S/C
HUMAN-LIKE									
Abominable Snowman	FUp,FYF	27-30	Cl	M/188	H/80	3.8	C	-	-
Ashmonger	Mus	23-25	Rp	M/195	H/80	3.7	C	1	S
Backwoods Marodor	Mal	39-43	St	M/188	H/80	3.3	S/S3	4	-
Blodfelag Captive	SvW	10	Cl	M/188	–	4.5	C	-	-
Blodfelag Dreng	SvW	14-16	St	M/188	H/85	3.6	S/S4	-	S
Blodfelag Haxa	SvW	19-20	Cl	M/188	H/85	4.0	C	-	S
Blodfelag Henchman	SvW	12-13	Lr	M/188	H/85	3.3	S/S3	-	S
Blodfelag Livvakt	SvW	20	Ch	M/188	H/85	3.0	S/T3	-	S
Blodfelag Oathbreaker	SvW	10-12	St	M/188	H/85	3.8	C	-	S
Blodfelag Partisan	SvW	13-15	Cl	M/188	H/85	3.6	S	-	S
Blodfelag Soothsayer	SvW	14	Cl	M/188	H/85	4.0	C	-	S
Blodfelag Svard	SvW	16-17	St	M/188	H/85	3.5	S/S4	1	S
Blodfelag Thralldriver	SvW	14-15	Cl	M/188	H/85	3.8	S	-	S
Blodfelag Tormentor	SvW	19-20	St	M/188	H/85	3.5	S	-	S
Blodfelag Windcaller	SvW	17-18	Cl	M/188	H/85	4.0	C	-	S
Blodfelag Wolfwarrior	SvW	18-19	Ch	M/188	H/85	3.0	S/T5	5	S
Bone-Eater Clanmother	FOG, FUp,FYF	42	Cl	M/188	H/80	3.8	S	-	S
Bone-Eater Eviscerater	FJM,FOG, FUp,FYF	41-42	Ch	M/188	H/80	3.0	S/S5	-	S
Bone-Eater Oracle	FJM,FOG, FUp,FYF	39-41	Cl	M/188	H/80	3.9	C	-	S
Bone-Eater Slayer	FJM,FUp,FYF	37-38	Ch	M/188	H/80	3.5	S/S2	-	S
B-E. Spine-Ripper	FJM,FUp,FYF	39-40	Ch	M/188	H/80	3.4	S/S3	-	S
Bone-Eater Warleader	FJM, FOG,FYF	45	Ch	M/188	H/80	3.4	S/S4	-	S
Bounty Hunter	Rau	55	Lr	M/188	H/80	3.7	S	-	C
Bounty Hunter Leader	Rau	57	Lr	M/188	H/80	3.7	S	-	C
Cave Ogre	DVC	29-30	Lr	M/192	H/70	3.7	S	-	S
Cave Trow	DSp	47	Cl	M/188	L/10	3.8	S	-	S
Cave Trow Trollkarl	DSp	48	Cl	M/188	L/10	3.8	C	-	S
Duegar Tjuv	DSp	37	Lr	M/188	L/3	3.8	T	3	-
Dverge Crackler	Mus	28	St	M/188	M/50	3.6	T/C15	5	C
Dverge Fire-Eater	Mus	30	St	M/188	H/80	3.6	T/C20	7	C
Dverge Igniter	Mus	25	St	M/188	H/75	3.6	C/S5	1	C
Dverge Sparker	Mus	24	St	M/188	H/75	3.6	C/S5	1	C
Elder Skogsfru	SkR	32	Cl	M/188	H/80	3.8	S	-	C
Escaped Thrall	Got,SvE	3	Cl	M/188	M/30	3.8	C	-	-
Fossegrim	FUp,FYF	29-31	Cl	M/185	–	3.8	C	-	-
Frostbite Wildling	FUp,FYF	27-29	FA	M/185	L/1	3.8	S	-	-
Goblin Guard	DVC	25-27	Ch	M/192	H/70	3.7	S	-	-
Gotawitch	Got	9	Cl	M/175	H/80	4.0	C	-	-
Half-Frozen Madman	FUp,FYF	25	Cl	M/180	H/80	4.1	C	-	-
Hill Person	VMu	6	Cl	M/188	M/40	3.8	C	-	C
Hobgoblin Biter	VMu	6	Cl	M/188	M/60	3.8	S	-	S
Hobgoblin Fish-Catcher	Got,Myr	0	Cl	M/188	–	3.8	S	-	S
Hobgoblin Pincher	Got,Myr	4	Cl	M/188	M/40	3.8	T	-	S
Hobgoblin Prankster	Got,VMu	3	Cl	M/188	–	3.8	S	-	S
Hobgoblin Prowler	Got,VMu	8	Cl	M/188	H/80	3.7	S/T1	-	S
Hobgoblin Snagger	Got,Myr	2	Cl	M/188	–	3.8	S	-	S
Hobgoblin Snake-Finder	Got,Myr, VMu	1	Cl	M/188	–	3.8	S	-	S
Huldu Hunter	Got,VMu	4	Cl	M/188	L/5	3.8	T	-	S
Huldu Lurker	Got,VMu	2	Cl	M/188	L/5	3.8	T	-	S
Huldu Outcast	Got,VMu	1	Cl	M/188	–	3.8	T	-	-
Huldu Stalker	Got,VMu	5	Cl	M/188	M/30	3.8	T	-	S
Isalf Abider	FYF	30	Lr	M/188	–	3.8	C	-	S
Isalf Blinder	FUp,FYF	34-35	Lr	M/188	L/5	4.0	C	-	S
Isalf Forayer	FJM,FOG,FUp,FYF	44	Ch	M/188	L/5	2.5	S/S2	-	C

Name	Zones	Lvl	Body Type	Spd	Agg	Atk Spd	Atk Type	Ev %	S/C
Isalf Icemage	FUp,FYF	32-34	Lr	M/188	L/5	4.0	C	-	S
Isalf Scryer	FUp,FYF	33	Lr	M/188	L/5	4.0	C	-	S
Isalf Snowtracker	FJM,FUp,FYF	35	St	M/188	L/5	3.6	T/S1	-	S
Isalf Surveyor	FUp,FYF	32-33	St	M/188	L/5	3.8	T	-	S
Isalf Warrior	FUp,FYF	35-36	Ch	M/188	L/5	3.3	S/S2	-	S
Lair Guard	DNL	10-11	Lr	M/175	H/90	3.7	S	-	-
Lair Patrol	DNL	9	Lr	M/175	H/90	3.7	S	-	-
Little Water Goblin	Got,SvE,VMu	2	Cl	S/150	–	3.8	S	-	-
Mad Kobold	DSp	42	Cl	M/188	L/25	3.8	C	-	-
Mindless Thrall	SvW	10	Cl	M/188	H/85	3.8	C	-	-
Minor Fideal	SvW	15-16	EW	M/188	H/80	3.8	S	-	-
Moss Maiden	SkR	24-25	Cl	M/188	H/80	3.8	S	-	-
Nordic Yeti	FJM,FOG,FUp,FYF	33-36	FA	M/188	H/80	3.8	C	-	-
Northern Ettin	FOG,FUp,FYF	25-27	Cl	M/188	H/80	3.8	C	-	-
Perfidious Pook	Got,SkR	10	Cl	M/188	H/80	3.3	S	7	-
Prisoner	DNL	0	Cl	2x/400	–	3.9	S	-	S
Roaming Thrall	SvE	7	Cl	M/188	H/70	3.8	C	-	-
Seithkona Initiate	Got	5	Cl	M/188	H/80	4.0	C	-	C
Sharktooth Whelp	Got	1	Cl	S/150	–	3.8	T	-	-
Sidhe Draoi	SkR	36-38	Cl	M/188	L/10	4.0	C	-	C
Skogsfru	SkR,SvW	13-14	Cl	M/188	H/80	3.8	S	-	C
Snowshoe Bandit	FJM,FOG, FUp,FYF	30-35	St	M/188	H/80	3.7	S	-	S
Snowshoe Bandit Mage	FJM,FOG, FUp	32-33	Cl	M/188	H/80	3.8	C	-	S
Stromkarl	FJM,FUp	38-40	Cl	M/185	L/5	3.8	C	-	-
Svartalf Arbetare	DSp	37	Cl	M/188	–	3.8	C	-	C
Svartalf Bloodbinder	Mal	51-55	Lr	F/225	H/80	3.4	T/T5	-	C
Svartalf Chanter	Myr,SvW	14-15	DV/Lr	M/188	H/85	3.8	C	-	C
Svartalf Foister	Mal	48-52	Lr	M/195	H/80	3.6	T/T1	-	C
Svartalf Foreman	DSp	39	Cl	M/188	–	3.8	C	-	C
Svartalf Guard	Got	10	Cl	M/188	H/80	3.6	S/S15	2	S
Svartalf Hunter	Myr,SvW	14-15	DV/Lr	M/188	H/85	3.3	T	1	S
Svartalf Infiltrator	Mal	45-49	Lr	M/192	H/80	3.8	T	-	C
Svartalf Merchant	Got	6	Cl	M/188	H/80	3.7	S	2	C
Svartalf Outcast	Got,Myr	8	Cl	M/188	H/80	3.7	S	2	S
Svartalf Predator	Myr	16	DV/St	M/190	H/90	3.1	S/T3	8	C
Svartalf Smith	Got	6	Cl	M/188	H/80	3.7	S	2	C
Svartalf Sorcerer	Myr	15	DV/Cl	M/188	H/90	4.0	C	-	C
Svartalf Thrall	DSp	36	Cl	M/188	–	3.8	C	-	C
Svartalf Watcher	Myr	13	DV/Lr	M/190	H/90	3.5	S/T2	3	C
Svartskogsfru	Myr	17	DV/Cl	M/192	H/80	3.7	S	-	S
Svendo	DVC	31-34	FA/Cl	M/192	H/70	3.7	S	-	S
Thrall	SvE	3	Cl	M/188	–	3.8	S	-	-
Tomte Aggressor	SvE	9	Lr	M/175	H/90	3.7	S	-	C
Tomte Caitiff	DNL	17	FA	M/188	H/80	3.5	S/S30	-	C
Tomte Captor	DNL	12	FA	M/175	H/99	3.7	S	3	C
Tomte Cutthroat	DNL	8	FA	M/175	H/80	3.7	S	3	-
Tomte Guard	DNL	16	FA	M/188	H/80	3.5	S/S30	-	-
Tomte Guard	DNL	17	FA	M/188	H/80	3.5	S/S30	-	S
Tomte Handler	DNL	10	FA	M/175	H/90	3.7	S	-	C
Tomte Hoodoo	DNL	13	FA	M/188	H/80	4.4	C	-	S
Tomte Jager	DNL	15	FA	M/188	H/80	3.5	S/S30	-	S
Tomte Pillager	SvE	8	Lr	M/175	H/80	3.7	S	3	C
Tomte Plunderer	SvE	10	Lr	M/175	H/99	3.7	S	3	C
Tomte Protector	DNL	13	FA	M/175	H/90	3.7	S	-	-
Tomte Runner	DNL	13	FA	M/175	H/90	3.7	S	-	-
Tomte Seer	DNL	18	FA	M/188	H/80	3.5	S/S30	-	C
Tomte Shaman	DNL	10	FA	M/188	H/80	4.4	C	-	-
Tomte Skirmisher	SvE	7	Lr	M/175	H/70	3.8	S	3	C
Tomte Thug	SvE	5	Lr	M/175	M/50	3.8	C	-	C
Tomte Zealot	DNL	16	FA	M/188	H/80	3.5	S/S30	-	S
Vendo Bone-Collector	VMu	13	FA	M/188	H/80	4.4	C	-	S
Vendo Flayer	VMu	15	FA	M/188	H/80	3.5	S/S3	-	S
Vendo Frightener	VMu	14	FA	M/188	H/80	3.5	S	3	S
Vendo Guard	DVC	22-25	Ch	M/192	H/70	3.7	S	-	S
Vendo Reaver	DVC	24-30	St	M/192	H/70	3.8	S	-	S
Vendo Savager	DVC	32-35	Pl	M/192	M/60	3.6	S	-	S
Vendo Shaman	VMu	10	FA	M/188	H/80	4.4	C	-	S
Vendo Stalker	VMu	12	FA	M/188	H/80	3.6	T/S5	2	S
Vendo Warrior	VMu	11	FA	M/188	H/80	3.6	S/C2	-	S
Vendo Yowler	DVC	28-31	Lr	M/192	H/70	3.8	S	-	S
Wildling	Got,SvE	0	FA	M/188	–	3.8	S	-	-

INSECT

Name	Zones	Lvl	Body Type	Spd	Agg	Atk Spd	Atk Type	Ev %	S/C
Arachite Greensilk	Myr	5	Sh	M/190	L/10	3.8	T	-	S
Arachite Grymherre	SkR,DSp	42	Sh	M/195	H/80	2.5	T/T8	-	C
Arachite Hatchling	Myr	1	Sh	M/170	–	3.8	T	-	S
Arachite Husker	DSp	38-39	Sh	M/195	H/80	3.3	T	-	C
Arachite Impaler	SkR,DSp	37-39	Sh	M/195	H/80	3.0	T/T1	-	C
Arachite Krigare	SkR,DSp	40	Sh	M/195	H/80	3.0	T/T5	-	C
Arachite Prelate	SkR,DSp	39-40	Sh	M/195	H/80	3.3	T	-	C
Arachite Priest	Myr,SkR	15-16	Sh	M/190	H/75	3.7	T	-	C
Arachite Shadowslinker	Myr	13-15	Sh	M/190	M/50	3.6	T/T1	2	C
Arachite Tunnelhost	DSp	36-37	Sh	M/195	H/80	3.3	T	-	C
Arachite Vakt	DSp	37-38	Sh	M/195	H/80	3.0	T/T1	-	C
Arachite Weblasher	Myr	14-16	Sh	M/190	H/80	3.6	T/T5	2	C
Army Ant Soldier	SvE	8	Sh	M/175	H/70	3.6	T/T4	-	S
Army Ant Worker	SvE	6	Sh	M/175	–	3.8	T	-	C
Carrion Crawler	Got,Myr	6	Sh	M/170	–	3.7	T/S10	-	-
Carrion Eater	Got,Myr	7	Sh	M/170	–	3.7	T/S10	-	-
Cave Crab	DCT	19-21	Sh	M/188	–	3.8	T/S20	-	-
Cave Spider	DNL	13-14	Sh	M/192	H/75	3.6	S	-	-
Chiseler	SvW,FUp,FYF	20-24	Sh	M/188	–	3.8	T	-	-
Corpse Crawler	DCT	21-23	Sh	M/188	M/50	3.7	S	-	-
Corpse Eater	Myr	11-13	Sh	M/188	–	3.7	S	-	-
Cursed Thulian	DSp	47	Sh	M/188	L/5	3.0	T	-	-
Death Spider	Myr	18	Sh	M/190	H/80	3.5	T/T2	5	-
Deeplurk Dissembler	DSp	47-49	Sh	M/195	H/80	3.0	T	-	S
Deeplurk Feeder	DSp	47	Sh	M/195	H/80	3.8	T	-	S
Deeplurk Manslayer	DSp	47-48	Sh	M/195	H/80	3.0	T/T3	-	S
Djupt Odjur	DSp	49	Sh	M/195	H/80	2.6	T/T3	-	S
Djupt Usling	DSp	48	Sh	M/195	H/80	2.6	T/T3	-	S
Djupt Vivunder	DSp	50	Sh	M/195	H/80	2.6	T/T3	-	S
Duegarhunter	DSp	36	Sh	M/200	L/1	3.8	T	-	-
Dungeon Chitin	DCT	22-23	Sh	M/195	L/20	3.5	T	-	-
Dungeon Crab	DCT	20-22	Sh	M/188	–	3.8	S/S20	-	-
Ekyps Gunstling	DSp	45	Sh	M/195	–	3.0	T	-	S
Ekyps Scavenger	DSp	42	Sh	M/195	–	3.5	T	-	-
Fire Ant Gatherer	Mus	21	Sh	M/188	L/10	3.8	T	-	S
Fire Ant Scavenger	Mus	20	Sh	M/188	L/10	3.8	T	-	S
Fire Ant Worker	Mus	22	Sh	M/188	L/10	3.8	T	-	S
Forest Spider	VnS	50-52	Sh	M/192	L/20	2.0	S	-	-
Forest Spider Queen	VnS	55	Sh	M/192	L/20	2.0	S	-	-
Forest Spider Runner	VnS	53	Sh	M/210	L/20	2.0	S	-	-
Frenetic Wolfspider	DVa	38	Sh	M/188	L/20	3.5	T/T3	-	-
Frosty Scuttlebug	FUp,FYF	23-24	Sh	M/188	–	3.8	S	-	-
Giant Snowcrab	FJM,FUp,FYF	33-34	Sh	M/188	–	3.8	S/S1	-	-
Giant Water Strider	SvE	5	Sh	M/175	M/65	3.8	T	-	C
Great Tingler	Myr,SkR	16-18	Sh	M/190	M/30	3.6	T	-	S
Harvestman	SvE	3	Sh	M/180	–	3.8	T	-	-

Monster	Zones	Lvl	Body Type	Spd	Agg	Atk Spd	Atk Type	Ev %	S/C
Husk	DSp	10	Soft	M/195	–	3.8	S	-	-
Icestrider Chiller	Rau,FUp,FYF	43-45	Sh	M/188	H/80	3.3	T	-	S
Icestrider Frostweaver	Rau,FJM,FOG,FUp,FYF	44-46	Sh	M/188	H/80	3.8	C	-	S
Icestrider Interceptor	Rau,FJM,FOG,FUp	47-51	Sh	M/188	H/80	3.1	T/T4	-	S
Large Wolfspider	DVa	28	Sh	M/188	–	3.5	T	-	-
Mud Crab	VnS	35	Sh	M/192	L/20	3.5	S	-	S
Mud Crab Warrior	VnS	36	Sh	M/192	L/20	3.5	S	-	S
Poisonous Cave Spider	DCT,DNL	15	Sh	M/192	H/75	3.6	S	-	-
Poisonous Cave Spider	DCT,DNL	23	Sh	M/192	H/75	3.6	T	-	-
Rock Crab	Got,SvE	7	Sh	M/190	L/10	4.5	S/S5	5	-
Soft-Shelled Crab	SvE	1	Soft	M/190	–	3.8	S	3	-
Soot Harvester	Mus	20-22	Sh	M/170	L/10	3.8	T/S2	-	-
Spider	DVC	25-28	Sh	M/192	H/70	3.8	S	-	-
Spindel	DSp	37	Sh	M/195	–	3.7	T	-	S
Spindel Layer	DSp	41	Sh	M/195	–	3.7	T	-	C
Spindel Silkster	DSp	39	Sh	M/195	–	3.7	T	-	S
Spindly Rock Crab	Got,SvE	9	Sh	M/190	L/5	4.0	S/S3	15	-
Stinger	DSp	37-39	Sh	M/190	L/5	3.3	S/T6	-	-
Sulphur Crab	Mus	20-22	Sh	M/170	L/10	3.8	T/S2	-	-
Terra Crab	DSp	38-40	Sh	M/185	–	3.3	S/S4	-	-
Tingler	Myr	12	Sh	M/190	L/20	3.7	T	-	S
Vein Spider	VMu	5	Sh	M/170	–	3.8	T	-	-
Vein Spiderling	Got,SvE,VMu	0	Sh	S/130	–	3.8	T	-	-
Venomous Tree Crawler	Mal	55	Sh	F/250	H/100	0.0	-	10	-
Water Strider	Got,SvE	1	Sh	M/188	–	3.8	T	-	S
Wolfspider	DVa	25	Sh	M/188	–	3.5	T	-	-
Wood-Eater	VMu	3	Sh	M/188	–	3.8	T	-	C
Wood-Eater Alate	VMu	7	Sh	M/210	–	3.8	T	5	C
Wood-Eater Hunter	SvE,VMu	5	Sh	M/188	–	3.5	T	2	C
Wood-Eater King	VMu	15	Sh	M/200	L/10	3.6	T/T20	-	C
Wood-Eater Queen	VMu	8	Sh	S/160	–	4.3	T	-	C
Wood-Eater Royal Guard	VMu	16	Sh	M/210	–	3.8	T	5	S
Wood-Eater Soldier	VMu	6	Sh	M/188	L/10	3.6	T/T20	-	S
Wood-Eater Worker	VMu	4	Sh	M/188	–	3.8	T	-	C

MAGICAL

Monster	Zones	Lvl	Body Type	Spd	Agg	Atk Spd	Atk Type	Ev %	S/C
Aurora	FJM,FOG,FUp	41-47	LE	M/188	–	3.8	S	-	-
Cold Light	SvW,FUp,FYF	20-25	LE	M/188	–	3.8	S	-	-
Crazed Lycantic	DVa	34	Cl	M/188	M/50	3.0	S/S1	-	S
Drakulv Armguard	Mal	42-46	FA-Rp	M/192	H/80	4.4	S	-	C
Drakulv Attendant	Mal	51-55	FA-Rp	M/192	H/80	4.8	S	-	S
Drakulv Axehand	Mal	48-52	FA-Rp	F/220	H/80	4.6	S	-	S
Drakulv Disciple	Mal	62-64	FA-Rp	F/250	H/80	5.4	S/C3	-	C
Drakulv Executioner	Mal	57-61	FA-Rp	F/245	H/80	5.2	S	-	S
Drakulv Klok	Mal	65	FA-Rp	3x/600	H/99	3.8	S	-	S
Drakulv Missionary	Mal	36-40	FA-Rp	F/250	H/80	4.0	S	-	C
Drakulv Prast	Mal	65	FA-Rp	3x/600	H/99	3.8	S	-	S
Drakulv Protector	Mal	54-58	FA-Rp	F/220	H/80	5.0	S/C4	-	C
Drakulv Riddare	Mal	65	FA-Rp	3x/600	H/99	3.8	S	-	S
Drakulv Sacrificer	Mal	45-49	FA-Rp	M/195	H/80	4.4	S	-	C
Drakulv Soultrapper	Mal	62-64	FA-Rp	F/248	H/80	5.2	S	-	C
Fenrir Guard	FJM,FOG,FUp,FYF	45	FA/Lr	M/188	H/80	3.6	S	-	C
Fenrir Mystic	Rau	57-60	FA/Lr	M/188	H/80	3.3	S/S3	-	C
Fenrir Prime	FJM,FYF	49	FA/Lr	M/188	H/80	3.3	S/S3	-	C
Fenrir Prophet	FJM,FOG,FUp,FYF	44-45	FA/Cl	M/188	H/80	4.0	S	-	C
Fenrir Shredder	FJM,FOG,FYF	45-46	FA/Lr	M/188	H/80	2.1	S/S10	-	C
Fenrir Snowscout	FUp,FYF	36-38	FA/Lr	M/188	H/80	3.5	T/S1	1	C
Fenrir Soldier	Rau	58	FA/Lr	M/188	H/80	3.3	S/S3	-	C
Fenrir Tracker	FJM,FUp,FYF	40-42	FA/Lr	M/188	H/80	3.6	T/S1	1	C
Ghost Light	Got,Myr	7	LE	F/220	–	3.5	S	-	-
Greater Fenrir	Rau	59-62	FA/Lr	M/188	H/80	3.3	S/S3	-	C
Icy Wisp	FJM,FUp,FYF	28-33	El	M/188	–	3.8	S	-	-
Minor Werewolf Noble	Myr,SkR	19-21	FA/Lr	M/192	H/90	3.3	S/S3	5	C
Mora Dancer	Myr	14-16	DV/Cl	M/195	H/80	3.4	S	3	S
Mora Rider	Myr	15	DV/Cl	M/195	H/80	3.4	S	3	S
Northern Light	FJM,FUp,FYF	25-30	LE	M/188	–	3.8	S	-	-
Patrolling Drakulv	Mal	39-43	FA-Rp	F/265	H/80	4.2	S	-	C
Seithr Orb	Got	9	ME	F/220	–	3.3	S	-	S
Shadow	Myr,SvW	10-11	DV	M/205	H/90	3.2	S	1	-
Soul Sinker	Myr	16	DV	M/192	H/90	3.4	C/C1	-	S
Werewolf	Myr,SkR	17	FA/Lr	M/192	H/90	3.3	S/S3	5	C
Werewolf Bodyguard	DVa	37	FA/Lr	M/188	M/50	3.3	S/S2	3	S
Werewolf Captain	SkR	37-38	FA/Lr	M/195	H/90	3.2	S/S16	6	S
Werewolf Churl	DVa	34	FA/Lr	M/188	–	3.8	S	-	S
Werewolf Commander	SkR	36	FA/Lr	M/195	H/90	3.2	S/S14	6	S
Werewolf Courier	SkR	27-28	FA/Lr	M/200	H/90	3.2	S/S1	6	C
Werewolf Grimnought	DVa	39	FA/Lr	M/188	L/25	2.9	S/S5	-	S
Werewolf Guard	SkR	31-33	FA/Lr	M/195	H/90	3.2	S/S10	6	S
Werewolf Lieutenant	SkR	33-34	FA/Lr	M/195	H/90	3.2	S/S12	6	S
Werewolf Noble	DVa	38	FA/Lr	M/188	L/20	3.6	S/S2	1	S
Werewolf Runner	SkR	21-22	FA/Lr	M/200	H/90	3.2	S/S2	6	C
Werewolf Scruff	DVa	35	FA/Lr	M/188	M/30	3.8	S	-	S
Werewolf Skulker	SkR	23-25	FA/Lr	M/195	H/90	3.2	S/S4	6	S
Werewolf Warder	SkR	27-30	FA/Lr	M/195	H/90	3.2	S/S6	6	C
Wolfaur Headsman	SkR	33-36	FA/Lr	M/195	H/90	3.2	S/S8	6	S
Wolfaur Lunarian	DVa	39	FA/Lr	M/188	L/1	3.8	S	-	C
Wolfaur Pragmatic	DVa	35	FA/Lr	M/188	–	3.6	S	-	C
Wolfaur Quixot	DVa	37	FA/Lr	M/188	L/1	3.4	S/S3	3	S

REPTILE

Monster	Zones	Lvl	Body Type	Spd	Agg	Atk Spd	Atk Type	Ev %	S/C
Aged Boreal Cockatrice	FJM,FOG,FUp	49	Rp	M/188	L/5	3.5	S	-	-
Alpine Cockatrice	FJM,FUp,FYF	32-33	Rp	M/188	L/5	3.5	S	-	-
Black Orm	VnS	36-38	Rp	M/192	M/50	3.0	T/T15	-	S
Blindsnake	DSp	37-38	Rp	M/180	–	3.8	T	-	-
Boreal Cockatrice	FUp,FYF	24-27	Rp	M/188	L/5	3.5	S	-	-
Carrion Lizard	Got,Myr,VMu	3	Rp	M/210	–	3.7	S	-	-
Cave Crawler	DVC	16-22	Rp	M/192	H/70	3.8	S	-	-
Cave Viper	DVC	25	Rp	M/192	H/70	3.8	S	-	-
Enslaved Orm	VnS	40	Rp	M/192	M/50	3.0	T/T15	-	S
Enslaved Orm Biter	VnS	44	Rp	M/192	M/50	3.0	T/T15	-	S
Enslaved Orm Runner	VnS	42	Rp	M/212	M/50	3.0	T/T15	-	S
Forest Viper	VnS	40-44	Rp	M/192	L/20	3.5	S	-	-
Frost Orm	FOG,FUp,FYF	35	Rp	M/188	L/15	3.8	T	-	-
Grass Viper	SvW	12	Rp	M/175	H/80	3.8	T	-	-
Green Orm	SkR	38-40	Rp	M/188	M/60	4.6	S	-	-
Green Serpent	Got,Myr,SvE	2	Rp	S/165	–	3.8	T	-	-
Hog-Nose Slither	Myr	0	Rp	M/170	–	3.8	T	-	-
Ice Lizard	FJM,FOG,FUp,FYF	32-34	Rp	M/188	–	3.6	T	-	-
Lake Serpent	SvW	10-11	Rp	M/175	–	3.8	T	-	-
Large Enslaved Orm	VnS	48-50	Rp	M/192	M/50	3.0	T/T15	-	S
Lg. Enslaved Orm Runner	VnS	48	Rp	M/212	M/50	3.0	T/T15	-	S
Lava Lizard	Mus	22	Rp	M/188	–	4.0	T	-	-
Mud Snake	SvE,VMu	0	Rp	S/130	–	3.7	T	-	-
Reincarnate Orm	VnS	45-55	Rp	M/192	M/50	2.5	T/T25	-	S
Small Black Orm	VnS	35	Rp	M/192	M/50	3.0	T/T15	-	S
Venomspitter	Myr	11-13	Rp	M/180	H/90	3.2	S	3	-
Water Snake	Got	0	Rp	M/180	–	3.8	T	-	-
Young Fire Wyrm	Mus	25-27	Rp	M/200	L/10	4.0	S/S10	-	-
Young Grendelorm	VMu	7	Rp	M/180	L/20	3.6	S	-	-

TREE OR PLANT

Monster	Zones	Lvl	Body Type	Spd	Agg	Atk Spd	Atk Type	Ev %	S/C
Fire Flower	Mus	20-22	TP	M/170	L/10	4.0	S	-	S
Frigid Broadleaf	Rau	57	TP	2x/350	H/99	3.8	C/S6	-	S
Sapherd	Got,Myr	5	TP	S/160	M/50	4.1	C	-	C
Shrieking Willow	Myr,SkR	18	TP	M/185	M/35	3.9	S	-	-
Treekeep	SkR	22	TP	M/188	M/50	4.0	C	-	C
Weeping Willow	Myr	12	TP	M/185	L/5	3.9	S	-	-
Whispering Willow	SkR	33-34	TP	M/188	–	4.2	T	-	-

UNDEAD

Monster	Zones	Lvl	Body Type	Spd	Agg	Atk Spd	Atk Type	Ev %	S/C
Acrid Ghoul	Mus	29	FU	M/188	H/80	3.6	C	-	-
Ashen Spirit	Mus	21-23	IU	M/170	L/10	3.8	C	-	-
Brittle Skeleton	Myr	0	BU	M/170	–	3.8	S	-	-
Burnt Skeletal Sentry	Mus	21	BU	M/170	M/30	3.7	T	-	C
Charred Skel. Warrior	Mus	23-25	BU	M/170	H/80	3.7	S/T10	4	C
Chattering Skeleton	FJM,FUp,FYF	32	BU	M/188	–	3.8	S	-	-
Chillsome Wight	Rau,FJM	51-52	FU	M/178	H/99	3.7	S	-	-
Cursed Mora	DCT	23-24	IU	M/210	L/20	3.0	T	3	C
Cursed Mora Dancer	DCT	25	IU	M/210	L/15	3.2	T	3	C
Cursed Mora Weeper	DCT	25	IU	M/210	L/15	3.2	T	3	C
Cursed Spirit	DCT	19-20	IU	M/188	M/50	3.8	C	-	S
Decaying Norseman	Myr	11	FU	M/175	M/30	3.8	C/C5	-	-
Decaying Troll	Myr	10	FU	M/175	M/30	3.8	C	-	-
Dishonored Hagbui	DCT	23-24	FU	M/188	H/80	3.8	S	-	S
Draugr Warrior	DCT	21-23	FU/Lr	M/188	H/80	3.8	C	-	S
Drifting Spirit	Got,SvW	12-14	IU	M/170	L/10	3.7	S	-	-
Drowned Soul	Got	3	IU	M/175	–	3.8	C	-	-
Dwarf Bone Skeleton	Got,SvE	5	BU	M/192	H/85	4.5	C	-	S
Enraged Mara	Mal	50	Rp	F/226	H/80	2.8	S	-	-
Entrancing Dirge	Myr	21	IU	M/170	M/60	3.8	C	-	-
Fallen Troll	FJM,FUp	44-45	FU	M/188	L/20	3.8	C	-	-
Fire Phantom	Mus	25	IU	M/188	H/80	3.7	S	-	-
Fragile Skeleton	Got,Myr,SvE	3	BU	M/170	–	3.8	S	-	-
Frore Lich	Rau,FJM,FOG	55-57	FU	M/175	H/99	3.7	S	-	S
Frost Spectre	FJM,FUp,FYF	45-46	IU	M/188	H/80	3.8	S	-	-
Ghastly Albion Invader	FJM,FOG, FUp,FYF	42-43	IU	M/188	L/20	3.8	S	-	-
Ghostly Hib. Invader	FJM,FOG, FUp,FYF	42-43	IU	M/188	L/20	3.8	S	-	-
Ghoulish Warrior	FJM,FUp	44-45	FU	M/188	L/20	3.8	S	-	-
Hagbui Berserker	VnS	50-51	IU/Lr	M/192	M/60	3.2	S	-	S
Hagbui Forge Tender	VnS	37	FU/Lr	M/192	–	2.1	S	-	-
Hagbui Guard	VnS	40-42	FU/Lr	M/192	M/60	3.2	S	-	S
Hagbui Herald	VnS	38	FU/Lr	M/192	–	2.1	S	-	-
Hagbui Page	VnS	36	FU/Lr	M/192	–	2.1	S	-	-
Hagbui Runemaster	VnS	42	IU/Lr	M/192	M/60	3.2	S	-	S
Hagbui Shaman	VnS	40	IU/Lr	M/192	M/60	3.2	S	-	S
Hagbui Spiritmaster	VnS	43	IU/Lr	M/192	M/60	3.2	S	-	S
Hagbui Squire	VnS	39	FU/Lr	M/192	–	2.1	S	-	-
Hagbui Swordbearer	VnS	35	FU/Lr	M/192	–	2.1	S	-	-
Hagbui Thane	VnS	53	IU/Lr	M/192	M/60	3.2	S	-	S
Haunt	Got,Myr,DNL	7	IU	M/190	L/15	3.9	C	-	-
Icy Skeleton	FUp,FYF	25	BU	M/188	–	3.8	S	-	-
Lost Hagbui	DSp	42	FU/Cl	M/175	H/80	3.8	C	-	S
Lost Spirit	DCT	19	IU	M/188	–	3.8	S	-	-
Magmatasm	Mus	29-31	IU	M/188	H/80	3.3	C	-	-
Meandering Spirit	Got,VMu	1	IU	S/150	–	3.8	S	-	-
Mephitic Ghoul	Mus	25-28	IU	M/188	H/80	3.7	S	-	-
Miserable Zombie	FJM,FOG, FUp,FYF	28-32	FU	M/175	L/1	4.0	S	-	-
Nordic Dirge	SvE	6	IU	S/150	M/60	3.8	C	-	-
Phantom Hound	Got,SvE,VMu	3	IU	M/200	–	3.8	T	-	-
Phantom Wolf	SvW	17-19	FU	M/210	H/99	3.0	T	3	-
Plasmatasm	Mus	23-25	IU	M/188	H/80	3.5	C	-	-
Pyrophantom	Mus	28-30	IU	M/188	H/80	3.4	S	-	-
Pyrotasm	Mus	35-42	IU	M/188	H/80	3.5	C/S5	-	-
Rattling Skeleton	Got,SvE,VMu	1	BU	M/170	–	3.8	S	-	-
Roaming Corpse	DCT	19-21	FU	M/174	–	3.8	C	-	-
Roaming Dirge	Myr,SvE	8	IU	S/150	H/80	3.8	C	-	-
Sanguinite Ghoul	SvW	13-14	FU	M/170	H/80	3.8	T	-	-
Seared Skeleton	Mus	27-29	BU	M/175	H/80	3.6	T	-	-
Shivering Presence	FJM,FUp,FYF	32-33	IU	M/190	L/1	3.8	S	-	-
Skeletal Oarsman	Got	5	BU	M/175	–	3.8	S/T5	-	-
Skeletal Seafarer	Got	4	BU	M/175	–	3.8	S	-	-
Spectral Bayer	Myr	13	IU	M/200	H/90	3.3	S	2	-
Spectral Hog	Got,Myr	2	IU	M/170	–	3.8	S	-	-
Spook	Got,Myr	6	IU	M/188	L/15	3.9	C	-	-
Sulphuric Ghoul	Mus	22	FU	M/188	H/80	3.7	S	-	-
Thawing Corpse	FUp,FYF	31	FU	M/170	H/99	3.8	C	-	-
Tomb Sentry	DCT	19-20	BU	M/188	H/75	3.8	C	-	-
Trapped Thrall	DCT	19-20	IU	M/170	–	3.8	C	-	-
Undead Explorer	Got,Myr	3	FU	M/170	–	3.8	C	-	-
Undead Troll Warrior	FOG,DSp	47	FU/Ch	M/188	L/20	3.8	C/C5	-	-
Undead Viking	FJM,FUp	44-45	FU	M/188	L/20	3.8	C	-	-
Undead Woodcarver	Myr	4	FU	M/188	–	3.8	C	-	-
Vapor Wraith	Mus	30	IU	F/240	H/80	3.0	T/S30	9	-
Vengeful Ghoul	DCT	23-24	FU	M/175	M/60	3.4	S	-	C
Way Keeper	DCT	19-20	BU	M/188	H/75	3.8	C	-	-
Wayward Ghoul	Myr,SvE, SvW,VMu	4	FU	M/170	–	3.8	S	-	-
Windswept Wraith	Rau,FJM,FOG	50-53	IU	M/200	H/80	3.3	S	-	S
Wintery Dirge	FJM,FOG,FUp,FYF	40-42	IU	M/188	H/80	3.8	S	-	-

Realm vs. Realm

ANIMAL

Monster	Zones	Lvl	Body Type	Spd	Agg	Atk Spd	Atk Type	Ev %	S/C
Demoniac Familiar (Boar)	RDF	30	FA	F/220	L/1	3.5	S	1	-
Demoniac Familiar (Cat)	RDF	21	FA	F/220	L/1	3.5	S	1	-
Demoniac Familiar (Dog)	RDF	33	FA	F/220	L/1	3.5	C	1	-
Demoniac Familiar (Horse)	RDF	27	FA	F/220	L/1	3.5	C	1	-
Demoniac Familiar (Lynx)	RDF	36	FA	F/220	L/1	3.5	S	1	-
Demoniac Familiar (Rat)	RDF	15	FA	F/220	L/1	3.5	T	1	-

DEMON

Monster	Zones	Lvl	Body Type	Spd	Agg	Atk Spd	Atk Type	Ev %	S/C
Ambassador Mannam	RDF	65	Lr	3x/650	H/80	4.0	S	-	S
Archivist Borath	RDF	35	Pl	2x/350	H/80	3.8	S	-	S
Avernal Quasit	RDF	25-27	Rp	F/250	H/80	3.9	T	3	S
Behemoth	RDF	65	EE	3x/650	H/80	4.0	C	-	S
Cambion	RDF	45-47	Rp	2x/450	H/80	3.0	S	-	S
Chaosian	RDF	55	Rp	2x/550	H/80	3.8	S	-	S
Chthonic Knight Absax	RDF	60	Pl	3x/600	H/80	4.1	S	-	S
Chthonic Knight Aciel	RDF	52	Pl	2x/520	H/80	4.1	S	-	S
Chthonic Knight Ain	RDF	52	Pl	2x/520	H/80	4.1	S	-	S
Chthonic Knight Azea	RDF	60	Pl	3x/600	H/80	4.1	S	-	S
Chthonic Knight Babyzu	RDF	52	Pl	2x/520	H/80	4.1	S	-	S
Chthonic Kn. Carnivon	RDF	54	Pl	2x/540	H/80	4.1	S	-	S
Chthonic Knight Exal	RDF	58	Pl	3x/580	H/80	4.1	S	-	S
Chthonic Knight Exte	RDF	50	Pl	2x/500	H/80	4.1	S	-	S
Chthonic Knight Ezpeth	RDF	56	Pl	3x/560	H/80	4.1	S	-	S
Chthonic Knight Fonath	RDF	64	Pl	3x/640	H/80	4.1	S	-	S
Chthonic Kn. Gaapoler	RDF	62	Pl	3x/620	H/80	4.1	S	-	S
Chthonic Knight Haag	RDF	62	Pl	3x/620	H/80	4.1	S	-	S
Chthonic Knight Ibeko	RDF	50	Pl	2x/500	H/80	4.1	S	-	S
Chthonic Knight Marbos	RDF	58	Pl	3x/580	H/80	4.1	S	-	S
Chthonic Knight Obarus	RDF	50	Pl	2x/500	H/80	4.1	S	-	S
Chthonic Knight Olov	RDF	64	Pl	3x/640	H/80	4.1	S	-	S
Chthonic Knight Prosel	RDF	54	Pl	2x/540	H/80	4.1	S	-	S
Chthonic Knight Ronoro	RDF	56	Pl	3x/560	H/80	4.1	S	-	S
Chthonic Knight Tamuel	RDF	64	Pl	3x/640	H/80	4.1	S	-	S
Chthonic Knight Ukobat	RDF	56	Pl	3x/560	H/80	4.1	S	-	S
Chthonic Knight Vosoes	RDF	62	Pl	3x/620	H/80	4.1	S	-	S
Chthonic Knight Zaeber	RDF	58	Pl	3x/580	H/80	4.1	S	-	S
Chthonic Knight Zafan	RDF	54	Pl	2x/540	H/80	4.1	S	-	S
Chthonic Knight Zagal	RDF	60	Pl	3x/600	H/80	4.1	S	-	S
Commander Abgar	RDF	61	Pl	3x/610	H/80	3.5	S/S1	-	S
Deamhaness	RDF	32-34	Rp	F/320	H/80	3.7	S	2	S
Director Kobil	RDF	50	Rp	2x/500	H/80	3.8	T	3	S
Duke Alloc	RDF	70	FA	4x/700	H/80	3.2	S/S5	5	S
Duke Aypol	RDF	70	Lr	4x/700	H/80	3.1	S	-	S
Duke Bimure	RDF	70	Lr	4x/700	H/80	3.0	S	-	S
Duke Eligar	RDF	70	Pl	4x/700	H/80	3.8	S/T1	-	S
Duke Harboris	RDF	70	Lr	4x/700	H/80	2.5	S	-	S
Duke Sallis	RDF	70	Pl	4x/700	H/80	3.4	S	-	S
Duke Satori	RDF	70	Rp	4x/700	H/80	3.9	T	2	S
Duke Zepor	RDF	70	Pl	4x/700	H/80	3.5	T	-	S
Earl Fenex	RDF	66	Rp	3x/660	H/80	4.3	C	-	S
Earl Glassalab	RDF	66	Rp	3x/660	H/80	3.8	S	2	S
Earl Ipostian	RDF	66	FA	3x/660	H/80	3.0	S/S5	5	S
Earl Mercur	RDF	66	Rp	3x/660	H/80	3.9	S	-	S
Earl Mermer	RDF	66	Pl	3x/660	H/80	3.5	S	-	S
Earl Oraxus	RDF	66	FA	3x/660	H/80	2.6	S/S5	5	S

Monster	Zones	Lvl	Body Type	Spd	Agg	Atk Spd	Atk Type	Ev %	S/C
Earl Vone	RDF	66	FA	3x/660	H/80	2.8	S/S5	5	S
Essence Shredder	RDF	48-50	Rp	2x/480	H/80	2.3	T/S3	-	S
Field Marshal Nebir	RDF	65	Lr	3x/650	H/80	3.1	S	-	S
Gatekeeper Dommel	RDF	45	Lr	2x/450	H/80	3.8	S	2	S
Grand Chancellor Adremal	RDF	74	FA	4x/740	H/80	4.0	C	-	S
High Lord Baelerdoth	RDF	72	EE	4x/720	H/80	3.8	C	-	S
High Lord Baln	RDF	72	Rp	4x/720	H/80	4.0	S	-	S
High Lord Oro	RDF	72	FA	4x/720	H/80	4.3	C	-	S
High Lord Saeor	RDF	72	Pl	4x/720	H/80	3.2	T/C1	-	S
Inquisitor Asil	RDF	56	Cl	3x/560	H/80	3.2	T/T1	-	S
Inquisitor Bor	RDF	60	Cl	3x/600	H/80	3.2	T/T1	-	S
Inquisitor Eciraum	RDF	56	Lr	3x/560	H/80	3.2	T/T1	3	S
Inquisitor Factol	RDF	60	Lr	3x/600	H/80	3.2	T/T1	3	S
Inquisitor Famuel	RDF	64	Cl	3x/640	H/80	3.2	T/T1	-	S
Inquisitor Haap	RDF	62	Cl	3x/620	H/80	3.2	T/T1	-	S
Inquisitor Hadis	RDF	54	Cl	2x/540	H/80	3.2	T/T1	-	S
Inquisitor Haimir	RDF	58	Cl	3x/580	H/80	3.2	T/T1	-	S
Inquisitor Hellos	RDF	52	Lr	2x/520	H/80	3.2	T/T1	3	S
Inquisitor Irawn	RDF	50	Lr	2x/500	H/80	3.2	T/T1	3	S
Inquisitor Kireasil	RDF	64	Lr	3x/640	H/80	3.2	T/T1	3	S
Inquisitor Lokis	RDF	50	Cl	2x/500	H/80	3.2	T/T1	-	S
Inquisitor Medebo	RDF	50	Cl	2x/500	H/80	3.2	T/T1	-	S
Inquisitor Morg	RDF	52	Lr	2x/520	H/80	3.2	T/T1	3	S
Inquisitor Morrian	RDF	52	Lr	2x/520	H/80	3.2	T/T1	3	S
Inquisitor Mucifen	RDF	54	Lr	2x/540	H/80	3.2	T/T1	3	S
Inquisitor Nej	RDF	58	Cl	3x/580	H/80	3.2	T/T1	-	S
Inquisitor Nifil	RDF	54	Cl	2x/540	H/80	3.2	T/T1	-	S
Inquisitor Niloc	RDF	56	Lr	3x/560	H/80	3.2	T/T1	3	S
Inquisitor Tlaw	RDF	60	Lr	3x/600	H/80	3.2	T/T1	3	S
Inquisitor Yonzael	RDF	64	Lr	3x/640	H/80	3.2	T/T1	3	S
Inquisitor Yor	RDF	58	Lr	3x/580	H/80	3.2	T/T1	3	S
Inquisitor Zaviben	RDF	62	Cl	3x/620	H/80	3.2	T/T1	-	S
Inquisitor Zazinol	RDF	62	Lr	3x/620	H/80	3.2	T/T1	3	S
Lecherous Gress	RDF	30	Rp	F/300	H/80	3.8	T	3	S
Lieutenant Gargantan	RDF	63	Lr	3x/630	H/80	2.9	S	-	S
Lieutenant Loran	RDF	63	Lr	3x/630	H/80	3.7	S	-	S
Lieutenant Persun	RDF	63	FA	3x/630	H/80	3.3	S/S5	5	S
Lilispawn	RDF	29-31	EE	F/290	H/80	4.0	C	-	S
Mahr	RDF	51	Rp	2x/510	H/80	3.8	S	2	S
Malroch The Cook	RDF	35	EE	2x/350	H/80	3.8	C	-	S
Marquis Almen	RDF	68	FA-Rp	3x/680	H/80	2.3	T	2	S
Marquis Chaosmar	RDF	68	FA-Rp	3x/680	H/80	3.3	T	2	S
Marquis Dortaleon	RDF	68	Lr	3x/680	H/80	3.0	S	-	S
Marquis Focalleste	RDF	68	Rp	3x/680	H/80	4.0	S	2	S
Marquis Haurian	RDF	68	Rp	3x/680	H/80	4.2	T	2	S
Marquis Sabonach	RDF	68	FA	3x/680	H/80	3.2	S/S5	5	S
Marquis Scottiax	RDF	68	Lr	3x/680	H/80	3.9	S	-	S
Marquis Valupa	RDF	68	Rp	3x/680	H/80	3.8	S	2	S
Molochian Tempter	RDF	40-42	Rp	2x/400	H/80	4.0	C	-	S
Mutilator Axa'Al	RDF	60	St	3x/600	H/80	2.5	C/C5	1	S
Mutilator Axalnam	RDF	58	St	3x/580	H/80	2.5	C/C5	1	S
Mutilator Axtanax	RDF	50	St	2x/500	H/80	2.5	C/C5	1	S
Mutilator Konapher	RDF	64	Ch	3x/640	H/80	2.5	C/C5	-	S
Mutilator Laicanroth	RDF	52	St	2x/520	H/80	2.5	C/C5	1	S
Mutilator Lazorous	RDF	54	Ch	2x/540	H/80	2.5	C/C5	-	S
Mutilator Marbozer	RDF	58	St	3x/580	H/80	2.5	C/C5	1	S
Mutilator Nianax	RDF	52	Ch	2x/520	H/80	2.5	C/C5	-	S
Mutilator Novinrac	RDF	54	St	2x/540	H/80	2.5	C/C5	1	S
Mutilator Okabi	RDF	50	St	2x/500	H/80	2.5	C/C5	1	S
Mutilator Oprionach	RDF	64	Ch	3x/640	H/80	2.5	C/C5	-	S

Monster	Zones	Lvl	Body Type	Spd	Agg	Atk Spd	Atk Type	Ev %	S/C
Mutilator Oronor	RDF	56	St	3x/560	H/80	2.5	C/C5	1	S
Mutilator Phaxazis	RDF	56	Ch	3x/560	H/80	2.5	C/C5	-	S
Mutilator Samiol	RDF	64	St	3x/640	H/80	2.5	C/C5	1	S
Mutilator Taboku	RDF	56	Ch	3x/560	H/80	2.5	C/C5	-	S
Mutilator Uxybab	RDF	52	Ch	2x/520	H/80	2.5	C/C5	-	S
Mutilator Vorazax	RDF	62	St	3x/620	H/80	2.5	C/C5	1	S
Mutilator Vozoaz	RDF	62	Ch	3x/620	H/80	2.5	C/C5	-	S
Mutilator Xaabaro	RDF	58	Ch	3x/580	H/80	2.5	C/C5	-	S
Mutilator Xagalith	RDF	60	Ch	3x/600	H/80	2.5	C/C5	-	S
Mutilator Xakanos	RDF	54	St	2x/540	H/80	2.5	C/C5	1	S
Mutilator Xazbalor	RDF	60	Ch	3x/600	H/80	2.5	C/C5	-	S
Mutilator Yooginroth	RDF	62	St	3x/620	H/80	2.5	C/C5	1	S
Mutilator Zurabo	RDF	50	Ch	2x/500	H/80	2.5	C/C5	-	S
Naburite Drinker	RDF	43-45	Rp	2x/430	H/80	4.0	T	-	S
Nightmare	RDF	61	Rp	3x/610	H/80	2.4	S	2	S
Pale Guardian	RDF	67	Rp	3x/670	H/80	4.6	C	-	S
Rocot	RDF	39-38	Lr	2x/360	H/80	3.5	S/T1	-	S
Soult. A. Alerion Knight	RDF	43	IU	M/188	L/5	3.6	T	-	-
Soult. A. Dragon Knight	RDF	50	IU	M/188	L/5	3.6	T	-	-
Soult. A. Eagle Knight	RDF	38	IU	M/188	L/5	3.6	C	-	-
Soult. A. Gryphon Knight	RDF	35	IU	M/188	L/5	3.6	T	-	-
Soult. A. Guardian	RDF	28	IU	M/188	L/5	3.6	T	-	-
Soult. A. Lion Knight	RDF	48	IU	M/188	L/5	3.6	S	-	-
Soult. A. Myrmidon	RDF	33	IU	M/188	L/5	3.6	S	-	-
Soult. A. Phoenix Knight	RDF	40	IU	M/188	L/5	3.6	S	-	-
Soult. A. Protector	RDF	25	IU	M/188	L/5	3.6	S	-	-
Soult. A. Unicorn Knight	RDF	45	IU	M/188	L/5	3.6	C	-	-
Soult. A. Warder	RDF	30	IU	M/188	L/5	3.6	C	-	-
Soult. H. Brehon	RDF	33	IU	M/188	L/5	3.6	T	-	-
Soult. H. Cosantoir	RDF	30	IU	M/188	L/5	3.6	S	-	-
Soult. H. Gilded Spear	RDF	45	IU	M/188	L/5	3.6	S	-	-
Soult. H. Grove Protecter	RDF	35	IU	M/188	L/5	3.6	C	-	-
Soult. H. Raven Ardent	RDF	38	IU	M/188	L/5	3.6	S	-	-
Soult. H. Savant	RDF	28	IU	M/188	L/5	3.6	C	-	-
Soult. H. Silver Hand	RDF	40	IU	M/188	L/5	3.6	T	-	-
Soult. H. Thunderer	RDF	43	IU	M/188	L/5	3.6	C	-	-
Soult. H. Tiarna	RDF	48	IU	M/188	L/5	3.6	T	-	-
Soult. H. Wayfarer	RDF	25	IU	M/188	L/5	3.6	T	-	-
Soult. N. Einherjar	RDF	50	IU	M/188	L/5	3.6	S	-	-
Soult. N. Elding Herra	RDF	45	IU	M/188	L/5	3.6	T	-	-
Soult. N. Elding Vakten	RDF	35	IU	M/188	L/5	3.6	S	-	-
Soult. N. Flammen Herra	RDF	43	IU	M/188	L/5	3.6	S	-	-
Soult. N. Flammen Vakten	RDF	33	IU	M/188	L/5	3.6	C	-	-
Soult. N. Isen Herra	RDF	40	IU	M/188	L/5	3.6	C	-	-
Soult. N. Isen Vakten	RDF	30	IU	M/188	L/5	3.6	T	-	-
Soult. N. Skiltvakten	RDF	28	IU	M/188	L/5	3.6	S	-	-
Soult. N. Stormur Herra	RDF	48	IU	M/188	L/5	3.6	C	-	-
Soult. N. Stormur Vakten	RDF	38	IU	M/188	L/5	3.6	T	-	-
Soult. N. Vakten	RDF	25	IU	M/188	L/5	3.6	C	-	-
Succubus	RDF	57	Rp	3x/570	H/80	3.1	S	2	S
Umbral Aegis	RDF	63	Sh	3x/630	H/80	4.2	S	-	S
Umbrood Warrior	RDF	59	Rp	3x/590	H/80	3.3	S	-	S

Monster	Zones	Lvl	Body Type	Spd	Agg	Atk Spd	Atk Type	Ev %	S/C

HUMAN-LIKE

Monster	Zones	Lvl	Body Type	Spd	Agg	Atk Spd	Atk Type	Ev %	S/C
Apprent. Necyomancer (F)	RDF	18	Cl	M/188	L/1	3.8	S	1	-
Apprent. Necyomancer (M)	RDF	21	Cl	M/188	L/1	3.8	T	1	-
Condemned Necyomancer	RDF	48	Cl	M/188	L/1	3.8	T	1	-
Cursed Necyomancer	RDF	42-45	Cl	M/188	L/1	3.8	C	1	-
Exp. Necyomancer (F)	RDF	36	Cl	M/188	L/1	3.8	S	1	-
Exp. Necyomancer (M)	RDF	39	Cl	M/188	L/1	3.8	T	1	-
Necyomancer (Female)	RDF	30	Cl	M/188	L/1	3.8	T	1	-
Necyomancer (Male)	RDF	33	Cl	M/188	L/1	3.8	C	1	-
Tormented Necyomancer	RDF	50	Cl	M/188	L/1	3.8	C	1	-
Young Necyomancer (F)	RDF	24	Cl	M/188	L/1	3.8	C	1	-
Young Necyomancer (M)	RDF	27	Cl	M/188	L/1	3.8	S	1	-

INSECT

Monster	Zones	Lvl	Body Type	Spd	Agg	Atk Spd	Atk Type	Ev %	S/C
Demoniac Familiar (Ant)	RDF	18	Sh	F/220	L/1	3.5	T	1	-
Demoniac Fam. (Scorpion)	RDF	24	Sh	F/220	L/1	3.5	T	1	-
Demoniac Fam. (Spider)	RDF	30	Sh	F/220	L/1	3.5	T	1	-

Appendix C: A Chat with Kirstena

When Prima suggested an atlas for Dark Age of Camelot, *we made a quick survey to see what players found useful in the maps that they used. More often than not, the answer was "look at Kirstena's maps, that's what we want." So we contacted Kirstena to see if she was interested in working with us. She's a busy woman, between real life,* DAoC *and making maps — but she agreed to help us out however she could, especially giving us the benefit of her experience in mapping out a world as extensive as* Dark Age.

-Melissa Tyler

Melissa: *So, why on earth did you take on a project as huge as mapping* DAoC? *I mean, IMGS got the monster locations handed to us on a platter, and it took us* forever *to get them all placed. You had to actually walk around and find the monsters yourself.*

Kirstena: I'm fairly new to gaming. I played *EQ* before *DAoC* and was spoiled by the plethora of maps available for my first online game experience.

I really didn't want to give up *EQ* when my fiancé (known to many as Caladin) brought home *DAoC* to try. We had 3 real-life friends that we started playing with. *Dark Age* quickly became my new addiction. Caladin kept suggesting that I make maps: "but you could do soooo much better than these, baby," with those cute puppy dog eyes.

So I made my first map. It really doesn't seem like it took much time to do, but I didn't try to do them all at once either. Starting out it took me probably three days or so to do a map; now if I really work at it I can sometimes do a map in a day. But I usually don't sit down and knock out an entire map. I have blanks that I sketch on, then draw up the basic terrain, then add the mobs. Mobs I take notes of as I travel or play.

Sometimes I go to a zone specifically to research mobs, but it's more fun if I can hunt as I map. I've gotten at least a level while mapping a zone before, *and* I find rarely hunted spawns that give good bonuses!

M: *Did you always intend it to be on a website?*

K: The website came about because I had software sitting at work that I had never used. I learn best while doing a project, so the site became my pet project. I talked to Caladin about it and he happened to have some web space that he's had for a long time — he offered to let me use it and that was that. I didn't want to bother with ads, and with Caladin's offer I didn't have to. Once I got the site up, I let my friends know about it. Cal had the idea of posting to VN boards, and from there it spread pretty much by word of mouth. Then Catacombs picked it up to include in their map links, I get a lot of feedback from people who found the site through them. Allakazam eventually picked it up also. By the time Kirstena — my character on Galahad — hit 50, I was getting tells in game from people asking if I was *that* Kirstena and telling me they liked my maps. I've learned a bit about creating, publishing and maintaining a website, not to mention setting up a good map template and honing it down to easily get to all the styles and icons I use.

M: *Is there information that you keep that you don't put in your maps?*

K: When I wander and note mobs for maps I usually note any info I notice about them — especially if they are neutral or hostile, if they BAF or Call or are connected together. I don't put that info on the maps because I haven't sat down and tackled that one yet. I'd probably key it in the moblist somehow.

When I started out, I did blanket mob groupings for some areas. I stopped doing that as I realized people wanted specific names for completing kill tasks quickly. So, while I don't list every instance of a mob, I list it in the area where it is found, no matter how many times it appears there — my rule of thumb is once every 5 to 10k on the grid. I have one source that sends me excellent information, but he includes *every* instance of a mob, so, in the end I tend to throw half the info out. It just won't fit.

I also abbreviated the grid numbers to the thousands to take up less room on the map and to make them less intimidating, plus when navigating in-game (except in dungeons) everyone almost always gives **/locs** rounded in thousands.

M: *Obviously, you're a big map user. How exactly do you use the maps to help you play* DAoC?

K: In a game I use maps for travel, hunting, locating certain types of merchants, planning, scribbling notes, kill tasks, quests, one-time-drop critters. I refer to maps to give directions and advice, and to avoid certain areas in RvR and when running for my life. I try to provide a couple of ways to orient myself to a map — the grid and landmarks/mobs. Terrain can be a third way, but I avoided it on mine, because it made the maps too busy to have it all together. The compass rose can help too.

When I'm traveling, taking my time, or looking for something, I tend to use the grid and **/loc** coordinates, backed up by landmarks. When running for my life, or giving chase, I use landmarks more, as the grid takes more time to read and absorb. Plus **/locs** fly by too fast (if much is going on near you) to use them on the fly in a pinch.

(I'm very much a "picture" oriented person as opposed to a word or number oriented person; those types would probably use the maps differently)

M: *So, did you scout out all these creatures yourself, or do you have help?*

K: I have help. Players send me info, and I've met a few people who have become very reliable sources. I do my best to confirm either in person (or through my reliable sources) the presence of every mob I put on the maps. If I'm not sure, I either include it with a question mark or leave it off and make a note to check it on my master set.

When I first started out I had five or more printed versions of each map floating around the computers ... now I date them and throw away everything but the current ones. I keep a master set where I scribble my notes, changes, corrections, additions so that when I have time to work on them it's all right there.

I checked out the Randomly maps (http://www.randomly.org/projects/mapper/) and find them very pretty, and great for showing terrain, but that's about it. Paths and marking stones are often lost or difficult to find and they don't always come across well in grayscale. I keep mine plain and simple, focused on displaying the most information as clearly as possible.

People also say they like mine because they can scribble on them!

M: *Well, we're intending to follow your example and have "clean" maps, but we're also running the terrain maps for people like me! However, we've tweaked the terrain maps so that all the landmarks show up as white, even though the map itself is gray.*

Kirstena's website is a wondrous aid; you can visit it at:

http://www.io.com/~caladin/kirstena/